Pension Reform

Issues and Prospects for
Non-Financial Defined Contribution (NDC) Schemes

Edited by
Robert Holzmann and Edward Palmer

THE WORLD BANK
WASHINGTON, D.C.

ISBN-10: 0-8213-6038-8
ISBN-13: 978-0-8213-6038-5
eISBN-10: 0-8213-6166-X
eISBN-13: 978-0-8213-6166-5
DOI: 10.1596 / 978-0-8213-6038-5

Library of Congress Cataloging-in-Publication Data
Pension reform: issues and prospects for non-financial defined contribution (NDC) schemes / edited by Robert Holzmann, Edward Palmer.
    p. cm.
Includes bibliographical references and index.
ISBN 0-8213-6038-8
    1. Defined contribution pension plans. 2. Pensions. I. Holzmann, Robert. II. Palmer, Edward. III. World Bank.

HD7105.4.P465 2005
331.25′22—dc22   2005045767

Cover photos: Curt Carnemark/The World Bank; Chris Stowers/Panos Pictures.

Contents

FIGURES

TABLES

BOXES

Preface

THE PREVIOUS DECADE HAS BEEN A DECADE OF PENSION REFORM throughout the world. In high income countries the driving force has been the threat that current systems will become unaffordable in coming decades, with demographic developments presenting a major risk. In another setting, countries in the process of transition from a command to a market economy are confronted with the challenge of introducing a public pension system that will provide social security in old age but that also supports the fundamentals of a market economy. In the latter sense, it is important to examine carefully the experiences of developed market economies. Even in these countries, the driving force behind reform is demographic change and affordability. In a third setting, middle and lower-middle income countries are faced with the question of what system will best serve the interests of their specific country goals for the future. In all of these settings "NDC"—non-financial defined contribution—pension schemes have been on the agenda in discussions of possible options.

Sweden is one of the handful of countries to have implemented an NDC scheme in the 1990s. The Swedish NDC pension reform has its roots in the work of a Working Group on Pensions that began its work at the end of 1991. After about two years of public discussion of the central ideas of the reform, following the Working Group's publication of the proposed framework of the reform in 1992, the final proposal was published in February 1994, and passed as legislation by the Parliament in June 1994. After a short political pause, following the election in the fall of 1994, the process of implementation began in 1996. This encompassed rewriting extensive benefit and tax legislation, including difficult transition legislation, as well as developing new information technology, a new annual statement for participants, and a new electronic information system for participants. The final conceptual bolt was put in place with the construction of a mechanism to assure long-run balance between assets and liabilities, the automatic balancing mechanism. Account statements were sent out for the first time in 1999. Benefits have been paid out according to the new rules since 2001. Now, in 2005, all of the nuts and bolts are in place and the system has been operating over several years.

Additionally, the political consensus behind the Swedish pension reform is as strong today, in 2005, as it was in 1994. From the mid-1990s, NDC came into its own as a concept and was implemented in four EU countries. Italy, Latvia, and Poland are the other three. Following these examples, NDC has become a reform option considered by many countries.

It is now safe to say that the reforms in the four original NDC countries in Europe generated considerable interest especially among European neighbors, but also world-wide. The interest generated in Europe is easy to understand since most of Europe has a pay-as-you-go tradition, and NDC constitutes a new way to "organize" a mandatory, universal pay-as-you-go pension system. And, the majority of European countries are discussing reform of their systems in one way or another. What's more, we now have some experience of NDC schemes implemented during the 1990s. Against this background, it felt particularly relevant for Sweden to host a conference devoted to discussing both the conceptual and institutional aspects of NDC. This would provide an opportunity for Swedish reformers to reflect over the design of the Swedish system in the presence of international pension experts, from both the academic and the policy communities. The goal was even more ambitious, however. The goal was to contribute to creating a synthesis of current knowledge on this new topic. This book is the realization of that goal.

The Swedish National Social Insurance Board was particularly pleased to organize the conference jointly with the World Bank, which served to broaden the discussion to encompass considerations of importance for World Bank client countries. The conference was held during two days in late September 2003 on the island of Sandhamn, one of the outermost islands in the Baltic Sea Archipelago outside Stockholm. The discussion of papers and ideas was spontaneous and challenging, with a whole room of experts from varying affiliations, regions of the world and intellectual "priors."

My experience is that intellectual reciprocity is a rare outcome of seminars and conferences, and that staying with one's own hobby-horse is the normal *modus operandi*. This was certainly not the case on Sandhamn, however. Here, experts were not only speakers; they were listeners. Ideas were exchanged and developed in a positive, collegial atmosphere. This gave the feeling of something happening in the room, the feeling that at the end a new and shared understanding had been reached. I believe that all the participants felt that they left the island of Sandhamn with the feeling that they had participated in a conversation that lifted their thoughts to a new level.

Although we didn't call it NDC in the initial years in Sweden, I have personally been on the NDC journey for well over a decade. From late 1991 to June 1994 I represented the Social Democratic Party in the Government's Working Group on Pensions, and then became responsible for the reform process as Deputy Minister for Social Insurance, following the election of 1994. In mid-1996, as Director General of the National Social Insurance Board, I became responsible for implementing the reform. Now, in 2005, over a decade after the historical decision of the Swedish Parliament, it is a pleasure for me to help provide a broad readership with the opportunity to share the fruits of the Sandhamn deliberations. And, I'm pleased to note that since the Sandhamn conference in autumn 2003, the contents of this book have developed considerably, not only with improved papers originally presented there, but with several new papers. I believe that this book will provide stimulating reading for pension experts and politicians representing both varied academic and country backgrounds.

Anna Hedborg

Acronyms and Abbreviations

ABM	automatic balancing mechanism
AEI	average earnings index
AF	adjustment factors
ATP	*allmänna tilläggspension* (earnings-related benefit in Sweden)
CNAV	*régime général* (basic general scheme in France)
CWB bonds	covered wage bill bonds
DB	defined benefit
DB-PAYG	defined-benefit pay-as-you-go
DC	defined contribution
EP	earnings points
EPC	Economic Policy Committee (European Union)
FDB	financial defined benefit
FDC	financial defined contribution
FEDEA	Fundación de Economía Aplicada (Spain)
FFS	fully funded schemes
FP	*folkpension* (flat-rate universal benefit in Sweden)
FRD	Demographic Reserve Fund (Poland)
FUS	Social Insurance Fund (Poland)
GRV	*Gesetzlich Rentenversicherung* (public retirement insurance in Germany)
IC	initial capital
IFM	integration to financial markets
ILO	International Labor Organization
INPS	Istituto Nazionale per la Previdenza Sociale (National Social Security Institute in Italy)
IRA	individual retirement account
IRR	internal rate of return
ISSA	International Social Security Association
IT	information technology
KNH	Kosei-Nenkin-Hoken (principal pension program for private-sector employees in Japan)
LE	life expectancy
LMW	Latvian Ministry of Welfare
MEA	Mannheim Research Institute for the Economics of Aging

MODPENS	Modelo de Pensiones (Spain)
NDB	non-financial defined benefit
NDC	non-financial defined contribution (also, *notional defined contribution*)
NIPSSR	Japanese National Institute of Population and Social Security Research
INE	Instituto Nacional de Estadística (National Institute of Statistics in Spain)
IRR	internal rate of return
OLG	overlapping generations
PAYG	pay-as-you-go
PDV	present discounted value
PPM	*Premiumpensionsmyndighet* (Premium Pension Agency, the public clearinghouse for the new FDC scheme in Sweden)
PROST	Pension Reform Options Simulation Toolkit
RPI	retail price index
SSA	U.S. Social Security Administration
TD	turnover duration
TFR	total fertility rate
TSSCI	total social security contributions index
VAT	value-added tax
ZUS	Social Insurance Institution (Poland)

Chapter 1

The Status of the NDC Discussion: Introduction and Overview

*Robert Holzmann and Edward Palmer**

PENSION REFORM IS A WORLDWIDE ISSUE. There is hardly any country in the world where the reform of the existing pension system is not on the reform agenda. The drivers behind the need to reform differ somewhat between countries and across regions, but they share three communalities: first, short-term fiscal pressures typically dictate immediate action, while the looming, much larger problems resulting from an aging population and insufficient long-term resilience of systems remain inadequately addressed. Second, socioeconomic changes demand a rethinking of the basic ideas behind pension system design, some dating back more than 100 years. Third, the challenges and opportunities of globalization require countries to pay more attention to the economic effects of pension schemes, including creating a larger risk pool that extends over occupation, branch, and sector, and enables easy portability of rights both within and across country borders.[1]

Against this background, in the 1990s a number of countries started comprehensive reforms of their pension systems, notably countries in Latin America and the transition economies of Central and Eastern Europe. These fundamental reforms were undertaken in an environment of difficulties in making parametric reform work, and they have aimed to at least put schemes on a financially sustainable basis. These systemic reforms have exhibited the potential as well as the limitations of moving toward comprehensive funded systems. Although the potential benefits of funding are high, so are the transition costs and the requirements for setting up these financial schemes. The need to address the demographic and economic reform pressures while avoiding creating additional burdens for future workers has generated international interest in a new genre of pension systems, non-financial or notional defined contribution schemes (NDCs).[2] NDCs address the fiscal, political, social, and economic needs of reform while keeping the fiscal burden of reform low. Yet, do NDCs offer a panacea for pension reform or are they merely the latest fad?

To address more systematically the question of what the NDCs bring to the pension reform table—their strengths and weaknesses—the World Bank and the Swedish National Social Insurance Board joined forces to organize an international conference, which was held October 2003 in Sandhamn, Sweden. The motivation for this conference was quite straightforward: The World Bank wants to know under what conditions and with what

* Robert Holzmann is director, Social Protection Department, at the World Bank and Edward Palmer is professor of social insurance economics at Uppsala University and Head of the Division for Research at the Swedish Social Insurance Agency.

limitations this approach can be proposed to its international cliental. Although the experience in Latvia and Poland is encouraging, the sample is still too small to draw general conclusions about implementing NDCs in transition countries. The Swedish reformers, who spearheaded this new reform approach, wanted to share their experience; but they wanted also to bring a group of experts together to discuss possible improvements in the design and implementation of this innovation.

This conference volume presents the result of the deliberations of a number of leading economists, pension specialists, and policy makers from around the world. It contains 24 chapters plus a number of prepared comments. The chapters cover conceptual issues as well as the specific reform experiences of "pilot" countries. Most of the chapters were papers presented at the conference, but they have undergone major revisions since then. Some new chapters have been added to the proceedings after the conference to broaden further the contents of the book, making it a primer on the theoretical underpinnings of NDC and practical issues involved in its implementation.

The structure of the remainder of the introduction is as follows: the first section outlines in somewhat more detail the background of the reform pressure and the promised advantages as well as drawbacks of NDC systems. The second section provides a short review of the individual chapters and their main findings. The final section sketches the outlook: the lessons so far, the potential of the NDC approach, and the main research gaps to be filled.

Reform Pressures and the Promises of NDCs

What are the main reform pressures on pension systems? What do NDCs offer to the toolkit of pension reform when viewed within a broader economic and political perspective? What do the chapters contained in this volume say about what the NDC framework has to offer in addressing these questions? Our point of departure in answering these questions is to elaborate briefly on the pressures confronting pension reform as we enter into the twenty-first century.

Fiscal pressures continue to be the trigger for the initiation of a pension reform. Reforms are inevitably driven by short-term budgetary pressure resulting from the increasing costs of what in the long-term are fiscally unsustainable public systems. The more important longer-term problems of sustainability due to population aging typically figure less prominently in the political debate and associated reform process.

The *short-term fiscal pressure* for pension reform is always budgetary. The diagnosis is almost invariably that there are too many recipients and too few contributors. The underlying problem in developed economies is system maturation resulting in increasing benefit levels mixed with decreasing *de facto* retirement ages, accentuated by population aging and the deterioration in demographic dependency ratios (the ratio of elderly to the working-age population). Countries are frequently strapped down with high levels of expenditures on benefits, reflecting low and inflexible retirement ages set in times when life expectancy was considerably lower and in an economic environment that was characterized by high economic growth and employment. Developing countries usually have the additional problem of a highly informal labor force, which prevents the translation of a rising labor force into a low system dependency ratio (the ratio of beneficiaries to contributors). On the contrary, the system dependency ratio is high as a result of closed systems (civil service) or strong incentives to stay in the informal economy, including design and implementation features of the pension scheme, or other obstacles to join the formal economy. Stop-gap emergency action may move the system closer to short-term financial balance, but this can be counterproductive by removing focus from design issues that need to be addressed to deal with the underlying long-term imbalances and the need to provide a country with a lasting and transparent set of rules for the public system.

The *longer-term fiscal pressure* is clearly linked to the aging of the population. All countries are more or less affected by this pressure as birth rates fall toward or below the level needed to reproduce the population and as falling mortality rates generate substantial increases in the longevity of the older population. It is not a question of whether this problem will become acute in a country, but when.

The need to act and the broader political and economic implications of different courses of action have come into sharper focus during the last decade. Three issues are of particular relevance for the design of pension systems: (1) Most of the future aging will take place in the developing countries where resources are scarcer. Careful design and cost-effective implementation are important for all countries, but the poorer countries are also less able to bear the fiscal burden of poor design. (2) Aging and population stagnation—and even decline—in the wealthier nations of the northern hemisphere will create arbitrage opportunities with the much younger and growing population in the developing nations of the southern hemisphere. This calls for a pension system that allows easy cross-border portability of acquired rights. (3) National interests are best served by managing population aging in a framework that supports efficient use of both capital and labor.

Socioeconomic changes are a second main reason for reform. The public provision of retirement income for workers in the private sector originated in the late nineteenth century in the now developed countries—as a political response to urbanization and industrialization. Schemes were based on the model of a working husband with a spouse responsible for the household and children, with a high probability of becoming a surviving widow, a probability that increased with age. The first aim of pension systems was understandably to provide some relief to surviving children and widows. It is noteworthy that the minimum retirement age in Europe was originally set high in systems originating around 1900, typically 67–70 years, an age only a small share of male contributors could expect to reach. Typically, in the 1960s and 1970s, politicians capitalized on the shared interests of unions and management and lowered the pension age in many developed economies without paying attention to the long-term costs. This vogue proved to be short-lived, as all these countries began to tighten age and other eligibility requirements in the 1990s, largely with ad hoc adjustments in the rules. To date, there seems to be no known limit on the improvement in healthy years of life. This trend alone calls for a system design that provides incentives for workers to stay longer in the labor market as improvements in health and working conditions lead to longer healthy lives—improving the individual prerequisites for working when older, but also as the decline in fertility contributes to increase the demand.

Toward the end of the twentieth century, two additional socioeconomic changes have altered the landscape: rising female labor force participation and changing family structures. High female labor force participation, high rates of divorce, and the formation of new partner alliances call for a rethinking of benefits for widows—one of the *raisons d'être* of the nascent public schemes of a century ago. Although these changes are most pronounced in the postindustrial countries, they are increasingly a part of the picture in the developing world, too.

Globalization, with the increasing integration of markets for goods and services, factors of production, and knowledge, requires changes in the way public programs operate, including pensions. Such reforms are needed not only to reap the benefits of globalization but also to deal with the challenges it creates, including profound shocks resulting from technical innovations and shifts in the demand and supply of goods and factors of production. This calls for pension systems that distort less decisions made on the labor markets; that support labor mobility across occupations, sectors, and countries; that are conducive to financial market development; and that support lifelong learning.

Against these diverse reform pressures, what are the promises of NDCs, and how are they put in perspective? But, before we get to these promises, very quickly: What is NDC? An NDC scheme is a pay-as-you-go scheme that by design mimics a financial defined contribution (FDC) scheme,[3] and in doing so has many of the features of an FDC scheme. Individual contributions based on a fixed contribution rate are noted on individual accounts. Accounts are credited with a rate of return. Account values continue to accumulate as long as the participant works and pays contributions. There is no "full-benefit" age, but instead all new contributions enhance the size of the individual's annuity once he or she claims it, or after a *minimum* pension age. The annuity is calculated by dividing the account balance with an estimate of life expectancy at retirement. Compared with an FDC scheme, the two most important differences are, first, that the internal rate of return in an NDC scheme is a function of productivity growth, labor force growth, and factors linked with contribution and benefit payment streams as opposed to "the" financial market rate of return. Second, the only financial saving that can occur is in the form of a reserve—or buffer—fund, as opposed to the prefunded character of FDC. The NDC buffer fund is necessary to save the surplus paid by larger cohorts to be paid out when they become pensioners, but the fund also has other buffer functions depending on specific system design.

Since the financial rate of return is generally expected to be higher than the rate of economic growth, NDC requires a higher level of contributions to achieve the same payout as an FDC scheme, and for this reason an NDC scheme is second best in economic terms. On the other hand, the appeal of NDC is that it does not involve the transition cost associated with introducing an FDC scheme where some form of pay-as-you-go arrangement already exists. NDC does not aspire to create financial saving, whereas FDC schemes may do this. Nevertheless, NDC can contribute *indirectly* to creating financial saving for retirement by clearly establishing the limit of the public pension commitment. NDC moves the focus to individual responsibility for providing for her- or himself in old age through work and accumulation of "funds" in individual accounts.

NDC has two desirable design features as opposed to the counterfactual design of a defined benefit scheme. First, NDCs are fair in the sense that two persons from the same birth cohort who make the same contributions into the scheme in the same period can expect to receive the same pension rights for these. Second, a generic NDC is, in principle, financially stable. The system is geared to maintain long-run equivalence between assets and liabilities at an unchanged contribution rate. This is accomplished in part through the dependence of annuities on life expectancy, in part by the fact that the internal rate of return reflects growth of productivity—and hence real wages—but also changing demographic conditions, the most important being declining fertility as propagated through the size of the labor force, and finally by designing the system to fulfill the long-term condition that assets be at least as great as liabilities.

As a result of these characteristics, a generic NDC promises to deal with the effects of the aging population more or less automatically and in the absence of political intervention. A generic NDC scheme maintains financial stability, with a given contribution rate, completely autonomously, based on legislated rules. It is accompanied by account information to participants, and a system financial statement can (should) be produced and made public annually. NDC provides no guarantee against political intervention, however, although it makes the results of political intervention more transparent than a conventional pay-as-you-go defined benefit scheme does. In practice, however, the transition from the previous regime to NDC may place some restrictions on the full-fledged implementation of generic NDC. For example, there may be a "tax overhang" from the old system in the form of commitments politicians choose to honor, even though they might be inconsistent with the logic of the new NDC regime.

There are features of NDC that promise to make it particularly attractive in terms of effects on the labor supply. First, NDC contributions can be perceived by the individual as premium payments into an insurance system—that is, NDC is like a career savings plan that is illiquid until retirement and then pays out in the form of an annuity. Second, NDC rules—together with tax rules that provide equal treatment of pensions and earnings—are neutral in this sense on the work–leisure decisions of older workers. Third, NDC accounts are "infinitely" devisable, which means that it is only practical considerations that determine what percent of a full annuity an individual can claim at any time—after reaching the minimum pension age. Older workers can continue to work, but less, and can change their minds about how much, since an annuity can always be recalculated—and new contributions can be included in the calculation. Fourth, accounts can be shared between spouses or cohabiting couples. Fifth, NDC (like FDC), by basing benefits on individual accounts, makes labor mobility easy. In the NDC (and FDC) world it makes no difference for a pension in which occupation, branch, region, or country one works. Portability is possible by definition, and there are no benefit conditions that lock workers into specific employment situations. Finally, in economic environments where informality is prevalent, NDC rewards those who choose to participate in the formal economy. This being said, however, it is important to recall the importance of supplementing an NDC scheme with some form of "top-up," which in very poor countries with a high degree of informality may be a main benefit for some time. What NDC provides in this context is an explicit structure for integrating an emerging formal sector into an earnings-related mandatory pension scheme.

In sum, NDC promises to address the issues confronting pension policy in the twenty-first century. How well it does this is the subject of this book.

The Structure of the Book and an Overview of the Contributions

The book is organized into two parts with two sections each. Part I presents the NDC concept and issues. Section 1 defines NDCs and focuses on conceptual questions. A set of broader conceptual, policy, and cross-country questions are the topics of section 2. Part II presents country experiences and prospects, with the chapters in section 3 reviewing the experience of countries that have actually introduced NDC schemes, while section 4 presents chapters on selected countries where NDC is being considered as an option for reforming the current defined benefit (DB) system.

Section 1 sets the stage for the book as it approaches the concept of NDC schemes from different angles as variations of a theme. The first chapter of this section defines generic NDC. It is intended to function as a "primer," providing a common ground and putting everybody on the same page. The second chapter addresses what NDCs can bring to pension reform strategies, and the third chapter assesses NDCs from the perspective of welfare economics. Following this, there are three pieces that are written comments emanating from an ad hoc panel discussion organized at the conference in Sandhamn. It adds further light and also conceptual shades on the discussion about the nature of NDCs and their role in pension systems and reforms.

Chapter 2, by *Edward Palmer*, sets the stage by defining a "generic NDC." He establishes and discusses a set of conditions characterizing a generic NDC scheme. As noted above,

NDC is like an individual saving scheme in which contributions on earnings are paid into an account, but NDC follows the principle of pay-as-you-go—that current contributions of workers finance the pensions of current retirees. An essential micro condition defining NDC is that the value of an individual account at any time is the present value of the participant's pension entitlement. The macro condition of NDC is that assets must be at least as great as liabilities, a condition that can be fulfilled in practice in a number of ways, which are discussed in the chapter. The chapter also discusses NDC in an intra- and intergenerational distributional context and examines the possibility of sharing accounts between spouses.

Chapter 3, by *Axel H. Börsch-Supan*, presents first the basic ideas underlying NDC systems and discusses their main advantages and disadvantages. He argues that an NDC system is mainly a political device. It makes parametric reform, badly needed to stabilize the pay-as-you-go (PAYG) pillars all over the world, easier because it exposes the trade-offs and clarifies concepts. It may also change the microeconomics of labor supply and savings. It does not, however, change the macroeconomics of PAYG systems and thus does not substitute for the introduction of prefunded second and third pillars. NDC systems can be installed as individual account systems, as is done most prominently in Sweden. However, Börsch-Supan argues that they can also be mimicked by a set of rules in a conventional defined benefit PAYG system, showing that NDC systems are more a political than an economic device. The second part of his chapter claims that the German pension reform proposals made in late summer 2003 effectively introduced an NDC-like system without explicit NDC-type accounting.

Chapter 4, by *Nicholas Barr*, offers an assessment of NDC pensions from the perspective of welfare economics, in terms of three questions: Is the particular feature an advantage? If so, is the advantage inherent in NDCs or could it be achieved by other arrangements? And is the advantage one of policy design or of political reality? The chapter argues that NDC pensions can facilitate desirable design features such as a flexible retirement age and automatic adjustment to rising life expectancy, enhance the ability to cope with risk and uncertainty, assist sustainability, enhance transparency, and reduce incentives to fraud. It also argues, however, that these advantages are not the sole property of NDCs, but could be achieved by other designs. The chapter goes on to discuss equivocal aspects of NDC pensions and their disadvantages. The final section offers three strategic conclusions: First, NDC pensions are not a theoretically dominant policy—they are *a* policy reform, not *the* policy reform; second, NDC schemes can take many guises—the case for NDCs is strongest as part of a wider pension system, rather than as a stand-alone design; third, NDC pensions do little to address the fundamental cause of unsustainability—the fact that earliest pensionable age is not related to life expectancy.

The presence of *Peter Diamond, Assar Lindbeck, and Salvador Valdés-Prieto* at the conference suggested the creation of a panel on the conceptualization and position of NDC among alternative pension systems. Their written contributions in chapter 5 emanate from this discussion and provide highly valuable insights into the conceptualization of pensions and the position of NDCs among alternative systems. All three start with the three-dimensional classification developed in Lindbeck and Persson (2003): (1) funded versus unfunded systems, (2) actuarial versus nonactuarial systems, and (3) DB (defined benefit) versus DC (defined contribution) systems. But they differ importantly on the interpretation of these characteristics and the position of NDCs in the spectrum of pension system. Although all three give the NDC system pretty good overall grades, they see also virtues in alternative system designs and put up a warning flag about "overselling" NDC.

Section 2 covers a broad spectrum of conceptual and policy questions related to reform needs and NDCs, including the role of demographics in pension systems, the internal rate of return in NDC, conversion from a PAYG-DB scheme to NDC, cross-country considerations such as the usefulness of NDC as a coordinated European pension system or the applicability of NDCs for middle- and low-income countries, and the politics of NDC pension reforms.

Chapter 6, the opening chapter of this section, by *Juha M. Alho, Jukka Lassila, and Tarmo Valkonen* approaches NDC by examining some of the demographic and economic "shocks" with which a generic NDC design would be confronted, but without applying all the tools of a truly generic NDC scheme. Hence, the chapter serves to illustrate the problems confronting the pension system reformer. The chapter combines stochastic population simulations with economic models, providing us with a new way to think about the sustainability of public welfare systems. The chapter discusses the expected change in the age distribution of Europe and consequences for Europe's pension systems. In addition, using four country examples, the authors demonstrate how demographic risks can be shifted in time and between groups.

Chapter 7 by *Ole Settergren and Boguslaw D. Mikula* presents a method for calculating the internal rate of return in PAYG pension systems in general. This generic method is most easily applicable in NDC schemes. They demonstrate that, in addition to the rate of growth of average covered earnings and the number of covered persons—as would be the case in a steady state—a third factor becomes important. This is the time structure of contributions and pension payments, which is labeled the *turnover duration* (TD)—the expected money-weighted average time from contributing to the system to receiving the pension. They show that at any given time assets can be valued as the product of the TD of contributions in the system and contributions actually paid in the period evaluated. Liabilities in the NDC scheme are the current value of all obligations. With the TD valuation of assets it is possible to estimate the (implicit) asset side of the balance sheet, making it possible to determine the ratio of assets in a given period over liabilities, that is, to determine whether the pension system fulfills the condition of financial balance.

Salvador Valdés-Prieto presents an alternative balancing mechanism to the Swedish automatic balancing mechanism (ABM) in chapter 8. When NDC design was adopted in the early 1990s it was known that, in addition to responding to the rates of growth of productivity and the labor force, NDC liquidity would be affected by the timing of payments—by the age-earnings distribution of contributions and age distribution of payments. Yet it was not clear initially how this knowledge could be incorporated into the formulas. Swedish policy experts responded to this challenge by formulating how the internal rate of return in a PAYG system could be represented, and using this knowledge, created the ABM, which is used to secure financial balance. This chapter proposes an alternative to the ABM that also endows NDC plans with automatic financial stability in the short run. This method is labeled integration to financial markets (IFM). In contrast to the ABM, the IFM proposal is based on financial-market-determined discount rates and trade of uninsurable risks with market investors, that is, agents who are neither participants in the scheme nor taxpayers. Relative advantages and risks of the IFM and the ABM are discussed.

Chapter 9 by *Edward Palmer* reviews the issues arising in converting a PAYG-DB scheme to an NDC scheme and presents models for conversion. The first one is based on the NDC formula and the second on the acquired DB rights. Adhering to the NDC formula requires (1) establishing how to approximate past earnings if there is not complete information; (2) what contribution rate should be set for past earnings if it is not to be the rate looking forward after the implementation of NDC; and (3) what the imputed rate of return on past contributions should be. The chapter also discusses how countries introducing NDC have dealt with acquired rights (including special privileges where they have existed), and how other components of DB schemes for low-income recipients' noncontributory rights and disability and survivor benefits are handled in conversion to NDC. Speed of transition and the consequences of complete and immediate transition (as in Latvia) contrasting with slow transition focusing largely (Italy) or solely (the Kyrgyz Republic) on new entrants are discussed. Slow transitions protect acquired rights in the old system, but are counterproductive in terms of the policy goals of the new NDC system. The balance of pros and cons, it is argued, favors rapid transition.

Florence Legros discusses similarities and differences between NDC and the French and German point systems in chapter 10. She focuses on how these systems differ when there is an external shock (demographic, economic, and so on) and discusses the possible consequences of moving from the point system to NDC. The French point system—with no automatism in its indexing device—can be regulated each year according to the forecasts. Legros concludes that this may be the best way to react to changes in the economic and demographic environment—but to do this also requires, first, reliable and frequent forecasts, and second, a total independence of the governing board of the scheme from the retiree and worker lobbies. She notes that although the second point can be handled with rules, as opposed to the present state of affairs, it is questionable whether the first point can be fulfilled. Germany has adopted a method to correct the excessive generosity of the scheme with what she calls a "return spring"—a mechanism in which the pension yield is lowered in relation to a desired contribution rate. This mechanism is reinforced by the "Rürup sustainability factor," which explicitly introduces the dependency ratio and accounts for life expectancy changes. She notes that with this strategy it is probable that the German scheme will move into surplus within some years, allowing for a reserve that might be needed for intergenerational transfers. She concludes by asking the question Why introduce NDC? Her answer is that FDC schemes promote individual responsibility while NDC maintains the principle of social cohesion in public pension schemes.

In chapter 11, *Robert Holzmann* (1) reviews the reform needs of pension systems in the member countries of the European Union for fiscal, economic, and social reasons; (2) makes the case for a move toward a more coordinated pension system in Europe; and (3) sketches what such a system may look like and how it may come about. The central claim and content of the chapter is that a multipillar system, with an NDC system at its core and coordinated supplementary funded pensions and social pensions at its wings, is an ideal system to deal with diverse fiscal and social reform needs. The approach would permit introducing a harmonized structure while allowing for country-specific preferences about coverage and contribution rate. Although the chapter focuses on the European Union, the arguments and proposed structure for a more harmonized system with some autonomy for subnational entities are also valid for other countries or integration areas such as China or Mercosur.

Chapter 12, by *David Lindeman, David Robalino, and Michal Rutkowski*, discusses the suitability of NDC for middle- and low-income countries. Much of the policy discussion to date so far has been focused on high-income countries such as Sweden and Italy. The authors' point of departure is the observation that middle- and low-income countries are characterized by less stable macroeconomic environments, a narrow and highly sensitive contributory base, a more uneven income distribution than in developed countries, and, in addition, they are often in the midst of a demographic transition. The chapter focuses on the general macroeconomic, demographic, and institutional variables that can affect the application and performance of the NDC concept. The chapter discusses the primary benefits from adopting the NDC concept in middle- and low-income countries in terms of reducing economic distortions and improving financial sustainability of PAYG pension schemes. The chapter identifies initial conditions and design factors that are likely to influence the realization of these benefits. It also addresses implementation issues, redistribution and poverty, institutional capacity requirements, and the political economy of NDC schemes in the middle- and low-income setting.

The point of departure of chapter 13 by *Annika Sundén* is that the shift to defined contribution schemes increases the need for general financial literacy. Both NDC and FDC schemes put more of the responsibility and need to plan for retirement on the individual participant. Studies of what people know indicate that they have poor knowledge about the conditions that determine their benefits, and that learning about pensions is difficult. This chapter discusses what people need to know and what surveys show they know, using data gathered for the new Swedish NDC scheme. The chapter concludes that information and education leading to participant understanding of the scheme and, generally, improved pension literacy is important, and that pension system design that makes understanding easy is important. The latter provides an argument against complicated rules, for example the rules for conversion to NDC that affect different cohorts or persons in the same cohort differently, and a need to create an understanding of the basic logic of NDC.

Chapter 14 by *Sarah M. Brooks and R. Kent Weaver* focuses on the political aspects of NDC. It begins by listing the positive policy arguments for NDC compared with the counterfactual policies of PAYG-DB and FDC schemes. The authors argue that the impression of "property rights" that NDC conveys has the negative feature of creating a "lock-in" effect. In the words of the authors, proponents argue that the political advantage of NDC is that it "absolve[s] politicians of responsibility for potential future benefit reduction," for example due to an aging population. Put differently, in adopting NDC, governments "lash themselves to the mast." The chapter addresses two questions: First, is NDC reform more likely to get onto the reform agenda in countries with certain characteristics? Second, does NDC really have the potential to absolve politicians of their responsibility, or will NDC schemes eventually spark resistance that undercuts their intended effects?

Section 3 contains a set of chapters that review the experience of countries that have actually introduced NDC schemes; more specifically these are countries that have reformed traditional non-financial—that is, PAYG—defined benefit (NDB) systems into an NDC system. The country set includes all the reform countries of a fully fledged NDC system: Italy, Latvia, Poland, and Sweden. Italy is even represented with two chapters.

Edward Palmer, Sandra Stabiņa, Ingemar Svensson, and Inta Vanovska present and analyze the Latvian NDC reform, which was implemented on January 1, 1996, in chapter 15. This was the first, and to date is the only, NDC reform covering *all workers from the first year of implementation*. The most difficult design issue was the conversion of rights acquired in the old scheme into NDC rights, because there were only historic service records and because the transition occurred during a period of general economic upheaval in the early years of transition. The pros and cons of the method chosen are discussed. The chapter also presents financial calculations for the coming three-quarters of a century under a variety of extreme economic and demographic assumptions. Initially, the NDC contribution rate was 20 percent, but the overall rate of 20 percent is being successively redistributed to an FDC scheme with a rate of 10 percent by 2010. The chapter illustrates the impact of moving into the financial account scheme and reducing the NDC rate to 10 percent. The introduction of the FDC scheme requires a tax to finance previous NDC commitments made with NDC contribution rates above 10 percent. Alternative estimates are provided for a less ambitious financial account pillar with a contribution rate of 6 percent rather than the scheduled 10 percent (leaving 14 percent for the NDC scheme). The chapter also shows that the NDC scheme per se is financially robust under a large variety of assumptions, even with the pessimistic assumption that the working-age population will decline by 50 percent in the coming half decade. The authors stress that the system design needs to be completed by formally implementing the reserve fund and producing more comprehensive financial accounts, including the tax-financed debt to the NDC scheme accompanying the introduction of the FDC scheme.

Chapter 16 by *Marek Góra and Agnieszka Chłoń-Domińczak* presents the new Polish pension system, which was introduced under the banner of "Security through Diversity," on January 1, 1999. It automatically replaced all previous legislation on old-age pensions for the majority of the working population as for all persons under age 50 in the year the reform the new scheme was introduced. The chapter presents the design of the Polish NDC scheme in the context of the framework of the entire pension system implemented in 1999, and it assesses the early experiences with implementation and discusses the future of the NDC pension system in Poland. The chapter also presents financial calculations over the coming 50 years, showing that the system moves into balance from a point of departure of substantial imbalance—and this is helped along by a gradual formalization of the economy that for a couple of decades counteracts a gradual fall in the working-age population. Though the general design of the Polish NDC scheme has remained unchanged, some elements of its original construction have become a subject of debate. One of the most important is the decision in the original legislation to allow women to retire at age 60, while men retire at age 65. In addition, the reform left farmers outside, which is likely to create a coverage problem for this segment of the population as they integrate into the formal economy. A major lesson to be drawn from the Polish experience is that the implementation needs good administrative support if major problems are to be avoided.

Chapter 17 by *Bo Könberg, Edward Palmer, and Annika Sundén* presents the Swedish NDC experience. The Swedish pension reform dates back to the summer of 1992 when the Parliamentary Working Group on Pensions published a "sketch" containing almost all the essential elements of the reform. In June of 1994, the Swedish parliament passed the reform legislation that was to be the Swedish NDC scheme. Implementation began in 1995 and moved forward in stages. This chapter discusses how the Swedish reform came about, what it is, its public image, and remaining issues. A driving force behind the creation of the Swedish NDC scheme was the goal of creating financial stability while using contributions per capita as the rate of return on accounts. This led to the creation of the automatic balancing mechanism (ABM). The authors discuss the fact that one of the remaining challenges is to create a popular understanding that the ABM is simply a component of the rate of return on NDC accounts. The authors highlight the idea that the potential risk for the autonomy of the system is the very mechanism that was designed to create autonomous financial balance—the ABM. They conclude by reflecting that Sweden had already accumulated large reserves in the old system to meet the demographic burden of the post-war baby boomers, which will help to provide payments when both the boomer and next boomer generation—the children of the postwar boomers—retire. This puts Sweden in a very favorable position compared with many countries considering introducing NDC. Calculations show that demography will stress finances in the 2040s, and this will be taken into consideration in solving the remaining problem of "balancing"—a method of determining when reserves are large enough to allow them to be distributed to the then-living participants. Finally, the authors conclude that what remain to be examined in greater depth are the implications of the construction of the balancing mechanism for the intergenerational distribution of resources.

The first case study of Italy is presented by *Daniele Franco and Nicola Sartor* in chapter 18. Since 1992, reform of the pension system has been at the core of the effort to consolidate Italian public finances. The reform process began in 1992 when a quarter of prospective public sector pension liabilities was abruptly cancelled. A second major reform in 1995 introduced NDC, but beginning with new entrants and with a pro rata formula for persons with fewer than 18 years of coverage. The authors provide and discuss empirical evidence on the results of the reform and conclude that the reform process is not yet finished. According to their analysis, further adjustments are required to: (1) accelerate the introduction of notional accounts; (2) avoid increases in the ratio of pension expenditure to GDP; and (3) strengthen the self-equilibrating mechanisms of the new pension regime, such as by moving to an annual revaluation of the life expectancy factor used in calculating newly granted NDC annuities. In the view of these authors, present problems derive from the fact that the 1995 reform was implemented without an extensive analysis and an open public debate. The lengthy and incremental process associated with the "unfinished reform"—following the first stage in 1992—has generated uncertainty, and, according to the authors, may limit the microeconomic benefits of the approach embodied in NDC. New reform proposals discussed after 1995 do not explicitly call into question the 1995 reform, but, generally, they have not been consistent with its underlying philosophy. The authors conclude that the future of NDC in Italy is therefore uncertain.

The second case study on Italy by *Sandro Gronchi and Sergio Nisticò* in chapter 19 compares the Italian and Swedish reforms. The point of departure is a theoretical framework that highlights the implications of the different ways in which Italy and Sweden implemented the NDC model. In particular, this chapter focuses in depth on the real growth norm factored into the life annuities in the Italian and Swedish NDC schemes—a feature no other country has implemented. The chapter is unique in providing an analysis of this feature. Like the Swedish annuity, the Italian annuity contains an economic growth factor—in Italy's case, a real growth factor of 1.5 percent per annum over the life of the annuity (in Sweden it is 1.6 percent). The main conceptual defect of the "Italian-style" NDC scheme is that the indexation of pensions should reflect the difference between the sustainable rate of return (with GDP growth as a proxy) and the value of 1.5 percent used in calculating annuities, which is the case in Sweden. The absence of this correction jeopardizes the objectives of sustainability and fairness. Other shortcomings and inconsistencies of the Italian reform are discussed. The authors conclude that, although blueprints have been available since 1995, successive governments have not taken the necessary step to form a committee of experts with a mandate to "bridge the gap between the theoretical foundations of the NDC scheme and the countless details that implementation would inevitably bring."

Section 4, the last section of the book, presents case studies for countries that are thinking about introducing NDC systems, or, at least according to the authors, should have a close look at NDC approach as a promising option for reforming the existing PAYG system. As to be expected, some country considerations are more advanced than others. Five country studies are presented: Austria, the Czech Republic, Germany, Spain, and Japan. The characteristic of all country cases is the size of the inherited Bismarckian-type retirement system, which ranges between 9 percent (Japan) and 15 percent (Austria) of GDP; the piecemeal approach of past parametric reforms, which has failed so far to put the public pension schemes on a sustainable basis; and implications of introducing NDCs for benefit levels for a given retirement age.

Austria competes with Italy, Poland, and Uruguay for the "world championship" in public pension expenditure. All countries have expenditures close to 15 percent of GDP, but some contenders start to fall back in the race as they have reformed their system (such as Poland). So far Austria is leading the race. Recent reforms have helped to reduce the sustainability problem but will not solve it, as is discussed in chapter 20 by *Bernhard Felderer, Reinhard Koman, and Ulrich Schuh*. This study demonstrates the impact of different scenarios on expenditures, revenues, and replacement rates through 2050. They present new evidence that confirms the need for a more fundamental reform of the Austrian pension system. In a second part, the chapter investigates the potential effects of moving from the current NDB to an NDC system. The results indicate that an NDC reform can put the public scheme on sustainable basis, but the arithmetic of pensions that the NDC approach forces to light exhibits the impact on replacement rates: For men, replacement rates would be reduced from some 80 percent (if unchanged but unsustainable) by some 20 and more percentage points (depending on the labor force scenario); for women, the replacement rates would be reduced from some 50 percent by similar dimensions. Based on these sobering calculations, the authors recommend introducing an additional fully funded, mandatory second pillar to a reformed NDC scheme to provide acceptable benefit levels for future retirees.

The Czech Republic shares many features with its southern neighbor, including the historical origins of the pension system. According to UN population projections,[4] population aging is projected to be even more pronounced than in previous projections and the Czech Republic—together with Greece, Italy, and Spain—is expected to have the highest share in the population of people 65 and older by 2050. The projected pronounced population aging in the coming decades makes a reform of the Czech pension system even more important to avoid a future financial crisis. Although various reforms have been undertaken in the course of 1990s, they are not sufficient to create financial stability, making more significant changes even more necessary. The authors of this case study (chapter 21)—*Agnieszka Chłoń-Domińczak and Marek Mora*—review the reform options and conclude that a move toward a mandatory funded pillar does not seem a viable option, as public finances would not be able to bear the costs of transition financing. Also, following relatively poor performance of the voluntary pension funds, there is little support among the politicians and the society generally for introducing a funded pension system. On the other hand there is increasing political resistance to another round of parametric reforms. Against this background the introduction of an NDC scheme provides a framework that joins the microeconomic incentives of the funded system with PAYG financing that does not imply transition costs. The chapter analyzes NDC as a viable option for reforming the Czech pension system, with particular focus on advantages and disadvantages of such an option from the perspective of the Czech Republic. The financial simulations that complement the analysis show that a mere move from the current two-tier PAYG system to an NDC scheme does not lead to financial sustainability. Such a move would have to go hand in hand with other changes, such as an increase (and equalization) of retirement ages for men and women and lower pension indexation.

Germany still has a very generous public PAYG pension system. It is characterized by early effective retirement ages and very high effective replacement rates. Most workers receive virtually all of their retirement income from this public retirement insurance. Costs are almost 12 percent of GDP, more than 2.5 times as much as the U.S. social security system). The pressures exerted by population aging on this monolithic system, amplified by negative incentive effects, have induced a reform process that began in 1992 and is still ongoing. This process is the topic of chapter 22 by *Axel H. Börsch-Supan and Christina B. Wilke*, and they proceed in two parts. The first part describes the German pension system as it has shaped the labor market until about the year 2000. The second part describes the three-staged reform process that will convert the exemplary and monolithic Bismarckian public insurance system after the year 2000 into a complex multipillar system in which the PAYG pillar will emulate an NDC system. The chapter assesses how far these reform steps will solve the pressing problems of a prototypical PAYG system of old age provision, it is hoped with lessons for other countries with similar problems.

Spain is another European country with pronounced projected population aging as a result—as elsewhere—of increasing life expectancy, but mixed with one of the lowest fertility rates in the world. Chapter 23 by *Carlos Vidal-Meliá and Inmaculada Domínguez Fabián* has two goals: first, to provide an objective technical assessment of the current situation of the contributory pension system in Spain and its prospects for the future, and second, to look at the issues surrounding the introduction of a system of notional defined contribution accounts. To this end the chapter sketches the basic elements upon which the current system is based, and highlights its main indicators before discussing some of its fundamental problems. These problems include equity issues resulting from highly unequal implicit rates of return in the different pension schemes organized according to occupational affiliation. The review of the set of forecasts of Spanish researchers and institutions all confirm the financial unsustainability of an unreformed system. When investigating the usefulness and applicability of the NDC approach for Spain (and its largest subsystem), the chapter has two interesting twists. It compares the replacement rates (and internal rates of return) of the current scheme with that of alternative NDC implementations using Spanish data. The reference benefit formulas are reforms in Sweden, Italy, Brazil, Poland, and Latvia. The result shows variations across the different benefit benchmarks, but across all benchmarks are clear signals that the current Spanish benefit formula is totally unsustainable because it is much too generous. As a second twist, the chapter takes an alternative realization of potential notional interest rate options for contributions and pensions and suggests which formula or group of formulas would best fit the profile of contributor-beneficiary risk and what the transition process would be.

Japan already has the oldest population in the world. Since 2001, the income statement of the principal pension program has turned into a deficit. Increasing drop out has been observed from the basic old-age income protection for nonsalaried workers. The generous pension program has to be reformed to be much more incentive-compatible. In this little note (chapter 24), *Noriyuki Takayama* claims that a reform of the Japanese PAYG system toward a Swedish-type NDC system would very much help Japan overcome a number of problems in its current schemes, including problems of incentive-compatibility. Japan faces the additional specific challenge of handling huge excess liabilities resulting from entitlements of past pension contributions, equivalent to 130 percent of GDP in 2004. If Japan were to move to an NDC system, the chapter suggests handling this legacy problem of excess liability through a budget mechanism such as an earmarked consumption tax or transfers from the general budget.

Summing Up and Research Outlook

As is evident from the summary of the contents of this book, the NDC conference held on the island of Sandhamn outside Stockholm resulted in a very rich conference producing important contributions on the topic of NDC. The contents of this book should be helpful for countries that want to investigate this approach to reform an NDB pillar that is not working, to readjust weights between unfunded and funded pillars, or to introduce an NDC scheme as the foundation, perhaps with a mandatory public and/or a private FDC scheme on top. NDC is worthy of a country's examination as a means of dealing with the financial instability accompanying the aging of the population. It provides a framework for dealing with most of the demands on a modern pension system. In some environments, it may be the best alternative where conditions are not ripe for the introduction of a financial account scheme.

The rich conference outcome provides some answers but, as should be expected, also poses many more questions that require the attention of policy makers and researchers. In addition, the relatively short experience of the little more than a handful of countries that can claim to follow an NDC-type approach is simply too short to draw strong conclusions. Nevertheless, there was definitely a clear agreement among the diverse group of researchers and policy makers at the Sandhamn conference that all countries are invited to have a close look at the NDC approach as a viable option for dealing with the diverse reform pressures of their pension schemes.

Against this background, we make no attempt to provide a detailed concluding summary. This said, there are three main themes that run across all the chapters. These lead to some conclusions, while at the same time they suggest questions for future research.

First, the conference outcome suggests that the conceptual promises of an NDC reform, in particular that of financial sustainability, can be fulfilled. Yet, as with other reform approaches, the challenge is in its implementation. More specifically, the experience of NDC reform countries suggests that NDC is not a foolproof approach, and it needs to be politically well managed. As in other reforms, communication with the stakeholders of the reform to get their buy in is crucial, and administrative preparedness is also crucial. The limited country experience also suggests that faster transition from the inherited DB system may have major advantages. Although the *concept* of the balancing mechanism intended to achieve financial sustainability seems to have been understood and embraced by experts, it may be difficult to implement, both for technical (data quality) and political reasons. In the one country where the automatic balancing mechanism has been implemented—Sweden—there is still no experience of the possible political repercussions of automatic balancing. But, perhaps most importantly, too little thinking has been given to the issue of "tax overhang," that is, the need for additional fiscal resources or reform measures to deal with transitory deficit resulting from past commitments that are not covered by the fixed NDC contribution rate.

Second, the short time period since the introduction of NDC (the longest period is nine years in Latvia) and interaction with other reform measures has not allowed for careful assessment of the economic effects of NDC reforms, and the distributive effects have not figured prominently in the political and academic discussions. As a result, too little is known, especially about the intergenerational distributive effects, and very little attention has been devoted to dealing with the spouse pension. We still have very little empirical evidence about the promised effects on labor supply, in particular the retirement decision, although the limited evidence from reform countries looks promising. As a result we do not know if individuals faced with a lower pension at early retirement age do sufficiently postpone their retirement decision or draw on a much lower pension, and how much this is influenced by overall system design issues (such as the minimum pension guarantee) or constraints imposed from outside the system.

Last but not least, there was a shared feeling at the conference that NDC schemes must be assessed as part of a broader (multipillar) pension concept and not (only) viewed in isolation. An issue that needs to be given more attention is the question of how to integrate occupational schemes into the overall pension framework. This may be relatively easy for, say, pensions of civil servants, but it is likely to require more thinking for, say, farmers or persons involved in the informal or semiformal agricultural setting in developing economies. As NDC systems apply the logic that benefits depend only on one's own contributions, and with life expectancy determining the size of the life benefit, for any given contribution rate and retirement age the benefit level will be lower—perhaps markedly lower—than under the old NDB scheme. Individuals may compensate with later retirement but they may also compensate with more individual savings—but in what form (mandated, voluntary), with what instruments (financial assets, annuities), under what form of supervision, and so on? Hence, opting for an NDC scheme also requires having a game plan for the (second or third) supplementary pillars, and there are many issues involved. What's more, as the NDC scheme has no distributive aspirations, the choice of overall framework also requires paying attention to the needs of basic income support to the needy elderly in a way that achieves the social objective while not unduly compromising the expected behavioral effects of NDC.

That we can pose these and other research questions at all, or at least much more clearly, is the result of the conference and of the chapters in the book. Enjoy the reading!

Notes

1. See Holzmann et al. (2005).

2. "Non-financial defined contribution" and "notional defined contribution" are used interchangeably in this book and should be understood to have the same definition.

3. Note that we adopt the terminology presented in Góra and Palmer (2004) that distinguished between defined benefit and defined contribution schemes on the one hand, and financial and non-financial schemes on the other. A *financial scheme* is a scheme the assets of which are held in financial market instruments, and a *non-financial scheme* is a scheme in which the assets are the fewer contributions of workers. This gives four distinct categories of pension schemes: Financial defined contribution (FDC), financial defined benefit (FDB), non-financial defined contribution (NDC) and non-financial defined benefit (NDB). FDC is what is called individual account schemes in some of the pension literature. Since NDC is also an individual account scheme, it seems more appropriate to distinguish between the financial and non-financial aspects of these in choosing the nomenclature.

4. See UN (1998).

References

Góra, M., and E. Palmer. 2004. "Shifting Perspectives in Pensions." IZA Discussion Paper 1369, The Institute for the Study of Labor, Bonn.

Holzmann, R., R. Hinz, and World Bank team. 2005. *Old Age Income Support in the 21st Century: An International Perspective on Pension Systems and Reform.* Washington, DC: World Bank.

Lindbeck, A., and M. Persson. 2003. "The Gains from Pension Reform." *The Journal of Economic Literature* 41(1): 74–112.

UN (United Nations). 1998. *World Population Prospect: The 1998 Revision.* New York: UN Population Division.

PART I

THE CONCEPT OF NON-FINANCIAL DEFINED CONTRIBUTION SYSTEM— VARIATIONS ON A THEME

Chapter 2

What Is NDC?

Edward Palmer*

IT IS ALWAYS A PRECARIOUS BUSINESS TO TRACE THE ORIGIN OF AN IDEA, but among the published works available to an international audience, Buchanan (1968) probably contains the first proposal that can be likened to what have emerged as notional—or non-financial defined—defined contribution (NDC) pension schemes.[1] A proposal in Boskin, Kotlikoff, and Shoven (1988) is also on this track, and the point systems of Germany and France certainly contain the embryo of an NDC system. Nevertheless, NDC as it is now known was not given a face until the arduous task of redesigning pension systems was taken on in a series of reforms in Europe in the 1990s.

It is probably safe to say that NDC has emerged as a result of the interchange of ideas and discussions among pension experts and politicians working on pension reform issues in those countries where NDC has been implemented. Since the mid-1990s, the exchange of ideas about the possible contribution of NDC to the pension policy toolbox has been truly international, with both avid proponents and a healthy number of skeptics. To date, however, ten years after NDC legislation was passed in two countries—Sweden and Italy—no paper has attempted to bring all the strands together to provide a cohesive technical framework. That is the ambition of this study.

In the general discussion in the next section, this study touches briefly on the differences in principle between NDC and alternatives for mandatory national pension schemes. The purpose of the study, however, is not to argue the comparative merits of alternative pension schemes, or to discuss what countries implementing NDC have done in practice. Instead, the aim of this study is to present what an NDC pension system is. The second section of the study briefly discusses efficiency and distribution with respect to NDC schemes.

In the third section the generic NDC scheme is presented. The fourth section deals briefly with considerations in integrating social policy into the NDC framework and touches upon some other issues that can arise in constructing an NDC scheme. The study closes with a brief summary and some final remarks.

---

* Edward Palmer is professor of social insurance economics at Uppsala University and head of the Division for Research at the Swedish Social Insurance Agency.

The author is grateful for comments on this chapter generously provided by Robert Holzmann.

A General Overview of NDC

A First Description of NDC

An NDC scheme is a *defined contribution*, pay-as-you-go (PAYG) pension scheme. Contributions are defined in terms of a fixed contribution rate on individual earnings. These contributions are noted on an individual account. As opposed to a financial defined contribution (FDC) scheme, the contributions of participants noted on individual accounts are not "funded." More specifically, individual account money is not invested in financial market instruments. Compared with an FDC scheme, where individual account money *is* invested in financial market assets, by definition, the pay-as-you-go individual account DC scheme is a *notional* DC scheme.

It can be argued that it is more precise to use the terminology "financial" and "non-financial"—that is, financial DC and non-financial DC—to distinguish these two types of defined contribution schemes, stressing the fact that money in accounts is invested in market assets in the FDC scheme, but not in the NDC scheme. Note that in the pension literature financial DC schemes are generally referred to as "individual account schemes." Given that an NDC scheme is *also* an individual account scheme, the use of the term "individual account scheme" to describe financial account schemes seems ambiguous. Góra and Palmer (2004) argue that financial individual account schemes should be called FDC schemes, and notional—or non-financial—account schemes should be called NDC schemes, which is the terminology used throughout in this study.

Before describing NDC in greater detail, two brief statements about the difference between NDC and FDC individual account schemes are helpful. First, they differ with respect to their (potential) contribution to national saving. An NDC scheme provides no direct contribution to saving, except through the possible mechanism of demographic saving. An FDC scheme contributes to national saving during the build-up phase to maturity, but thereafter the potential effect on national saving will depend on the demography of the scheme participants. Furthermore, it is a well-discussed caveat in the economic literature on pensions that the net overall effect of mandatory pension schemes on national saving depends on private and government offsetting behavioral responses. Second, NDC and FDC differ with respect to the system rate of return. Participants in an FDC scheme earn a financial market rate of return, whereas participants in an NDC scheme earn an internal rate of return, which is determined by factors underlying the development of the economy. The next section discusses potential economic consequences of the differences between NDC and FDC schemes in greater depth.

Now, what is an NDC scheme? A general description follows. In the next section, more precise criteria for a generic NDC scheme are developed. Basically, in an NDC scheme, participants—or employers on their behalf—pay contributions on earnings during their whole working career. Although there is a minimum age at which an annuity can be claimed, there is no "pension age." As long as people continue to receive earnings from work, these earnings generate contributions to individual accounts. This is true even if the individual is already drawing on a partial or full annuity after the minimum age to claim the annuity. Once again, each period's contributions are *noted* on an individual account. This notional individual account grows with new contributions and is credited with a rate of return. In the generic NDC scheme, the rate of return is the internal rate of return.

The NDC benefit is a life annuity. It can be claimed at any time from the minimum retirement age. The generic NDC annuity embodies a rate of return based on the same internal rate of return that is credited accounts during the accumulation phase and, importantly, cohort life expectancy at the time the annuity is claimed. Since newly granted annuities reflect life expectancy, in principle, NDC is an actuarially fair pension system.

Thus an NDC scheme distributes *individual* resources over the life cycle, but within the framework of a countrywide (universal) PAYG insurance scheme. In this sense it can be likened to an illiquid, individual cash balance scheme, with the important difference that it is an *insurance* scheme: that is, it redistributes the capital of the deceased to the survivors in the scheme. It fulfills the function of insuring against the individual risk of outliving the average participant.

Because the NDC benefit is based on individual contributions from individual earnings, it may not provide sufficient coverage in old age for everyone because, for one reason or another, some individuals will not have had sufficient earnings before retirement to provide a sufficient benefit in old age. This is not a problem inherent to NDC; rather, it is a characteristic of any earnings-related benefit. As opposed to many possible defined benefit (DB) formulas, the pension formula in an NDC scheme contains no built-in redistribution of the system's revenues. Thus an NDC scheme must be supplemented with some form of low-income support scheme, in the form of minimum income or minimum benefit guarantee. NDC accounts can also be supplemented with noncontributory rights, e.g., for childcare years. What is essential is that these be financed with revenues exogenous to the NDC scheme, i.e., general tax revenue.

Efficiency and Distribution

Both NDC and defined benefit pay-as-you-go—that is, non-financial defined benefit—schemes differ from financial schemes in terms of economic efficiency. The relevant discount rate for money set aside today to pay for consumption tomorrow is the financial market rate of return. In terms of this metric, a pension scheme that gives a risk-adjusted rate of return below the risk-adjusted financial market rate creates a tax wedge, and this means participants would attain a higher level of lifetime consumption with the counterfactual financial market rate of return.

Rated in terms of efficiency, non-financial pension schemes, among these NDC schemes, are only potentially at least as efficient as financial pension schemes. They would be as efficient as financial schemes in a steady-state (closed) Golden Rule economy[2] but otherwise not necessarily so. If the rate of return on assets, r, traded in the financial market dominates the growth rate of the economy, $\lambda + g$, where λ is population (labor force) growth and g is productivity growth or, more exactly, the internal rate of return (IRR) of the NDC scheme (see the next section),[3] then financial schemes dominate non-financial schemes in terms of efficiency. Nevertheless, although empirical evidence from the past century suggests this is the case, at least if the account portfolio includes equities,[4] it need not always be the case in specific country settings and specific periods.

Although $r >$ IRR means, ceteris paribus, that an FDC scheme dominates an NDC scheme, by linking individual benefits solely to individual contributions, an NDC scheme does not have the tax effect inherent in a DB-PAYG scheme. However, in the final analysis one should take into account the effects of the tax regime.[5] For example, a country's taxes on earnings and capital may differ.

In addition, although by definition the IRR of an NDC scheme depends on the development of the country's economy, in a comparison with an FDC counterfactual, it is important that two other considerations are kept in mind. First, an FDC scheme with a portfolio dominated or exclusively invested in home country debt is exposed to home country risk, just as NDC is. Second, an FDC scheme counterfactual, also holding only or mainly government bonds, can be likened to an NDC scheme fully monetized with Buchanan bonds. However, if the government bond rate is greater than the IRR, this "advantage" will be paid for through taxes levied on the same countrywide insurance collective, that is, the recipient of the higher return; although there are likely to be tax-distributional effects that distinguish these two approaches.

The expected value of an NDC pension in any period t is exactly the amount in an individual account at that time. This amount, in turn, has, been determined by the individual's contributions and the rate of return on his or her account. This is just another way of saying that in a generic NDC scheme there is no built-in mechanism—either explicit or implicit—to redistribute income, as opposed to a DB scheme. A DB scheme involves at least some within-scheme redistribution, by definition.

Furthermore, an NDC scheme differs from defined benefit pay-as-you-go (DB-PAYG) schemes in how it deals with the effects of changing demographic and economic factors. In an NDC scheme, the effects of economic and demographic fluctuations are accommodated endogenously, as the NDC internal rate of return adjusts account values during both the accumulation and the payout phases, and as annuities adjust to changes in birth cohort life expectancy at retirement.

In a DB-PAYG scheme, benefits are fixed by "contract"—at least in principle—and system adjustments to exogenous economic and demographic shocks are accommodated through changes in the contribution rate. Obviously, this approach to dealing with exogenous economic and demographic risks can generate very different distributional outcomes from NDC, which adapts by adjusting accounts.

Because an NDC scheme has a constant contribution rate over time, successive generations of participants can expect to pay the same fixed percentage of their earnings into the scheme. If this property is chosen as a definition of intergenerational fairness, then an NDC scheme is intergenerationally fair. Each generation will pay a fixed percent of lifetime earnings into the scheme and can expect to receive a stream of benefits, determined by these individual payments and the system rate of return.

NDC schemes can nevertheless give varying outcomes *across cohorts*. This is because the value of individual benefits depends on the intertemporal rate of return, which will vary from period to period. This is true of any pension scheme, however. Individual outcomes are a function of either the market rate of return (financial schemes) or some form of indexation (non-financial schemes), and the distribution of individual outcomes over time will be a function of either the development of the financial market or the economy, respectively, with the exact outcome depending on how the system rules link the scheme to either of these. Variation in the NDC intertemporal rate of return means that outcomes for given amounts of real valued contributions can vary over cohorts, and even over persons in the same birth cohort, depending on when they enter and exit the labor force.

A generic NDC scheme distributes the resources of the scheme through the time dimension of the IRR, to be defined more precisely in the next section. In addition, it is important to note that, to date, all country designs of NDC have included a transfer mechanism through the actual annuity formula employed, through the application of unisex life expectancy. Furthermore, taxes and transfers reenter the picture indirectly through the external (to the NDC scheme) tax and transfer system, since the government can transfer general tax revenues to the accounts of the NDC participants.

It follows then that what the NDC scheme does in practice is to provide a setup for transparent accounting of the flows of money into the overall system and the sources of finance for these flows. NDC does not eliminate the political risk in this sense, but it provides a transparent framework for weighing the pros and cons of political decisions on taxes and transfers regarding a nation's pension system.

In sum, an NDC scheme is dominated by or is at least as good as an FDC scheme on the basis of efficiency. Whether a particular FDC counterfactual dominates a generic NDC scheme in practice will depend on the investment portfolio of the FDC scheme and the tax-regime backdrop. In addition, dominance is not only dependent on these institutional considerations, it is also time-dependent, as the relation between the financial market rate of return and the IRR is dependent on the home economy—and indirectly, on the international economy, and the domestic and international financial markets. By definition, pay-as-you-go DB schemes include intra- and intergenerational tax distortions through internal redistribution not embedded in a generic NDC scheme—but NDC is not necessarily free of distributional effects, either. Also, by maintaining a constant contribution rate, an NDC scheme means all generations pay the same percent of earnings into the scheme. The value of these contributions depends, however, on the economy-determined rate of return, but this is also true of DB-PAYG schemes. Finally, for the same intragenerational distributional goals, an NDC scheme also dominates defined benefit schemes by making any form of distribution and the financial sources for this transparent.

Generic NDC

Design
The central component of the NDC scheme is the individual *lifetime* account. This section describes how account values arise and how annuities are calculated. It begins with the concept of notional capital. Note that the entire discussion is in terms of *real* values. In practice, however, the system is inflation-neutral since it is set up in terms of *nominal* values.

NOTIONAL CAPITAL

According to the NDC formula, for an individual, i, paying contributions on wages (or earnings), w, during an accounting period, t, with contribution rate, c, notional capital at the end of any period, T, is

$$K_{i,T} = \sum_{t=1}^{T} c\, w_{i,t}\, I_t\,,\tag{2.1}$$

where $cw_{i,t}$ denotes the individual's contributions in period t. Note that usually a ceiling will be set on earnings giving rights in the system.

I_t is an index, calculated from an internal rate of return, α_t:

$$I_t = \prod_{t+1}^{T-1} (1 + \alpha_t)$$
$$I_T = 1.\tag{2.2}$$

The internal rate of return is discussed in greater detail below, but for now it is sufficient to say that it is the rate of return that maintains financial balance over time, for a given contribution rate.

Some participants will not live long enough to claim a benefit, and this creates "inheritance capital," which in a closed system will be distributed to the account values of the survivors in the insurance collective. In practice, this can be done on a birth cohort basis, and in accordance with the individual's share of capital in the cohort's total capital. The inheritance capital is distributed in conjunction with some set age, such as the minimum age at which an annuity can be claimed. This adds another component to individual capital at retirement, increasing the return on capital.

THE ANNUITY

Total capital at retirement, beginning in period τ, is the sum of capital accredited the individual's account prior to the period of retirement. Total capital at the end of the period prior to retirement, $K_{\tau-1}$, divided by an annuity factor, G, gives the initial value of the annuity, P_τ, for pensioner j, from birth cohort κ

$$P_{j,\tau} = \frac{K_{j,\tau-1}}{G\left[LE_\kappa, \alpha\left(LE_\kappa\right)\right]} \qquad (2.3)$$

The annuity is a function of two factors. The first is cohort-based life expectancy, LE, for cohort κ at retirement. The second is the internal rate of return, α, computed over the same period. The latter becomes an indexation formula in practice.

The life expectancy factor. In principle, men and women would have separate LE factors. However, in countries where NDC schemes have been introduced, the annuity is calculated using unisex life expectancy. The use of unisex life expectancy in calculating the annuity introduces an explicit redistribution from those who live a shorter life to those who live a longer life, for this reason, given current longevity patterns and a unisex LE factor that entails a transfer from men to women.

The rate of return and the life annuity. An NDC scheme provides a life annuity that encompasses a real rate of return—determined by the internal rate of return, discussed below.

The rate of return for the period over which the annuity is to be paid out is only known ex post, whereas the annuity is calculated ex ante. This means that in practice a computational rule is required to determine how α is to be entered into the annuity formula.

One procedure is to include an ex ante value of α in the formula. In practice this could be any value reasonably close to the expected internal rate of return. This approach requires a second rule for dealing with the deviation of the actual outcomes from the α included ex ante in the formula used to compute the annuity. A convenient method is to adjust (for example, annually) for the difference between the rate of return included in the annuity, which can be called the *norm*, and the actual rate of return determined on an ex post basis (annually). If the actual return is less than the norm used in the annuity, a negative correction is called for, and vice versa.[6]

In practice, use of formula 2.3 "frontloads" the annuity and, in economic terms, creates a higher annuity in the beginning of the total payout period compared with straight-forward yearly indexation, but at the expense of a lower annuity (compared with straight-forward annual indexation) in the latter segment of the payout period. This is consistent with assuming that the time preference of individuals is weighed in favor of more consumption now than in the future, and creating the annuity to reflect this assumption.

The alternative to including the rate of return in the annuity is to *index the annuity annually*, still with the internal rate of return. This form of real indexation gives higher consumption for each year into the future—as long as there is real growth—but at the expense of a lower initial value. This is because the individual lifetime pension-benefit stream available to distribute is fixed. This in turn means that if the annuity is higher from the beginning, by including a norm in the calculation of the initial benefit, then benefit-based resources available for consumption when young are also higher. However, since there is a fixed sum of money to distribute over the lifetime for the individual, resources will be lower (relatively to a contemporaneous wage earner's earnings) when older.

Note also that the individual account is an entity that exists until death. This is a convenient property, for two reasons. First, in practice, it is always possible to continue to work and pay contributions on earnings, even after a full annuity has been claimed. Additional work and contributions always enhance account values. Second, an annuity can always be converted into an account value and vice versa, using formula 2.3, at any time after retirement, using the expected payout period to make the conversion. Note also that it is possible to grant partial annuities—of any percentage—since it is technically easy to convert annuities back into account values and vice versa. This feature of the NDC scheme makes it very suitable for combining work and pensions in any proportion, enabling gradual retirement from the labor force.

In sum, the lifetime capital of an individual j from retirement is determined by his or her account at retirement, cohort life expectancy at retirement, and the internal rate of return, expressed as a norm based on the internal rate of return (with the deviation correction factor) or in the form of annual indexation with the internal rate of return. What's more, total (available) individual lifetime benefit payments in the NDC scheme can be distributed over the life cycle of the retiree, either weighting them more heavily toward the beginning of the retirement period or allowing them to increase gradually as the country's prosperity increases during the life annuity period.

THE INTERNAL RATE OF RETURN AND FINANCIAL BALANCE

The internal rate of return is the rate of return required to keep the scheme in financial balance, where financial balance is defined as the state where the present value of overall system assets $PV(A_t)$ equals the present value of total system liabilities $PV(L_t)$: that is,

$$PV(L_t) = PV(A_t). \tag{2.4}$$

System liabilities at any time t are the sum of all NDC commitments to all living participants, both workers and pensioners. Where the liability to worker i is $K_{i,t}$ and the liability to pensioner j is $P_{j,\tau}$ (where, for simplicity, τ denotes the date when members of cohort κ became pensioners)[7] total liabilities are

$$PV(L_t) = \Sigma K_{i,t} + \Sigma P_{j,\tau,t} \tag{2.5}$$

at time t. The present value of assets is the present value of the stream of future contributions for all workers in period t plus funded (technical) reserves. This can be expressed as

$$PV(A_t) = TD * \sum_{i=1}^{\psi} cw_{i,t} + Fund_t \tag{2.6}$$

where TD denotes the turnover duration of contribution assets. TD is a density function, developed and described in Settergren and Mikula (2006). In discrete terms, the density function in period t is the product of the earnings-weighted average number of years participants have worked based on the age-earnings profile in period t and the payment weighted average number of years payments have to be made in year t based on the payment profile in period t. The turnover duration of the contribution asset is the average time a unit of money (such as a dollar or a euro) is in the system. In a discrete time frame, TD represents a static time cross-section density of money flows in the system, as seen at time t. With each new period t there is potentially a new density of money flows, thus generating a new value of TD.

In the generic NDC model, both the accounts of workers during the accumulation period and the accounts of pensioners—converted into annuities—earn the same rate of return in a given period t.

In a steady state, defined by a fixed workforce-age-wage-distribution and fixed age-mortality rates, an NDC rate of return based on the (instantaneous) rate of growth of the contribution base is sufficient to maintain financial equilibrium. The rate of return is determined by the rate of growth of productivity, g, and the population, or more specifically in the actual pension context, the labor force, λ. In a steady state, the latter is determined by the rate of growth of the working-age population, and is what Samuelson (1958) called the biological rate of return.

The rate of return of $\lambda + g$ is not sufficient to maintain financial equilibrium[8] under various circumstances. Given any rate of economic growth—that is, $\lambda + g$—different distributions of contribution and benefit payment flows will affect the NDC scheme's ability to maintain temporal balance between assets and liabilities. In insurance terms, the *time* money remains in the system before it has to be paid out affects the instantaneous liquidity of the system. This is shown in Settergren and Mikula (2006) in the context of a more-than-two generation model, since two-generation models are not sufficient to bring out this feature.

If it were known in period t that a unit of money were to remain in the system some duration of time so that TD_t is greater or less than TD_{t-1}, then the value of assets according to expression 2.6 would change solely as a result of this, and this change would constitute a component of the internal rate of return

$$\rho = [\mathrm{PV}(A_t)/\mathrm{PV}(L_t)] - 1. \tag{2.7}$$

In the generic NDC scheme, this gives an internal *real* rate of return,

$$\alpha = g + \lambda + \rho, \tag{2.8}$$

also derived in Settergren and Mikula (2006). The component ρ constitutes an adjustment of the well-known real growth criterion, $g + \lambda$, which can arise in nonsteady state. In practice, an operative procedure has to be developed to determine the value of ρ, based on an estimate of liabilities and assets (see below). Also in practice, ρ will consist of a pure payment timing component and a component that picks up what can be called system "noise": that is, design features that can lead to a less than "ideal" outcome.

There is a market-based financial alternative to determining the internal rate of return. This would be for the government to issue Buchanan bonds to cover the liabilities of the system. Full market monetiziation of an NDC scheme through the issuance of Buchanan bonds can be criticized on two counts, however. First, if the wage sum, which using the terminology here is $\Sigma\, w_{i,t}$ (from equation 2.1) is proportionate to national income, or approximately so over the long run—which would be the case if the share of profits in income were constant over time—then contributions, which constitute new account assets, would also be a constant proportion of national income and the tax base. This means that new Buchanan bonds earn a government decreed rate of return, equal to growth of income, $\lambda_t + g_t$, and that the ratio of government Buchanan bond liabilities to national income could grow at the rate $\lambda_t + g_t$ for any given contribution rate, c, (and any given profit ratio). However, if the government were to set a rate of return on the Buchanan bonds of $\lambda_t + g_t$, this would be tantamount to running a nonmonetized NDC scheme with internal rate of return $\lambda_t + g_t$ but with a deadweight loss required to cover market issuance and transaction costs. This makes the nonmonetized NDC scheme more efficient.[9] In addition, this procedure would not account for the possible effects on system finances of the factor ρ.

Second, if the bond (which over time would have to be a series of bonds) were to be a normal government bond(s), the rate of return would depend on the government's status as a borrower on the market. In such a set-up, if the rate of return on bonds is greater than the rate of growth, the money transferred to NDC accounts through this mechanism would be financed by a tax on the same persons who are the workers and pensioners in the NDC scheme. This not only introduces transaction costs, but also rate of return and a time-related distributional profile that depend on the government's creditworthiness and market evaluation of government policy.

Properties of NDC

NDC is identified through a set of properties, which are satisfied by setting up the system as described above. These properties are:

Property 1. *At any time the present value of an individual's lifetime benefit equals the individual's account balance.*

For each participant and at all times, the amount in the account, K, is the present or expected value of his or her benefit. The value of the account is determined by the individual's own contributions and the system's internal rate of return. This is a first property of an NDC scheme. It can be stated (where E denotes the expected value) as

$$E(P_t) = K_t. \tag{2.9}$$

This is a property of a defined contribution system. Note that it has an important economic implication: Contributions constitute a payment for the individual's *own* pension, similar to premium payments to a financial account system. Fulfillment of this property is a necessary condition for a scheme to be called an NDC scheme.

Property 2. *To maintain a fixed contribution rate, total NDC system assets must equal or be greater than total liabilities.*

In the generic system, set out above, assets always equal liabilities. This gives a second property defining an NDC scheme

$$A_t \geq L_t. \tag{2.10}$$

Fulfillment of this property is necessary to maintain a constant long-term contribution rate. This is also a property that is consistent with a financial defined contribution scheme, where $A = L$. The process of individual account valuation distributes the returns among the participants in the generic NDC system, fulfilling the equality 2.10. In practice, design issues impose various constraints. As long as $A > L$, NDC schemes other than pure generic NDC schemes can also be called NDC schemes according to this definition.

Property 3. *The NDC benefit is constructed as a life annuity reflecting life expectancy at retirement.*

A key feature of an NDC scheme is that the annuity is based on life expectancy. A correct valuation of life expectancy leads to a correct valuation of the liabilities associated with annuity payments. Even if a lump-sum payment were theoretically possible, it is not a desirable feature of a mandatory system that aspires to protect people in old age (and tax-payers) from the temptations of short-sightedness or the results of otherwise poor planning or management of money.

> **Property 4**. *Financial balance in the generic system requires that accounts be valued at the internal rate $g + \lambda + \rho$.*

If in practice the rate of return is set lower, for example, by not factoring full real growth into the annuity, which may be the result of a policy restriction during the implementation phase[10] than compared with the counterfactual of generic NDC, a surplus arises—and if it is used for purposes other than accrediting accounts, then it should be viewed as a tax. If the system is monetized with Buchanan bonds, then the monetization process gives rise to transaction costs, which is also a tax, albeit a tax whose financial source is exogenous to the NDC system. In this case, it does not impede upon the function of the internal rate of return.

RESERVE FUND

All other things equal, if the NDC scheme is not monetized with Buchanan bonds, the occurrence of large and small fluctuating birth cohorts means that, ceteris paribus, contributions of large cohorts should be funded and paid out when the large cohorts become pensioners. If this is not done, there will be a tendency for the system to be out of financial equilibrium. For example, in a two-or-more-cohort world with a large and small cohorts, this would result in a situation where $L > A$ when large cohorts are working, with the difference between this outcome and $A = L$ being the amount of the "missing fund." With automatic balancing (see discussion below) the automatic balance would be triggered to restore the condition $A = L$. Also, the rate of return on reserves must be at least equal to the internal rate of return.

The reserve fund serves the purpose of collecting and disbursing the demographic balance. It would be difficult, if not impossible, to do this without the institution of the reserve fund. More generally, the reserve fund is a general buffer fund. Its sources of funds and withdrawals will depend on the exact design of the system.

A number of examples can be given of how design affects the reserves. One is that accounts can be augmented with noncontributory rights. These must have a source of financing, such as general tax revenues or a special contribution rate earmarked for this purpose, and these revenues should be transferred to the reserve fund. The financial source is the asset counterpart of the liability to the account holder. This money should also earn at least the rate of return accredited individual accounts of workers. A second example is a "tax overhang" from the old system, to be elaborated upon below, which should be quantified and funded—in the sense that it also needs to earn the internal rate of return.

A third example of the use of the reserve fund is the Swedish reform principle, which uses g to index accounts and benefits, based on the principle that the value of benefits should increase at the rate of growth of the per capita covered wage. A liquidity band is defined between the value $A/L = 1$ and some value greater than unity. As long as A/L remains within the band, the surplus remains as liquidity in the system, and the system is "insulated" from changes in $\lambda + \rho$ in expression 2.8. Liquidity in excess of the band ceiling is distributed according to a rule, and the automatic balancing mechanism (see below) balances the system for $A < L$. Within the band, no reserves are disbursed.

In practice, reserves are needed for other reasons, as will be discussed in the next section.

An NDC system is self-adjusting financially and can run without external intervention. The generic system is autonomous by construction, which is a result of fulfillling properties 1 through 4, and maintaining a reserve fund. Of course, whether politicians will let the system run free from intervention is another question.

Finally, no country has introduced the generic model as it is presented here. Design in implementation varies considerably among countries that have implemented varieties of NDC schemes. Where they generally differ is in the indexation rules chosen, and to date, only Sweden has legislated an ABM. There are many reasons for the deviations from the generic model. These include the transitional considerations of phasing in the indexation of new NDC benefits with the already existing stock of pension benefits at the time of implementation (Palmer 2006), political goals, and data and information requirements.

Automatic Balancing

Because system designs deviate from the generic model, in practice, equation 2.7 will encompass all design deviations from the generic model. Hence in practice, equation 2.7 yields

$$b_t = [\text{PV}(A_t)/\text{PV}(L_t)] - 1 \qquad\qquad (2.11)$$

where $b_t = \rho_t$ if the model is generic, but otherwise not. The value b_t is the factor with which the accounts of workers and annuities of pensioners needs to be adjusted to maintain balance. This is the automatic balancing mechanism (ABM).

The ABM mechanism is described as follows. If $\text{PV}(A_t) < \text{PV}(L_t)$, regardless of the cause, account values of workers and annuities of pensioners will have to be given a lower rate of return to bring the system back into financial equilibrium. On the other hand, the system can distribute a higher rate of return to participants if $\text{PV}(A_t) > \text{PV}(L_t)$. The ABM is used in the country in which it was conceived, Sweden.[11] Other countries adopting NDC have relied on system design that can be expected to give $A > L$ primarily as a result of not distributing all possible internal returns. This is tantamount to imposing a tax on returns and using the revenues for other purposes.[12]

Some examples of the most common sources of generic design deviations follow. One is that ex post mortality rates can deviate from the ex ante values used to compute life expectancy for newly granted annuities. Another is that annuities may cost more (or less) than thought ex ante. For example, persons with higher than average incomes (and contributions) may live longer, and the annuity factor may not be designed to account for this, or if it is, it might not do the whole job. Another form of generic deviation would be the choice to use the per capita rate, g, as the rate of return, rather than a measure closer to the internal rate of return. This choice can be motivated by the goal of maintaining a constant ratio of an average pension to an average wage. Yet another form of generic deviation is the choice of the wage sum rate $g + \lambda$ for indexation, instead of $g + \lambda + \rho$. Note also that, ceteris paribus, the choice of $g + \lambda$ for indexation would be the same as using g together with a balancing mechanism without the proposed Swedish liquidity interval.

There are more examples of how financial imbalance can arise. A rate of return on reserves that deviates from the rate accredited individual accounts also creates imbalance. Potential imbalance is also caused by the fact that in practice indices used to compute the rate of return need to be based on historical data, and probably a smoothing mechanism, which means they are always one or more periods behind. This may be no or only a small problem for random positive and negative fluctuations, but it can become a serious problem for negative trends, especially in λ, if g is the chosen system rate of return. Finally, there may be a liability overhang after conversion from the old DB to the new NDC scheme, with unfinanced liabilities. How a tax overhang should be dealt with is discussed below.

Valdés-Prieto (2006) presents an alternative to the ABM. He envisages market determination of the balancing mechanism through the issuance of a limited number of bonds with *property rights*, which he labels integration to financial markets, or IFM. He argues that full coverage of NDC debt is not essential to its valuation, and that a limited issuance of debt would be sufficient to enable the NDC rate of return to be determined by the market. It is not evident, however, why this rate of return would be preferable to $λ + g + ρ$.

Computing Life Expectancy

Some procedure must be adopted to compute life expectancy at retirement. At least three procedures can be employed in practice. These are described and discussed briefly in this section.

One approach is to form a committee of demographic experts, charged with the responsibility of performing analyses that lead to official cohort projections. Their proceedings, analytical report, and minutes from deliberations would be published to assure that the process is as transparent as possible. Revisions can be made annually, but with relatively accurate long-term projections from the outset, only small, infrequent revisions would be needed. Revisions would always apply to nonretired cohorts and would be greater the farther from retirement age the cohort is. The transparent process would support system autonomy from political interventions in the projection process.

A second approach is to base the estimates of birth-cohort life expectancy on known ex post cross-sectional survival data. This provides stronger protection from political intervention since it involves no process of judgment. However, inherent in this procedure is the almost certain risk that projections will lag behind reality, systematically creating higher than warranted annuities for older workers, ceteris paribus, shifting costs to future cohorts. This financial strain on the system is eventually rectified if the system design includes automatic balancing, but a distributional effect remains. Furthermore, all other things equal, this procedure yields an unfinanced deficit.

A third alternative is to use current (ex post) cross-sectional data and regularly adjust the benefits of all retirees in accordance with new life expectancy tables as they are revised. Compared with trying to get the projection right from the beginning, as in the first alternative, or burying the problem in the general error-correction mechanism, as in the second, the naked perpetual change model, although right on target, is nevertheless the least appealing for the policy maker. All other things equal, it means that the administrator will be constantly decreasing the value of the benefits of retirees of all ages as new life expectancy statistics become available. For some longer-lived pensioners, this process of benefit deflation could go on for over a quarter of a century. This method shares the ceteris paribus disadvantage of the second method, where the automatic balancing mechanism performs the task of balancing all possible causes of a deviation between assets and liabilities, including errors in projecting life expectancy.

On balance, the first and third approaches explicitly fulfill the criterion of financial balance, whereas the second and third provide greater autonomy, at least in principle, since they are based on actual outcomes, which presumably cannot be influenced by politicians. The first approach has a good chance of being autonomous, however, if its operation and proceedings are made transparent for the public.

Converting to NDC with a "Tax Overhang" from the Old DB Framework

A country may wish to introduce NDC but is confronted with what we will call a "tax overhang" from the previous system. A tax overhang can be defined vis-à-vis the counterfactual of having had an NDC scheme from the very outset, including a contribution rate fixed at some specific level. This is obviously a controversial statement, but the logic in it is that if the policy maker has decided that NDC is the best option, then it is consistent to view old pay-as-you-go commitments that cannot be financed by the contribution rate chosen for the NDC scheme as a tax overhang.

An example of a tax overhang would be the failure to create a fund for a large birth cohort of persons for whom most of their working careers have lapsed at the time of conversion to NDC. Another example would be old-system commitments that are more generous than those the NDC formula provides, and which the government decides to honor as a part of the transition to NDC. In principle, the tax overhang can be estimated and the government's commitment to honor it can be made transparent by including the debt to the system as a fund asset in equation 2.11, which defines total assets.

To finance the overhang, the government could transfer money or issue bond(s) to be held by the pension fund, yielding the internal rate of return, and which would be monetized at a pace needed to finance tax-overhang commitments. Alternatively, the amount owed would be kept on the books, and the government would finance the amount owed (with the internal rate of return) as payment commitments occur, through a tax levied as the liabilities have to be honored. In practice, there is no difference between these two methods, although issuing a bond has the formal advantage of being a more steadfast commitment.

NDC and Social Policy Considerations

The Scale of the System

The introduction of NDC does not mark the downfall of social policy. On the contrary, it provides a means for separating the goals of social policy from the goal of smoothing out individual consumption over the life cycle with the aid of a mandatory insurance scheme.

A first consideration is that the scale of the NDC scheme—like any other mandatory pension scheme—should be set so as not to impose unjustifiably on individual preferences regarding the time preference of consumption. For example, in poorer societies, a large pension in the future paid at the expense of current consumption can easily conflict with the obvious time preference of persons living in poverty who would prefer higher consumption in the present. This suggests a lower scale for the system and a high minimum pension age. On the other hand, in richer societies, many people—but never all—can prefer a lower scale to leave room for individual choices for work and saving over the life cycle. A reasonable scale goal in a developed market economy is to provide an adequately dimensioned NDC benefit in old age for the normal worker retiring at or close to the minimum retirement age, but leaving room for individual choice regarding consumption and leisure. The minimum retirement age needs to be set so that people cannot claim a benefit at an age that by definition gives an annuity that on average is too low, given that benefits are based on life expectancy from retirement.

Generally speaking, the size of an annuity is determined by individual preferences between work and leisure. In an NDC scheme, individuals themselves determine the timing and scope of their withdrawal from the labor market. If the tax rules provide equal treatment of pensions and earnings, an NDC scheme is neutral in the work-leisure decisions of older workers (at least above the guarantee level).

Also, NDC accounts are "infinitely" devisable. This means that only practical consider-ations determine what percent of a full annuity an individual can claim at any time—after reaching the minimum pension age—and it is possible to combine work and a pension in any proportions and at any age. Finally, NDC (like FDC), by basing benefits on individual accounts, facilitates labor mobility between occupations, branches, sectors of the economy, and regions of the country, or for that matter, between countries.

Minimum Pension Income—for the Elderly

By definition, although an NDC scheme provides some benefit for all who work and con-tribute to the scheme, it will not necessarily provide a benefit that gives sufficient income for all to live on. There will always be some in the population whose genetic and human capital—or other individual characteristics or circumstances—will lead to an insufficient NDC benefit.

Continuing with the discussion in the previous section, generally speaking, it is impor-tant to emphasize that the sufficiency of the NDC benefit depends on the minimum pen-sion age. Data on national pension systems reveal that people tend to exit the labor force at the minimum possible age, even though this may give them a low lifelong benefit. Part of the essence of the mandatory scheme is protect people from their own bad judgment in this sense. Also, the practice of setting lower pension ages for women, whose exit from the labor force may be timed to coincide with the exit of her (often older) spouse, itself can lead to poverty in old age for surviving women. Finally, it is reasonable to adjust (index) this age, once thoughtfully set, to changing longevity.

Given a reasonably set minimum pension age, some form of minimum income floor (for example, a guarantee or flat rate) is unavoidable. For various reasons, there will always be a certain part of the older population that will not have a sufficient contribution-based pension to live on. Therefore an NDC scheme will always need to be supported at the "zero" level by some form of external transfer paid by general tax revenues.

Finally, given some form of minimum income transfer floor for the worst-off in society, a threshold effect will occur at this floor level that may mean that additional contributions to the NDC scheme in old age will not have a counterpart in a benefit, in the sense that they do not bring the contributor above the guarantee level. Remaining in the formal labor force may nevertheless be worthwhile given individual preferences on work and leisure—or necessary, because of dire circumstances. In countries where the informal market is an important feature of the economic landscape, people may take their minimum benefit and (continue to) work informally. This could be regarded as an informal counterpart to flexi-ble retirement in a formal market economy.

Putting Distributional Policy into NDC

It is possible to supplement NDC (and FDC) schemes with noncontributory rights. What is essential, to maintain financial stability, is to finance these as they are granted, since these represent liabilities that need to have an asset counterpart in the financial balance. Since all contributions to the NDC scheme on earnings give rights directly to the contributing par-ticipant, there is no room to finance noncontributory rights from individual NDC contri-butions. Instead, these will have to be paid from other sources of public revenues.

The financing of noncontributory rights in the same accounting period in which they are granted keeps order in the system. The alternative would be for the accounting system to record a claim on the state budget (including the internal rate of interest), with the state making partial payments on this debt sometime in the future when it becomes time to honor the commitments. This creates a different payment distributional profile. In the worst case, a future government can decide not to honor these rights.

Finally, the principle of separating distributional aspects of policy from the pure NDC insurance system has the advantage of creating transparent distributional policy. All decisions to introduce a new distributional right must be specified clearly, including the source of finance identified.

The Connection to Disability Benefits

In most social insurance pension systems devised during the past century, disability benefits have been a part of the overall pension package. This is not true of an NDC scheme, which is an old age insurance scheme. Because of this, integration of disability into the NDC framework is an important issue. Before receiving disability, a worker will normally have had an account in the NDC system. In principle, the straightforward way to handle disability and NDC is to devise a rule for paying—that is, financing externally to the NDC scheme—contributions for the disabled during the remaining period up until the minimum pension age (or some other age at which a disability benefit is replaced by an old age benefit), and then to replace the disability pension with an old age benefit from the NDC scheme. The contribution rule chosen for financing the disability benefit will determine the coverage earned during the disability period.

Sharing NDC Accounts between Spouses

It is possible to share accounts between spouses in NDC. The principles of legal codes governing the financial affairs of spouses could also be extended to NDC accounts. The discussion that follows describes how this might work in practice. In doing so, it is important to distinguish between the accumulation period and the annuity period.

During the accumulation period, NDC capital earned prior to marriage (or some form of legal cohabitation, depending on national legislation) could remain with the individual, whereas capital earned during a marriage would be shared equally between the spouses. This capital would also be retained upon divorce, and would remain the individual's own capital upon entering into a new marriage.

Here two considerations are important. The first is whether the account division rule should be mandatory or voluntary, and the second is whether the default option should be joint accounts or single accounts. A main argument against mandatory sharing of accounts in a country where cohabitation is legally recognized is that persons uninterested in sharing accounts would choose not to marry, whereas some married people might even choose divorce plus cohabitation as a means to get around a mandatory system upon its introduction. The latter means that a cohabitation rule would also have to be devised, or that this behavior would have to be accepted.

Because of these possible behavioral responses, voluntary sharing of accounts can seem more appealing. Then the question is whether independent accounts should be the default, with a positive decision of both spouses required to enter into shared accounts, or whether shared accounts should be the default, requiring a joint decision to create separate accounts. Making joint accounts the default option certainly agrees well with other joint property arrangements for spouses. Joint accounts would always be to the advantage of the spouse with lower earnings and would help compensate for more time spent in non-market activities.

The next question is, should a joint annuity for spouses (cohabitants) be mandatory, voluntary, or not permitted at all in NDC? The goal of a joint annuity is to provide a better annuity in old age for the surviving spouse, generally women. Would this be fulfilled by entering into joint annuities? The answer to the question is empirical. If unisex life expectancy is used in computing the individual annuity, it is possible to find examples where women would lose with a joint NDC annuity.

To illustrate this, assume that women have on average lifetime earnings that are 80 percent of those of men, that unisex life expectancy is used in calculating the annuity, and that women have an expected (average) 15 percent transfer from men due to the difference in longevity. Sharing accounts equally would lead to a benefit for a woman based on 90 percent of her spouse's life income. However, if the single benefit alternative means that the average woman would receive a transfer that raises her benefit by 15 percent, due to the difference in the average life expectancy of men and women, she would receive a benefit amounting to $(0.8 \times 1.15) = 92$ percent of her spouse's income, which is superior to the benefit based on a straightforward splitting of pension rights. Generally speaking, shared accounts are to the disadvantage of women if their life earnings are close to or surpass those of men, but become advantageous as the lifetime earnings gap becomes large.

This illustration suggests that what seems to be a simple question turns out not to be so simple. A *mandatory* system requiring joint annuities at retirement could actually work against the goal of providing better benefits for many women. Seen over the long run it could also become counterproductive, as the gender earnings gap becomes small. A *voluntary* rule would provide an opportunity for spouses with relatively large lifetime earnings differences to share accounts, thereby providing an opportunity for the spouse with lower life earnings to secure a better benefit. A voluntary arrangement requires the consent of both spouses: that is, including the spouse with the higher life earnings. This sometimes may not give the desired result, but as a rule, it would be socially desirable. In sum, voluntary sharing of accounts, with sharing as the default, is an alternative in the accumulation period that reflects most country's legal arrangements for sharing of property between spouses; however, it requires special rules for cohabiting couples. Voluntary sharing of annuities is preferable to mandatory sharing of annuities, but the default should be chosen with respect to who the winners are expected to be. This is because the closer the earnings of women come to those of men, single annuities calculated with unisex life expectancy will be to the advantage of surviving women—who constitute the likely survivors.

Final Remarks

This study has established a generic conceptual framework for NDC pension schemes, an innovation that emerged as recently as the mid-1990s. Important design issues have been discussed. Still, it remains to continue to identify issues and improve our engineering as we gain experience.

Notes

1. "Notional defined contribution" and "non-financial defined contribution" should be understood to have the same definition.

2. See Samuelson (1958).

3. This is an accepted tenant of economics. See, for example, Lindbeck and Persson (2003); Valdés-Prieto (2006).

4. See, for example, Burtless (2003).

5. See Diamond (2003).

6. To date, two countries, Italy and Sweden, have included a rate of return in the annuity. Both use per capita covered income as the norm, rather than the internal rate of return (see below). Sweden applies the type of correction procedure described here. Italy has no legislated correction procedure.

7. Cohort κ is implicitly assumed to either all become pensioners in τ or to be normally distributed around τ so that it would be a "money-weighted" average date of retirement.

8. See, for example, Palmer (1999) and Valdés-Prieto (2000).

9. See Góra and Palmer (2004).

10. See Palmer (2006).

11. The ABM was first presented in the international literature in Settergren (2001).

12. For example, Latvia is using this tax to help finance the introduction of a mandatory individual financial account scheme.

References

Boskin, M., L. J. Kotlikoff, and J. Shoven. 1988. *A Proposal for Fundamental Social Security Reform in the 21st century*. Lexington, Mass.: Lexington Books.

Buchanan, J. 1968. "Social Insurance in a Growing Economy: A Proposal for Radical Reform." *National Tax Journal* December 21: 386–97.

Burtless, G. 2003. *Asset Accumulation and Retirement Income Under Individual Retirement Accounts. Evidence from Five Countries*. Washington, DC: The Brookings Institute.

Diamond, P. 2003. *Taxation, Incomplete Markets, and Social Security*. Munich Lectures in Economics—Center for Economic Studies. Cambridge, Mass. and London, England: MIT Press.

Góra, M., and E. Palmer. 2004. "Shifting Perspectives in Pensions." Institute for Study of Labor (IZA) Discussion Paper 1369. Bonn, Germany.

Iyer, S. 1999. *Actuarial Mathematics of Social Security Pensions*. Geneva: International Labour Office (ILO).

Lindbeck, A., and M. Persson. 2003. "The Gains from Pension Reform." *Journal of Economic Literature* XLI (March): 74–112.

Palmer, E. 1999. "Individual Decisions and Aggregate Stability in a NDC PAYG Account Scheme." Avaliable on: www.rfv.se/english.

———. 2000. "The Swedish Pension Reform Model: Framework and Issues." Social Protection Paper 0012, *Pension Reform Primer*. Washington, DC: World Bank.

———. 2006. "Conversion to NDCs—Issues and Models." *In Pension Reform: Issues and Prospects for Non-Financial Defined Contribution (NDC) Schemes*, ed. R. Holzmann and E. Palmer, chapter 9. Washington, DC: World Bank.

Samuelson, P. 1958. "An Exact Consumption-Loan Model of Interest With or Without the Social Contrivance of Money." *The Journal of Political Economy* 6 (December): 467–82.

Settergren, O. 2001. "The Automatic Balance Mechanism of the Swedish Pension System: A Non-technical Introduction," *Wirtschaftspolitishe Blätter* 4/2001: 339–49.

Settergren, O., and B. D. Mikula. 2006. "The Rate of Return of Pay-As-You-Go Pension Systems: A More Exact Consumption-Loan Model of Interest." In *Pension Reform: Issues and Prospects for Non-Financial Defined Contribution (NDC) Schemes*, ed. R. Holzmann and E. Palmer, chapter 7. Washington, DC: World Bank.

Valdés-Prieto, S. 2000. "The Financial Stability of Notional Account Pensions." *Scandinavian Journal of Economics* 102 (3): 395–417.

———. 2006. "A Market Method to Endow NDC Systems with Automatic Financial Stability." In *Pension Reform: Issues and Prospects for Non-Financial Defined Contribution (NDC) Schemes*, ed. R. Holzmann and E. Palmer, chapter 8. Washington, DC: World Bank.

Chapter 3

What Are NDC Systems?
What Do They Bring
to Reform Strategies?

*Axel H. Börsch-Supan**

THE PRESSURES EXERTED BY POPULATION AGING, amplified by the negative incentive effects that induce early retirement, make public pension systems unsustainable all over the world. The demographic pressures are strong in Europe because Europe's population is already relatively old. Demographic change is occurring particularly quickly in Asia. Japan shares both the European level and the Asian speed, an especially dangerous combination. Population aging is not sparing the more youthful United States, but the speed and level is slower. Aging also affects the developing countries and adds to their difficult economic and political problems. It comes as no surprise that pension reform is on the agenda in almost all countries of the globe.

Pension reforms seem to follow a wave-like pattern. After a wave of reforms and reform attempts with a strong stress on prefunding, not the least precipitated by the World Bank's 1994 book, *Averting the Old-Age Crisis: Policies to Protect the Old and Promote Growth*, the newest wave of reforms fashion "notional defined contribution" (NDC) systems.[1] This study's aim is to make a systematic assessment of such a reform strategy, in both economic and political terms.

This study poses two questions: what are NDC systems, and what do NDC systems bring to pension reform? It may come as a surprise that the second question in the title has more quickly been answered (and often with more confidence) than the first question.

This chapter goes back to square one. It begins with the first question. While there are large differences between a Beveridgian defined benefit (DB) pension scheme and an NDC system, and large differences between an NDC system and a prefunded defined contribu-

* Axel H. Börsch-Supan is director of the Mannheim Research Institute for the Economics of Aging (MEA) and professor of macroeconomics and public policy at the University of Mannheim, Germany.

This study takes as its point of departure and owes much in the way of intellectual debt to Disney (1999). This analysis has profited from Richard Disney's detailed comments, as well as those of Peter Diamond, Ed Palmer, Anette Reil-Held, and Christina Wilke, and from the lively discussion during and after the Sandhamn conference. Special thanks go to Nick Barr, Anna Hedborg, Robert Holzmann, Assar Lindbeck, Michal Rutkowski, and Salvador Valdés-Prieto. The German National Science Foundation (DFG) and the Gesamtverband der Deutschen Versicherungswirtschaft (GDV) provided additional financial support. The usual disclaimer applies.

tion (DC) system, the difference between Bismarckian DB pension schemes and NDC systems is less clear-cut, in terms both of the underlying economic substance and the perception in the political arena.

This study thus provides a taxonomy of pension systems that helps structure answers to both questions. The analysis shows how blurred the distinction between conventional DB and NDC systems can become, and tries to condense the economic meaning of NDC.

Our answer to the second question follows the same line. Properly designed NDC systems can contain very powerful economic and political mechanisms that may facilitate pension reform, such as transparency and accountability. Cleverly designed DB systems, however, may often do the same job—and in some circumstances may be even better. Whether NDC systems bring new life into the pension debate is therefore a question of the historical path and the nature of the debate in each country.

The second section sets the stage by stressing the most important challenges that NDC systems are supposed to master. The third section is conceptual and devoted to the first question in the chapter. It defines an NDC system on the mechanical level and then proceeds to extract its economic and political core. The study contrasts this to DB and FDC schemes. The fourth section answers the second question. It discusses the pros and cons of an NDC system in terms of economics, the perception of workers and pensioners, and the political process. The fifth section provides a real-life example of a well-known conventional DB system, which almost perfectly mimics an NDC system. This is the German "point system" augmented by a so-called sustainability factor as proposed by the German government's reform commission for the "sustainability in financing the social insurance systems." The sixth section concludes and picks up the challenges described in the second section: which of those challenges can be mastered by NDC systems, and which challenges must be addressed by other economic and political mechanisms, notably prefunding?

The Challenges

The first and foremost challenge to pension systems around the globe is *population aging*, long ago heralded by often-cited publications such as OECD (1988) and World Bank (1994). The consequences of demographic change have now reached many countries in a perceptible way. Population aging is becoming one of the secular "mega trends" of the new century.

Demographic change has two distinct components: a decline in fertility and an increase in longevity. The fertility decline is most pronounced in Europe and occurred as a historically unparalleled and in many countries rather sudden sequence of the baby boom in the late 1950s and early 1960s, followed by the baby bust in the 1970s. In the developing countries, fertility decline has been less sudden, but is still steady and incisive. The secular increase in life expectancy is largely due to the progress in medical technology. With an unchanged or even declining retirement age, the increase in longevity has led to a massive expansion of pension systems.

Coping with these two demographic developments requires two strategies. To deal with the sudden decline in fertility due to the baby boom/baby bust transition, a reduction of the pay-as-you-go (PAYG) replacement rate for the baby boomers and, simultaneously, an increase of privately financed prefunded pensions substituting for part of the PAYG pensions seems unavoidable in those countries that already have very high payroll taxes. Increasing longevity, in turn, is most naturally addressed by an increase of the length of working life: that is, a higher retirement age.

Demography is, however, not the only challenge to current pension systems. The European economies—and not only they—face two deeply routed macroeconomic problems:

poor growth and *high unemployment*. The most pressing goal of economic policy is therefore to increase employment (and thereby growth), not the least in order to provide the economic base that should support the social security systems in general, and the pension system in particular. If at least a part of pension contributions is perceived as distortionary taxes, the demographic and macroeconomic challenges interact with each other through the wedge that pension contributions drive between total labor costs paid by employers and net earnings received by employees. Germany is a striking example of a country where population aging and macroeconomic weakness combine to create serious economic problems. Germany has the lowest economic growth rate among all European Union (EU) countries. At the same time, Germany has by far the highest labor costs (total hourly labor compensation) within the EU.[2] Much of the thinking of current German pension reform is guided by the conviction that the goal of more growth demands more employment, and more employment demands at least a stabilization of—or better yet, a reduction of—payroll taxes and tax-like contributions.

Stabilizing or reducing contribution rates, however, requires cost cutting. This can be done by shifting the retirement age or by reducing pension benefits. Both reform strategies cut deeply into existing claims. It is an illusion to sell the necessary structural reform steps as a "win-win" situation. Neither a reduction of the replacement rate nor an increase of the retirement age is popular. To minimize negative coalitions against reform, employees should therefore be able to choose as flexibly as possible between the two unpopular options.

Many people, particularly in Europe, view pension systems as social achievements that one must defend, no matter how much the demographic and macroeconomic environment has changed. Hence a change of paradigm is necessary from thinking what one wishes to claim toward thinking what can be financed. This requires a change in the rhetoric of our pension systems; it also requires a transparent statement of the costs of the current systems that support this rhetoric.

There are further *political challenges*. Confidence in the PAYG pension systems has been steadily declining during the past two decades (Börsch-Supan and Miegel 2001). This poses a huge political challenge since every reform must prove that things will eventually get better than without reform. Rhetoric alone will not bring confidence back, in particular because it has been discredited in the past. What is needed—not only for a change of paradigm, but also to restore confidence—is transparency and a credible reform process. Adjustment processes should be gradual. Any kind of emergency operations undermine credibility. The recent history of German reform provides bad examples. These include the 2000 unexpected discretionary indexation rule change and the 2002 contribution rate hikes. These occurred after much of the liquidity reserve had been given up during the last business cycle upturn, exposing the pension system to sudden changes and thereby further undermining confidence in the PAYG system.

Another challenge consists in the many *bad microeconomic design features* in existing PAYG systems that create negative incentive effects. DB systems that base benefits solely on the final year of earnings, for example, do not reward additional years of work and yield incentives for strongly backloaded earnings. Other examples are systems that provide benefits that are not actuarially related to retirement age. There is strong evidence that the negative incentive effects exerted by such systems have shifted the effective retirement age to substantially earlier ages, and thus contributed to the financial pressures on PAYG systems.[3] In Germany, early retirement makes up for almost 25 percent of the old-age pension budget, corresponding to almost 5 percentage points of the contribution rate.[4]

Negative labor supply incentives are an important reason to make contributions closely reflect pension benefits (the "equivalence" or "insurance principle"). This will minimize the tax-character of contributions. Ideally, a fully equivalent pension system with an internal rate of return equal to a suitably risk-adjusted capital return has no tax-character at all. In turn, violating the equivalence principle, providing relatively low rates of return, and a lack of credibility all add to the tax-character of contributions and thus to labor market distortions. In a similar vein, flexibility to choose the date for retirement entry and the abolition of earnings tests minimize distortions in the choice between labor and leisure and should therefore also minimize tax-like distortions.

In summary, the challenges are manifold. Population aging creates financial pressures on pension systems, requiring unpopular cuts in benefits and the duration of retirement. Macroeconomic growth and employment problems are amplified by pension systems if and when pension contributions are perceived as distortionary taxes. Reforms may lack political credibility in the same way as the underlying PAYG systems have lost their credibility. A host of bad design elements on the microeconomic level requires fixing to minimize negative incentive effects.

Notional Defined Contribution Systems

NDC systems are supposed to address these economic and political challenges. Proponents argue that NDC systems make a large step to solve all these problems in one big stroke. [5] Skeptics argue that they add little that is new but may distract from deeper reform.[6]

NDC systems were legislated in 1994 in Sweden and in 1995 in Italy, among other countries. In Sweden, the new system was introduced for all employees with a 15-year transition period. It will be fully implemented within a few years from now. Palmer (2000) provides a good description of the Swedish NDC system and its introduction. In Italy, the NDC system was introduced as part of the so-called Dini-Reform with a very long transition period. It will be relevant only for workers who are younger than the baby boom generation. Franco and Sartor (2006) provide a critical evaluation. While Sweden and Italy are the most cited examples of NDC systems, Latvia and Poland have actually served as trial grounds for these reforms.[7] What are NDC systems? What are their mechanics, and what is the economic essence of NDC systems?

The Mechanics of an NDC System

NDC systems are accounting devices that treat a PAYG system like a DC system. Pension benefits are paid out of current contributions, as in a conventional PAYG system; however, the link between benefits and contributions is individualized and defined by the NDC accounting mechanism. Later this study will describe a "pure" NDC system as a special form of a "pure" PAYG system. In real life, almost all PAYG systems, and especially NDC systems, have a buffer fund, which make them "mixed" PAYG-funded systems.

Like any other DC system, the system starts with the individual contributions to the pension system, which are credited to, and accumulated on, individual accounts kept by the pension system. The balance is fictitious (or "notional"), since no capital is accumulated. The accumulated sum represents the fictitious (or "notional") pension wealth.

The balance earns interest at some rate of return. The magnitude of this return is a central parameter of the NDC system. Since no capital is accumulated and the claims on the balance are not traded, there is no market-mechanism to determine the rate of return.[8] Viewed from a macroeconomic perspective, the "natural" rate of return for an NDC system is the implicit return of a PAYG system: that is, the growth rate of the contribution bill. However, some NDC systems—such as the Swedish system—have chosen rates of return, which are higher under current circumstances, such as the rate of wage growth.

When entering retirement, the notional pension wealth is converted into a lifelong pension ("*annuitized*") according to actuarial rules. The annual pension benefit depends on three variables:

- The notional pension wealth (proportionality guarantees equivalence)
- The interest rate used to compute the annuity (using the implicit rate of return from the PAYG system guarantees equivalence within each birth cohort), and
- Life expectancy at retirement (using up-to-date cohort-specific life tables guarantees actuarial sustainability).

The two last elements are often combined and referred to as "annuitization divisors" or "G-values" in Sweden and Latvia.[9] In Italy, these values have been tabulated. Benefits B are then

$$B = PW/G,$$

where NPW denotes the notional pension wealth.

Including the implicit rate of return from a PAYG system and including the expected length of retirement in the benefit calculation links pension benefits to the demographic and employment parameters of the macroeconomic environment. This makes NDC systems more sustainable than conventional DB systems in the sense that changes in the demographic and macroeconomic environment automatically lower benefits.

Including the remaining life expectancy links benefits to the retirement age at the individual level. This makes NDC systems actuarially neutral (at the employed rate of interest).

Since the present discounted value (PDV) of pension benefits is independent from the actual retirement age, the financial burden of the younger generation is fixed for each cohort and determined by the G-value: that is, the notional interest rate and the expected average duration of retirement.

The actual properties of an NDC system depend on many detailed design features. They are discussed below. At this point, three features are worth noting. First and foremost, the determination of the "notional" interest rate is central since it governs both the demographic and macroeconomic sustainability of the system and the microeconomic incentive effects. Second, it makes a big difference which life tables are used. Third, the extent to which retirees are protected from future shocks is an important parameter potentially conflicting with financial sustainability.

NDC accounting systems do not change the mechanics of PAYG systems: that is, the necessity to adapt either the contributions or the replacement rate (or both) to changes in the demographic or macroeconomic environment. This is an important point. The current young generation pays the current old generation. The determination of the notional interest rate and the estimated remaining life expectancy amounts to the specification of the link between benefits (represented by some replacement rate) and contributions (represented by some payroll-tax rate). By changing this link, the system can shift the burden of population aging between the younger and the older generation. A pure NDC system, however, is still financed purely PAYG, and thus cannot mimic a prefunded system in the sense that the financial burden of a cohorts' worth of pension benefits will be carried by that same cohort.

The significance of this point is most clearly seen in the sudden transition from a thick baby boom to a thin baby bust generation. If the thick baby boom generation should finance a major part of their retirement income out of their own income, rather out the income of the much thinner baby bust generation, the baby boomers need to give up some consumption early in life and transfer the corresponding resources to their postretirement period. This requires saving and the build-up of a real capital stock by the baby boomers. A notional capital stock cannot serve this purpose because the annuities computed from the national wealth accumulated by the baby boomers have to be financed by the contributions of the baby bust generation.

The Economic Essence of an NDC System

Stripped down to its economic essence, there are three crucial mechanisms that make a PAYG system an NDC system:

1. An accounting mechanism that credits all lifetime earnings
2. A mechanism linking the final balance with the demographic and macroeconomic environment
3. An actuarial rule converting the final balance into an annuity.

To emphasize the last point made in the preceding subsection, a fourth element can be added, which distinguishes pure notional from fully funded DC plans:

4. Claims on future benefits are not collaterized with real capital but promises by a (almost always) government-related entity.

The first mechanism is realized by crediting all lifetime contributions to an individual account, just like funded DC plans. In many respects, this parallels the German and French point systems, except that the unit of credit is currency (euros), not earnings points.[10] It differs substantially from the many pension systems in which only the X best years are credited (at the extreme, only the earnings of the final year of work), and of course from Beveridgian systems that provide flat benefits.

The second mechanism is realized in NDC systems by the notional interest rate—if chosen to be the internal rate of return of a PAYG system—that reflects demographic changes, employment changes, and productivity changes, since the contribution bill grows with the rate at which the number of contributors and their labor productivity increases. This mechanism parallels the indexation rules of conventional DB systems. Most pension systems index their benefits at retirement to the current wage level. Most conventional PAYG systems add discretionary adaptations of the replacement rate to demographic changes; one of the main features of NDC systems is the direct and automatic linkage to demography once the notional interest includes the growth rate of the contribution base. In funded DC plans, the demographic and macroeconomic environments enter benefits through exactly the same mechanism as in NDC systems: namely through the rate of interest—although the applicable rates of interest are generally different.

The third mechanism is the essence of the $B = NPW/G$ rule. Proportionality between B and NPW and an actuarially correct determination of the G-values makes an NDC system actuarially neutral and, within each cohort, also actuarially fair (see Disney 2003 for this taxonomy). Some conventional PAYG systems have actuarial adjustments, notably the U.S. social security system between age 62 and 65. Most funded DC plans are automatically actuarially neutral, since conversion to an annuity takes place at actual retirement. Many DB-type PAYG systems, however, have no or little linkage between annual benefits and retirement age.[11]

A Taxonomy of Pension Systems

How close are NDC systems to funded DC systems? And how close are they to conventional PAYG-financed DB systems? The taxonomy in table 3.1 serves to clarify matters. It distinguishes pension systems by four dimensions that are closely related to the four elements listed in the preceding subsection. The many possible design features in real life, however, add additional complexity to these four dimensions. We do not claim that all dimensions are covered (such as voluntary vs. mandatory).[12]

One of the main features of table 3.1 is that all the dimensions provide a continuum of allocations within each dimension. NDC systems often enforce an extreme position along a dimension, but conventional DB systems may come close in some of the dimensions of table 3.1.

In terms of *crediting contributions*, NDC systems do indeed take an extreme position: contributions are credited on a lifetime basis and earlier contributions get a higher weight according to the rate of interest. While the German point system also credits all lifetime contributions, the point system weights all contributions equally, independent of time. This corresponds to ignoring compound interest (see below). The French point system credits only the best 25 years. The U.S. social security system permits taking out the five worst years, which creates less labor supply disincentives than the French system. Many systems in developing countries use earnings only from the final year of work.[13] In strictly Beveridgian systems such as the Dutch or British base pensions, credits do not play a role in the determination of benefits at all since benefits are flat.[14]

NDC systems feature a "natural" *accrual of interest* through the crediting mechanism. However, the conversion factor between benefits at retirement and the sum of contributions over the working life can be interpreted as crediting all accrued interest at the time of retirement.[15] While the latter mechanism ignores compound interest because it does not matter when contributions are paid over the working life, there is no other genuine difference between NDC systems and a DB formula that (implicitly) credits the accrued interest at retirement. The determination of the rate of interest is another matter. In a funded system, the internal rate of return is r, the market rate of interest. In a PAYG system, it is $n + g$, where n is the rate of growth of the contribution base, and g is the growth rate of labor productivity. In Sweden, the government chose g as the notional rate of interest, leaving out a

Table 3.1. Dimensions of Pension Systems

1. Credits for contributions

Base:	Life-long . . . . Best X years . . . . Final salary . . . . Flat
Weights:	Early contributions earn interest . . . . Equal (point system)

2. Accrual of interest

Rate:	r (market) . . . . g (wages) . . . . $n + g$ (Aaron-Samuelson)

3. Conversion to benefits

Conversion:	Linear (equivalence) . . . . Concave (redistributive)
Indexation:	NDC: $B = NPW/G$ . . . . DB: $B =$ f(credits, other; accrual rate)
Actuarial:	Neutral at retirement (at the margin) . . . . Flat
Risk:	Benefits frozen at retirement . . . . Indexation rules . . . . Fully adjustable

4. Funding

Extent:	No fund at all . . . . Reserve buffer . . . . Fully funded
Collateral:	None . . . . Government bonds . . . . Commercial bonds/stocks

Source: Author's compilations.

direct link of accruing interest to demography.[16] In an aging population, $n + g$ tends to be smaller than g since n is negative, and it is in most circumstances much smaller than r.[17]

The third dimension relates to the *conversion* of the accumulated notional wealth *into benefits* at and after retirement. There are four elements in that conversion. First, how are individual credits related to individual benefits? NDC systems use simple proportionality by applying the $B = NPW/G$ rule. Some DB systems have the same proportionality, such as the point systems in France and Germany or systems with a simple accrual rate rule. The U.S. social security system credits additional contributions at a decreasing value; the system redistributes through a concave linkage function between contributions and benefits. In a strictly Beveridgian system, credits play no role at all, as mentioned before.

This third dimension includes an important aspect of practical pension policy: namely, how strictly these rules are adhered to. The Swedish NDC and the German DB system attempt to avoid discretionary decisions. In both countries, the benefit rules are actually written into the law as mathematical formulae. So far, this attempt has been successful in Sweden, and also in Germany, with some notable exceptions between 1999 and 2001. Discretionary deviations have taken place more often in the French point system. The Italian NDC system leaves ample room for discretionary adaptations to the political climate. The future has yet to show whether the political risk is smaller in NDC systems than in conventional DB systems.

The second element in this third dimension is how benefits are related to the demographic and macroeconomic environment. In NDC systems, this is expressed in the G-values. Conventional DB systems usually have benefit indexation rules that link the benefits at retirement to the current wage or earnings level, and then continue to index benefits to prices, wages, or a combination of the two during the retirement period.[18] They fail to include demographic factors directly, although there may be indirect linkages. Indexation to net wages, for instance, where net means net of taxes and contributions, entails an indirect linkage since rising contributions, precipitated by population aging, will also reduce benefits. There is nothing, however, to prevent DB formulae from including direct linkages to demography to increase the elasticity of benefits with respect to demographic changes. This study presents a concrete example below.

The third element is the relation between retirement age and benefits. NDC systems are automatically actuarially neutral in the sense that the PDV of benefits is not affected by the actual retirement age if the PDV is computed at the internal rate of return of the NDC system. However, workers may use a different rate of interest when they are computing the PDV in order to make retirement decisions. This difference then creates a wedge between actuarial neutrality and the absence of labor supply disincentives. The latter is defined as the case in which the PDV of benefits is independent of the retirement age, if the PDV is computed using the personal discount rate of workers. The crucial question is then, what is the personal discount rate of workers? If it is the market rate of interest, then it is usually larger than the internal rate of return of the NDC system, especially in times of aging populations.[19]

This is an important point: NDC systems may be actuarially neutral, but they may still create substantial labor supply disincentives. The root cause for this distinction is the difference in the discount rates that are applied to the actuarial adjustment. There are at least three candidates: (1) the internal rate of return, which is $n + g$ in a PAYG system, independent of whether it is NDC or conventional DB; (2) the market rate of interest r, which is also the internal rate of return of a funded system; and (3) the rate of time preference of the employees who make the retirement decision. As noted, the market rate of interest r tends to be higher than $n + g$. While one may argue that the average rate of time preference should be approximately equal to the market rate of interest, the empirical evidence shows that the workers' rate of time preference, guiding their retirement behavior, is even larger than r.

Hence NDC systems may be more incentive-neutral, when they apply large discount rates, than DB systems, which apply very small adjustments of annual benefits to retirement age. For example, the adjustment in Germany is 3.6 percent per year phased in after 2001; see discussion below. NDC systems are certainly less distortionary than systems in which annual benefits are completely independent of retirement age (such as the German system before 2001). On the other hand, NDC systems may distort the retirement decision more than DB systems that apply rather large adjustments (such as the UK system, with adjustments of 9 percent per year, which is likely to be closer to the personal rate of time preference). NDC systems may provide a most "natural" way to compute retirement-age specific adjustments; but again, there is nothing intrinsic in this respect that distinguishes NDC from DB systems with actuarial neutral (or larger) adjustments such as the U.S. social security system at age 62 to 65.

The fourth element is the indexation of benefits *after* retirement (different from the indexation, or anchoring, of benefits *at* retirement). Conventional DB systems index benefits after retirement to cost of living (United States, Italy's new system) or net wages (France, Germany) or some combination in between (Switzerland). In funded DC systems, this is represented by the type of annuity (real or nominal, or any other schedule). The Swedish NDC system freezes the benefits in real terms, corresponding to a cost-of-living indexation, but other NDC systems have other indexation mechanisms. Again, NDC systems provide no special features in this respect.

By now, it should be clear that NDC systems are accounting devices with properties that can be introduced in DB systems as well (although that may not be easy politically). They may serve to provide more transparency and credibility because some features come more "naturally" in an NDC system than through complex formulae in a DB system; however, it is more rhetoric than economic substance that distinguishes NDC and DB systems. In fact, there are conditions under which NDC and DB schemes are mathematically equivalent, as Lindeman, Robalino, and Rutkowski show (2006).

The discussion below presents the example of the new German DB system, which almost perfectly mimics an NDC system. Table 3.1 has shown the complexity by which pure PAYG systems may differ from one another, and the distinction between NDC systems and "modern" DB systems is much smaller than between "modern" and "traditional" DB systems.

How is NDC different from a funded DC plan? This is addressed in the fourth dimension of table 3.1. Most PAYG systems have some reserve fund, although the size of it varies greatly. The Swedish reserve fund amounts to some five years of expenditures, while the German system's reserve fund is minimal, with a few days worth of expenditures. The crucial question, however, is whether the accumulated balances are collateralized and which claims represent the collateral. NDC systems are "notional" in the sense that there is no collateral at all. Balances are claims against future taxpayers, and they are not backed by a financial instrument.[20] Funded DC plans are usually understood as being collateralized against physical capital, mostly through financial instruments such as commercial bonds or stocks. We use the word "funded" only for these plans. Some authors also call those DC plans that are collateralized with government bonds "funded." We think that this is a misuse of the word "funded." Although benefit claims of such plans are marketable and yield a well-defined rate of interest, they do not represent claims on physical capital. NDC systems may permit a "natural" way to make the implicit debt of a PAYG system explicit by linking the NDC balances to government bonds, and the resulting insights about future benefits and contributions may create saving incentives on the microeconomic level.[21] However, NDC systems and conventional DB systems share the crucial macroeconomic features of PAYG systems: NDC systems do not accumulate savings in real assets with the potential beneficial side effects on the national saving rate, capital market development, and growth.[22] NDC systems are therefore no substitute for prefunding.

Pros and Cons of Notional Defined Contribution Systems

Now consider the chapter's second question: what do notional contribution systems bring to pension reform? What are their advantages and disadvantages? As the preceding sections showed, NDC systems can almost perfectly be mimicked by conventional DB systems. Thus this discussion focuses on the psychological and political aspects of a new rhetoric. This does not mean that this study ignores the microeconomic implications of transparency and credibility. This study will stress that they are important for pension reform. They are, however, sometimes quite subtle and indirect.

Advantages

An NDC system has many advantages:

- It adapts itself automatically through an internal interest mechanism to the changed balance of contributors to pensioners (*baby boom/baby bust problem*) without the necessity to intervene in a discretionary way.
- It adapts itself automatically to changed life expectancies (*longevity problem*) through the actuarial conversion of the notional pension wealth into a lifelong pension. Reductions for early retirement result automatically and are automatically adapted to the demographic situation. (This adaptation is incomplete when benefits are frozen at retirement and pensioners are effectively insulated against subsequent changes of longevity.)
- It avoids *arbitrariness* of benefit indexation rules, adjustment factors, and so on, the change of which have undermined the *credibility* of many unfunded DB systems.
- It strengthens the *equivalence principle* and for this reason minimizes the wedge between gross and net income, which results from the distortionary impact of taxes and tax-like contributions.
- It adds *transparency* to the PAYG pillar by clearly identifying individual contributions and the resulting benefit claims, helping to regain credibility.
- It strengthens the principle that pensions are based on *lifelong earnings*, and honors employees who enter the labor market early.
- It allows *transfer mechanisms* to be easily identified as in-lieu contributions: notably tax-financed credits for higher and vocational education and similar credits for educating children.
- It creates a framework that can consistently be enlarged to a *general "accounting system"* of all PAYG subsystems. The advantages and disadvantages of joining subsystems (such as civil servants and the self-employed) will become immediately obvious in such an accounting system.
- It produces a suitable framework for *independent pensions of spouses*.
- It creates a *homogeneous paradigm* for the first, second, and third pillar of a multiple-pillar system; hence, it may increase the acceptance of the second and third pillar,

which are regarded as "alien" system components in those countries that used to have a monolithic first-pillar dominated pension system.

- It permits a considerable amount of *flexibility* for employees in choosing their retirement age; makes the inflexible and politically problematic fixation of a "normal" retirement age superfluous; and exposes the trade-off between accumulated contributions and retirement age in an internally consistent fashion.
- It permits easy *portability* of pension rights between jobs, occupations, and sectors.

Disadvantages

One of the main strengths of NDC systems, namely transparency, comes with some obvious disadvantages in the political realm:

- The financial situation of an unsustainable PAYG system becomes more obvious since workers "see" their declining benefits (while contribution rates are increasing) on their own accounts—thereby translating a general knowledge about the financial situation of the pension system into a personal concern. This is the flip side of the advantage of transparency: it may turn into a disadvantage because this may undermine confidence even further.
- If the contribution rate is fixed, the replacement rate becomes uncertain since it is dependent on the future development of earnings and demography. The replacement rate cannot serve any longer as a political instrument. This is of course the essence of a defined contribution system, including a notional one, but the uncertainty will become painfully visible in an NDC accounting system.
- The system does not change the tension between declines in business cycle-related earnings and long-term spending commitments. Therefore, a genuine liquidity reserve is necessary. In countries where it has been depleted, it must be rebuilt, even if this means sacrificing lower contribution rates or installing higher ones, especially during business cycle upswings. Some countries, such as Sweden, have the historical gift of a buffer fund that is sufficiently large to mitigate even a substantial part of the demographic shock in the decades to come.
- If the annuity is frozen at the beginning of retirement, a stabilizing feedback mechanism is missing if there is an unexpected rise in life expectancy. With a fixed contribution rate, the system will not automatically obey the annual budget restriction of a conventional PAYG system.[23] In Sweden, a complex "automatic balancing mechanism" was introduced to overcome this problem.[24]
- Discretionary decisions are not absent; they are simply more hidden. They take place at the choice of life table, computation rules (such as the averaging) for the internal rate of return, the determination of a minimum retirement age, and so on.
- The system does not change the fact that only prefunding can change which generation pays for a given pension benefit. If one wants to have the workers of generation X at least partially pay for their own pension, rather than their children in generation X + 1, some extent of prefunding is necessary. An NDC system is no replacement for such partial funding. It is only an optimization of the PAYG pillar.

Design Details

This is not the place to discuss the many design issues that must be resolved in order to establish an NDC system.[25] Only some especially important ones are discussed below:

- Like any other PAYG system, a *minimum age* must be established when healthy workers may begin to receive a pension. Such a minimum retirement age is necessary unless one makes the participation in the PAYG system optional—which is not a sta-

ble solution, especially in times of population aging. None of the existing NDC systems has an automatic adjustment of the minimum retirement age to longevity.
Hence the existing systems respond only partially to demographic changes.

- Specification and updating of life tables have immediate consequences for benefits.
  Most countries so far have adapted *unisex life tables* based on cross-sectional data.[26]
  What is actuarially correct are cohort tables, with some projection for changes in life
  expectancy. Many countries do not have a reliable mechanism to compute such
  tables. An independent board of actuaries should supervise the construction of such
  tables, and the life tables should be consistent with those used in the private pension
  sector.

- The *internal interest of the contributions* (growth rate of the contribution bill) must be
  smoothened over time. Several models are on hand. A moving average across a business cycle seems to be the natural choice. Peaks should be leveled off to flow into the
  liquidity reserve, used for the troughs of a cycle. Designing such smoothening mechanisms is not trivial since the amplitude and duration of a business cycle is not
  known in advance, and there is no foolproof mechanism to distinguish trends from
  cycles.

- Since the internal rate of return of a PAYG system is in general substantially lower
  than the workers' discount rates, *incentive effects to retire early* may still be large if later
  pension uptake is governed by actuarial neutrality. From a macroeconomic point of
  view, it is not obvious whether actuarial neutrality (using the internal rate of return
  of the PAYG system) or absence of incentive effects (using the workers' discount rate)
  is welfare maximizing.

- There are many ways to design the *annuities*. They can be chosen to rise with inflation
  or with wages, or any other schedule; the initial level is adjusted accordingly, holding PDV over expected duration constant. The freedom to choose is probably more
  important than potential problems with adverse selection. However, there is little
  experience around the world so far with such trade-offs.

- Benefits are determined at the beginning of retirement, but the demographic and
  economic environment may unexpectedly change after such determination. If the
  growth rate of contributions, measured in nominal terms, is very low, pensions may
  fall in real terms, which is politically unattractive. Some adaptation to the new environment is probably optimal, but pensioners seem to value protection quite highly.
  The overall welfare-maximizing policy is not known so far. As emphasized earlier, if
  pensioners are fully protected from demographic and economic changes taking place
  after they entered retirement, NDC systems lose an important feedback mechanism,
  which may undermine long-run financial sustainability. If pensions are protected by
  a floor (for example, never to fall in real or nominal terms), the system can become
  financially unbalanced because expenditures and contributions are treated asymmet-
  rically: Expenditures cannot fall below a certain floor, while contributions can.

- The *rules for the transition period* should follow the Swedish model, not the Italian
  one.[27] The extremely lengthy Italian transition time does not permit the NDC system to address the most urgent financial problem: the strain on the pension budget that will occur when the baby boom generation retires. A more difficult
  question is the extent to which existing pensions should be protected. "Natural"
  transition paths can be constructed when benefits are defined pro rata in proportion to the time spent under current and new law. The transition can be faster if
  important design elements of an NDC system are already in place. In Germany,
  for instance, a relatively short transition period (from 2005 through 2020) would

be possible because the existing point system has an important feature of NDC systems already in place.

A Blend of DB and NDC: The German Point System and the Sustainability Indexation

This final section uses the proposed new German public pension system as an example of a DB system that quite closely mimics an NDC system. There are three main elements of the German public pension system: the point system of credits, the actuarial adjustments, and the benefit indexation formula. During the recent pension reform process,[28] these elements have been changed consistently in the direction of NDC-type pensions.

The *point system*, described in detail further below, has been a feature of the German pension system since its conversion to a PAYG system in 1957. *Actuarial adjustments* were legislated by the 1992 reform; they have been phased in since 1997, with the bulk of adjustments in force by 2007. As a result, effective retirement ages are expected to increase by about two years within the next ten years.[29] In 2001, the so-called Riester reform made a first step from a purely pay-as-you-go to a capital-funded pension system. It established upper limits to the contribution rate, discontinued the benefits indexation formula, and substantially lowered pension levels. At the same time, the Riester reform introduced state-subsidized supplementary private pensions ("Riester pensions") to fill the upcoming pension gap. However, these reforms did not suffice to stabilize public pension finances. In late fall of 2002, the government established a reform commission to achieve "sustainability in financing the social insurance systems." A broad majority of this commission took the view that the upper limit of the contribution rate legally anchored by the Riester reform must be adhered to, and consequently changed the *benefit indexation formula* to follow an income-oriented policy. This change has been approved by the government and passed the Bundestag in first reading in fall 2003. Details of this new indexation mechanism are described below. This was the last step that in effect turned the German DB system into an NDC-type pension system.

The German Point System

The German public pension system computes benefits according to the following formula:

$$B_{t,i} = PV_t * EP_i * AA_i$$

where

$B_{t,i}$ = Benefits of pensioner i in year t,

PV_t = Current pension value in year t,

EP_i = Number of individual earnings points collected by pensioner i until his retirement, and

AA_i = Actuarial adjustment, dependent on the retirement age of pensioner i.

Benefits therefore have a simple structure: an individual component $EP_i * AA_i$ determined by each person's earnings history and retirement age, which stays fixed for the entire retirement period, and an aggregate component PV_t, which adjusts benefits over time equally for all pensioners.

EP_i represents the "point system" and AA_i is determined by actuarial accounting rules (see below). A typical worker who works for 40 years and who earns the average labor income in each of these 40 years receives 40 earnings points. If this worker retires at age 65, no actuarial adjustments take place ($AA = 1$). In the second half of 2002, the current pension value PV_t was 25.86 euros.[30] Hence this typical worker receives a pension of 1,034.40 euros per month. A worker who has worked for 20 years at average earnings, or a worker who has worked for 40 years at 50 percent of average earnings, will receive half these pension benefits, while workers who earn twice the average labor income for 40 years will receive twice as much as the 40-year average earner.

The Actuarial Adjustments

Before 1992, adjustment of benefits to retirement age was only implicit via additional earnings points. For a worker with 40 years of service at the average earnings level, an additional year of service would therefore increase the annual pension benefit by 2.5 percent. There were no further actuarial adjustments. The 1992 reform changed this, and the changes are currently being phased in.[31] Age 65 will then act as the "pivotal age" for benefit computations. Benefits will be reduced by 3.6 percent (maximum 10.8 percent) for each year of earlier retirement. The 1992 reform also introduced rewards for later retirement: for each year of postponement, benefits increase by 6 percent. There is some debate whether these percentage adjustments are actuarially neutral.[32] The German Reform Commission took a cautious position by stating that "the adjustments are low, but probably sufficiently close to actuarial neutral."[33] At conventional discount rates, they still exert considerable negative incentives to retire early.[34]

The Benefit Indexation Formula

Each year, currently on July 1, the current pension value PV_t is recalculated with the aid of the benefit indexation formula. Until recently, this benefit indexation formula was essentially a simple indexation rule, increasing pensions by the growth rate of net earnings:

$$PV_t = PV_{t-1} * \frac{ANW_{t-1}}{ANW_{t-2}}$$

where

PV_t = Current pension value in year t, and

ANW = Average earnings of all employees subject to compulsory insurance, net of taxes and social insurance contributions.

Since the current pension value PV_t has a direct influence on every individual pension, the benefit indexation formula is a critical determinant for the well-being of pensioners and the amount of money spent by the public pension scheme. However, the benefit indexation formula gives no direct reference to the demographics of the system nor to the number of employed persons, although there is a feedback through net earnings. Higher contributions dampen net earnings, and thus pension benefits, incorporating a kind of burden-sharing between generations. The limitations of this feedback mechanism are one reason for the unsustainability of the German pay-as-you-go system.

Starting in 2005, the benefit indexation formula will be augmented by a "sustainability factor" that incorporates demography and employment into the German benefit indexation formula. Specifically, it also indexes benefits to the numbers of contributors and pensioners. The relative number of contributors to pensioners, the so-called system dependency ratio (PQ), is the most important long-term determinant of pension financing:

$$PV_t = PV_{t-1} * \frac{ANW_{t-1}}{ANW_{t-2}} * \left[\left(1 - \frac{PQ_{t-1}}{PQ_{t-2}} \right) * \alpha + 1 \right]$$

where

PV_t = Current pension value in year t,

ANW = Average earnings net of public and private pension contributions,[35] and

PQ = System dependency ratio [pensioners/(contributors + unemployed)].

Incorporating the sustainability factor in the benefit indexation formula links annual increases in pensions to productivity growth and the growth of the contribution base. The weighting factor α gives weight to each of these two determinants; it effectively spreads the financial burden among contributors and pensioners. If α equals zero, the current benefit indexation formula would remain unchanged and the financial burden generated by a higher proportion of pensioners in the population would mainly be shouldered by the labor force. The condition α equals one implies a purely receipts-oriented pension expenditure policy. The German Reform Commission has set α to 1/4 to target the contribution rates anchored in the Riester reform (contribution rate below 20 percent until 2020, and under 22 percent until 2030).

The NDC Characteristics of the German Pension System

While there is no perfect equivalence, the three main elements of the German public pension system (the point system of credits, the actuarial adjustments, and the indexation to both earnings and system dependency) mimic the essential features of an NDC system.[36]

The *point system* includes all earnings over the lifetime; almost all redistributive features of the German old-age pension system take the form of earnings points credited without actual earnings (for example, years of unemployment, years of higher education, years of educating a child, in each case valued at an imputed earnings level). The equivalence between the point system and an NDC system is not perfect since all earnings points count equally in the German point system, while in an NDC system the earnings necessary to gain one such earnings point are valued more when earned earlier in life, due to compound interest.[37]

One deviation from equivalence is the fact that the *actuarial adjustments* in the German system are not directly linked to life expectancy. The actual adjustment rates are somewhat arbitrary, probably too small, and certainly controversial.[38] One of the advantages of an NDC system is to automatically generate the adjustment rates by the annuitization mechanism.

The *benefit indexation formula* of the German DB system, with its indexation to earnings growth and changes in the system dependency ratio, approximates the effect of the accumulated interest in an NDC system, in which the internal rate of interest is the growth rate of the contribution bill $(1 + n)*(1 + g)$.

This is easy to see in the most stylized case when all contributions (normalized to one unit) are credited upfront. In this stylized NDC case, the notional pension wealth after T years is $T*(1 + n)^T*(1 + g)^T$. The pension benefit is therefore $P = T*(1 + n)^T*(1 + g)^T/G$ where G denotes the annuity factor (or "G-value"). In the German DB system, this average worker earns T earnings points. During these T years, the average pension value PV will increase with the rate of wage growth (g) and the growth rate of the dependency ratio (n, if the number of pensioners remains constant): $PV_T = PV_0*(1 + n)^T*(1 + g)^T$. Hence, the pension benefit is $P = T*PV_0*(1+n)^T*(1+g)^T$, proportional to the NDC value.

This stylized comparison may ignore many differences in detail. Nonconstant contributions will have a differential impact on the two formulae; net wages are likely to grow at a different rate than gross earnings; the system dependency ratio is likely to shrink faster than the labor force. The principles, however, are the same. What a country prefers as a pension policy—an almost textbook-like NDC system as in Sweden or a demography-indexed DB system as in Germany—is probably more dependent on the historical path of a country and the specific circumstances of the political debate than on abstract economics.

Conclusions: Can NDC Systems Master the Challenges?

This summary starts with three claims about NDC systems that are not true. NDC systems are *not automatically balancing*: they do not automatically fulfill the PAYG budget constraint when economic parameters change. In particular, automatic balancing will not hold if annuities are frozen at retirement and the contribution rate is fixed since there is no feedback mechanism if longevity of current pensioners increases unexpectedly. Second, an NDC system is *not automatically sustainable* unless the contribution rate is fixed and the rate of return equals the contribution bill (or the system follows an equivalent trajectory). Third, an NDC system is *no substitute for prefunding*. An NDC system does not change the basic PAYG mechanism in which the children pay for the pensions of their parents, and it does not create savings unless it generates a benefit cut, which in turn precipitates savings.

However, if correctly designed, an NDC system will automatically respond to changes in the demographic and macroeconomic environment because benefits are indexed to longevity (due to the annuitization mechanism), fertility, and employment (through the notional rate of interest, if indexed to the contribution bill).

Moreover, an NDC system has potentially important microeconomic effects. It will create a sense of *actuarial fairness* (because annual benefits are in line with lifetime contributions) and *actuarial neutrality* (because the system creates automatic adjustments to retirement age). It exposes redistribution because any noncontributory credits appear clearly marked on the account statements.

An NDC system changes the *rhetoric of pension systems*. It makes people think in terms of accounts rather than entitlements and thus may make the transition to partial funding psychologically easier. Moreover, by exposing the dwindling balance of first pillar pensions, it may actually create incentives to save in the second and third pillar. An NDC system makes workers and administrators think in terms of "pension wealth," which may ease portability both within a country and between countries. It enables interpersonal transfers (for example, between husband and spouse) and eases replacement of survivor pensions by independent pension claims.

An NDC system also takes certain issues out of the political agenda, potentially easing reform. It minimizes the role of the "normal retirement age" and permits a more flexible choice between consumption (work longer) and leisure (get lower replacement rate). This flexibility finds its limitations in the conflict between actuarial neutrality and absence of labor supply disincentives and the necessity to establish an early retirement age. NDC systems also create a new set of "parameters," another aspect of the new rhetoric, which may make reform more palatable. It permits redefinitions and readjustments and changes the focus of debate from parametric reform to the introduction of "a new system" (while this is not the case with respect to economic substance), thus enabling parameter change. This point is not without some irony, and even more so, because we claimed that NDC systems strengthen credibility through transparency, while we now use it as a device to deflect emotional opposition by using a new rhetoric.

The usage as a rhetorical and psychological device, however, should not be belittled, and insights among workers and pensioners precipitated by a new rhetoric may have real economic effects. By exposing the economics of a pay-as-you-go system, by visualizing the budget constraint of a pension system, and by making the trade-off between retirement age and replacement rate concrete, NDC systems may induce economic reactions, such as later retirement or higher saving rates.

In addition, the new rhetoric may help to get a pension reform process going because it provides a framework to introduce actuarial adjustments (since they come "automatically"), a framework to diffuse the explosiveness of changes in the retirement age (since a flexible choice of retirement age minimizes opposition), and a framework to change intergenerational redistribution in a genuine sense if, and only if, NDC systems make workers save more.

Coming back to the challenges posed in the second part of this study, NDC systems are well positioned to manage the *challenge of longevity*. They are also well set up to react to slow *changes in fertility*, if the internal rate of interest is properly defined as the growth rate of the contribution bill. Sudden changes of fertility, however, such as the sudden baby boom/baby bust transition, are not well manageable in NDC systems. Countries in which the younger generation is simply overwhelmed by the financial burden of pensions need prefunding, enabling the members of the older generation to carry part of the pension burden themselves.

Design flaws of current DB systems (such as labor supply disincentives) are relatively well manageable in NDC systems; changing the rhetoric may be instrumental here. We have, however, already stressed the important distinction between absence of labor supply effects and actuarial neutrality.

NDC systems are only indirectly devices to foster growth, savings, and improvements in capital market performance. Since NDC systems are still PAYG devices, they do not alter the macroeconomic mechanisms at all; by changing the microeconomic incentives, at least by psychological means, they precipitate substantial real effects after all—through later retirement and higher savings. To alter the growth path of an economy, NDC systems therefore must be coupled with a strengthening of second and third pillar pensions. This combination of NDC with prefunding looks like one of the most fruitful paths of pension reform.

Notes

1. "Notional defined contribution" and "non-financial defined contribution" should be understood to have the same definition.

2. See IW (2003).

3. See Gruber and Wise (1999); Börsch-Supan and Schnabel (1998, 1999); and Börsch-Supan (2000).

4. See Börsch-Supan, Kohnz, and Schnabel (2003); Börsch-Supan, Schnabel, Kohnz, and Mastrobuoni (2003).

5. See Palmer (2000); Chłoń, Góra, and Rutkowski (1998).

6. See Disney (1999); Valdés-Prieto (2000)

7. See Rutkowski (1998); Góra and Rutkowski (1998); Fox and Palmer (1999); Chłoń-Domińczak and Góra (2006).

8. Valdés-Prieto (2003) suggests a potential trading mechanism.

9. In Sweden, the G-value is the remaining unisexual life expectancy at retirement age, reduced by the effect of compound interest during retirement. The assumed interest rate is 1.6 percent. This is modified if the growth of contributions is unusually low, by the "automatic balancing mechanism." For details. see Settergren (2001).

10. See Legros (2006).

11. See Gruber and Wise (1999).

12. See the textbooks by Homburg (1988) and Valdés-Prieto (1998).

13. See Börsch-Supan, Palacios, and Tumberello (1999).

14. This is strictly true only in citizenship- or residence-based flat benefit systems, such as in Australia. In the United Kingdom, a minimum number of credits determines eligibility.

15. See Ruland (2000).

16. Demography enters directly through longevity-dependent annuities and indirectly through feedbacks that change g, such as through age-specific productivity. Sweden also has a rebalancing mechanism that will respond to demography once the current system fails (see Settergren 2001).

17. The theoretical relation between r and $n+g$ in and out of steady state and its relation to dynamic efficiency fills volumes and is not the subject of this study. See Valdés-Prieto (1998). For some enlightening empirical results, see Schnabel (1998).

18. Note this distinction between the initial indexation at retirement for the flow of new entrants and the indexation of benefits after retirement for the stock of existing retirees.

19. Empirically measured personal discount rates tend be even larger than r, and by a substantial margin. See the survey by Frederick, Loewenstein, and O'Donoghue (2002).

20. This could be changed by converting the implicit claims on the contributions of future workers in explicit claims on future taxes backed by government bonds (see Valdés-Prieto 2003).

21. See Góra and Palmer (2003).

22. See Holzmann (1997); Schmidt-Hebbel (1998); Börsch-Supan and Winter (2001).

23. For a clearly stated mathematical exposition of this point, see Valdés-Prieto (2000).

24. A detailed description can be found in Settergreen (2001).

25. See Palmer (2003) for many of such details.

26. An exception is Latvia, which applies a cohort life-table.

27. The transition rules in Latvia and Poland are similar to the Swedish rules, while Kyrgyzstan's transition rules are similar to Italy's.

28. Börsch-Supan and Wilke (2003) present a detailed description of the pension reform process.

29. Econometric estimates are provided in Berkel and Börsch-Supan (2003).

30. This value was determined by the goal to provide a 70 percent ratio between the average pension and the average earnings level (see discussion below).

31. See Berkel and Börsch-Supan (2003) for details of the transition process.

32. There is a controversial discussion about the correct actuarial adjustment rate in the German public pension system. See Ohsmann, Stolz, and Thiede (2003) vs. Börsch-Supan (2000).

33. Kommission für die Nachhaltigkeit in der Finanzierung der Sozialen Sicherungssysteme (2003).

34. Börsch-Supan (2000); Börsch-Supan and Schnabel (1998, 1999); Börsch-Supan, Schnabel, Kohnz, and Mastrobuoni (2003); Börsch-Supan, Kohnz, and Schnabel (2003).

35. The careful reader may note the difference in the *ANW* definitions. We choose to ignore these here since we want to focus on the NDC characteristics. The current formula does *not* net out taxes and social insurance contributions other than taxes, but *does* net out

contributions to second and third pillar pensions at an imputed rate. It also computes the system dependency ratio using full-time equivalents for workers and pensioners. For these computational details, see Börsch-Supan and Wilke (2003).

36. Ruland (2000) has succinctly expressed the relationship between earnings points and current pension value by regarding earnings points as "shares" in the "financial assets" held by the pension fund. The current pension value corresponds to the current "share price."

37. Note that the metric is earnings points. If the metric is euros, the relation is reverted.

38. See the review in Berkel and Börsch-Supan (2003).

References

Berkel, B., and A. Börsch-Supan. 2003. "Pension Reform in Germany: The Impact on Retirement Decisions." MEA Discussion Paper 31-03, Mannheim Research Institute for the Economics of Aging, Mannheim University, and NBER Working Paper 9913, National Bureau of Economic Research, Cambridge, Mass.

Börsch-Supan, A. 2000. "Incentive Effects of Social Security on Labour Force Participation: Evidence in Germany and Across Europe." *Journal of Public Economics* 78: 25–49.

Börsch-Supan, A., and M. Miegel, eds. 2001. *Pension Reform in Six Countries.* Heidelberg, New York, Tokyo: Springer.

Börsch-Supan, A., and R. Schnabel. 1998. Social Security and Declining Labor Force Participation in Germany. *American Economic Review* 88 (2): 173–178.

———. 1999. "Social Security and Retirement in Germany." In *International Social Security Comparions,* ed. J. Gruber and D.A. Wise, Chicago: University of Chicago Press.

Börsch-Supan, A., and C. Wilke. 2003. "The German Social Security System: How it Was and How it Will Be." MEA-Discussion Paper prepared for the MRRC-Conference on Social Security, May 2003, Washington, DC.

Börsch-Supan, A. and J. Winter. 2001. "Population Aging, Savings Behavior, and Capital Markets." Working Paper 8561, National Bureau of Economic Research (NBER), Cambridge, Mass.

Börsch-Supan, A., R. Palacios, and P. Tumberello. 1999. *Pension Systems in the Middle East and North Africa: A Window of Opportunity.* Pension Reform Primer. Washington, DC: World Bank.

Börsch-Supan, A., S. Kohnz, and R. Schnabel. 2003. "Micro Modeling of Retirement Choices in Germany." In *Incentive Effects of Public Pension Systems,* ed. J. Gruber and D. Wise. Chicago: University of Chicago Press, in press.

Börsch-Supan, A., R. Schnabel, S. Kohnz, and G. Mastrobuoni. 2003. "Budget Effects of Pension Reform in Germany." In *Budget Effects of Reforming Public Pension Systems,* ed. J. Gruber and D. Wise. Chicago: University of Chicago Press, in press.

Chłoń, A., M. Góra, and M. Rutkowski. 1999. *Shaping Pension Reform in Poland: Security through Diversity.* Social Protection Discussion Paper 9923, World Bank, Washington, DC.

Chłoń-Domińczak, A., and M. Góra. 2006. "The NDC System in Poland: Assessment after Five Years." In *Pension Reform: Issues and Prospects for Non-Financial Defined Contribution (NDC) Schemes,* ed. R. Holzmann and E. Palmer, chapter 16. Washington, DC: World Bank.

Disney, R. 1999. "Notional Accounts as a Pension Reform Strategy: An Evaluation." Social Protection Discussion Paper 9928, World Bank, Washington, DC.

———. 2003. "Are Contributions to Public Pension Programmes a Tax?" Paper prepared for the Fourth Annual CeRP Conference, Turin, September 16.

Fox, L., and E. Palmer. 1999. "Latvian Pension Reform." Social Protection Discussion Paper 9922, World Bank, Washington, DC.

Franco, D., and N. Sartor. 2006. "NDCs in Italy: Unsatisfactory Present, Uncertain Future." In *Pension Reform: Issues and Prospects for Non-Financial Defined Contribution (NDC) Schemes*, ed. R. Holzmann and E. Palmer, chapter 18. Washington, DC: World Bank.

Frederick, S., G. Loewenstein, and T. O'Donoghue. 2002. "Time Discounting and Time Preference: A Critical Review." *Journal of Economic Literature* 40: 351–401.

Góra, M., and E. Palmer. 2003. "Shifting Perspectives in Pensions." Revised version of working paper published by CASE in Warsaw, 2002. National Social Insurance Board, Stockholm.

Góra, M., and M. Rutkowski. 1998. *The Quest for Pension Reform: Poland's Security through Diversity*. Social Protection Discussion Paper 9815, World Bank, Washington, DC.

Gruber, J., and D.A. Wise, eds. 1999. *Social Security and Retirement Around the World*. Chicago: University of Chicago Press.

Holzmann, R. 1997. "Pension Reform, Financial Market Development, and Economic Growth: Preliminary Evidence from Chile." *IMF Staff Papers* 44 (2): 149–78.

Homburg, S. 1988. *Theorie der Alterssicherung*. Berlin, Heidelberg, New York: Springer.

IW (Institut der deutschen Wirtschaft). 2003. *Deutschland in Zahlen*. Köln: Deutscher Instituts Verlag.

Kommission für die Nachhaltigkeit in der Finanzierung der Sozialen Sicherungssysteme. 2003. Abschlußbericht. Bundesministerium für Gesundheit und Soziale Sicherheit. Berlin. http://www.bmgs.bund.de/deu/gra/themen/sicherheit/kommission/index .cfm.

Legros, F. 2006. "NDCs: A Comparison of the French and the German Point Systems." In *Pension Reform: Issues and Prospects for Non-Financial Defined Contribution (NDC) Schemes*, ed. R. Holzmann and E. Palmer, chapter 10. Washington, DC: World Bank.

Lindeman, D., D. Robalino, and M. Rutkowski. 2006. "NDC Pension Schemes in Middle- and Low-Income Countries." In *Pension Reform: Issues and Prospects for Non-Financial Defined Contribution (NDC) Schemes*, ed. R. Holzmann and E. Palmer, chapter 12. Washington, DC: World Bank.

OECD (Organisation for Economic Co-operation and Development). 1988. *Ageing Populations: Social Policy Implications*. Paris: OECD.

Ohsmann, S., U. Stolz, and R. Thiede. 2003. Rentenabschläge bei vorgezogenem Rentenbeginn: Welche Abschlagssätze sind "richtig"? *Die Angestelltenversicherung* Heft 4, 119–124.

Palmer, E. 2000. "The Swedish Pension Reform Model: Framework and Issues, Social Protection." Discussion Paper 0012, World Bank, Washington, DC.

Palmer, E. 2003. "Conversion to NDC—Isssues and Models." Paper presented at World Bank and Swedish Social Insurance Agency Conference on NDC Pensions, Sandhamn, Sweden, September 28–30.

Ruland, F. 2000. *Neugestaltung der Rentenformel im bestehenden Umlageverfahren*. Vortrag bei Speyerer Sozialrechtsgesprächen. www.vdr.de.

Rutkowski, M. 1998. "A New Generation of Pension Reforms Conquers the East: A Taxonomy in Transition Economies." *Transition* 9 (4, August): 54–76.

Schmidt-Hebbel, K. 1998. "Does Pension Reform Really Spur Productivity, Saving, and Growth." Working Paper 33, Central Bank of Chile, Santiago.

Schnabel, R. 1998. "Rates of Return of the German Pay-As-You-Go Pension System." *Finanzarchiv* 55 (3): 374–99.

Settergren, O. 2001. "The Automatic Balance Mechanism of the Swedish Pension System." *Wirtschaftspolitische Blätter* 2001/4.

Valdés-Prieto, S. ed. 1998. *The Economics of Pensions: Principals, Policies, and International Experience*. Cambridge: Cambridge University Press.

————. 2000. "The Financial Stability of Notional Account Pensions." *Scandinavian Journal of Economics*, 102, 385–387.

World Bank. 1994. *Averting the Old-Age Crisis: Policies to Protect the Old and Promote Growth*. New York: Oxford University Press.

Chapter 4

Non-Financial Defined Contribution Pensions: Mapping the Terrain

*Nicholas Barr**

The Backdrop

This chapter offers an assessment of notional defined contribution (NDC) pensions from the perspective of welfare economics, with a brief discussion of management and implementation.[1] The opening section sets out the objectives of pension schemes, the idea of NDCs, and the simple economics of pensions. The second section assesses NDC pensions in terms of policy design. Is the aspect under discussion an advantage? If so, is the advantage specific to NDCs, and is it one of policy design or political reality? The third section briefly discusses the institutional prerequisites necessary if a country is to introduce NDC pensions effectively. The final section offers three conclusions. NDC pensions are not a theoretically dominant policy, but one with pros and cons that need to be compared with those of other designs. The case for NDCs is strongest as part of a wider pension system, rather than as a stand-alone construct. The NDC approach does little to address the central problem of pension finance—the age at which people are first eligible to claim their pension.

Objectives of Pension Schemes

From the viewpoint of the individual, pensions have two purposes:

- *Consumption smoothing* over the life cycle, and
- *Insurance*, notably in respect of the longevity risk.

Public policy has additional objectives:

- *Poverty relief.* This is necessary if someone is poor for his or her lifetime as a whole and, as a practical matter, is needed to address transient poverty.
- *Distributional objectives.* Governments may also have broader distributional objectives. They frequently wish to protect the pension rights of people with caring responsibilities and they may wish to subsidize the consumption smoothing of people whose earnings are above the poverty line, but not by much.

---

* Nicholas Barr is professor of public economics at the London School of Economics and the author of numerous books and articles, including *The Economics of the Welfare State* (OUP, 4th edition, 2004).

These four elements are the primary objectives of pensions. The analysis, particularly in the second section, considers the extent to which different types of NDC arrangements do, or do not, contribute to their achievement. There is also an important constraint—*sustainability*—that recurs in the discussion below.

NDC Pensions

The basic idea of NDC pensions is to separate the state pay-as-you-go (PAYG) scheme into two components: a strictly actuarial element (the NDC pension), operating on a PAYG basis but mimicking a funded defined contribution scheme; and a redistributive element financed from general taxation.[2]

The actuarial element is calculated in the following way:

- A contribution of x percent of a person's earnings is credited to a notional individual account: that is, the state "pretends" that there is an accumulation of financial assets.
- The cumulative contents of the account are credited periodically with a notional interest rate.
- At retirement, the notional account is converted into an annuity.

Thus NDC pensions mimic conventional (funded) defined contribution schemes by paying an income stream whose present value over the person's expected remaining lifetime equals his/her accumulation at retirement.

QUESTIONS ABOUT THE DESIGN OF STATE PENSIONS

Policy makers face a series of issues. How large should the state pension be; how redistributive from richer to poorer; and should benefits be defined contribution or defined benefit (defined and discussed shortly)? Further, if a new pension system, such as an NDC arrangement, is introduced, how will the transition be financed? Moreover, there is a range of questions specific to the design of NDC pensions:

Question 1. What is the minimum pension? Is it paid in addition to the NDC pension, or does it take the form of a guarantee that is paid only if the NDC pension falls below a predetermined minimum level? If the former, is the minimum flat rate or with an earnings-related element? Is it minimal or larger?

Question 2. Is there a maximum NDC pension?

Question 3. Is minimum pensionable age unconstrained, with full actuarial adjustment of the pension to a person's age at retirement? Or is there a legally defined minimum age, with actuarial adjustment for retirement at a later age? And/or is there a minimum age that rises according to some functional relationship with life expectancy?

Question 4. Is the accrual rate during working life based on earnings growth per worker, and hence unaffected by unemployment, or on earnings growth in aggregate, and hence lower in years when unemployment is higher? Separately, is the pension formula adjusted for life expectancy? Several NDC schemes have an accrual rate equal to

$$\frac{\text{Rate of growth of}}{\text{the contributions base}} = \text{productivity growth} + \text{employment growth.}$$

Most schemes, being new, include an adjustment for life expectancy.

Question 5. Is the annuity, once in payment, adjusted annually in line with changes in consumer prices, or with real wage growth?

DEFINED CONTRIBUTION AND DEFINED BENEFIT PENSIONS: A BRIEF COMPARISON

In a defined contribution (DC) scheme, a person's pension is an annuity whose size, given life expectancy and the rate of return on pension assets, is determined only by the size of his lifetime pension accumulation. Thus the approach leaves the individual to face the risk that his pension portfolio might perform badly. Under a defined benefit (DB) scheme, often run at the firm or industry level, a person's pension is based on his wage and length of service. Thus his annuity is wage-indexed during working life, and the risk of varying rates of return to pension assets falls on the employer, and hence on some combination of the industry's current workers (through effects on wage rates), its shareholders and the taxpayer (through effects on profits), its customers (through effects on prices), and/or its past or future workers, if the company uses surpluses from some periods to boost pensions in others.

The debate between DC and DB pensions is often posed as one between polar opposites, a strictly actuarial DC scheme being compared with a final salary DB scheme. The reality is more subtle, as Diamond (2002, 55–57) points out. Suppose a person's earnings in a particular year are 70 percent of average earnings that year; call that variable x. Call the average value of x over n years, $\bar{X}$, which is thus a measure of the person's earnings each year indexed by the rate of wage growth. Then $\bar{X}$ is the earnings base on which a person's pension in a DB scheme is determined. If n relates to earnings in the last year before retirement, the scheme is a final-salary DB scheme. In contrast, if n spans an entire working life, the scheme is a DB scheme in which pensions are based on lifetime contributions compounded each year by the rate of wage growth. In a funded DC scheme, annual contributions are compounded by the return on assets (for short, the interest rate), again over a person's working life. If the rate of interest and the rate of wage growth are similar, the difference between DC and DB is minor; and the difference is even smaller between a lifetime DB scheme and an NDC scheme with an accrual rate equal to wage growth.

In the limit, suppose that a DB scheme bases benefits on a person's entire working life; has an accrual rate that is age-related (that is, contributions in early years have a heavier weight, as with compound interest); and offers an annuity rate that is announced only at the time that a person retires. In that case, DB and DC converge.

Thus DB schemes can be very different, and hence have very different economic impacts; the same is true of NDC regimes. The analysis that follows tries to be clear which type of scheme is being compared with which.

The Simple Economics of Pensions

A final piece of background before turning to specific assessment of NDC pensions is the simple economics of pensions, which can be confusing because the literature tends to focus on financial aspects such as analysis of portfolios of financial assets. This discussion tries to simplify matters by concentrating on the essential economic issues: namely, the production and consumption of goods and services.

There are two (and only two) ways of seeking security in old age.[3] It is possible, first, to *store current production* by storing part of current output for future use. Though this is the only way that an individual such as Robinson Crusoe could guarantee consumption in retirement, the method in practice has major inefficiencies. It is costly; it does not deal with uncertainty— for example, how one's tastes or constraints might change; and it cannot be applied to services deriving from human capital, medical services being a particularly important example. With few exceptions, organizing pensions by storing current production on a large scale is therefore a nonstarter.

The alternative is for individuals to exchange current production for a *claim on future production*. There are two broad ways in which a worker might do this: by saving part of his wages each week, he could build up a pile of *money* that he would exchange for goods produced by younger people after his retirement; or he could obtain a *promise*—from his children, or from government—that he would be given goods produced by others after his retirement. The two most common ways of organizing pensions broadly parallel these two sorts of claim on future output. Funded schemes are based on accumulations of financial assets, PAYG schemes, including NDC schemes, on promises.

Given the deficiencies of storing current production, the *only* way forward is through claims on future production. Thus the central variable is the level of output after a worker has retired. The point is fundamental: pensioners are not interested in money (colored bits of paper with portraits of national heroes on them), but in consumption—food, heating, medical services, seats at football matches, and so on. Money is irrelevant unless the production is there for pensioners to buy.

The discussion thus far suggests a series of propositions against which an NDC (or any other) pension scheme should be assessed.

- From the point of view of sustainability, the central variable is the level of national output, not the specific method by which pensions are financed. Since NDC pensions *per se* do not increase output, the main contribution to sustainability is if they facilitate lower pensions, later retirement, and/or an increase in contributions.
- The design of the state scheme matters. If the state scheme is unsustainable, the *only* solution is to fix the state scheme. Thus a move to NDC pensions may make it possible to reduce pensions to sustainable levels and/or to make it possible to remove or reduce special benefits for particular groups.
- Insurance, consumption smoothing, and poverty relief are all important. A pure NDC pension is concerned only with insurance and consumption smoothing, with implications, which this study explores, for the broader design of a pension system.

Assessing NDC Pensions

In assessing NDCs, it is useful to distinguish different questions:

- Is the particular feature under discussion an advantage?
- Is the advantage inherent in the NDC design or could it be achieved by another arrangement?
- Is the advantage one of policy design or of political reality?

A final question, discussed in the concluding section, is whether NDC pensions are a dominant policy.

Advantages

This section assesses a series of advantages that are claimed for NDC pensions.

ASSIST CLEAR THINKING

It is useful to distinguish three elements of pensions that are often conflated: public or private; PAYG or funded; DC or DB. The NDC approach reminds us that public + PAYG + DC is a possible option: in other words, that PAYG does not *automatically* mean DB. This reminder is helpful.

FACILITATE DESIRABLE FEATURES OF PENSION DESIGN

NDC pensions facilitate a number of desirable design features.

A flexible retirement age is welfare-improving because it increases the range of individual choice over consumption smoothing. This advantage can, however, be a feature of other types of schemes. In terms of the retirement decision, what is needed is an actuarial relationship between contributions and pensions at the margin, but not necessarily across the entire contributions record.[4]

A flexible combination of work and retirement, again, increases individual choice between both work and leisure and over the time path of income. Again, however, this is possible with other pension arrangements, such as a state scheme offering defined benefits from the age of 65 but with actuarial adjustment for delayed retirement and options for combining work with receipt of pension.

Automatic adjustment to rising life expectancy. Given the sustained increase in life expectancy, this feature of NDC pensions is essential for long-run viability. But it could equally be a feature of other pension arrangements: for example, if the age at which the pension is first payable rises according to an explicit relation with life expectancy. If NDC pensions have any advantage in this respect, it is that the politics of adjustment might be easier, rather than a design feature possible only with NDCs.

ENHANCE THE ABILITY TO COPE WITH RISK AND UNCERTAINTY

Risk and uncertainty lower the welfare of risk-averse individuals (proof: the amount that people spend on voluntary insurance). Consumption smoothing is thus more efficient if people can be protected from excessive risk and uncertainty. The distinction is important: with risk, the probability of the occurrence of the insured event is known; with uncertainty, it is not. Risks can be covered by actuarial insurance. With uncertainty, in contrast, ignorance of the underlying probability distribution makes it difficult or impossible to assess an actuarial premium; hence uncertainties are generally covered badly, if at all, by actuarial insurance. In the case of pensions, the estimates of life expectancy have a sufficiently small variance that annuities are possible. With inflation, in contrast, the variance of future rates is so high that fully inflation-proofed private pensions are hard to come by and expensive. In short, it is no accident that it is possible to buy life insurance but not inflation insurance.[5]

What risks and uncertainties can hamper consumption smoothing? All pension schemes face macroeconomic shocks, demographic shocks, and political risks. Private, funded schemes face additional risks:

- *Management risk.* This can arise through incompetence or fraud, which imperfectly informed consumers cannot monitor effectively.
- *Investment risk.* Pension accumulations held in the stock market are vulnerable to stock market fluctuations. At its extreme, if a person is required to retire on the day of his sixty-fifth birthday, there is a lottery element in his pension accumulation.
- *Annuities market risk.* For a given accumulation, the value of an annuity depends on remaining life expectancy and on the rate of return the insurance company can expect over those years. Both variables face both risk and significant uncertainties.

NDC pensions avoid some of the risks that private pensions face, notably management risk and investment risk. They may also reduce annuities market risk, if only because with a single, nationwide annuities pool, the law of large numbers will reduce the variance facing the insurer (that is, the state). This is an unambiguous advantage. However, the advantage is inherent in state-run PAYG schemes generally, rather than NDC schemes specifically.

Less stringent demands on private sector institutional capacity. Private pensions make considerable institutional demands on both the public and the private sector. The latter will be absent in poorer countries. Even where it is present, private pensions may not be the most welfare-enhancing use for scarce private sector skills, which might better be used in building up productive capacity. NDC pensions make no demands on the private sector, though that advantage is inherent in all state pensions. As discussed in the third section, however, NDC pensions make heavier demands on public institutional capacity than state schemes with a less tightly defined relation between contributions and benefits.

Capacity to cope with uncertainty, not just risk. With social insurance, the contract is not fully specified. Precisely for that reason, social insurance can adjust to changing conditions and unforeseen contingencies. Atkinson (1995, 210) points out that "the set of contingencies over which people formed probabilities years ago may have excluded the breakdown of the extended family, or the development of modern medicine, simply because they were inconceivable." Thus social insurance, in sharp contrast with actuarial insurance, can address not only *risk* but also *uncertainty*.

Thus NDC pensions have the potential to ameliorate uncertainty in ways that private schemes do not. The ability to pay fully indexed pensions once a person has retired is one example; the capacity to protect the pension rights of people with caring responsibilities (which is not an insurable risk) is another. This is a significant advantage—again, however, one that resides in social insurance generally, rather than the NDC design specifically.

ASSIST SUSTAINABILITY

If an NDC scheme is genuinely actuarial, then future expenditure is by definition equal to revenues, so that the scheme—again by definition—is sustainable. This feature, however, is not exclusive to NDCs. Consider a balanced PAYG scheme, where:

$$sWL = PN \qquad (4.1)$$

where

s = the PAYG social security contribution rate,

W = the average real wage,

L = the number of workers,

P = the average real pension, and

N = the number of pensioners.

If the social security act specifies a pension formula in which

$$P = sWL/N \qquad (4.2)$$

again, expenditure = revenue by definition.

Thus sustainability is not specific to the NDC design. It may be, however, that the politics are easier with NDCs.

ENHANCE TRANSPARENCY

The argument is that NDC pensions have explicit rules and therefore that the system is transparent in two ways: individuals know the basis on which their pension will be calculated; and any attempts by government to alter the scheme are visible. These features are important, but not exclusive to NDCs. The U.K. system prior to 1975 was highly transparent, with a flat rate contribution for all workers giving entitlement to a flat rate benefit. Another example of transparency is a PAYG scheme with defined benefits, but with retirement age explicitly related to life expectancy, significantly reducing the need for other parametric change. A final salary scheme is also transparent to the recipient, and government attempts to change the benefit are *very* visible.

REDUCE INCENTIVES FOR FRAUD

In an NDC scheme, like all PAYG schemes, the only pot of money is the current year's contributions: that is, the *flow* of contributions, not the stock. Thus there are few assets for the state or private actors to pillage. Separately, if the state wants to increase the taxation of pensions, it can do so only on benefits in payment, not on the fund, since there is no fund. Both features, once more, are inherent in PAYG generally rather than in NDC design specifically.

NDC schemes thus have advantages, but almost all of them are features of state pensions generally, rather than exclusive to the specific design of NDCs. Separately, any advantage of principle may impose a heavy requirement in terms of government capacity, a topic to which the third section returns.

Equivocal Aspects

Some features of NDCs can be regarded either as advantages or disadvantages, depending on views about theory, empirical facts, or values.

NONDISTORTIONARY

In discussing the impact of pensions on labor market decisions, it is helpful to distinguish two statements: badly designed pensions cause labor market distortions; and fully actuarial pensions minimize such distortions. This chapter argues that the first statement is true, but the second does not follow.

Badly designed pensions undoubtedly cause labor market distortions in terms of both retirement decisions and responses earlier in life. [6] If the concern is the retirement decision, pensions should be related at the *margin* to individual contributions. The argument is important. It is open to policy makers to have a pension formula that is redistributive in the sense that worker A, with twice the earnings of worker B over his working life, gets a pension which is higher than B's, but less than twice as high. However, if either A or B retires early, his pension would be actuarially reduced relative to the pension he would have received at age 65. In contrast, earlier labor market decisions depend not only on the marginal relationship between contributions and benefits, but also on the effect of an increase in earnings on the total pension package. In this case, it is necessary to consider a fuller actuarial relationship between contributions and benefits.

How do these arguments apply to fully actuarial pensions like NDCs? Badly designed state pensions cause major distortions. However, state schemes, whether NDC or DB, avoid one important distortion—the labor immobility problem caused by private DB schemes. In addition, DB schemes with long averaging periods are less distortionary than with a short period and, as discussed earlier, can be very similar to a DC scheme. More fundamentally, the next section argues that fully actuarial benefits are not optimal in a second-best world.

A second reason why a fully actuarial design might not be optimal is that minimizing distortions is only part of the story. The argument implicitly assumes that all that matters is labor supply. But it can be argued that what really matters is economic welfare. It may be, for example, that a defined benefit scheme reduces labor supply at the margin; but if

the loss of utility resulting from lower output is more than offset by the utility gain resulting from greater certainty about consumption smoothing, then defined benefit arrangements may be welfare-improving, notwithstanding reduced labor supply. At a minimum,
the welfare gains from greater certainly should be set against any costs of reduced labor
supply.

Thus the argument that NDC pensions minimize distortions is far from definitive. If the
argument is true, then it is also true of other schemes in which contributions bear an actuarial relationship to contributions, for instance a scheme with flat rate contributions and
flat rate benefits, such as in the United Kingdom between 1948 and 1975. The desirability,
or otherwise, of actuarial benefits is taken up in the next section.

EQUITABLE

The argument that actuarial benefits are equitable rests on the belief that redistribution
should apply only to poverty relief and to credits in specific instances such as caring for
small children. A contrary view is that the state pension should include redistributive
assistance for consumption smoothing as well as for poverty relief. It can also be argued
that, though NDC pensions help to cope with risk and uncertainty, they continue to face
the individual with significant risks associated with the variability of earnings; other
approaches, for example, DB, share risks more broadly, as discussed in the first section.

Thus NDC pensions do not have a unique claim to equity. They are inequitable if policy
makers or the electorate believe that social insurance has a redistributive role broader than
poverty relief and/or if policy makers want risks to be shared more broadly than is possible with actuarially based benefits.

TIES THE HANDS OF GOVERNMENT

The proposition is that NDC pensions, being actuarially based, constrain the government's freedom of action. Two sets of questions arise.

Does the NDC design really tie the government's hands? In theory, the contract is fixed;
but government could change the contract. Second, is tying the government's hands welfare-improving? At the core of this question lie two further sets of questions. The first is an
empirical issue about the competence and motivation of government, about which people
may take different views, and about which conclusions might differ for different countries.
Some writers are sceptical about government, arguing that politicians award concessions to
special interests in exchange for short-run political support, leaving the costs of those concessions to future taxpayers, at a time when the politicians who have granted them have
long since retired. The contradictory argument is that a *disadvantage* of NDCs is that they
reduce policy flexibility by adopting a fully specified contract, and thus forgo options for
enhancing consumption smoothing by reducing the uncertainty faced by the individual. A
second question concerns the trade-off between the certainty of a supposedly rigid scheme
versus the greater options for risk-sharing that can occur with a more flexible scheme.

If tying the hands of government is thought an advantage, is this possible only with
NDC pensions? In principle the answer is no: NDC schemes are based on a social security
law just like other PAYG schemes. It is true, however, that it might be harder politically to
change NDC pensions.

Disadvantages

Alongside their advantages and equivocal aspects, NDCs have two significant sets of disadvantages: they are not efficient, and they are suboptimal in welfare terms.

Inefficient

A central objective of pensions is to allow each person to make efficient choices about the time path of his or her consumption. Such a system of consumption smoothing should minimize distortions.

On the face of it, this suggests that a strictly actuarial system would be efficient. Indeed, Góra and Palmer (2003, 15–16) write:

> In the NDC and FDC [funded defined contribution] framework there is no redistributive ambition, other than redistribution over the individual's own lifecycle from working years to years of retirement. Instead, the government's redistributive policy . . . is financed through explicit taxes from general revenues. . . . In this way, insurance and its source of financing and social policy and its means of financing are kept separate, enhancing transparency.

The approach gives rise to a number of queries. First, why is it efficient to have both first- and second-tier pensions organized on a DC basis? More fundamentally, though a strictly actuarial scheme may be efficient in a first-best world, policy design needs to cope with serious market imperfections.

People can be myopic and/or imperfectly informed, giving a justification for compulsion. The problem is nontrivial, and means that the simple assumption of rational utility maximization may not hold. New (1999) makes the useful distinction between an information problem and an information-processing problem. An information problem can be resolved by providing the necessary information, such as the capacity of different computers, after which the individual can make his or her own choices. With an information-processing problem, in contrast, the problem is too complex for agents to make rational choices, even if the necessary information is provided. The problem can arise where the time horizon is long, as with pensions; or where the good or service involves complex probabilities, including, for example, life expectancy (the failure in this case is an inability to process probabilities); or where the information is inherently complex, as with complicated pension products.

A second problem is missing markets. The market for indexed contracts, for example, is thin, to say the least.

Progressive taxation is a third deviation from first-best. Diamond argues that in the comparison between defined contribution and defined benefit schemes, "there is no simple dominance of one over the other in the presence of other labor market distortions" (2002, 57). Assuming that the rate of interest exceeds the rate of wage growth over the longer term, he continues:

> Indeed, with a progressive annual income tax and age-earnings profiles that are generally increasing in real terms, the marginal income tax rate is rising with age, on average. Thus, a well-designed DB system may well have better labor market outcomes since the overall tax burden, income tax plus net tax from social security, will vary less over the life-cycle. That is, income taxes are lower on the young and net social security taxes are higher. Therefore, without a detailed calculation, one cannot reach an efficiency conclusion. In any case the difference is likely to be much smaller than the difference between DB systems with long and short averaging periods.

Formulating the issue as an optimal taxation problem would make it clear that in a second-best world, a scheme that is strictly actuarial is not, in general, efficient.

SUBOPTIMAL IN WELFARE TERMS

Consumption smoothing is one objective of pensions but, as discussed at the start of the chapter, there are others, including reducing the risk people face (implicit in both the consumption smoothing and insurance objectives), poverty relief, and distributional objectives (which may include subsidizing consumption smoothing by people only slightly above the poverty line). A strict adherence to actuarial benefits may provide consumption smoothing, but sets aside the others.

Proponents of NDC pensions then argue that the NDC pension provides consumption smoothing, and other instruments provide poverty relief and distributional goals. But—going back to a point I learned so many years ago as a graduate student—if there are three targets, three instruments are needed to achieve them. The optimal solution, however, is normally *not* a single one: one relationship between each instrument and a particular target. The NDC arguments are tidy in this respect and, on that account, rather appealing. But that does not make them right—as an optimal tax formulation would make clear.

Prerequisites for Implementation

The previous section asked whether NDC pensions are desirable. This section considers very briefly the parallel question: are they feasible?

An initial question for policy makers concerns the level and distribution of income. If the country is poor, the poverty line, which determines the minimum pension, is relatively close to average earnings. Hence there is little gain from an earnings-related pension in general, and NDC pensions in particular. Thus a prerequisite for NDC pensions is sufficient disparity in the earnings distribution to make consumption smoothing relevant.

A second central issue is that contributory pensions in general, and NDC pensions in particular, require considerable government capacity. The government needs to have sufficient *economic capacity* to maintain macro stability, sufficient *political capacity* to make long-term pension promises credible, and sufficient *basic institutional capacity* to collect contributions, to account for them in each year, and to cumulate records across years. The last of these conditions is particularly important for NDC arrangements, where every cent of every contribution counts toward a person's final pension. For NDC pensions, government also needs *advanced institutional capacity* for monitoring changes in life expectancy and for maintaining the long-run balance of the scheme, for example, the capacity to run a reserve fund effectively. Merely to state these requirements makes it clear that NDC arrangements impose particularly heavy demands on public sector capacity. Where this capacity is absent, NDC pensions should be regarded as future option rather than current policy.

Conclusion

Góra and Palmer (2003) talk about the need to "create new concepts" (p. 2) and about the "design of a new vehicle for efficient accumulation over the life cycle" (p. 27). Palmer's work has mapped out the idea of NDCs—in terms both of policy and implementation—much more fully than previously. This is a considerable advance. NDCs remind us that state PAYG pensions can be as much or as little actuarial as we want: in other words, social insurance is not *necessarily* redistributive. Thus the approach is important because it reminds us of an important but often forgotten truth, but is not itself new. As I wrote in 1987 (and others had doubtless written before), "[Redistribution] is not *inevitable*, since a PAYG scheme could be organized to pay actuarial benefits" (Barr 1987, 222, emphasis in original).

Conclusion 1: NDCs Are Not a Dominant Policy

Put another way, NDCs are *a* design for state pensions, not *the* design. Except in a world that is first-best and where policy makers are indifferent about distributional matters, a strictly actuarial relationship is not an optimum. That is stated as a proposition in theory. It implies that we cannot say that a strictly actuarial relationship is always and necessarily the best way to design pensions; indeed, it will generally not be optimal.

Put another way, the theoretical conclusion leaves it open to people to take different views about pension design. Thus it is entirely sensible, coherent, and defensible to advocate NDC pensions. But since they are not a theoretically dominant policy, there are other sensible, coherent, and defensible policies: for example, a pension design that includes redistribution not just for poverty relief but also for consumption smoothing. Sweden, with its NDC system, offers an important example. But so do other countries, such as Australia (noncontributory, income-tested, first-tier pensions plus mandatory DC second-tier pensions), the Netherlands (tax-funded citizens' pensions plus mandatory, largely occupational second-tier pensions), and the United States (contributory DB first-tier pensions plus voluntary DC third-tier accumulations). In short, there is room for different views about preferred pension design.

On what basis should different policies be assessed? Much of the issue depends on the answers to the following questions:

- *Question 1.* Is policy flexibility an advantage or a disadvantage? This is the old rules-versus-discretion debate. The answer depends on empirical views about the effectiveness and probity of government, and will therefore vary from person to person and by country.
- *Question 2.* Is a wholly actuarial system (for example, NDC first tier + funded DC second tier) efficient? As discussed earlier, the answer is generally no; but the extent of welfare loss will depend, among other things, on the extent of risk aversion in the population (the welfare gains from greater certainty being higher the greater the degree of risk aversion).
- *Question 3.* Are actuarial benefits equitable or not? This ultimately is a value judgment about whether redistribution is or is not properly limited to poverty relief.
- *Question 4.* Would NDC be more sustainable than a defined benefit scheme? Note that we are comparing current defined benefit schemes as they are, with lots of barnacles, with a perfect, pristine NDC scheme. The answer is probably more political than economic.
- *Question 5.* Is the scheme cost-effective? The answer will depend on objective factors such as the level of income in a country, and on empirical judgments about whether or not the relevant supporting institutions are sufficiently developed.

Conclusion 2: It Depends on What You Mean by NDC

NDCs can take many guises. Two polar cases are particularly relevant.

- *Case 1.* The pension system is NDC plus a minimal guarantee. Such a system comes close to being strictly actuarial, and hence offers insurance in respect of the longevity risk and consumption smoothing, but only minimal poverty relief and vertical redistribution. This is a corner solution, and hence can be criticized for being inefficient and also, depending on one's perspective, inequitable.
- *Case 2.* The pension system has two elements: a tax-funded pension that can either be flat rate or with an earnings-related component, and an NDC element. The latter may include tax-funded credits, for example, to recognize caring activities. This arrange-

ment offers poverty relief, insurance, and consumption smoothing. If the tax-funded element has an earnings-related component, there is a redistributive element in consumption smoothing.

The latter construct contains a richer array of policy options. But in this case the NDC pension is not the first tier, but the second. It amounts to a pension system with a tax-funded first tier and an NDC second tier. NDC is no longer *the* pension, but an element in a wider system.

Finally, as discussed earlier, a state-run DB scheme with accrual over a full working life, an age-related accrual rate, and annuities determined ex post is formally identical to an NDC scheme based on earnings growth per worker.

Conclusion 3: NDC Pensions Do Little to Address the Central Funding Issue

The root of long-term unsustainability is that in virtually all countries pension schemes incorporate a retirement age of 60 or 65, which remains largely fixed as life expectancy rises. Rising life expectancy is a source of joy; the problem is having a fixed age at which the pension first becomes payable.

NDC pensions address the problem in a formal sense by reducing the accrual rate. But unless people retire later, this approach on its own risks pensioner poverty. That is, sustainability is in conflict with sound social policy. In the absence of any constraints, the endogenous variable is not the minimum pensionable age but the size of the pension. In a world of rationality and perfect information, this would face each person with an actuarial budget constraint against which to make his or her optimal choice about when to retire. But if people have a personal discount rate higher than the interest rate used for actuarial adjustment, they will tend to retire as soon as possible, with progressively larger actuarial adjustments as life expectancy increases. In the limit, this pulls everyone down to the minimum pension. One of the conclusions to emerge from Gruber and Wise (1998, 2002) is that many people retire as early as they are allowed. "The collective evidence from all countries combined shows that statutory social-security eligibility ages contribute importantly to early departure from the labor force" (Gruber and Wise 1998, 161). Thus a minimum age at which a person may first receive a pension is an important element in pension design.

Given these arguments, my own view is that a minimum pensionable age that rises over time is an essential ingredient in the policy maker's armory. A more comprehensive solution has five elements:

- Policy makers should set an initial pensionable age at a point that makes it fiscally feasible to provide a genuinely adequate state pension. In the absence of a normative theory, a pragmatic approach would be to work out the maximum fiscal envelope for pensions, and the minimum genuinely adequate pension. Together, these determine the maximum number of pensioners that can be supported. That figure, combined with the age distribution, determines the initial pensionable age.
- Deviations from that pensionable age should be roughly actuarial.
- Over time, the minimum pensionable age should increase in line with rising life expectancy in a way that is rational and transparent, so that people know a long time in advance when (in broad terms) they will be able to retire.
- Labor market reform should introduce flexibility to allow people to move from full-time work toward full retirement along a phased path of their choosing. The design of pensions will need to support these choices.
- Government should strengthen its efforts to increase public understanding of the simple economics of pensions.

Notes

1. "Notional defined contribution" and "non-financial defined contribution" should be understood to have the same definition.

2. Pay-as-you-go pensions are paid (usually by the state) out of current tax revenues. With funded schemes, pensions are paid from a fund built over a period of years from the contributions of their members.

3. See Barr (2001), chapter 6.

4. The question of whether pensions should be actuarial at the margin or across a person's entire contributions record is discussed in subsequent sections.

5. See Barr (2004), chapter 9.

6. See Gruber and Wise (1998, 2002).

References

Atkinson, A. B. 1995. *Incomes and the Welfare State: Essays on Britain and Europe.* Cambridge: Cambridge University Press.

Barr, N. 1987. *The Economics of the Welfare State.* London: Weidenfeld; and Stanford, Calif.: Stanford University Press.

———. 2001. *The Welfare State as Piggy Bank: Information, Risk, Uncertainty and the Role of the State.* Oxford and New York: Oxford University Press.

———. 2004. *The Economics of the Welfare State* (4th ed.). Oxford: Oxford University Press; and Stanford, Calif.: Stanford University Press.

Diamond, P. 2002. *Social Security Reform.* Oxford and New York: Oxford University Press.

Góra, M., and E. Palmer. 2003. "Shifting Perspectives in Pensions." Paper prepared for the "Conference on NDC Pensions," Sandhamn, Sweden, September 28–30. http://www.rfv.se/konferens/docs/shifting_perspectives_in_pensions.pdf.

Gruber, J., and D. Wise. 1998. "Social Security and Retirement: An International Comparison." *American Economic Review* 88 (2, May): 158–63.

———. 2002. "Social Security Programs and Retirement Around the World: Micro Estimation." Working Paper W9407, National Bureau of Economic Research, Cambridge, Mass.

New, B. 1999. "Paternalism and Public Policy." *Economics and Philosophy* 15: 63–83.

Chapter 5

Conceptualization of Non-Financial Defined Contribution Systems

*Assar Lindbeck**

WHEN COMPARING ALTERNATIVE PENSION SYSTEMS, it is useful to rely on a three-dimensional classification: funded versus unfunded systems, actuarial versus nonactuarial systems, and defined benefit (DB) versus defined contribution (DC) systems (see Lindbeck and Persson 2003).

The basic distinction between funded and unfunded (PAYG) pensions is that pension benefits in funded pension systems are financed by the return in financial markets on earlier accumulated pension funds, but in unfunded (PAYG) systems they are financed by the current flow of contributions (taxes) from the active population. In the context of the box (trapezoid) in figure 5.1, where funding is depicted on the vertical axis and actuarial fairness on the horizontal axis, variations in the degree of funding are illustrated as vertical movements. It is also useful to distinguish between "broad funding," when the build-up of pension funds is associated with increased national saving, and "narrow funding," when this is not the case.

The second dimension of pension systems, actuarial versus nonactuarial arrangements, refers to the link between the individual's own contributions and his or her future pension benefits. The strength of this link may be characterized as an expression of the degree of actuarial fairness. A pension system is completely nonactuarial if there is no link at all. By contrast, a link is "actuarially fair" if the capital value of the individual's expected pension benefits is equal to the capital value of his or her own contribution—also on the margin (that is, when the individual varies his or her hours of work during his lifetime). This is the only type of pension system in which there is no labor market distortion. Variations in the degree of actuarial fairness, and hence in the labor market distortion, are schematically depicted as horizontal movements in the figure. Thus not only the funding dimension but also the actuarial dimension is a continuous variable.

In principle, all pension systems covered by the two dimensions depicted in figure 5.1 could be either DC or DB. This aspect of pension systems is then a third (orthogonal) dimension (not depicted in the figure). I define a DC system as one where the contribution rate is fixed, which means that the pension benefits must be (endogenously) adjusted from time to time to ensure that the pension system remains financially viable. In a DB system,

---

* Assar Lindbeck is professor of international economics at the Institute for International Economic Studies (IIES), Stockholm University, and at the Research Institute of Industrial Economics (IUI).

Figure 5.1. A Taxonomy of Social Security Systems

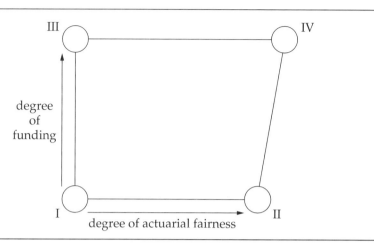

Source: Lindbeck and Persson (2003).

by contrast, the individual is promised either a lump-sum pension benefit or a specific relation between earnings and subsequent pension benefits (often expressed as a promised replacement rate). The contribution rate then must be (endogenously) adjusted from time to time to ensure financial balance.

The taxonomy may be illustrated by considering the extreme points I–IV in the figure. A tax-financed lump-sum pension benefit, equal for all pensioners, is the prototype of a non-actuarial unfunded system (position I in the figure). In the context of a simple overlapping generations model, where the individual's lifetime is divided into two periods—work and retirement—the average return on previously paid contributions is then equal to the growth rate of the tax base, G, while the marginal return is zero.

Position III in the figure instead depicts a nonactuarial, fully funded system, where the average return is the return in financial markets, R, and the marginal return is zero. In position II, with the maximum degree of actuarial fairness for a PAYG system, both the average and the marginal return is G. Finally, position IV depicts an actuarially fair fully funded system where both the average and the marginal return is R. Since the average and marginal returns in position II differ from the corresponding returns in position IV (the former are usually lower), I call a system in the former position "quasi-actuarial" rather than actuarially fair.

In the context of this classification of pension systems, a "notional defined contribution" (NDC) system is simply a quasi-actuarial system (position II in the figure) of DC type: that is, a system with an exogenous contribution rate. The individual's pension wealth may then be registered in an abstract ("notional") account—rather than in a factual financial account as in fully funded, actuarially fair systems.[1]

Although the entire contribution rate, τ, constitutes a marginal tax wedge in a completely nonactuarial system (positions I and III in figure 5.1, as well as in between them), the wedge falls when the system becomes more actuarial (that is, by a move to the right in the figure). For instance, a horizontal move from position III to position IV reduces the marginal tax wedge from τ to zero. The consequences for the marginal tax wedge of a move from I to II are slightly more complex. While the marginal tax wedge in the case of a lump-sum pension (position I) is τ, in a quasi-actuarial system (position II), it may be written as follows in a two-period overlapping generations model (Lindbeck and Persson 2003):

$$\tau(R-G)/(1+R) \equiv \tau\left[1-(1+G)/(1+R)\right] \tag{5.1}$$

The equation says that the individual's income loss from having to pay the contribution rate τ in a quasi-actuarial system is equal to (the discounted value) of the difference between the market return, R, and the return in the PAYG system, G, multiplied by the contribution rate, τ. (The individual is forced to save the fraction τ of his earnings at the return G rather than at the market rate R.)[2] Thus a shift from a completely nonactuarial PAYG system to a quasi-actuarial system implies a reduction in the marginal tax wedge from τ to the expression in equation 5.1. For instance, if the contribution rate is 20 percent, such a shift may cut the marginal tax wedge by approximately half—with realistic assumptions about the number of years in work and retirement, respectively, and with reasonable assumptions about G and R.[3] This would amount to a nontrivial reduction in the tax distortion of work. Since there is no income effect in this case (the *average* return is G both before and after the reform), the individual is encouraged to choose more hours of work, a longer working life, more investment in human capital, more effort to be promoted, more geographical mobility, and so on—provided he understands that the marginal tax wedge has been reduced considerably.

This schematic calculation has assumed that the original pension system was completely nonactuarial. If, instead, the original PAYG system has some actuarial elements—if it is located somewhere between positions I and II in figure 5.1—the reduction in the marginal tax wedge would, of course, be smaller. Indeed, simply basing the pension benefits in a DB system on more years of earnings than the current scheme may reduce the marginal tax wedge. In the limiting case, when the pension benefit is based on an individual's lifetime earnings, the implicit marginal tax wedge could, in fact, be the same as in the expression in equation 5.1, provided yearly earnings are indexed by the same factor as the return factor in the NDC system. Thus an earnings-based DB system may mimic the work incentives in an NDC system. The reason for claiming that the DB system then mimics an NDC system, rather than the other way around, is that the latter type of system is by its very nature quasi-actuarial, while the degree of actuarial fairness varies in DB systems. Indeed, in many countries, the degree of actuarial fairness in DB systems is quite modest, since such systems are designed to ensure income protection (hence to guarantee an accustomed income level) and to redistribute income across income classes.

Earnings-based DB systems may also mimic other typical features of NDC systems. One example is automatic reductions in pension benefits in proportion to increased average life expectancy for each cohort. Such adjustments are also an inherent ("natural") feature of NDC systems, which are designed to include strong actuarial elements. Although the same mechanism can be introduced in earnings-based DB systems, this would be less self-evident since actuarial features are not emphasized in such systems.

Another difference between DB and NDC systems concerns the *international transferability* of pension benefits. Such transferability is also an obvious element in NDC systems, since an individual's pension wealth consists of personal accounts based on contributions paid earlier by the individual. Thus the wealth in a notional account is in a natural way regarded as the individual's property. Such transferability is a less obvious feature of DB systems, where pension benefits have traditionally been tied to citizenship or residence in a specific country. Moreover, international complications are bound to arise if international transferability is allowed in today's DB pension systems. The reason is that such systems are often tied to earnings over a limited number of years. Without intergovernment coordination of pensions systems, some individuals may lose their pension benefits when they move to another country (because of too few years of work to be eligible for pension benefits). In other cases, the sum of pension benefits from different countries may add up to a larger amount than an individual would have accumulated if he or she had lived in one country during his or her entire working life. (Only if all years of earnings would count, as is automatically the case in NDC systems, could this problem be avoided in an earnings-based DB system.)

DB and NDC systems may also differ with respect to their *financial viability*. A crucial issue in this context is whether it is politically easier, or more difficult, to adjust the pension benefits in NDC systems than to adjust the contribution rates in DB systems. Historically, it has certainly turned out to be politically feasible to raise the contribution rates gradually over the years in DB systems—from a few percent of earnings to 15 to 25 percent in most developed countries. The situation may be different today in the sense that voters and politicians may regard contribution rates as so high that further increases are not politically feasible. Indeed, ambitions to avoid further increases in contribution rates are an important background for recent attempts to freeze the contribution rates in DB systems. Again, this would mean that a typical feature of NDC systems is introduced into a DB system.

How financially stable then are NDC systems compared with DB systems? This depends, of course, on exactly how the systems are designed. In principle, to be financially stable, pension benefits in an NDC system should ideally be gradually adjusted throughout an individual's retirement period in response to variations in the growth rate of the tax base of contemporary workers and expected remaining longevity of retired individuals. This would obviously require a *variable* rather than a fixed annuity. (The need for such adjustments of annuities could be reduced, however, if the systems had buffer funds that smooth the benefit payments over time, although this would make the pension system less actuarial.)[4]

The distributional effects also tend to differ between DB and NDC systems. In principle, an NDC system reflects no particular distributional ambitions, either within or across generations, since the system is supposed to be quasi-actuarial. DB systems have no such distributional limitations, and they have traditionally been regarded as legitimate and useful tools for both inter- and intragenerational redistribution. Like other PAYG systems, earnings-based DB systems redistribute income in favor of the first generation of pension beneficiaries, which also implies subsidization of the labor supply (another example of a labor market distortion). Intragenerational redistributions are more ambiguous. For instance, although floors and ceilings on benefits (without corresponding arrangements in the case of contribution rates) tend to redistribute income in favor of low-income groups, rules according to which pension benefits are based on earnings during the best x or last y years usually favor relatively affluent individuals. The net effect on the redistribution of lifetime income among income classes within generations usually seems to be rather modest in real world systems.

Although "pure" NDC systems are void of redistributional ambitions, real world NDC systems are often *combined* with policy measures designed to bring about intragenerational redistribution. Obvious examples are specific tax-financed pension benefits for military service, childcare, sickness, and unemployment. In other words, redistributional elements are often *added* to pure NDC systems, so that the distributional consequences become more like DB systems. In this special sense, NDC systems may mimic the distributional features of DB systems. If politicians are anxious to maintain the "purity" of an NDC system itself, such tax financing may be kept outside the NDC system. Nevertheless, such complementary arrangements have to be considered when analyzing the consequences of shifting from DB to NDC systems.

DB and NDC systems also have different implications for intergenerational *risk sharing*. Mature DB and NDC systems distribute income risk differently in response to disturbances of various types. In principle, in DB systems, the "burden" of unexpected changes in the growth rate of aggregate earnings (and hence the tax base) is borne by active generations, in the form of variations in contribution rates. In NDC systems, by contrast, this risk is shared between generations, since pension benefits will change for both pensioners and workers (in the future). Current employees, of course, also experience a change in earnings.

The distribution of income risk also differs in response to changes in life expectancy. If pension annuities in NDC systems are adjusted gradually (for instance, every year) during the retirement period (a variable annuity), pensioners bear the entire income risk. In NDC systems in the real world, however, the adjustment often takes place only at the time of retirement. If no further adjustment occurs during an individual's retirement period in response to changes in remaining longevity (a fixed annuity), such disturbances may impair the financial viability of an NDC pension system. Subsequent generations then have to bear this risk in one way or another. In the real world, politicians often try to create financial viability by combining reduced benefits and increased contributions, presumably to force active generations and pensioners to share the risk.

To summarize: Even if DB systems may mimic typical features of NDC systems (and in some cases, vice versa), the systems differ in their *general philosophy*. Some features "fit" better in NDC systems than in DB systems—and vice versa. The systems also have different distributional consequences, within as well as across generations, and they tend to distribute income risk differently. Moreover, they differ with respect to the ease of allowing pension benefits to be transferable across countries. It is also likely that the "property rights" of pension benefits are more robust politically in NDC systems.

Notes

1. "Notional defined contribution" and "non-financial defined contribution" should be understood to have the same definition.

2. However, the implicit tax wedge will be higher in early than in late working life, since in the former case the contributions are locked in (at a low yield) over a longer period than in the latter case; see Lindbeck and Persson (2003, p. 85).

3. The calculation is based on the assumption that the value of the contributions accumulates, on average, for 32 years, which means that equation 5.1 may be rewritten $\tau[1 - (1 + G_1)^{32}/(1 + R_1)^{32}]$. I also assume that $G = .02$ and $R = .04$.

4. The Swedish system is unnecessarily unstable because the return is tied to average real wages rather than to the wage sum, and changes in life expectancy do not result in changes in pensions during the course of the retirement period. This is the background for the introduction of a special "balancing mechanism" in the Swedish system.

Reference

Lindbeck, A., and M. Persson. 2003. "The Gains from Pension Reform." *Journal of Economic Literature* 41 (1): 74–112.

Conceptualization of Non-Financial Defined Contribution Systems

Peter Diamond*

IN THEIR PAPER IN THE *JOURNAL OF ECONOMIC LITERATURE*, Assar Lindbeck and Mats Persson (2003) provide a three-dimensional classification of pension systems. One dimension is seen in the contrast between defined contribution (DC) and defined benefit (DB) systems based on adjustment methods to financial realizations. DC systems adjust benefits, while DB systems adjust revenues. This distinction is really a continuum in that one can adjust a combination of the two. This could be done as part of automatic adjustment, as has been proposed for the United States by Peter Diamond and Peter Orszag (2004), who proposed that roughly half the automatic adjustment for the impact of life expectancy increases on social security finances be accomplished by benefit reductions and roughly half by payroll tax rate increases. Or a combined approach can be used in the course of legislation, as in the 1983 reform of U.S. social security (see Light 1985). When it is done by legislation, then the picture can become even more complicated, in that benefits for some can be increased while the general level of benefits is decreased. In addition to arguing that this dimension be considered a continuum, I wonder if it might not be better to use the phrase "adjustments to stochastic realizations," recognizing that pure DC and pure DB systems are just two points in this continuum.

Lindbeck and Persson's second dimension is the degree of funding, which is a continuous variable as well. This dimension is also more complex in that there is the important distinction made by the source of the funding. Analysts are very aware of the difference between assets that are politically committed to paying for benefits and assets that also have been accumulated in a way that contributes to national savings. Thus there is further complexity in this dimension, as well.

They refer to their third dimension as actuarial—the extent to which there is a tight link between paying taxes and getting benefits. This is clearly tied to labor market incentives and is also more complex than they describe. One can think of a system that is a combination of a flat benefit and a benefit proportional to the accumulation of taxes paid. Then the relative sizes of the two portions indicate how distortive the labor incentives are (distortive in the sense that this would interfere with the fundamental welfare theorem if there were no other violations of the conditions needed for the theorem to hold). This example makes it clear that, as with the other two dimensions, there is no sense that "more actuarial" is necessarily better (since income distribution matters as well as efficiency), just as there is no sense in which "more funded" is necessarily better or further along on the DB, DC dimension (in one direction or the other).

But there are other ways in which the determination of benefits can differ from a DC system (which may not be distortive in the sense I used the term above). There is the issue of the weights on different years of earnings in determining benefits—the differ-

---

* Peter Diamond is an institute professor at Massachusetts Institute of Technology.

76

ence between accumulating at a market interest rate in a DC system and an internal rate of return in an NDC system. Actually this comparison needs to be adjusted if it is to be orthogonal to the other dimensions. That is, the comparison ought to be performed holding constant the present value budget constraint for a given cohort. In this case, the NDC approach is expected to weight earlier years less than the market interest rate does and weight later years more than the market interest rate does. Use of the market interest rate involves no distortion if the cohort breaks even on taxes and benefits, there is no redistribution within the cohort, and there are no other labor market distortions. But these conditions do not hold generally. Indeed, the use of progressive annual income taxes would make the NDC approach less distortive since it would tend to balance the rise in marginal income taxes that comes with the usual age-earnings profile. That is, with an upward sloping age-earnings profile and progressive annual income taxes, the sum of explicit income tax and implicit social security tax can well be smoother with NDC than with DC.

It is common to observe that the redistribution to earlier cohorts distorts the labor supply of later ones. In a two-period overlapping generations (OLG) model where the first generation gets a surprise benefit after retirement and all later cohorts pay for it, this is the full story. In practice, early generations are treated more generously over an extended period, thereby affecting labor supply of both recipients and payers of intergenerational redistribution. That is, early cohorts get their labor supplies subsidized, while later ones get them taxed. Given a presumption of a preference for relatively stable tax rates, this is suggestive of a distortion, but a more complex one than in the simple two-period model.

The same issue arises in systems that use a shorter averaging period—the last n years rather than all years, for example. Then, with a break-even comparison, there is taxation of earnings in earlier years that do not count for benefits, and subsidization in later years, which produce so much in benefits as to more than offset the taxes paid. The story becomes even more complex in a setting of individual uncertainty and the use of some measure of highest earnings rather than last earnings. That is, different benefit rules, combined with different stochastic structures on earnings possibilities, will yield different degrees of uncertainty about retirement benefits. I am not convinced that *actuarial* is a good term for this dimension since it is an intervention in the labor market that affects efficiency, individual insurance, and redistribution. Such a term is not used in considering the degree of progressivity of the income tax and it is not clear it is helpful to do so here. This is not to suggest a disagreement with Lindbeck and Persson's identification of labor market incentives as a very important third dimension when classifying systems—just that this dimension, like the other ones, is itself multidimensional, not a single point in a one-dimensional scale. Perhaps "labor market incentives" is a better phrase than "degree actuarial."

Thus I would rename their three dimensions, with new names of "adjustments for stochastic realizations," "degree of funding," and "labor market incentives." Renaming is essentially agreeing with the value in this tripartite way of approaching the effects of social security designs.

In this setting, a pure NDC does all its adjustments on the side of benefits and none on the side of taxes, has limited funding through its buffer stock of assets, and has good labor market incentives. Where each of these three choices is, relative to optimality for some particular country's initial position, is a hard question to answer. There is no basis for claiming a general optimality for any of the positions of a pure NDC system in any of the three dimensions.

To put an NDC system into context, let us briefly review how other systems work. If there is no system, an individual who is doing life cycle optimization saves, with different savings rates at different times; invests in some combination of assets; and at some time purchases an annuity of some form, with at least some of the accumulation. (Rolling purchase of annuities would be better insurance if available at equivalent pricing.) Such a person adjusts the level of savings over time in response to both the realizations of returns on assets and the realized earnings levels.

A mandatory DC plan preserves the individual character of budget balance and the reliance on market pricing of assets and annuities and the bearing of the risk in both asset returns and earnings trajectories. A mandatory DC system does not typically attempt to adjust the savings rate to realizations. The uniform savings loses out on both the liquidity needs behind an ex ante plan of varying savings rates and the ability to adapt savings to experience. But there is room for varying savings if the mandatory rate is not too high—below a savings level adequate for financing all of appropriate retirement income. Redistribution can be combined with this, either through a separate arrangement (such as minimum incomes) or within the system by transferring between accounts.

A corporate DB plan typically relates benefits to a history of earnings and uses projected needs to determine assets to be accumulated. If there is government regulation of financing, it does not apply to an individual but to the plan as a whole. Contribution rates would be continuously adjusted if there was a serious attempt to preserve full funding. In practice, corporations adjust both benefit formulae and contribution rates in response to realizations of both corporate earnings and pension system experience. Moreover, the wage levels themselves are among the candidates for responding to the risks in both pension experience and corporate earnings, subject of course to labor market responses.

A mandatory national DB often differs from corporate DBs in the formula chosen for relating benefits to the history of earnings, although it need not (some corporate plans use the entire history of earnings in determining benefits). It also can differ from a regulated corporate plan in the target level of funding. Put differently, the risk implications of the level of funding are different for corporate and national plans since conditions leading to corporate bankruptcy are different from conditions resulting in countries repudiating benefits.

An NDC is a hybrid with two creative innovations. One is that benefits depend on taxes paid, not earnings. The second is that the NDC plan is discussed in terms of a DC vocabulary, not a DB vocabulary. In the context of an unchanging tax rate, the first innovation is of little significance. The second innovation must have been helpful in achieving political consensus for reform in Sweden, but Axel Börsch-Supan, (2006) has argued that it would not have been helpful in Germany.

If followed closely, a pure NDC has one less degree of freedom than does a similarly constructed DB. An NDC is supposed to provide benefits for different cohorts that have a present discounted value (PDV) that equals the value of the account, using the internal rate of return (IRR) for a discount rate. A DB system could adjust benefits for successive cohorts that followed a similar rule for relating relative benefits to relative life expectancies. But it has a degree of flexibility in setting the relationship between benefits and earnings. In practice, the Swedish NDC used a degree of flexibility in choosing to use period mortality tables rather than cohort ones, either projected or adjusted based on experience, as does a (CREF) annuity pioneered by TIAA-CREF in providing annuities for university employees. Instead, the Swedish system does its adjustment in two ways. One is the level of assets to provide the system at the start. The other is the automatic adjustment mechanism.

In contrasting a well-designed DB or NDC system with a DC system, we see the potential in the DB to improve social welfare by redistributing income and providing insurance for earnings through a progressive benefit formula. (Differently designed redistribution is potentially present in both DC and NDC, but is more in keeping with the approach of a DB.) We see the potential in both the DB and the NDC to provide more within-cohort risk sharing by relying less on rates of return, (rates of return also being earned on individually held assets). We see differences among the three in the weighting of earnings in different years in the determination of benefits. There is no sense in which an NDC is better than a well-designed DB. Instead I think of it as a way to get a DB system that is better designed than many current or former DB systems.

There is wide agreement on several properties of a good system. A country should have one system—not separate systems for separate groups, with political power affecting the relative treatment of different workers. Benefits should be based on at least a large fraction of a career. A system should preserve projected balance, either through fully automatic adjustments or some combination of some automatic adjustments and periodic legislation.[1] A system also needs to have a reliable process for projecting the future workings of the system—both its financial position and its fulfillment of its social insurance goals. And not too much of the cost of reaching balance should be shifted onto generations in the distant future. Does an NDC help countries not meeting these conditions meet them? It may, but it need not.

It has been claimed that it is a virtue of the Swedish system that there is no reliance on forecasts. I think this is not necessarily a virtue. In a fully privatized system, the market engages in projections when deciding how to price annuities and when committing to rates of return on long-lived investment options that have given rates of return. I see nothing inherently problematic in using projections in determining a balance between benefits of different cohorts. I also note that with a private market system with sensible workers, workers would be adjusting their savings rates to realizations of their experience in financing retirement incomes. Moreover, the adjustment rules that do not use an explicit forecast can be seen as merely relying on a naïve forecast.

It should be noted that the value of one kronor in an NDC account is not equal to the value of one kronor in a funded DC account. Since the NDC kronor is earning a lower rate of return than the DC kronor, it is worth less. Thus the claim that workers know the value of their accounts is wrong. It is good for workers to be informed about anticipated monthly benefits. Since there is speculation that workers overvalue lump sums relative to the flows they can finance, more information is definitely useful. Moreover, the dependence of the value of the accumulation in an NDC account on future legislated returns means that accounts with the same accumulation would have different values in countries with different anticipated growth rates. Thus wider use of NDC does not provide ready transfers between countries without detailed actuarial calculations of assets that would need to be transferred to accompany a transfer of liabilities.

An NDC system faces a choice between how it allocates risk to different participants at different times and how likely it is to have a need for an adjustment. For example, recognizing the higher risk aversion of retirees than of workers, it makes sense to have benefits in force not fully subject to the fluctuations in taxable earnings.

In sum, an NDC system is likely to be pretty good—serving its social insurance goals well. It leaves open several choices about design, choices that should be based on the consequences of choice, not some notion of an ideal NDC in light of NDC philosophy. The choices in the design of benefits may be particularly important—single or joint-life annuities, choice of indices for adjusting benefits, and the time shape of benefits more generally.

These choices should reflect both the impact on retirees and the labor market incentives. On a break-even basis, steeper benefits that start lower may be particularly useful for discouraging retirements if they are thought to be occurring too early. Related is the choice of whether to have a retirement test for a few years after initial eligibility for retirement benefits. Such a test affects the time shape of consumption beyond the early entitlement age as well as retirement decisions. Although an NDC is likely to be a pretty good system, it does not make sense to oversell it, claiming excessive virtues relative to alternatives.

Note

1. For discussion of different ways of achieving balance—of allocating the risk associated with realizations of economic equilibria—see Diamond (2004).

References

Börsch-Supan, A. 2006. "What Are NDC Systems? What Do They Bring to Reform Strategies?" In *Pension Reform: Issues and Prospects for Non-Financial Defined Contribution (NDC) Schemes*, ed. R. Holzmann and E. Palmer, chapter 3. Washington, DC: World Bank.

Diamond, P. A. 2004. "Social Security." *American Economic Review* 94 (1): 1–24.

Diamond, P. A., and P. R. Orszag. 2004. *Saving Social Security: A Balanced Approach.* Washington: Brookings Institution Press.

Light, P. C. 1985. *Artful Work: The Politics of Social Security Reform.* New York: Random House.

Lindbeck, A., and M. Persson. 2003. "The Gains from Pension Reform." *Journal of Economic Literature* XLI (1, March): 74–112.

Conceptualization of Non-Financial Defined Contribution Systems

*Salvador Valdés-Prieto**

THE FIRST SECTION OF THESE COMMENTS SHOWS where the notional defined contribution (NDC)[1] design stands regarding funding method and benefit formulae. The second section shows that most NDC plans allocate the outcomes of risk in a way that is fundamentally different from fully funded defined contribution (DC) plans (which are mutual funds), and in this sense most NDC plans are not really defined contribution. The third section argues that the NDC design should not be allowed to have a role in first-pillar and in third-pillar policies. The final section argues that notional accounts (NA) plans can and should provide some liquidity for their members, illustrating that the room for improvements of NDC plans is significant.

Mapping the NDC Family

The three main dimensions of pension plan design are the degree of financial funding of the plan, the type of benefit formula offered to members, and the method used by the plan to allocate the outcomes of aggregate plan risk.[2] It is generally agreed that NDC combines a benefit formula that uses "actuarial" formulae, with a low degree of financial funding: that is, it approaches pure pay-as-you-go finance.

Adoption of the NDC design seems driven by the wish to attenuate initially very high labor distortions, and by the inability of the adopting country to overcome the transition cost toward partially or fully funded alternatives. These issues relate to the first two of the main design dimensions, not to the third.

Degree of Funding

Consider the degree of "financial" funding of the plan, which is the same as the "narrow funding" mentioned by Assar Lindbeck in this roundtable. This degree of funding is obtained by dividing the market value of the pension fund by the expected discounted value of accrued liabilities at the same date. What economic assets are part of the pension fund? Possible assets include not only financial securities, but also land, real estate, and even precious metals owned by the plan. On the other hand, the present expected value of government subsidies and other donations to the plan do not belong in the pension fund because those policies can be modified and those donations can stop. It follows that a pension fund is the set of payment promises in favor of the plan that are protected by property rights, defined in turn by protections spelled out in the constitution (Valdés-Prieto 2002).

* Salvador Valdés-Prieto is professor of economics at Catholic University of Chile and researcher at the Centro de Estudios Públicos, Santiago.

Robert Holzmann provided excellent comments on the final draft. Reactions at the conference by Axel H. Börsch-Supan and Elsa Fornero were also very useful in preparing this written version.

There is another aspect of funding, referring to economywide savings. The degree of "ultimate" or "broad" funding is the degree to which individual wealth is backed by physical assets and net foreign assets. The degree of broad funding is a function of the size of the public debt and of publicly financed infrastructure, and not only of the funding status of the national pension plan. In fact, intergenerational transfers in health subsidies, in education, and in the stock of knowledge can back substantial amounts of individual wealth,[3] influencing the degree of broad funding.

Which of these two is most relevant? It is not appropriate to characterize a pension plan by the features of the economy in which it operates. Therefore, the degree of broad funding of the economy cannot be one of the defining characteristics of a pension plan.[4] Consider an economy where credit card securitization is introduced, allowing an expansion of the stock of consumer credit outstanding and a transitory increase in the flow of consumer expenditures. As the economy's stock of national saving has fallen, the degree of broad funding of the economy has fallen. However, if a fully funded pension plan buys these securitized bonds, any observer will ascertain that the plan itself remains fully funded. As shown by Bernheim and Shoven (1988), there is no link between aggregate savings and changes in the funding status of a pension plan. In conclusion, what matters for labeling the funding status of a pension plan is its degree of "financial" funding.

A pension plan's impact on aggregate national saving may be positive, but it depends heavily on how much other components of savings adjust when the pension plan changes its degree of narrow funding. Raising the degree of "financial" funding of a plan does have two desirable consequences, even if national saving is unaffected. First, the plan gets the additional protection of property rights over the future cash flows produced by the assets. Second, a higher share of plan assets can be traded in financial markets, and this allows the plan to gain from trade, benefiting members. In contrast, raising the size of national savings may or may not be desirable after the transition cost is taken into account.

Benefit Formulae

Benefit formulae are functions that link the amount of benefits received by an individual member during the passive phase of life with that same member's circumstances during the active phase of life. There are two main classes of benefit formulae. The "actuarial" class is based on the amount contributed when active, uses individual account balances, interest is credited to the accounts and uses annuity conversion factors to transform the balance in an annuity. This class includes deferred annuities purchased by installments and variable annuities. The other main class of benefit formulae is built around "years of service" and "revalued career average salary." There are other benefit formulae outside these two classes, such as the Brazilian *"fator previdenciario"* introduced in 1999. Under some parameter configurations, a years-of-service benefit formula can be almost equal to an actuarial benefit formula, but they always differ in one aspect: the response of benefits to increases in contribution *rates* is positive for actuarial formulae and is zero for years of service formulae.

It was suggested in the conference that NDC plans introduce no tax wedge on labor decisions because they use an actuarial benefit formula. I disagree, because a benefit formula may be actuarial but can use nonmarket parameters. Examples of parameters are the interest rate credited to individual accounts and the annuity conversion factors that set the amount of the pension. The link between individual contributions and the expected present value of additional benefits may be far from the analogous link offered by financial market prices, despite the mathematical shape common to all actuarial formulae.

Consider NDC plans. The fact that they use pay-as-you-go (PAYG) finance fixes the direction of the deviation between the link provided by the financial market and the link provided by the benefit formula, at least for steady states. Consider a situation where GDP and the covered wage bill grow at a constant rate g, where the internal rate of return (IRR) offered by the NDC plan's benefit formula is g, and where the real rate of return on a balanced portfolio of investments and insurance contracts available in the financial market is r, after adjusting for risk differences. Asset market equilibrium requires that $r > g$ in the long run. If not, it would be possible for any infinitely lived agent whose income grows in proportion to the economy to borrow at rate r and roll over its debt indefinitely without ever paying interest, and the total debt would still fall over time relative to assets (Tirole 1985). In addition, the empirical evidence supports the hypothesis that $r > g$ in most actual economies most of the time (Abel et al. 1989). It follows that $r > $ IRR. Therefore, the wedge introduced by an actuarial benefit formula with rate g is a tax, not a subsidy, in the long run. Two important labor decisions that are distorted by this hidden tax in NDC plans are:

- Retirement at earlier ages—the fact that IRR $< r$ creates an economic incentive to start a NDC pension as early as allowed, and
- Joining covered employment at older ages—the fact that IRR $< r$ gives an incentive to the young to prolong their studies and ramblings and to engage in uncovered work for a longer period. This may prevent some of them from getting crucial on-the-job training at the most appropriate age.

There are two other good reasons to avoid attaching efficiency, equity, and insurance implications to pension plans that use "actuarial" benefits formulae, as some authors did in the conference. One is that the plan's incentives may be irrelevant in the wider economic context in which the individual operates. The other is that the plan's incentives might be highly correlated with the incentives provided by other government policies that affect the individual.

To see this, consider the efficiency of the labor market decisions made by active workers, such as hours, effort, and participation. These decisions depend on net taxes on earnings. These net taxes, in turn, depend on both the marginal and the average link between contributions and the risk-adjusted expected present value of benefits in this particular pension plan. However, labor incentives also depend on other pension plans in which the individual may participate (say an occupational plan), on the income tax schedule, and on the marginal and average link between contributions and the expected value of benefits offered by mandatory health insurance and unemployment insurance. If a pension reform raises the marginal link between benefits and contributions in the pension plan, the impact on labor choice may be small or zero, if the other programs maintain or increase their tax wedges.

Now consider a case where the current pension plan is fully funded, but it replaced an older PAYG financed plan that was solvent, that is, financially balanced. Assume that the contribution rate to the new funded plan was cut to take advantage of the higher return ($r > g$). Assume also that the transition cost was financed by issuing new public debt and by introducing a new explicit and permanent tax on earnings to finance interest payments on that new public debt, equal to $(r - g) \times$ (New Debt). This new tax collects revenue that is just enough to prevent the ratio of new debt to GDP from exploding in the long run (Auerbach and Kotlikoff 1987). Then changes in the tax wedge of the mandatory plan—currently zero—are fully *negatively* correlated with the total explicit tax rate on earnings. In fact, the overall tax rate on covered earnings is the same as it was under the old PAYG-financed plan.

The impact of the wider economic context should also moderate statements about the impact of pension reforms on insurance and income redistribution. Consider a comparison between a defined benefit (DB) plan that offers implicit insurance for an unexpectedly short working life through a less-than-actuarial reduction to early pensions, such as the U.S. social security program, and a simple NDC plan. It is standard practice to attach insurance advantages to the DB plan over the NDC plan, without checking if the personal tax system in the second country includes implicit insurance for a short working life. This insurance will be offered if the income tax schedule on pension income is progressive, because those who start their pension younger—say, due to an unexpectedly short working life—will receive a smaller pension and therefore will pay lower tax rates, achieving a less-than-actuarial cut on after-tax early pensions. Moreover, if the country with the DB plan exempts pensions from personal income taxes, and the second country does not, total insurance for a short working life may be larger in the second country, despite a plan that does not offer that type of insurance.

From the two features of NDC—an actuarial benefit formula and a low degree of funding—it follows that NDC is a label that covers a wide set of pension designs. For instance, if the notional interest rate credited in individual accounts during the active phase of life is the growth rate of average wages minus 1.6 percent per year, as in Sweden, the financial behavior of the plan and its implications for members are bound to be quite different from those of another NDC plan where the notional interest rate is 6 percent real per year, as was proposed in Brazil during the debate leading to the *"fator previdenciario"* reform of 1999.[5] The use of actuarial benefit formulae still allows for substantial differences in parameters, which may create large differences in the labor market incentives, insurance, and redistributional impacts.

NDC and Redistribution

It is useful to distinguish between three types of redistributive policies. The first supports the poor, including the elderly poor, with resources from the rest of society. The second redistributes income among the employed middle classes, say from professionals with higher earnings toward menial workers with lower earnings. The third type taxes the owners of capital to support the working classes.

Consider the following policy of the second type: concentrating the redistribution among the middle classes in the tax system versus dispersing such redistribution among a variety of pension, health, housing, education, and unemployment insurance programs, in addition to the tax system. If concentration is chosen, then this type of redistribution can be designed in more encompassing ways than if these redistributive policies are dispersed and embedded in several sectoral policies. When the trade-off between redistribution and efficiency is presented globally to public opinion, transparency increases, because the debate is freed from the complicated aspects of sectoral policies that raise the cost of communication.

Some may believe that policies should be made *less* transparent to enable experts to escape the manipulations introduced by politicians seeking reelection through pork rather than through the production of desirable public policies. This can be the case in some countries and episodes. However, experts also have an interest in gaining access to the broad picture when they design policies that redistribute income within the middle classes.

Concentration implies that redistribution within the middle classes ceases to be one of the purposes of pension policy because that goal is served by overall tax policy. Of course, redistribution continues to be important, but it is pursued more comprehensively. A major advantage of adopting NDC is that it facilitates concentration, allowing an increase in the transparency of the overall redistribution policy.

The overall degree of redistribution also implies a degree of partial insurance of disposable income, because taxes fall when income falls. If pension amounts reflect lifetime income better than annual income, then let fiscal policy impose a different set of income tax rates on pension income than on other sources of annual income. The same logic is used in most countries to set special tax rates on the capital gains that occur when a family sells their house.

Another advantage of concentration is that tax rates on pension income can be designed to take into account income from third-pillar pension contracts and from capital.

Method Used to Allocate the Outcome of Aggregate Plan Risks

Casual observers tend to believe that the method used by a plan to allocate the outcomes of aggregate risks is set by the benefit formula. For example, it is thought that actuarial benefit formulae come together with the DC method used by mutual funds. It is also believed that years-of-service benefit formulae always allocate aggregate risks with the DB model. Two examples show that this association is invalid. Consider first an annuity contract. As the life insurance company guarantees a certain benefit amount regardless of shocks to investment returns and to the life tables, this contract is appropriately described as a defined benefit. However, its benefit formula is actuarial. In the opposite extreme, consider a plan that uses a years-of-service benefit formula to set the initial pension for each member, but indexes subsequent pension payments to the actual observed growth rate of contribution revenue, in a PAYG context. This plan uses a method to allocate aggregate risks that transfers them in full to older members, so it is not DB.[6]

The method for allocating aggregate plan risks is heavily influenced by other aspects of the plan, too. These other aspects can be rules for adjusting plan parameters (if such rules exist), the rules for the use of credit lines from sponsors (such as the treasury), and the rules for trading the uninsurable component of aggregate risk in the financial markets. Risk can be allocated by discretion as well. Discretion is what happens when the allocation of aggregate financial losses and gains is decided ex post by a designated set of people—say, members of parliament, members of a board of elders, or a minister of finance. Such authorities may also limit the pension plan's access to credit. In practice, successive layers of rules for adjusting parameters blend gracefully into discretion. These other aspects turn the risk allocation method into a design dimension that is effectively independent from the benefit formula, as emphasized by Lindbeck and Persson (2003).[7]

Risk may be created, destroyed, or transferred. Badly designed rules and discretion can create risk. Consider a hypothetical NDC plan whose factor for converting account balances to annuities is a fixed function of the returns earned by a relatively small buffer fund that is partly invested in equities. That rule is a bet that *creates* risk, making the plan operate as a casino, which would be Pareto-dominated by other rules unless some members are risk lovers. Now consider risk creation by a plan whose parameters are set by parliament according to the electoral needs of a changing majority. This plan may turn into a *political casino*. A partial-equilibrium model of optimal life-cycle consumption calibrated with data for Germany and the United States finds that political risk creates a welfare loss equivalent to between 1.7 percent and 3.6 percent of the pension amount (Holst 2005).

These examples show that the set of possible risk allocation methods that may be used by a pension plan is wider than the conventional distinction between defined benefit and defined contribution. This fact raises two challenges: the first is to classify the options in a useful way, and the second is to develop welfare criteria to identify the optimal option in a given environment.

Classifying the Options

One of the most useful classifications of risk allocation methods was presented above: rule-based versus discretionary. Another common distinction is between DC and DB.

These distinctions are independent, so we have a two-way classification of risk allocation methods. In one axis is the degree to which aggregate risk is allocated by rules versus discretion. The other axis contains pure DB, pure DC, and combinations such as portfolios that change risk in response to the member's age.

Consider the precise meaning of pure DC. The origin of the expression *defined contribution* is legal: the obligations of the sponsor are limited to the obligation of paying the agreed contribution, and are *defined* by this limit. When considering the economic meaning of DC, it cannot be that the contribution rate is fixed over time because when that rate has been changed in fully funded DC plans, those plans have not lost their DC character.[8] DC cannot mean that the contribution rate is not adjusted in response to realizations, because the mutual fund, which is the original DC design, does not change its DC nature when a member adjusts her contribution rate in response to realizations.[9] I offer the following economic definitions (Valdés-Prieto 2002, p. 717):[10]

> DC: *When the risk allocation method transmits all the plan's aggregate financial risk to current members only, and it does so in proportion to the capital value of the accrued rights to pension benefits owned by each member.*

This definition of DC is a summary description of the standard mutual fund. This is the natural benchmark because of its widespread use in financial markets. A mutual fund allocates risk by defining the price of each share as the market value of assets divided by the number of shares (the value of liabilities is this price times the number of shares). The number of shares varies with inflows and outflows valued at yesterday's share price.[11] The proposed definition of DC allows some leeway because the method for calculating capital value is not specified. It is quite different to discount future expected benefits at market interest rates than to discount them at the internal rate of return of the plan, which may be quite lower,[12] because the pro-rata shares for allocating the aggregate outcomes of risk are distributed among plan members in a different way.

> DB: *When the risk allocation method does **not** transmit any portion of the plan's aggregate financial risk to pensioned members.*

Shielding pensioners from aggregate risk implies that risk must be allocated to other plan members, or to a bond issuer (who pays a fixed amount in most states of nature), or to a sponsor (as in annuities, where the life insurance company takes the risk), or to taxpayers (as in discretionary DB, where parliament can pass the risk to taxpayers and beneficiaries of government transfers).

Optimal policy can be analyzed after the options have been outlined. Automatic financial stability in the short run is a valuable property for a pension plan because it prevents insolvency. International experience shows that discretion has failed to provide automatic financial stability in the pension policy area, in contrast to the case of central banks and monetary policy. This evidence suggests that rules are better than discretion in pension policy.

Which is the optimal rule? Economic theory shows that to maximize welfare, a plan should trade risk with the rest of the economy at market prices, and the uninsurable risk that remains should be shared among members in proportion to individual risk tolerance.[13] Empirically, the predicted risk tolerance of a member is a function of the volatility of labor earnings, the presence of other wealth, access to insurance and credit lines, and age. Pure DB (as defined above) cannot be socially optimal, because it is unlikely that all pensioners have zero risk tolerance.[14] Even among aged members, risk tolerance is likely to be higher than zero for a subset of members. In the same way, a DC plan with a single portfolio is not optimal either. In contrast, a DC plan where members are allowed to choose among a set of balanced portfolios with different risk levels appears closer to optimality, because adaptation to individual risk tolerance is allowed. Moreover, a portfolio designed to serve those who plan to start a pension in a given date (say in 2020) can provide a valuable service to its members: change the level of risk slowly as they age, moving toward portfolios more heavily invested in bonds. Bond portfolios are DB as well because the issuers of the bonds absorb 100 percent of the underlying economic risks.

Implications for NDC Plans

An NDC plan that indexes pensions to price inflation is DB because pensioners are exempt from sharing in the plan's aggregate financial risk. In contrast, when an NDC plan indexes pensions to GDP growth (as in Italy) or to the growth rate of average covered wages (as in Sweden), the plan does not guarantee a fixed standard of living to pensioners, and therefore is neither DC nor DB. Those designs allow pensioners to share in the economy's growth or in the growth of average wages. However, they do so *regardless* of whether the plan is experiencing an aggregate actuarial surplus or deficit in the present. For example, if unemployment rises due to a drop in labor demand for menial jobs, the Swedish rule registers that average wages rise while slower employment growth may push plan assets below liabilities. The ensuing increase to pensions (triggered by the increase in average wages) raises liabilities, exacerbating the financial imbalance. This NDC rule may be foisting risks on members when aggregate risk is zero, a situation that may be described as risk creation or wagering.

In contrast, if the origin of the faster growth in average covered wages is an across-the-board increase in labor productivity, then this rule can be defended on the grounds of intergenerational risk sharing. Policy makers should check how rules respond to a wide variety of shocks, to avoid risk creation.

Now consider rules for active members. Most NDC plans are less financially stable than fully funded DC plans because all deviations from steady state growth create actuarial surpluses and deficits (see Settergren and Mikula 2006, and a proof in Valdés-Prieto 2000). Moreover, reliance on credit lines from the treasury means that these plans create risk for the treasury, or require taxation of past generations to endow the plan with a buffer fund. If parliament makes the final decision but organized members respond with political activism, the plan may come to be seen by some as a political casino.

The *creation* of risk for active members is a trick that a truly DC rule, as the one used by mutual funds, is unable to pull. A truly DC rule transmits all aggregate risk to current plan members, without creating risk. Thus, the NDC design is fundamentally different from DC, in the sense defined above. For this reason, I subsequently refer to the Italian, Polish, and Swedish plans as "notional accounts" (NA), rather than NDC.

The Swedish plan's original rules were to credit notional capital of active workers at the growth rate of contribution revenue, and to adjust pensions in payment by the growth rate in average wages minus 1.6 percent per year. However, since May 2001, a different rule applies: When the plan's liabilities exceed assets, the notional interest rate credited to active members and the rate of adjustment of pensions in payment are both cut, to equal the growth rate of average wages minus the growth rate in liabilities plus the growth rate in assets (Settergren 2001). This mechanism might endow the Swedish NDC plan with automatic financial balance in the short run and might prevent the creation of risk for the treasury. However, a further twist was introduced in the 2001 reform. Even if subsequent liabilities are surpassed by assets, the lower notional interest rate and the lower rate of indexation of pensions remain in force, until the original ratio of average pensions to average wages is restored. No symmetric rule for the case when assets exceed liabilities is in place. This asymmetry may produce permanent cash surpluses, which would strengthen the treasury at the expense of plan members.

This discussion suggests that sponsors of NA plans have much work to do improving risk allocation methods. This task requires the development of a more comprehensive framework to define optimality.

The Role of NA in Pillars One and Three

Let us discuss first the role of the NA design in third-pillar policy. I define *third-pillar policies* as those that introduce fiscal or regulatory incentives, but not mandates, to induce improvident people in the middle classes to save more for old age on a voluntary basis.[15]

PAYG finance allows workers to invest in an implicit security whose dividend is a share of the human capital returns (earnings) of future generations of covered workers.[16] Assume that this security should have pride of place in most people's long-term portfolios.[17] It follows that any financial services company should consider offering an NA plan to clients who save for old age induced by fiscal incentives. For example, banks and mutual funds that offer IRAs and 401(k) plans may want to offer an NA plan on a voluntary basis.

However, third-pillar plans that are NA are likely to enjoy an undeserved marketing bonanza in their introductory phase. This is because PAYG finance offers net subsidies to the initial generation. But when PAYG finance matures, it must create a tax on members to remain financially independent. It will be difficult to find new members in the long run, in the absence of a mandate to future workers to join the plan. An example is the pyramid pension plan that appeared in Paraguay in 1985, which grew for at least 10 years thanks to the subsidies offered to the initial members.[18] Therefore, investor protection criteria suggest that financial firms should be banned from offering voluntary NA plans.

For a related reason, the state should beware of mandating an NA plan on a class of firms or on a sector of economic activity. Although a new NA plan can pay subsidies to the initial generation, which will help attract workers into this sector, in the long run the tax hidden in mature PAYG finance is likely to scare them away. In that case the plan will default on promised pension amounts. At that point, the losing members are likely to remember the sectoral mandate and demand compensation from the government.

Now consider the role of NA in *first-pillar* policy, which I define as the set of government programs that provide support to the old poor. The aim of such programs is to provide *more* subsidies to those people who are poorer—and who are precisely those who contribute less. Given the fact that NA plans use actuarial benefit formulae, which pay *less* benefits to those who contribute less, it is obvious that NA plans contradict the aim of first-pillar policy.

Poor pensioners are likely to be relatively more risk-averse, because of their closeness to perceived subsistence consumption levels. The fact that NA plans are not DB means that the old poor are allocated an excessive share of the plan's aggregate financial risk. Moreover, an NA first-pillar program may subject poor pensioners to the bets embedded in the risk allocation method. It follows that NA should not be used in first-pillar programs.

NA Plans and Partial Liquidity for Mandatory Saving

Mandatory plans where member wealth is illiquid create efficiency costs when the member values liquidity. Only those members who own substantial voluntary liquid assets are exceptions. Even provident members respond to illiquidity by modifying their labor choices in order to minimize this perceived cost. Mandatory plans that freeze accrued pension rights into an illiquid claim are also likely to be inequitable. The reason is that workers who own negligible amounts of precautionary savings are likely to be the poorest. The illiquidity of pension claims may force these poorer workers to sacrifice too much consumption in order to build up a stock of precautionary savings, or to depend too much on the emergency loans provided by close kin or loan sharks. These problems besiege all mandatory plans, including fully funded, NA, and traditional designs.

An interesting claim made in this conference is that in an NA plan, benefits are as illiquid as in fully and partially funded plans. Pension plan liquidity refers to giving members the option of getting immediate access to a limited portion of their claims on old age benefits in response to an emergency, ideally defined by members themselves. Partial liquidity holds the promise of mitigating the efficiency costs and the inequities caused by imposing a mandate to save at a flat rate, disregarding individual liquidity needs.

Partial liquidity is a real possibility in fully and partially funded plans, which can sell some assets to give credit to members. As international experience shows, recovery of liquidity loans can be ensured by possessing a number of pension payments starting at the date of pension issue, delaying effective pension age.[19] The amount of such loans should be capped with methods that create incentives to repay.[20]

Now consider an NA plan, financed with the PAYG method. Can it offer the option of providing partial liquidity to its members? If members are allowed to make partial withdrawals, the plan has to finance the aggregate net flow by issuing debt in the financial market. To break even, the plan must charge members a market interest rate (plus administrative costs).[21] However, this option is not available to all NA plans: the plan must enjoy enough financial stability to be creditworthy.

Thus, NA plans that wish to offer partial liquidity to their members face one more requirement than those faced by fully funded plans. They must be creditworthy, despite being financed with the PAYG method and being subject to some political discretion.[22]

Summing up, the NA design is very attractive for initial conditions characterized by highly inefficient benefit formulae and fiscal constraints that prevent a transition to full funding. However, much remains to be done to improve this promising design.

Notes

1. "Notional defined contribution" and "non-financial defined contribution" should be understood to have the same definition.

2. This three-way classification, used by many, including Lindbeck and Persson (2003), is more useful than the older two-way classification that merged together the benefit formula and the method for allocating the outcome of aggregate risks.

3. See Lee (1994).

4. In this we differ from Lindbeck and Persson's taxonomy (2003, p. 75).

5. That proposal was rejected because 6 percent real was far *below* market interest rates in Brazil at the time.

6. There is no suggestion that any of these risk allocation rules is optimal.

7. One may also consider defining DC as a combination of a certain benefit formula (actuarial) and some risk allocation property. That approach would fail to build upon the orthogonality between benefit formulae and the risk allocation method, and would fail to manage the different ways in which a plan may deal with risk.

8. On this point, I disagree with Assar Lindbeck, in this roundtable.

9. On this I disagree with Peter Diamond, in this roundtable.

10. This definition of DC fulfills the principle enunciated by Settergren (2001, p. 4, footnote 9): "In a DC plan uninsurable risks must be assumed by the pension level, rather than by the contribution rate."

11. The use of daily prices to value the accrued rights of members transmits any short-term volatility contained in market prices to the value of accrued rights. To prevent the transitory component of that volatility from creating unwarranted worries among members with limited financial experience, it may be wise to report accrued values using averages over reasonable periods.

12. For example, Sweden discounts liabilities and assets at the growth rate of average covered wages, which is below market interest rates in the long run.

13. See the summary of "Syndicate Theory" provided by Kreps in his textbook, *A Course in Microeconomic Theory* (1990, pp. 169–74).

14. Merton (1983) stated this point more than 20 years ago.

15. Provided that the fiscal incentives are more generous than those given to savings not oriented to cover old-age needs. The fiscal incentive may be flat rate, progressive (as in the Czech Republic's 1995 program), or regressive (as in deductions from income tax in the United States).

16. The word *security* implies that the owner is protected by property rights. This is usually not the case for claims on a share of the future earnings of workers.

17. For example, see Merton (1983) and Dutta, Kapur, and Orszag (2000).

18. See "Voluntary participation in a pay as you go plan," in Valdés-Prieto (2002, box 10.2, p. 516–7).

19. This repossession method is used successfully in the Philippines by the Employees Provident Fund (EPF). The critical requirement for economic efficiency is that the cost of nonpayment remains with the individual, as if the loan were deducted from the individual account balance, not from a collectively owned fund. One requirement for political sustainability of liquidity loans is that repossession does not reduce the pension amount, and this justifies a preference for raising the effective pension age. See a summary of international experience in Valdés-Prieto (2002, chapter 4, section 4.4).

20. A recent proposal is to cap the loans outstanding at, say, 70 percent of the sum of contributions made during the last 36 months. This works like airline frequent-flyer miles. It ensures that 100 percent of the contribution is saved for old age after 3 years and 30 percent is saved immediately. As the option of drawing a liquidity loan is valuable, many are unlikely to remain fully indebted most of the time. See Beyer and Valdés-Prieto (2004) for a recent proposal for Chile.

21. In PAYG-financed plans in steady state, this interest rate will be above the IRR offered by the plan to its members.

22. An NA plan can become creditworthy thanks to a credit line from the treasury, but in this case the scheme should be described as engaging the treasury in consumer finance. The interesting case is where partial liquidity is provided without guarantees from the treasury.

References

Abel, A., G. Mankiw, L. Summers, and R. Zeckhauser. 1989. "Assesing Dynamic Efficiency." *The Review of Economic Studies* 56 (1): 1–20.

Auerbach, A. and L. Kotlikoff. 1987. *Dynamic Fiscal Policy.* New York: Cambridge University Press.

Bernheim, D., and J. Shoven. 1988. "Pension Funding and Saving." In *Pensions in the U.S. Economy*, ed. Z. Bodie, J. Shoven, and D. Wise, 85–114. Cambridge, Mass.: National Bureau of Economic Research, University of Chicago Press.

Beyer, H., and S. Valdés-Prieto. 2004. "Análisis de la situación de trabajadores con baja densidad de cotizaciones y propuestas para corregir esta situación." Report to *Servicio Nacional de la Mujer*, Santiago, Chile, March.

Dutta, J., S. Kapur, and M. Orszag. 2000. "A Portfolio Approach to the Optimal Funding of Pensions." *Economic Letters* 69: 201–6.

Holst, R. 2005. "Policy Risk: Some Evidence, its Relevance and Welfare Costs in Retirement Programs." Dept. of Economics, University of Chicago, March.

Kreps, D. 1990. *A Course in Microeconomic Theory.* Princeton, N.J.: Princeton University Press.

Lee, R. 1994. "Population Age Structure, Intergenerational Transfer and Wealth: A New Approach, with Application to the U.S." *Journal of Human Resources* 29 (4): 1027–63.

Lindbeck, A., and M. Persson. 2003. "The Gains from Pension Reform." *Journal of Economic Literature* XLI (March): 74–112.

Merton, R. 1983. "On the Role of Social Security as a Means for Efficient Risk Sharing in an Economy where Human Capital is not Tradeable." In *Financial Aspects of the U.S. Pension System*, ed. Z. Bodie and J. Shoven. Cambridge, Mass.: National Bureau of Economic Research, University of Chicago Press.

Settergren, O. 2001. "The Automatic Balance Mechanism of the Swedish Pension System: A Non-Technical Introduction." *Riksförsäkringsverket* (August). www.rfv.se/English.

Settergren, O., and B. D. Mikula. 2006. "The Rate of Return of Pay-As-You-Go Pension Systems: A More Exact Consumption-Loan Model of Interest." In *Pension Reform: Issues and Prospects for Non-Financial Defined Contribution (NDC) Schemes*, ed. R. Holzmann and E. Palmer, chapter 7. Washington, DC: World Bank.

Tirole, J. 1985. "Asset Bubbles and Overlapping Generations." *Econometrica* 53 (6): 1499–1527.

Valdés-Prieto, S. 2000. "The Financial Stability of Notional Account Pensions." *Scandinavian Journal of Economics* 102 (3): 395–417.

———. 2002. *Políticas y Mercados de Pensiones: Un Texto Universitario para América Latina.* Santiago, Chile: Ediciones Universidad Católica. mriverv1@puc.cl

PART II

CONCEPTUAL ISSUES OF DESIGN AND IMPLEMENTATION

Chapter 6

Demographic Uncertainty and Evaluation of Sustainability of Pension Systems

Juha M. Alho, Jukka Lassila, and Tarmo Valkonen[*]

POPULATION AGING IN EUROPE IS MORE COMPLEX than is generally recognized. The uncertainty in demographic projections is also larger than is usually assumed. This makes the assessment of long-term characteristics of pension systems challenging. Since different pension policy instruments react in different ways to demographic developments across cohorts and over time, the risk characteristics of the existing policies and proposed alternatives should be investigated and "crash-tested" under a wide range of realistic alternatives.

Because of the complexities of changing age structures, neither individuals nor firms nor administrators of pension systems can easily see what will happen to pensions and contributions if unlucky demographics materialize. Thus it is difficult for anyone to design and apply their risk strategies efficiently. "Crash testing" provides one way of addressing the problem. The broader conclusion is that for a pension strategy to be sustainable, it should explicitly state what actions are to be taken if the population and the economy do not evolve as expected. For example, while the notional defined contribution (NDC) system[1] in Sweden provides an exceptional degree of transparency in this respect, the challenge of quantifying and communicating the risk characteristics of the system to the population at large remains.

This study combines stochastic population simulations with an overlapping generations (OLG) model that assumes perfect foresight from the agents. We view this as a first step toward a more comprehensive model, in which future uncertainty is handled in a more advanced manner. Yet even the current models provide novel insights. New questions can be formalized and new strategies entertained. We suggest areas for future research that are relevant for pension policy design.

* Juha M. Alho is professor of statistics at the University of Joensuu, Finland; Jukka Lassila is research director and Tarmo Valkonen is head of the Unit in Public Finance Research at the Research Institute of the Finnish Economy.

We thank Edward Palmer and Sergio Nisticò for comments. We also acknowledge the financial support of the European Commission for two underlying research projects: DEMWEL "Demographic Uncertainty and the Sustainability of Social Welfare Systems" (QLK6-CT-2002-02500), and UPE for "Uncertain Population of Europe" (HPSE-CT-2001-00095).

Uncertainty Caused by Lack of Sustainability

A well-known definition of the sustainability of fiscal policies is the view of the Organisation of Economic Co-operation and Development (OECD): "Sustainability is basically about good housekeeping. It is essentially about whether, based on the policy currently on books, a government is headed towards excessive debt accumulation."[2] More precisely: "Fiscal policy can be thought of as a set of rules, as well as an inherited level of debt. And a *sustainable fiscal policy* can be defined as a policy such that the ratio of debt to GNP eventually converges back to its initial level."[3] The forecasts for spending and transfers are taken as given. This is close in spirit to generational accounting.

In the case of pension systems, the OECD view requires that the current contribution rate suffice to finance benefits and that the possible fund stays at a reasonable level compared with the size of the system. However, other aspects merit attention. In particular, a contributor may consider a system sustainable even if rules are changed or pensioners suffer but the contribution rate does not change too much. A pensioner may consider the system sustainable as long as the pension is as expected, even if this requires changing the rules and the contributors suffer. In either case the risk is that, because of future developments, the system puts an unexpected strain on one party or another. If the likelihoods of the various risks were known, the agents could prepare for them in a rational manner. Reducing the scope of the unexpected seems to be a natural aspect of sustainability.

In game theory, a *strategy* is a set of rules, defined for the present and the future, stating what action will be taken under all states of the world.[4] In the case of pensions, a *sustainable policy strategy* is a set of rules such that both the contributors and the pensioners know, beforehand, what will be done in any reasonable future circumstance, and they accept the future actions, or at least cannot force a change of the system.

The difference between a policy and a policy strategy is a very practical one. Considerations about sustainable pension policies are usually based on one set of base assumptions about key factors such as future demographics, productivity, and interest rates. In contrast, considerations about sustainable pension strategies must be based on a large number of possible states of the world that cover a realistic range of economic and demographic developments.

The whole Swedish NDC system may be thought of as a step toward implementing a strategy rather than merely being a set of policy instruments. It is "designed to be financially stable, that is, regardless of demographic or economic development it will be able to finance its obligations with a fixed contribution rate and fixed rules for calculating benefits."[5] Adjustment mechanisms have been defined; even a "brake" has been established, to be activated if things go badly.[6] Whether the strategy is sustainable depends on its operating characteristics. Will the contributors and pensioners accept the outcomes that come of the new legislation, under different future circumstances? The time horizon may also be important. Valdés-Prieto (2000) suggests that long-term financial stability is irrelevant if the rules allow imbalances that continue long enough so that the political process is likely to intervene.

In practice, one cannot know with certainty how future workers and pensioners will react to the system. The designers of new policies tend to emphasize the most likely future developments, when they argue for the reform. Opponents try to imagine circumstances in which one or another aspect of the system would cause it to crash. Our proposal is to provide realistic descriptions of the future contingencies in a probabilistic fashion. Conventional "high" and "low" scenarios that have been used for this purpose have had little or no effect on policy recommendations. Without any probabilities attached to the alternatives, their importance is suspect and the results are difficult to interpret. Analyses based on expected or "most likely" assumptions have dominated.

For an individual contributor or a pensioner, sustainability is related both to trustworthiness and predictability. Can the level of future contributions and future pensions be known with sufficient accuracy, so that a choice can effectively be made between supplementary savings or consumption (or leisure time)? To have operational counterparts, this study will approach "trust" by defining thresholds for a change in contribution rates and replacement rates. These thresholds form a politically viable region within which the rates can change without leading to system reform.[7] "Predictability" requires a known or estimated distribution of outcomes in the viable region. In the Swedish case, for example, it would be desirable to produce estimates of the likelihood of having to use the "brake."

What is said above concerning an individual can be said for a firm, as well. In decisions concerning which country to invest in, it helps if the firm has a realistic view about indirect labor costs in the future. Unrestricted pension contribution rates can be a major source of risk.

Aspects of Future Fertility and Mortality in Europe

Age Structure and Negative Growth

The *total fertility rate* of year t is defined as the expected number of children a newborn baby girl is expected to have, under the fertility and mortality regimes of year t. About 105 boys are born for every 100 girls, so if all women would survive to the end of child-bearing ages, a total fertility rate of 2.05 would suffice for internal population renewal. Allowing for mortality, a somewhat higher value, about 2.07, is sufficient in Europe. In year 2000, Iceland had a total fertility of 2.07. The remaining European countries have below replacement fertility. Belgium, France, Luxembourg, the Netherlands, the Nordic countries, Portugal, and the United Kingdom had a total fertility in the range [1.51, 1.89]. Austria, Germany, Greece, Italy, Spain, Bulgaria, Hungary, Poland, and Romania form a low fertility group with fertility in the range [1.24, 1.36]. It is well known that these are exceptionally low values, in historical perspective. What has received less attention is the implication of fertility on the age distribution.

In Finland, the total fertility rate in 2000 was 1.7. If this level were to persist, the population would start to *decline* at the rate of about 0.63 percent per year. Figure 6.1 tries to put this into a perspective. The solid curve corresponds to the age distribution of a closed stationary population (in which births equal deaths) whose mortality equals that of the Finnish women of the late 1990s. The dashed curve is based on the same survival probabilities, but with births exceeding deaths by a constant ratio. The ratio has been chosen so that the resulting rate of increase (= 0.0065) equals the average growth of the Finnish population during the 20th century. The dotted line has the corresponding age distribution when the rate of decline is negative (= –0.0065). This happens to be almost exactly the asymptotic rate of decline implied by the current Finnish fertility. The declining stable population has a *much older* age distribution than the stationary one, let alone the growing population from which we derive our understanding of the world. *This form of population aging derives from fertility alone*, since we are keeping mortality fixed.

In general, convergence to stability might take over a century, so stable populations have not received much attention in past years. However, the solid line with squares in figure 6.1 gives the current age distribution of Finland. In about 10 to 15 years' time, the Finnish age distribution will be quite close to the asymptotic stable age distribution that

Figure 6.1. Age Distribution: Actual and Three Scenarios

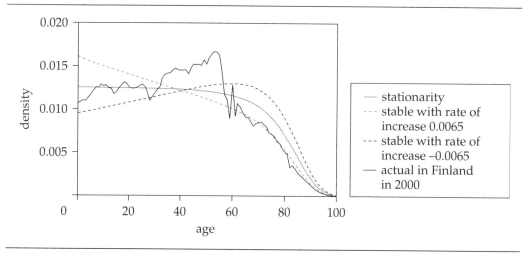

Source: Authors' calculations.

would result from constant schedules of fertility and mortality. The conclusion is that barring large changes in fertility or migration, the Finnish population will resemble its stable equivalent quite soon. A similar conclusion probably holds for most European countries, but with variations in timing, and with due allowance for differential migration.

Although much of current aging discussion involves future prospects of mortality, the major determinant of population aging is fertility, both via the current low level that leads to negative growth, and via the large baby boom cohorts that will begin to retire soon.

The decrease in mortality does have an important effect on the sustainability of the pension systems. Vaupel and Oeppen (2002) have presented evidence of the development of the "best practice life expectancy." This is the life expectancy of the country that at any given time has the longest life expectancy. Vaupel and Oeppen show that for women the curve goes almost linearly from the value of 45 years, observed in Sweden in 1840, to 85 years, observed in Japan in 2000. Accordingly, the best practice life expectancy has improved by approximately 0.25 years annually for 160 years.

In individual countries the development has been quite erratic, however. In Finland, for example, female life expectancy increased by 24 years (81 years – 57 years) from 1930 to 2000, or by 0.34 years annually. During the first 40 years, the increase was 0.45 years annually. During the latter 30 years, the increase was 0.20 years annually. Finland is not alone in this respect. Female data from 19 industrialized countries (Austria, Australia, Belgium, Canada, Denmark, Finland, France, Iceland, Ireland, Japan, Luxembourg, the Netherlands, New Zealand, Norway, Sweden, Switzerland, the United Kingdom, and the United States) from 1950 to 2000 show that Japan's improvement is much higher than that of the other countries. During the first half of the 50-year period the average improvement of the remaining 18 countries was 0.23 years annually, but during the latter half it was 0.18 years annually, and in the 1990s it was only 0.15.

It is difficult to say how the development should be interpreted. One can argue that as the leading country demonstrates that the improvements are possible, this will lead to policy responses in other countries to catch up. However this may be, the example of Denmark shows that such a response may take a long time. Fifty years ago Denmark was almost at the best practice line, but now it is six years behind. Pessimistic forecasters would suggest that improvements in European mortality are becoming smaller. Even if this view agrees with the most recent data, we note that a diminishing returns hypothesis has been repeatedly advanced in the past, but in retrospect, it has been the major source of error in mortality forecasts.

A compromise between the optimistic and pessimistic views is to assume the continuation of past trends, but to quantify the variations about the declining trend. This can be particularly important for individuals making their career plans. Decisions about how much and how long to work may depend on how the level of pensions is viewed relative to the wages one might earn and the savings one might have. If, in addition, the pensions are lowered—assuming a fixed retirement age—as a response to improvements in life expectancy (as is the case in Finland), decisions about saving may become more important than before.

Quantifying Uncertainty

Past forecasts can be analyzed to assess how accurate they have been. The difficulty in doing this in practice is that the number of past forecasts is small for all European countries. Reliable estimates are hard to obtain. Statistical time-series models can also be used, but it is difficult to find a compromise between overfitting on the one hand, and ignoring substance knowledge on the other. An intermediate way of assessing the uncertainty of forecasting is to consider the so-called naive or baseline forecasts. There is evidence that forecasts in the United States for total fertility have essentially assumed the current value to persist indefinitely.[8] This has later been observed in many other (post-demographic transition) countries, as well. If total fertility were a random walk (or more generally, a martingale), then such a forecast would be optimal. Indeed, the autocorrelations of first differences of the total fertility suggest that a random walk provides a rough approximation.

For countries with long data series available, one can determine how large errors such baseline forecasts would have had in the past, had they been systematically made every year (Alho 1990). In considering past errors, this study concentrated on the absolute value of the relative error and used the median to describe central value because this automatically eliminates the effects of outliers that were caused by wars or famines. Figure 6.2 (from Alho 2003) shows estimates from the Netherlands, Denmark, Norway, Finland, Iceland, and Sweden (here listed from the largest to the smallest in terms of forecast error). The differences between the countries are considerable, but the order of magnitude is similar. This is to be expected due to the high autocorrelation of the errors. To appreciate the order of magnitude, note that 0.10 in the log-scale corresponds to an expected median error of 10 percent. Under a normal (Gaussian) model of relative error, this corresponds to a standard deviation of 0.15, or 15 percent.

A similar analysis was carried out for mortality. Long data series from nine European countries (Austria, Denmark, France, Italy, the Netherlands, Norway, Sweden, Switzerland, and the United Kingdom), in ages 50–54, 55–59, . . . , 90–94, were analyzed much the same way as fertility data. The difference was that in this case, the baseline forecast assumed that the decline observed during the most recent 15 years would continue indefinitely. Such a forecast would be optimal, if the actual development would be a random walk with a drift, and 15 years worth of data were available. Lee and Carter (1992) have shown that models of this type have considerable empirical support. The data were aggregated over age groups for each country. Figure 6.3 shows the relative error. Comparing with figure 6.2, we find, surprisingly, that *the relative error one can expect in age-specific mortality forecasts is almost equal to that of total fertility*. We have no explanation for the close

Figure 6.2. Median Relative Error of Fertility Forecast

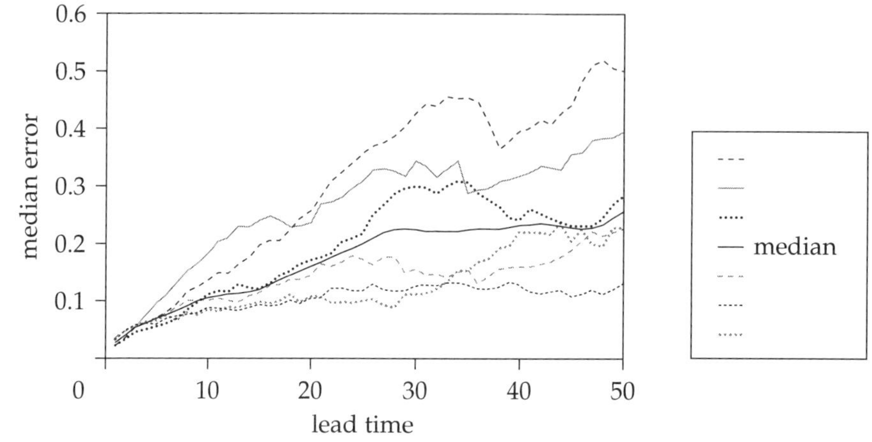

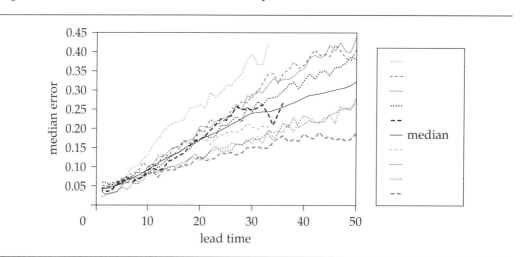

Source: Authors' calculations.

Note: The figure shows the median relative error of fertility forecast as a function of lead time for six countries with long data series, and their smoothed median (circle).

agreement of the two estimates. One should note, however, that the *probability of survival* can be forecast much more accurately. If one makes a large relative error in forecasting a mortality rate that is of the order of 1 percent, then the relative error in the number of survivors is about one-hundredth of that.

Estimates such as those displayed in figures 6.2 and 6.3 can be coupled with point forecasts of age-specific demographic rates, and translated into statistical models that can be

Figure 6.3. Median Relative Error of Mortality Forecast

Source: Authors' calculations.

Note: Relative error is forecast as a function of lead time for nine countries with long data series, and their smoothed average.

used in simulation. A number of additional parameters for correlations across age and over time are needed in this. In our practical work, we have used the program PEP (Program for Error Propagation) written at the University of Joensuu.[9]

Demographic Uncertainty, Pensions, and Public Finances

In the past, the volatility of demographics has often been underestimated, and economic analyses have concentrated on other uncertainties that are essential in population aging research. Research results obtained thus far unequivocally show that demographic uncertainty must not be neglected. Its magnitude should make us humble when recommending policies to avoid bad and unsustainable outcomes caused by aging. However, this does not mean that inactivity in policies is recommended. Quite the contrary, uncertainty is an extra reason for activity. As Auerbach and Hassett (2001) point out, for a risk-averse population the cost of future outcomes worse than expected outweigh the benefits of outcomes better than expected. Wise aging policies should be especially robust against a worse demographic future than the expected one.

The discussion below presents examples of how stochastic population simulations have been used with economic models to analyze pensions in Europe. We look at projections of pension outcomes and the effects of single policy instruments. We hope to address explicit pension policy strategies, consisting of contingent use of several instruments, in future studies.

Although our main goal is to throw light on the sustainability of pension systems, it is useful to keep in mind that there are other social systems that compete for the same economic assets. The costs of health care, schools, and social services are financed essentially by pay-as-you-go (PAYG) systems that aggravate the fiscal burden of the economically active population, in addition to pensions, for some potential future population paths; for other paths, they may bring relief.[10] This chapter will not discuss these aspects further.

Economic Calculations Subject to Exogenous Demographic Uncertainty

The following two tables summarize the effects of the current policy, and four alternative pension policies, to contribution rates in Lithuania.[11] The study used an OLG model for Lithuania.[12] The demographic population paths were generated as described in Alho (2001). They were treated as being exogenous to the economic system. The results have been obtained by simulating the population 100 times and solving the OLG model in each case. A number of technical issues had to be solved to be able to carry this out. For example, arranging the population paths in a suitable manner helped in achieving convergence faster. The results were stored so that their statistical characteristics can be examined using standard statistical programs.

The old-age pension system in Lithuania consists of the basic pension and the earnings-related supplementary component. The pension system is purely pay-as-you-go. Contributions are collected from the wage bill. The basic pension is almost flat, and it depends only to a minor extent on a person's insurance period. The supplementary pension component depends on the number of years the insured person has worked according to social insurance records and income. Pension benefit is fully indexed to average wage income.

Table 6.1 presents statistical summaries of the predictive distribution of the social security contribution rate, under each of the four policies. In Lithuania, social security contributions consist of a 31 percent employer contribution on the wage bill, plus a 3 percent employee contribution on individual wages. These are used to finance pensions (old-age, disability, and survivorship), short-term benefits (sickness and maternity), as well as unemployment and health insurance partially. The contribution rate of 28 percent in 2000

Table 6.1. Distribution of the Social Security Contribution Rate in Lithuania (percent)

Policy measure	2000	2030			2050		
		Median	50%	80%	Median	50%	80%
Current system	28	29.41	28.49	27.46	35.70	33.31	30.19
			30.40	31.39		38.05	42.69
Wage-bill indexation	28	28.43	27.64	26.64	32.10	30.39	28.29
			29.42	30.15		34.25	36.55
Longevity adjustment	28	29.16	28.34	27.42	34.84	32.90	29.96
			30.19	31.20		37.17	42.01
Retirement age increase	28	25.05	24.20	23.31	29.83	28.06	25.24
			25.78	26.84		31.77	35.51

Source: Authors' calculations.

Note: The table shows the median and 50 percent and 80 percent predictive limits.

is the employer rate where the health insurance is excluded. In the future the contribution rate is assumed to endogenously adjust so that the benefits are financed each period. Table 6.2 presents summaries of the predictive distribution of policy effects: that is, the difference between the contribution rate under an alternative policy and the current policy.

The width of the 80 percent predictive interval for the contribution rate is 4 percentage points in 2030 and 12 percentage points in 2050. Ranges of this sort are not atypical. As shown in the previous section, demographic uncertainty is of the same order of magnitude in different countries, and the closer a pension system is to a PAYG system the closer it replicates the underlying demographics. These estimates suggest what can be expected about the accuracy of our aging projections—and this is just the demographic component.

Tables 6.1 and 6.2 show that pension policies have effects on both the location of the distribution of outcomes and its scale. Indexation of benefits to total wages, instead of average earnings, cuts the expected contribution rate by 3.6 percentage points in 2050 and narrows its 80 percent predictive range from 12 to 6 percentage points. This instrument is analyzed more closely in the discussion below on wage-bill indexation. Longevity adjustment of future pension benefits was applied only partially, and has very small effects on outcomes, perhaps because of problems related to the quality of old-age mortality statis-

Table 6.2. Distribution of Policy Effects on the Social Security Contribution Rate (percent)

Policy measure	2030			2050		
	Median	50%	80%	Median	50%	80%
Wage-bill indexation	−0.84	−0.38	0.22	−3.00	−1.74	−1.17
		−1.62	−2.35		−5.38	−7.46
Longevity adjustment	−0.18	−0.12	−0.04	−0.47	−0.13	0.25
		−0.29	−0.39		−0.82	−1.19
Retirement age increase	−4.38	−4.18	−4.07	−5.64	−5.22	−4.96
		−4.64	−4.98		−6.48	−7.23

Source: Authors' calculations.

Note: The table shows the median and 50 percent and 80 percent predictive limits.

tics in Lithuania. The next section considers the likely effects of the longevity adjustment in Finland. Increasing the retirement age also effects both the location and the scale of the predictive distribution of outcomes, but it is not directly linked to demographics, and this study will not discuss it in more detail.

Predictive Distribution of Longevity Adjustment

An increase in life expectancy can put a strain on the finances of a defined benefit pension system. In a PAYG system this means increasing the contribution levels of the current workers. In anticipation of future gains in life expectancy, a law was passed in Finland that automatically adjusts pensions if life expectancy changes. The aim is to preserve the expected present value of future pensions.

Define $p(x)$ as the conditional probability of surviving to age $62 + x$ given survival to age 62. Let 0.02 be the discount rate. Suppose a pension is paid continuously, at the rate of one euro per year. Then the Finnish law stipulates that the expected net value of the pension that forms the basis of life expectancy adjustments is

$$\xi = \int_0^\infty p(x)e^{-0.02x}dx. \tag{6.1}$$

In practice, estimates of expected net values are computed based on past data. Consider the cohort of individuals who become 62 years old during a calendar year $t = 2009$. To calculate the expected present value for year t, denote it by $x(t)$, mortality data from the five-year period $[t - 6, t - 2)$ is used to calculate $p(x)$. Thus there is no element of forecasting in the calculation, but the expected net value does not correspond to the actual cohorts of pensioners either. This aspect has been analyzed more closely in Lassila and Valkonen (2003), showing that the use of forecasts may mitigate the adjustment factor.

The life expectancy adjustment is then defined as $A(t) = \xi(2009)/\xi(t)$. Or, the pensions of those who became 62 years old in year t are multiplied by $A(t)$. If mortality decreases from the year 2009 onward, $A(t) < 1$, so pensions would be cut.

Since the future level of mortality cannot be known with certainty, the values of $A(t)$ cannot be known accurately at the present time. However, in the interest of showing what one might expect, we can provide a probabilistic description of how the $A(t)$'s are likely to behave, since a predictive distribution of future mortality is available. Without going into details, we note that a number of technical issues must be resolved in any such calculation. For example, since a unique adjustment factor is used for males and females, a combined measure of mortality is used. This depends on the shares of women and men, in ages $x \geq 62$, in the future. Various approximations were used to obtain the results shown here.

The practical calculations were carried out via stochastic simulation using the program Minitab. The median, the first and third quartiles, and the first and ninth deciles, for the predictive distribution of the adjustment factors in 2030 and 2050, are as follows:[13]

Year	d_1	Q_1	Md	Q_3	d_9
2030	0.86	0.88	0.92	0.95	0.99
2050	0.78	0.81	0.87	0.92	0.98

We expect the adjustment factor to decline to about 0.87 in 2050, with an 80 percent prediction interval [0.78, 0.98]. These intervals are valid provided that the volatility of the trends of mortality during the next 50 years does not exceed the volatility of mortality during 1900–94. In view of the discussion above, an optimist in mortality reduction who believes in a reversal of the recent slowdown might use the first decile (0.78 for year 2050) as a benchmark to consider how to adjust the predictive distribution to better match his or her beliefs.

Wage-Bill Indexation

Studies of the type presented in the previous two sections can be criticized because they do not incorporate the notion of sustainability or system reform in any way. The current (or alternative) rules are assumed to apply, irrespective of how the population or the economy develops. Addressing this issue in full generality is vastly beyond current analytical capabilities. Yet some aspects of a more realistic analysis can be easily introduced in the existing modeling framework via thresholds.

In Lithuania, the earnings-related pension benefit is fully indexed to average wage income. Alho et al. (2003) studied an alternative indexation, where the benefit follows the weighted average of the average wage income (with a weight $1 - \alpha$) and the total wage bill in the economy (with a weight α). The rationale of wage-bill indexation is that it would provide automatic relief to the working population should, as expected, the share of pensioners in the population increase.

In the spirit of the previous two sections, figure 6.4 shows how the situation would change by 2050, in the polar cases of $\alpha = 0.0$ (left-hand side) and $\alpha = 1.0$ (right-hand side). The scatter plots are based on 300 population paths, each producing a dot on the (c, r) plane. First, we see that increasing α tilts the scatter cloud from a horizontal position downward. Second, with current indexation, there are some extremely high contribution rates by 2050. A high degree of wage-bill indexation effectively cuts down the most extreme contribution rates, but even at $\alpha = 1.0$ the contribution rate can reach values above 0.4 with nonnegligible probability. Third, the control of contribution rates is accomplished by accepting a lower replacement rate.

Figure 6.4. Replacement Rates and Contribution Rates in Lithuania in 2050, with $\alpha = 0$ (left) and $\alpha = 1$ (right)

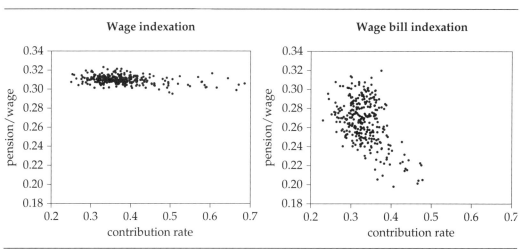

Source: Alho et al. (2003).

As pointed out by Edward Palmer, a crucial assumption in these calculations is that the retirement age is kept fixed, even though life expectancies vary between population paths. Assuming, for example, a constant retirement/work ratio would certainly produce smaller declines in replacement rates, and further analysis should take this into account. At present this cannot be done properly because, as noted in connection with table 6.2, variation in longevity appeared modest, perhaps due to quality problems of old-age mortality data in Lithuania.

In an effort to address the sustainability issue, Alho et al. (2003) approximate the complex political process by postulating bounds for the contribution rate, c, and the replacement rate, r, that cannot be violated. They assume that there is an *upper bound* $c^* > 0$ such that values $c > c^*$ would not be considered politically acceptable for the working population, and institutional arrangements would be changed instead. Similarly, they assume that there is a *lower bound* $r^* > 0$ such that replacement rates $r < r^*$ would lead to a system reform. The set $\{(c, r) \mid c \leq c^*, r \geq r^*\}$ is the *viable region* of the policy.

Neither c^* nor r^* can be known with certainty. Alho et al. (2003) consider a range of values for both bounds, in an effort to get a feeling of how likely it is that the indexation rule might survive in future political process. Using these bounds, they try to find a suitable degree of indexation. Table 6.3 replicates some of their results for one value of c^*.

The limit $c^* = 0.38$ represents a 10 percentage point increase in the contribution rate. Many countries face the prospect of such increases in their payroll taxes, and it is exactly these projections that have led the experts and decision makers to pay attention to the aging problem and seek ways to avoid such increases.

The rightmost column of table 6.3 shows that the replacement rate is below 33 percent in all alternatives. The **values in bold italics** are maximum probabilities of staying in the viable region that can be achieved by choosing α optimally, for the specific combinations of c^* and r^*. For example, should one think that the replacement rate has to be at least 30 percent and the contribution rate must not rise more than 10 percentage points from the current level (or it stays at or below 38 percent), then it is best to stick with the current indexation system where $\alpha = 0$. With this policy, the probability of staying in the viable region is 63 percent. If one would accept a replacement rate as low as 29 percent, choosing $\alpha = 0.2$ would produce a probability of 68 percent of staying in this viable region, whereas sticking with the current policy ($\alpha = 0$) would have lower probability of being sustainable, or 63 percent.

Table 6.3. Joint Probabilities of the Contribution Rate Being Lower Than c^* and the Replacement Rate Being Higher Than r^* in 2050

α	$c^* = 0.38$							
	$r^* = 0.20$	0.25	0.26	0.27	0.28	0.29	0.30	0.33
0	0.63	0.63	0.63	0.63	0.63	0.63	*0.63*	0
0.2	0.70	0.70	0.70	0.70	0.70	*0.68*	0.44	0
0.4	0.77	0.77	0.77	*0.77*	*0.72*	0.52	0.22	0
0.6	0.83	0.83	*0.81*	0.71	0.56	0.32	0.13	0
0.8	0.86	*0.83*	0.72	0.58	0.39	0.23	0.09	0
1	*0.90*	0.74	0.62	0.47	0.30	0.17	0.07	0

Source: Alho et al. (2003).

Note: The table is for $c^* = 0.38$ and selected values of r^* and for different values of the indexing parameter α.

Other measures for operationalizing sustainability can be developed based on the minimal r and maximal c over the forecast horizon (2001 to 2050), for example. Yet even the simple analysis that concentrates on year 2050 adds an aspect of realism to the study of sustainability that is absent from statistical summaries such as the expected values, variances, or fractiles.

Fertility-Dependent Prefunding

The following example is based on the partially funded defined benefit (DB) private sector pension system (TEL) in Finland. In this statutory system, funding does not affect pension benefits at all; it affects only the timing of contributions. This cohort-specific forced saving makes current workers partially pay their own future pensions. It is an open issue whether this increases total saving in the economy or whether people counter it by saving less privately. What it definitely does is to smooth the changes in pension contribution rate that are due to demographic developments. That is the main aim of funding in Finland; the issue is how efficiently this aim is fulfilled.

Lassila and Valkonen (2001) showed that to reduce the effect of the expected aging of the population on the contribution rate, increasing the level of prefunding is a sensible policy. Yet there is a clear danger of prefunding too much, in the sense that current workers pay unnecessarily high contributions and future workers will face lower contributions. Utilizing fertility data in setting the funding level is a promising approach to increase funding and avoid excesses. The discussion that follows elaborates on this idea.

Prefunding in a DB system reduces the risk caused by changing fertility on contribution rates. The risk reduction is obtained, in part, by introducing new risks through uncertain investment performance. Since the funding rate is far from full (no target is set for the funding rate in the Finnish system, but currently it is roughly one-quarter), the funding rules can potentially be improved by considering the future size of the working cohorts.

The current prefunding rule is as follows. Every year t, new pension rights accrue at a rate k for each worker. A share a of the present value of the accrued right, to workers aged $i = 23, \ldots , 54$, is put in the funds. The present value is calculated from age 65 to a maximum age, denoted here by M. Let $g(t,i)$ be the labor income of the individual in age i during year t. For prefunding purposes, the magnitude of this right is evaluated ignoring all future changes due to wage or price developments. An interest rate r is administratively set. Suppose the proportion $S(i,j,t)$ of those in age i at t is expected to be alive at age j. Then, the following amount is prefunded for the worker in age i during period t,

$$h(i,t) = a \sum_{j=65}^{M} kg(i,t)S(i,j,t)/(1+r)^{j-i}. \tag{6.2}$$

We propose to amend the rule so that, for each funding cohort (those aged 23 to 54), the share funded also depends on the size of the cohort at birth $B(t)$ relative to the size of the later born cohorts. The idea is that we can estimate from the size of recently born cohorts the size of the work force in those future periods when the funding cohort is retired. Or we propose to multiply $h(i,t)$ by

$$b(i,t) = B(t-i) / \sum_{j=0}^{i-1} w(j,i)B(t-j-1), \tag{6.3}$$

where $w(j,i) \geq 0$ add up to 1 for each i. The weights are calculated so that they approximate the shares of the various cohorts in the working-age population, when the funding cohort (those in age i at t) has retired. This fertility effect on funding varies between cohorts, and for each cohort it varies in time. If the funding cohort is bigger than the younger cohorts are, b exceeds unity and thus funding is increased. If fertility increases and younger cohorts are bigger, funding declines compared with current rules.

Under current pension rules the contribution rate is expected to stay close its current level of 21.5 percent over the next 10 years, and then rise to about 30 percent. Uncertainty increases with the time horizon, and in the 2060s the 80 percent predictive interval is 12 percentage points wide. These estimates were obtained by simulating the population 100 times, and solving the Finnish OLG model in each case. The demographic population paths were generated as described in Alho (2002).

A fertility-dependent funding rule would narrow the predictive intervals from the 2050s onward. The cost of this is that the intervals before the 2050s become slightly larger. Doubling the current funding degree would restrict the future variability sooner, but it would also increase the variability in the near future. Thus funding in general shifts demographic risks in time. Figure 6.5 shows this in the form of standard deviations, calculated each period from the contribution rates in each of the 100 population paths.

With a fertility-dependent funding rule, the median contribution would be first slightly higher and later somewhat lower than with current rules, but the distributions would be

Table 6.4. Pension Contributions during Selected 10-Year Periods in the Finnish TEL System (fractiles of the predictive distribution)

	2005–14				
Prefunding rule	d_1	Q_1	*Md*	Q_3	d_9
Current rules	21.,4	21.6	21.9	22.0	22.2
Fertility-dependent funding	22.2	22.5	22.8	23.0	23.3
Funding doubled	24.8	25.1	25.6	25.9	26.1
	2030–39				
	d_1	Q_1	*Md*	Q_3	d_9
Current rules	27.7	28.6	30.0	30.7	31.9
Fertility-dependent funding	27.0	28.4	29.9	31.2	32.1
Funding doubled	28.5	29.4	30.6	31.2	32.3
	2050–59				
	d_1	Q_1	*Md*	Q_3	d_9
Current rules	26.8	28.4	30.4	32.7	34.7
Fertility-dependent funding	26.2	28.0	29.7	32.2	33.5
Funding doubled	25.0	26.2	27.8	29.6	31.3
	2060–69				
	d_1	Q_1	*Md*	Q_3	d_9
Current rules	26.4	28.5	31.3	35.1	38.4
Fertility-dependent funding	26.2	28.3	30.2	33.0	34.7
Funding doubled	24.2	25.9	28.3	31.2	33.9

Source: Authors' calculations.

Figure 6.5. Standard Deviation in 100 Simulations of Pension Contribution Rate in the Finnish Private Sector TEL System under Alternative Funding Rules

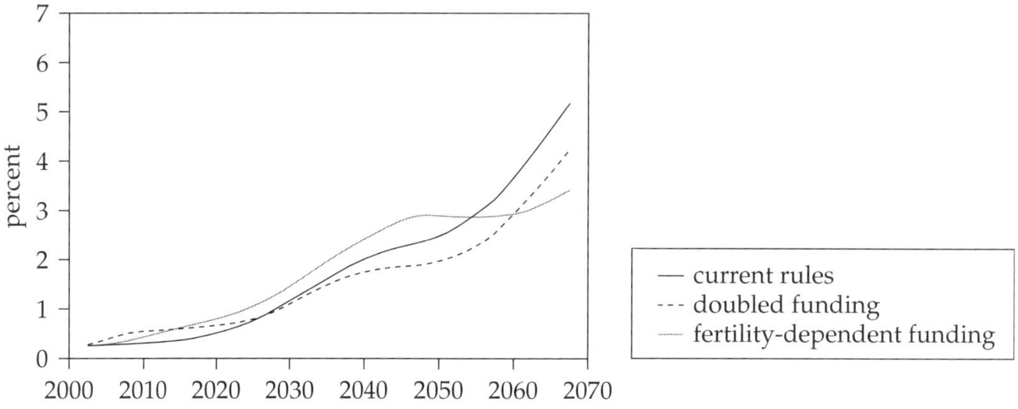

Source: Authors' calculations.

markedly different. The 80 percent predictive interval in 2060–69 would be about 26 to 35 percent instead of 26 to 38 percent. The slight increase in variability in some earlier periods seems a price worth considering for reducing the third quintile value by 2 percentage points and 9th decile value by close to 4 points in 2060–69. Figure 6.6 compares the contribution rates under a fertility-dependent rule with those under the current rule in each of the 100 population paths.

Funding too little and funding too much are not symmetric cases. Increasing funding requires unpopular decisions of increasing contributions, and smaller increases are easier to accept. Thus in the future, looking back to the present time, we would probably be happier for not prefunding too much. This provides another tool for comparing different funding rules. The simulations suggest that excess funding has taken place if somewhere in the future the contribution rate declines significantly. Different threshold values for "significant" can be used. Table 6.5 shows the share of cases in the 100 population paths where excess funding was observed, with five different threshold values. The unit period in calculations is five years, so qualifying for "excess" requires that there is a pair of five-year periods, not necessarily successive but both within the total period of 2005–69, where the contribution rate in the earlier period exceeds the latter period's contribution rate by at least the threshold value.

Table 6.5 shows that small decreases in the contribution rate have a probability of one-third with current pension and funding rules. With fertility-dependent funding, that probability will be slightly larger. But looking at decreases over 2 percentage points, or 3 or 5, note that with fertility-dependent rules, the probability of overshooting in funding would be reduced markedly compared with current rules.

A permanent increase in the funding degree does not seem a good choice because it does not adjust to demographics. The gains are there from 2050 onward, but they are partly in the form of very low contributions. The price to pay, higher contributions in the near future, is high. Excess funding would become much more likely.

Figure 6.6. Pension Contributions in the Finnish Private Sector TEL System

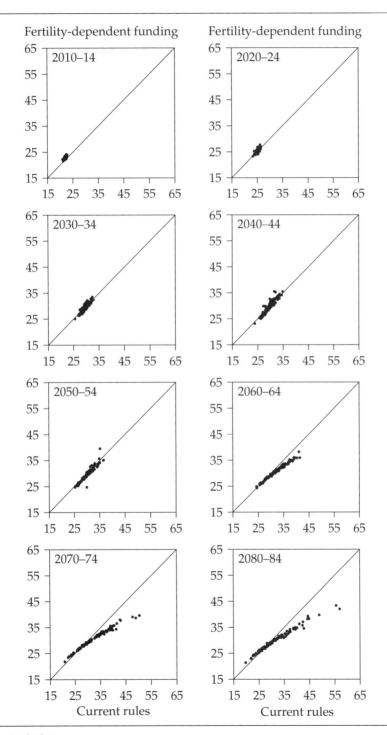

Source: Authors' calculations.

Note: Each of the 100 dots represents one population path.

Table 6.5. Probability of Excess Funding during 2005–69

Threshold value	1	2	3	5	10
Current rules	35	17	13	5	0
Fertility-dependent funding	44	12	5	0	0
Funding doubled	94	77	56	21	0

Source: Authors' calculations.

Note: Share of cases where the pension contribution rate decline, in some subperiod of 2005–69, exceeds the threshold value. Threshold expressed as percentage points.

Future Directions

The need for sustainable financing strategies is not confined to pensions. Publicly financed health care and long-term care are another area where the tools described above can be used.[14] These areas are correlated: demographic paths that are costly from the pension point of view are likely to be costly in terms of health care.

The pension examples above seem relevant also for NDC systems, although both Lithuania and Finland have DB pension systems. Longevity adjustment and wage-bill indexation are by nature NDC instruments,[15] and funding, at least in buffer form, is required to keep contributions fixed and prevent the necessity of using brake-type arrangements continuously.

The Swedish NDC concept has strong strategy features, especially the aim of keeping contributions fixed in all states of the world. It seems like a major improvement compared to the many current PAYG defined benefit systems. Yet the system has not been crash-tested, and it is conceivable that it may not be sustainable in all realistic circumstances. There may also be other systems with comparable risk characteristics.

We view the combination of stochastic population simulations and a numerical OLG model as a first step toward a more comprehensive model. Stochastic population simulations for all EU countries and some other European countries are being produced in the European Union's fifth framework research project, Uncertain Population of Europe (UPE). In another EU project, Demographic Uncertainty and the Sustainability of Social Welfare Systems (DEMWEL), several European research institutes are working together to create models where future uncertainty is handled in a more advanced manner. But even with current models many aspects of uncertainty in the economic consequences of population aging can be explored, and that is also the aim in DEMWEL.

In future work, it might be useful to extend the notions of sustainability and sustainable strategies into a probabilistic direction, complemented with a "viability" concept with soft or unknown limits of acceptability. A theoretical challenge is to achieve a better concordance of the demographic and economic models. Alternative descriptions of how uncertainty is taken into account in actual practice, when it is not clear what the relevant decision horizon might be, is one aspect of such work.

Creating pension strategies more sustainable than the current ones is important. As Disney (1999) argues, if the future paths turn out to be unsustainable, there are stark choices left: to adjust other public finances or to change the rules ex post. Stochastic simulations with models combining the economic and demographic ingredients of the pension system can be used to crash-test the current systems and reveal the circumstances where their potential weaknesses become crucial. Similarly, the simulations will help to design alternative, and possibly very complicated, pension policy strategies, and test their consequences both at the system level and the individual level.

Notes

1. "Notional defined contribution" and "non-financial defined contribution" should be understood to have the same definition.
2. See Blanchard et al. (1990, p. 8).
3. See Blanchard et al. (1990, p. 11).
4. See, for example, Rasmusen (1989, p. 17).
5. See Settergren (2001, p.1).
6. See Könberg, Palmer, and Sundén (2006).
7. For more on viability theory, see Aubin (1991).
8. See, for example, Lee (1974).
9. For a description, see Alho (1998) or visit http://www.joensuu.fi/statistics/juha.html.
10. See Alho and Vanne (2001).
11. See Alho et al. (2002).
12. See Jensen and Lassila (2002).
13. See Alho (2003).
14. See Lassila and Valkonen (2004).
15. See Palmer (2000).

References

Alho, J. M. 1990. "Stochastic Methods in Population Forecasting." *International Journal of Forecasting* 6 (4): 521–30.

———. 1998. "A Stochastic Forecast of the Population of Finland." *Reviews 1998/4.* Statistics Finland, Helsinki.

———. 2001. "Stochastic Forecast of the Lithuanian Population 2001–2050." Unpublished report, September 25. http://www.etla.fi/lithuania.

———. 2002. "The Population of Finland in 2050 and Beyond." Discussion Paper 826. ETLA (The Research Institute of the Finnish Economy), Helsinki.

———. 2003. "Predictive Distribution of Adjustment for Life Expectancy Change." Working Paper 3, Finnish Centre for Pensions, Helsinki.

Alho, J. M., and R. Vanne. 2001. "On Predictive Distributions of Public Net Liabilities." Paper presented at "International Meeting on Age Structure Transitions and Policy Dynamics: The Allocation of Public and Private Resources Across Generations," Taipei, December 6–8.

Alho, J. M., S. E. H. Jensen, J. Lassila, and T. Valkonen. 2003. "Controlling the Effects of Demographic Risks: The Role of Pension Indexation Schemes." Discussion Paper 2003-12, Centre for Economic and Business Research, Copenhagen.

Alho, J. M., S. E. H. Jensen, J. Lassila, R. Lazutka, A. Morkūnienė, and T. Valkonen. 2002. "The Economic Effects of Population Ageing and Demographic Uncertainty in Lithuania: Summary, Conclusions and Recommendations." Research report, downloadable from www.etla.fi/lithuania.

Aubin, J. 1991. *Viability Theory*. Basel: Birkhäuser.

Auerbach, A. J., and K. Hassett. 2001. "Uncertainty and the Design of Long-Run Fiscal Policy." In *Demographic Change and Fiscal Policy,* ed. A. J. Auerbach, and R. D. Lee. Cambridge: Cambridge University Press.

Auerbach, A. J., and L. J. Kotlikoff. 1987. *Dynamic Fiscal Policy.* Cambridge: Cambridge University Press.

Blanchard, O., J. C. Chouraqui, R. P. Hagemann, and N. Sartor. 1990. "The Sustainability of Fiscal Policy: New Answers to an Old Question." *OECD Economic Studies* 15 (Autumn): 7–36.

Disney, R. 1999. "Notional Accounts as a Pension Reform Strategy: An Evaluation." Social Protection Discussion Paper 9928, World Bank, Washington, DC.

Jensen, S. E. H., and J. Lassila. 2002. "Reforming Social Security in a Transition Economy: The Case of Lithuania." *Journal of Policy Reform* 5 (1): 17–36.

Könberg, B., E. Palmer, and A. Sundén. 2006. "The NDC Reform in Sweden: The 1994 Legislation to the Present." In *Pension Reform: Issues and Prospects for Non-Financial Defined Contribution (NDC) Schemes*, ed. R. Holzmann and E. Palmer, chapter 17. Washington, DC: World Bank.

Lassila, J., and T. Valkonen. 2001. "Pension Prefunding, Ageing, and Demographic Uncertainty." *International Tax and Public Finance* 8 (4): 573–93.

———. 2003. "Ageing, Demographic Risks and Pension Reform." In *Social Security and Pension Reform,* ed. Martin Weale, Occasional Paper No. 56, NIESR (The National Institute of Economic and Social Research), London.

———. 2004. "Prefunding Expenditure on Health and Long-term Care under Demographic Uncertainty." *Geneva Papers on Risk and Insurance: Issues and Practice* 29 (4): 620–39.

Lee, R. D. 1974. "Forecasting Births in Post-transition Populations: Stochastic Renewal with Serially Correlated Fertility." *Journal of the American Statistical Association* 69: 607–17.

Lee, R., and L. Carter. 1992. "Modeling and Forecasting U.S. mortality." *Journal of the American Statistical Association* 87 (14): 659–71.

Lindbeck, A., and M. Persson. 2003. "The Gains from Pension Reform." *Journal of Economic Literature* Vol. XLI (March): 74–112.

Palmer, E. 2000. "The Swedish Pension Reform Model: Framework and Issues." Social Protection Paper 12, World Bank, Washington, DC.

Palmer, E. 2002. "Swedish Pension Reform: How Did It Evolve, and What Does It Mean for the Future?" In *Social Security Pension Reform in Europe,* ed. M. Feldstein and H. Siebert. NBER conference volume. Chicago: University of Chicago Press.

Rasmusen, E. 1989. *Games and Information.* Oxford: Blackwell.

Settergren, O. 2001. "The Automatic Balance Mechanism of the Swedish Pension System: A Non-Technical Introduction." *Riksförsäkringsverket* (August). Downloadable at http://www.rfv.se/english/publi/index.htm.

Valdés-Prieto, S. 2000. "The Financial Stability of Notional Account Pensions." *Scandinavian Journal of Economics* 102 (3): 395–417.

Vaupel J. W., and J. Oeppen. 2002. "Broken Limits to Life Expectancy." *Science* 296: 1029–31.

Discussion of "Demographic Uncertainty and Evaluation of Sustainability of Pension Systems"

Sergio Nisticò*

THE CHAPTER BY ALHO, LASSILA, AND VALKONEN succeeds in showing how stochastic population simulations could assist the main agents (individuals, firms, policy makers) in dealing with the lack of reliable information about the strains demography is exerting on pension systems. More specifically, the aim of the chapter is to show that it is possible to enforce sustainability of defined benefit (DB) pay-as-you-go systems by providing all agents with a "sustainable policy strategy...[that is,] a set of rules such that both the contributors and the pensioners know, beforehand, what will be done in any reasonable future circumstance, and they accept the future actions." The authors rightly emphasize the importance for agents to know "the likelihood of the various risks" because "without any probabilities attached to the alternatives, their importance is suspect and the results are difficult to interpret." This is why stochastic demographic simulations in conjunction with appropriate economic models can certainly help policy makers evaluate the likely impact of alternative policy measures on the key parameters of those pension systems on which demography puts a strain.

Although in a pure DB scheme the burden of adjustment entirely falls on contribution rates—in that if benefits are defined there are no means to contain pension expenditure—in actual (spurious) DB schemes, all parameters can undergo possible revisions: accrual rates (through longevity adjustments), indexation of already awarded pensions, and retirement ages. Alho, Lassila, and Valkonen provide some very interesting stochastic exercises showing the comparative impact on contribution rates in Lithuania of continuing the current policy as opposed to the three alternative parametric reforms. They convincingly suggest that a widespread diffusion of this kind of information can help agents foresee what policy will actually be enforced in a context in which the "rules of the game" allow for various policy measures.

However, it should be added that NDC schemes are precisely designed to provide individuals with that set of rules the authors argue will stem from good demographic information. As discussed by Gronchi and Nisticò (2006), the NDC scheme is endowed with a sort of automatic pilot that intervenes promptly on expenditure, avoiding the usually protracted waiting period necessary before governments resign themselves to the necessity of sustaining the electoral cost of altering the award parameters and unions assume the responsibility of agreeing to such changes. The NDC's intervention is not only prompt but also, more importantly, perfectly predictable. This contrasts with DB schemes, wherein the outcome of the political process leading to parametric reforms is not only delayed but also uncertain.

---

* Sergio Nisticò is professor of economics at the University of Cassino (Italy) where he teaches Microeconomics, History of Economic Thought, and Social Insurance Economics.

Take as an example the argument the authors develop in the section of their chapter focusing on alternative possible adjustments of indexation for pensions already awarded. The authors rightly emphasize that the domain within which indexation will ultimately fall is "constrained" by the contribution rate, which cannot exceed a given ceiling, and the replacement rate, which cannot fall below a given floor. In this respect, the authors show that, within DB schemes, good forecasting of possible demographic scenarios becomes crucial for the identification of a sustainable indexation: that is, for an indexation compatible with admissible levels of contribution and replacement rates. Again, the NDC adjustment mechanisms solve this dilemma through an automatic, predictable, and fully transparent mechanism. Once the contribution rate is freely chosen, the policy maker has a "lever" to solve the trade-off between the first pension annuity (the replacement rate) and the indexation of future installments. The lever is the return on pensioners' account balances that can be "prepaid" ("imputed," in Swedish terminology): that is, devoted to increasing the first installment. Indexation of subsequent installments will, each year, equal the sustainable return minus the prepaid return. (This is why in chapter 19 the prepaid return is referred to as the "deviation rate" between the sustainable return and the indexation.) This "endogenous" indexation, which Italy has awkwardly failed to adopt, ensures the sustainability of the NDC scheme. The lower the prepaid return (the replacement rate), the better indexation will perform in adverse economic and demographic scenarios. This is why Sweden has probably prepaid an excessively high return (1.6 percent).

The difference between the DB and NDC adjustment mechanisms also has important consequences on the distribution of the burden of adjustment among generations. The authors argue that within a DB scheme "to reduce the effect of the expected aging of the population on the contribution rate, increasing the level of prefunding is a sensible policy." Also on this respect, good demographic forecasting is essential to convince active generations not to shift the entire burden of adjustment on future generations and to pay a contribution rate that is above its equilibrium level. It is hard to ask current workers to fund the system on the basis of "weak" predictions: that is, when the risk of overshooting is not negligible. Funding is generally possible only in the face of good demography: that is, by keeping the contribution rate unaltered when it could be lowered. Again, the authors hit the target when they emphasize that information is essential for fine tuning the policy mix within a DB setting to guarantee, at the same time, both sustainability and fairness (in this case, intergenerational). On the other hand, it is common to misinterpret the ability of NDC systems to be self-sustainable for any given contribution rate, as if pensioners only were asked to bear the burden of balancing the system. According to this view, NDC schemes would suffer from an intergenerational unfairness, which is symmetric to that characterizing pure DB schemes, wherein active workers only bear the burden of adjustment. However, one should consider that the prompt intervention of the "automatic pilot" has the twofold form of slower indexation of old pensions and reduction of the contribution balances being formed (thus containing future pension awards), so that the sacrifice is imposed at the same time on pensioners and active workers.

Good demographic information is obviously also essential to NDC schemes, though not as a direct support to the provision of alternative policy measures, but rather to provide individuals with some important pieces of information needed to respond to demographic trends. The flexibility in retirement age is one of the most important features of NDC schemes. Postponing retirement age is the main instrument at individuals' disposal to offset the effects of a bad demographic scenario. Good predictions about longevity, when collected, filtered, and synthesized by signals (such as the expected levels of the annuitization divisors and of the sustainable return) that are easy to be perceived and interpreted by individuals will play a fundamental role in this respect.

The authors conclude by asserting that the NDC system "has not been crash-tested and it is conceivable that it may not be sustainable either in all realistic circumstances." This is true, but no pension scheme can survive in any demographic scenario that is seriously negative. However, when something can be done for public pension schemes to survive, NDC does it in a prompt and fair way; and good demographic forecasting will help.

Reference

Gronchi, S., and S. Nisticò. 2006. "Implementing the NDC Theoretical Model: A Comparison of Italy and Sweden." In *Pension Reform: Issues and Prospects for Non-Financial Defined Contribution (NDC) Schemes*, ed. R. Holzmann and E. Palmer, chapter 19. Washington, DC: World Bank.

Chapter 7

The Rate of Return of Pay-As-You-Go Pension Systems: A More Exact Consumption-Loan Model of Interest

Ole Settergren and Boguslaw D. Mikula*

Paul Samuelson's well-known article, "An Exact Consumption-Loan Model of Interest With or Without the Social Contrivance of Money," published in 1958, has been interpreted as showing that the rate of return of pay-as-you-go (PAYG) pension systems—that is, unfunded pension schemes—is the growth in the contribution, or tax, base of the system. In the absence of technological progress and with a constant number of hours worked per person, the growth in the contribution base is equal to the growth in population, or what Samuelson calls the "biological interest rate."

Several researchers have pointed out that the two-age overlapping generation (OLG) model used by Samuelson cannot explain the dynamics of the equilibrium interest rate in a world of more than two-age OLGs. Arthur and McNicoll (1978) and Willis (1988) have demonstrated that in a more than two-age OLG model, changes in the differential between the ages at which the average income is earned and consumed is a critical factor in determining equilibrium interest rates. Likewise, Keyfitz (1985, 1988), as well as Lee in numerous works (1980, 1988a, 1988b, 1994a, 1994b, 2000), showed that the amount consumed at some or all ages is affected by changes in this age differential. However, statements that the rate of return on PAYG financing is equal to the growth in the contribution base are surprisingly common.[1] Rarely are such claims accompanied by the necessary qualification that they are valid only in a two-age OLG model or in the equally unrealistic case of an economy and demography characterized by a steady state.[2]

The common assumption that the rate of return of PAYG pension systems is equal to the growth in the contribution base is rarely an efficient simplification. Recent experience in

* Ole Settergren is the director of the Pensions Department at the Swedish Social Insurance Agency and Boguslaw D. Mikula is a researcher in the Division for Analysis at the same agency.

We are grateful to Sergio Nisticò and Edward Palmer for their valuable comments. Special recognition goes to Hans Olsson. Without his early support, experience, and hard work preceding the decision by parliament in 1998, when it settled for an asymmetric design of the indexation of the new system's pension benefits and implicit pension liability, the ideas presented here would probably not have survived their infancy and become Swedish legislation.

With the permission of the World Bank, this chapter was published in the *Journal of Pension Economics and Finance*, volume 4, issue 2, July 2005.

Sweden indicates how poor that assumption can be. The increase in life expectancy in Sweden from 1980 to 2001 made the income-weighted average age of retirees increase from 72 to 75 years, while the income-weighted average age of contributors to the system remained relatively stable at 43 years.[3] Thus the increase in life expectancy made the differential between the average age at which contribution was paid to the system and the average age at which pension was paid from it grow from about 29 to 32 years. This represents close to a 12 percent increase, which added roughly 0.4 percentage units to the annual real rate of return on contributions to the PAYG system during this period. As the average annual growth in the contribution base over the same period was only 0.3 percent, the common simplification that the rate of return equals the growth in the contribution base revealed less than half of the true return.

Thus one consequence—and perhaps a counterintuitive one—of increases in life expectancy is that it adds to the rate of return of PAYG pension systems. This indicates an even more serious drawback with the simplified view than its low precision. The assumption that the rate of return of PAYG financing is the growth rate of the contribution base hides a structure vital to understanding the financial dynamic of PAYG pension systems. Possibly the simplification is so frequent because it is assumed that, without it, the analysis becomes prohibitively complex for making statements about the system's cross-section internal rate of return (IRR).

The aim of this study is to demonstrate that there is a simple method for estimating the cross-section internal rate of return on contributions to PAYG pensions systems, even as the two-age OLG restriction, and the steady state restriction, is canceled. The method entails a procedure for valuing the contribution flow of PAYG financing and identifies the complete set of factors that decides the cross-section IRR. The procedure makes it possible to apply the algorithm of double-entry bookkeeping in PAYG pension systems.

The method presented here for calculating the rate of return of PAYG pension financing, including the valuation of the contribution flow and the use of double-entry bookkeeping in a PAYG context, is a result of the research undertaken to deal with some conflicting ambitions of the new Swedish pension system.[4] This method for solving, or rather managing, this conflict was reached in ignorance of the research cited above by Arthur and McNicoll, Willis, Keyfitz, and Lee.[5]

In this text, the phrase *cross-section* IRR is used to indicate a measure distinct from the more familiar *longitudinal* IRR measure, which informs the rate of return that equates the value of the time-specific contributions with the benefits to an individual or a group of individuals. The cross-section IRR is the return on the pension system's liabilities that keeps the net present value of the pension system unaltered during a period of arbitrary length. However, to derive the cross-section IRR, a continuous time model is used. The expression *cross-section internal rate of return* is abbreviated below to *rate of return,* while we sometimes use the abbreviation IRR. We also use the terms *contribution base, contribution rate,* and *contributions,* where some would prefer *tax base, tax rate,* and *taxes.*

In the next section, a method for estimating the value of the contribution flow to PAYG pension systems is presented. In the following section, this method is used to obtain a formula for calculating the cross-section IRR on contributions to such systems. The final section concludes by commenting on the results. In annex B, the methods used to value the contribution flow and the definition of the cross-section IRR are illustrated by means of simple numerical examples. Some readers will probably find it helpful to read the numerical examples before they read the second and third sections.

The Value of the Contribution Flow

PAYG financing implies that the flow of future contributions is used to finance a pension liability that has already accrued.[6] It is probably a matter of personal preference whether one considers that a PAYG system, by definition, has a deficit equal to this liability, or accepts that its net present value is zero if contributions match pension payments. Here the latter view is taken and *financial balance* is defined as

$$Assets - Liabilities = 0. \tag{7.1a}$$

This standard definition of financial balance is unconventional for PAYG pension systems. The commonly performed projections of cash flows to and from PAYG pension systems used to evaluate their financial situation have traditionally not been presented in the form of assets and liabilities, as the methods used does not allow this.[7] As already indicated, it seems reasonable to consider that a PAYG pension system whose contributions and benefits match have a zero net present value and subsequently to conclude that its liability is matched by an implicit asset, below referred to as a *contribution asset*. In another context, Lee (1994 and later) calls a corresponding concept *transfer wealth*.

Often PAYG systems are considered to be defined by the absence of any funded assets. In practice, however, there is normally a transaction account, and sometimes there are substantial funded assets. Systems without any funded assets are only a special case of the general description that follows. Hence equation 7.1a can be re-expressed as

$$CA(t) + F(t) - PL(t) = 0, \tag{7.1b}$$

where

$\qquad CA$ = contribution asset,

$\qquad F$ = buffer fund,

$\qquad PL$ = pension liability, and

$\qquad t$ = time.

In a steady state, contributions will equal pension benefits, thus $CA(t_{ss}) = PL(t_{ss})$, and $F(t_{ss})$ = 0. For each income and mortality pattern and set of pension-system rules, there is a unique value for the pension liability. Equations 7.2 through 7.4 give an expression for this value in steady state.

In the case of a stable population—that is, a population with constant mortality rates and constant population growth—the age distribution of the population can be expressed as

$$N(x) = N(0) \cdot l(x) \cdot e^{-\gamma x}, \tag{7.2}$$

where

$\qquad N(x)$ = number of persons of age x,

$\qquad x$ = age,

$\qquad \gamma$ = the rate of fertility-driven[8] population growth, and

$\qquad l(x)$ = life table survival function.

In this system, the indexation of benefits can have any relation to the growth in average wage. Thus the pension benefit may vary in size relative to this average wage at different ages. If, for example, pensions are indexed by the change in consumer prices, and average wages grow at a faster rate, the average pension benefit per birth cohort will be lower for older cohorts than for younger ones. The distribution of pensions within a cohort is ignored, since it has no relevance for the system-level rate of return.

The pension liability, V, is defined as the present value of future pension benefits to all persons to whom the system has a liability at the time of evaluation minus the present value of future contributions by the same individuals,

$$V = \int_0^m population(x) \int_x^m PV[pensions(u) - contributions(u)]du\ dx\ , \qquad (7.3)$$

where

> m = maximum age, and
>
> x, u = age; both are variables of integration.

Discounting payments to and from the pension scheme by the growth in the contribution base, the pension liability can be re-expressed as:

$$V = \int_0^m \underbrace{N(0) \cdot l(x) \cdot e^{-\gamma \cdot x}}_{population,\,age\,x} \int_x^m \underbrace{\frac{l(u)}{l(x)}}_{survivor\,rate} \cdot \underbrace{e^{-\gamma \cdot (u-x)}}_{discounting} \cdot \left[\overbrace{\underbrace{k \cdot \overline{W} \cdot e^{\varphi \cdot u}}^{average\,pension,\,age\,u} \cdot R(u)}_{pension\,payments} - \underbrace{c \cdot \overline{W} \cdot W(u)}_{contributions} \right] du\ dx\ , \qquad (7.4)$$

where

> $W(x)$ = wage pattern—that is, the average wage for age group x, as a ratio of the average wage for all age groups,
>
> $\overline{W}$ = average wage in monetary units per unit of time,
>
> c = required contribution for a financially stable PAYG pension system,
>
> φ = the rate of pension indexation relative to the rate of average wage growth,
>
> $R(x)$ = number of retirees as a ratio of the number of individuals in age group x, and
>
> k = constant determining the pension level (equals the replacement rate if $\varphi = 0$).

The rate of discount is the product of the growth in average wages times the rate of population growth. As both wages and benefits grow with the average wage growth, the growth in average wage falls out of the equation and leaves the population growth rate as the effective discount rate, γ. It would be inappropriate to use a market rate of return on capital as a discount rate. The return on capital has no impact on the financial balance of a PAYG pension system, disregarding its effect on the buffer fund if there is one.

For a stable population with stable income patterns, the contributions, C, are generated by the size of the population by age, $N(x)$; the wage pattern, $W(x)$; the average wage, $\overline{W}$; and the required contribution rate for a financially stable system, c.

$$C = \int_0^m N(x) \cdot c \cdot \overline{W} \cdot W(x) dx. \qquad (7.5)$$

In a steady state, the contribution rate that satisfies the financial-stability criteria of equation 7.1 is also the contribution rate that makes contributions equate with pension payments in every period. Thus c is calculated as

$$\underbrace{\int_0^m N(0)\cdot l(x)\cdot e^{-\gamma\cdot x}\cdot k\cdot \overline{W}\cdot e^{\varphi\cdot u}\cdot R(x)\,dx}_{\text{pension payments}} = \underbrace{\int_0^m N(0)\cdot l(x)\cdot e^{-\gamma\cdot x}\cdot c\cdot\overline{W}\cdot W(x)\,dx}_{\text{contributions}}\ ,$$

$$c = k\cdot\frac{\int_0^m e^{-(\gamma-\varphi)\cdot x}\cdot l(x)\cdot R(x)\,dx}{\int_0^m e^{-\gamma\cdot x}\cdot l(x)\cdot W(x)\,dx}\ . \tag{7.6}$$

It is possible to get a form of measurement of the pension liability, in steady state, that is independent both of the size of the contribution base and of the contribution rate simply by dividing the pension liability by contributions paid per time unit. Thus equation 7.4 is divided by equation 7.5, where equation 7.6 is substituted for c. Rearranging and integrating by parts, this simplifies to

$$\frac{V}{C} = \underbrace{\frac{\int_0^m x\cdot\left[e^{-(\gamma-\varphi)\cdot x}\cdot l(x)\cdot R(x)\right]dx}{\int_0^m \left[e^{-(\gamma-\varphi)\cdot x}\cdot l(x)\cdot R(x)\right]dx}}_{\text{average age of retirees}} - \underbrace{\frac{\int_0^m x\cdot\left[e^{-\gamma\cdot x}\cdot l(x)\cdot W(x)\right]dx}{\int_0^m \left[e^{-\gamma\cdot x}\cdot l(x)\cdot W(x)\right]dx}}_{\text{average age of contributors}}\ . \tag{7.7}$$

The intermediate steps of the simplification are presented in annex C.

Equation 7.7 informs the conceivably intuitively reasonable fact that in steady state, the liability divided by contributions is equal to the time differece between the average age of retirees (the first term of the right-hand side), and the average age of contributors (the second term of the right-hand side). Both ages are money-weighted. However, this is not evident from the expression, as the average wage is a part of contributions, C. This leaves equation 7.7 with only the age patterns. The age difference between the average contributor and retiree is a measure of the duration of the pension liability. We call it *turnover duration (TD)*.

$$\frac{V}{C} = A_r - A_c = TD \tag{7.8}$$

where

> A_r = money-weighted average age of retiree, and
>
> A_c = money-weighted average age of contributor.

The top half of figure 7.1 illustrates the age structure for average wage, $W(x)$; a certain life-table, $l(x)$; a population growth trend, γ; and rules for indexation of pensions, φ. It also illustrates the retirement pattern, $R(x)$. The bottom half of figure 7.1 illustrates the resulting age structure for the contribution base and the pension payments. The resulting age-differential between the money-weighted average age of retirees, A_r and contributors, A_c is also shown.

Hence, for a stable population with stable income patterns, the factors determining the size of the pension liability can be separated into a volume component that is *contributions*

Figure 7.1. Illustration of Equations 7.7 and 7.8

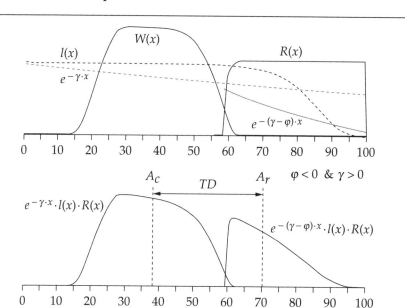

Source: Authors.

and a structural component that is the *turnover duration*. Turnover duration is a useful concept that sums up the factors that determine the scaleless size of the pension liability: *scaleless* refers to disregarding the size of contribution rate and contribution base. The present value of the pension liability for a stable population with stable income patterns is expressed in years of contributions:

$$\frac{V}{C} = TD \iff V = TD \cdot C. \tag{7.9a}$$

The separation of the steady state pension liability into a volume and a structural component also has a temporal aspect. Except in a steady state, there will be no definite value for the turnover duration; however, the current economic and demographic patterns can be used to measure the *expected* turnover duration. It is expected in the same sense as the common measure of life expectancy; that is, it uses current observations to calculate a value that will turn out correct ex post only if observed patterns remain constant. The probability that any generation will live according to any published life table is virtually zero. Nevertheless, life tables are relevant and useful. Repeated estimations of the expected turnover duration[9] will reflect the changes in the financially relevant patterns and thus yield new estimates of the contribution asset, which are infinitely unlikely to produce the ex post correct figure. This procedure of repetitive revaluation of the contribution asset is not so different from the recurring revaluation of funded assets by the market.[10] For these reasons we find it appropriate to define the value of the contribution flow as the current turnover duration times the current contributions:

$$CA(t) = TD(t) \cdot C(t). \tag{7.9b}$$

The turnover duration indicates the size of the pension liability that the present contribution flow can finance, given the present income and mortality patterns and the population growth rate. As economic and demographic patterns change, the new value of the contribution flow can be estimated. The inverse of the turnover duration is a computable discount rate for the contribution flow, a measure of the current internal time preference of the PAYG pension scheme. This time preference is a function of the system design with respect to the rules that govern the indexing of pensions, the income and mortality patterns of the insured population, and the population growth trend. Annex C provides rough estimates of the turnover duration for 41 countries from Settergren and Mikula (2001). The country-specific turnover duration varies from 31 to 35 years; thus, with the internal time preferences of the hypothetical pension system in the estimate, the discount rates for contributions vary between approximately 2.8 and 3.2 percent. These rates are interestingly close to the frequently assumed real interest rate of about 3 percent.

The usefulness of the turnover duration for valuing the contribution flow is critically dependent on its volatility. In many countries, perhaps most, the volatility of the turnover duration can be anticipated to be moderate to low. The stem-and-leaf exhibit in figure 7.2 presents estimates of the annual percentage change in the turnover duration in Sweden in the period 1981–2003.[11] The average increase was 0.4 percent, most of it attributable to the increase in life expectancy; the average, money-weighted age of contributors remained closely around age 43, with no clear trend. The maximum one-year increase in turnover duration was 2.1 percent; the maximum annual decrease was 0.5 percent. More than half, 12, of the annual changes were between zero and 0.5 percent, and the standard deviation of the 23 observations was 0.6.

In the next section, the above method for estimating the value of the contribution flow is used to derive an expression for the rate of return of PAYG pension systems, and the application of double-entry bookkeeping for such systems is outlined.

Figure 7.2. Turnover Duration in Sweden, 23 Annual Changes, percentages 1981–2003

```
    2  |  1
    1  |  8
    1  |  11
    0  |  865
    0  |  4443220000
   -0  |  234
   -0  |  5
```

The stem-and-leaf diagram is read as follows:

```
   ...  |  ...
    1   |  11   = 1.1% and 1.1%
    0   |  865  = 0.8%, 0.6% and 0.5%
   etc. |
```

Source: Riksförsäkringsverket (2003, 2004).

The PAYG System's Rate of Return

Financial balance can be ensured by adjusting the size of the pension liability: that is, by adjusting the value of present and or future benefits, or by adjusting the contribution rate—the size of the contribution asset as defined by equation 7.9b—or by doing both. Irrespective of the type of tuning, the financial-balance requirement of equation 7.1b, a net present value of zero, applies. To continue the derivation of the IRR, equation 7.1b is rephrased to

$$TD \cdot C + F - PL = 0, \qquad (7.10)$$

where

F = buffer fund, and

PL = pension liability.

Equation 7.10 implies that both negative and positive funded assets are allowed, and in some situations necessary, to comply with the definition of financial balance.[12] Annex B presents numerical examples that illustrate this point.

The rate of return of the pension liability that yields a net present value of zero is, by definition, the rate of return on contributions to the system. The formula for the rate of return of a PAYG pension system follows from differentiating equation 7.10 with respect to time

$$\frac{d(TD \cdot C + F - PL)}{dt} = TD \cdot \frac{dC}{dt} + \frac{dTD}{dt} \cdot C + \frac{dF}{dt} - \frac{dPL}{dt} = 0. \qquad (7.11)$$

The change in pension liability is a function of the rate of return of the liability and of the difference between payment of contributions and disbursements of pensions, as shown in equation 7.12

$$\frac{dPL}{dt} = PL \cdot IRR + (C - P), \qquad (7.12)$$

where

IRR = internal rate of return, and

P = pension payments in monetary units per unit of time.

The IRR may turn up in two different forms: *implicit* and *explicit*. The *implicit* rate of return is a function of the impact of changes in mortality on the pension liability, and of any divergence between new pension obligations and contributions paid. In addition, changes in the rules of the system will normally alter the value of the pension liability, producing an implicit effect on the IRR. The *explicit* rate of return is the result of any explicit rules for indexing the liability—that is, the benefits to present and future retirees.

The net difference in payments to and from the pension system is captured by the buffer fund, if there is one. In addition, the value of the fund is changed by the return on its assets, as shown in equation 7.13

$$\frac{dF}{dt} = F \cdot r + (C - P), \qquad (7.13)$$

where

r = rate of return on the buffer fund.

Depending on its sign and magnitude, the return on the buffer fund may increase or decrease the rate of return of the PAYG pension system. Equation 7.11 can then be re-expressed as

$$TD \cdot \frac{dC}{dt} + \frac{dTD}{dt} \cdot C + F \cdot r - PL \cdot IRR = 0 \,. \tag{7.14}$$

Finally, the IRR, separated into its components, is

$$IRR = \underbrace{\frac{TD \cdot \dfrac{dC}{dt}}{PL}}_{i} + \underbrace{\frac{\dfrac{dTD}{dt} \cdot C}{PL}}_{ii} + \underbrace{\frac{F \cdot r}{PL}}_{iii} \,. \tag{7.15}$$

Thus the rate of return of a PAYG system is a function of:

i	*Changes in contributions*	This component consists of Samuelson's biological interest rate, changes in labor force participation, average wage growth, and changes in the contribution rate.
ii	*Changes in turnover duration*	This component consists of changes in income and mortality patterns and in the fertility-driven growth rate of the population.[13]
iii	*Buffer fund return (interest)*	This component consists of the return (interest) on any assets (debt) in the system.

The part of the IRR that is caused by mortality changes and any divergence between new pension obligations and contributions paid, or by changes in the system rules, can be considered an implicit indexation of the pension liability. The IRR reduced by the rate of implicit indexation is the rate of available indexation of the pension liability. Thus,

Rate of available indexation = i + ii + iii – rate of implicit indexation. (7.16)

In practice, the indexation rules, or the adjustment of the contribution rate or other system rules, are not necessarily such that they distribute all the available indexation each time period. The applied indexation will differ temporally from what is available. The difference is the net income or loss to the system during the measured time period.

Rate of available indexation – rate of explicit indexation = system net income. (7.17)

The accrued value of such net income or losses gives the opening surplus or deficit for the next period.

How does the expression for the cross-section IRR of PAYG pension systems in equation 7.15 relate to the longitudinal IRR on contributions? For individuals, this calculation becomes possible at the time of death. For a birth cohort, it is possible when everyone in the cohort has died; for the pensions system, it is possible when it has been closed down. Such delays of information are, indeed, impractical. Both participants and policy makers want regular information on financial position and development. In order to produce this information, cross-section rate of return measures must be adopted, for which there is only imperfect information. In the business world, the problem is similar. The true rate of return can be calculated only when all payments to and from the business entity have been made. As business stakeholders need regular information on the rate of return, accounting principles are developed for an ongoing business. It is well known that accounting measures of the rate of return—basically business net income—are subject to some degree of arbitrariness. Therefore, the preferred choice of method is a matter for debate.

For PAYG pension systems, it is possible to envisage other accounting procedures than the one described here, and other measures will normally yield a different rate of return for a specific period. By our method, the contribution flow is valued according to the turnover duration with cross-section observations at the time, while the pension liability is estimated with an actuarial projection that may or may not imply changes in future turnover duration. Such differences will have an impact on the trajectory of the measured rate of return, but not on the aggregate rate of return as the system approaches a hypothetical steady state.

Conclusions

The rate of return on contributions to PAYG pension systems is not only a function of the growth in the contribution base of the system. It is also a function of changes in income and mortality patterns and in the trend of population growth. These three factors cause changes in the average age at which contributions are paid and pensions received: that is, they cause changes in *turnover duration*. Further, if there is a buffer fund in the system, the return on that fund will influence the rate of return on contributions. The rate of return can be implicitly distributed through the effects on the pension liability from mortality changes and also by differences between contributions paid and new pension liabilities. The difference between the rate of return and the implicitly distributed return is the rate of available indexation—the explicit indexation of the pension liability, which must be made to keep the systems net present value unaltered.

The turnover duration provides an estimate of the discount rate for the contribution flow to systems, which finances obligations with a zero prefunding requirement, that is, PAYG systems. This makes it possible to apply a form of double-entry bookkeeping. With the double-entry algorithm, the financial position of these schemes can be reported by means of a balance sheet, as summarized in equation 7.10, and changes in the financial position can be reported by means of an income statement, summarized in equation 7.17.[14] We would argue that extending the field of double-entry bookkeeping to PAYG pensions systems has the potential of improving the quality and transparency, and thus the understandability, of financial information on these important transaction systems over the different measures of actuarial balance used today. Disentangling the components of the rate of return also adds options for the design of PAYG pension systems. In particular, the forms of indexing pensions can be given a more efficient design.[15]

Annex 7A. A Bibliography of the Legislative History
of the Income Index and the Automatic Balance Mechanism

Settergren, O. With the assistance of H. Olsson. 1997. Kapitel 5 Inkomstindex "Inkomst-grundad ålderspension—finansiella frågor m.m.," Ds 1997:67. Socialdepartementet, Stockholm. (Chapter 5 The Income Index in "Income-Related Old-Age Pension—Financial Issues etc." Ds 1997:67, Ministry of Health and Social Affairs, Stockholm.)

———. 1998. Chapter 16 Inkomstindex, "Regeringens proposition 1997/98:151 Inkomst-grundad ålderspension, m.m.," Riksdagen, Stockholm. (Chapter 16 The Income Index in "The Government Bill 1997/98:151 Income-Related Old-Age Pension etc." Swedish Parliament, Stockholm.)

———. 1999. With the assistance of H. Olsson and D. Sundén. "Automatisk balansering av ålderspensionssystemet—regler för avsteg från inkomstindexeringen inom ålderspen-sionssystemet," Ds 1999:43. Socialdepartementet, Stockholm. (Automatic Balancing of the Old-Age Pension System—Rules for Deviating from the Income Indexation within the Old-Age Pension System." Ds 1999:43, Ministry of Health and Social Affairs, Stockholm.)

———. 2000. With actuarial modeling and calculations by B. D. Mikula, N. Holmgren, and J. Leander. "Automatisk balansering av ålderspensionssystemet—redovisning av regeringens beräkningsuppdrag," RFV Analyserar 2000:1 Riksförsäkringsverket, Stockholm ("Automatic Balancing of the Old-Age Pension System—An Account of the Calculation Assignment from the Government." RFV Analysis 2000:1).

———. 2001. "Regeringens proposition 2000/01:70 Automatisk balansering av ålderspen-sionssystemet," Riksdagen, Stockholm. (The Government Bill 2000/01:70 Automatic Balancing of the Old-Age Pension System." Swedish Parliament, Stockholm.)

Annex 7B. Numerical Illustrations in an Overlapping Generation Model

A three-age overlapping generation (OLG) model is used to illustrate the impact of changes in the average ages at which income is earned and consumed. Three is the minimum number of ages needed for changing the differential between the ages at which the average income is earned and consumed. This age differential is called *turnover duration*, and is formally derived in equations 7.1–7.9. To demonstrate the effects of changes in mortality on the rate of return, the model is extended from three to four ages.

In the model, the life of an individual is divided into three (four) periods of equal length. All individuals work for exactly two periods, at ages 1 and 2, and they are all retired for the entire third (and fourth) period, age 3 (and 4). All are born on the first day of each period; all birth cohorts are of equal size; there is no fertility-driven population growth, no migration, and no preretirement mortality. And everyone in retirement dies on the last day of their final period. There is no technological progress. Under these assumptions, the contribution base for the pension system is constant. All financial transactions are made at the end of each period. To avoid the complication that changes in contribution rate have on the internal rate of return (IRR) (see equation 7.15) the examples are constructed so that the system in all examples can finance its pension payments with an unchanged contribution rate—25 percent—for every period in all examples.

The effects on IRR from shifts in income and mortality patterns are described for certain alternative pension-system rules. The reason for this is to illustrate that:

- The system's cross-section IRR is not a function of system design[1]
- The distribution of the IRR over cohorts, the "longitudinal IRR,"[2] is a function of system design
- The timing of cash flows is a function of system design, even when designs are equally financially stable in the sense that they all produce a zero net present value as defined in equation 7.10.

Although the numerical examples are straightforward, the somewhat complex feature of OLG, in combination with the detailed account of the effects of the shifts in income and mortality patterns, may make it tedious to work through the examples. However, this effort can be well invested as the examples, once grasped, clearly reveal structures that are vital for understanding important aspects of PAYG financing.

Example 1. A Shift in Income Pattern

Summary of what the example illustrates. In the following example, the income pattern shifts—the income of older workers increases relative to that of younger workers, so that the income-weighted average age of contributors increases. The example shows how this change decreases the turnover duration and leads to a negative IRR. The effects of the negative IRR are illustrated for a pension system where the rules are such that this specific shock will result in a *rate of implicit indexation* equal to the negative IRR. In example 1.1 below, the effects of the same shift in income pattern are illustrated for a system where the rules are such that this specific shock will result in a rate of implicit indexation equal to zero. Thus in example 1.1, to maintain a zero net present value, the negative IRR must be distributed through *explicit* indexation equal to the IRR. The subsequent effects on the cash flow, buffer fund, and so on of the system are illustrated with an income statement and a balance sheet.

The shift in income pattern. Up until and including period 1, the wage is 48 for the older working cohort and also 48 for the younger. In the period 2, the income pattern is changed.[3] From then on, the wage is 72 for the older cohort and 24 for the younger. Thus the wage sum, equal to the contribution base, is constantly 96. The average wage for workers in general also remains unaltered; only the distribution of the average wage between the age groups has shifted.

The rules of the pension system. The pension system is designed to pay a benefit that is 50 percent of the gross average wage of all wage earners—admittedly an awkward rule, but here it serves our purpose.

The effects of the shift in income pattern. Table 7B.1 illustrates that this system will result in contributions of 24 that perfectly match pension benefits of 24 before and after the shift in income pattern. Cohort B, the only cohort whose lifetime income is altered by the change in income pattern, will receive a pension of 24, whereas it paid contributions of 30, the sum of 25 percent of wages 48 and 72, respectively. As the pension received is only 24, this cohort will receive 6 less than they paid, a periodically compounded rate of return of roughly –15 percent. The computation is

$$0.25 \times 48 \times r^2 + 0.25 \times 72 \times r = 24 \Rightarrow r - 1 \approx -15\%.$$

The effect of the change in income pattern on the system's cross-section rate of return is the monetary effect, –6, relative to the systems pension liability[4] of 36. Thus the cross-section rate of return is –1/6. Table 7B.1 shows that the cross-section rate of return is equal to the relative decrease in the money-weighted average difference in time between the payment of contributions and the collection of benefits, that is, the decrease in turnover duration from 1.5 to 1.25. From table 7B.2 it is also clear that the change in turnover duration makes the con-

Table 7B.1. Effect of a Shift in Income Pattern on Cohort Contributions and Benefits

Cohort / Period	0	1	2	3	4	Cohort total Contributions	Pensions
A	48	48	**24**			24	24
B		48	72	**24**		30	24
C			24	72	**24**	24	24
D				24	72	24	..

Period total		0	1	2	3	4
	Wage sum	..	96	96	96	..
	Contribution rate	25%	25%	25%	25%	25%
	Contributions	..	24	24	24	..
	Pensions	..	..	**24**	**24**	**24**

Source: Authors.

Note: The central box shows wage sums in normal type and **pensions in bold face**, per period, for each cohort.

Table 7B.2. Effect of a Shift in Income Pattern on Turnover Duration and Pension Liability

	Before shift	After shift	Relative change
Average age of retiree, $\bar{A}_R$	3[a]	3[a]	—
Average age of contributor, $\bar{A}_C$	1.5[b]	1.75[c]	+1/6
Turnover duration, TD, $(\bar{A}_R - \bar{A}_C)$	1.5	1.25	−1/6
Contribution asset, $TD \times$ contributions	36	30	−1/6
Pension liability, PL	36[d]	30[e]	−1/6
IRR (Monetary loss / PL)[f]		−6/36	−1/6

Source: Authors.

Note: In explanations b, c, d, and e, contributions are shown in normal type, **pensions in bold face**, *ages in italics*. For explanation of pension liability, brackets [ ] are used to group money flows from and to the same cohort. Figures relating to cohorts are presented in order from oldest to youngest.

a. All pensions are paid at *age 3*.
b. $(48 \times 2 + 48 \times 1) / (48 + 48)$.
c. $(72 \times 2 + 24 \times 1) / (72 + 24)$.
d. **[24]** + **[24** − 12].
e. **[24]** + **[24** − 18].
f. The monetary loss occurs "at" the shift, indicated by the placement of the number between the "before shift" and "after shift."

tribution asset, which is calculated as the contribution flow times the turnover duration, decrease and that this decrease is equal to the monetary loss incurred by cohort B.

As a combined effect of the shift in income pattern and the rules of this pension system, the pension liability decreases to the same extent that the value of the contribution flow is reduced by the shorter turnover duration. Before the shift the pension liability was 36; after the shift the pension liability is 30. Owing to this implicit negative indexation of the pension liability, the net present value of the system is consistently zero throughout the shift. The shift in income pattern in combination with the rule that says that pensions are 50 percent of average income of all wage earners implicitly distributes the negative IRR to cohort B. However, the negative IRR itself was not a consequence of the system's rules, as will be illustrated in the following example.

Example 1.1 Same Shift in Income Pattern, Different Pension System Rules

The rules of the pension system. The same shift in income pattern is now applied in a pension system designed as a so-called notional defined contribution (NDC) system. The rules of such a system imply that each cohort is to be repaid an amount equal to their contributions indexed at some rate, positive or negative. Initially, the indexing rules of the system are assumed to provide that notional pension capital and pensions are to be revalued at the growth rate of the contribution base, which in the example is zero for every period.

The effects of the shift in income pattern. Up until and including cohort A and period 2, this system will yield an identical result as the first set of rules: zero cross-section and longitudinal IRRs. But when cohort B retires, it will have accumulated a notional pension capital of 30, equal to what it has paid in contributions. As the flow of contributions is constant at 24, the system can only repay cohort B their notional pension capital by incurring a deficit of 6—a figure familiar from example 1. This deficit is caused by the same reduction in turnover duration as in example 1. However, in the NDC system the same negative IRR causes a cash deficit since the rate of (implicit) indexation is zero, while in Example 1 the rate was −1/6, thus distributing the negative IRR.

The shift in income pattern does not immediately reduce the pension liability of the notionally defined contribution system; this liability remains at 36 in period 2,[5] while the shorter turnover duration—just as in Example 1—has decreased the value of the contribution flow to 30. To be financially stable, the notional defined contribution pension system must explicitly distribute the negative IRR by reducing the pension liability. One way to accomplish this is to index the system's total pension liability by the "rate of available indexation," (see equation 7.16). Table 7B.3 shows the development of the income statement and balance sheet of the NDC system, which applies explicit indexation at the available rate, here equal to the IRR.

Indexing cohort B's and C's notional pension capital of 30 and 6,[6] respectively, by the available rate of 5/6 reduces it to 25 and 5, respectively. Thus the total pension liability of

Table 7B.3. Example 1: Income Statement, and Balance Sheet

	Period				
	1	2[a]	2	3	4
Income statement					
Contributions	24	24	24	24	24
Pensions	−24	−24	−24	−25	−23
= net cash flow (a)	0	0	0	−1	1
Change in contribution asset (b)	0	−6[c]	−6[c]	0	0
New accrued pension liability[b]	−24	−24	−24	−24	24
Paid-off pension liability[b] (= paid pension benefits)	24	24	24	25	23
Indexation of liability[b]	0	0	6	0	0
= change in pension liability (c)	0	0	6	1	−1
Net income/ −loss, (a) + (b) + (c)	0	−6	0	0	0
Balance sheet					
Buffer fund	0	0	0	−1	0
Contribution asset	36	30	30	30	30
= total assets (d)	36	30	30	29	30
Pension liability, age 3	0	0	0	0	0
Pension liability, age 2	24	30	25[d]	23[e]	24
Pension liability, age 1	12	6	5[e]	6	6
= total liability (e)	36	36	30	29	30
Net present value of system (d) − (e)	0	−6	0	0	0

Source: Authors.

a. Values before indexation with the available rate of return.
b. A negative number denotes an increase in the pension liability and thus a cost. A positive number denotes a decrease in the pension liability and thus an income.
c. $-0.25 \times 24 = -6$ {change in $TD \times$ [contributions (t) + contributions $(t-1)$]/2}.
d. $12 + 18 \times 5/6 = 25$ [cohort B's period 1 contribution + cohort B's period 2 contribution $\times$ IRR].
e. $6 \times 5/6 + 18 = 23$ [cohort C's period 2 contribution $\times$ IRR + cohort C's period 3 contribution].

the system is reduced from 36 to 30—equal to the new shorter turnover duration of the system (1.25) times the contribution flow (24). This implies that the system has regained its zero net present value. Nonetheless, the shift in income pattern and the negative indexation of the pension liability will affect the system's cash flows. Period 3 pension payments to cohort B will be 25. As system income is 24 every period this will result in a deficit of 1. In period 4, pension payments to cohort C will be 23 (5 + 18); thus a cash flow surplus of 1 will arise and close the deficit.[7] The systems total assets period 3 are 29, that is the sum of the buffer fund period 3 is –1 and the contribution asset is 30. The total assets are equal to the system's pension liability, and the system's net present value is consistently zero.

Example 2. A Shift in Mortality Pattern

Summary of what the example illustrates. In example 2 the mortality pattern changes—life expectancy shifts upward—so that the money-weighted average age of retirees increases. The example shows how this change increases the turnover duration and results in a positive IRR. The effects of the positive IRR are illustrated for a pension system where the rules are such that the rate of implicit indexation equals the positive IRR. In example 2.1 the effects of the same shift in mortality pattern are illustrated for a system where the rules are such that the rate of implicit indexation is zero. Thus in example 2.1, to maintain a zero net present value, the positive IRR must be distributed through *explicit* indexation equal to the IRR. The subsequent effects on the cash flows, buffer fund, and so on of the system are illustrated with an income statement and a balance sheet.

The shift in mortality pattern. The shift in mortality occurs—simply, though unrealistically—through a one-time increase in life span. After one period of retirement, no retiree in cohort B dies; instead, after the third period, all retirees in the cohort continue to live for exactly one more period. Subsequent cohorts also live for exactly two periods as retirees.

The rules of the pension system. In the example, we keep the contribution rate fixed at 25 percent. Thus average pension benefit must be halved after the first cohort with a longer life expectancy received its first pension payment. Cohort B's pension is thus 24 in their first period as retirees and 12 in their second. Cohort C, the second cohort with a longer life span, will receive a pension of 12 in each period, as will subsequent cohorts.

The effects of the shift in mortality pattern. Table 7B.4 illustrate that the system will result in contributions of 24 that perfectly match pension benefits of 24 before and after the shift in mortality. However, cohort B, the first to benefit from the longer life span, will receive a total pension of 36, whereas it paid only 24 in contributions, for a periodically compounded rate of return of approximately 25 percent. The computation is

$$0.25 \times 48 \times r^3 + 0.25 \times 48 \times r^2 = 24 \times r + 12 \Rightarrow r - 1 \approx 25\%.$$

The effect of the change in mortality pattern on the system's cross-section rate of return is cohort B's monetary gain, 12, relative to the systems pension liability 36. Thus the cross-section rate of return is 1/3. Table 7B.5 shows that the cross-section rate of return is equal to the relative increase in the money-weighted average difference in time between the payment of contributions and the collection of benefits—that is, the increase in turnover duration from 1.5 to 2. The reason for the positive return is the longer time span between the average wage-weighted age of contributors and the average benefit-weighted age of retirees resulting from the shift in mortality pattern, the increase in turnover duration. With the longer turnover duration, the value of the contribution flow increases from 36 to 48.

The system is financially balanced throughout the shift since the pension liability increases to the same extent as the value of the contribution flow. The positive return of 12 is implicitly distributed to the cohort whose initial pension was calculated on the basis of

Table 7B.4. Effect of a Shift in Mortality on Cohort Benefits

Cohort \ Period	−1	0	1	2	3	4	Cohort total Contributions	Cohort total Pensions
A	48	48	**24**				24	**24**
B		48	48	**24**	12		24	**36**
C			48	48	**12**	12	24	**24**
D				48	48	**12**	24	...
Period total — Wage sum	..	96	96	96	..	..		
Period total — Contribution rate	25%	25%	25%	25%	25%	25%		
Period total — Contributions	..	24	24	24	..	..		
Period total — **Pensions**	..	..	**24**	**24**	**24**	**24**		

Source: Authors.

Note: The central box shows wage sums in normal type and **pensions in bold face**, per period, for each cohort.

Table 7B.5. Effect of a Shift in Mortality Pattern on Turnover Duration and Pension Liability

	Before shift	*After shift*	*Relative change*
Average age of retiree, $\overline{A}_R$	3[a]	3.5[f]	+ 1/6
Average age of contributor, $\overline{A}_C$	1.5[b]	1.5[b]	—
$\overline{A}_R - \overline{A}_C$, turnover duration, TD	1.5	2	+ 1/3
Contribution asset, $TD \times$ contributions	36	48	+ 1/3
Pension liability, PL	36[d]	48[g]	+ 1/3
IRR (monetary gain / PL)	12/36		+ 1/3

Source: Authors.

Note: See table 7B.2 for explanation of the use of normal type, **bold-face,** and *italics.*
a., b., d: see table 7B.2.
f. $(\mathbf{12} \times 4 + \mathbf{12} \times 3) / (\mathbf{12} + \mathbf{12})$.
g. $[\mathbf{12}] + [\mathbf{12} + \mathbf{12}] + [\mathbf{12} + \mathbf{12} - 12]$.

the previous life expectancy. This can also be illustrated by placing the numbers in the example into equation 7.16

$$[\text{rate of available indexation}] = [i] + [ii] + [iii] - [\text{rate of implicit indexation}].$$
$$0 = 0 + 1/3 + 0 - 1/3$$

The positive return resulting from an increase in life expectancy is due neither to the design of the pension system nor to the imperfect knowledge of life expectancy assumed in the example. If cohort B's life span had been known ex ante and the benefit had been reduced to 12 already in cohort B's first period of retirement, there would have been a surplus of 12 in period 2. Equation 7.16 would then read as follows

$$[\text{rate of available indexation}] \;=\; [\text{i}] \;+\; [\text{ii}] \;+\; [\text{iii}] \;-\; [\text{rate of implicit indexation}].$$
$$1/3 \;=\; 0 \;+\; 1/3 \;+\; 0 \;-\; 0$$

If the available indexation is not used to increase the pension liability, the identity requirement for financial stability—a zero net present value—is not met since an undistributed surplus then arises. Example 2.1 illustrates the effects of one rule for distributing this surplus.

Example 2.1 Same Shift in Mortality Pattern, Different Pension System Rules

The rules of the pension system. We now again assume an NDC system. This NDC system indexes its liability by the available rate of return. In the example, this return will equal the IRR since we assume perfect information on life expectancy. In such a system and with this information, the surplus of 12, representing a rate of available indexation of 1/3, will be distributed through indexation of the pension liability in period 2.

The effects of the shift in mortality pattern. Before the shift, pension payments and contributions will both be stable at 24. Periods 3, 4, and 5, pension payments will be 16, 30, and 26, respectively. Pension payments will be back at 24 as from period 6. Periods 3 and 4, the buffer fund, will thus stand at 8 and 2, respectively, and be back at zero as from period 5. (Readers are encouraged to verify these calculations.) The positive fund is necessary to balance the pension liability, which will temporarily exceed the contribution asset by the same magnitude as the value of the fund. Assuming revaluation of the pension liability at the rate of available indexation and, more realistically, imperfect information on life expectancy, the flow of payments will be different. Still, the system will maintain a zero net present value at all times and in a steady state end up with a zero buffer fund.

Summary of What the Examples Show

For financially stable PAYG pension systems, the examples showed that the cross-section IRR, regardless of system design and ability to forecast life span, is affected identically by changes in income and mortality patterns. We also learned that the distribution of the IRR among cohorts depends on system design and ability to forecast mortality. Furthermore, the principle of double-entry bookkeeping in PAYG pension systems has been illustrated.[8]

Notes

1. However, if the rate of return on buffer fund assets or the interest rate on a buffer fund deficit differs from the growth rate in the contribution base, the design of the PAYG system as one with or without buffer fund will have a (small) impact on the system's cross-section IRR.

2. See the first section of this chapter for a definition of *cross-section* and *longitudinal* IRR.

3. *Income pattern* is defined as the ratio of the average wage for each age group to the average wage for all age groups. A stable income pattern exists when this ratio is constant over time for all age groups.

4. *Pension liability,* or *PL*, is defined in equation 7.3 as the present value of future pension benefits to all persons to whom the system has a liability at the time of evaluation, minus

Table 7B.6 Example 2.1: Income Statement and Balance Sheet

	Period					
	1	2[a]	2	3	4	5
Income statement						
Contributions	24	24	24	24	24	24
Pensions	−24	−24	−24	−16[g]	−30[h]	−26[i]
=net cash flow (a)	0	0	0	8	−6	−2
Change in contribution asset (b)	0	12[c]	12[c]	0	0	0
New accrued pension liability[b]	−24	−24	−24	−24	−24	−24
Paid-off pension liability[b](= paid pension benefits)	24	24	24	16	30	26
Cost of / income from indexation of liability[b]	0	0	−12	0	0	0
= change in pension liability (c)	0	12	−12	−8	6	2
Net income /−loss (a) + (b) + (c)	0	12	0	0	0	0
Balance sheet						
Buffer fund	0	0	0	8	2	0
Contribution asset	36	48	48	48	48	48
= total assets (d)	36	48	48	56	50	48
Pension liability, age 3	0	0	0	16	14	12
Pension liability, age 2	24	24	32[d]	28[f]	24	24
Pension liability, age 1	12	12	16[e]	12	12	12
= total liability (e)	36	36	48	56	50	48
Net present value of system (d) − (e)	0	12	0	0	0	0

Source: Authors.

Note: NDC system and indexing at the available rate, in the example equal to the IRR.
a., b., see table 7B.3.
c. $0.5 \times 24 = 12$ {change in $TD \times$ [contributions (t) + contributions $(t-1)$]/2}.
d. $(12 + 12) \times 4/3 = 32$ [(cohort B's period 1 contribution + cohort B's period 2 contribution) × IRR].
e. $12 \times 4/3 = 16$ [cohort C's period 2 contribution × IRR].
f. $(12 \times 4/3) + 12 = 28$ [(cohort C's period 2 contribution × IRR) + cohort C's period 3 contribution].
g. $32 / 2 = 16$ (cohort B's notional pension capital period 2 / life expectancy).
h. $16 + (28 / 2) = 30$ (cohort B's pension period 4 + cohort C's pension period 4).
i. $14 + (24 / 2) = 26$ (cohort C's pension period 5 + cohort D's pension period 5).

the present value of future contributions by the same individuals. As there is neither population growth nor technological progress, the contribution base will be constant; thus, the discount rate will be zero.

5. Pension liability to cohort B is 30, and to cohort C it is 6. Only after cohort B has passed through the system will the total pension liability drop to the new sustainable level of 30—disregarding the deficit of 6 caused by the shift in income pattern.

6. The total wage of cohort C period 2 is 24; with the contribution rate of 25 percent this will make cohort C's contribution and notional capital equal 6 this period.

7. The return on the buffer fund assets is assumed to equal the growth in contribution base which is zero.

8. The accounting standard used is a simplified version of the format developed and used since 2001 for the Swedish public pension system.

Annex 7C. Intermediate Steps before Equation 7.7

$$\frac{V}{C} = \frac{N(0)\cdot\overline{W}\cdot k\cdot\int_0^m\int_x^m l(u)\cdot e^{-\gamma\cdot u}\cdot\left[R(u)\cdot e^{\varphi\cdot u}-W(u)\cdot\dfrac{\int_0^m e^{-(\gamma-\varphi)\cdot a}\cdot l(a)\cdot R(a)da}{\int_0^m e^{-\gamma\cdot a}\cdot l(a)\cdot W(a)da}\right]du\,dx}{N(0)\cdot\overline{W}\cdot k\cdot\int_0^m l(x)\cdot e^{-\gamma\cdot x}\cdot W(x)\cdot\dfrac{\int_0^m e^{-(\gamma-\varphi)\cdot a}\cdot l(a)\cdot R(a)da}{\int_0^m e^{-\gamma\cdot a}\cdot l(a)\cdot W(a)da}dx}\ \dots$$

The expression above can easily be reduced by elementary algebraic manipulations. However, to make it simpler, the following substitutions will be useful:

$$\begin{cases} F_R(a)=e^{-(\gamma-\varphi)\cdot a}\cdot l(a)\cdot R(a) \\ F_W(a)=e^{-\gamma\cdot a}\cdot l(a)\cdot W(a) \end{cases}$$

$$\dots = \frac{\int_0^m\int_x^m l(u)\cdot e^{-\gamma\cdot u}\cdot\left[R(u)\cdot e^{\varphi\cdot u}-W(u)\cdot\dfrac{\int_0^m F_R(a)da}{\int_0^m F_W(a)da}\right]du\,dx}{\int_0^m F_W(x)\cdot\dfrac{\int_0^m F_R(a)da}{\int_0^m F_W(a)da}dx}$$

$$= \frac{\int_0^m\int_x^m l(u)\cdot e^{-\gamma\cdot u}\cdot\left[R(u)\cdot e^{\varphi\cdot u}\cdot\int_0^m F_W(a)da-W(u)\cdot\int_0^m F_R(a)da\right]du\,dx}{\int_0^m F_R(a)da\cdot\int_0^m F_W(x)dx}$$

$$= \frac{\int_0^m\left[\int_0^m F_W(a)da\cdot\int_x^m l(u)\cdot e^{-\gamma\cdot u}\cdot R(u)\cdot e^{\varphi\cdot u}\,du-\int_0^m F_R(a)da\cdot\int_x^m l(u)\cdot e^{-\gamma\cdot u}\cdot W(u)du\right]dx}{\int_0^m F_R(a)da\cdot\int_0^m F_W(x)dx}$$

$$= \frac{\int_0^m\left[\int_0^m F_W(a)da\cdot\int_x^m F_R(u)du-\int_0^m F_R(a)da\cdot\int_x^m F_W(u)du\right]dx}{\int_0^m F_R(a)da\cdot\int_0^m F_W(x)dx}$$

$$= \frac{\int_0^m F_W(a)da\cdot\int_0^m\left[\int_x^m F_R(u)du\right]dx-\int_0^m F_R(a)da\cdot\int_0^m\left[\int_x^m F_W(u)du\right]dx}{\int_0^m F_R(a)da\cdot\int_0^m F_W(x)dx}$$

$$= \frac{\int_0^m\left[\int_x^m F_R(u)du\right]dx}{\int_0^m F_R(x)dx}-\frac{\int_0^m\left[\int_x^m F_W(u)du\right]dx}{\int_0^m F_W(x)dx}\ \dots$$

For the next step, the following identity is needed:

$$
\left.\begin{array}{l}
\int_0^m \int_x^m f(u)du\,dx = \int_0^m x \cdot f(x)dx \\[2mm]
\text{proof:} \\[2mm]
\int_0^m \int_x^m f(u)du\,dx = \left[x \cdot \int_x^m f(u)du \right]_0^m - \int_0^m x \cdot (-f(x))dx \\[2mm]
= m \cdot \int_m^m f(u)du - 0 \cdot \int_0^m f(u)du + \int_0^m x \cdot f(x)dx = 0 + 0 + \int_0^m x \cdot f(x)dx
\end{array}\right\} \;.
$$

Thus

$$
\ldots = \frac{V}{C} = \frac{\int_0^m x \cdot F_R(x)dx}{\int_0^m F_R(x)dx} - \frac{\int_0^m x \cdot F_W(x)dx}{\int_0^m F_W(x)dx} = \frac{\int_0^m x \cdot e^{-(\gamma-\varphi)\cdot x} \cdot l(x) \cdot R(x)dx}{\int_0^m e^{-(\gamma-\varphi)\cdot x} \cdot l(x) \cdot R(x)dx} - \frac{\int_0^m x \cdot e^{-\gamma \cdot x} \cdot l(x) \cdot W(x)dx}{\int_0^m e^{-\gamma \cdot x} \cdot l(x) \cdot W(x)dx}
$$

QED.

Annex 7D. Rough Estimate of Turnover Duration in 41 Countries

Individuals who are not in the labor force and are 55 years or older are assumed to receive benefits from the pension system that on average amount to 50 percent of the average wage. Pensions are assumed to be indexed by the growth in the average wage, thus $\varphi = 0$.

Country	Year	Estimated population growth, $\gamma - 1$ (percent)	Turnover duration (years)
Tajikistan	1991	3.8	35.3
Argentina	1990	1.5	34.1
Spain	1990	0.2	34.1
New Zealand	1990	0.8	34.0
Australia	1994	0.3	34.0
Kyrgyz Republic	1995	2.8	33.7
Israel	1994	1.8	33.6
Portugal	1992	0.1	33.3
Canada	1992	−0.1	33.3
Chile	1997	1.5	33.2
Romania	1992	0.5	33.2
Italy	1994	−0.3	33.2
United States	1995	0.2	33.1
Austria	1996	−0.4	33.1
Belgium	1994	−0.1	33.1
Ireland	1990	0.9	33.0
France	1995	0.2	33.0
United Kingdom	1996	−0.1	32.9
Hungary	1996	−0.1	32.8
Greece	1995	−0.1	32.8
Kazakhstan	1996	1.4	32.7
Slovak Republic	1995	0.8	32.7
Denmark	1994	−0.4	32.7
Sweden	1996	−0.3	32.7
Netherlands	1995	−0.3	32.7
Latvia	1996	−0.1	32.6
Norway	1996	0.1	32.6
Armenia	1993	1.6	32.5
Czech Republic	1996	−0.1	32.1
Slovenia	1993	−0.2	32.0
Estonia	1996	0.0	31.9
Belarus	1996	0.1	31.9
Poland	1996	0.4	31.8
Russian Federation	1995	−0.1	31.7
Germany	1994	−0.8	31.7
Bulgaria	1993	−0.2	31.6
Japan	1990	−0.4	31.6
Finland	1996	−0.4	31.6
Korea, Rep. of	1991	0.9	31.5
Ukraine	1993	−0.1	31.3
Moldova	1994	0.8	31.2

Source: Authors' calculations, based on UN and ILO statistics. For details, see Settergren and Mikula (2001).

Notes

1. While many examples could be cited to illustrate this point, here are just two of them: "As Paul Samuelson showed 40 years ago, the real rate of return in a mature PAYG system is equal to the sum of the rate of growth in the labor force and the rate of growth in productivity" (Orszag and Stiglitz 1999, p. 15). "The rate of return in a notional system can only be the rate of growth of the tax base that results from rising real wages and increasing numbers of employees (Samuelson 1958)" (Feldstein 2002, p. 7).

2. In the context of pensions, a *steady state* is defined as a situation where the average wage at each age, relative to the average wage for all ages, is constant over time and where the number of retirees at each age, relative to the total number of retirees, is constant over time: that is, where mortality rates are constant. Thus the definition of steady state is consistent with population growth (or decline) if the change rate remains constant over time.

3. See Riksförsäkringsverket (2004). To be more precise, the average ages refer to the *expected* average ages. The expected ages will correspond with actual average ages only if fertility-driven population growth, income, and mortality patterns are stable: that is, if they are in a steady state.

4. See the legislative history of the indexation of the Swedish pension system and Settergren (2001, 2002).

5. This ignorance is clear from the legislative history of the Swedish pension reform (annex A), as well as Settergren (2001). It is evident that we were not alone in being unaware of the works, or of their implications, that "explore the interface of richer demographic models and the overlapping generation models of economists" (Lee, 1994a). An example is Valdés-Prieto (2000), who observed that changes in income and mortality patterns influence the financial balance of a "notional defined contribution" PAYG pension scheme. However, Valdés-Prieto does not explain his observations by the effects that changes in income and mortality patterns have on the money-weighted age difference between the average ages when income is earned and consumed.

6. Pension liability is defined as the present value of future benefits to all persons to whom the system has a liability at the time of evaluation, minus the present value of future contributions by the same individuals (equation 7.3), sometimes also referred to as the implicit pension liability (see also Iyer 1999). The practical problems of measuring pension liability in PAYG schemes are often substantial. Depending on the system design, and the quality and availability of data, the estimate of pension liability may indeed be so uncertain that it is practically useless. This chapter does not deal with these important practical obstacles for applying the method suggested for estimating IRR and applying double-entry bookkeeping.

7. An example of the conventional presentation of financial status in a PAYG pension system is the analysis in the Annual Report of the Board of Trustees in the Federal Old-age and Survivors Insurance and Disability Insurance Trust Funds (2003).

8. The expression could be extended also to incorporate the effects of migration on the expected contribution-weighted average age of contributors. See Settergren and Mikula (2001) for such an extended interpretation of γ.

9. Below we will not use the full expression *expected turnover duration* to indicate that the turnover duration is measured outside of a steady state, but will refer only to *turnover duration*.

10. An obvious difference between repetitive re-evaluation of the contribution assets and recurring re-evaluation of funded assets is that funded assets are tradable, which make their prices much less "implicit." However, their valuation is inevitably hypothetical to some degree as long as they are not sold off.

11. The data for the estimate are the annual individual earnings and benefit records for all persons covered by the national pension scheme in Sweden from 1981 through 2003.

12. To get a zero buffer fund in steady state, either the steady state rate of return on the buffer fund or the interest rate paid on a deficit must equal the growth in the contribution base or the valuation of the fund must reflect an assumption of a return on capital different from the growth in the contribution base.

13. Note that since the turnover duration is affected, however mildly, by changes in the fertility-driven growth rate, γ, the IRR may differ from the contribution base growth even in the unrealistic case of constant mortality and income patterns. This points out the short-comings in the two-age OLG model: it cannot represent the relevant geometry of the problem.

14. In practical applications equation 7.17 should be extended to accommodate the possibility of an opening surplus or deficit—that is, a difference between assets (buffer fund assets and contribution asset) and liabilities.

15. Whether or not the claim that double-entry accounting provides better information than traditional measures of actuarial balance is correct can, perhaps, be judged from the Annual Reports of the Swedish Pension System, which have been published every year since the 2001 report, published in 2002. The design of the index in the new Swedish public PAYG pension system indicates that separating the components of the IRR adds new options for designing the indexation of pensions. See the legislative history of the income index and automatic balance mechanism in annex A and Settergren (2001, 2002).

References

Aaron, H. J. 1966. "The Social Insurance Paradox." *Canadian Journal of Economics* 32 (August): 371–74.

Arthur, W. B., and G. McNicoll. 1978. "Samuelson, Population and Intergenerational Transfers." *International Economic Review* 10 (1): 241–46.

Buchanan, J. 1968. "Social Insurance in a Growing Economy: A Proposal for Radical Reform." *National Tax Journal* 21: 386–95.

Disney, R. 1999. "Notional Accounts as a Pension Reform Strategy: An Evaluation." Social Protection Discussion Paper 9928, World Bank, Washington, DC.

Federal Old-Age and Survivors Insurance and Disability Insurance Trust Funds, Board of Trustees. 2003. *2003 Annual Report of the Board of Trustees of the Federal Old-Age and Survivors Insurance and Disability Insurance Trust Funds.* Washington, DC: U.S. Government Printing Office.

Feldstein, M. 2002. "Introduction, an American Perspective." In *Social Security Pension Reform in Europe*, ed. M. Feldstein and H. Siebert, 1–8. National Bureau of Economic Research. Chicago: The University of Chicago Press.

Iyer, S. 1999. *Actuarial Mathematics of Social Security Pensions.* Geneva: International Labor Organization.

Keyfitz, N. 1985. *Applied Mathematical Demography.* Berlin and Heidelberg: Springer Verlag.

———. 1988. "The Demographics of Unfunded Pensions." *European Journal of Population* 1: 5–30.

Lee, R. D. 1980. "Age Structure, Intergenerational Transfers and Economic Growth: An Overview." *Revue Economic* 31 (6): 1129–56.

———. 1988a. "Induced Population Growth and Induced Technological Progress: Their Interaction in the Acceleration Phase." *Mathematical Population Studies* 1 (3): 265–88.

———. 1988b. "Intergenerational Flows of Time and Goods: Consequences of Slowing Population Growth." *Journal of Political Economy* 96 (31): 618–51.

———. 1994a. "The Formal Demography of Aging, Transfers, and the Economic Life Cycle." In *The Demography of Aging*, ed. L. Martin and S. Preston, 8–49. Washington, DC: National Academy Press.

———. 1994b. "Population Age Structure, Intergenerational Transfer, and Wealth: A New Approach, with Application to the U.S." *Journal of Human Resources* 29 (4): 1027–63.

Lee, R. D., and H. Yamagata. 2003. "Sustainable Social Security: What Would It Cost?" *National Tax Journal* 56 (1, part 1): 27–43.

Orsag, P., and J. Stiglitz. 1999. "Rethinking Pension Reform: Ten Myths About Social Security Systems." Paper presented at World Bank conference "New Ideas About Old Age Security," Washington, September 14–15.

Riksförsäkringsverket. 2002. The Swedish Pension System Annual Report 2001. Stockholm.

———. 2003. The Swedish Pension System Annual Report 2002. Stockholm.

———. 2004. The Swedish Pension System Annual Report 2003. Stockholm.

Samuelson, P. 1958. "An Exact Consumption-Loan Model of Interest With or Without the Social Contrivance of Money." *The Journal of Political Economy* 6 (December): 467–82.

———. 1975a. "The Optimum Growth Rate for Population." *International Economic Review* 16 (3): 531–38.

———. 1975b. The Optimum Growth Rate for Population: Agreement and Evaluations. *International Economic Review* 17 (2): 516–525.

Settergren, O. 2001. "The Automatic Balance Mechanism of the Swedish Pension System— A Non-technical Introduction." *Wirtschaftspolitishe Blätter* 4: 339–49.

———. 2002. "Financial and Inter-Generational Balance? An Introduction to How the Swedish Pension System Manages Conflicting Ambitions." *Scandinavian Insurance Quarterly* 2: 99–114.

Settergren, O., and B. D. Mikula. 2001. "Financial Balance & Inter-Generational Fairness in Pay-As-You-Go Pension Systems—Empirical Illustrations in an Alternative Framework." Paper prepared for presentation at the meeting of the Old-age, Invalidity and Survivors' Benefits Technical Commission held during the General Assembly of the International Social Security Association in Stockholm, September.

Valdés-Prieto, S. 2000. "The Financial Stability of Notional Accounts Pensions." *The Scandinavian Journal of Economics* 102 (3): 395–417.

Willis, R. J. 1988. "Economics of Changing Age Distribution in Developed Countries." In *Life Cycles, Institutions, and Population Growth: A Theory of the Equilibrium Interest Rate in an Overlapping Generations Model. International Studies in Demography*, ed. R. Lee, 106–138, Oxford: Oxford University Press.

Discussion of "The Rate of Return of Pay-As-You-Go Pension Systems: A More Exact Consumption-Loan Model of Interest"

Ronald Lee*

WHAT RATE OF RETURN IS EARNED BY PARTICIPANTS in a pay-as-you-go (PAYG) pension system? We all know that in steady state, the rate of return equals the population growth rate plus the rate of productivity growth, or equivalently the rate of growth of the tax or contribution base, or the rate of growth of the economy. But many of us casually replace the qualifying condition "steady state" with the condition "mature," and conclude that the pension programs of most industrial nations should yield this rate of return since most cover the great majority of workers and are therefore mature.

Not so, the authors of this chapter tell us. Mature pension systems depart from the steady state characterization for many reasons, including changes in population age distributions, ages at retirement, ages at beginning work, mortality, rates of productivity growth, and the age structure of wages. Mortality has been declining for more than a century in the industrial nations, and most analysts expect these declines to continue. Even if most other aspects of the pension program were in steady state, this one factor would mean that the effective rate of return earned by each generation in a strict PAYG system would exceed the growth rate of the contribution base. Each generation of workers would pay taxes to cover the retirement costs of generations whose retirements are cut short by mortality at earlier ages than will be true for the generations of workers when they themselves retire several decades later. For this reason, their rate of return will exceed the growth of the contribution base. Of course, to fund this lengthening retirement and higher rate of return, the contribution rate must be rising over time. The effect of declining mortality on the generational rate of return is quite noticeable in the U.S. social security system, adding perhaps 0.3 to 0.5 percent per year to the implicit rate of return, a little realized fact.

The rate of return earned by any particular generation can always be calculated ex post, once its last members have died. But the last members of a generation will not have died until it is well over 100 years old, and by then the question will be of only historical interest. For practical purposes, we may want a measure of the system's rate of return based on its circumstances and performance today.

The chapter addresses this problem by constructing a measure of the implicit rate of return to a PAYG pension system. The authors first develop a measure for the steady state context, deriving and interpreting an accounting identity. This part of the chapter builds

* Ronald Lee is director of the Center on the Economics and Demography of Aging, University of California at Berkeley.

   Research on which this comment was based was supported by a grant from the National Institute of Aging, R37-AG11761.

on an existing literature describing an accounting framework for intergenerational transfers in general. The accounting identity states that the implicit debt of the system, V, or equivalently the present value of the system's current net liabilities, is equal to the annual flow of contributions, C, times the difference between the average age at which a pension payment is received, minus the average at which a contribution (payroll tax) is paid. The authors call this age difference the turnover duration, or TD. The TD synthesizes into a single number a great deal of information about the system's rules, the age distribution of the population, age patterns of labor supply and earnings, and survival. Note that the TD will be greater when pension benefits are indexed to rise with wage growth following retirement than when they are indexed only to inflation, as in the United States. TD would be shorter for a NDC program in which the beneficiary received a lump-sum payment on retirement, and then converted this to an annuity through the private sector. In these and many other ways, the TD will reflect the details of the particular pension plan.

Annex D of the chapter presents rough estimates of the TD for 41 countries, based mainly on their labor force participation rates. These 41 countries, with very different demographic situations, retirement ages, and age profiles of earnings, have remarkably similar TDs, all falling between 31 and 35 years. I find this very surprising, but perhaps the similarity reflects the strong simplifying assumptions used for the calculation. The number given for the United States, 33 years, is right on target, which I know from my own detailed calculations.

We can try out this simple equation for the United States, using the age difference of 33 years. Social security benefit payments (for pensions, survivors, and disability insurance, OASDI) in 2004 amounted to 4.33 percent of GDP, and in a pure PAYG system, this would also be the share of payroll tax payments.[1] The cross-sectional estimate of net pension obligations, or implicit debt for current participants, is therefore 33*4.33 percent of GDP, or 1.43 times GDP. This comes out to US$16.5 trillion, from which the trust fund of US$1.5 trillion should be subtracted to get US$15 trillion.This is considerably greater than the US$11.2 trillion reported by the actuaries in the Trustees Report (2005: Table IV.B8) as the unfunded obligation for past and current participants. However, the actuaries use a much higher discount rate than the population growth rate which is implicitly used in this cross-sectional calculation and which is probably responsible for most of the discrepancy (see Lee 1994 for a similar estimate for the United States).

The authors suggest that the turnover duration can be interpreted as a measure of the time preference of the pension program, and that its inverse is a measure of the discount rate for contributions. Based on the range of values described above, the implied discount rate would be between 2.8 and 3.2 percent per year. I found this idea puzzling, and would be interested to see the authors develop it further and explain it more clearly.

The results in the first part are interesting and conceptually useful, but they are of limited practical use since actual systems are not in steady state. The results reveal the parameters upon which financial stability is dependent, within the framework of a continuous financial balance sheet. What is unique is that this method of presentation of the framework follows a traditional "business" financial balance, while it introduces the economist's or economic demographer's way of describing this balance. To use this framework for actual, nonsteady state situations, we have to imagine stopping time at two intervals and using a comparative static comparison between them. This is the approach developed by the authors in the second part of the chapter. If we consider a simple special case of their more general equation, in which the trust fund is zero, then the steady state identity can be written $PL = TD*C$, where PL is pension liability (which I have been calling the implicit debt owed to current participants), TD is the turnover duration just discussed, and C is the annual flow of contributions to the system. They argue that the rate of return on contributions to the system (in a cross-sectional sense) is the rate of return at which the change in *PL* is zero over time. I would have liked to see more discussion of this point. In a growing economy, fixing the size of the *PL* would mean that pension wealth would decline relative to GNP, which does not seem right. In any event, setting equal to zero the time derivative of the equation just given, their result implies that the IRR of the system equals the exponential rate of growth of contributions, *C*, plus the exponential rate of change of the turnover duration, *TD* (for the special case in which there is no trust fund balance).

In the steady state case, the rate of growth of contributions will just equal the rate of population growth plus the rate of growth of productivity, while the rate of change of TD would be zero. This gives the well-known steady state rate of return for a PAYG system. However, out of steady state, the growth rate of *C* will also depend on demographic fluctuations rippling through the labor force, changes in the age structure of earnings, changes in retirement age, and changes in the age at starting work, in addition to productivity growth and general population growth.

Similarly, out of steady state, TD will vary due to changes in many of the factors just mentioned, plus changes in survival in old age. For example, if life expectancy is rising so that retirees continue to receive pensions at higher ages, then the average age of receiving pensions will increase and so will TD, and therefore the IRR received through the pension system will rise as well. If life expectancy ceases to rise, then TD will stop rising, and the rate of return will drop back down again. TD will also be changing in other ways due to rising life expectancy, depending on the details of the program. If benefits are indexed to mortality, then younger generations of retirees will receive lower benefit flows, altering TD, for example. To take another example, if the peak of the cross-sectional age-earnings profile shifts to older ages reflecting an increasingly educated labor force, that would raise the age of paying contributions, leading to a reduction in TD and a lower rate of return. All these year-to-year changes are reflected in the suggested calculation, in addition to the standard rate of growth of contributions. The cross-sectional rate of return measure is affected only so long as these changes are occurring. Once the changes stop, the rate of return will also tend to go back to its steady state level, which is unaffected by the level of the TD.

This general approach, and its strengths and hazards, are familiar to demographers who confront similar issues when measuring fertility or mortality. There is a straightforward measure that can be calculated at the end of the reproductive years, completed cohort fertility, and another that can be calculated after all in a generation have died, the average age at death or cohort life expectancy. But for obvious reasons, we would like a measure of fertility and mortality that describes the current situation. Demographers construct synthetic cohort measures, or period measures, that summarize the current situation by imagining that a generation lives its entire life experiencing the age-specific rates of a given year. In the case of fertility, this yields the most commonly used measure, the period total fertility rate (TFR). For mortality it yields another most commonly used measure, period life expectancy. However, there has been intense controversy about these measures, particularly the TFR, because it provides a distorted indication of the completed fertility of any cohort when the timing of fertility in a woman's life cycle is changing—the "tempo" effect—as opposed to the "quantum" of completed cohort fertility. In Europe, the mean age at first birth has been rising by about 0.2 years of age per calendar year for several decades, which depresses the TFR by about 20 percent or nearly 0.4 births relative to the likely eventual completed cohort fertility. Many demographers have suggested adjustments to the period TFR to make it a better indicator of cohort completed fertility.

In the case of the proposed cross-sectional measure of the rate of return to pension participation, similar issues are bound to arise, but have not yet been deeply explored. However, this chapter makes a very promising and enlightening start on addressing this problem in its second part. We can think of the change over time in the turnover duration as introducing a kind of tempo distortion. When the turnover duration is increasing, for example, we would expect that the current rate of benefit payments would be temporarily reduced, and the reverse when the duration is contracting. The rate of change in the contribution rate will likewise be affected by transitory changes in the age of starting or ending work, which come on top of the effects of productivity growth and in a sense distort it. These effects are correct for the cross section, but may be misleading when we try to draw inferences from the cross-sectional rate of return about the longitudinal or long-run rate of return.

In an NDC system, changes across generations in age at retirement and in life expectancy would presumably have no effect on the generational rate of return, since NDC is actuarially fair. But such changes would affect the timing of the payment of contributions and the timing and level of benefits, and these timing changes would be reflected in a changing cross-sectional TD, and thus in the cross-sectional rate of return. The trick is to choose an accounting method, whether cross-sectional or longitudinal, that treats the different generations fairly in a nonsteady state system, avoiding the kinds of inequities that are illustrated clearly in the very helpful annex B.

The chapter is relatively brief, even including its useful appendices, and many details are not spelled out. Discussion toward the end suggests that the cross-sectional pension liability that they have in mind, $PL(t)$, is actually based on an actuarial projection into the future. I found this confusing because there is also a cross-sectional measure of PL, based on the contributions from and benefit payments to the synthetic cohort, and I don't understand why this is not used instead. Similarly, the measure of transfer duration is referred to as "expected" TD toward the end of the chapter, which suggests again a longitudinal and projected aspect, whereas there is a purely cross-sectional measure of TD that does not involve expectations. Because of these details, I do not fully understand the calculations or their underlying logic. Doubtless most of these issues could be resolved through discussion with the authors.

In other places, I had difficulty following because of unfamiliarity with some of the terms and phrases used. This was particularly true of the important discussion toward the end of the "rate of available indexation," "rate of implicit revaluation," "rate of explicit indexation," and "system net income." I am not clear about the relation of these terms and phrases to the IRR, the main topic of this paper. I believe, however, that these terms refer to a kind of residual correction to the cross-sectional estimate of the rate of return.

The method described in this study appears to be a powerful tool for assessing the performance of PAYG pension systems. However, questions remain, and we will need to see a more complete exposition of this approach, and perhaps a more complete analysis, before fully understanding what is being proposed for the rate of return out of steady state. Proper evaluation of the proposed procedure can come only after a more complete understanding of it by the research community. This is quite possibly just a matter of fuller exposition.

In my view, the authors are too modest about their contribution on this topic. While the literature they cite, including my own contributions, is certainly highly relevant, most of it takes a comparative steady state approach and does not deal with nonsteady situations, and none of it addresses the specific problem of how to measure the rate of return to a nonsteady state PAYG pension system. The work in this chapter is an important application that will, I hope, lead to a series of articles by the authors and by others that further develop these ideas and probe their limitations and uses.

Note

1. See Board of Trustees (2005).

References

Board of Trustees. 2005. *The 2005 Report of the Board of Trustees of the Federal Old-Age and Survivors Insurance and Disability Insurance Trust Funds.* Washington, DC: United States Government Printing Office.

Lee, R. 1994. "The Formal Demography of Population Aging, Transfers, and the Economic Life Cycle." In *The Demography of Aging,* ed. L. Martin and S. Preston, 8–49. Washington, DC: National Academy Press.

Chapter 8

A Market Method to Endow NDC Systems with Automatic Financial Stability

Salvador Valdés-Prieto*

PENSION PLANS THAT ARE FINANCED WITH THE PAY-AS-YOU-GO (PAYG) METHOD, but that have an actuarial benefit formula that includes individual accounts, have been spreading in Europe since the end of World War II. These plans have been recently named *notional defined contribution* (NDC).[1] A more apt name is *notional accounts* (NA), since such plans can also offer defined benefits, as shown below.

An important property of a pension plan is its degree of automatic financial stability in the short run. It is normally considered valuable to insulate the government's finances from the shocks that impinge on the pension plan, and to insulate the pension plan from the shocks that affect the treasury because it destroys the risk created by random parliamentary delays in parameter adjustment to shocks—that is, it minimizes political risk.

Insulation in this sense is not an absolute concept. Fiscal policies can always be used ex post by parliament either to subsidize or to tax pension income. Insulation adds value because it gives parliament the opportunity to debate possible fiscal policies in response to shocks, free from the pressure coming from the insolvency of the pension plan.

A major precondition for mutual insulation is that the parameters of the plan are such that, if no more shocks arrive in the future, the plan would be able to meet its payment promises for the indefinite future. Call this characteristic initial financial independence, or initial solvency. Many pay-as-you-go-financed plans are currently insolvent in this sense, and for them, the issue of financial stability is simply a far-off aspiration.

For initially solvent plans, the issue of financial stability is renewed over time, as uninsurable shocks arrive and add their aggregate financial impact. These shocks can be demographic (longevity and fertility), economic (changes in average taxable income of covered workers, variations in employment), and financial (changes in stock and bond prices, which affect the fund portion in partially funded plans). The aggregate financial impact is the difference between the impact on plan liabilities and the impact on plan assets. The benefit formula of the plan, whatever it is, controls the liability side and normally specifies

* Salvador Valdés-Prieto is professor of economics at Catholic University of Chile and researcher at the Centro de Estudios Públicos, Santiago.

This chapter is related to a quite different earlier paper circulated at the Swedish Social Security Fund–World Bank Conference on Notional Defined Contribution Pension Systems, September 29–30, 2003, Sandhamn, Sweden. Comments are welcome at svaldes@faceapuc.cl.

adjustments to the benefits of the individual member. For example, if taxable earnings and contributions drop, promised pension amounts drop in all earnings-related plans. Adding these adjustments across all individual members yields the aggregate financial conse-quence of the shock on the liability of the pension plan. Independently, the shock has an impact on the assets of the plan. The difference between both impacts is the aggregate financial impact of the shock. This impact may be relatively large in the short run.[2] An example is an increase in unemployment in an initially solvent defined benefit (DB) plan financed with the pay-as-you-go (PAYG) method.

This chapter discusses alternative ways in which a plan adjusts to aggregate financial shocks. In general, adjustment depends on four sets of rules, which operate in successive layers: (1) the benefit formula of the plan, which links individual contributions with indi-vidual benefit amounts; (2) the rules for adjusting parameters of the plan; (3) the rules for the use of eventual buffer funds and credit lines offered by a sponsor; and (4) the rules governing the exercise of discretion ex post by a set of people, say members of parliament, members of a public board governing the plan, civil servants who control deeper technical parameters, and finance ministers who retain the right to limit the plan's access to credit lines or to buffer funds. The financial stability of a pension plan can be described as "auto-matic" when layers (3) and (4) are avoided in almost all states of nature (except war and the like) because layers (1) and (2) are able to cope with most shocks by themselves.

The literature has proved that NA plans that use any of a set of simple benefit formulae that were adopted in Europe in the 1990s do *not* enjoy automatic financial stability in the short run in the face of demographic and economic shocks.[3] In an NA plan, the benefit for-mula comprises the individual account of active members, the formula used to set the notional interest rate credited to those accounts, the factor to convert the account balance at retirement into the initial pension, and the formula for indexing pensions in payment. Consider the case where the instantaneous notional interest rate credited to individual accounts is the instantaneous growth rate of contribution revenue, where pension pay-ments are indexed to the growth rate of contribution revenue, and where the conversion factor at pension age is an adequate function of this same growth rate and expected longevity. Even in this case, which is more favorable to automatic financial stability than others, a permanent drop in the population growth rate triggers a long wave of cash deficits that lasts up to 80 years.[4] These deficits are due to discrepancies in the timing of the expenditure and revenue changes triggered by this shock. The discrepancy is significant: for a permanent drop in the population growth rate of just 0.5 percent per year, in a plan where the contribution revenue is 10 percent of GDP, the present discounted value of these cash deficits discounted at 3 percent real and located in the year of maximum deficit is about 9 percent of GDP.

In contrast, rule-based and contract-based plans such as defined contribution (DC) plans (mutual funds) and defined benefit annuities offered by life insurance companies always achieve automatic financial stability in the short run merely by using layers (1) and (2). Consider the mutual fund formula, invented in Boston in 1924, that underlies DC plans. Each individual member has a number of shares of the mutual fund, and its price is adjusted daily in the following way: the new price is the new value of assets (at forward-looking market prices) divided by the number of shares outstanding. It may be argued that rule-based and contract-based plans are irrelevant, because they require a costly tran-sition to full funding (see definition in box 8.1). This is incorrect, as shown by Valdés-Pri-eto (2005), because the transition can be costless and immediate.

In 2001, the Swedish authorities devised an alternative path to reach automatic financial stability in their NA plan. The original rules were to credit notional capital of active work-ers at the growth rate of contribution revenue, and to adjust pensions in payment by the

Box 8.1. What Is Meant by *Funding*

The issue of whether a pension plan is "funded" or not is controversial because there are three meanings of the term. In the fiscal meaning, the pension fund is the financial securities, real estate, and other rights owned by the plan. In contrast, the present expected value of government subsidies to the plan is not a part of the pension fund, because the law can be modified and these donations can stop. These donations can be explicit subsidies, as when notional plans receive a regular budget transfer, or can be implicit subsidies such as the net lifetime tax implicit in mature PAYG finance as described in the main text. Therefore this critical revenue source is not part of the pension fund either. Generalizing, a *pension fund* is defined as the set of payment promises in favor of the plan that are protected by property rights.[5] The *degree* of funding in the financial sense is a ratio obtained by dividing the market value of the pension fund by the expected discounted value of accrued liabilities at the same date.

In its *fiscal* meaning, funding is the degree to which changes in benefit liabilities bring about changes in the net fiscal debt, or affect the riskiness of the payment profile of the net public debt. For this purpose, the "net public debt" is the standard public debt, minus publicly owned assets, plus the implicit fiscal debt to insolvent health and old-age benefit programs. The fiscally costly "transition costs" are caused by restructuring of fiscal funding, not by changes in the degree of financial funding.

There is another meaning of *funding*, which refers to the impact of the plan on the volume of economywide savings. This "macro," "ultimate," or "broad" funding is not a feature of the plan itself but of the wider macroeconomic context. The degree of broad funding is a function of private savings, national debt policy, the degree of Ricardian equivalence, and the presence of other state-sponsored transfer programs such as health subsidies for the old, student loans, and the pension plan. Broad funding is a characteristic of the economy, not the plan.

As pension plans should not be labeled on the basis of something not related to them, the meaning of *funding* should be restricted to the financial definition (the first one). The IFM reform discussed in this chapter does not affect the economy's degree of funding. However, it increases the plan's degree of financial funding because it grants the plan property right protection over the revenue of the tax implicit in the contributions extracted from future contributors who are forced to remain in or join the plan.

growth rate in average wages minus 1.6 percent per year. However, since May 2001, a different and highly creative rule—called the automatic balance mechanism (ABM)—was adopted. When the plan's liabilities exceed assets, the notional interest rate credited to active members and the rate of adjustment of pensions in payment are both cut, to equal the growth rate of average wages minus the growth rate in liabilities plus the growth rate in assets.[6] The ABM seems to endow the Swedish plan with automatic financial stability.

This chapter discusses an alternative response, which also endows NA plans with automatic financial stability in the short run, by adopting a rule-based method to allocate aggregate risk. I call it "integration to financial markets" (IFM) for reasons to be explained below. In contrast to the ABM, the IFM method is based on discount rates determined by the financial and capital markets, and thus relies on objective projections. This also allows the IFM to be decentralized, reducing the risk of political and bureaucratic interference, an aspect that might increase the confidence of members in the plan. It is also important to stress that as the IFM relies on asset values, it adjusts using rational expectations rather than slow-moving averages. In addition, the IFM method allows the plan to trade part of the uninsurable risks that it faces with other investors and internationally, creating scope for substantial economic gains.

In most NA plans, the value of the pension fund is negligible as a proportion of liabilities. Even in the case of the Swedish plan, which is endowed with a large buffer fund, the pension fund was about 10 percent of liabilities in 2001, under current accounting rules.[7] Therefore, most of the assets of a NA pension plan are the present expected value of the net lifetime tax on labor earnings that future members will have to bear. This tax revenue is not owned by the pension fund in the legal sense because the law can be modified to stop this cash flow. For example, a future law may allow Swedish workers to divert part of those contributions to the PPM (a financial DC plan). Access of the NA plan to most of the economic assets that back its promises is not protected by property rights.

Consider endowing NA plans with property rights over the net lifetime tax revenue that future covered workers will yield, followed by securitization of these cash flows and by trade of at least a few of these new securities in the financial markets. The new securities are called *covered wage bill* securities, or CWB securities (see Valdés-Prieto 2005). This chapter compares the resulting pension plan with the ABM system. It stresses that the market prices that emerge for these new securities will be forward-looking, and that these prices contain the discount rates needed to ascertain the assets and liabilities of the plan. Therefore, feeding these discount rates back into the benefit formula of the NA plan— specifically, making the notional interest rate equal to the rate of return on CWB securities observed in the financial market and adopting the mutual fund rule to determine the balance of the individual accounts—endows the plan with automatic financial stability in the short run. This stability is different from the one produced by the ABM, because it is based on forward-looking prices.

The chapter proceeds as follows. The next section summarizes the proposal to create CWB securities, to endow the NA plan with them, to trade some of them, and to insert the resulting market prices into the NA benefit formula. The third section compares this method to achieve automatic financial stability with the automatic balance mechanism adopted by Sweden in May 2001 in its pure form. The final section offers concluding comments.

Endowing a Solvent NA Plan with Automatic Financial Stability

This section summarizes the proposal to modify an NA plan that is initially solvent to endow it with automatic financial stability. These steps are developed and justified in detail by Valdés-Prieto (2005).

The Economic Asset That Backs PAYG-Financed Pension Promises

Every pension plan has a liability given by the expected present value of its commitments to pay pensions to its *current* members. The plan does not yet owe anything to future members, since they have not contributed. The size of the existing liability is set by the current benefit formula—which may be based on individual accounts or years of service—by the history of taxable salaries or contributions of current members, by pension ages, and by the formula that indexes pensions in payment.[8] The size of this liability does not depend on the financing method used by the plan.

A solvent pension plan is defined as one that does not require financial support from its sponsor, nor will pay a profit to it, in present expected value. An initially solvent plan financed with "pure" PAYG does not own financial assets or real estate in any measure comparable to its liabilities. It may seem that this plan has no assets but has a large liability, so that a large negative net worth would be needed to respect the balance sheet identity. But the cash flow in this plan is balanced at zero by the assumption of initial solvency. This implies that the net worth of the plan for its sponsor is zero, not negative. The answer to this riddle is that the pension plan holds a special economic asset, in addition to whatever pension fund it may own.

Lee (1994) has argued that the present value of expected future transfers to be received, minus transfers to be made, is a form of wealth that is held by individuals in modern economies—and by institutions such as pension plans. He also points out that when a transfer system can obligate people as yet unborn to make future transfers to members of the current population, aggregate "transfer wealth" may be positive for the current population, and negative for the yet unborn generations.

Consider the difference between the present value of contributions and the present value of benefits promised to each future generation of members. For example, consider an overlapping-generations (OLG) economy populated by agents whose lives last two periods, young and old, with probability 1, and where the old do not work. Each worker active at date t earns covered labor income in amount y_t. The number of workers that are active in date t is N_t. Assume that plan parameters are in a steady state where contributions are paid at rate θ_O percent of labor income, while in old age benefits are received at a level such that β percent of the earnings of the previous period are "replaced." The real discount rate after inflation, given by alternative investments of the plan in the financial market or in real estate, is r percent per period.

The difference between the contributions and the present value of benefits promised in exchange to that same generation is, in the aggregate and as of young age:

$$T_t \equiv \theta_0 \cdot y_t N_t - \frac{\beta \cdot y_t N_t}{1+r} = \left(\theta_0 - \frac{\beta}{1+r} \right) \cdot y_t N_t \equiv \tau \cdot y_t N_t \,, \tag{8.1}$$

where T_t is the "lifetime hidden tax" on that generation of members. T_t is not zero unless $\beta = \theta_O \cdot (1 + r)$: that is, unless $r = (\beta/\theta_O) - 1$. The internal rate of return (IRR) of pure PAYG finance in steady state is the growth rate of the contribution base, which is also the growth rate of the economy (GDP): say, g percent real, given by the sum of population growth and labor-augmenting productivity growth. In hypothetical "golden rule" economies, the real interest rate earned by physical capital is $r = g$.[9] Box 8.2 argues that g must be *smaller* than the real interest rate available in the financial markets before taxes (and earned by pension funds invested in financial instruments or in physical assets) after discounting for risk.

It turns out that for two-period lives and pure PAYG finance, the IRR for members of the plan is IRR = $(\beta/\theta_O) - 1$. In a steady state where the plans keeps a constant share of the overall economy, IRR = g. Therefore, the condition $r > g$ (see box 8.2) implies that the discount rate for plan liabilities must be $r >$ IRR. Given this, the tax T_t defined by equation 8.1 must be *positive* (see proof in Sinn 1999). One intuition for a positive tax T_t is that it is the counterpart of the gift granted to the initial old generation when PAYG finance was introduced, which is positive. This result generalizes to out-of-steady-state situations, to the partially funded case and to the uncertainty case, but refers now to the average tax paid by all generations (see proof in Valdés-Prieto 2005). However, the tax can be negative for a few generations, depending on the plan's rule for adjusting to shocks, as shown by Settergren and Mikula (2006).

Define the PAYG asset as the expected present value of the hidden taxes that the plan expects to collect from its future members, who have not yet joined the plan, for the infinite future. This is just another way to write the "expanded" balance sheet for an ongoing pension plan. The expanded balance sheet adds to the asset side the expected present discounted value of the contributions that all future generations will pay, and adds to the accrued liabilities the expected present discounted value of benefits for all future genera-

Box 8.2. Why the Rate of Return on Capital Must Be Larger Than the Growth Rate

There is abundant empirical evidence in favor of this hypothesis for developed countries (Abel et al. 1989). Moreover, there is by now a well-developed theory that explains why this inequality must be a feature of any market economy.

In the presence of assets that are infinitely durable, such as land, whose ownership is widely dispersed in many societies, it has been shown that $r > g$ in macroeconomic equilibrium (Scheinkman 1980; Richter 1993). One simple way to explain this reasoning is as follows: If land is in fixed supply and yields a rent of 1 unit of output per year, and the economy grows at rate g, and the share in consumption of land-based goods is constant, then the price of a unit of land output must grow at rate g. The present value of this rent, discounted at the real interest rate r, is \$1$/(r - g)$. Therefore, if $r = g$ as in golden rule economies, the value of land would be infinite. As land ownership attracts part of the portfolio of households, they would cease to hold other physical capital (machinery). However, a fall in the supply of other physical capital would raise its return, until $r > g$.

Confirming this result from another direction, Tirole (1985) showed that the inequality $r > g$ also follows from the need to prevent arbitrage by entities that are infinitely lived and whose income grows at rate g. Examples of such entities are governments that can issue debt, dynasties that earn a wage bill that grows at rate g and may issue debt, pension plans, and health plans for the old.

The following "slow Ponzi scheme" is possible for each such entity when $r = g$: issue \$1 million of financial debt at interest rate $r = g$, and when interest and principal comes due, refinance *both* at rate $r = g$. Although the size of the new debt grows exponentially at rate g, the ratio of the new debt to current income is fixed at a constant number, because current income also grows at rate g. Therefore, the entity remains solvent in the sense of ability to repay all its debts on time forever. Thus the entity can distribute \$1 million in dividends to its owners now, without demanding any compensating cuts in dividends in the future. Put another way, when $r = g$ in the long run, such entities are not subject to a budget constraint, and even less so if $r < g$. As owners still attach a positive marginal value to extra wealth, the supply of debt explodes to infinity when r falls so low as to equal g. This increase in the demand for credit must raise interest rates until $r > g$.

The inequality $r > g$ also implies that the economy is dynamically efficient in the sense that it would *not* be better off by destroying physical capital. Given these facts, golden rule economies where the real interest rate earned by physical capital is $r = g$ are only hypothetical.

tions. If this latter liability is written as a negative asset, the difference between these two expected present discounted values appears as the PAYG asset.[10]

As the average hidden lifetime tax is positive, the PAYG asset is positive too (given initial solvency). Therefore, this is an asset for the plan, not a liability. This is a real asset for the plan, which collects real revenue, as long as it is reasonable to expect that future contributors will continue paying the net lifetime tax embedded in their contributions. The PAYG asset is used by the plan to back its accrued liabilities to current members.

Valdés-Prieto (2002, chapter 8) proved that if the plan is initially solvent, the size of the PAYG asset will be just enough to fill up the asset side of the balance sheet of the plan. This proof has been extended to the uncertainty case (Valdés-Prieto 2005). Therefore, the PAYG asset can be calculated with a simple rule: take liabilities and subtract the pension fund, if partially funded.

However, this is not true if the plan is not solvent initially. When projections show that the present value of cash flow is negative—that is, when the plan is initially insolvent—

the PAYG asset is not large enough to cover the plan's liabilities at current values for the parameters of the benefit formula. Insolvency does not imply that the pension plan is illiquid. Its cash flow may be positive for the next 10 or 20 years. Insolvency means that financial independence is unsustainable in the longer run if current parameter values are not modified.

Let us review some implications. Young and future members are taxed because the rate of return on saving through this plan is below the rate of return offered by investment in the financial market or in physical capital. The ratio $\tau = (T_t/y_t N_t)$ is the *rate* at which the hidden tax is levied on covered labor earnings.[11] The hidden tax rate τ always meets the condition $\tau < \theta_O$ for workers who are forward-looking or "provident" regarding old age, because each one sees that he will recover a portion of contributions as pension benefits.

Relabel the Cash Flows

Consider a reform that comprises several steps. First, the tax hidden in PAYG finance is made explicit. One way to do this is to split the initial mandatory contribution rate θ_0 into a new (smaller) contribution rate θ' and a new residual payroll tax on covered earnings, levied at rate τ, where τ is equal to the estimated rate of the hidden tax in the initial situation. In our model of two-period lives for a plan that is initially solvent, this implies

$$\theta_0 = \theta' + \tau, \quad \text{where} \quad \tau \equiv \theta_0 - \frac{\beta}{1+r} > 0. \tag{8.2}$$

Second, a law endows the plan with the revenue collected by the new residual payroll tax on covered earnings. However, this law can be changed by another law in the future, and in that event, the plan will not have a right to claim any compensation for expropriation. Thus the plan does not yet enjoy a property right over this tax revenue.

These two steps merely relabel existing cash flows. The sum of income flows received by the pension plan does not change, the take-home earnings of workers do not change, and firms' labor costs do not change. The only difference so far is that the IRR earned by plan members on their new contributions (just θ') rises to r. Meanwhile, the IRR earned on the residual payroll tax component drops to zero. This expresses in yet another way the budget identities summarized by Lindbeck and Persson (2003).

Make the PAYG Cash Flow Tradable

In this step, a law grants the plan property rights, in the standard legal sense, over the cash flows indicated previously by T_t. It was already pointed out that a future law could repeal this law, totally or partially. As long as this remains possible, the plan will not have a "real" property right over the PAYG asset.

The standard approach to this problem—which affects all private property rights as well—is for the courts to enforce a "property right." Most judicial systems (courts or constitutions) specify that in case of expropriation of something covered by property rights, the previous owner is entitled to *compensation* at market value, paid by the state. This is the current legal status of government debt securities and the legal status of *all* private property, since it is always subject to the possibility that a new tax in the future may cut a large part of its value to the owner.

To protect plan ownership over the revenue T_t, the analogous approach is proposed: The law that grants the plan the revenue T_t must declare that it is *owned* by the plan, and must add that if some future government wishes to withdraw part or all of the residual payroll tax in the future, or if that government taxes or otherwise ceases to pay the tax collection to the plan in the future, then the plan will be considered an expropriated owner, just like any other owner. This clause must be written in a way that is clear for the local courts. Of course, the courts must be independent from the executive power for property rights to exist. The objective of spelling out such details is to minimize the risk that procedural objections by a cash-strapped state may devalue the plan's property right over the hidden tax revenue in a significant amount.

It turns out that the resulting commitment does not reduce the freedom of future politicians to modify the rate and the base of taxes on covered earnings, and thus engage in welfare-improving tax policy in the future. Parliament keeps the freedom to replace the residual payroll tax at rate τ by other substitute revenue sources, such as an increase in value-added tax (VAT). This can be done by using the extra revenue from VAT to finance a permanent subsidy to covered workers that defrays the cost of the residual payroll tax for workers. The only requirement imposed so far is that any new policy that imposes losses on the plan by diverting its cash flow must compensate the plan. Of course, the plan may remain publicly managed at this stage (but see Valdés-Prieto 2000 for the longer term).

Securitize the New Cash Flows Owned by the Plan

Securitization is defined as a process that transforms an illiquid asset into a set of securities that are standardized at small enough sizes to make them tradable, which can be sold to investors in the financial markets.[12]

Consider transforming the PAYG asset into a tradable financial asset, by creating CWB securities. The dividend of CWB securities is T_t. The financial design of CWB securities can be uniform, consisting of a simple pro rata share of the revenue from the residual payroll tax to be received in the future. Alternatively, these shares can take different shapes over time and over states of nature, provided that the sum of all CWB dividends in each and every contingency and time period add up to total tax revenue available at that contingency and time period.

In a standard case, the volume of CWB securities is a vast proportion of GDP (if this securitization is applied to all the earnings-related NA plan). For example, if T_t is a revenue of 3 percent of GDP, the real interest rate is about 3 percent per year, and the expected growth rate of covered earnings is 1 percent per year, then the value of all CWB securities is 3 percent$/(0.03 - 0.01) = 150$ percent of GDP. Note that the market discount rate on CWB securities must be larger than the growth rate of the covered wage bill, because the dividend T_t grows at rate g. If the market discount rate were equal to g, then the market value of a CWB security would be infinite.

CWB securities differ from public debt in a fundamental way: CWB securities are not owed by the government. They are owed by future contributors to the pension plan, despite the fact that the state does force them to join and pay the residual payroll tax. In addition, CWB securities have a payment profile that is like equity, in the sense that it varies directly with fluctuations in fertility, labor force participation, and real earning trends. In contrast, public debt makes a fixed nominal (or CPI-indexed) payment. The owners of CWB securities take 100 percent of the loss when dividend growth falls below expectations, and also reap the gains when the dividend T_t rises faster than expected.

The amount of CWB to be sold in the market by the pension institution can take two very different values. On the one hand, some small amount must be sold to obtain a market valuation of CWB securities. Achieving sufficient trades for this purpose requires a modest sale of CWB securities compared with the total available. A schedule of weekly sales of CWB securities adding up to, say, 0.3 percent of GDP per year for the first 10 years may be enough to free the market valuation from liquidity penalties.

On the other hand, the pension institution may attempt to abandon its inherited portfolio and move toward the risk-return frontier, creating substantial economic gains. This requires exchange of much more substantial amounts of CWB securities, say 30 percent of the total, for corporate securities, both national and foreign.[13] Valdés-Prieto (2005) argues that it will not be in the interest of pensioners for the plan to exchange much more than this because many are likely to prefer the safety of CWB securities.

Adapt the Benefit Formula of the NA Plan

In order to endow the NA plan with automatic financial stability, its benefit formula must adopt a rule that ensures that the current value of liabilities tracks the market value of plan assets on a daily basis.

One rule-based benefit formula expresses the notional account balance of each individual member as a number of *shares* in the assets of the plan. The price of each share is set daily by dividing the value of plan assets by the number of shares outstanding, just as mutual funds do. Then the notional interest rate credited to active members' account balances is chosen: the rate of change of the price of shares. The resulting rule for allocating aggregate uninsurable risk is "defined contribution."

Rule-based defined benefits can also be arranged, as follows. The plan buys fixed annuities from a life insurance company, which in turn would back those promises by purchasing a separate portfolio made up of long-term fixed-income bonds. The pension institution would purchase these annuities with the proceeds of sales of CWB securities in the same amount as the account balance of the retiring members. In addition, the owners of the life insurance company must put up some capital as a guarantee of their promise to take losses if the portfolio falls in value. (If the portfolio rises in value, the owners take the gains.) This insurance function could be performed by the pension institution itself if it had some capital, but this would have to be supplied by the state.

Of course, the supply of an adequate volume of fixed-income bonds at reasonable prices can be a problem. This problem is solved if the CWB securities are created in two different classes, the first one paying a dividend indexed to average wages and the other paying as dividend the remaining cash from T_t, (which tracks demographic and participation risks). Life insurance companies would be happy to buy the wage-indexed CWB securities and offer wage-indexed variable annuities to retiring members. The second class of CWB securities, with returns linked to demography and participation, would be held by the more risk-tolerant investors, including younger workers.

In both cases, the NA plan will have been endowed with rules that provide automatic financial stability in the short run. This follows from the use of either the mutual fund formula (defined contribution) or the hiring of a sponsor that guarantees a wage-indexed annuity (defined benefits). Let us explain the term *integration to financial markets*: Although the basic purpose of rule-based benefits is to destroy political risk by attaining automatic financial stability in the short run, a side benefit is that members become able to direct the funds in their individual account toward the portfolios available in the financial markets. Active members are likely to differ in their degree of risk tolerance. For example, those near retirement may seek a high degree of certainty about the interest rate that will be credited in the future to their individual account balance. The plan should respond by offering several balanced portfolios with different levels of uninsurable risk to active members, and also should offer to purchase deferred annuities for those members who fear a rise in annuity prices for the year in which they plan to start a fixed annuity. At least one of these portfolios should be a fixed-income one, such as the Thrift Savings Plan offered by the U.S. government, which has 3.2 million members.[14] To create each portfolio, the plan would mix CWB securities with equities and fixed-income, long-term bonds in the financial market (purchased with the proceeds of sales of some CWB securities) in the same amount as the account balance of the members that choose the associated portfolio.

Comparison between this Proposal and the Swedish ABM

Consider as a starting point a country with a two-pillar pension policy. The first pillar comprises solidarity programs that help the old poor. The second pillar is a set of mandatory savings and insurance plans that pay earnings-related pensions. The aim of these plans is to help the improvident or myopic members of the middle class save for old age more than they would have saved on their own. An example is the two-plan second-pillar created in Poland in 1997. Assume that one of these plans is an NA plan, financed by (almost) pure PAYG finance. The other plan is a fully funded defined contribution (DC) plan.

At least two methods to endow the NA plan (in the second pillar) with automatic financial stability can be considered. The first is the ABM method, which was adopted by Sweden in May 2001. This mechanism relies on accounting measures of plan assets and plan liabilities. The "pure" version of the ABM method works as described below.

Assume that at some point the plan's measured liabilities exceed assets. Then, the notional interest rate credited in this period to active members and the rate of adjustment of pensions in payment are both set to equal the original notional interest rate, minus the growth rate in liabilities from the previous period, plus the growth rate in assets from the previous period. The conversion factor that turns an account balance into an annuity is *not* modified.[15] The second way to reach automatic financial stability is the rule-based IFM method, described in the previous section. Summarizing, the IFM method relabels contribution flows into a new contribution rate θ' and a residual payroll tax at rate τ, such that $\theta_o = \theta' + \tau$; endows the NA plan with property rights over the revenue of this new tax on earnings; creates new securities (CWB securities) out of this cash flow; trades a small share of the new securities in the financial market to obtain market valuation; and crucially, adopts a rule-based benefit formula.

There are many similarities between the two methods. For example, both adjust the value of liabilities automatically toward asset values, using either a rule-based benefit formula (IFM) or an adjustment to the notional interest rate and indexation rule (ABM). Another similarity is that neither tries to increase national savings or to reduce taxes on labor. On the other hand, the following differences between these two approaches are apparent and interesting:

1. The IFM method values the plan's assets at prices and implicit discount rates determined objectively by transactions of CWB securities in the financial markets. There, many different participants, presumably guided by the profit motive, compete to make accurate projections of dividends and apply discount rates that take into account the cost of risks that impinge on these cash flows, including their correlations with other cash flows available in the local and world economy. In contrast, the ABM method leaves valuation of the plan's assets to a single team of civil servants. This team is supervised by the political leadership, by the press, and by

public opinion, including interested academics. However, the tightness of this vigilance is bound to be quite different from the one produced by multiple participants in the financial markets.

2. The discount rate used by the ABM method to value assets is the growth rate of the economy, g. This is clear from Settergren (2001) and Settergren and Mikula (2006). They follow the tradition started by Arthur and McNicoll (1978) and summarized by Lee (1994), which analyzes asset valuation in hypothetical golden rule economies where the real interest rate earned by physical capital is $r = g$. In contrast, the IFM method values CWB securities at a discount rate actually set by the financial markets. As explained in box 8.2, this discount rate must be above the growth rate of GDP to avoid an infinite price for CWB securities. This difference in discount rates implies that the capital values of account balances, overall liabilities, and overall plan assets will be different between NA plans that adopt the IFM method rather than the ABM. This implies that the ABM method contains implicit taxes and subsidies between members that do not arise in the IFM. These taxes and subsidies have an impact on both equity and efficiency. For example, since high-earners live longer on average, they benefit on average from an implicit subsidy because the duration of their pension rights is longer and therefore the liabilities owed to them are overvalued in the ABM, compared with market discount rates.

3. The difference between discount rates also affects intergenerational distribution. Adopting the ABM method implies assigning a higher pro rata share of assets to plan members who hold longer-lived rights to benefits at any given point in time: that is, a higher pro rata share is assigned to the younger (active) members than to older (pensioned) members.

4. Valuation can produce surprises in the ABM. Valuation in the ABM is as follows: If there were just \$1 in lifetime tax revenue paid by the initial generation, and growing at rate g, then the present value of all these lifetime taxes would be $\$1/(g-g)$, infinite! On the other hand, when $r = g$, the tax T_t is zero, so the numerator in this expression is also zero. Both effects cancel each other in the limit as the discount rate falls toward g, yielding a finite asset for the ABM method. This limiting amount is the product of the current contribution revenue (a flow) and the average difference between the timing of contributions and the timing of liabilities (usually about 30–40 years). This valuation formula for assets is not valid out of steady states, so its application in an uncertain world can create surprises. For example, assume that the unemployment rate rises because of a fall in international demand, which is only transitory. The ABM valuation formula takes the fall in revenue as permanent. The asset is estimated to fall in the same percentage in which revenue fell (the average difference in timing is essentially constant). This translates into a large cut in the notional interest rate credited to active members and a drop in pensions. When the shock reverses, the notional interest rate rises and the drop in pensions is recovered. In contrast, the IFM method takes the change as transitory and the price of CWB securities is almost unaffected. The account balances are not affected. In this example, the ABM valuation method creates risk.

5. Valuation of assets in the ABM is not affected, but the valuation of liabilities is affected when the rate of economic growth changes. Consider a case where the projected economic growth rate falls slightly but permanently. Because market interest rates are fixed by international capital mobility, and because the dividend payout of a CWB security grows less rapidly, the value of CWB securities falls,

say, by 2 percent. Consider the impact on active members (workers). In the IFM method, the price of shares is cut by 2 percent in the following day and individual account balances are cut in the same proportion. Newly issued pensions will be 2 percent *smaller*. In the ABM method, the valuation of assets is not affected (it does not depend on the growth rate), but the value of accrued liabilities rises. The net impact is an actuarial deficit, so the notional interest rate will be cut and pension amounts must fall gradually. The time-phasing of this fall is different from the one in the IFM method. There, a person about to retire whose pension rights are fully invested in CWB securities takes a 2 percent cut in pensions and future generations buy CWB securities at reduced prices so are not affected. In the ABM, the same person would take a very limited immediate cut, given by a drop in the notional interest earned in the last year. That person would also take additional cuts as each year's rate of pension indexing is below the original path, as long as she lives. A share of the loss would be passed on to future generations, because those generations would be credited a smaller notional interest rate despite the fact that market interest rates have not changed (by assumption).

6. In an uncertain world, the discount rate assigned by the financial market to CWB securities is stochastic as well. If this discount rate changes, the ABM method leaves account balances and pensions unaffected because financial prices do not enter its valuation formulae. In contrast, the IFM method appears to transmit this risk to active members (assuming average wages are not affected, pensioners with wage-indexed annuities will not be affected either). For example, if the discount rate on CWB securities rises, active members will suffer a cut in their account balances. However, the dividend payout of CWB securities is not affected by changes in the discount rate, and pensions are financed mostly from this payout.[16] This creates a sort of immunization: a member just about to retire would *not* be affected by a rise in the discount rate if he wanted an annuity indexed to average wages. If the insurance company offers such annuities and backs it with the first tranche of CWB securities (which are perpetuities), it would earn a higher interest on this portfolio after the rise in discount rates. Thus, annuity *prices* should drop in the same proportion as the drop in the member's account balance, allowing the member to purchase an annuity of the same size as before the shock. The difference, however, is that in the IFM method the contributions made after the rise in discount rates would earn a higher return, while in the ABM method they would still earn the growth rate g, which did not change.

7. Regarding the allocation of the plan's aggregate uninsurable financial risk *among* plan members, in the ABM method all members get a single level of uninsurable risks. In contrast, the IFM method allows the plan to offer several balanced portfolios with different levels of uninsurable risk, allowing each member to self-select according to his or her risk tolerance. The ABM method must offer a single portfolio to all its members. Therefore, the IFM method can do better by recommending a portfolio to each member as a function of the determinants of the member's predicted risk tolerance, such as the presence of other wealth, earnings variability, and access to insurance and credit lines, in addition to age.

8. Adopting the ABM method does not allow the plan to trade uninsurable risks with other participants in the financial markets, such as other institutional investors, owners of firms, and foreigners. The IFM method allows this. This option is

especially valuable for smaller countries, which place a greater value on international risk diversification.

9. Distributional impact of changes in corporate risk premia. Consider a case where some members have chosen a balanced portfolio where corporate securities (bonds and equities) have a substantial weight, and their risk premia rise but the discount rate on CWB securities remains constant. In the IFM method, only the more risk-tolerant members who chose the balanced portfolios with corporate securities are affected. They should respond to the losses by increasing their saving rate and by working more hours per year, if still active, and by cutting lifetime consumption. To compare this outcome with the one occurring under the ABM method, assume that the plan is partially funded and holds such corporate securities in the same total amount. In this case, the rise in risk premia cuts the value of the plan's fund, and this translates into a cut to the notional interest rate for *all* active members and into a cut in the indexation rate for *all* pensions in payment. The more risk-averse members are not spared.

Concluding Comments

It has been shown that an NA plan can be endowed with automatic financial stability in the short run. This feature is appreciated because it helps insulate the government budget from demographic pressures and in the future would insulate the pension budget from fiscal pressures. However, the literature proved that the initial generation of benefit formulae did not achieve automatic financial stability in the short run in the face of demographic and economic shocks. Sweden responded to this challenge by creating an ABM, which was legislated in May 2001.

This study discusses an alternative response, which also endows NA plans with automatic financial stability in the short run. The method is presented in more detail in Valdés-Prieto (2005) and labeled here *integration to financial markets* (IFM). In contrast to the ABM, which relies on asset valuations made by a single group of civil servants supervised by politicians and the press, this proposal bases asset valuation on market-determined discount rates set by multiple investors, presumably guided by the profit motive. In this dimension, the difference boils down to private versus public management. Both have well-known advantages and disadvantages, the magnitudes of which differ across countries.

Another important difference is that the discount rate used by the ABM method to value assets is the growth rate of the economy, g. This is appropriate for asset valuation in hypothetical golden rule economies where the real interest rate earned by physical capital is $r = g$. In contrast, the IFM method values the PAYG asset at the discount rate actually set by the financial markets. These market discount rates come from real economies where infinitely lived assets pay a return that is higher than g, and provide the efficient incentives.

A critical difference is that the IFM method allows the pension institution to abandon its corner portfolio and move toward the risk-return frontier, creating substantial economic gains. The participation in the financial market also allows the offer to individual members of a set of, say, five balanced portfolios, permitting a better adaptation of the pension plan to individual circumstances. This would also create immediate social gains.

It is apparent that the choice between the ABM and IFM methods merits attention from policy makers. This choice has many facets. The weights that should be granted to each one are likely to differ across economic and political settings, and therefore across countries. It is possible that advanced nations that have an independent judiciary, well-regulated financial markets, and are well integrated to international capital markets can gain relatively more by having their pension plan engage in international risk diversification through the IFM method.

Notes

1. "Notional defined contribution" and "non-financial defined contribution" should be understood to have the same definition.

2. It is important to be precise about the meaning of "short" run. For our purposes in this chapter, the "short" run is an election cycle. This is the maximum time available for adjustment before politicians respond to an aggregate deficit in the plan with legal reforms, taxes, subsidies, and other discretionary measures taken ex post. In most well-functioning democracies, political response can be faster.

3. See Valdés-Prieto (2000). The paper by Arthur and McNicoll (1978) does not discuss the issue of financial stability. On the contrary, that paper restricts itself not only to the case of steady state growth but, within that, it considers only the case where the growth path meets the "golden rule" condition (marginal productivity of capital equal to the growth rate of the economy), which implies dynamic inefficiency.

4. The original paper by Valdés-Prieto (2000) made the mistake of stating that in that event, there would be a cash *surplus* rather than a cash *deficit* (table 1 in that paper). Professor Friedrich Breyer spotted this mistake. His correction and my response are available in the *Scandinavian Journal of Economics* (see Breyer 2004 and Valdés-Prieto 2004).

5. See Valdés Prieto (2002, pp. 391–3).

6. See Settergren (2001).

7. See Settergren (2001).

8. With lives spanning two or more active periods, some current plan members have not yet completed their career at any given reform date. To measure the plan's liability to them, it is necessary to determine the "recognition bond" that the plan's charter grants to members who leave the plan at mid-career. This recognition might equal past contributions plus interest, or, alternatively, might equal the present value of future expected benefits for a full career minus future expected contributions. Which approach is used is important out of steady state.

9. Such economies were labeled "golden" by an earlier literature that compared steady states without taking into account the cost of moving from one steady state to another. Rate g can be positive, zero, or negative.

10. The PAYG asset differs from a Buchanan bond—a type of public debt that pays a rate of return equal to the growth rate of national income—in two fundamental ways (see also Góra and Palmer 2004). The Buchanan bond is a debt of the state, serviced by the treasury, and its holders are protected by property rights against expropriation. In contrast, the PAYG asset is a debt of future members of the pension plan (the present value of the lifetime taxes they will pay), not the state. Morever, its holder, the pension institution, is not protected by property rights because if future legislation allows contributors to quit the plan (and, say, contribute instead to a mutual fund), or cuts the coverage of contributions, the pension institution does not have the right to claim compensation in the courts. In addition, there is a financial difference: the rate of return of the PAYG asset differs from the rate of growth of national income almost surely due to variations in average taxable wages, coverage, benefits, and longevity.

11. This definition of τ assumes that the tax rate hidden in PAYG finance is applied to earnings, when the member is active.

12. See Kendall and Fishman (1996). For example, securitization can transform assets such as the accounts receivables of a telephone company into securities that can be traded in a stock exchange.

13. Asset exchanges between the pension institution and foreign residents have no impact on the exchange rate because international capital inflows and outflows balance exactly.

14. For details of the TSP plan, see www.tsp.gov. The TSP plan is available for complementary tax-favored savings for employees at the federal, state, and municipal levels in the United States, and offers five balanced portfolios, including international and national equities and bonds.

15. The factor used by the current ABM method to convert individual account balances into annuities is not sensitive to the extent by which liabilities exceed assets because it always uses a discount rate of 1.6 percent. This small divergence could be overcome in a more advanced version of the ABM method.

16. See Valdés-Prieto (2005).

References

Abel, A., G. Mankiw, L. Summers, and R. Zeckhauser. 1989. "Assesing Dynamic Efficiency." *The Review of Economic Studies* 56 (1), 185, January: 1–20.

Arthur, W. B., and G. McNicoll. 1978. "Samuelson, Population and Intergenerational Transfers." *International Economic Review* 10 (1): 241–6.

Breyer, F. 2004. "Comment on S. Valdes-Prieto, 'The Financial Stability of Notional Account Pensions.'" *Scandinavian Journal of Economics* 106 (2): 387–88.

Góra, M., and E. Palmer. 2004. "Shifting Perspectives in Pensions." Discussion Paper 1369, IZA Institute for the Study of Labor, Bonn (October), http://www.iza.org.

Kendall, L., and M. Fishman. 1996. *A Primer on Securitization.* Cambridge, Mass.: MIT Press.

Lee, R. 1994. "Population Age Structure, Intergenerational Transfer and Wealth: A New Approach, with Application to the U.S." *Journal of Human Resources* 29 (4): 1027–63.

Lindbeck, A., and M. Persson. 2003. "The Gains from Pension Reform." *Journal of Economic Literature* XLI (March): 74–112.

Richter, W. 1993. "Intergenerational Risk Sharing and Social Security in an Economy with Land." *Journal of Economics (Zeitschrift für Nationalökonomie),* Suppl. 7: 91–110, Springer Verlag.

Scheinkman, J. 1980. "Notes on Asset Trading in an Overlapping Generations Model." Dept. of Economics, University of Chicago, unpublished.

Settergren, O. 2001. "The Automatic Balance Mechanism of the Swedish Pension System: A Non-Technical Introduction." *Riksförsäkringsverket,* August. www.rfv.se/English.

Settergren, O., and B. D. Mikula. 2006. "The Rate of Return of Pay-As-You-Go Pension Systems: A More Exact Consumption-Loan Model of Interest." In *Pension Reform: Issues and Prospects for Non-Financial Defined Contribution (NDC) Schemes,* ed. R. Holzmann and E. Palmer, chapter 7. Washington, DC: World Bank.

Sinn, H. W. 1999. "Why a Funded Pension is Useful and Why It is Not." CESifo Working Paper 195, Institute for Economic Research, Munich. (Also printed in *International Tax and Public Finance* 2000 (7): 389–410.)

Tirole, J. 1985. "Asset Bubbles and Overlapping Generations." *Econometrica* 53 (6): 1499–1527.

Valdés-Prieto, S. 2000. "The Financial Stability of Notional Account Pensions." *Scandinavian Journal of Economics* 102 (3): 395–417.

———. 2002. *Políticas y Mercados de Pensiones.* Santiago, Chile: Ediciones Universidad Católica.

———. 2004. "Response to Breyer." *Scandinavian Journal of Economics* 106 (2): 387–90.

———. 2005. "Pay-As-You-Go Securities." *Economic Policy* 42 (April): 215–51.

Discussion of "A Market Method to Endow NDC Systems with Automatic Financial Stability"

*Marek Góra**

THE CHAPTER ADDRESSES A VERY IMPORTANT ISSUE, namely short-run stability of unfunded pension plans. The focus of analysis is on non-financial defined contribution (NDC) systems. The author provides a set of arguments to support the view that pension systems that are not backed with financial assets are potentially unstable. More precisely, even if they are automatically solvent over the long term, they do not have the property of short-run stability. The arguments provided in the chapter are strong and lead to clear conclusions.

The author suggests creating a mechanism called *integration to financial markets* (IFM) that will impose more financial stability in NDC systems. The idea—similar to various types of buffer fund existing in countries running NDC—is interesting, and worth further discussion and possibly implementation.[1]

Valdés-Prieto's chapter is not only technical, but it is also a very inspiring background for a broader discussion on pension systems and their reforms. The discussion starting from this chapter can lead to various specific issues. I shall address only some of them.

The arguments supporting the key thesis of the chapter, namely the possible lack of stability of NDC, can also be applied to pension systems using financial markets (financial defined contribution, FDC) that are not pure savings plans but are saving plans in the activity period and are turned into insurance after retirement. So arguments should take into account the method of annuitization in NDC versus annuitization in FDC. Full obligatory annuitization of account values irrespective of their type is natural if pension systems are a part of social security.

This leads to a very important point. Does implementing individual accounts mean privatization of the pension system (whatever this means) or creating public-private partnership based on public (social) goals and private management (using financial markets) of the system? We can assume that defined contribution (DC) is a voluntary savings plan or a forced private savings plan that is treated as a voluntary one, even if it is mandatory. However, we can also assume that a DC regime applied to a pension system is just a method leading to stabilization in economy. The chapter assumes the first, while for instance the design of the new Polish pension system—both the NDC and FDC part—assumes the latter. So different understanding of the issues discussed in the chapter may stem from deep differences in assumptions.

Defining key concepts helps the discussion. Valdés-Prieto provides a clear definition of funding. The term is often broadly used, referring to all types of savings in the economy, including ones based on political decisions. By contrast, Valdés-Prieto prefers to use the narrow definition of funding that is based on property rights. The difference between the two definitions and its consequences lead to an interesting multifold problem.

---

* Marek Góra is professor of economics at the Warsaw School of Economics.

Property rights are needed to protect pension rights against political manipulation. They are needed for two reasons. The first is to reduce the tax wedge; the second is to contribute to economic stability. The latter needs explanation. Traditional mandatory pension contributions, although perceived as "robbery" (leading to an increased tax wedge), are in fact "charity," since participants typically receive more, or even much more, than the present value of contributions paid.

Implementation of individual accounts leads to actuarial neutrality. This means reduction of pension rights: that is, the amount of pension if compared with prior law is reduced. The reduction is socially just if the welfare of each subsequent generation is equally valued. The political manipulation that societies need to be protected against is an attempt to finance inflated pension rights at the expense of lower remuneration of production factors.

The successful implementation of the new pension system in Poland was based— among other factors—on the common feeling that the old system cheated people. In fact, it paid out too much. The new one (NDC + FDC) will generate much lower replacement rates. So both effects will be achieved: namely, reduction of the part of GDP allocated to the entire retired generation (GDP^R), and reduction of the contribution of the reduced GDP^R on the tax wedge.

Promoting property rights within NDC does not need to be restricted to IFM. Upon first thought, the most straightforward idea that comes to mind would be to give the NDC rights the same legal protection as they would have if they were FDC rights, based on government bonds with explicit property rights. From an economic viewpoint, this would be natural. In both cases, namely NDC and FDC based on government bonds, running the system is just rolling debt. It is easier to understand the similarity when the institution administering NDC is split into two parts. The first collects contributions and passes them to the budget; the other pays out benefits, receiving money from the budget. FDC based on government bonds can be described in the same way. The only difference— and it is an important one—is the property right. So why not turn NDC liabilities into legally protected rights? The only thing preventing that is accounting procedures. A country that drew the logical conclusion from the economic similarity of NDC and FDC would show huge deficits. In Europe, this would violate the Stability and Growth Pact. In the whole world, this would be badly perceived by financial markets—although economically neutral. So NDC is used as a clever trick to avoid the accounting problem, rather than to achieve full DC purity.

Valdés-Prieto's definition of funding in the narrow sense provokes an important question. Is a funded system possible if it covers entire population? The answer "yes" is possible only if government debt is assumed to be economically identical with private debt/investment. From the economic viewpoint, this is not necessarily true. Discussing this issue goes beyond the scope of my comment. The discussion should take into account not only FDC but also NDC.

Commenting on Valdés-Prieto's chapter is difficult because it needs a much broader discussion that can be offered here. So I shall address only one additional issue: the argument that the market rate of return, r_F, is larger than the economic growth, g. There are both theoretical and empirical arguments to support that view. Irrespective of that discussion, it is interesting to discuss the consequences of $r_F > g$.

The pension system is an institutional framework for intergenerational exchange. Irrespective of whether participation is voluntary or mandatory, current GDP is divided between the working and the retired generation. This is done with or without the intermediation of financial markets. The latter method has a lot of advantages but eventually leads to the same qualitative result. Proportions of the division are subject to the market or implicit rate of return. Actually, both can be—and often are—"too" high. Traditional pension systems must increase contributions to pay out pensions inflated by promises that are too high (implicit rate). We can also imagine a funded pension system based on government bonds that are overvalued by markets (the reason for this does not matter). Individual accounts receive high rates of return. However, the result will be higher taxes. This is the problem of fiscal policy, but the pension system—as a large share of nations' economies—can accelerate the problem.

The pension system, especially the one that covers the entire population, is a large part of the economy. What really matters is the stability of the entire economy. The stability of a pension system can contribute to economic stability—or just the opposite. A poorly designed pension system that generates ever-increasing costs can destabilize the economy. The key goal for pension reform is to stop the increase of GDP^R/GDP (the pension system consuming too large a portion of GDP).[2] From that viewpoint, NDC can be as effective as FDC, even if one of them or both are not perfectly stable themselves. Actually, NDC can do the job quicker since the rate of return it generates, r_N, is close to if not equal to the GDP growth rate.[3] Both NDC and FDC can lead to reintroducing intergenerational equilibrium, which means keeping GDP^R/GDP constant over the long term.

Equilibrium could be reached even without involving financial markets. However, it would be more difficult because for ordinary people, investing in financial markets is based more on intuition than on a grasp of macroeconomic fundamentals. So if their contributions are managed in financial markets in a way similar to their other financial resources, they will feel more comfortable and accept the concept of individual accounts. Without financial markets, the reform would be less understandable, and hence less acceptable for the public. Financial markets play a "demonstration" role.

However, NDC has a very good property: namely, $r_N = g$. This prevents inflation of pension rights, which will have to be financed out of real GDP—irrespective of the type of the system. Here we could suggest extending the definition of funding formulated in the chapter. The very narrow definition of funding would refer to this part of funding, in the narrow sense that is not based on government bonds. In spite of the privileged legal status (property rights) of the government bonds, tax revenues are needed to turn them into income-financing consumption. The IFM (buffer fund)—being a short-run concept—can be less strict. Valdés-Prieto's narrow definition of funding is especially appropriate for designing the IFM financing.

NDC could replace FDC in the part that is based on rolling government bonds. At the same time, NDC should be limited to the level that cannot or should not be spent on private investment instruments. FDC can be more efficient because it is much more rooted in thinking of economists, policy makers, and general public. So coming back to Valdés-Prieto's idea, making NDC more like FDC is really a good one. However, one of the preconditions for property rights within NDC would require some modernization of procedures applied to national accounts (the calculation of the deficit and debt in the economy). This modernization is needed anyway, since without it, pension reforms will not be manageable, irrespective of their designs. So it probably will be possible to implement the idea of endowing NDC with at least some property rights.

Notes

1. In the new Polish system the buffer fund has been designed in a similar way to the concept of IFM. The fund is invested in financial markets.

2. The scale of the share of GDP^{Rt} to GDP does not matter for aggregate demand, but it does for supply.

3. Technically, this can be another rate converging to g.

Chapter 9

Conversion to NDCs—
Issues and Models

*Edward Palmer**

NON-FINANCIAL (NOTIONAL) DEFINED CONTRIBUTION (NDC) SCHEMES began to take shape on the drawing boards in the 1990s, and were implemented for the first time in practice in a handful of countries from the mid-1990s. The conceptual development of NDC has gone hand in hand with the emergence of implementation issues and other technical challenges. The implementation of the first NDC schemes involved addressing a large number of design issues that had never been confronted within the traditional pay-as-you-go (PAYG) context. The initial decade of work on design of NDC schemes helped to clarify some of these issues.

One of the most important design issues in introducing an NDC scheme is the conversion of rights acquired from the previous system—normally a defined benefit PAYG system—into NDC account values. This is the topic of this study. The study provides a systematic framework for thinking about conversion from PAYG defined benefit to NDC and identifies and discusses issues that arise in implementation. The study also examines what countries have done in practice and discusses the implications of the methods chosen in terms of the more generic, theoretical framework.

To begin with, briefly, what is an NDC pension scheme?[1] An NDC pension scheme can be likened to a lifetime savings plan where individuals regularly contribute a percentage of their income until retirement and then draw on their account throughout their retirement period. An NDC scheme is more than a savings scheme, however, since the capital of the deceased becomes available for distribution among the survivors, as in any typical pension insurance scheme.

In an NDC scheme, an amount equal to the contributions paid by or on behalf of the participant is credited to an individual account in each accounting period. In addition, the account is credited periodically with a rate of return, based on what the system can afford—the internal rate of return (IRR). The account value constitutes a claim on future resources. Based on the account value and cohort life expectancy at retirement, from some stipulated minimum age, the NDC benefit is calculated as a life annuity.

As opposed to a financial account scheme, where the assets are all held in financial market instruments, the assets in an NDC scheme are the future contributions of workers: that

* Edward Palmer is professor of social insurance economics at Uppsala University and head of the Division for Research at the Swedish Social Insurance Agency.

The author is grateful to Agneta Kruse for comments on an earlier draft of this study.

is, financing is on a PAYG basis. As opposed to a defined benefit (DB) scheme, where the contribution rate adjusts to accommodate the scale of overall benefit payments, in an NDC scheme the contribution rate is fixed and the rate of return credited accounts is that which upholds long-term financial stability, which is a function of the development of the contribution base. Since the assets are not held in financial market instruments, the scheme is *non-financial*. For this reason, it is more appropriate to call NDC a *non-financial defined contribution scheme*.

Personal account schemes, whether they are non-financial (NDC) or financial defined contribution schemes (FDC) schemes,[2] require a full working life to introduce. However, since accounts are not financial in the NDC framework, it is possible to convert rights acquired from previous years of coverage in a pay-as-you-go (PAYG)—non-financial, defined benefit (NDB)—scheme directly into NDC rights. This means that in practice—given a conversion rule—an NDC scheme can be introduced fully at any time. This is in fact one of the appealing features of converting from a PAYG-DB scheme to NDC, compared with the counterfactual of introducing a financial account scheme.

It follows that an issue that must be dealt with in conversion from a PAYG-DB scheme to an NDC scheme is the issue of how rights acquired in the old system are to be recognized. This raises the related questions of what are acquired rights and what constitutes fair treatment of these. The point of departure in this study is a discussion of the question of fairness in the context of converting a public PAYG pension system from a defined benefit (NDB) to defined contribution (NDC) scheme.

In the 1990s, a handful of countries—as diverse as Italy, the Kyrgyz Republic, Poland, and Sweden—began gradual transitions from mandatory PAYG-DB schemes to NDC schemes for the working population. Latvia was the first to make a total conversion for all workers, which it did in 1996. Many more countries are now considering implementing NDC.[3] This study draws upon the experiences of the original five NDC countries in discussing how countries have dealt with acquired rights in conversion to NDC.

The remainder of this study is organized as follows. The next section discusses acquired rights and fairness. Two principles of fairness are presented and discussed in this context. The third section presents and discusses the merits of several approaches for calculating initial capital, and relates these to the principles of fairness. The fourth section discusses issues in determining the speed of conversion. The fifth section presents examples of how countries have made the conversion in practice. The sixth section discusses other important related issues that can arise in conversion from a PAYG-DB scheme to NDC, namely disability and survivor benefits. The last section presents some final remarks.

Transition to NDC—What Is Fair Treatment of Acquired Rights?

Some Introductory Remarks

By way of background, there is a whole body of literature on the more general topic of the distribution and redistribution of resources between individuals. In the literature, various principles are developed and employed to determine the fairness of a redistributional policy for individuals or groups of individuals, as well as the effect on overall social welfare. As is well known, what is fair depends on the definition of fairness, which is a rather circular but unavoidable approach.

Perhaps the most frequently employed definition of fairness is the Kaldor-Hicks criterion, in which a redistribution of resources between individuals is acceptable if total welfare is at least as great with the redistribution and where the winners could compensate the losers. This implies that if NDC dominates NDB alternatives in terms of potential effects on economic growth, conversion to NDC can fulfill the Kaldor-Hicks criterion, even if the redistribution accompanying the conversion to NDC creates losers.

In the context of this discussion, if a country has a PAYG pension scheme—of any sort— a redistribution of resources has *already* taken place in accordance with the rules and design of the particular scheme. All PAYG-DB schemes create a transfer of resources between individuals, the exact outcome of which, however, may be known only *ex post*, when individuals have retired and benefits have been calculated according to the rules of the scheme. If in a given scheme, the present value of the expected stream of an individual's benefits is greater than the present value of his or her expected contributions, he or she is the recipient of a positive transfer to lifetime resources.

According to standard economic consumer theory, individuals experiencing an exogenously determined increase in individual lifetime income will be inclined to spend more time in leisure over the life cycle—including earlier retirement—and to save less and consume more prior to retirement. NDC aspires to be neutral in this sense.

The underlying principle of an NDC scheme is that the amount on the individual's account reflects only his or her own contributions and an IRR granted the accounts of all participants.[4] In this sense, then, an NDC scheme can yield a higher level of national welfare than NDB schemes that result in less individual labor supply and saving.

There is a built-in "conflict" when NDC replaces some set of PAYG-DB rules, since the implication is that individual advantages gained under the DB scheme will be lost as a result of the transition. Of course, the nearer NDC the actual DB scheme is that is to be replaced, the smaller this conflict will be. Generally speaking, the winners under the DB scheme are the potential losers in a transition to NDC, whereas the DB losers are likely to be the winners.[5]

To judge the overall effect of a reform introducing NDC, one must also take into consideration the low-income guarantee that must accompany an NDC scheme, and which by definition will function as a progressive tax. There are various ways of designing the guarantee, but these will not be discussed in this study. Instead, the discussion that follows assumes that the floor in the pension system consists of some form of guarantee, which has the clear objective of transferring public revenues to the *needy* elderly, but no further reference is made to a guarantee.

Comparison of Two Principles

The two principles for conversion of rights in a PAYG-DB scheme to an NDC scheme that will be examined here are the *acquired rights principle* and the *contribution principle*. There is a definition of fairness implicit in each:

> Principle 1. *Acquired rights principle*. A fair transition to a new system preserves acquired rights.

> Principle 2. *Contribution principle*. A fair transition to a new system gives rights based on individual contributions already paid, including a relevant rate of return.[6] This is the NDC principle.

These two principles also represent the two possible generic models for converting rights in a PAYG-DB scheme to NDC. They are analyzed and discussed in this section.

Application of the two principles in converting rights from the old DB scheme will lead to very different results. This is illustrated with the help of an example presented in table 9.1. In the example, a DB scheme that in many ways resembles an NDC scheme is chosen to show how different the outcomes are, despite the fact that the design of the DB scheme is close to an NDC scheme.[7]

Table 9.1. Varying Results over Time of a DB Scheme that Resembles an NDC Scheme

Year of retirement	Year 1 (1960)	Year 40 (2000)	Year 80 (2040)
Life expectancy (P) from age 60 = years with benefit	17 years	21 years	25 years
Years of work (L)	40 years	40 years	40 years
Replacement rate (average benefit/average wage, (b/w)	0.5	0.5	0.5
Contribution rate	21.25	26.25	31.25

Source: Author's calculations.

Note: See the text for details.

In the example, the defined benefit to be replaced by an NDC benefit is based on individual contributions. Forty years of coverage are required to claim a full benefit in the DB scheme, and a benefit can be claimed at age 60. The contribution rate is computed as $b \cdot P/w \cdot L$, where b is the benefit, w the wage, L is years of work, and P is life expectancy as a pensioner. The ratio b/w is the individual replacement rate.

With 40 covered years, a full benefit in the DB scheme replaces 50 percent of income from retirement at age 60. The individual in the example is an average worker who receives the average wage. For simplicity, all individuals are assumed to earn the average wage, which is set to unity in the absence of wage growth and which would grow with the rate of technical progress with growth. The only factor that changes in the example is life expectancy P at age 60, which is assumed to increase at the rate of one year for every ten years of time that lapse.

By definition, the DB scheme generates increasing costs for all future birth cohorts of workers because the retirement age is fixed at 60 with forty years of work, whereas the benefit period is increasing with increasing pensioner longevity at the rate of one year for every ten years that lapse. As a result, the ratio of years of work to years of retirement is declining (for the whole country), which means that younger birth cohorts of workers must pay a higher contribution rate to support a fixed benefit here assumed to equal 50 percent of the wage.

In the beginning, the contribution rate needed to finance this DB scheme is 21.25 percent. Eighty years later it is 31.25 percent, due solely to the additional costs created by increasing longevity.[8] This can be thought of as a DB scheme implemented in 1960, and where costs have already gone up to 26.25 percent by the year 2000—with further expected increases to 31.25 percent in 2040. Since the example is constructed assuming a fixed population and constant labor force participation patterns, the cost increase is driven solely by the aging population through the increase in the dependency ratio.

To illustrate the difference between the two transition principles, assume that policy makers decide to discontinue the DB scheme in year 20 and convert acquired rights in the old scheme into NDC rights. The difference in the outcomes of the two principles can then be illustrated for a person with 20 years of coverage in the "old" DB scheme.

ACQUIRED RIGHTS PRINCIPLE

The acquired right (the life stream of benefits) the individual can expect from the DB scheme cannot be known *exactly* until he or she—or the relevant birth cohort—has died. There are two obvious reasons for this. The first is that the benefit the individual is entitled to under the DB scheme will typically require x years for a full benefit, in the example 40. More generally, the size of the benefit may be determined by some number of years y, which is less than or equal to x, or on final salary. The second is that longevity determines the payout period, and, typically, defined benefit schemes do not take projected cohort longevity into account in determining the size of the benefit.

There are two logical possibilities for calculating the acquired right at the time of conversion to NDC:

> Alternative 1. *Wait until the worker retires to compute the acquired right*, using the "best possible" cohort projection of life expectancy at age 60 for the birth cohort.[9] In this example, the individual has worked 20 years of the necessary 40, and his or her acquired right is equivalent to half a full right at retirement in year 40 (for example, the year 2000, if the starting point is 1960). This gives a benefit of 5.25,[10] based on a period of 21 years of pension payments from retirement at age 60.

> Alternative 2. *Compute the acquired right at the time of conversion*. This alternative uses the life expectancy estimate at the time the conversion from the DB to the NDC scheme is to be made. In the example, this gives 19 years of pension payments instead of 21, and an acquired right of 4.75.[11]

CONTRIBUTION PRINCIPLE

This principle honors *contribution payments actually made* prior to the time of conversion. By design, the example in table 9.1 avoids the important question of how past contributions should be indexed. However, since by assumption in this illustration. there is neither positive nor negative labor force growth, nor are there any changes in the density of contribution or pension payments, this is no problem.[12] According to the contribution principle, initial capital in the new NDC scheme equals what individuals have paid in contributions. Given the assumptions of the example, these are valued in terms of the current wage at the time of valuation.[13]

Initial capital is calculated as $IC = \Sigma C_t$, where C_t denotes contributions paid during t years. The wage is set equal to unity in the example, but in practice account values would be indexed to the development of the average contribution wage, giving a present value equivalent to a current wage. Using the contribution principle, initial capital is 4.5, which is lower than in the acquired right calculation.

THE DIFFERENCE BETWEEN PRINCIPLES

The DB scheme embodies a tax on future generations generated by steady increase in longevity. The acquired right principle honors this tax. The question is whether this is "fair," since it honors a transfer of resources that has little to do with a transfer from the rich to the poor—a more acceptable criterion for redistribution—but rather involves a general transfer from younger to older cohorts. In addition, it is inconsistent with the decision to introduce NDC, which embodies a decision to abolish the tax on future generations arising due to increasing life expectancy.[14]

In terms of honoring the DB "contract" reigning prior to the introduction of NDC, Principle 1, the acquired rights principle, can be said to be fair. According to this measuring stick, Principle 2 is not. Of course this reasoning presumes there is reason to believe that the first contract would have been honored. The obvious question is whether future workers will honor the contract. In other words, are workers in 2040 willing to pay the contribution rate of more than 31 percent needed to continue to honor the "contract" (which they were not a part of drawing up)? As this example has been designed, the terms of the contract imply that transfers will increasingly subsidize the leisure of successive younger generations—it has nothing to do per se with a transfer of resources from the rich to the poor. So, where does the tolerance of future younger generations for transferring resources to subsidize the leisure of the previous generation (with increasingly better health) stop? Ex ante, decision makers can only make a *qualified guess* about the willingness to pay of future generations. Furthermore, for the terms of the contract to be forever valid, all future generations must believe that workers coming after them will be willing to pay more pro-portionally than they have to continue to honor this fixed DB contract for them. What is almost certain is that eventually coming generations will whittle away—with ad hoc changes now and then—the terms of the contract.

In sum, straightforward application of the *NDC principle* for conversion is neutral vis-à-vis future generations. It contains no implicit intergenerational tax and abolishes the intra and intergenerational taxes typically embedded in the reigning DB commitment. On the other hand, application of the *acquired-rights principle* adheres to "the contract," but in doing so preserves intra and intergenerational taxes inherent in the DB rules. The follow-ing sections discuss how the NDC principle can be applied in practice, drawing on the experiences of countries implementing NDC as examples. We return to the acquired rights principle in a later section in a discussion of the implementation of reforms, using the Pol-ish model as an example of a possible implementation technique.

Calculating Initial Capital in Applying the NDC Framework

This section begins by describing a generic model of initial capital based on the NDC prin-ciple—the contribution principle discussed in the previous section. This model is used to discuss the pros and cons of various implementation strategies. The subsections then go step-by-step through many of the issues arising in applying this model.

A Generic Model of Initial Capital

The point of departure is a generic formula for initial capital (IC) based on past individual wages, w, a contribution rate, c, applied to these to derive imputed contributions and an index, I_t, encompassing the rate of return on contributions made prior to time t and indexed up to this time. The time at which initial capital is calculated and credited to the individual account is T. The generic formula is

$$IC_{i,T} = \sum_{t=1}^{T} c^{IC} w_{i,t}^{IC} I_t^{IC} ,$$

(9.1)

and

$$I_t^{IC} = \prod_{t+1}^{T-1}(1+\beta_t)$$

$$I_T^{IC} = 1.$$

(9.2)

β_t is the rate of return in period t used to establish a value for accounts in the accounting period t.

Total capital at retirement, K_{T^*}, is thus the sum of initial capital, accredited individual accounts for pension contributions made prior to the introduction of NDC, and NDC capital earned thereafter. The benefit calculated at retirement is based on this capital, distributing it over a full life in accordance with cohort-based life expectancy at retire-ment.

There are three variables that need to be considered in determining initial capital: the contribution rate, c^{IC}, past earnings, w^{IC}, and the rate of return, β. These are discussed below one at a time.

Application of the Generic NDC Model: Earnings Histories

The models presented in this section for the determination of initial capital are based on either actual records of individual earnings, or on countrywide macro statistics on earnings that enable creation of an acceptable proxy on which to base initial capital. They all embody an assumption that rights earned prior to the introduction of the NDC scheme are valued in terms of the growth of wages per capita. The internal rate of return in an NDC scheme is a function of more than the wage per capita, however. The consequences of using the per capita wage as the internal rate of return in computing initial capital are discussed in a separate section below.

The following models are possible to employ in determining initial capital:

Model 1. *Use actual contributions paid historically.* If this model is chosen, then what remains is to determine the valuation of these contributions: that is, the indexation factor. The logic of this model is that workers get entitlements in relation to what they have already paid. The drawback is that this is likely to give a low level of coverage in a situation where the contribution rate has increased considerably over a short time. The closer the historical contribution rate is to the current one, the easier it becomes to implement this model.

Model 2. *Use actual individual earnings histories combined with the forward-looking contribution rate to be employed in the new NDC scheme.*[15] If earnings histories are available, these can be used directly to compute initial capital, together with the current contribution rate and indexation principle for historical earnings. The same rate can be used both ex poste to compute initial capital and ex ante to compute future notional capital.

Model 3. *Use of individual service years.* Assume that there is no reliable historical information on the exact values of individual earnings or contributions at the time implementation is being considered, but that there are reliable records of years in which individuals have worked and paid contributions. This situation was typical in the countries of the former Soviet Union and Central and Eastern European transition countries. These years are called service years.[16] Records of these years can be used to compute initial capital.

Use of individual service years in computing initial capital, *per se*, takes individual labor force participation into account, and, indirectly, age-gender participation, as well. What remains is to choose an acceptable method of determining the individual wage for years with participation.

Model 3a. *Combine data on individual service years with the known average wage for all covered participants at the time of implementation.* The simplest procedure is to use the average covered wage for all participants the year prior to the introduction of the NDC scheme. This has the advantage of starting the scheme out on a scale in line with the actual development of *average* covered earnings.

Model 3b. *Combine data on individual service years with an average—historical or current—age- and gender-related wage distribution.* This model can be designed to give the same macro result as Model 3a. Whether it gives more precision depends on the actual situation.

Model 3c. *Combine data on individual service years with the individual's own average wage based on an available series of actual outcomes immediately prior to and/or following the implementation of the NDC scheme.* This model attempts to reflect the past distribution of individual earnings and contributions based on the individual's own *current* status. This is fair to the extent that current individual earnings relative to other workers reflect the past pattern of relative earnings.[17] Note, also, that it discriminates in favor of persons in the formal sector. If applied in countries where informality is a property of the labor market, using actual outcomes following implementation puts a premium on reporting and paying contributions on earnings after the conversion.

In sum, if previous contributions or earnings are not used to compute initial capital, due either to inadequate information or for reasons of policy, or if there are no or only inadequate historical individual earnings data available, the earnings component in the calculation of initial capital can be approximated using one of the above models, and an appropriately chosen contribution rate and rate of return. In the end, since different models involve different potential advantages and deficiencies, policy makers will have to defend the arguments favoring their chosen model. The political decision should be based on analysis of available data, supported with a view of what is "fair"—given the political-economic environment.

Finally, regardless of the model chosen, if some rights granted under the conversion rule are *not* financed within the generic NDC framework, a "tax hangover" is created. This tax hangover should be identified and a means of financing it externally should be specified explicitly—as a component of the conversion.

Application of the Generic Model: The Contribution Rate

The contribution rate determines the scale of the system. There are two approaches to determining the contribution rate. The first and most straightforward approach is to employ a model to determine initial capital that is based on actual contributions paid, that is, model 1 above. This approach may not be desirable, however, since it may not reflect the scale of the system desired by the policy maker.

Use of actual contribution histories links initial capital to what people have actually contributed, but this may not be a desirable policy. Why? If the contribution rate has been increasing over time historically, this procedure would be expected to yield lower benefits for older workers precisely because they paid contributions that were lower than what they would have had they paid according to the contribution principle. In other words, it may be a desirable policy to set a higher contribution rate for determining initial capital and to calculate—and earmark finances—for the tax overhang generated by this decision.

The example in table 9.1 above can help illustrate how the policy maker can approach the problem of determining the size of the contribution rate and, by doing this, the scale of the system. In the example, the contribution rate needed to finance the DB scheme increased from 21.25 to 26.25 percent, solely because of an increase in the life expectancy of the retired over a period of 40 years: for example, between the years 1960 and 2000.

The first important point is that, in the example, the country is currently paying benefits based on a contribution rate of 26.25 percent. The contribution rate could be fixed "forever" at the rate that is required to finance the DB system at the time the NDC scheme is to be introduced. In the example, 26.25 percent. An obvious drawback of this approach is that the policy maker may consider the current rate to be too high, in which case a lower conversion rate could—or should—be set.

If the forward-looking NDC contribution rate is to be set below the existing DB rate then a tax overhang will arise. It will no longer be possible to finance the existing benefits with a lower contribution rate. The tax overhang will require a source of tax financing external to the NDC scheme. In practice, this could continue to be a contribution rate that is higher than that attributed NDC accounts, which would decline with time as the system converges to the NDC rate.

Note that the lowering of the contribution rate with the introduction of the NDC scheme might be a part of a larger policy package: for example, increasing the minimum age at which a pension can be claimed. This leads to an increase in the average (macro) replacement rate, which can help to moderate the effect of introducing the NDC life expectancy adjustment of benefits.

In sum, application of the same contribution rate in the computation of both initial capital and future contributions yields internal time consistency. For political or other reasons this may not be desirable or possible, however. If the same contribution rate is not applied to both past and future earnings, everything else equal, under-financing or over-financing may occur, depending on the choice made—but also depending on the rate of return to be applied in the calculation, which is the topic of the next section. The extent of under-financing—the tax hangover—should be estimated and a means of financing identified. This is required to maintain system financial stability within the NDC scheme. Both under-financing and over-financing lead to a redistribution of resources over birth cohorts of the population, the result of which can be studied empirically in the process of making the policy decision.

Application of the Generic Model: The Rate of Return

All the models for computing earnings presented above are based on individual earnings. The rate of growth of the average covered wage is a logical choice for indexing benefits up to present values in computing initial capital because it adjusts rights in accordance with actual growth of the average covered wage.

The rate of growth of the average covered wage is only one of the components of the IRR, however. What are the arguments for and against taking other components into account? An important component of the IRR, together with the average wage, is the rate of growth of the covered population. Together, the rate of growth of the average covered wage and the number of covered participants determine the growth of the contribution base, and, hence, the funds available to finance NDC benefits. Figure 9.1 illustrates the development of the contribution base with a per capita (covered) wage growth of 3 percent and a growth/decline in the covered population of 0.3 percent per year, respectively. The latter constitutes a strong, although not entirely unrealistic, "band" around the rate of growth of the real wage rate. With steady growth, the contribution base, and ceteris paribus, the 20-year rate of return is 10 percent higher than the rate that would be ascribed accounts with the earnings models discussed above, and with a decline in the covered population 10 percent lower.

The positive labor force growth scenario suggests that the affordable scale of the scheme is higher than that given by the per capita earnings model. If the NDC scheme had been running from the outset, instead of the DB scheme, ceteris paribus, per capita wage indexation would have generated a system surplus. A difficulty arises, however, with a decline in the labor force. The NDC scheme was not running during this time, however. Instead, there was a DB scheme that at the point of introduction of the NDC scheme cost exactly the amount of the sum of all individual contributions paid at the point of introduction. This suggests that in terms of covering acquired rights in the old DB scheme, which is

Figure 9.1. Contribution Base Growth with Wage Per Capita Growth of 3 Percent and Labor Force Growth/Decline of 0.3 Percent

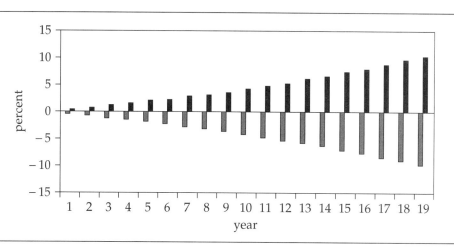

Source: Author's calculations.

the goal of creating initial capital for the NDC scheme, the combination of the actual con-tribution rate at the time of introduction and indexation of historical rights with the aver-age wage index will cover rights acquired in the old scheme up to the point of introduction of the NDC scheme.

Ceteris paribus, use of the average contribution wage to value acquired rights at the point of introduction of the NDC scheme can be viewed as starting the system with one large increment value of first period earnings, given the contribution rate. This means that past earnings are given their current average value. This is also the value of individual ini-tial capital that corresponds to the NDC principle. Whether initial capital computed according to the above formula exactly covers the acquired DB rights depends in practice on the parameters chosen to make the conversion.

Acquired Rights "Revisited" in the Context of Demography

The demographic history of a country is itself an important issue in the implementation of NDC. If the working birth cohorts nearest retirement are larger than younger birth cohorts, then the system is starting with a demographically generated deficit. This is also a tax overhang from the old system, unless a reserve has already been built up in the old sys-tem that covers this overhang. What can be done about this?

In principle, one can conceive of different time profiles for the payment of a tax to finance a demographic overhang. These would affect different generations differently, beginning with the current pensioners and continuing through different generations of current or future workers. Ceteris paribus, the fairest tax model—it could be argued—is to impute the tax and charge it to the "big" cohort of workers, whose total rights have not been funded in advance. After all, this was a generation whose past consumption was "too high" given what they should have paid in the NDC framework to acquire NDC rights. This could be done by reducing their initial capital accordingly.

If there is no historically accumulated reserve and if the tax is not levied specifically on the "big" cohort in the form of lowering their initial capital, then there is an implicit tax accumulated from previous times, the payment of which has to occur in the future. Alternatively, if the NDC system is equipped with an automatic balancing mechanism,[18] then imbalance between system assets and liabilities will eventually occur and cause internal adjustment *within* the NDC pension system. In sum, there is a time—and hence generational—difference associated with different approaches.[19]

Demographic Funding

The conversion of rights from the "old" PAYG DB scheme to NDC account values is a necessary condition for creating an NDC scheme, but it may not be sufficient to fulfill the condition of long-term financial stability. The main reason for this is that NDC also requires that a financial reserve be built up for relatively large cohorts of workers to help finance their pensions. The reserve fund is a practical institution that acts as the system's piggy bank. It ensures that there is "money in the bank" when it is eventually needed to meet the commitments to relatively large cohorts. It also ensures that the "right" generation pays for its own commitments.

A Tax Overhang from the Old System

The unfinanced demographic bubble passed on from the old system is an example of a tax overhang, as has already been discussed. There are others. Two others that typically arise in the DB setting are associated with financing old-age commitments for the disabled and financing survivor benefits. A third tax overhang that can arise is the one created by the need to phase out special privileges.

In the NDB framework, liabilities to future old-age pensioners "presently" covered by disability or survivor benefits are covered by the wages of future workers: that is, those who are in the work force when the disabled and survivors become old-age pensioners. However, survivor benefits should be kept outside the NDC scheme; these benefits are discussed in a separate section below.[20]

A tax overhang will arise with the introduction of NDC if, before the NDC scheme is introduced, there is no financial transfer into the NDC scheme to cover old-age pension rights of persons on disability. This tax overhang is just the overhang that existed anyway and would have to be paid once persons on disability benefits became old-age pensioners. In the new NDC scheme, the old-age pension accounts of the disabled have to be accredited with capital financed by a transfer into the system. The overhang rights earned prior to the introduction of NDC will exist until the old commitments are phased out.

In many countries, various groups of workers have been granted special privileges within the defined benefit context. These must be financed, but as in the case of disability, since they are DB benefits, the intention was not to provide financing until sometime into the future, when benefits were claimed. These will either be phased out or made external, perhaps through occupational arrangements, with the introduction of the NDC scheme. This study returns to survivor, disability, and special benefit rights in the context of transition in a separate section below.

Speed of Conversion, Acquired Rights, and Fairness

The simplest form of transition from a PAYG-DB scheme to an NDC scheme is to start with new entrants into the labor force. The "new entrant model" takes decades until it is fully implemented, however, and for this reason a faster transition will usually be desirable. This section begins with a discussion of the new entrant model and concludes with a more general discussion of the pros and cons of different speeds of transition into NDC.

Conversion Beginning with New Entrants into the Labor Force

If NDC covers only new entrants into the labor market, then no estimate of initial capital is needed. By definition, the rights acquired in the "old system" are preserved, since only new entrants are covered by the new rules. For this reason, at first glance this form of implementation looks fair. Upon further consideration, there are potential drawbacks with this approach, depending on how it is formulated.

For the sake of illustration, assume two identical twins, A and B. Assume also that they both have unit wages over their entire lifetimes, so that their benefits depend only on years of work, *t*, and the benefit rules in the old DB scheme and the new NDC scheme. Assume that the DB rule is such that with 35 years of contributions or more, it gives the same benefit as the lifetime-earnings-based NDC scheme does for a full earnings career from normal entrance age 20. Now assume that twin A enters the labor force at age 29 and twin B at age 30, but after the introduction of NDC with the new entrant rule. Twin A is covered by the DB scheme and twin B is covered by the NDC scheme.

Comparing the two schemes, all other things equal, twin B's benefit will be about 78 percent of twin A's if twin B retires at age 65. This is because in the NDC scheme, the benefit is based on 35 of 45 possible years of contributions from age 20 to age 65, whereas 35 years were sufficient in the DB scheme for a full benefit. This sort of discrepancy will arise as long as the new entrant rule is not set at the first possible age from which pension rights can be acquired. Also, the NDC life expectancy factor may lead to an even greater difference.

What can be said about fairness in this case? If fairness is defined as straightforward adherence to contracts, the results of the above application of the new entrant rule are fair, by definition. Twin A continues to be covered by the contract of the old system, while Twin B is covered by the NDC contract. However, if what we mean by fair is that the size of the benefit should be linked to the contributions, the unfair outcome is a result of the generosity of the DB scheme—not the conversion to the NDC scheme.

In sum, for the new entrant rule to be fair in terms of treating twins equally, it must be implemented so that it applies from the *youngest age* at which pension rights can be earned. This gives the twins the same information and same benefit criteria from the start, and an equal opportunity to take this information into consideration in formulating life plans for work and leisure. In terms of the broader question of fairness, couched in terms of the "contractual right" to tax future birth cohorts of workers embodied in the DB rule, it can be argued that twin B is, in fact, being treated fairly, and the introduction of NDC discontinues the unfair "advantage" of the DB legislation that favors twin A.

Speed of Conversion to NDC: General Considerations

The above example illustrates a more general problem associated with the speed of conversion. To begin with, equality of opportunity requires that the rules of a regime apply to all, whereas the very fact of change means that different agents will have to operate under different rule sets. In this sense, any regime change is unfair, regardless of what it entails—and regardless of whether it happens in an existing NDB scheme or in conversion to NDC. On the other hand, in this discussion, regime change is associated with a move from a regime that passes a tax forward to future generations of workers, which can be considered unfair to a regime that does not.

In terms of the twins' example above, generations covered by the NDC scheme will not be creating and passing on new taxes, whereas as long as the DB scheme operates, a tax is created. One can argue that the higher the tax in the old regime, the more unjustifiable the redistribution of individual resources is under the old system and the more important it is for the conversion to occur and to be speedy.

In sum, a slow transition prolongs the life of a tax that itself may be considered unfair to pass on to future workers, and an immediate transition puts an end to the creation of unfinanced rights—or identifies a tax source to pay for these. On the other hand, the introduction of NDC will be accompanied by a redistribution of pension rights, given the replaced DB scheme as the counterfactual. The further from the contribution principle the DB scheme is, the greater this redistribution is likely to be.

Speed of Conversion and the Replacement Rate

IMMEDIATE TRANSITION

An immediate transition has the advantage of breaking clearly with the past and marking the beginning of a new system. It reduces the potential prolongation of the "twin effect" discussed above, while making it possible to reap the advantages of NDC from the outset. However, the distribution of rights will change. An immediate transition is likely to emphasize this otherwise generic NDC effect compared with the DB counterfactual. The dimension of the effect will depend on the "distance" between the NDC and counterfactual scheme.

GRADUAL TRANSITION

A gradual transition can take one of several forms. One form would be to introduce an immediate conversion, but beginning with a birth cohort that at the time of implementation is x years from the normal (minimum) retirement age. However, if the overall effect of the transition on older cohorts is expected to be small, there is really no reason to wait to begin to compute benefits according to the new rules. In fact, waiting may simply lead to a pronounced difference between the two future birth cohorts retiring immediately before and the other after the date set for the conversion.

The larger the expected immediate change in individual outcomes due to the introduction of NDC, the more justifiable it may be to construct a gradual conversion. This suggests another form of gradual transition, which takes a weighted average of a benefit computed according to the old and new rules for a "transition generation."[21]

The advantage of a "long" gradual transition is that it reduces the effect on "losers": generally speaking, persons with shorter working careers inherited from the NDB regime.[22] Of course, it also reduces the potential positive effect for "winners": persons with long contribution careers. Nevertheless, the gradual transition inadequately addresses the most justifiable reason for having a long transition: the fact that in terms of giving people equal opportunities, the transition should cover workers beginning with the first age at which pension rights can be earned, as discussed above. The disadvantage of the "long" transition is the fact that it *is* long, and prolongs the period during which the old system creates a tax to be passed on to future generations—and generates unjustifiable financial costs. In sum, the arguments for a fast transition appear, on balance, to outweigh the arguments against it.

Country Examples

The implementation of NDC introduces at least two sets of problems. The first is the decision of how to deal with acquired rights under the old regime, which has thus far been the topic of this chapter. The second is how to phase in the NDC scheme smoothly, given that at the outset the entire collective of existing pensioners is still subject to the rules of the old system. The rate of return on NDC annuities is especially problematic in practice, since the method of indexation applied in the scheme being replaced may not coincide with what is desirable within the framework of NDC, whereas a good policy can be considered to give both old system and new system pensioners the same rate of indexation of pension benefits. A third design issue has to do with special rights. These issues are discussed below, drawing on the experiences of countries that introduced NDC in the 1990s as illustrations of possible approaches. Tables 9.2 and 9.3 provide a summary overview of how countries have dealt with various issues.

Acquired Rights and Transition

Table 9.2 provides an overview of how the five countries that introduced NDC in the 1990s dealt with the issue of acquired rights. Two of the countries, Poland and Sweden, created initial capital and converted relatively rapidly, while one country, Latvia, created initial capital and converted immediately to NDC. Two other countries, Italy and the Kyrgyz Republic, have not created initial capital and have chosen a slow pace of transition. These groups are discussed separately.

COUNTRIES THAT DID NOT CONVERT ACQUIRED RIGHTS INTO INITIAL NDC CAPITAL

Both the Kyrgyz Republic and Italy have pro rata models to combine rights in the old and new regimes. For this reason, transition into full NDC is much longer in Italy and the Kyrgyz Republic than in the other three countries. In the Kyrgyz Republic, everyone has had an NDC account based on contributions made since 1996—but not for previous years. In Italy, persons with fewer than 18 years of coverage before 1996 are covered by NDC; persons with 18 or more years are not. Notional accounts were first established in 1996.

Italy. The Italian reform breaks with the NDC principle in that both employees and the self-employed are accredited with capital based on a contribution rate that is higher than

Table 9.2. Transition Models for Initial Capital and Introduction of NDC

Calculation of initial capital				
Country	Earnings (W^{IC})	Rate of return (β)	Contribution rate (c^{IC})	Transition model
Italy	No initial capital. The conditions of the pre-NDC DB formula were tightened in 1992. With the introduction of NDC, persons with 18 or more years of contributions in 1995 remained in the old system, with the benefit rule prior to 1992.	—	—	Persons with fewer than 18 years of contributions in 1995 receive a benefit based on a pro rata formula, combining the old and new schemes. New entrants covered only by NDC.
Kyrgyz Republic	No initial capital. Total benefit during the transition to full NDC: Benefit = DB transition benefit (based on service years – max 30 prior to 1996 and best yearly earnings in 1991–95) + NDC (based on earnings from 1996) + universal flat rate (12% of average wage).	—	—	Earnings 1996 and after are covered for the *entire population.*

Table 9.2. (continued)

Calculation of initial capital				
Country	Earnings (W^{IC})	Rate of return (β)	Contribution rate (c^{IC})	Transition model
Latvia	Initial capital calculated as recorded service years *and* for persons retiring in 1996: average wage of the covered population 1995 1997: the individual's wage in 1996 if over the average for all individuals in 1996, or guarantee 1998: the average of individual's wage 1996–97 if more than the average for all individuals, or guarantee 1999: the average of individual's wages 1996–98 if over the average for all individuals, or guarantee. *Guarantee wage for initial capital 1997–99*: If 30+ covered years, the overall average wage for the covered population in the relevant period. 2000–200X: the average of the individual's covered wage 1996–99, or 40% of average of all covered wages for all years from 1996 up to the year a pension claim is made. From 200X, straightforward rules (X is still to be determined).	Average covered earnings	20%	Initial capital is calculated for *all workers* claiming a benefit in 1996 or after. Generally, this means NDC capital is calculated for women born 1940 and later and men born 1936 and later (given the pension age in 1996 of 56 for women and 60 for men).
Poland	Initial capital = present capital value of acquired rights from the old system calculated as of December 31, 1998, the day before implementation of the new scheme on January 1, 1999. New rights are based on a contribution rate of 12.22%.	—	—	NDC applies to all employees and non-agricultural self-employed workers born 1949 and after.
Sweden	Initial capital based on individual earnings histories from 1960, for everyone born 1938 and after. Contribution rate of 18.5% through 1994; 16.5% for 1995–97; and 16% beginning 1998.	Average covered earnings	18.5% for earnings through 1995.	Persons born 1938: 4/20 of benefit with new and 16/20 with old rules, etc. Persons born 1954 + later, full NDC.

Source: Author's compilations.

Note: — denotes that initial capital was not computed in the introduction of NDC.

the one they actually pay (table 9.2). This means the system is creating liabilities that are not covered by contemporary assets. Thus, as it is currently set up, the system can not become internally self-financing, even after persons with pre-1992 benefits have left the scene. Instead, a tax has been created for payment in the future. In addition, using GDP for the rate of return is only an approximation of the IRR that the scheme can pay. There is no mechanism that ensures that assets are at least as great as liabilities, the way there is in Sweden.

In Italy, pension payments were about 16 percent of GDP in 1999 and are likely to rise to around 17.5 percent of GDP by 2015.[23] These figures are high by international standards. The Italian NDC scheme appears to stabilize outlays in the coming half century, but at a high level. Italy's slow transition into NDC is a prime reason for this. The slow transition means that a large percentage of the labor force around 2000 will retire with non-NDC benefits. For example, Franco (2002) notes that about 40 percent of the labor force in 2000 will retire with benefits calculated according to the pre-1992 pension formula. In addition, the pronounced difference in treatment of persons who in 1992 and 1995 had small differences in contributory records raises a question of equity. This concern is consistent with the analysis presented in the first half of this study. What's more, Franco concludes that the length of the transition period and other aspects of the reform may significantly reduce its microeconomic effects.

The Kyrgyz Republic. The Kyrgyz Republic's scheme is for new entrants and is incompletely designed, especially regarding the rate of return used. With the slow transition, it will take until 2039 before the first person retires with a benefit based on the NDC formula, given entry at age 21 in 1997 and retirement at age 63. It will take until around 2060 for the entire population to be covered by NDC. With only partial wage indexation of notional capital accounts, replacement rates will decline. Furthermore, benefits are to be indexed ad hoc. There is no legislated rule for indexation. With only sporadic indexation of benefits, the share of pensions in GDP is likely to decline from an already low level of just over 4 percent.[24] In sum, the Kyrgyz NDC reform will take a half century to emerge, and more work is required to bring it closer to true NDC, where the rate of return is a crucial parameter to design correctly.

COUNTRIES THAT CONVERTED ACQUIRED RIGHTS INTO INITIAL CAPITAL

The slow-transition models of Italy and the Krygyz Republic can be contrasted with the conversion in Latvia, wherein January 1996 the NDC rules *completely* replaced rights acquired in the existing DB scheme for the entire work force at that time. In Sweden, with a slower rate of transition, all newly granted benefits are based 100 percent on NDC from 2017, and over 50 percent determined by NDC from 2007 (with an assumed retirement age of 63).

The models chosen for the three countries converting acquired rights into initial capital are very different. Sweden based initial capital on earnings histories from 1960. Latvia and Poland had service books from the pre-1991 regimes with good records of years of service (including "non-contributory" periods); however, these did not provide any useable information on earnings. Hence, Latvia and Poland had to devise rules accommodating this reality to compute initial capital.

Sweden. Sweden had computerized records of earnings from 1960. These were used to create notional accounts from earnings histories, using a contribution rate close to the one required to pay old-age commitments in the DB system that was being replaced at the time of reform.[25] In computing initial capital, Sweden used an index based on the covered wage per capita to create account values, and a contribution rate of 18.5 percent applied for historical accounts from 1960 though 1994. The Swedish reform also encompassed the introduction of a mandatory financial account (FDC) scheme, with contributions set aside for this in 1995. The contribution rate to the FDC scheme was increased to 2 percent and then 2.5 percent, and the NDC rate was the difference between the total mandatory rate of 18.5 percent and the amount set off for the FDC scheme. The long-run NDC contribution is 16 percent. Sweden also increased the minimum pension age from 60 to 61, but most workers wait longer in practice to claim an old-age benefit. Under the old system, people viewed 65 as the normal pension age, owing to a considerable reduction in a benefit claimed early from both the public scheme and occupational supplements.[26]

Latvia. Initial capital in Latvia is computed according to the general formula: IC = individual covered earnings × individual service years × 0.20. The latter is the contribution rate used to compute both initial capital and capital from 1996 with the implementation of the NDC scheme. This rate was lower than the contribution rate needed to cover actual old-age pension payments at the time, and was set so consciously to bring down the level of commitments.

Earnings in the formula for initial capital are determined by the product of recorded service years and an individual-based covered wage. The original rule used to determine the individual's covered wage was: the average covered wage for *all* participants in 1995 for persons retiring in 1996; the individual's own average covered wage in 1996 for retirees in 1997; the individual's own average covered wage in 1996–97 for retirees in 1998; the individual's own average covered wage in 1996–98 for retirees in 1999; and the individual's average covered wage in 1996–99 for persons claiming a benefit in 2000 and later.

The choice to use the individual's *own* wage after 1995 as the basis for conversion of pre-reform service years to initial capital was aimed at creating a strong incentive to report income—and penalize evasion.[27] This method had its drawbacks, however, as is discussed extensively in Palmer et al. (2006). Briefly, the timing and length of the period used to compute this wage proved to be a problem for persons who genuinely had a poor footing in the labor market in the 1990s.[28] For this reason, a transition guarantee and additional transitional rules were adopted for computing initial capital. These were adopted in parliament in 1996 and will be in force through 2010.

The Latvian transition-guarantee rule applies to persons with at least 30 years of service (or who were registered as unemployed during 1996–99). According to the guarantee, initial capital is based on the best of either the individual's earnings according to the main law, or an amount based on the average wage for all participants in the years 1996–99.[29] For all others, initial capital is computed as the best of either the computation using the individual's own earnings or an amount based on 40 percent of the average covered wage, which is approximately the level of the minimum wage. Hence, in practice, the *minimum* guaranteed amount of initial capital based on service years prior to 1996 is that which corresponds to the minimum wage. As time passes, the importance of initial capital will decline. Total notional capital will depend more and more on actual individual earnings and contributions, and less on pre-1996 service years and the transition rule.

Latvia also increased the minimum pension age (gradually) from 55 for women and 60 for men to 62 for men in 2003 and for women in 2008.

Poland. Poland chose to compute the capital value of commitments earned under the old scheme "as if" these were to be paid out on December 31, 1998, and used these values for initial capital.[30] However, initial capital is calculated to deliver the same pension benefit as the old system formula (adjusted for age and contribution years), if everyone had retired December 31, 1998. The contribution rate used is 24 percent, which was approximately the cost of old-age pensions at the time of the reform.

Poland chose this path for three reasons.[31] First, no individual contribution or earnings data were available. Second, recalculating the accrued rights to the initial capital allows smoothing the transition. Third, this procedure provided no incentives or disincentives in the choice given workers between participation solely in the NDC scheme or both the NDC and FDC schemes in the new system, as workers received exactly the same pension rights for past years, regardless of their choice.[32]

The Rate of Return

In principle, the NDC rate of return is the rate of return that equates system assets with system liabilities over the long run. Assets grow with the growth of the contribution base. The valuation of assets will depend, in addition, on changes in the income and mortality patterns of the working population, because these—together with the money-weighted length of the payout period—determine the duration of time a unit of money is in the system, called the *turnover time*.[33] The contribution base changes with the rates of growth in the covered per capita wage and the number of covered persons. Note that system reserve funds (for example arising due to demographic swings or transfers from the state budget for noncontributory rights) are also system assets. The IRR embodies all these components.

Sweden uses the per capita wage as the rate of return for notional capital and annuities. This means that if one of the other factors determining the value of assets (for example, the rate of growth of the covered population, the turnover duration as determined by changes in earnings and mortality patterns, or the return on the reserve fund) or liabilities (poor life expectancy projection) causes the present value of liabilities to surpass the present value of liabilities, then the automatic balancing mechanism is triggered—and the rate of return is decreased—until balance is restored. Likewise, if the ratio of the present value of assets to liabilities surpasses a threshold value, there will be grounds to distribute the "surplus" in the system. In this sense, the Swedish NDC scheme can be said to resemble a traditional financial insurance scheme.

Participants in the Swedish NDC scheme receive a rate of return on accounts determined by the nominal covered wage per participant, possibly adjusted downward for "negative" balancing, or upward for "positive" balancing. Negative balancing arises when the value of system assets is less than the value of liabilities at the end of an accounting period, and—in principle—the opposite occurs when a surplus is large enough to be distributed, according to a rule. The Swedish NDC annuity is calculated from the outset with an expected rate of wage growth of 1.6 percent, called the *norm*. Indexation of an annuity includes the rate of inflation plus or minus the difference between the outcome for wage growth and the norm. Hence, the annuity is indexed solely to inflation if growth follows the norm and if system assets are greater than liabilities—but under the level justifying the distribution of a surplus. Even the benefits of persons who retired under the *old rules* are adjusted with deviations from the norm, in order to give both old-system and NDC pensions the same indexation.

The use of the norm made it possible to grant a higher initial annuity, but at the expense of a declining relation between a fixed real-valued annuity in relation to the average wage of contributors. This is equivalent to the result obtained when a defined benefit is price indexed, all other things equal. The alternative to this procedure would have been straightforward wage indexation, but from a lower initial annuity value.

Italy's scheme also embodies a norm in the calculation of the annuity,[34] using a value of 1.5 percent, and based on the growth of GDP. GDP growth is a proxy for the growth of the system's contribution base and using GDP growth implies an assumption of a fixed ratio of the wage sum (and, hence, profits) to GDP. It also implies that the GDP measure of the wage sum is a sufficient measure of covered earnings, which in economies with a large degree of informality will not be the case.

System design in the other original NDC countries—the Kyrgyz Republic, Latvia, and Poland—differ from the Swedish model in various ways. First, for example, notional capital in Latvia earns a rate of return determined by the rate of growth of contribution wages (contributions), while Poland uses 75 percent of contribution wages and the Kyrgyz Republic 75 percent of the average covered wage. The lower-than-100-percent rates of return have been set purposely by politicians to hold down pension costs.[35] An alternative would have been to set a lower contribution rate for notional capital, which would have established a lower scale for the scheme—instead of "taxing" the return—by setting indexation below 100 percent. The latter yields unnecessarily low pensions, for example, compared with a financial scheme where there is no such tax. Clearly, a tax of this nature will undermine support for the NDC scheme.

Second, none of these countries has full wage (or wage sum) indexation of *benefits* because at the point of conversion to NDC, practically all benefits were determined by the previous DB scheme, and were price indexed. No country has found it plausible to give price indexation to one group of pensioners and wage indexation to another. For this reason, wage indexation is also a transition issue. A country can afford to do this as the NDC scheme increases its share in total benefit payments.

Third, if, ceteris paribus, the growth path of the labor force—and covered participants—is negative, a need for "negative" balancing will accompany the decline if indexation is based on the covered per capita wage rather than the development of the contribution wage sum, that is, the combined effect of the development of the per capita labor force. In this respect, the effect of balancing will be the same as applying a wage sum index, all other things equal. All other things are not equal, however, and in practice balancing will depend also on other factors affecting the value of system assets and liabilities in the accounting period, such as the value of a reserve fund. Furthermore, the balancing mechanism designed for Sweden requires sophisticated data, which are still not available in countries like Latvia, the Kyrgyz Republic, or Poland. Perhaps when data are available, these countries will choose to convert to this more sophisticated procedure.

Finally, none of the other countries had the large-scale reserve fund that Sweden had at the point of introduction of NDC. This means that if negative labor force growth is likely from the time of introduction,[36] the scales are tipped in the direction of continuous negative balancing due to the effect of negative labor force growth on the contribution base—and hence contribution assets. Wage-sum indexation of notional capital performs this balancing function in practice in Latvia and Poland, although both countries have chosen not to apply this indexation mechanism to pensions.

Special Rights

In principle, special rights, if they exist, need external financing. Special rights can even occur in the NDC system, but they require external financing to maintain the financial stability of the system. Special rights will be tax-financed either over the budget, or by necessitating a higher contribution rate than that accredited to accounts. Italy is a special case. It introduced *unfinanced* special rights (see column one of table 9.3) when it introduced NDC. These will create taxes on future workers.

Table 9.3. Other Transition Issues

Country	Occurrence of "unfinanced" special rights	Rate of return on notional capital	Rate of return on annuities	Reserve fund
Italy	The contribution rate for employees is 32%, but 33% is used to calculate account values; for the self-employed, the contribution rate is 15%, but 20% is used to calculate account values.	GDP index	GDP index	No
Kyrgyz Republic	Special rights from the old regime were reduced by about 70% in legislation from 1997.	75% of wage growth	Indexation by ad hoc political decision	No
Latvia	Account values for persons with special rights under the old regime are adjusted according to specific formulas, and all special rights are phased out under the new NDC law. Beginning in 2003, "special rights increments" are financed from general state budget revenues.	Covered wage sum	Inflation adjustment 1996–2002, and inflation adjustment plus 25% of the real wage sum from 2002, and 50% real wage sum from 2011	Not at time of implementation, but reserves are projected to turn positive from ~2005
Poland	Farmers are excluded from the NDC scheme, but are covered by a separate scheme, approximately 95% subsidized by general tax revenues. Bridging pensions were created for persons with special rights, and are financed with state budget revenues.	75% of the covered wage sum	Inflation adjustment plus at least 20% of real wage growth, the latter by ad hoc political decision	A contribution rate was earmarked to build up reserves, but general budget deficits have thus far prohibited this in practice
Sweden	No special rights in either the old or new NDC scheme.	Covered contributions per participant + automatic balancing	Covered contributions per participant + automatic balancing	Large reserve fund from the outset

Source: Author's compilations.

Reserve Funds and Other Considerations

As already noted, Sweden is the only country introducing NDC that came into the transition with a reserve fund. This fund is especially important for demographic reasons, for, among other things, the large birth cohorts from the 1940s will retire around 2010–15, using some of the reserves. Sweden had a reserve fund in the old PAYG scheme that was sufficient at the time of transition to pay approximately three years of current benefit payments (even after transferring about 40 percent of the fund to the general budget as a part of the conversion from the old to the new regime). The eventual demographic overhang from the old system is a part of the overall liability of the PAYG scheme, encompassing old and new NDC benefits, while the inherited fund is a part of the overall assets.

Italy has no reserves, and current calculations show that, instead, the contribution rate will have to be increased (see the discussion above) to cover increased benefit outlays. The Kyrgyz Republic should develop reserves in the next decade, given that it has no pension indexation rule and the minimum pension age progressively increases to 63. On the other hand, these reserves will increase the scope for better indexation of and all PAYG benefits, including gradually rising NDC benefits, continuing the transition process. Poland introduced an earmarked contribution rate to contribute to the accumulation of a reserve fund. Because a large deficit in the state budget arose from around the time the NDC scheme was introduced, to date, the government has not allowed these reserves to develop.

Latvia will develop positive reserves in the overall PAYG system from around 2005, calculations indicate.[37] These will be needed around 35 years later to finance the Latvian baby boomers, born around the late 1980s.

Latvia also introduced a mandatory financial account scheme in 2002, with a contribution rate of 2 percent in 2002–6, decreasing the contribution rate for the NDC scheme to 18 percent.[38] A further exchange of up to 10 percent each for the NDC and FDC schemes is scheduled in the legislation. All other things equal, since many workers have notional capital based on a rate of 20 percent, this decease in the NDC contribution will create a financial deficit that has to be tax-financed. However, calculations show that because of the increase in the minimum pension age for women from 55 and for men from 60 to 62, considerable room is created for introducing the mandatory financial scheme[39] without creating a serious transitional financial deficit. Whether a serious financial deficit arises depends on the scale of the FDC scheme together with the degree of indexation of NDC benefits. A contribution rate to the mandatory financial scheme that surpasses 6–7 percent creates a tax on the transition generation that increases with the scale of the FDC scheme,[40] whereas a lower contribution rate to the FDC scheme leaves more room for eventually increasing the scale of wage indexation in the direction of 100 percent, and finishing the NDC transition in this respect.

Other Important Issues in the Overall Conversion to NDC

Disability Benefits

In the DB framework replaced by NDC, the old-age commitments to recipients of disability benefits are paid by workers when the disabled have reached and have passed the age of retirement. In this context, costs associated with today's decisions to grant disability benefits carry a commitment to pay benefits in old age. NDC does not work this way. Instead, what is consistent with the NDC framework is the idea that contributions should be paid into the old-age scheme to finance disability benefits on a current account basis. In principle, this means money should be transferred to NDC accounts to cover the old-age pension rights of recipients of disability benefits on a regular—for example yearly—basis.

Two models of dealing with disabled persons have been employed in countries converting to NDC. One has been for the disability system to make contributions (through state general revenues) to the accounts of disabled persons, based on imputed earnings during the time of disability. The other is to base the transfer to the accounts of the disabled persons on some general rule applied to all, without taking individual foregone earnings careers into account. The first is more in line with the insurance idea, and has been applied in Sweden, for example.

A related issue is whether the disability recipient should be allowed to continue to receive a disability benefit on a lifelong basis, to receive the best of either the disability or old-age benefit, or should be restricted to taking the old-age benefit from a specific age. Different models are currently employed in different countries.

If people are allowed to keep the best of a disability benefit or an old-age benefit based on notional capital accounts, in principle, there should be financial transfers arranged from the disability to the old-age scheme(s). If the disability benefit is higher than the old-age benefit, and the claimant is allowed to retain the higher of the two, this is equivalent to granting a special right and the extra amount should be financed by a transfer from the disability scheme into the old-age scheme(s).

A third issue involves the timing of the conversion from disability to an old-age benefit. In principle, this should be at the minimum age to claim an old-age benefit. This is the case in Latvia, for example, but not in Sweden. In Sweden, the conversion occurs at age 65. This means that it is normally to the advantage of individuals to be on disability before they turn 65, rather than to claim an actuarially fair old-age benefit from age 61.

Survivor Benefits

The death of workers in an NDC scheme leaves an "inheritance gain": that is, an undistributed amount of money. This can be distributed to surviving workers in the old-age scheme, on a birth cohort basis and at the minimum age for claiming a benefit. This creates a better benefit for all who survive to the age of retirement. The alternative is to use this surplus for some other purpose. One example would be a benefit for a surviving caregiver with children. Another example would be to create a traditional survivor benefit.

There is a question of principle regarding creating a survivor benefit along traditional lines, however. A survivor benefit for a spouse (not caring for children) puts single persons and couples on different statuses and, more generally, can be argued to be inappropriate in a county where the goal is gender equality. A surviving spouse if working is no different from any single person working, and a surviving spouse not working is, in principle, no different than any other person who is not working. For this reason, it is not clear why a working surviving spouse should receive the inheritance gain, rather than the whole collective of working participants in the pension scheme. One might argue for some form of short-term adjustment benefit to help make the transition from married to single—although even here, the problem is hardly different from that arising in a divorce. Generally speaking, one can only argue that is justifiable to compensate time spent at home caring for younger children. This time can be compensated for using noncontributory childcare rights. Any other financial support provided to survivors with children should be arranged outside the pension system.

In sum, it is difficult to argue for a traditional survivor benefit where gender equality is an explicit goal. The traditional spouse benefit for working-age persons is from a time when women were not expected to participate in market work. Finally, it is also difficult to find a fair rule for splitting NDC accounts between spouses. If the argument against a general (traditional) survivor benefit is accepted, then what remains is to calculate acquired rights for survivors under the old regime and to phase out this benefit. Of course, the alternative of creating a traditional survivor benefit using the inheritance gains will always be a possible choice for a country that does not accept the above argument.

Final Remarks

This study has examined issues occurring in the transition to NDC. A major conclusion is that Sweden is an outlier in the process of conversion to NDC, and because of this has been able to fulfill all conditions for NDC. Perhaps the most advantageous feature of the pre-reform landscape was the existence of a large reserve fund. The Swedish reform also had the advantage of a relatively fast and total transition to NDC. As opposed to Sweden, Italy has moved forward in a piecemeal fashion, and because of this, discussion about reform is an ongoing feature of the political landscape.

As in Sweden, the reforms in Latvia and Poland have been overall reforms, although transition issues remain concerning the formulation of the rate of return and the creation of reserves. This is not the result of oversight, but a function of the realities of transition, some political and some due to circumstances. The most important restriction on the rate of return on annuities in the NDC scheme is the indexation formula for current pensioners, whose pensions were granted according to the old regime. However, it is possible to achieve a better return as the NDC scheme grows.

The introduction of NDC in the Kyrgyz Republic is in a nascent phase. It will be so for some time to come because it only applies to earnings from 1996. By contrast, Latvia, Poland, and Sweden began by computing values of initial capital for current workers. Nevertheless, the model employed in the Kyrgyz Republic is one of many possible models of introducing NDC. That said, it is important to point out that the Kyrgyz model needs further development if participants are to receive a good replacement rate. Even Poland's NDC scheme is suffering from the decision to give notional accounts 75 percent rather than 100 percent of a possible rate of return: that is, the decision to "tax" accounts.

These experiences show that it is important to set the NDC framework—the contribution rate and rate of return—so that the resultant income replacement rate is reasonable, given other mandatory schemes. For example, Latvia, Poland, and Sweden have all introduced mandatory financial account schemes to supplement NDC. It is the overall package—the expected replacement rate from the mandatory schemes, including the variation in rates of return—that is important. Finally, even the room left above the ceiling in the mandatory scheme will determine the room left for development of individual, private coverage. In sum, in system design it is important to leave room for private initiative, while at the same time satisfying a need to provide good mandatory coverage for the average wage earner.

Notes

1. See Palmer (2006), for a more thorough definition of an NDC scheme.

2. This study employs the terminology developed in Góra and Palmer (2004) to distinguish between financial and non-financial schemes, depending on whether they are financed through purchases of financial market assets or through the future contributions of workers, and are defined benefit as opposed to defined contribution schemes. This leads to four possible schemes: Financial defined contribution (FDC), which in much of the literature is loosely called "individual account" or "privatized" schemes; non-financial defined contribution schemes (NDC); financial defined benefit schemes (FDB); and non-financial defined benefit schemes (NDB), loosely called "public" schemes or pay-as-you-go schemes. The point of this dichotomy is to focus on the importance of distinguishing clearly between NDC and NDB as two forms of *non-financial* schemes, with very different economic logic, and between FDC and FDB as two forms of *financial* schemes, with potentially very different contractual logic.

3. See Felderer, Koman, and Schuh (2006) for Austria; Chłoń-Domińczak and Móra (2006) for the Czech Republic; Börsch-Supan and Wilke (2006) for Germany; Domínguez-Fabián and Vidal-Meliá (2006), and Takayama (2006) for Japan. Also, in 2002, Russia introduced a version of NDC.

4. As is also generally recognized, NDC is still, however, only second best in terms of economic efficiency.

5. The same discounting factor applies to both a traditional PAYG-DB and an NDC scheme, so that in a comparison, this factor can be disregarded.

6. The IRR is the rate of return the system can afford, given the present value of contributions and benefit liabilities. This concept will be elaborated on in the context of conversion below.

7. Account values and benefits can be viewed as arising in a steady state world with or without technical growth. In the latter case, accounts and benefits are indexed with average wage growth. An alternative assumption that would yield the results in table 9.1 is that of a point system, where each year individuals get accredited with a point that is the ratio of their own covered wage to the average covered wage. Individuals earn the average wage and account values are valued at retirement by the average wage of all contributing participants at the time the valuation is made. Benefits continue to be indexed by the average covered wage. If the size and composition of the labor force are unchanged, financial balance "simply" requires forever increasing the contribution rate in line with what is required to finance the system with increasing life expectancy.

8. An obvious "fix" for this DB scheme would be to introduce a life expectancy indexation of the full benefit pension age. This would bring it closer to the NDC scheme. To exactly create NDC from this scheme, one will still have to go to *lifetime* accounts, together with an annuity based on life expectancy at retirement and indexation with the internal rate of return.

Demographers and actuaries have notoriously underestimated the future development of life expectancy in their projections.

10. The full benefit equals 0.5 times the unit wage and is paid out over 21 years of retirement: that is, $B1 = 0.5 \times (0.5 \times 1 \times 21) = 5.25$.

11. That is, $B1^* = 0.5 \times (0.5 \times 1 \times 19) = 4.75$.

12. The next section of this chapter deals with the more complicated question of indexation of past rights. The more general framework of NDC is important in this context.

13. This would be exactly what the accounts in a point system indexed to the growth of the contribution wage would yield. The difference between the NDC and point system, given that the point system also employs cohort employees life expectancy at retirement to calculate the life annuity, would then rest upon whether (how) the macro financial condition—that system assets should be at least as great as system liabilities for a given contribution rate—is fulfilled in the point system.

14. Note that there is an opportunity for policy makers to use the tax implicit in the DB scheme for another purpose, for example, to retarget resources to needy elderly instead of providing a general "longevity dividend" for everyone.

15. This is the model employed in Sweden and is discussed below in the section on what countries have done.

16. Workbooks with recorded service years were kept in the former Soviet Union and Central and Eastern Europe transition countries prior to the fall of communism and the emergence of independent states.

17. This is the approach adopted by Latvia in 1996. Exactly how this approach was designed and the pros and cons of applying it are discussed at length in Palmer et al. (2006).

18. Readers not familiar with this concept are referred to Settergren (2003), Settergren and Mikula (2006) or Palmer (2006) to understand its construction and role in the NDC framework. Basically, given an estimate of system assets, A, and liabilities, L, it adjusts

account values automatically when assets fall short of liabilities and can be used to increase liabilities (indexation) when assets are greater than liabilities.

19. For the big cohort the question is whether they should bear the whole burden through a reduction in initial capital, or share the burden when they become older and retire with younger generations of workers.

20. There is a separate issue as to whether notional accounts could (should) be split between spouses. In considering this issue, one has to consider whether it should be mandatory or voluntary: if it is voluntary (with both parties agreeing), at what point a decision has to be made (at the time of marriage, declared cohabitation, or another time, and whether a decision can be reversible), and what the consequences are at separation prior to retirement due to death or divorce. Many problems arise, and to date, no country has legislated a mechanism for sharing accounts.

21. See the example of Sweden below.

22. Note, however, that countries introducing NDC systems have created special rights for parents (mothers) for years of child care immediately following childbirth, which are financed externally.

23. See Franco (2002).

24. Based on data from IMF (2003) and the Kyrgyz Pension Fund.

25. Childcare credits were almost exclusively accredited mothers and were also imputed retroactively on the basis of historical records.

26. This is the age at which a full occupational supplement to the old DB scheme applied. Following the reform of the public system, the majority of occupational schemes have also converted to defined contribution, but claiming a benefit before age 65 gives a much poorer outcome. In addition, the minimum guarantee can be claimed first at age 65, which has the effect of keeping healthy low-income workers in the labor force until this age.

27. An alternative, the use of the overall average wage for all contributors, would have favored low-income earners and penalized high-income earners. In this sense, it would also have been unfair. Unfortunately, some people were in a position to gain from these transition rules by negotiating with their employers to declare higher wages during this short period.

28. See Vanovska (2004).

29. Note, however, that this guarantee also covers persons who consciously evaded making full contribution payments. This is an inadvertent consequence of having such a rule.

30. See Chłoń-Domińczak and Góra (2006) for a more in-depth discussion.

31. See Chłoń-Domińczak and Góra (2006).

32. This can be compared with the reform in Hungary, where people traded rights in the old system to participate in the new financial account system.

33. See Settergren and Mikula (2006).

34. See Gronchi and Nisticó (2006).

35. See Chłoń-Domińczak (2002) for the experience in Poland.

36. The Kyrgyz Republic had a period fertility rate 2.1 or higher in the 1990s. However, there is a net outflow of workers to Russia and other neighboring countries, according to national statistics. Latvia's fertility rate is expected to remain well below 2.1 per woman over the coming half century, combined with a net outflow of working age persons (Latvian Ministry of Welfare 2003).

37. See Palmer et al. (2006).

38. The financial account scheme is mandatory for persons under 30 years of age July 1, 2002 and is voluntary for others up to 50 years of age in 2002. Participation was relatively

small at the outset because of little voluntary interest. The contribution rate to the financial account (FDC) scheme is scheduled to increase again in 2007 to 4 percent, and possibly up to 10 percent thereafter.

39. See Latvian Ministry of Welfare (2003) and Palmer et al. (2006).

40. See Latvian Ministry of Welfare (2003).

References

Börsch-Supan, A. and C. B.Wilke. 2006. "The German Public Pension System: How It Will Become an NDC Look-Alike." In *Pension Reform: Issues and Prospects for Non-Financial Defined Contribution (NDC) Schemes*, ed. R. Holzmann and E. Palmer, chapter 22. Washington, DC: World Bank.

Chłoń-Domińczak, A. 2002. "The Polish Pension Reform of 1999." In *Pension Reform in Central and Eastern Europe* Volume 1, ed. E. Fultz. Budapest: International Labour Organisation (ILO).

Chłoń-Domińczak, A., and M. Góra. 2006. "The NDC System in Poland: Assessment after Five Years." In *Pension Reform: Issues and Prospects for Non-Financial Defined Contribution (NDC) Schemes*, ed. R. Holzmann and E. Palmer, chapter 16. Washington, DC: World Bank.

Chłoń, A., M. Góra, and M. Rutkowski. 1999. "Shaping Pension Reform in Poland: Security Through Diversity." Social Protection Discussion Paper 9923. World Bank, Washington, DC.

Chłoń-Domińczak, A., and M. Mora. 2006. "The NDC Reform in the Czech Republic." In *Pension Reform: Issues and Prospects for Non-Financial Defined Contribution (NDC) Schemes*, ed. R. Holzmann and E. Palmer, chapter 21. Washington, DC: World Bank.

Domínguez-Fabián, I. and C. Vidal-Meliá. 2005. "The Spanish Pension System: Issues of Introducing NDCs." In *Pension Reform: Issues and Prospects for Non-Defined Contribution (NDC) Schemes*, eds. R. Holzmann and E. Palmer, chapter 23. Washington, DC: World Bank.

Felderer, B., R. Koman, and U. Schuh. 2006. "Investigating the Introduction of NDCs in Austria." In *Pension Reform: Issues and Prospects for Non-Financial Defined Contribution (NDC) Schemes*, ed. R. Holzmann and E. Palmer, chapter 20. Washington, DC: World Bank.

Franco, D. 2002. "Italy: A Never-Ending Pension Reform." In *Social Security Pension Reform in Europe,* ed. Martin Feldstein and Horst Siebert. Chicago: University of Chicago Press.

Góra, M., and E. Palmer. 2004. "Shifting Perspectives in Pensions." Institute for Study of Labor (IZA) Discussion Paper 1369. Bonn, Germany.

Gronchi, S. and S. Nisticò. 2006. "Implementing the NDC Theoretical Model: A Comparison of Italy and Sweden." In *Pension Reform: Issues and Prospects for Non-Financial Defined Contribution (NDC) Schemes*, ed. R. Holzmann and E. Palmer, chapter 19. Washington, DC: World Bank.

IMF (International Monetary Fund). 2003. *Kyrgyz Repubic: Selected Issues and Statistical Appendix.* IMF Country Report No. 03/53. IMF, Washington, DC.

Kotlikoff, L. J. 2004. "Generational Policy." In *The Handbook of Public Economics*, Second Edition, ed. Alan J Auerbach and Martin S. Feldstein. Amsterdam: North Holland.

Latvian Ministry of Welfare. 2003. *The State Social Insurance System in Latvia, Financial Analysis 2002–2070*. Riga: Latvian Ministry of Welfare.

Lindbeck, A., and M. Persson. 2003. "The Gains from Pension Reform." *The Journal of Economic Literature* 41: 74–112.

Palmer, E. 1999. "Individual Decisions and Aggregate Stability in the NDC System." World Bank, Washington DC. Processed.

———. 2000. "The Swedish Pension Reform Model: Framework and Issues." Social Protection Discussion Paper 0012, World Bank, Washington, DC.

———. 2002. "Swedish Pension Reform: How Did It Evolve and What Does It Mean for the Future?" In *Social Security Pension Reform in Europe*, ed. Martin Feldstein and Horst Siebert. Chicago: University of Chicago Press.

———. 2006. "What Is NDC?" In *Pension Reform: Issues and Prospects for Non-Financial Defined Contribution (NDC) Schemes*, ed. R. Holzmann and E. Palmer, chapter 2. Washington, DC: World Bank.

Palmer, E., S. Stabina, I. Svensson, and I. Vanovska. 2006. "NDC Strategy in Latvia: Implementation and Prospects for the Future." In *Pension Reform: Issues and Prospects for Non-Financial Defined Contribution (NDC) Schemes*, ed. R. Holzmann and E. Palmer, chapter 15. Washington, DC: World Bank.

Samuelson, P. 1958. "An Exact Consumption-Loan Model of Interest with or without the Social Contrivance of Money." *Journal of Political Economy* 68 (6): 467–82.

Settergren, O. 2001. "The Automatic Balance Mechanism of the Swedish Pension System— A Non-technical Introduction." *Wirtschaftspolitishe Blätter* 4/2001: 339–49.

Settergren, O., and B. Mikula. 2006. "The Rate of Return of Pay-As-You-Go Pension Systems: A More Exact Consumption-Loan Model of Interest." In *Pension Reform: Issues and Prospects for Non-Financial Defined Contribution (NDC) Schemes*, ed. R. Holzmann and E. Palmer, chapter 7. Washington, DC: World Bank.

Takayama, N. 2006. "Reforming Social Security in Japan: Is NDC the Answer?" In *Pension Reform: Issues and Prospects for Non-Financial Defined Contribution (NDC) Schemes*, ed. R. Holzmann and E. Palmer, chapter 24. Washington, DC: World Bank.

Valdés-Prieto, S. 2000. "The Financial Stability of Notional Account Pensions." *Scandinavian Journal of Economics* 102 (3): 395–417.

Vanovska, I. 2004. "Pension Reform in Latvia: Achievements and Challenges." *Reforming Public Pensions. Sharing the Experiences of Transition and OECD Countries.* Paris, OECD.

Discussion of
"Conversion to NDCs—Issues and Models"

*Marek Góra**

ALTHOUGH ONLY A FEW COUNTRIES (LATVIA, POLAND, AND SWEDEN) have fully introduced non-financial defined contribution (NDC) schemes,[1] and a few others have introduced them to an extent, the NDC concept is increasingly considered in discussions and reform proposals all over Europe and elsewhere. This is the case for a number of reasons, including relatively easy conversion to NDC from defined benefit (DB) pay-as-you-go (PAYG) plans. It is true that introducing NDC is easier than introducing financial defined contribution (FDC). This does not mean, however, that NDC does not need a deliberate approach. A number of options can be applied both at the general and technical level. Edward Palmer's study is probably the most comprehensive, critical presentation and discussion of options available in the course of conversion to NDC. In his chapter, Palmer also compares the experience of countries that have introduced NDC to their pension systems. He highlights the pros and cons of various ways of conversion to NDC. The chapter can serve not only as an economic analysis but also as a "manual" for those who consider conversion to NDC as an option for other countries.

Palmer provides the reader with a very clear view on NDC and its implementation. In this particular study, however, Palmer does not address the economic nature of NDC. In this regard, the following questions are pertinent. How does conversion to NDC differ from conversion to FDC? More generally, what is the key difference between the two options: namely, introducing individual retirement accounts in a non-financial way (with the returns stemming directly from real economy growth) or in a financial way (with the returns stemming from real economy growth via financial markets)? The questions are beyond the scope of Palmer's chapter. However, the problem of whether to convert all or part of DB-PAYG into NDC (or FDC, or a combination of the two) is crucial for pension reform. Two factors are probably the most important for the decision. First is the "fairness" of the change of the regime (whatever "fairness" means). The second is the "transition cost." How do these two issues differ, depending on whether NDC or FDC is to be implemented?

The chapter broadly discusses the fairness of conversion. However, whatever the definition of fairness used, it applies to conversion to NDC and to FDC in exactly the same way. This message is important for the reader, especially for a policy maker involved in public debate about the reform options. It makes sense to formulate this conclusion explicitly in the "manual."

The chapter does not address the issue of transition costs. However, that issue is clearly one that should be discussed in a broader context of conversion from the traditional approach (DB-PAYG) to a modern approach (NDC, FDC). Palmer's chapter is a very good starting point for such a discussion. The study provides readers with a number of indirect

---

* Marek Góra is a professor at the Warsaw School of Economics.

hints—that the difference between conversion to NDC and to FDC stems from accounting standards, to a large extent. Actually, NDC is a clever "trick" to solve a fundamental economic problem, namely converging to intergenerational equilibrium, without generating problems related to accounting conventions. The guidelines Eurostat, the statistical agency for the European Union (EU), has recently formulated for EU countries on how to account flows through FDC-type individual accounts formally do not apply to NDC. They are not, which is bad news (economic inconsequence) and good news (fewer short-term problems for reformers) at the same time. I do think that both types of individual accounts differ from each other. That is why Poland has followed a well-balanced approach and combined NDC and FDC, and has chosen the largest share of FDC in the entire old-age pension system among countries that have also introduced NDC. The difference, however, has little to do with the way government's deficit and debt are accounted. This is the message that matters for implementation of pension reforms.

Returning to Palmer's chapter, the study compares implementation approaches in five countries (Italy, the Kyrgyz Republic, Latvia, Poland, and Sweden) and concludes that the Swedish approach is the most sophisticated. It is difficult to disagree with this conclusion. For many reasons, including less-developed data processing and unavailability of reserves left by the previous system, the Swedish approach to balancing the newly introduced NDC was not applicable in countries such as Latvia and Poland. However, is the less-sophisticated approach really worse? Should it, as Palmer suggests, be changed for the more sophisticated one? The simple approach, precisely because it is simpler, is easier for the participants to understand. It is also more transparent. Isn't the simple (straightforward) approach more suitable for NDC?

Note

1. "Non-financial defined contribution" is alternatively called "notional defined contribution" should be understood to have the same definition.

Discussion of
"Conversion to NDCs—Issues and Models"

*Elsa Fornero**

AS DEBATE AND EMPIRICAL WORK ON PENSION SCHEMES PROGRESS, transition phases stick out as the really important element at the level of economic policy. This is true for two reasons. First, transition phases last so long that they outlive politicians, and it is hard for politicians to set themselves goals that will deliver benefits they will hardly be able to see. Second, during transition phases, a highly critical redistribution element is unavoidable. So, how can these phases be controlled? Are rules possible or must politicians be left without guidance and able to act on whim? Economists are normally very good at designing steady state solutions; it goes to Edward Palmer's great credit that he is not afraid to grapple with the far more messy and less gratifying issue of transition.

The transition that he is interested in is the one from a defined benefit (DB) to a defined contribution (DC) pay-as-you-go (PAYG) system, the so-called notional defined contribution (NDC)[1] or *Bismarckian* scheme, characterized by pension formulae that, as a general rule, correlate benefits with payroll taxes paid over the *whole working career* and with *retirement age.*

Palmer introduces readers to a very detailed menu of transitional issues, which he discusses according to two criteria: *recognition of acquired rights* and *acknowledgment for contributions paid.*

Before commenting briefly on his points, I will observe that his presentation implies that at least two *preliminary questions* have been answered. Is a NDC scheme preferable to a DB one? Doesn't it impose too much risk on workers? The implied answers are "yes" to the first question, and "no" to the second.

Although I broadly agree with these answers, I do not think they are obvious. In my view, and maybe also in Palmer's, a DC scheme is preferable to a DB one because—at a properly defined internal rate of return—it ensures both a stable financial equilibrium and a "fair" treatment, within and between cohorts. Of course, one feature is the mirror of the other, provided the definition of what is "fair" rests on the concept of *actuarial fairness* as the basic principle for calculating benefits. This means that lifetime payroll taxes are "notionally" accumulated, earn a return equal to (an average of) the growth rates of either the wage bill or GDP, and are converted at retirement into an annuity according to mortality tables.

This method has many advantages, but is far from optimal. The possibility of achieving an almost automatic financial equilibrium reduces the need for politically determined corrections. The uniformity of treatment avoids the maze of schemes characteristic of many PAYG systems in Europe, with various privileges accorded to more influential categories. A flexible contribution rate and a flexible retirement age—which are more easily accom-

---

* Elsa Fornero is professor of economics at the University of Turin and director of CeRP (Center for Research on Pensions and Welfare Systems, Turin).

modated in a DC scheme than in a DB one—are more in line with a life cycle perspective than a constant payroll tax and a mandatory age. The direct link between age of retirement and the level of benefits avoids the bias toward early retirement normally associated with DB formulae.

On the other hand, although the definition of what is "fair" is always subjective, the definition I just referred to implies that it is fair to offer each worker the rate of return corresponding to the rate of growth of aggregate earnings. It could be objected that this is too restrictive a definition, and that fairness should imply some kind of explicit redistribution toward the less fortunate members of society (in terms of working career, earnings, and hardship). The experience of many countries shows, however, that a DB scheme may redistribute very heavily but also very unjustly, with DB rules used to favor steep earnings careers as opposed to flat ones, workers in "rich" industries as opposed to workers in "poor" ones, the relatively young retirees as opposed to the older ones, the self-employed as opposed to the employees, and public as opposed to private employees. In all these comparisons, redistribution is very often not from rich to poor, but the other way round.

It would therefore seem that one of the main advantages of a DC scheme is to eliminate all these kinds of misdirected (and often hidden) redistributive flows. Its superiority derives then as much from tight economic reasoning (financial equilibrium and a good incentive structure) as it does from its ability to withstand politicians' attempts to use it for their own interests due to the greater transparency of its rules.

Moreover, the separation of insurance from redistribution need not be complete, as some kind of redistribution, if desired, can be easily superimposed on a DC scheme. A guaranteed floor, a rate of return decreasing with income, survivors' and disability benefits, and the like may all be adapted to a DC scheme with an appropriate correction to the basic rate of return. This somewhat blurs the general picture, but leads to much clearer and more just results in terms of *fairness*.

Now to the question about risk. The coverage offered by a DC scheme depends, roughly speaking, on the rate of growth of the economy. The welfare of pensioners is therefore linked to the welfare of the rest of the community. Is this unfair? The alternative solution— to isolate pensioners by offering them a predetermined rate of return—implies shifting the risk to the working generation. In the latter case, if growth is slow, workers suffer twice, both because their income is static and because they must pass a higher fraction of it to the pensioners. If, instead, income growth is rapid, pensioners perceive a greater gap vis-à-vis the young. True, the demographic risk still rests on the workers, unless the state is ready to transfer (part of) it to taxpayers—which again shows that the goal of a complete separation between insurance and redistribution is illusory.

The separation is even more difficult to achieve in the transition phase, which brings us to the core of Palmer's chapter. This is because there are costs in the transition even to a *notional* fund; they are higher when the initial conditions involve a very large "implicit debt" and even higher when building a *real* fund is also an objective of the new design. The political process that brings about the change in the design is thus very difficult because it normally requires a much larger redistribution both between and within generations than the one implicit in the previous steady state.[2]

Abstracting from political difficulties, Palmer examines the key decision points of the implementation process, presents possible solutions, and evaluates them according to the two principles mentioned above—acquired rights and contributions paid. In more detail, he discusses how to calculate the "initial capital" to be recognized when the system is applied to all workers (irrespective of their seniority in the past system). This entails a three-step process: reconstructing the individuals' earnings histories, assigning contribu-

tion rates, and crediting a rate of return. He also examines the *speed of transition*, with political options ranging from the slowest phasing in (new entrants only) to an immediate
application of the new system, passing through a gradual solution, as when a pro rata
mechanism is applied, with the new rules valid only for future seniority (the Italian case).
He also considers the treatment of *supplementary benefits* (survivor and disability benefits),
as well as issues such as pension indexation mechanisms and ways to increase the effective retirement age, even if they seem more pertinent to the question of reform design than
of its implementation.

The chapter examines three models for the reconstruction of earnings under the
hypothesis—particularly relevant for Eastern European countries—that individual
records are either not available or missing: the nationwide average wage; the age- and
gender-related average wage; and a rough estimate of the individuals' earnings profile,
given the earnings of a few reference years at the time of the implementation. All three
models involve some degree of redistribution. Palmer notes that "policy makers will have
to defend the arguments favoring their chosen model. The political decision should be
based on analysis of available data, supported with a view of what is "fair"—given the
political-economic environment."

Of course, by choosing solutions that are more favorable to current retirees and workers
already in the system, the implicit debt that was involved in the past system is simply
rolled over, and may even be increased, which means a more prolonged transition.

Palmer is very accurate in identifying the various "tax overhangs" that can derive
from the (necessarily imperfect) practical implementation of the NDC principle, also
showing how to "factor" them in the entitlements initially recognized or in the return to
be awarded, in order to maintain it as nearly as possible to the "true" internal rate of
return. This can diverge for various reasons from what is formally awarded, as when a
demographic cycle temporarily changes the underlying trend, making it more difficult
to identify the contribution by population growth to the system's return, or when, for
political reasons, it is decided that the first pension is calculated by assuming a positive
fixed rate of return, which nicely increases the first pension, but may not correspond to
the internal rate, requiring subsequent corrections. In all cases, Palmer's preferred solutions are those that appear to be more coherent with the steady state, perhaps not surprisingly once one accepts his premises, discussed above, for the very introduction of
the NDC system.

Given this, I agree with most of his propositions, which are quite sensible in the
adopted framework. However, I have two main reservations. The first is about the possibility that the two principles he refers to (acquired rights and contributions paid) are not
enough for guiding the practical implementation of the reform. The second is about the
treatment of families, as opposed to individuals, in pension systems. I will now consider
these two caveats in turn.

Logical consistency would require that, if the new system to be implemented is judged
better than the previous one, the conversion should be undertaken as quickly as possible
and, in any case, by choosing at any point of the decision tree the option that appears to be
more in line with the adopted NDC principle. In the extreme, this would mean an immediate application of the DC formula to all cohorts, and a strict adherence to Palmer's second principle, the "contributions paid" criterion. In practice, there are at least two kinds of
limitations to this radical scenario: group pressures to maintain "acquired rights" and a
shared view of "social justice," with particular reference toward the worst-off individuals
of society. However, if one of the main advantages of the NDC system rests in the abolition

of previous privileges, the "acquired rights" criterion will very likely freeze them for the current generation and impose a highly unbalanced transition, with costs to be borne mainly by the poor, as well as the young. On the other hand, the "contributions paid" criterion will distribute more evenly across generations but will leave the poor equally or even more exposed.

In this context, just as the NDC system is normally integrated by a minimum pension provision (possibly financed through general taxation), an external criterion could be required to guide the transition, such as the "Rawlsian principle" of sustainable maximum.[3] To give this discussion a more concrete content, consider the case of Eastern European countries, many of which have already implemented an NDC system, or are about to do so. Given that typically these countries do not have the earning histories, in calculating the "initial capitals" to be recognized for past seniority, they could certainly refer to Palmer's criteria, with the risk, from a social point of view, of postponing the previous structure of privileges or excessively penalizing the poor according to whether the first (acquired rights) or the second (contributions paid) criterion is chosen. In these historical circumstances, the fact that the older generations had little or no choice in the previous political regime deserves perhaps more consideration than the two principles advocated by Palmer could allow.

The second caveat concerns the treatment of families, as opposed to individuals. Under the heading of survivors' benefits, Palmer seems to suggest the opportunity of using differential conversion factors for women and men according to their specific longevity, thus eliminating the implicit subsidy to women that derives by the use of unisex mortality tables. He also argues, on the basis of the "gender equality" principle, against maintaining survivor benefits within the NDC scheme. In an ideal world, where gender equality in the job market and in the family were effectively realized, he would be right in both claims. There would be no point in objecting to the use of gender-specific mortality rates, just as nobody objects to insurance companies developing and selling products for the individual and pricing them according to their cost, and thus differentiating private pensions with respect to the different mortality patterns that characterize genders, cohorts, and professions. Along the same reasoning, survivors' benefits for spouses, even when properly priced, would probably be obsolete.

The reality is different. On the one hand, the fact that in many countries survivors' benefits have greatly helped to prevent poverty among widows is an undoubted achievement of the traditional social security systems. Moreover, families are still typically made up of a working man, a woman whose working life outside the family is shorter and more discontinuous, and one or more children. The question therefore is whether the family instead of the individual should be the proper unit of reference for a public pension system, even of the NDC type.[4] There are surely some insurance opportunities within the family that would be lost in a system centered on the individual. Indeed, typically the public system offers survivors' coverage without either charging higher contributions or reducing the benefits paid to the male as long as he survives. Disregarding the less typical situations, in this case social security, as compared with an actuarially fair system, taxes both single men and single women in favor of families, in the sense that these supplementary benefits are not paid for on an individual basis. Is this fair? The answer is probably yes, if bearing and rearing children is considered a socially relevant duty. A favorable treatment by social security is an offset (and only a very partial one) to the financial and non-financial costs involved. Aspects of this risk sharing within the family should be maintained, in my view, in the pension system, whether or not it is NDC.

Notes

1. "Notional defined contribution" and "non-financial defined contribution" should be understood to have the same definition.

2. See Diamond (2001).

3. See Schokkaert and Van Parijs (2003).

4. See Diamond (2004).

References

Diamond, P. 2001. "Towards an Optimal Social Security Design." CeRP Working Paper 2, Center for Research on Pensions and Welfare Policies, Turin. http://cerp.unito.it

———. 2004. "Social Security." *American Economic Review* 94 (1): 1–24.

Schokkaert, E., and P. Van Parijs. 2003. "Debate on Social Justice and Pension Reform." *Journal of European Social Policy* 13 (3, August): 246–63.

Chapter 10

NDCs: A Comparison of the French and German Point Systems

Florence Legros[*]

IN RECENT YEARS, MANY COUNTRIES HAVE TAKEN STEPS to increase the age at which individuals receive benefits from their retirement programs. This is supposed to shift the incentives in the right direction: that is, to keep workers in the workforce longer than they have been in recent decades. Notional defined contribution (NDC) pension plans have been considered one of the best means to increase the effective retirement age because they take into account the individuals' whole career, from the first day to the last. From this point of view, they are closer to actuarial fairness than traditional pay-as-you-go (PAYG) defined benefits (DB) pension plans.[1] This is probably one reason why NDC has received increasing attention during the last years, even if the ability to increase the labor force participation rates for older workers has probably been oversold.

Other reasons why NDC has received attention recently are qualities such as transparency, flexibility, adequacy of provided pensions, and robustness: that is, the ability to resist various economic and demographic shocks.

This study focuses on the feature of robustness and assesses it by analyzing the Swedish system (as a benchmark) and comparing it with the German and French schemes that often have been claimed to be NDC variants.[2]

To this end, the chapter is organized as follows. The next section briefly describes the French and the German pension schemes. It then considers key points of NDC and actuarial fairness: how pure NDC guarantees actuarial fairness both at the margin and on average, and how this is reflected in the role of the life expectancy in the parameters of NDC pension schemes. In the third section, the study focuses on the conceptual equivalence among the French, German, and Swedish systems and highlights the differences in their design and in their evolution policies. This leads to a discussion of how the reactions of these systems differ when there is an external shock (demographic, economic, or other). The chapter concludes with a discussion about the possibility (and opportunity) of moving from a point scheme toward an NDC scheme (whether pure, with a minimum pension

---

[*] Florence Legros is professor of economics at the University Dauphine in Paris.

I thank Robert Holzmann for helpful discussions and valuable comments. An acknowledgment is also due to Jean-Louis Guérin for the fruitful discussions we had during our co-authorship of a paper dealing with actuarial fairness (Guérin and Legros 2003). Any remaining errors are fully mine.

scheme, or some combination). The conclusion considers the redistributive impacts of such a transition between generations and inside a generation.

A Quick Description of French and German Pension Schemes

French and German pension schemes have a component that uses points: that is, part of these schemes provides a pension that depends on the individuals' whole career.

France

This section focuses on the main French pension scheme: the compulsory pension scheme that provides pensions to employees in private enterprises, including white-collar workers, about 61 percent of the working population. There are plenty of other schemes. Some run like the basic French pension scheme, the *régime général* discussed below. Some run like the private sector pension scheme. Previous schemes include both a scheme that is close to the *régime général* and a scheme with points.

For the private sector, French pensions rely on two pillars. The basic general scheme (*régime général*, or CNAV) offers benefits corresponding to the share of the wages below the social security ceiling (TRanche A, or TRA) equal to €2,516 per month, for the year 2005). The complementary schemes include AGIRC (the Association Générale des Institutions de Retraite des Cadres) for executives, for the fraction of their wages over TRA; and ARRCO

Table 10.1. Schemes and Contributions in the Main French Pension Scheme

Considered wage share	Below TRA	Up to three times TRA	Up to eight times TRA
Population			
Nonexecutives	CNAV Workers: 6.55%[a] Firms: 8.2% [a] Total: 14.75% [a]		
	CNAV: + Firms: 1.6% ARRCO Workers: 2.4% Firms: 3.6% Calling rate: 125%[b] Effective rate: 7.5% [a]	ARRCO Workers: 6.4% Firms: 9.6% Calling rate: 125%[b] Effective rate: 20% [a]	
Executives	CNAV Id. nonexecutives ARRCO Id. nonexecutives	AGIRC Workers: 6% Firms: 10% Calling rate: 125%[b] Effective rate: 20% [a]	AGIRC Workers: 6% Firms: 10% Calling rate: 125%[b] Effective rate: 20%

Source: Author's compilations.

a. Contribution rates are applicable to the gross wage in the defined interval (below the TRA).
b. The calling rate is a multiplicative factor that is applied to the contractual contribution rate to increase the schemes' resources (below the TRA, workers are supposed to contribute up to 2.4 percent of their gross wage—contractual rate—but pay in reality 125 percent of 2.4 percent—that is, 3 percent—while they accumulate their rights proportionally to the contractual rate).

(the Association des Régimes de Retraite Complémentaires), for the other workers, based on their total wage, and for executives, for wages below TRA. These plans are summarized in table 10.1.

At the beginning of 2003, the CNAV pension, P_{cnav}, was computed as follows

$$P_{cnav} = w * \alpha * \text{Min}[1, (T/37.5)],$$

where w is the yearly gross reference wage average of the 25 best wages for the generation born after 1948.[3] The rate of pension, α, is

$$\alpha = 0.50 * [1 - 0.10 * \text{Min}[40 - T; 65 - A)],$$

where T is the number of contributing years and A is the retirement age.

The last reform (approved on August 21, 2003) will progressively affect the formula as follows. The full rate contributing period (40 years, currently) will increase according to the gain in life expectancy (one quarter a year between 2009 and 2012, to increase to 42 years in 2012). The discount rate, which is currently 0.10, will decrease step by step to reach 0.05 in 2013. The $T/37.5$ term's denominator (currently 37.5, corresponding to the full rate contributing period before the previous reform in 1993) will increase by two quarters a year to reach $T/40$ in 2008 ; at this period it will be equal to the full rate contributing period (40 years). After 2008, it will increase by one quarter a year and reach 42 years in 2012. If the corresponding full rate is denoted by T', the contributing period in the above formula becomes

$$P_{cnav} = w * \alpha * \text{Min}[1, (T/T')], \text{ and}$$

$$\alpha = 0.50 * [1 - 0.05 * \text{Min}[T' - T; 65 - A)].$$

Note the existence of a minimum pension provided by CNAV. It reaches €6,935 per year for a single person and €12,440 for a cohabiting or married couple.

The complementary pension schemes are fully contributory schemes. The first pensions after retirement, P_{comp}, are computed according to a system of points, which are the pension basic units. These are "sold" when people retire at the age of A (after a career of length T) at the price that prevails during the year $C + A$ (C being the cohort generation, that is, the birth year). Thus the value of the point, VP, a virtual price at which individuals transform their virtual capital—corresponding to the sum of the points that are accumulated during the working period—into a yearly pension, is expressed as VP_{C+A}.[4]

$$P_{comp,C+A} = \left[\sum_{T} \text{points} \right] * VP_{C+A}$$

During any year t, during the working period, the flow of accrued points can be computed as follows for nonexecutives

$$\text{points}_t = \text{points}_{ARRCO,t}$$

$$\text{points} = [\tau_{ARRCO,TRA} * w \le TRA + \tau_{ARRCO,TRB} * TRA < w \le TRB]/PP_{ARRCO},$$

for executives

$$\text{points} = [\tau_{ARRCO,TRA} * w \le TRA]/PP_{ARRCO} + [\tau_{AGIRC} * TRA < w \le TRC]/PP_{AGIRC},$$

where $\tau_{ARRCO,TRA}$, $\tau_{ARRCO,TRB}$, and τ_{AGIRC} are the "contractual contribution rates" or "facial contribution rates" of the regimes (respectively, 6 and 16 percent in 2005); TRB and TRC are equal to three and eight times TRA (€7,548 and €19,456 per month, respectively, in 2005). PP_{ARRCO} and PP_{AGIRC} are the "purchasing" price of a point.

Note that during the retirement period, while basic pensions (CNAV) are revalued at the inflation rate, complementary pensions are revalued at the point's value, VP_t.

One of the ways to handle the resources of the schemes is a coefficient, the "calling rate," that applied to the facial contribution rate, increases the schemes' resources. For example, the flow of income of ARRCO is given by

$$\text{Resource}_{ARRCO} = [\tau_{ARRCO,TRA} * coeff] * w \leq TRA + [\tau_{ARRCO} * coeff] * TRA < w \leq TRB.$$

With the current *coeff* equal to 125 percent, that leads to the effective contribution rates of 7.5 and 20 percent. This coefficient (the calling rate) is an important means to manage the scheme, like the price and the value of the point. This rate was lower than one during the first decades of existence of the system and now increases more or less regularly.

Simplifying matters,[5] the French complementary pensions by points are computed according to the following formula for an individual i who retires at age A after a contribution period lasting from t_0 to $A - 1$:

$$P^i_{C+A} = \sum_{t=t_0+1}^{A} \frac{\tau_{t-1} * w^i_{t-1}}{PP_{t-1}} * VP_{C+A} .$$ (10.1)

This is the pension that the pensioner gets when aged of $A + C$, while the resources of the scheme in t are

$$R_t = \sum_i \tau_t * w^i_t * coeff_t .$$

Note that although pensions are indexed on prices after A, PP and VP are changed regularly by the boards of the schemes according to the forecasts about the pension schemes. Also note that AGIRC and ARRCO are private associations linking together sectoral pension schemes. This is because when the schemes were created, each economic sector had its own pension scheme. French complementary pension schemes are fully contributive and proportional schemes (according to their Bismarckian origin), compared with the basic scheme that only partially relies on the career and that includes a flat part. They are managed by trade unionists with the help of retirement specialists, including actuaries and financial investors. They were created in 1945, and were designed by insurers. They became compulsory in 1972. The accounts are held by individuals.

The management of the executives' pension scheme, AGIRC, serves as an example of the piloting of such schemes. Since the first oil shock in 1974, a decrease in the pensions' yield has been scheduled. The analysis of AGIRC data shows the prevailing, discrete, and progressive mechanism based on the price of the point (PP). This is because as soon as PP increases more quickly than the contributors' average wage, the number of points earned decreases. In 1970, a share contribution of 13.9 percent of the taxable wage provided 1,000 points, while the same contribution rate would have provided only 850 points at the end of the 1990s.[6] The trade-off between the price increase, the value decrease, and the calling rate management is a result of the burden-sharing between retirees and contributors. Until 1976, the AGIRC point value was the result of an automatic adjustment by comparing for the next 10 years the expected contributions' flows to the expected pensions' flows (and taking into account the buffer fund balance).[7] In 1976, the point value was forecast to drop sharply and the pensions' schemes' board chose to favor the retirees and to employ the calling rate.

Germany

The German pension scheme (described, for example, in Queisser 1996 and Vernière 2001) seems simpler since it relies on only a single point scheme that covers not only the employees of the private enterprises but also certain self-employed and some other specific parts of the population, some 85 percent of the active population.

In fact, as it includes an early retirement pension scheme, the qualifying conditions are quite complex. Note that this is not the case in France, where, by law, early retirement does not exist. "Old workers"—that is, workers just below the retirement age—are exempted from searching for a job that they would not find anyway and do draw pensions that are generally funded either by unemployment schemes or by disability insurance. This "tool" has been used greatly by firms to decrease their wage bill when necessary.

Compared with the French pension schemes, the contributory ceiling in the German system is rather low. As noted, in France, workers must contribute until their wage reaches eight times the social security ceiling (€20,128): that is, 8.5 times the average wage. In Germany, the contributory ceiling is 1.8 times the average wage. This has implications that will be discussed in the next section of this chapter.

There is no minimum contributory wage in Germany, but very low pensions are scaled up if people have contributed for at least 35 years. In this case, the personal points can be multiplied by 1.5, up to a maximum of 75 percent of the value of contribution for average earnings of all insured persons. Since the 2001 reform[8] there has been a minimum pension, which helps very low income pensioners. On the other hand, there are noncontributory additional rights for part-time working women and for children's care.

Like the French pension point schemes, each working period provides pension rights according to the wage earned by the contributor. The gross pension is given by the following formula

$$P^i_{C+A} = \sum_{t=t_0}^{A} \frac{w^i_{t-1}}{\overline{w}_{t-1}} * \alpha^i * VP_{C+A} . \tag{10.2}$$

The notations are the same as for France in equation 10.4: $\overline{w}_t$ is the gross average wage in t, α is the entry factor corresponding *grosso modo* to the French rate of pension, and w^i_t is the part of the wage under the ceiling.

$$\alpha = 1 - [0.003(780 - A(12)], \text{ where } A(12) \text{ means age } A \text{ in months.}$$

This means that there is a discount equal to 0.003 per month in case the pension is drawn before age 65.

Most of the adjustments rely on the value of the point VP.

The 2001 reform deeply changed the parameters in the indexation formula,

$$VP_t = VP_{t-1} * \frac{\overline{w}_{t-1}}{\overline{w}_{t-2}} * \frac{x - \tau_{t-1} - \mu_{t-1}}{x - \tau_{t-2} - \mu_{t-2}} . \tag{10.3}$$

The indexation coefficient, x, was supposed to change. Between 2001 and 2010, $x = 1$, meaning a full indexation on net wages. After 2010, $x = 0.9$, meaning partial indexing.

The variable μ is the contribution rate to the voluntary additional private pension scheme sponsored by the fiscal chapter of the reform. What is called here *net wage* is in fact the wage net of all contributions dedicated to pension schemes (but containing the personal income tax).

In the forecasting exercises, the value of μ was supposed to increase between 2001 and 2008, from 0.5 to 4 percent, and remain stable after 2008. It corresponds to the value that binds the fiscal constraint.

This reform has quickly been judged as inefficient.[9] The so-called Rürup report led in October 2003 to another indexing formula, which will hold until 2010

$$VP_t = VP_{t-1} * \frac{\overline{w}_{t-1}}{\overline{w}_{t-2}} * \frac{x - \tau_{t-1} - \mu_{t-1}}{x - \tau_{t-2} - \mu_{t-2}} * SF_t . \qquad (10.4)$$

SF is the sustainability factor, defined as

$$SF_t = \left(1 - \frac{s_{t-2} * N_{t-3} \Big/ N_{t-2}}{s_{t-3} * N_{t-4} \Big/ N_{t-3}} \right) * 0.25 + 1$$

where $s_{t-2} * N_{t-3}/N_{t-2}$ is the sociodemographic dependency ratio: that is, the ratio of the retirees (in $t-2$, those who were active in $t-3$ and living in $t-2$) to those active in $t-2$.

That means that—in the long run, with a constant demographic structure—the pensions will increase like the gross wages. In the transition period (the demographic shock), the pensions will increase like net wages minus the 25 percent of the demographic drift (that is, 25 percent of the demographic drift will be "paid" by retirees).

As in the French scheme, life expectancy does not appear explicitly in the pensions' formula. It is implicitly introduced by two means: by the scheme equilibrium that links the contribution rate to the dependency ratio; and by means of the dependency ratio, which strongly depends on the retirees life expectancy.

If it is assumed that the fiscal resources of the pension scheme (ecotax, the German energy tax program dedicated to limit the industrial consumption of polluting energy, 32 percent of the scheme resources) remain constant, and/or that, in the long run, this tax is a share of the wage bill, which is a constant share of the national income, resources can be derived as

$$R_t = \sum_i \tau_t * w_t^i .$$

NDC and Actuarial Fairness

In both countries, many individuals used to quit their job five years before the legal pensionable age. To provide incentives to delay this retirement, actuarial fairness at the margin is a concept that must be explored. The following section shows that even if one ignores the value of leisure, actuarial fairness at the margin is very difficult to implement and can lead myopic individuals to poverty. It is why actuarial fairness on average is a preferable concept. It provides every generation a pension strictly equivalent to its contributions; it spontaneously leads to NDC. Unfortunately, the second part of this section shows that this collective concept can be unfair overall for individuals with low life expectancies.

Actuarial Fairness at the Margin: An Individual Concept

Actuarial fairness at the margin works along those lines: early retirement is swapped against a proportional reduction of the pensions' benefits during the whole retirement period. If the agent decides to postpone retirement (after a legal minimum retirement age, for example) and does not retire at date $t-1$ and age A, but waits until date t and age $A+1$, he or she will pay contributions for the longer time and will benefit from a higher pension. On the other hand, if the worker retires early, benefits will be reduced by a fraction d during the entire retirement (this reduction is called "decrual"). By retiring early, the agent will save contributions and benefit from a longer period of leisure.

That actuarially fair decrual in pension is measured in such a way that the choice of the agent does not threaten the budgetary equilibrium of the system. If the decrual rate is set at a higher value, early retirement will improve the financial situation of the system; if it is less, the opposite applies. Whatever the case, the decrual will have an impact on agents' behavior. In the first case, if the decrual is high, it is costly for an agent to leave early and few workers are likely to make that choice. In the second, if the decrual is low, early retirement benefits the pensioners and the attractiveness of that formula will help degrade the budgetary balance of the system.

It should be noted that the decrual/accrual rate depends on individual career's profile: if two agents are considered, each having earned the same rights to pension benefits, but with different wages for the last year of activity, the value of the decrual must be higher for the one having the largest wage. Intuitively, that agent must be rewarded by a higher premium if he or she delays the retirement decision.

With the same logic, it can be inferred that if pensions are indexed on gross wages, the accrual/decrual has to be higher than if they are indexed on prices. (For a formal demonstration, see the annex.)

From a very simple model (see the annex), where ρ is the individual discount rate, r, the interest rate, and ℓ_{t-1}^A, the income equivalent of the leisure associated with leaving activity one year early,[10] the following results can be derived:

- If $\rho = r$ and $w_{t-1}^A = \ell_{t-1}^A$, then the worker is indifferent between ceasing work early or delaying retirement.
- If $\rho = r$ but $w_{t-1}^A < \ell_{t-1}^A$, then the worker draws a high satisfaction from leisure, and he or she will opt for an early retirement, with the actuarially fair decrual in benefits.
- If $w_{t-1}^A < \ell_{t-1}^A$ and $\rho < r$, then because his or her discount rate is high, the individual prefers to retire early, as he or she does not give much weight to the loss in income induced by an early retirement.
- If $w_{t-1}^A > \ell_{t-1}^A$ and $\rho < r$, then the individual opts for a postponed retirement, but if $w_{t-1}^A > \ell_{t-1}^A$ and $\rho > r$, then the individual's preference for the present is so high that the financial gain induced by actuarial fairness at the margin does not mean much to him or her, and the agent retires early.

So the efficiency of the system's parameterization strongly depends on individual preferences: most importantly on the taste for leisure and on the preference for the present. On a general note, it can be assumed that there is a high probability that high taste for leisure and preference for the present are true for aging workers. Many reasons can be given for that point: residual life expectancy is lower; the number of healthy years left is reduced; the higher uncertainty prevailing about life expectancy increases preference for the present.

The value of the actuarially fair decrual rate changes with the indexing rule. (This holds as well for an indexing on the net wages.) It rises with the interest rate and the contribution rate, and decreases in line with life expectancy, the inflation rate, technical progress, and the replacement rate. It is worth noting that with realistic data and even without giving any value to the leisure, the decrual will have high values: 6.6 percent with indexed pensions on prices and 7.1 percent in the case of indexed pensions on gross wages. As can be seen, for a standard Bismarckian, PAYG pension system, actuarial fairness at the margin implies a high value of the decrual, far from the values given by a linear calculus. (A replacement rate of 60 percent after 40 years of work gives an accrual rate of 1.5 percent.) Thus it is necessary to have a bend in the accrual curve of benefits. In other words, the concept of actuarial fairness at the margin can apply only to a part of the age distribution. In concrete terms, because of the indexing rule on the net wages (even in case of partial adjustment), Germany should have a more steeply sloping curve than France. This implies also that because productivity gains change every year, the benefits accrual curve has to change as well.

Now consider the case of a system displaying both Beveridgian and Bismarckian elements. Every pensioner earns a pension compounded of two parts. One is proportional to his career (as previously) and one is a lump sum fixed independently of his career profile, not subject to the decrual. Such a system cannot be actuarially fair to every member simultaneously, as the benefits decrual rate is now a function of the wage and so depends on the wage profile of the individual. Because such minima exist in both the German and the French systems, actuarial fairness for the whole system is only a desideratum and cannot be reached.

The existence of a contributory ceiling is another point that moves the schemes away from actuarial fairness at the margin. This is particularly the case in Germany, assuming that a worker has a nonnegligible probability of attaining this wage level by the end of his working life and that postponing retirement has a very weak return. That means that when this is the case—that is, when the contributory ceiling is rather weak—the accrual is nearly zero.

Another consideration is the cost of actuarial fairness at the margin. If leisure is valued highly, the value of the decrual (or the accrual) should be higher than the values given previously. That means that there is an infinite number of decruals/accruals, which provides actuarial fairness. A financial level with a null value of leisure insures the financial equilibrium of the scheme. An individual level, with a bigger value of leisure, insures personal optimality. This is because, first, it is generally assumed that there is a decreasing relationship between life expectancy and value of leisure;[11] second, there are non-Bismarckian elements in the pension scheme that imply a decreasing relationship between the individual wage and decrual. For these reasons, the optimal decrual for low incomes will be higher than the optimal decrual for high incomes. Thus if the government's wish is to retain high and low incomes on the labor market (which pools the longevity risks, as can be seen in table 10.2), the decrual should be quite high but very costly.

Actuarial fairness at the margin is costly and rather difficult to implement as soon as the life expectancy has to be taken into account, as correlated with the value of leisure.

To combine individual freedom, incentives, and financial equilibrium for all the ages, actuarial fairness on average seems to be a better concept than actuarial fairness at the margin. In this case, the acquisition of rights is a continuous unbroken straight line, which is the condition for uniqueness of the PAYG yield. This relationship is supposed to lead to

Table 10.2. Life Expectancy at Age 60, by Socioprofessional Categories, in Years (the case of France)

Category	Men	Women
Executives, self-employed	22.5	26.0
Intermediate profession (technicians, etc.)	19.5	25.0
Artisan, shopkeepers, firm managers	19.5	25.0
Employees	19.0	24.0
Workers	17.0	23.0

Source: Mesrine (1999).

pure actuarial fairness. It has certain advantages but its labor incentive character is less distinct than in the case of actuarial fairness at the margin.

NDC: *Actuarial Fairness on Average*

In an actuarially fair system on average, the discounted sum of contributions for every individual must be equal to the discounted sum of benefits. In addition, the discount rate is the same for every member of a cohort. As can be seen, the presence of Beveridgian elements in a pension system prevents the existence of such characteristics. In the same way, the existence of specific contributory advantages or of a ceiling on benefits is outside that logic. Those systems are left aside in the following analysis. As soon as the pension system allows for full freedom in retirement age, the respect of actuarial fairness on average necessarily implies the respect of actuarial fairness at the margin. In the steady state, with invariant demographic and economic structures, if all workers earn back what they contributed, the financial balance of the system is ensured. But the respect of actuarial fairness on average does not imply budgetary balance in case of a demographic or economic shock.

Two kinds of pension systems can aim to attain that notion of actuarial fairness on average: the fully funded schemes and the notional accounts or the system by points. The latter differ from pure fully funded schemes by their financing (the vast majority of such systems are PAYG systems), but also by the virtual nature of the acquired benefits. Every contributor has a personal account that records all of his or her pension contributions over his or her active lifetime. The hoarding of those contributions constitutes virtual capital, increased according to a specific rule of indexing. On the date of retirement, that virtual capital stock is converted into annuities according to a transformation coefficient that depends on the liquidation age and retirement life expectancy. In sharp contrast to the notion of actuarial fairness at the margin, fairness on average takes into account the whole career profile of the agent, without focusing on the last years of activity.

Of course that concept must be considered at the collective level, given the uncertainty prevailing on individual life expectancy. The most important defining parameter of such a system must be the rate of discount (or rate of return) used to compare past paid contributions and future earned benefits.

With the same notation as above, and taking into account the average life expectancy of the cohort in question, the internal rate of return of the system ρ can so be defined as

$$1 + \rho_t = \frac{P^i_{t+1} \, {}^* s_{t+1}}{\tau_t w_t} \, ,$$

where s_{t+1} is the portion of period $t + 1$ that is to be lived by the average retired individual

$$s_{t+1} = \frac{\sum_i s_{t+1}^i}{N_t} \, .$$

The value of that rate, as well as the contribution rate, are assumed to be the same for all the agents at the given date.

Of course, for an individual, one is able to compute his or her own personal internal return rate

$$1 + \rho_t^i = \frac{P_{t+1}^i * s_{t+1}^i}{\tau_t w_t^i} \, .$$

As soon as the system is of a PAYG nature, the earnings at date t of the system can be written as

$$R_t = \sum_i \tau_t w_t^i \tag{10.5}$$

and the benefits paid amount to

$$E_t = \sum_i P_t^i * s_t^i, \tag{10.6}$$

with i denoting the individuals (active or pensioners).[12] The budgetary balance of such a system depends on the indexing rule, which sets the internal rate of return and the evolution of pension benefits. That rule is generally given by the evolution of an economic parameter.

Consider the conditions in which an ex ante equilibrium can be reached by the system, denoting g_t the indexing rate of the pensions between t and $t + 1$

$$P_{t+1}^i = P_t^i (1 + g_t);$$

$$E_{t+1} = \frac{s_{t+1}}{s_t}(1 + g_t)\sum_i p_t^i s_t^i = \frac{s_{t+1}}{s_t}(1 + g_t) E_t;$$

$$R_{t+1} = \frac{\tau_{t+1}}{\tau_t}\sum_i \tau_t \frac{w_{t+1}^i}{w_t^i} w_t^i = \frac{\tau_{t+1}}{\tau_t}\frac{\sum_i w_{t+1}^i}{\sum_i w_t^i} R_t$$

as in a PAYG pension scheme, $E_t = R_t$,

$$E_{t+1} = R_{t+1} \Leftrightarrow E_{t+1} = \frac{s_{t+1}}{s_t}(1 + g_t)\frac{\tau_t}{\tau_{t+1}}\frac{\sum_i w_t^i}{\sum_i w_{t+1}^i} R_{t+1} \, . \tag{10.7}$$

As soon as the pension scheme contribution rate does not vary (which is generally the purpose of the switching from a "usual" PAYG toward an NDC PAYG), the indexing rule will try to provide an automatic stabilizing device to the pension scheme. At first glance, there is no NDC or point pension scheme providing this kind of automatic stabilizer, with the single exception of Sweden. Italy uses the total wage bill as an indexing device, France relies on inflation, and Germany on net wages.

There is a huge difference, on the one hand, between a simple comparison of the ability of different factors to achieve the stability of the scheme and, on the other hand, the expectation about the ability of the system to stabilize ex ante. In other words, even if the stabilizer is adequate, it can be inefficient or even incapable of playing its role.

NDC and Resistance to Various Shocks

As a consequence of the above developments, actuarial fairness on average, which is **very close** to pure NDC, can be a source of unfairness. Moreover, it has no automatic stabilizing device. In other words, if the stabilization of this type of scheme is discretionary (for example, decreasing pension benefits to avoid imbalances) the condition of actuarial fairness is broken. This implies a perfect forecasting—that is, no discretionary adjustments once the unbalance cannot be avoided but a perfect planning of future variables.

As shown, there is a need for a "zero pillar" (Holzmann 2006) to provide some redistribution toward the poorest.

A pure NDC—actuarially fair on average—is then far from being ideal. This chapter considers two actual cases, the French and German systems, to which, as a benchmark, is added the Swedish system, often presented as an ideal NDC.

Consider first the Swedish system: a PAYG scheme with virtual funding.

The basis of such a scheme is "virtual" capital, K, which arises through the accumulation of pension rights through contributions. This capital is re-evaluated each period at the rate r, while A is the age when retiring, and C is the birth date, which identifies the cohort C. K_t^C can be written as follows

$$K_t^C = K_{t-1}^C(1+r_{t-1}) \quad \text{or} \quad K_A^C = \sum_{t=t_0}^{A-1} \tau w_t (1+r)^t \; .$$

Note that to be closer to the effective scheme, the contributing period can be divided into subperiods t. The virtual capital, K_t^C, comes from the past flows of contributions during the entire contributing period. At age A, an individual can draw a pension, which is supposed to be re-evaluated during the pension period (whose length is the cohort's life expectancy at retirement). This—initial—actualized pension, P_A^C, is the capital divided by s_A^C, the life expectancy of cohort C when age A, which appears in this type of scheme as a central management parameter. This yields

$$(1+g)^{D-A} * P_A^C = \frac{K_A^C}{s_A^C}, \quad \text{and} \quad P_{t+1}^C = (1+g)P_t^C \text{ after retirement.}$$

In the Swedish pension scheme, $r = 1.6$ percent. This is a parameter of a "yield in advance" given to the contributors, representing a benchmark of economic growth. During the pension period, the index g is close to the nominal growth rate of the per capita GDP, from which this yield in advance is derived. Without any loss, is it later assumed that $r = 0$ and g equals the nominal growth rate of the per capita GDP. With the same simple mathematical manipulation as above, it is rather easy to lead to

$$E_{t+1} = R_{t+1} \Leftrightarrow E_{t+1} = \frac{s_{t+1}}{s_t}(1+g_t)\frac{\tau_t}{\tau_{t+1}}\frac{\sum_i w_t^{ic}}{\sum_i w_{t+1}^{ic+1}} R_{t+1} \, ,$$

where it is not only the period that is in equilibrium but the cohort as well. Thus the equilibrium is both in time and in space. The $C + 1$ factor means that the cohorts have aged by one unit of time, say, one year. The two-period model provides helpful information—and also an optical illusion: in fact, a perfect NDC scheme would require a yearly adjustment to the evolution in the life expectancy, including an adjustment for all pensions that have already been drawn, and not only for pensions of new pensioners.

In addition, the fact that the index g is the nominal growth rate of the per capita GDP implies that there is an "automatic adjustment" only when the share of the wages in the GDP is constant and if the active population remains constant—which is precisely the problem in case of fall in the fertility rate. In the former case, a high GDP growth with a slack wage growth would be a source of financial unbalances, since the PAYG resources are wages and social income.

The same type of calculation in the French case provides different insights. Without any loss in the argument, let us denote the contribution rate as τ (instead of $\tau * coeff$, which means to replace the contractual rate multiplied by the calling rate by a single rate). In this case, equations 10.5 and 10.6 still hold. In addition to equation 10.1 and taking into account the indexing rule to the value of the point, the previous equation becomes

$$E_t = \sum_i \sum_{t=t_0+1}^{A} \frac{\tau_{t-1} * w_{t-1}^j}{PP_{t-1}} * VP_t * s_i^t$$

and then

$$R_{t+1} = E_{t+1} \Leftrightarrow E_{t+1} = \frac{s_{t+1}}{s_t} * \frac{VP_{t+1}}{VP_t} \sum_t \frac{\tau_t/PP_t}{\tau_{t-1}/PP_{t-1}} * \frac{\sum_i \sum_t w_t^i}{\sum_i \sum_t w_{t-1}^{i-1}} * \frac{\tau_t \sum_i w_t^i}{\tau_{t+1} \sum_i w_{t+1}^{i+1}} * R_{t+1} \ .$$

$$\frac{VP_{t+1}}{VP_t} \sum_{t=t_0}^{A} \frac{\tau_t/PP_t}{\tau_{t-1}/PP_{t-1}}$$ represents the adjustment parameters of the scheme.

Some remarks are in order:

- First, there are three parameters: the contribution rate, the price of the point, and the value of the point. The transformation of one wage unit into n units of pensions depends on the relative evolution of the three parameters.
- The parameters can be changed every year, but the burden will not fall on the same persons. Changing the contribution rate, the price of the point, or both will affect both the contributors and the pensioners (such as a change in the contribution rate in a "normal" PAYG pension scheme); however, the "old" contributors will be affected during a shorter period. Changing the value of the point will affect both the young retirees (those who just retired during the last years) and the contributors, whose pension will be changed by this decrease or increase (this can be compared with a change in the replacement rate).
- These changes are deterministic. There is no explicit rule, but they rely on the long-run forecasts done by actuaries.
- The fact that the changes in these parameters can be annual and that they are more or less deterministic means that it is rather easy to adjust them, especially if some fore-

casting errors were made. The bigger the errors, the greater the changes and the more difficult the adjustments are to implement. In the past, the adjustments have been made in the correct time intervals. As a result, the French complementary pension schemes AGIRC and ARRCO enlarged by €40 billion in provisions.

- The above result shows the need for yearly adjustments. The first term represents the change in life expectancy between two cohorts and may be rather weak. The terms

$$\frac{\sum_i \sum_t w_t^i}{\sum_i \sum_t w_{t-1}^{i-1}}$$

and

$$\frac{\tau_t \sum_i w_t^i}{\tau_{t+1} \sum_i w_{t+1}^{i+1}} ,$$

respectively, represent the change in the contribution base between the two cohorts and the opposite of the change in the pension rights between the two cohorts.

In the German pension scheme, two equations remain

$$P_{C+A}^i = \sum_{t=t_0}^{A} \frac{w_{t-1}^i}{\overline{w}_{t-1}} * \alpha^i * VP_{C+A}, \text{ and}$$

$$VP_t = VP_{t-1} * \frac{\overline{w}_{t-1}}{\overline{w}_{t-2}} * \frac{x - \tau_{t-1}}{x - \tau_{t-2}} * \left(1 - \frac{s_{t-2} * N_{t-3} / N_{t-2}}{s_{t-3} * N_{t-4} / N_{t-3}}\right) * 0.25 + 1 ,$$

without any change in the reasoning (provided we take into account the fact that the contributions to the additional pension fund are exogenous, that the sensitivity of a fully funded scheme [FFS]) to the demographic shocks is the same as the sensitivity of a PAYG to the same shock, or both. This leads to consider τ instead of $(\tau + \mu)$.

That implies the following

$$P_{t+1}^i = P_t^i * \underbrace{\left[\frac{\overline{w}_t}{\overline{w}_{t-1}} * \frac{x - \tau_t}{x - \tau_{t-1}} * \left(1 - \frac{s_{t-1} * N_{t-2} / N_{t-1}}{s_{t-2} * N_{t-3} / N_{t-2}}\right) * 0.25 + 1\right]}_{(1+g_t)}.$$

In other words, this yields the same NDC scheme as the one described in the second part of this chapter. It leads to a corroboration

$$E_{t+1} = R_{t+1} \Leftrightarrow E_{t+1} = \frac{s_{t+1}}{s_t}(1+g_t) \frac{\tau_t \sum_i w_t^i}{\tau_{t+1} \sum_i w_{t+1}^i} R_{t+1} , \tag{10.8}$$

with

$$(1+g_t) = \frac{\overline{w}_{t-1}}{\overline{w}_{t-2}} * \frac{x-\tau_{t-1}}{x-\tau_{t-2}} * \left[\left(1 - \frac{s_{t-1}/(1+n_{t-2})}{s_{t-2}/(1+n_{t-3})} \right) * 0.25 + 1 \right].$$

On the surface, this analysis leads to a notional interest rate, which is the growth rate of the net average wage. In fact, this formula deserves a rather long comment. First, g_t depends on τ_t, which depends on the PAYG equilibrium in t, which mainly comes from g_{t-1}, yielding P_t. Intuitively, there is a huge difference between the French and the German pension schemes. Any change in VP in the French pension scheme is a burden for contributors (as future pensioners—and not for those who have already retired whose pension has not been changed). By contrast, a change in VP in the German pension scheme is a burden shared between pensioners and contributors, since any change in τ_t will imply a change in g_t. In other words, if the increase in the point value VP between t and $t + 1$ is too great, the PAYG is unbalanced and is rebalanced by an increase in τ_{t+1} (a burden for the contributors), which decreases g_{t+1} (a burden for both contributors and retirees, that is, for current and future retirees). This mechanism will later be called the *return spring mechanism*. It corresponds to the left-hand side of the equation.

Second, the Rürup formula[13] explicitly introduces the demographic ratio, which becomes quite easily a ratio depending on life expectancy, s, and labor force growth rate, n. How does that change if we compare the new formula (Rürup's) with the Riester formula? First, it explicitly introduces demography: until now, the burden was shared between contributors and retirees, as described above. Now, the retirees pay 25 percent of the burden. This will limit the increase in g, and thus in τ. A second point is linked with the way the retirement pensions schemes are funded in Germany. With the previous formula, it would have been possible to increase the fiscal part of the funding, leaving constant the contribution rates with no change in the point growth rate. Now, because exogenous data hold, this full "fiscalization" of the deficit is not possible.

The problem now is to explain two matters:

- How does the return spring work?
- How is the balance in PAYG achieved—specifically, what are the links to financial stability of the NDC scheme?

How Does the Return Spring Work?

Consider the left-hand side of the equation, yielding $(1 + g_t)$. Roughly speaking, the return spring mechanism is the following

$$\left. \begin{array}{c} \tau_t \\ \tau_{t-1} \end{array} \right\} \to 1+g_t \to VP_{t+1} \to E_{t+1} \to \tau_{t+1} \to g_{t+1} .$$

In its current formulation, it has two limits:

Limit 1. Manipulating the previous equations, and taking into account the PAYG equilibrium (with the fiscal resources denoted T):

$\tau_t * \overline{w}_t * N_t + T_t = \overline{P}_t * s_t * N_{t-1}$, where $\overline{P}_t$ is the average pension in t. This implies

$$1 + g_t = \frac{\overline{w}_t * x - \overline{P}_t * s_t / (1 + n_{t-1}) + T_t / N_t}{\overline{w}_{t-1} * x - \overline{P}_{t-1} * s_{t-1} / (1 + n_{t-2}) + T_{t-1} / N_{t-1}}.$$

This shows that the notional interest rate is the rate of increase in the average wage, a rate of increase that is adjusted in two ways:

- First, it is diminished by a share of the average pension. This share is the ratio of the probability of surviving when retired to the increase in the labor force, n. In other words, the "reimbursed" share of the average pension increases when the life expectancy increases and it decreases when the labor force increases.[14] Each time the average pension, or the life expectancy, or both increases (compared with the increase in the labor force), the return spring plays its part and the indexing is less favorable.
- Second, it is increased by the per capita fiscal part of the pensions scheme resources. This plays the exact opposite part compared with the average pension: the taxation allows a "neutral" increase in the indexing rate.

Limit 2. Again, the main problem is hidden in the use of the two-period model. The life expectancy of the retired persons is given as s_t. In fact, it is a weighted average of all the life expectancies of all the cohorts of retirees s. In other words, this inertia sentences the scheme to deficit and thus to an increase in the contribution rate.

This outcome helps partially answer the second question:

How Is the Balance in PAYG Achieved: That Is, How Does It Bear on the Financial Stability of the NDC Pension Scheme?

As noted, the notional interest rate depends partly on past life expectancies while ensuring that the financial equilibrium of the NDC would introduce the future life expectancies as well as the expected increase in the total amount of contributions (that is, the wage bill multiplied by the contribution rate). That would imply taking into account a change in the wage bill, which obviously does not appear in the indexing rate formula. With respect to this remark, assumptions about the automatic stability are in conflict with a change—that means a change either in the labor force or in the wages. Their realism is therefore questionable.

Conclusion: Nobody Is Perfect

One can clearly see the potential contradiction between the aims of actuarial fairness (insurance logic) and redistributive goals, since life expectancy strongly differs between socioprofessional groups. Taking into account the average life expectancy of one population, the NDC obviously favors financial equilibrium over social equilibrium, as life expectancy is highly correlated with income.

On the other hand, for a social reason, all these schemes have introduced either minimum pensions (as in Sweden and Germany) or are "only" complementary schemes. For example, in France, there is a basic scheme offering the possibility of a minimum pension. In Sweden, there is double protection against poverty in old age for unemployed or socially subsidized people. In addition to a minimum pension provided by the scheme, the social income (unemployment, disability subsidies, or other sources) provides contributions to the pension schemes and then provides supplementary rights. In the end, these arrangements are not pure NDC schemes.

Even though these schemes are supposed to offer a high degree of freedom for individuals to choose their own retirement age, they cannot escape fixing a minimum retirement age. With absolute freedom, the agents would not be very protected against the bias in their decision making arising from uncertainties or unrestrained optimism concerning life expectancy—situations all the more dangerous if pensions are no longer indexed to wages and/or if the pensions are low according to an early chosen retirement age.

In addition, the application of NDC to a real economy under uncertainty is problematic. That uncertainty is a major problem in the context of pensions is well known. Various reports are full of illustrations of such uncertainty. In the German case, for example, forecasted contribution rates through 2004 can vary by 15 percent depending on the assumptions about active population,[15] birth rates,[16] and life expectancies.[17]

Of course, the schemes can be periodically regulated according to changes in the forecasts.

In the French case, this is done yearly. This requires two things: the first are reliable and frequent forecasts (which are problematic, according to Lassila and Valkonen 2002). The second is total independence of the boards from retirees and even wage earners' lobbies. The German return spring, strengthened by the Rürup sustainability factor, is another mechanism in which the pension yield is lowered by the current contribution rate, which is a way to shift the burden on both the active and the retired population. In both cases, the periodic changes in the parameters of the schemes obviously break the actuarial fairness.

A precautionary strategy would be to use the less favorable assumptions in order to adapt the parameters of the schemes. With such a strategy, it is probable that the scheme will get into surplus within some years. In this case, these surpluses would be helpful by becoming a buffer fund, which has been demonstrated to be a useful tool for bringing about intergenerational equity.

To sum up, a pure NDC plan would be actuarially fair on average. An ideal NDC plan would provide redistribution, incentives to work longer, transparency, and automatic stabilizing. The chapter pointed out the lack of distibutive properties of a pure NDC, the lack of actuarial fairness of the considered schemes, the need for a zero pillar and for a precautionary buffer fund, and the fact that the economic and demographic uncertainties lead to break the actuarial fairness—that is, any revision in the parameters induce a different individual balance. Thus an ideal NDC cannot be a pure NDC.

Then why promote NDC? If pensions schemes are made to promote individual responsibility, the preferred schemes are FFS. If, in addition, the purpose is to promote social responsibility, a favorite choice is NDC schemes.

Annex A: Actuarial Fairness at the Margin

In the following simple model, the contribution rate is τ. If an agent who would be allowed to retire decides to postpone his retirement decision by one year, he renounces retiring at date $t - 1$ and age A, but waits until date t and age $A + 1$, he will pay his contributions, τw_{t-1}^A—that is, the contribution rate τ multiplied by his wage w in $t - 1$, and will benefit from a full pension, with liquidation rate p. On the other hand, if he retires early, his benefits will be reduced by a fraction d during his entire retirement.

That may be summed-up by the following equation

$$-\tau w_{t-1}^A + \sum_{j=1}^{N} \frac{1}{(1+r)^j} \cdot p_{t+j-1}^{A+j} = \sum_{j=0}^{N} \frac{1}{(1+r)^j} \cdot (1-d) p_{t+j-1}^{A+j}, \tag{10A.1}$$

where d denotes the actuarially fair decrual in benefits and N is the last age of pension earnings while j is the time index.

To keep things simple, omit the uncertainty prevailing over life expectancy. Taking it into account would lead to multiplying both sides of the equation by survival probabilities. That operation would not modify the accounting reasoning. However, risk-averse agents factor life expectancy uncertainty into their choices and behavior: whatever the decrual/accrual rate in pensions benefits associated with early/late retirement, an increase of this uncertainty has the effect of moving forward the retirement date.

The left-hand side of equation 10A.1 is the sum of discounted pensions benefits at rate r received from date t by an agent if he retires at age $A + 1$. The right-hand side is the sum of discounted pension benefits received from date $t - 1$ by the agent if he retires at age A, reduced by a fraction d.

The choices made by the workers depend on their individual preferences. Let $R^{(1)}$ and $R^{(2)}$ stand for income equivalents of the welfare of agents in situation 1 (delayed retirement) or 2 (early retirement)

$$R^{(1)} = w_{t-1}^A \cdot (1-\tau) + \sum_{j=1}^{N} \frac{1}{(1+\rho)^j} \cdot p_{t+j-1}^{A+j}, \tag{10A.2}$$

with ρ the discount rate of the individual considered,

$$R^{(2)} = (p-d.p)_{t-1}^A + \sum_{j=1}^{N} \frac{1}{(1+\rho)^j} \cdot (p-d.p)_{t+j-1}^{A+j} + \ell_{t-1}^A, \tag{10A.3}$$

with ℓ_{t-1}^A the income equivalent of the leisure associated with retiring one year earlier.

Let π stand for the inflation rate, and θ, the productivity gains of the economy—gains supposed to pass on to real wages. Nominal wages then increase at the rate $\rho + \theta$. As done in Artus (2000), pensions benefits are assumed to be indexed at the rate $\pi + x\theta$, a rate that covers all potential indexing rules. If $x = 0$, pensions are indexed on inflation; if $x = 1$, they are indexed on gross wages. This upgrading rate is generally also the rate applied to activity wages for calculating pension benefits.

The replacement rate of gross wage, noted β, has the following value

$$p_t^{A+1} = \beta . w_{t-1}^A . (1 + \pi + x.\theta).$$

Equations 10A.2 and 10A.3 become

$$R^{(1)} = w_{t-1}^A.(1-\tau) + p_{t+j-1}^{A+1} \sum_{j=0}^{N-1} \frac{(1+\pi+x.\theta)^j}{(1+\rho)^j}$$

$$= w_{t-1}^A.(1-\tau) + \beta.w_{t-1}^A \sum_{j=1}^{N} \left(\frac{1+\pi+x.\theta}{1+\rho} \right)^j \qquad /10A.2'/$$

$$R^{(2)} = \beta.(1-d)w_{t-1}^A.\frac{1+\pi+x.\theta}{1+\pi+\theta}.\sum_{j=0}^{N} \left(\frac{1+\pi+x.\theta}{1+\rho} \right)^j + \ell_{t-1}^A. \qquad /10A.3'/$$

In addition, the actuarial fairness condition /1/ can be rewritten

$$-\tau w_{t-1}^A + \beta.w_{t-1}^A \sum_{j=1}^{N} \left(\frac{1+\pi+x.\theta}{1+r} \right)^j = \beta.(1-d).w_{t-1}^A \frac{1+\pi+x.\theta}{1+\pi+\theta} \sum_{j=0}^{N} \left(\frac{1+\pi+x.\theta}{1+r} \right)^j. \qquad /1'/$$

Along with equations 10A.2' and 10A.3', it leads to the following, under the following assumptions:

- If $\rho = r$ and $w_{t-1}^A = \ell_{t-1}^A$, then $R^{(1)} = R^{(2)}$ and the worker perceives no difference between the early or delayed retirement. Either option, under the assumption of an actuarially fair scale at the margin, provides the same satisfaction.
- If $\rho = r$ but $w_{t-1}^A < \ell_{t-1}^A$, then $R^{(1)} < R^{(2)}$. In that case, the worker draws a high satisfaction from leisure and will opt for an early retirement, with the actuarially fair decrual in benefits.
- If $w_{t-1}^A < \ell_{t-1}^A$, what are the determinants of the retirement decision? Equations 10A.2' and 10A.3' yield equation 10A.4

$$R^{(1)} - R^{(2)} = -\tau.w_{t-1}^A + \beta.w_{t-1}^A.\sum_{j=1}^{N} \left(\frac{1+\pi+x.\theta}{1+\rho} \right)^j - \beta.(1-d)w_{t-1}^A \frac{1+\pi+x.\theta}{1+\pi+\theta} \sum_{j=0}^{N} \left(\frac{1+\pi+x.\theta}{1+\rho} \right)^j$$

$$= -\tau.w_{t-1}^A + \beta.w_{t-1}^A.\sum_{j=1}^{N} \left(\frac{1+\pi+x.\theta}{1+\rho} \right)^j - \left[-\tau.w_{t-1}^A + \beta.w_{t-1}^A.\sum_{j=1}^{N} \left(\frac{1+\pi+x.\theta}{1+r} \right)^j \right]. \qquad (10A.4)$$

As soon as $\tau < \beta$, the contribution rate is less than the replacement rate, which is always the case, and then $R^{(1)} > R^{(2)}$. In other words, when individuals have a high time discount rate, they prefer to retire early, as they do not give much weight to the loss in income induced by an early retirement.

- If $w_{t-1}^A \neq \ell_{t-1}^A$, actuarial fairness at the margin gives

$$R^{(1)} - R^{(2)} = \left(w_{t-1}^A - \ell_{t-1}^A \right) + w_{t-1}^A \beta \left(1 - (1-d)\frac{1+\pi+x\theta}{1+\pi\theta} \right) \sum_{j=1}^{N} (1+\pi+x\theta)^{j-1} \left[\frac{1}{(1+\rho)^j} - \frac{1}{(1+r)^j} \right].$$

If $w_{t-1}^A > \ell_{t-1}^A$ and $\rho < r$, then $R^{(1)} > R^{(2)}$. But if $w_{t-1}^A > \ell_{t-1}^A$ and $\rho < r$, then is $R^{(1)} < R^{(2)}$ as the second part of the right-hand side is always negative and lower in absolute value than w_{t-1}^A. In other words, the individual's preference for the present is such that the financial gain induced by actuarial fairness at the margin does not mean much to him or her, and the agent retires early.

Notes

1. "Notional defined contribution" and "non-financial defined contribution" should be understood to have the same definition.

2. See Valdés-Prieto (2000) and World Economic Forum (2004).

3. The 1993 reform changed this point: previously the reference wage was computed as the average of the 10 best indexed wages. The number of years increased by one a year since 1993. The reform will fully hold for the 1948 cohort.

4. The first of July, 2005, the value of the point is 1.1104 euros for an ARRCO point and 0.3940 for an AGIRC point. The purchasing prices are, respectively, €12.6600 (ARRCO) and €4.4163 (AGIRC).

5. These simplications include ignoring the "comp" index and considering a weighed average for the contribution rate as for the price and value of the point.

6. See Hamayon (1995).

7. Both schemes have permanent buffer funds. In 2004, these amounted to 30 billion euros for ARRCO (to cover a 28 billion euro annual payment of pensions) and 10 billion euros for AGIRC (to cover a 14 billion euro annual payment of pensions).

8. See Veil (2003).

9. For example, in the long run—with constant contribution rates for both PAYG and funded schemes—the formula leads to a gross wages indexing rule.

10. See Guérin and Legros (2003),

11. There is obviously a link between ρ (the internal rate of return of the system) and the life expectancy; it is included in the relationship between ρ and the value of leisure.

12. This analysis follows Valdés-Prieto (2000), but adds the consideration of life expectancy.

13. The mechanism of "return spring" is thus a sort of a balancing mechanism, reacting to potential disequilibria by feedback.

14. The Rurup report (summarized in Börsch-Supan 2003) also suggests an increase in the pensionable age; here we discuss only the point mechanism.

15. For example, the French Council for Retirement Schemes' forecasts for 2040 are based on an assumption in which the active population was to increase by 10 million, while the forecasts of the Centre d'Etudes Prospectives et d'Informations Internationales (CEPII) rely on an increase of only 1 million.

16. That will affect the entire active population. In this area, divergences in statistical estimations worldwide are enormous.

17. See Konrad and Wagner (2000).

References

Artus, P. 2000. "Quelques résultats de base, préalables à la réflexion sur les retraites." *Flash CDC-Marchés* 2000-17 (January letter).

Börsch-Supan, A. 2003. "The Rurup Commission's Pension Reform Recommendations." *MEA (Mannheim research institute for the Economic of Ageing) Newsletter* 6 (June): 1–4.

Bundesministerium für Gesundheit und Sociale Sicherung. 2003. *Achieving Financial Sustainability for the Social Security Systems*. Report by the Commission, A319, Berlin: Edition of the Bundesministerium für Gesundheit und Sociale Sicherung.

COR (Conseil d'orientation des retraites). 2001. *Retraites: renouveler le contrat social entre les générations*. Premier rapport du conseil d'orientation des retraites. Paris: La Documentation Française.

Guérin, J.-L., and F. Legros. 2003. " Neutralité actuarielle: un concept élégant mais délicat à mettre en œuvre." *Revue d'économie financière* (68): 79–90.

Hamayon, S. 1995. "Perspectives du système de retraite en France." In *Les retraites, genèse, acteurs, enjeux*, ed. B. Cochemé and F. Legros. Paris: Armand Colin.

Holzmann, R. 2006. "Toward a Coordinated Pension System in Europe: Rationale and Potential Structure." In *Pension Reform: Issues and Prospects for Non-Financial Defined Contribution (NDC) Schemes*, ed. R. Holzmann and E. Palmer, chapter 11. Washington, DC: World Bank.

Konrad, K., and G. Wagner. 2000. "Reform of the Public Pension System in Germany." Discussion Paper 200, DIW (Deutsches Institut für Wirtschaftsforschung), Berlin.

Lassila, J., and T. Valkonen. 2002. "Retirement Age Policies and Demographic Uncertainty in Lithuania: A Dynamic CGE Analysis." Paper prepared for the workshop sponsored by ENEPRI (European Network of Economic Policy Research Institutes) on Welfare and the Labour Market, Marseilles, October 25–26.

Mesrine, A. 1999. "Les différences de mortalité par milieu social restent fortes." *Données Sociales*, INSEE, Paris, 228–35.

Queisser, M. 1996. "Pensions in Germany." Policy Research Working Paper 1664, World Bank, Washington, DC.

Valdés-Prieto, S. 2000. "The Financial Stability of Notional Account Pensions." *Scandinavian Journal of Economics* 102 (3): 395–417.

Veil, M. 2003. "La réforme des retraites, premiers pas, débats, interrogations." *Chronique internationale de l'IRES* 82 (May): 3–16.

Vernière, L. 2001. "Allemagne, la réforme 2002 du système de retraite." *Question retraites, document de travail CDC (Caisse des dépôts et consignations, Paris)* 2001-41.

World Economic Forum. 2004. "Living Happily Ever After: The Economic Implications of Ageing Societies." A report of the World Economic Forum Pension Readiness Initiative developed in partnership with Watson Wyatt Worldwide, Watson Wyatt ed., Geneva.

Discussion of "NDCs: A Comparison of the French and German Point Systems"

Marek Góra*

THE CHAPTER BY FLORENCE LEGROS presents a very interesting overview and comparison of the French and the German pension systems. Legros focuses on vital elements of the systems and mechanisms behind them. The chapter provides the reader with arguments to confirm that the two crucial features of both systems analyzed are the complexity of regulations ruling participation in the system and the system itself, and exposure to discretional adjustments.

These features are not exclusive to the French and the German systems. They are found in the majority of systems, especially in continental European pension systems (I call them traditional systems). These features did not appear by chance. These are the most crucial features of traditional pension systems. Without detailed regulations and without discretional decisions, traditional pension systems—including point systems—will crash.

The growing popularity of notional defined contribution (NDC) is leading to an overuse of its name. In many cases, including Legros's chapter, NDC is understood in a very broad sense: namely, as any pension arrangement that assumes some linkage between contributions and benefits. In her chapter, Legros discusses practical cases of NDC arrangements that have been implemented. The discussion leads her to the conclusion that "a pure NDC does not exist." The conclusion is probably correct, but the same type of conclusion can be reached regarding other types of pension arrangements. However, this type of approach locks us into a very conservative conceptual framework. In phenomena like pension systems, the aim is not to seek purity. I would rather suggest seeking concepts that can help us understand the nature of the systems. NDC combines features of different pension arrangements, which opens the door for possibly fruitful research that can contribute strongly to the development of pension economics.

NDC has features that are opposite to the ones highlighted in the case of the French and the German point systems. NDC is very easy to describe and understand, and is transparent. The shortest possible description of participation in NDC is the following:

> At the moment of retirement, participants receive from the system (in the form of an annuity) the present value of contributions they have paid throughout the working period. The discount factor is the GDP growth rate, or is close to it.

The above is an ex ante arrangement that cannot only be understood but also internalized by the participants.

NDC has built-in automatic stabilizers. The system adjusts revenues and expenditure without discretional intervention from outside (that is, it is an endogenous arrangement,

---

* Marek Góra is a professor at the Warsaw School of Economics.

or ENDO). In practical application, this can be less than 100 percent effective; however, it is close to 100 percent. This does not ensure complete resistance to politicians' attempts to manipulate the system. Such an arrangement cannot exist in reality. This point also applies to financial defined contribution (FDC) plans. Nonetheless, NDC is much less exposed to political manipulation than any system that cannot function without intervention from outside. Both the French and German pension systems require interventions (or exogenous arrangement, EXO).

Is automatic adjustment a desirable feature of a pension system? Interventions from outside can at best reach the solution that individual accounts (ENDO) lead to automatically. The challenge is counteracting the ever-growing burden put on each successive generation of workers, who are increasingly discouraged in their labor supply and productivity growth. A good pension system should lead to a stable division of GDP between generations. The shares are subject to public choice. Once chosen, they should be kept stable. Individual accounts of both types—NDC and FDC—are endogenous arrangements, which lead to intergenerational equilibrium. Being in equilibrium, a pension system is economically neutral. This means remuneration of production factors is not affected by declining proportions of the retired and working generations, which leads ceteris paribus to the strongest possible growth of welfare of each generation being first a working one and then a retired one. Traditional EXO arrangements would not lead to this outcome unless proper decisions are taken. However, they are notoriously postponed. The growth in pension systems' debts, which slow down economic growth, clearly prove that.

In Legros's chapter, as is common in pension literature, NDC is reduced to a tricky way to balance defined benefit (DB) pay-as-you-go (PAYG) schemes. We are hostages of terminology inherited from social policy and finance. From the economic viewpoint, NDC is neither DB nor PAYG. Instead, in a very broad sense NDC is similar to a universal FDC scheme that spends the entire sum of contributions paid into it in buying government bonds and keeps them until maturity, and receiving a rate of return equal to economic growth rate. Discussing this issue in detail goes beyond the scope of this short discussion.

Being so similar, NDC and FDC fit each other very well. Latvia, Poland, and Sweden not only implemented NDC in their pension systems but also terminated EXO arrangements entirely. They have systems entirely based on individual retirement accounts: NDC and FDC. This is the revolution in European pensions, even if some technical elements that are not "pure" remain.

Chapter 11

Toward a Coordinated Pension System in Europe: Rationale and Potential Structure

*Robert Holzmann**

THE NEED FOR A RAPID AND COMPREHENSIVE REFORM of the pension systems in most current and future member countries of the European Union (EU) is increasingly acknowledged by pension scholars and politicians. While a few countries have recently undertaken major reforms to make their pension systems financially sustainable, in the majority of European countries the reform efforts are still insufficient. Although national efforts can now draw support on intensified EU cooperation based on the Open Method for Coordination, this method takes the diversity of European pension design as a given, and much of the reform debate is still limited to fiscal issues at national levels. There is little discussion about a reform need beyond fiscal consideration. There is no discussion (anymore) about a reform move toward a more coordinated pension system within the European Union, and how such a system may look and come about. That is the topic of this chapter. To this end, it progresses in four sections. The second section reviews the reform needs of the pension systems for fiscal, social, and economic reasons. The third section makes the case for a move toward a more coordinated pension system in Europe. The fourth section sketches how such a system may look and come about. The central claim of the chapter is that a multipillar system, with a non-financial (or notional) defined contribution (NDC) system at its core and coordinated supplementary funded pensions and social pensions at its wings, is an ideal approach to deal with diverse fiscal, social, and economic reform needs. The approach would also introduce a harmonized structure while allowing for country-specific preferences with regard to coverage and contribution rate. Such a reform approach may lead to a Pan-European reform movement as a number of countries have already or plan to introduce NDCs, and others may easily convert their point system into an NDC structure.

* Robert Holzmann is director, Social Protection Department, at the World Bank.

Revised study prepared for the joint Watson Wyatt & Deutsches Institut fuer Wirtschaftsforschung (WW-DIW) Lecture on Issues in Pension Reform, Berlin, September 26, 2003, and the NDC Conference in Sandhamn, Sweden, September 28–30, 2003. The draft and the revisions have benefited from valuable comments and suggestions by lecture and conference participants, in particular Bernd Marin and Edward Palmer, a presentation at the EU Commission in Brussels on October 31, 2003, discussions with World Bank staff, and able research support by Kripa Iyer. This paper has not undergone the review accorded to official World Bank publications. The findings, interpretations, and conclusions reflected herein are those of the authors and do not necessarily reflect the views of the International Bank for Reconstruction and Development/The World Bank and its affiliated organizations, or those of the Executive Directors of the World Bank or the governments they represent.

The Need for Pension Reform in EU and EUA Countries

There are three main reasons[1] why EU countries and the new EU accession countries (EUA) in Central, Eastern, and Southern Europe need rapid and comprehensive reforms of their national pension systems:[2] First, the current high expenditure level and related budgetary pressure will only worsen given the projected further aging of populations. The national systems need to be reformed to handle aging in a manner consistent with individual preferences and macroeconomic constraints. Second, ongoing socioeconomic changes are rendering current retirement income provisions inadequate at the social and economic level. Third, globalization creates opportunities and challenges, and to deal with them effectively requires, inter alia, benefit and tax regimes that improve the functioning of factor markets.

The *expenditure level for public pensions* in most Western European countries is well above that of other highly industrial and postindustrial countries at a similar income level. The average of public pension expenditures as a percentage of gross domestic product (GDP) for the 15 EU countries in 2000 amounted to 10.4 percent (this is a low estimate because it includes only the expenditure under the projection exercise of the Economic Policy Committee 2001). The Organisation for Economic Co-operation and Development (OECD) estimate is about 1.3 percentage points higher (OECD 2002). The average for the non-European and affluent OECD countries—Australia, Canada, Japan, New Zealand, the Republic of Korea, and the United States—in 2000 was about 5.3 percent: that is, roughly half. In the EU, only Ireland (4.6 percent) and the United Kingdom (5.5 percent) have similar levels. This difference is also shared by the accession countries in Central and Eastern Europe. Except Romania (5.1 percent), all others have expenditure shares close to the EU

Figure 11.1. Pension Expenditure in EU and EUA Countries (plus Croatia), 2000 or latest (percentage of GDP)

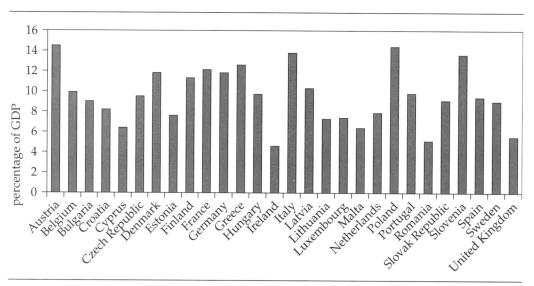

Source: EPC 2001; Palacios and Pallares-Miralles 2000, updated; World Bank 2003b.

Note: Croatia data from World Bank 2003b.

average (and in Croatia, Poland, and Slovenia, well above) and hence much higher than non-European OECD countries, despite an income level of one-quarter and less. Poland's public pension expenditures, at close to 15 percent of GDP, rival that of Austria and Italy for the world championship (see figure 11.1). The gap between these expenditure levels and those in non-European OECD countries is only partially explained by differences in population age structure. Rather, it reflects differences in the public/private mix of provisions and in the benefit levels and the effective retirement age in the public systems. The replacement rate is generally much higher as public (largely unfunded) pensions are little supplemented by private and funded arrangements (except in Denmark, Ireland, the Netherlands, and the United Kingdom). The effective retirement age is typically low as a result of disincentives to work longer in current public schemes, special options for early retirement, and past labor market policy that deliberately attempted to keep the unemployment rate low by allowing older workers to exit prematurely. Yet the demographic component in pension expenditure is going to increase under unreformed systems as aging in Europe accelerates.

In Europe, the total fertility rate has been below replacement level (approximately 2.1) since the 1970s in the West and since the 1980s in the East, and there are few signs of a rebound from the current low levels. On the other hand, life expectancy is likely to increase during the next 50 years by 4.2 years for women and 5 years for men. As a result, for the EU15, the old-age dependency ratio is projected to increase from 27.7 percent (2000) to 53.4 percent (by 2050) (see table 11.1), based on rather optimistic assumptions with regard to total fertility rate (assumed to rise again to 1.8 in most countries) and life expectancy (assumed to rise less than in the past). The projections for the EUA countries are very similar (United Nations 2002); actually the projected pace of aging in the EUA is faster. Based on this projected change in the old-age dependency ratio in the East and the West, and in a no-reform scenario, expenditures would roughly double.

Of course, such a radical expenditure increase would not necessarily materialize because some reform measures have already been enacted, and system dependency ratios (beneficiaries to contributors) may not deteriorate to the same extent as old-age dependency ratios. Greater labor force participation by women is likely and that of both older (55+) men and women may increase as well. This, at least, is the scenario put forth by the Economic Policy Committee of the EU, and the country projections for the period 2000 to 2050 (EPC 2001; see table 11.2).[3] As a result, the average EU public pension expenditures (captured under this exercise) are projected to increase "only" from 10.4 percent of GDP in 2000 to a peak of 13.6 percent around 2040 (with a projected fall from 5.5 to 4.4 percent for the United Kingdom, but almost a doubling for Spain from 12.6 to 24.8 percent). This moderate projected 30 percent increase of the average expenditure level (compared with a pure demographically induced increase of some 70 percent) is estimated as a result of lower benefit ratios (average benefits compared to GDP per capita) and higher employment ratios (employment to population aged 15 to 64). However, this modest increase in EU average public pension expenditure levels will require major changes in the pension schemes and their incentives for enhanced labor market participation and delayed retirement decisions. Put differently, a further major increase in pension expenditure can be prevented only if major reforms take place.

No similar and coordinated projection exercise has been undertaken for the new EU member states, but existing projections clearly paint a two-class picture (EPC 2003): In countries that have undertaken major reforms—such as Hungary and Poland—the expenditure share remains largely unchanged (and a similar path can be conjectured for reformed systems in Estonia and Latvia). In countries where a major reform is still out-

Table 11.1. Projections of Old-Age Dependency in EU and EUA Countries, 2000–50 (ratio of people aged over 64 to working age population, percent)

Country	2000	2010	2020	2030	2040	2050
Austria	25	29	32	44	55	55
Belgium	28	29	36	46	51	50
Denmark	24	27	34	39	45	42
Finland	25	28	39	47	47	48
France	27	28	36	44	50	51
Germany	26	33	36	47	55	53
Greece	28	32	36	42	51	59
Ireland	19	19	25	30	36	44
Italy	29	34	40	49	64	67
Luxembourg	23	26	31	40	45	42
Netherlands	22	25	33	42	48	45
Portugal	25	27	30	35	43	49
Spain	27	29	33	42	56	66
Sweden	30	31	38	43	47	46
United Kingdom	26	27	32	40	47	46
EU average	**27**	**30**	**35**	**44**	**52**	**53**
Bulgaria	24	24	29	34	41	53
Cyprus	18	20	26	32	34	39
Czech R.	20	22	32	38	47	59
Estonia	23	25	30	36	42	57
Hungary	21	23	29	33	40	50
Latvia	23	26	29	37	44	56
Lithuania	21	24	26	35	40	43
Malta	18	22	32	39	40	46
Poland	18	18	26	33	37	50
Romania	20	20	24	26	36	45
Slovak R.	16	17	23	30	36	47
Slovenia	20	24	32	44	53	64
EUA average	**20**	**22**	**28**	**35**	**41**	**51**

Sources: EU countries—EPC (2001); EUA countries—UN (2002).

standing, the expenditure share in percentage of GDP is projected to increase dramatically: to almost double in Cyprus and the Czech Republic, and to increase further from an already high level in Slovenia. World Bank internal projections are largely consistent with this picture.

Even if the budgetary and demographically induced pressures did not exist, there still would be a major need for most European countries to reform their public pension systems to better align them with socioeconomic changes. Three changes stand out: increasing female labor force participation; high divorce rates and changing family structures; and the rise in atypical employment. Furthermore, rising life expectancy and other changes also call for a rethinking of the design of disability benefits.

In the EU countries, the *labor force participation* of women has increased substantially over recent decades. In the former centrally planned countries, it was very high, but it decreased during the transition period of the 1990s (see table 11.3). The decrease for women followed that of men and was in some countries even less pronounced (World Bank 2003a). Although there are differences among EU countries (for example, in Italy,

Table 11.2. Public Pension Expenditure in EU and EUA Countries in 2000–50 (percentage of GDP)

Country	2000	2010	2020	2030	2040	2050
Austria	14.5	14.9	16.0	18.1	18.3	17.0
Belgium	10.0	9.9	11.4	13.3	13.7	13.3
Denmark[1]	10.5	12.5	13.8	14.5	14.0	13.3
Finland	11.3	11.6	12.9	14.9	16.0	15.9
France	12.1	13.1	15.0	16.0	15.8	—
Germany	11.8	11.2	12.6	15.5	16.6	16.9
Greece	12.6	12.6	15.4	19.6	23.8	24.8
Ireland[2]	4.6	5.0	6.7	7.6	8.3	9.0
Italy	13.8	13.9	14.8	15.7	15.7	14.1
Luxembourg	7.4	7.5	8.2	9.2	9.5	9.3
Netherlands	7.9	9.1	11.1	13.1	14.1	13.6
Portugal	9.8	11.8	13.1	13.6	13.8	13.2
Spain	9.4	8.9	9.9	12.6	16.0	17.3
Sweden	9.0	9.6	10.7	11.4	11.4	10.7
United Kingdom	5.5	5.1	4.9	5.2	5.0	4.4
EU	**10.4**	**10.4**	**11.5**	**13.0**	**13.6**	**13.3**
Cyprus	8.0	—	—	11.9	—	14.8
Czech Republic[4]	7.8	—	—	—	—	14.6
Estonia	6.9	—	—	—	—	—
Hungary[4]	6.0	—	—	—	—	7.2
Latvia[3]	9.8	—	—	—	—	—
Lithuania	5.3	—	—	6.0	—	7.0
Malta	5.4	—	—	—	—	—
Poland	10.8	—	—	9.6	—	9.7
Slovakia[3]	7.9	—	—	—	—	—
Slovenia	13.2	—	—	19.7	—	18.1
Bulgaria	9.1	—	—	—	—	—
Romania	6.4	—	—	7.8	—	8.2
EUA	**8.05**	—	—	**11.0**	—	**11.4**

Source: EPC (2001), except as indicated.

Note: For most EU member states, these projections include most public replacement income for persons aged 55 and over. — = not available.

1. For Denmark, the results include the semi-funded labor market pension (ATP).
2. Results for Ireland are as percentage of GNP, not GDP.
3. Source is Gesellschaft fur Versicherungswissenschaft und -gestaltung e. V. (which in turn draws on national statistics).
4. Source is OECD 2002.

female labor force participation in the age group 15–64 in 2000 stood at a low 46 percent, in contrast to Denmark where a 77 percent female participation rate is close to that of men), a further increase is projected for all countries. The EU average for women in the age group 15–54 is projected to increase from 63 to 76 percent, whereas that for men is projected to remain largely constant at around 85 percent. So far this change in female labor force participation is little reflected in countries' pension benefit structures (see table 11.4). The benefit rules still largely reflect the traditional image of a working husband and a child-caring housewife who needs a widow's pension for her protection in

Table 11.3. Labor Force Participation, Male and Female, in EU and EUA countries, 1960, 1980, 2000, and 2050 (percent)

| | Male | | | | | | | | Female | | | | | | | |
| | 15–64 | | | | 65+ | | | | 15–64 | | | | 65+ | | | |
Country	1960	1980	2000	2050	1960	1980	2000	2050	1960	1980	2000	2050	1960	1980	2000	2050
Austria	90.1	84.9	74.4	79.3	15.0	4.5	2.0	6.0	53.0	54.4	57.7	67.8	7.0	2.6	1.0	5.0
Belgium	85.9	79.7	71.7	71.9	9.5	4.6	1.4	1.3	30.5	41.2	58.6	67.8	3.3	1.3	0.5	0.6
Denmark	92.3	88.3	85.1	81.8	32.6	15.4	9.4	8.1	42.8	71.3	77.3	80.5	8.0	5.2	2.7	2.4
Finland	87.3	79.3	74.8	73.9	31.7	6.8	4.0	2.5	55.5	69.4	73.0	74.7	12.0	3.0	1.4	1.0
France	88.9	81.5	75.6	75.1	26.0	5.8	2.1	1.7	43.6	55.1	62.2	70.0	10.2	2.9	1.2	1.0
Germany	91.0	83.2	80.7	80.1	24.0	8.9	4.5	2.4	50.4	51.9	64.7	71.3	8.0	4.2	1.7	1.1
Greece	90.1	83.5	76.7	76.6	45.0	27.0	9.6	7.9	26.3	31.8	46.7	67.0	8.7	6.1	3.7	3.2
Ireland[3]	90.9	85.0	87.8	87.3	54.0	26.8	13.6	11.7	31.1	34.7	56.4	75.8	15.0	6.0	2.4	2.0
Italy	89.2	79.0	73.0	76.1	27.5	12.4	5.5	3.7	30.4	38.4	46.4	66.9	5.6	3.5	1.5	1.4
Luxembourg[1]	88.7	82.3	113.8	148.4	—	—	—	—	30.8	39.0	74.3	115.0	—	—	—	1.0
Netherlands	90.9	77.6	77.4	76.2	19.9	4.8	1.0	1.0	24.9	36.1	55.2	70.9	2.5	1.0	1.0	1.0
Portugal	93.5	87.1	87.5	87.2	62.9	29.7	16.7	14.3	18.4	52.4	66.4	81.5	11.0	8.4	7.1	6.5
Spain[3]	92.8	86.4	83.6	85.5	56.6	12.3	2.8	2.8	20.3	32.9	54.7	75.2	9.4	4.1	1.1	1.1
Sweden	88.8	87.9	81.3	83.3	27.6	10.4	6.8	7.2	38.0	75.3	76.5	82.6	4.5	2.6	3.5	3.9
United Kingdom[3]	94.6	89.2	87.6	85.9	26.6	11.0	6.8	5.8	43.6	57.0	69.9	75.5	5.4	4.1	2.7	2.4
EU	90.3	83.7	82.1	84.6	32.8	12.9	6.2	5.5	36.0	49.4	62.7	76.2	7.9	3.9	2.3	2.3
Bulgaria	88.4	82.7	77.2	77.2	38.3	18.8	10.1	8.6	68.9	70.4	71.4	68.8	8.5	3.9	3.0	2.5
Cyprus	91.7	88.6	88.0	86.1	53.0	35.7	20.5	0.2	42.0	46.7	56.9	59.1	17.6	11.8	7.8	6.3
Czech R.	86.5	84.8	83.0	80.6	24.4	18.8	11.7	10.3	61.6	75.0	75.0	71.7	9.2	7.1	4.9	4.5
Estonia	87.2	85.4	81.7	81.5	20.5	17.5	23.0	22.4	67.3	79.2	74.0	74.0	6.8	9.5	13.3	13.4
Hungary	91.7	84.8	78.7	76.2	57.0	3.8	0.9	0.9	46.9	62.0	61.1	60.5	20.0	3.0	0.2	0.2
Latvia	84.8	84.8	82.2	83.0	24.3	22.4	20.2	19.2	64.3	77.9	74.2	75.4	12.8	12.3	11.3	10.8
Lithuania	83.3	83.0	81.2	81.7	32.0	19.4	12.3	11.0	61.3	74.8	70.8	71.7	9.5	7.8	6.5	5.9
Malta	88.0	85.7	78.8	76.3	27.3	14.3	5.0	4.0	17.2	22.5	30.2	34.6	0.0	0.0	0.0	0.0
Poland	89.8	84.2	77.9	77.4	57.5	30.0	24.1	21.3	62.1	67.7	66.2	66.4	30.0	17.5	15.3	13.8
Romania	93.0	83.6	76.8	76.7	62.6	11.4	4.9	3.9	72.4	69.0	61.2	61.4	30.0	8.9	4.2	3.5
Slovak R.	86.5	83.5	82.1	81.8	30.9	19.8	11.0	9.6	47.4	69.3	74.6	72.7	7.7	4.7	4.2	3.6
Slovenia	89.9	81.9	76.0	74.1	57.1	19.0	11.8	10.2	44.3	67.0	66.5	64.9	13.5	10.0	8.6	8.0
EUA[2]	88.4	84.4	80.3	79.4	40.4	19.2	13.0	10.1	54.6	65.1	65.2	65.1	13.8	8.0	6.6	6.0

Sources: EPC (2001); OECD (2003); ILO (2003); UN (2002).

Note: — = not available.

1. Estimates for Luxembourg assumes increase in cross-border workers, which explains the high rate.
2. Projections for EUA countries are for the year 2010.
3. Population aged 20–64.

Table 11.4. Pension Arrangements for Widows/Widowers and Divorcees in EU and EUA Countries around 2000

Country	Widow/widower's benefit		Divorcee's benefit	
	Elgibility	Benefits	Eligibility	Benefits
Austria	Deceased met insurance or contribution requirements for disability pension or was a pensioner.	Up to 60% of deceased spouse's pension, income tested. Rates below 60% may be increased depending on beneficiary's income.	—	—
Belgium	Those aged 45+, or disabled, or caring for a child. Should have been married for at least 1 year at the time of spouse's death. Conditions are waived if child born out of marriage or in case of accidental death.	80% of deceased spouse's pension. Minimum 9,102.11 euros/year if worker was fully insured; if not, then reduced. If widow(er) receives other pension, receives survivor pension only for 12 months and total pension benefits may not exceed 110% of own pension.	Special pension at age 60.	37.5% of former spouse's earnings during period of marriage less pension earned in own right during the same years.
Bulgaria	Deceased had 5 years of service, or 3 years if aged 20–25 or was a pensioner.	Minimum pension for each survivor is 90% of social pension. One survivor, 50% of deceased's pension; if 2, 75%; if 3 or more, then 100%.	—	—
Cyprus	Conditions same as for old-age pension, lump sum paid if conditions not met. Payable to widow or dependent disabled widower.	Same as old-age pension + 60% supplementary pension. Widow may substitute husband's coverage record for her own for period prior to his death.	—	—
Czech Republic	Deceased met pension conditions or was a pensioner.	Basic amount of 1,310 koruny plus 50% of deceased's pension, payable to all widow(er)s for 1 year, thereafter only to widow(er)s aged 55(58), or any age if disabled or caring for disabled/dependent child or disabled parent.	—	—

Table 11.4. (continued)

Country	Widow/widower's benefit		Divorcee's benefit	
	Eligibility	Benefits	Eligibility	Benefits
Denmark	Survivor pension eliminated as of 1984.	Lump sum paid to widow(er) and children under 18 of deceased; amount depends on pension of the deceased.	—	—
Estonia	Widow(er) not capable of gainful activity; deceased had 1–14 years of coverage depending on age.	One survivor, 40% of deceased's pension entitlement; 2 survivors, 70%; 3 or more 100%.	—	—
Finland	Under age 65 if caring for a child; if childless then at least age 50 at time of spouse's death and must have been married for at least 5 years, residing in Finland.	Universal pension awarded for first 6 months after spouse's death, thereafter becomes income-tested.	Eligible for survivor's pension if not remarried; pension proportionately divided if more than one surviving spouse.	—
France	At least 55 years and married for 2 years. Conditions are waived if child from marriage or if widow(er) and deceased were disabled. Personal income must be less than 13,874 euros/year and must not have remarried.	54% deceased spouse's pension, income-tested, payable for 2 years. If beneficiary is age 50, payment extended until 55.	Former spouse eligible for survivor's pension. Amount split between widow(er) and former spouse according to length of marriage.	54% deceased spouse's pension.
Germany	Deceased had 5 years of coverage, or was a pensioner.	100% of deceased's pension for first 3 months; 55% if aged 45+, disabled, or caring for a child; otherwise 25%.	—	—
Greece	Eligible for survivor's pension for 3 years, those above 40 continue to receive it provided they do not work or receive any other pension.	Full pension paid if disabled. Those who work or receive other pension get 50% of normal survivor pension. When survivors reach age 65 they are paid full pension, if receiving other pension at 65+ then they get 70% of normal pension.	—	—

Country	Qualifying conditions	Benefit		
Hungary	Deceased was pensioner or met requirements for pension at death.	50% of insured's pension paid to widow(er) who at the time of death was 55(60), disabled, or caring for 2 children, paid to other widow(er)s for 1 year only.	—	—
Ireland	Annual average of at least 39 weeks paid or credited in last 3 or 5 fiscal years prior to date spouse died or attained age 66, at least 24 weeks for minimum pension.	Contributory pension: up to 123.30 euros/week (144.80 euros if aged 66+), noncontributory pension: up to 118.80 euros/week (134.00 euros if age 66+).	—	—
Italy	Deceased was a pensioner or had 5 years of contribution of which 3 years were in the last 5 years.	60% of insured's pension, 80% if 1 child, 100% if 2 or more children; lump sum paid if conditions for survivors pension not met; must have paid at least 1 year's contribution in last 5 years.	Separated spouse eligible for survivor's benefit.	—
Latvia	Deceased was insured or was a pensioner.	50% of insured's pension, 75% if 2 survivors, 90% for 3 or more.	—	—
Lithuania	Deceased must have been a pensioner or had adequate coverage for disability pension at the time of death. Widow(er) who has reached old age or is disabled is eligible.	20% of deceased's benefit, 25% for each child, total may not exceed 80% of deceased's pension.	—	—
Luxembourg	Insured had 12 months of coverage in 3 years prior to death or was a pensioner.	100% of insured's basic old age pension plus 75% of increment earned by insured, payable without regard to personal income.	Divorced spouse eligible.	Amount depends on years of marriage, not on personal income.
Malta	Deceased paid 156 weeks of contribution with annual average of 50 weeks, paid or credited, reduced pension awarded for less coverage, earned income of widow(er) must not exceed minimum wage. Widows under age 60 with children under 16 qualify regardless of income.	Benefit varies depending on whether contributions were made before or after January 22, 1979. Earnings-related benefit that can be as much as 70.72 liri/week are 5/9th yearly average of best 3 consecutive years of last 10 years before husband's death or retirement. Upon remarriage, widow forfeits benefit from previous marriage and receives lump sum equal to 52 weeks pension.	—	—

Table 11.4. (continued)

| Country | Widow/widower's benefit | | Divorcee's benefit | |
	Eligibility	Benefits	Eligibility	Benefits
Netherlands	Residents eligible. Payable to widow(er)/unmarried permanent partner.	Income-tested for those born before 1950, those 45% disabled, 932.38 euros/month for those caring for child under 18, benefit reduced by survivor's income from employment. No benefits if income > 2,002.54 euros/month.	—	—
Poland	Deceased was a pensioner or met employment requirements for old-age pension or disability benefits.	One survivor, 85% of deceased's pension; 2 survivors, 90%; 3 or more, 95%.	—	—
Portugal	Deceased met pension requirements or was a pensioner.	60% of insured's pension. Payable for 5 years only unless beneficiary over 35, disabled, or caring for a child.	—	—
Romania	Insured met pension requirements or was a pensioner at the time of death. Widows must fulfill certain age conditions and also duration of marriage requirements. No prior requirements if death was by work accident, occupational disease, or tuberculosis.	Limited benefit paid for 6 months to low-income spouse caring for child under age 7 who does not meet eligibility conditions. 50% of deceased's old-age pension; 2 survivors, 75%; 3 or more, 100%.	—	—
Slovak Republic	Deceased met pension requirements or was a pensioner.	60% of insured's pension payable to widows for 12 months, thereafter only to widows aged 50; aged 45 if she has reared 2 or more children; aged 40 if husband died in occupational accident; any age if disabled, caring for a child, having cared for 3 or more children; widowers pension 1,977 koruny/month.	—	—

Slovenia	Deceased met pension (old age or disability) requirements or was a pensioner and had 5 years of coverage and contribution; widow(er) must be at least 52(53) as of 2003.	70% of insured's pension; 2 survivors, 80%; 3 survivors, 90%; 4 or more, 100%.	—
Spain	Deceased had 500 days of contribution in the last 5 years, was pensioner at time of death, or had 15 years of contribution.	46% of either the deceased's or survivor's benefit base, whichever is higher, for income below a particular level—50%, 70% if there are dependents.	Ex-spouse not eligible for old-age pension once remarried unless 61+ at time of marriage, 65% disabled or survivor pension is 75% of pensioner's total income.
Sweden	Residents eligible. Deceased must be credited with pension points for at least 3 years or have 3 years coverage.	Benefit payable for 6 months if married or cohabiting for at least 5 years, under certain conditions. Payable for as long as living with child under 12. Special pension paid if unemployment or illness prevents self-support.	—
United Kingdom	Deceased met coverage requirements or was a pensioner.	Weekly allowance to those above age 45 without dependent children payable for 52 weeks after death of spouse. Amount depends on age at widowhood. Widow aged 18–59 with dependent children gets weekly allowance of 53.05 pounds plus 31.45–32.25 pounds for each child minus amount of other benefits/income.	—

Source: United States Social Security Adminstration (2002).

old age. Only a few countries, such as Denmark and Sweden, have fully moved toward independent pension rights and eliminated the traditional widow's pension (Denmark in 1984 and Sweden in 1991). As a result, there is often underprovisioning for young widows with children, and overprovisioning for widows with their own pensions—the latter group now includes widowers. To ensure gender neutrality, survivor's pensions in many countries have been extended to male spouses and the budgetary consequences are increasingly attempted to be curtailed by ceilings and tapers.

Furthermore, eligibility for survivor's pensions is complicated by the rising divorce rate. In a number of countries the divorce rates are more than 50 percent of the rates of marriage per 1,000 inhabitants (see table 11.5), which means that in many countries more than 50 percent of marriages will not survive, including second or third marriages. Countries with a more conservative divorce behavior, such as Italy and Ireland, can be expected to catch up quickly. But only a few countries have moved in the direction of establishing

Table 11.5. Changing Family Structures: Divorces and Marriages in EU and EUA Countries around 2000 (per 1,000 people)

Country	Divorces (per 1000 people)	Marriages (per 1000 people)
Ireland	0.7	5.1
Italy	0.7	4.9
Greece	0.9	5.4
Spain	1.0	5.2
Portugal	1.8	5.7
France	2.0	5.1
Luxembourg	2.3	4.5
Netherlands	2.3	5.1
Germany	2.4	4.7
Sweden	2.4	4.0
Austria	2.5	4.2
Finland	2.6	4.8
United Kingdom	2.6	5.1
Denmark	2.7	6.6
Belgium	2.9	4.2
EU average	**1.9**	**5.1**
Bulgaria	1.3	—
Cyprus	1.7	—
Czech Republic	2.9	—
Estonia	3.1	—
Hungary	2.4	—
Latvia	2.6	—
Lithuania	2.9	—
Poland	1.1	—
Romania	1.4	—
Slovakia	1.7	—
Slovenia	1.1	—
Malta	—	—
EUA	**2.0**	—

Sources: EU countries—EU (2003); U.K. Office of National Statistics, Inc. (2001). EUA countries—Americans for Divorce Reform (2003); UN (2001); Council of Europe (2001).

Note: — = not available.

independent rights for spouses (and even less for partners): that is, the individualization of pension rights. In many countries, benefit traps for women still exist: that is, incentives against rejoining the labor market or remarrying when eligibility for a survivor's pension has been achieved.

Another and more recent development concerns the rise in *atypical employment*: that is, the reduction in full-time salaried employment and the increase in part-time employment, self-employment, and temporary employment (see table 11.6). This development may be ascribed to globalization and competitive pressure that makes full-time employment and a life career with the same employer less dominant than it used to be; it may also be linked to more self-selected flexibility in the labor market (including the choice of retirement provisions). Data for OECD countries suggest that coverage under public pension schemes is decreasing (Holzmann 2003). Whatever the reason, these atypically employed people do not fare well under some pension schemes, which are based on the full-time employment fiction. In many current systems, the atypically employed fare extremely well, which limits their incentives to contribute on a continued basis. Again, this situation calls for reforms (and a stricter contribution-benefit relationships).

Socioeconomic changes also call for a review and redesign of disability benefits, including the delinking of design, delivery, and financing of old-age benefits. At the start of the Bismarckian-type pension scheme, disability benefits were much more important for individuals than old-age benefits as only one in six workers could expect to reach the advanced retirement age of 70. Old-age pensions then can be conceptualized as generalized or cate-

Table 11.6. Selected Work Arrangements in Europe, 1988 and 1998 (percent of total employment)

Country	Total employment (000s)		Self-employment (including family workers)		Part-time employment		Temporary employment[1]	
	1988	1998	1988	1998	1988	1998	1988	1998
Austria	—	3,626	—	13.8	—	15.8	—	6.8
Belgium	3,483	3,857	18.0	17.4	9.8	15.7	4.5	6.4
Denmark	2,683	2,679	11.0	9.7	23.7	22.3	10.2	9.1
Finland	—	2,179	—	14.6	—	11.7	—	15.1
France	21,503	22,469	16.2	12.5	12.0	17.3	6.6	12.2
Germany	26,999	35,537	11.5	11.0	13.2	18.3	10.1	10.9
Greece	3,651	3,967	49.5	43.4	5.5	6.0	8.8	7.4
Ireland	1,090	1,496	25.3	20.2	8.0	16.7	6.8	6.1
Italy	21,085	20,357	29.5	28.7	5.6	7.4	4.1	6.1
Luxembourg	152	171	11.2	9.4	6.6	9.4	3.3	2.4
Netherlands	5,903	7,402	12.1	11.6	30.3	38.8	7.7	11.2
Portugal	4,427	4,764	30.9	28.2	6.5	11.1	12.6	12.4
Spain	11,709	13,161	29.1	23	5.4	8.1	15.8	25.3
Sweden	—	3,946	—	11.4	—	23.9	—	11.4
United Kingdom	25,660	26,883	12.7	12.5	21.9	24.9	5.2	6.1
EU	**128,345**	**152,494**	**19.1**	**16.6**	**13.2**	**17.4**	**7.8**	**10.6**

Source: Holzmann (2003).

Note: — = not available.

1. Dependent employees, including apprentices, trainees, and research assistants.

gorical disability pensions: that is, insuring much the same risk. Nowadays an old-age pension is a life-annuity paid with accumulated funds or acquired rights and insures against the uncertainty of death. Conceptually, it is totally delinked from failing work capacity. But the original design of disability pensions and the close link to old-age pensions still prevail in many of the European pension systems, and the mixed design has also helped the use of disability pensions as a form of unemployment benefits in many countries. Furthermore, sport and car accidents instead of general incapacity have become a major reason for the granting of disability benefits, in particular at younger ages. As a final argument, disability benefits—insurance-based and means-tested—need to be reviewed and integrated into the design of an overall work/benefit package for the disabled (OECD 2003).

Last but not least, *globalization*—understood as high and increasing integration of markets for goods and services, factors of production, and knowledge—calls for changes in the way public programs operate, including in the area of pension provision. Such reforms are needed not only to reap the benefits of globalization but also to deal with challenges that include profound shocks resulting from technical innovations and shifts in the demand and supply of goods and factors. This calls, inter alia, for more flexibility across labor markets, improved financial markets, and lifelong learning.

A main conjecture about the fate of nations and their economic performance in a globalized world is their capacity to deal with shocks, in particular those that require the existing economic structure to adjust. It is claimed that the more flexible and adjustable an economy is in reacting to such shocks, the better it will fare. Such *flexibility* comprises mobility of individuals across professions, including between the public and the private sector. In most European countries, such mobility is hampered by separate pension schemes between both sectors that limit if not eliminate any movement between them. Moreover, separate schemes render the application of some reform measures difficult or counterproductive. For example, increasing the retirement age for all primary school teachers to, say, 67, may not be in the best interest of all concerned, but it is feasible if a teacher can move easily to a related or different profession.

The integration of countries into the world economy is importantly linked with their own *financial sector development*. A developed domestic financial market is a main ingredient for full capital account convertibility, including the capacity to diversify pension assets internationally.[4] International diversification is, perhaps, the only free lunch in the world, and it promises major welfare effects as long as national and international rates on return of retirement assets (beyond shares) are little correlated. This requires, however, that some minimum domestic financial market exists. Forcing individuals to hold most or all of their pension assets in illiquid pay-as-you-go (PAYG) assets is not an optimal strategy for dealing with diverse risks to which individuals are exposed and is clearly not welfare enhancing. Restricting a country solely to PAYG is truly an example of taking the risk of putting all pension eggs into one basket. Pension reforms that include introducing or strengthening a funded pillar allow such a risk diversification and at the same time can importantly contribute to development of the domestic financial market. Well-developed domestic financial markets are a critical pillar of a market-based economy as they mobilize intermediate savings, allocate and price risk, absorb external financial shocks, and foster good governance through market-based incentives. The level of financial market development is positively linked to output level and quite likely also to economic growth paths.[5] Such effects are crucial for the EUA countries and are likely to be important for various current EU member states as well.

Last but not least, to handle aging through prolonged labor market participation, to provide labor market flexibility in a socially acceptable manner, and to contribute to knowledge and skill formation as a major ingredient for economic growth, a pension system that supports *lifelong learning* is required. Too many pension schemes today are still based on the strict separation of education, work, and retirement leisure. But a modern economy and the need for lifelong learning require a pension scheme in which the mixing of the three activities is encouraged and not impeded—for example, going back to school after years of work, bringing forward (retirement) leisure, or taking up work again after retirement (say, from ages 70 to 72). Such flexibility is discouraged in most current pension schemes.

To deal with aging, socioeconomic changes, and globalization, a reform approach is required that moves toward a more actuarial system structure that better links contributions and benefits and includes more individualization to handle professional and family mobility and also some funding to allow more individual decision and choices. The approach must go beyond a parametric adjustment of existing schemes. For most old EU member countries, this contrasts with the adopted reform approach so far, while new EU member countries have shown more inclination to adopt a paradigmatic shift in pension provision,[6] yet with stronger differentiation in system design compared with Latin America.[7]

Reforms in the 1990s and early 2000s in the EU countries were essentially of a parametric nature—with Sweden and partly Italy as the only exceptions. The reform package typically included a combination of the following elements: reduction or elimination of early retirement provisions, an increase in the retirement age or related indirect measures to this effect, reduction in the annual accrual factor, further changes in indexation, and introduction or enhanced support of a funded voluntary pillar. Only a few countries started toward more harmonized national systems (for example, Austria and partially France). Most countries ignored the nonfiscal reform needs except, perhaps, for reasons of political economy.[8] While essentially all these reforms move in the right direction, even from a fiscal point of view more is needed and rapidly.[9]

The Need for a Better-Coordinated Pension System in an Integrated Europe

While there is increasing support for national pension reforms in old and new EU member countries, and despite agreement with some or perhaps all of the arguments advanced above, there is little understanding of and support for a Pan-European approach that should lead to a coordinated pension structure. Pension systems are considered—like other parts of social policy programs—as a national agenda item with little indication that member countries see a necessity for more coordination, and even less harmonization. Astonishingly, neither does the Commission of the European Union, which in many other areas often sees the need for such coordination, or even harmonization, and pushes accordingly. The EU approach of "Open Coordination" of the reform efforts by member countries is viewed as a benchmarking device, not a harmonizing one.[10]

This section argues that a major impetus for a Pan-European pension reform approach resides in European economic integration, and the objective of common markets for goods, services, and factors of production under a common currency—the euro. This objective has implications for the provision of retirement income: budgetary implications, the need for more labor market flexibility, and the need for enhanced labor supply in an aging population.

The concept of a stable common currency in Europe is linked with the Maastricht fiscal criteria to keep the fiscal deficit below 3 percent and public debt below 60 percent of GDP. Although the selection of the criteria may be questioned,[11] the objective is sound: to avoid excessive and opportunistic fiscal expansion by some member countries at the detriment of the internal and external value of the euro. To comply with the related growth and stability pact, the 12 "Euroland" members engage to achieve a structural budget deficit of zero percent (to allow for fiscal expansion when cyclically needed). But many countries will not be able to achieve a zero budget deficit in a sustainable manner unless the pension system is reformed and the explicit or implicit transfers from the budget are curtailed. In Austria, as an extreme example, the pension-related deficit amounts to almost 5 percent of GDP. And all current and future member countries are exposed to enhanced fiscal pressure of population aging in the main public programs—pensions and health—in addition to the not yet fully grasped expenditure pressure in long-term care programs or infrastructure.

Room for budgetary expansion (and contraction) is needed in a common currency area because exchange rate and interest rate policy are lost and few other instruments are available to deal with asymmetric shocks hitting some member states and not others. Given the limited effectiveness of fiscal policy in an integrated economic area resulting from high leakages to other regions or compensating private sector savings, the other main policy instrument has to come into play: *labor market flexibility* through wage flexibility and migration.

Empirical evidence for the United States suggests that although wage adjustment during regional crises is important, the main adjustment mechanism is migration from (temporarily) contracting to expanding regions.[12] This can be contrasted with the European experience, in which both wage flexibility and migration have had little importance;[13] actually the international and inter-regional mobility in Europe during recent decades has been very low.[14] For Europe, both adjustment mechanisms are likely to remain less important than in the United States because of more rigid labor markets, and cultural and linguistic barriers; the last two restrictions also translate into a larger loss of social capital when moving.[15] However, both wage adjustment and migration mechanisms need to be strengthened if sluggish adjustments after demand or supply shocks are to be avoided, along with their economic and social consequences.

A particular recent drastic example of the consequences of delayed structural adjustment and lack of mobility in resource reallocation under a common currency-type arrangement is Argentina. The introduction of the currency board with the national currency pegged to the U.S. dollar was motivated by many episodes of hyperinflation and the expectation that the tight monetary corset would help to push through reforms in the goods and factor markets. But these reforms (including reforms in the labor market) did not come through as expected, which left the country very vulnerable when shocks hit the world economy and neighboring countries.

One important mechanism to support a common currency and adjustments after shocks is a pension system that does not lock persons into sectors and countries, but instead supports full labor mobility across professions and states—a requirement that is far from reality in the European Union. In many European countries, different pension rules for public and private sector workers impede mobility between the sectors. Mobility between states exists notionally for public schemes (less in reality), but full portability for corporate and voluntary funded systems is still under construction. As a result, the European Union does not have a coordinated—and even less a harmonized—pension system, which characterizes other economically integrated areas under a common currency (such as Australia, Brazil, Canada, Switzerland, and the United States). These federations or confederations exhibit many differences at state or provincial levels (including income taxes or short-term social benefits), but they have one thing in common—a public retirement income scheme across states.

A third main argument for a more coordinated Pan-European pension system resides in the need for more *labor market integration* that goes beyond the requested labor market flexibility. A strand of international economics suggests that free trade in goods and services or alternatively free capital flows may be sufficient to lead to equalized factor prices and maximize welfare. However, in the real world of externalities and imperfect competition, quite likely the performance of all markets, including the labor market, needs to be improved and integrated more strongly to maximize welfare.[16] Full integration of the European labor market requires full portability of pension rights between countries.[17]

Finally, the long-term *external value of the euro* is likely to be determined or at least co-determined by the growth expectation of Europe (compared with the United States or other currency areas). Current-period balances or imbalances in flows of goods and services or even the net-asset positions of countries are increasingly conjectured to lose their importance in determining the relative price of a currency under globalization. Productivity growth can only compensate partially for the effects on GDP growth of projected population decline in the EU15 (13 percent between 2000 and 2050, compared with an expected increase in the United States of 50 percent or more; see Holzmann and Muenz 2004)—and higher productivity requires mechanisms to reallocate workers from shrinking to expanding sectors and regions. If falling population and aging are not better compensated for through increased labor supply resulting from higher labor market participation, delayed retirement, and increased external migration, the impact on GDP growth will be substantial. The weakness of the euro until recently (compared with the U.S. dollar) may be explained by expectations of the financial markets about the relative growth of these two currency areas. Enhanced labor force participation and delayed retirement, however, require major changes in age management practices in work places and labor markets, as well as appropriately reformed retirement income schemes.

Clearly, although a Pan-European pension system would help remove current constraints on labor mobility, in and by itself it is not sufficient. It would help as it reduces the transaction costs for people wanting to move between member states. These costs can be very high and, in consequence, mobility very low, as suggested by migration research. But uncoordinated pension systems are not the only source of transaction costs. Other national social programs need to be adjusted in order to enhance mobility—most importantly, health care financing, and in particular the private/supplementary health care programs. And there are nonmonetary costs as a result of culture and language barriers. The latter will be gradually reduced as younger people and the more educated population are increasingly more proficient in other European languages or use English as lingua franca. Open borders with more travel, more inter-European marriages, and the emergence of a European identity will also reduce actual or perceived cultural barriers.

Potential Structure of Pan-European Pension System and Transition Issues

What structure could or should a more coordinated Pan-European pension system have? And if an appropriate steady-state system were to emerge from the discussion, what are the transition issues the approach would encounter? And how could they be solved? This section suggests answers to these questions. Issues of the political economy and how to get there will be addressed in the concluding remarks in the last section. This section starts out by outlining the general and specific main objectives a Pan-European pension system should have, before reviewing which of the main three options fits best. The proposed Pan-European system consists of a mandatory first pillar NDC plan, a (voluntary) funded pillar with occupational and individual retirement plans, and a basic (or zero) pillar of social or noncontributory pensions providing minimum income support for the very vulnerable elderly. All elements are discussed in turn, with main emphasis on the NDC pillar. The proposed structure has highly attractive features against a Pan-European objective, but is also suggested to be an extremely powerful reform option for the many ailing pension schemes in Europe and beyond.

Demands on a Reformed and Coordinated Pan-European Pension System

What objectives should such a reformed system fulfill? A presentation of these desiderata should allow for a transparent and objective discussion and an easy comparison with alternative reform proposals. Two sets of objectives are suggested: generic objectives that all modern pension systems worldwide should fulfill, and specific objectives that result from the EU background.

The generic objectives are the ones developed and proposed by the World Bank in a recent policy position report, and two levels of goals—primary and secondary—are distinguished.[18]

The primary goal of a pension system should be to provide adequate, affordable, sustainable, and robust old-age income, while seeking to implement welfare optimizing schemes in a manner appropriate to the individual country.

- An *adequate* system is one that provides benefits to the full breadth of the population that are sufficient to alleviate old-age poverty on a country-specific absolute level, in addition to providing a reliable means to smooth lifetime consumption for the vast majority of the population.
- An *affordable* system is one that is within the financing capacity of individuals and the society: one that will not displace other social or economic imperatives or lead to untenable fiscal consequences.
- *Sustainable* refers to the financial soundness of a pension system and its capacity to be maintained over a foreseeable horizon under a broad set of reasonable assumptions.
- *Robust* refers to the capacity to withstand major shocks, including those coming from economic, demographic, and political risks.

The secondary goal of mandated pension provisions (and their reform) is to create positive output effects by minimizing negative impacts, such as on labor markets, while leveraging positive impacts, such as on financial market development. This secondary goal is important since all retirement incomes—whether funded or unfunded—are essentially financed out of the country's output. The centrality of output for pension systems[19] for delivering on the primary goals makes it imperative that the design and implementation of pension systems are checked for their economic output level and growth effects.

The suggested specific objectives of a Pan-European pension system, to be used as criteria for selection and choice, are: mobility, national preferences, solidarity, and feasible transition.

- First, the system should allow for *easy, most unrestricted mobility* between professions, sectors, and regions and also between stages of the life cycle (school, work, and leisure) and family structures.
- Second, the system should be consistent with the (European) concept of *solidarity*, understood as a mechanism of risk sharing among and between generations, redistribution of income from the life-time rich to life-time poor, and open risk coverage.

- Third, the system should allow for *national preferences* of target levels of (mandated) benefits or contributions, and the redistributive allocation of resources toward the poor or specific groups or activities.
- Finally, the proposed future system should involve a *feasible system transition* from the current national systems for the largest possible number of member countries.

Potential Structures of a Pan-European Pension System

There are three main options for a future Pan-European pension system that aims to fulfill the objectives set out above: a basic pension plus a mandated fully funded pillar (Beveridge for all); an unfunded defined benefit system plus voluntary fully funded pensions (Bismarck for all); and a basic or noncontributory pillar plus an NDC pillar plus a voluntary (or mandated) funded pillar.

The first option—a basic pension in the form of demogrant or means-tested social pension plus a mandated fully funded pillar providing defined contribution (DC) benefits—would be consistent with all objectives, except most importantly the one on easy transition. Such a system may be structured in such a way as to target all primary and secondary goals, and if well done it may achieve these goals pretty well. Namely, such a system can ensure mobility, allow for national preferences (for example by country-specific levels of basic pensions and contribution rates for the funded pillar), and can be structured to ensure solidarity: for example, through a central public pension fund that pays one rate of return (hence pooling of risks across individuals) and through explicit budget transfers to individual accounts to deal with low income or periods of unemployment (as in Mexico). A main obstacle is (easy) transition. Abstracting from political problems to find consensus for such an Anglo-Saxon approach in continental Europe, the main obstacle is fiscal. It is well known that such an approach makes the implicit debt that pension promises constitute explicit, and the level of this implicit debt is in the range of 200–300 percent for most European countries.[20] Repayment of such an amount is beyond political and economic reach, and for a broad range of assumptions not Pareto-improving.[21] Although a repayment of the debt may not be necessary to achieve the social policy objectives, it can be doubted that international markets are willing to live with such an explicit debt level of the European Union without consequences for interest rate and exchange rate of the euro.

Under the second option, a future pension system would expand the dominant Bismarckian approach of an unfunded and publicly managed defined benefit (DB) system to the whole European Union. Supported by social pensions and voluntary funded pensions, such an approach can also achieve many but not all objectives. Well structured, it can achieve all the primary goals, and very well structured it may even support the secondary goals of a pension scheme. But as experience with such systems throughout the world indicates, it will be difficult to make such structural reforms happen (and agreed at European level). With regard to the specific EU objectives, an inconsistency between the mobility goal and national preferences emerges. For example, with different accrual rates or additions for, say, childcare under another identical DB structure, it would be difficult but not totally impossible to move from one profession or member country to the next, but the administrative efforts to emulate such a mobility would be gigantic while not fully successful. Last but not least, the transition would first require a consensus on a DB structure (and there are many), and a second consensus on complicated rules of transitions.

The third option, the proposed structure of a (mandated) first pillar NDC plan, a (voluntary or mandated, if so desired) funded pillar with occupational and individual retirement plans, and a basic pillar of social/noncontributory pensions that provides minimum income support for the very vulnerable elderly, is claimed to fulfill all objectives—generic and specific, primary, and secondary.[22] Of course, there is room for design and implementation specificities to make a future structure fit very well or less well. The following subsections outline the basic structures and design elements to make it fit well.

The Crucial (First) Pillar: Non-Financial or Notional Defined Contribution Plan

To motivate the choice of NDC as the crucial pillar of a future Pan-European pension system, this subsection progresses in three parts: outlining the basic structure of an NDC system, highlighting its capacity to deal with system objectives and reform needs, and presenting the ease of transition for most (but not all) EU member countries.[23]

BASIC STRUCTURE OF IDEAL NDC[24]

One main attraction of an NDC system is the simplicity of its basic structure if one follows the rule book: that is, if it is seen as a system that makes the algebraic and economic logic and constraints of an (unfunded) pension system explicit. Simply put, an NDC system consists of an individual account system to which contributions by individuals (and their employers) are earmarked, notional interests paid, and at retirement the accumulated (notional) amount used to determine the level of annuity based on the residual life expectancy (and the notional interest rate). As a result, the system should be quasi-actuarially fair at the margin and on average.[25] Crucial elements for design and implementation are:

- The choice of a notional interest rate consistent with internal rate of return of a PAYG scheme: that is, growth rate of aggregate (covered) wage sum. Per capita rates of wage or GDP growth or contribution revenue will not do the trick if the contribution rate is constant, but the discussion about the (most) appropriate notional interest rate choice is far from over.[26]
- The choice of remaining life expectancy. Politically determined underestimation (for example, by taking the cross-section life expectancies instead of estimated cohort life expectancies) to deliver higher annuities will also jeopardize financial sustainability.
- The indexation of benefits. Although indexation beyond price adjustments is feasible, in principle, keeping benefits constant in real terms allows higher initial benefits. A temporary underindexation compared with a steady state also allows building up a reserve fund.[27]
- Although a reserve fund is not strictly needed in an NDC system to guarantee balancing the pension budget in every period—that is, to make it fully immune against economic and demographic risks[28]—it avoids extreme fluctuation in benefit levels.[29]

Other important basic design elements, which are discussed below, concern the minimum eligibility age to own pension and to minimum pension, if any; the introduction of redistributive elements; and transition rules to new NDC benefits. This and other design elements are discussed in more detail in Palmer (2006a; 2006b).

DEALING WITH SYSTEM OBJECTIVES AND REFORM NEEDS

An NDC pillar (together with a well-designed basic plus voluntary pillar) is able to achieve all reform needs outlined in the second and third sections, and to fulfill all system objectives. The discussion that follows concentrates on a subset for reasons of space and importance: financial sustainability, changing family structure and establishing own pension rights, mobility across professions and across states, and national preferences and solidarity.

Achieving financial sustainability, in particular under conditions of an aging population, is one of the trademarks of an NDC system, albeit it is not fully automatic. As life expectancy increases, individuals receive a lower pension benefit for a given retirement age, for which they can compensate by extending their labor force participation (or additional individual savings). Hence the system encourages behavior that deals with aging in a consistent and balanced manner: namely, splitting the increase in life expectancy between more work and more retirement leisure. Earlier or later retirement for a given age is sanctioned (rewarded) by quasi-actuarial decrements (increments) consistent with a PAYG scheme. But financial stability cannot be achieved automatically in all periods[30] without the use of a balancing approach.[31] A reserve fund is needed to fund the contributions of relatively large cohorts, as well as external financing to cover possible noncontributory risks. It is also a general buffer that helps stabilization of a number of key variables.

Dealing with increasing female labor force participation, changing family structures, and rising divorces is easy under an NDC system, as it allows individualization of pension rights, together with considerations of fairness and efficiency. For example, marriage and separations over the life cycle can be easily handled by splitting the accumulated (notional) amounts (contributions and interests) of the time together. But even if the marriage lasts until retirement, one can imagine a splitting of benefits at retirement (as unisex survival probabilities may be applied anyhow). Also survivorship can be handled in an easy manner: for example, widows/ers with very young children receive a generous transitory pension until, say, the children enter school, and the split accumulations from prior marriage help build her (or his) own pension account and eliminate any pension benefit trap. Since in most European countries accumulated financial and physical assets during marriage are split at divorce, it would be inconsistent not to split the accumulated pension rights.

Mobility across professions can easily and quickly be established, as an NDC plan allows immediate harmonization of pension schemes with few technical problems. Take civil servants pensions to be integrated into a national NDC pillar. For those already retired, nothing changes. For those with accumulated pension rights, these rights can be estimated with high precision, transformed into a present value, and credited to an individual (notional) account. The next month (or year) this individual gets credited the unified contributions and notional interests as everybody else. As a result, for those very close to retirement, little change in the pension amount takes place, while for those with only a few years of work record, the new system dominates by far. Quite likely such a reform will need to be accompanied by a review of the overall compensation package of the public sector, leading to changes in earnings profile or, perhaps, introduction of supplementary but funded pensions of DC type.

The mobility across EU member countries can also be made very easy under an NDC plan. Albeit the accumulated amounts are only notional, they are very precise and allow an easy aggregation across countries with two main approaches. Under a *transfer approach,* a worker moving from, say, Germany to France would take his accumulated amount along (that is, the German social security scheme would need to make a cash transfer to the French social security scheme). The pension would be calculated and disbursed in the country when the worker stops his or her activity and applies for a pension. From a national point of view, only the balance for all labor market migrants (to and from the country) need to be transferred, which is likely to be modest. Under the alternative *preservation approach,* each worker would keep his or her account and continue to receive national notional interests until retirement. Then the individual would receive partial pensions from as many countries as he or she has worked in. The second approach seems more transaction-cost intensive (unless administrated under a Pan-European clearinghouse) and may create a problem in case minimum pensions are granted (unless delivered in each country through top-ups and based on residency). Of course, social arbitrage is not excluded under the first approach, as individuals may be tempted to move before retirement to a country with high minimum pension, low remaining life expectancy, and low income tax rates.

But incentives for social arbitrage will always exist in case of national preferences and different depth of national solidarity across member countries, and NDCs cum social pensions/top-ups allow for national preferences. For example, one country may prefer a frugal mandated pension for its residents and prescribe a low NDC contribution rate (say 10 percent) and expect more voluntary contributions to well-regulated funded schemes (say also 10 percent). Another country may prefer a high target replacement rate and mandate a higher contribution rate accordingly (say 20 percent), but expect few people to contribute to a funded pillar. Individuals moving between these two countries would not fare too differently. The NDC approach exhibits national solidarity through its pooled rate of return approach—one single notional interest rate—and the sharing of economic and demographic risks. The second element of solidarity—redistribution—can also be easily introduced in NDC systems, but requires direct payments from the budget at the time of granting. For example, low-income workers can be provided a copayment to their contribution or for periods of recognized unemployment. The contributions to the NDC system are paid in cash by the unemployment benefits system.

DEALING WITH TRANSITION ISSUES ACROSS MEMBER COUNTRIES

The previous subsection has already highlighted that a transition across earnings-related and unfunded pension regimes within a country is technically but not necessarily politically easy. The same applies to countries that start from different systems. In the discussion that follows, such transition issues are discussed by country groupings.

Coordinating among the existing NDC countries. Four EU countries have already introduced NDC systems: Italy (1995/96), Latvia (1995/96), Poland (1998/99), and Sweden (1994/99). The first date refers to the year of legislation and the second date to the first year of payment into NDC. Although these countries share the broad system design of NDC, there are major differences in some design and implementation elements.[32] For example, the countries use different notional interest rates, different ways to determine the residual life expectancy, or different transition rules to the new system. This raises two general issues: to what extent must or should a Pan-European NDC system have the same system design and implementation features (and hence be fully harmonized, except, say the contribution rate levied); and to what extent must or should the transition rules be harmonized?

For example, using different notional interest rates is primarily an issue of financial sustainability for the national scheme. Assuming that the choice of the rate of aggregated wage growth provides sustainability but the per capita average wage growth is too high, a country that chooses the latter would need to balance through other means (such as annual benefit indexation) or find additional budgetary resources. A priori there is no reason why such national preferences should not be granted.

There are more arguments for some harmonization of transition from the old to the new system. For example, Italy and Sweden will only gradually phase in the NDC system over the next decades, while Latvia has moved all workers in one stroke to the new system. If mobility across professions and countries is the main goal of a Pan-European reform, it is the latter approach that is needed—an approach that, however, allows for the expression of national preferences, in particular concerning the generosity of the transition rules at the detriment of financial sustainability.

Transitioning quasi-NDC countries. Two countries have unfunded DB systems that almost mimic NDC systems and hence should be easy to transit: Germany and France. A DB system that uses lifetime income revalued with national wage growth and actuarially determined annuities based on yearly revisions is algebraically similar (but not equivalent) to an NDC system.[33] In reality, sizable differences do exist,[34] which may not prevent a transition toward a common NDC design but would make such a transition not different from that of other earnings-related schemes.

Transitioning other Bismarckian systems. The transitioning of the many other current and future EU countries with a typical unfunded and earnings-related social insurance scheme for old age is, in principle, very simple and equivalent to transitioning civil servants benefits to NDC (discussed above)—calculate the acquired pension rights and transform them into the present value: that is, a lump sum amount to be credited to the individual account. The alternative approach would be to use past contribution records and past notional interest rates to determine the initial amount. In an actuarially fair scheme, the result would be the same. Under current conditions in a number of countries, the first approach may be cheaper for governments, as it will capitalize on the recent reforms that have reduced the present value of pensions (via increase in retirement age, change in indexation, and so on).[35] Hence, for fiscal reasons, a substantive parametric reform prior to a move toward NDC makes sense. This will be the case for Austria, which just did such a parametric reform and which is discussing a move toward NDC/individual accounts. An NDC reform is also under discussion in Hungary and the Czech Republic, and proposed by researchers in countries such as Belgium, Germany, Greece, Portugal, and Spain (see, for example, Vidal-Meliá and Domínguez-Fabián (2006).

Transitioning the European outliers. Although Bismarckian-type systems by far dominate the European scene by the number of population covered, four main countries have a more Beveridge-type system, for which a transition toward NDC would constitute a main policy change. Ireland has a flat-rate contributory and noncontributory system. The United Kingdom has a flat-rate contributory plus an earnings-related system (SERPS), with opting-out options to private sector arrangements for the latter. Denmark and the Netherlands have universal pensions, which are flat in Denmark, and prorata with regard to residency in the Netherlands (see EPC 2001). The new EU member countries in Central and Eastern Europe have inherited a pension system that is typically earnings-related. This was not changed during the economic transition (except the reforms moving toward a multipillar structure; see annex to Holzmann, MacKellar, and Rutkowski 2003).

If a transition/nontransition were to be envisaged, what would be the approach? For a typical universal and basic system plus a quasi-mandated funded scheme, such as in Denmark, one solution to achieve some coordination with regard to mobility would consist in providing a buy-in option to the universal pension as well as funded scheme by transfers of an accumulated NDC amount, or the reverse when migrating from Denmark.

The Funded—Second or Third—Pillar in a Pan-European Pension System

With a well-designed Pan-European NDC scheme that allows for national preferences, what is the role of a funded pillar, what structure should it have, and what needs to be done to make it work well? All current and future EU member countries already have funded pillars at different levels of importance and sophistication. These will need some adjustment and coordination to achieve the objectives of a Pan-European pension system (table 11.7).[36]

Table 11.7. Scope of Funded Pensions in EU and EUA Countries around 2002

Country	Mandated second pillar	Description	Contribution rate	Share of covered LF as %	Funded pension as % of retirement income[3]	Funded pension assets as % of GDP
Austria	no	n.a.	n.a.	n.a.	3.0	2.6
Belgium	no	n.a.	n.a.	n.a.	0.5	4.8
Bulgaria[2]	yes	Supplementary mandatory pension funds; not less than 50–100 leva for farmers and 200 leva for self-employed; maximum monthly income 1,000 leva, current contribution 2% but planned increase to 5%; no reserves.	2% payroll	48.4	Close to nil	Close to nil
Cyprus	no	Supplementary earnings-related contributions/benefits. Voluntary coverage for formerly covered persons and for Cypriots working abroad for Cypriot employers. Employer contributes 6.3% (voluntarily covered 10%), employee 6.3%, and state 4%.	n.a.	n.a.	Modest	Modest
Czech R.	no	n.a.	n.a.	n.a.	Low	3.4
Denmark	yes	Privately administered defined contribution scheme; civil service pension scheme (defined benefit) for public sector employees.	n.a.	82.0	16.0	21.5
Estonia	yes	Employer contributes 4%, employee 2% to funded system; no ceilings. Pension fund management companies maintain individual accounts and must make quarterly contributions to a guarantee fund.	6% payroll	60.0	Close to nil	0.13
Finland	no	n.a.	n.a.	n.a.	38.6	n.a.
France	no	n.a.	n.a.	n.a.	Low	5.6
Germany	no	n.a.	n.a.	n.a.	13.0	3.3

Country		Description	Contribution			
Greece	no	n.a.	n.a.	n.a.	Low	11.9
Hungary	yes	Contribution to grow to 8% by 2004; employee contribution ceiling 250% average wage in 2003; no ceilings on employer contribution, maintained as individual accounts, 0.4% of contributions go toward guarantee fund.	6% payroll	45.0	Low	5
Ireland	no	n.a.	n.a.	n.a.	High	High
Italy	no	n.a.	n.a.	n.a.	4.2	3.2
Latvia	yes	Current contribution 2% but rate expected to increase to 9%; maximum income from which contributions are paid is 18,400 lats.	2% payroll	72.0	Close to nil	0.4
Lithuania	no	n.a.	n.a.	n.a.	Close to nil	Close to nil
Luxembourg	no	n.a.	n.a.	n.a.	Low	Low
Malta	no	n.a.	n.a.	n.a.	Low	Low
Netherlands[1]	yes	Not mandatory but schemes set by industrial agreements; 95% of schemes are defined benefit; occupational pensions integrated with public pension schemes.	n.a.	91.0	19.0	85.6
Poland	yes	DC individual account schemes in which employees choose the fund. Employees contribute half and not less than minimum wage, maximum for employers and employees 250% average wage (annually): guarantee fund is 0.1% pension assets; backed up with state budget guarantee.	7.3% of total social security contribution	70.0	Low	3.0
Portugal	no	n.a.	n.a.	n.a.	Low	12.0
Romania	no	Partially legislated then questioned; second pillar decided on principle; adoption depends on future fiscal condition.	8% payroll	75.0	Close to nil	Close to nil
Slovak R.	no	n.a.	n.a.	n.a.	Close to nil	1.0

Table 11.7. (continued)

Country	Mandated second pillar	Description	Contribution rate	Share of covered LF as %	Funded pension as % of retirement income[3]	Funded pension assets as % of GDP
Slovenia	no	n.a.	n.a.	n.a.	Close to nil	0.0
Spain	no	n.a.	n.a.	n.a.	Low	2.1
Sweden	yes	Premium Pension Authority maintains the individual accounts of the system; workers choose from several hundred privately managed funds for investment of their capital.	2.5% payroll	100.0	Moderate	32.6
United Kingdom	yes	Mandatory pension component covers defined benefit and defined contribution schemes; some components run by state, some by employers and some by financial services companies.	17.5%–40% earnings—varies with age	High	High	83.7

Sources: OECD (2000); World Bank (2003c); Luxembourg Income Study (2003); ISSA and INPRS (2003); Blommestein (2000); Whitehouse (2000, 2001); Palmer (2000); Denmark Ministry of Social Affairs (2002); Holzmann et al. (2003); Chloń-Domińczak (2003).

Note: n.a. = not applicable.

1. The second pillar in the Netherlands is quasi-mandatory, based on collective labor contracts. Data on pension as a percent of retirement income not available so capital income as % of retirement income has been used.

2. For Bulgaria, the share of covered labor force column gives data on proportion of participants in funded systems as a percent of total contributors.

3. Includes total population, as specific data for age group 65+ is not available. In the qualitative and author-based assessment, "close to nil" refers to > 1%; low to 1%– 5%, moderate to 5%–15%, and high to < 15% of funded pension income in retirement income of current population.

The role of a funded pillar is essentially fourfold. The first main purpose is consumption smoothing beyond NDC benefits. Although an NDC system can provide generous replacement rates if the contribution is sufficiently high, as a mandated, general scheme, it should not do so. A very high mandated contribution rate under an NDC scheme would resemble a labor tax rate with all the known negative social and economic effects, in particular for credit constrained individuals;[37] albeit the incidence effects on wage levels seem to be lower if the reciprocity between contributions and benefits is stronger.[38] An actuarially fair funded pillar allows better consumption smoothing according to individual preferences and has less distortionary effects on individual labor supply and savings decisions.

The second main purpose is to support retirement flexibility in an aging society. NDC as a quasi-actuarial scheme encourages later retirement with high decrements for early leavers. To compensate for future lower pensions at early age, individuals need to plan to stay longer in the labor market or to save more under a funded pillar. The alternative of voluntary NDC contribution to finance an earlier retirement is possible but must be weighted against the third main purpose—risk diversification. As funded and unfunded pension pillars have a different exposure to economic, demographic, and political risks, and as their rates of return are little correlated, diversifying pension benefits from two different pillars is welfare enhancing. It is often claimed that risks will increase in an aging and globalizing world that is subject to technological and many other changes, making risk diversification even more important (see, for example, Bovenberg 2003).

Last but not least, funded pillars are important to support Pan-European mobility and beyond. In the proposed more coordinated but not harmonized Pan-European pension system, differences would still exist. Their mobility-reducing effects, however, can be limited with a strong (voluntary or mandated) funded pillar. Furthermore, labor mobility with the rest of the world is also bound to increase, with Europeans working some part of their lives abroad, and migrants from developing countries working part of their lives in Europe. Again, a strong funded pillar that can easily be taken back home would make life for migrant workers, and host and sending countries, so much easier.

A number of choices need to be made to achieve a good Pan-European structure of a funded pillar. First, the issue of a mandated or voluntary pillar, a corporate (second), or an individual (third) pillar.[39] Mandating the second pillar at the explicit detriment of the first NDC pillar raises the issue of transition costs, and the assessment by many pension economists is likely to be that it is not worth the effort. In addition, it can be argued that the economic rationale for mandating a high replacement rate is decreasing because of reduced myopia of individuals and better financial retirement instruments. What can and should be considered is to transform existing and mandated severance payments, which exist in all EU member states, into funded unemployment benefit cum retirement benefit accounts, as some countries have started to do.[40] Hence I would argue that (newly) funded pillars should, in principle, be voluntary and the regulation should allow for both corporate and individual pensions in a well-designed but simple manner.

Second, the issue of DB or DC plans emerges. While as individuals we are likely to prefer a DB plan best in the form of the final salary-scheme type, economic rationale and recent trends tend to speak in favor of DC schemes. It is the least distortionary scheme with regard to individual labor supply decisions, including retirement, and it provides the required mobility across professions and states.

Third, simplicity and transparency of the approach will be of importance: that is, the structure of the retirement products should be simple and there should be at least one set of instruments that is standardized across the European Union. The suggested instruments are some kind of individual or personal retirement account, as well as some corporate pension account offered by the employer as they exist with a relatively simple structure in, say, the United States and Canada. Complicated structures à la Germany, which try to achieve too many objectives at the same time, should be avoided. The mandated annuitization of the accumulated retirement saving is not suggested, at least as long as the NDC account allows the financing of a minimum pension.

Finally, funded pillars as part of a Pan-European pension scheme also have coordination requirements at the level of regulation, supervision, and taxation that are likely to be difficult to fulfill. At the level of regulation and supervision, the question of mutual recognition versus more centralized approaches emerges. At the level of taxation, the issues of consistency of taxation (income versus consumption-type taxation, and in the latter case whether it is back-loaded or front-loaded) and recognition of tax deduction for contribution to funded pillars across Europe emerge. Although progress has been made toward harmonization of tax treatment by EU directives, the launch of new infringement procedures against Belgium, France, Italy, Portugal, and Spain, and pushing forward existing cases against Denmark, signal that more needs to be done. The Pension Directive that emerged in 2003 after 10 years of preparation and discussion seemingly needs time to be digested by financial market institutions and multinational enterprises before a judgment can be made.[41]

The Social Pension Pillar: A Strengthened Social or Noncontributory Pension in EU Member Countries

All current and future EU member states have some income provisions for the elderly poor, at least in the form of general social assistance, but increasingly also in the form of a (partially or fully) means-tested social pension, and a few in the form of a universal demogrant (table 11.8). It is strongly suggested that a Pan-European pension system will need to strengthen the social pillar (or zero or noncontributory pillar), which deals with the vulnerable elderly in Europe, for reasons of social objectives and system consistency.

The main argument for a strengthened social pension pillar is twofold. First, having under the new structure a quasi-actuarial NDC system as the first pillar and actuarial funded second and third pillars tends to increase the efficiency in the labor market but reduces the redistribution of income toward the poor. Shifting from a nonactuarial to an actuarial system can result in Pareto improvement but will require (keeping or introducing) a minimum benefit.[42] Second, income support for the very vulnerable elderly to prevent old-age poverty is part of the adequacy objectives of any pension system. A strengthened social pillar can be motivated by the increase in vulnerability of the elderly as aging progresses, and by the solidarity objectives of the European Union. With incomplete and perhaps falling coverage under earnings-related schemes, one can conjecture that poverty incidence will increase as the increase in life expectancy continues.[43]

With regard to how such a strengthened social pension pillar should be structured, three main issues emerge: Should there be a minimum pension in the NDC system in addition to a social pension pillar? How is this related to the social pension? And what eligibility criteria and level should be applied? First, there are a few good arguments for a minimum pension under the NDC system. Most importantly, it strengthens incentives for formal labor force participation. However, in order not to contradict the neutrality objective of the NDC structure with regard to the individual retirement decision, eligibility needs to be restricted. For example, while allowing individuals to retire from the age of, say, 60 onward, it may be required to have a minimum accumulated notional amount equivalent to 100+ percent of the minimum pension or else the need to reach the standard

Table 11.8. Scope and Form of Social Pensions in EU and EUA Countries around 2002

Country	General	Elgibility	Nationality/ residency requirements	Benefits	Percent share of elderly (65+)[i]	Social assistance expenditure as % of GDP	Comments
Austria	General assistance, supplementary pensions, minimum pension of 630.92 euros for an individual.	General assistance covers those unable to maintain minimum standard of living and age > 19. Older people (above retirement age) whose insurance pensions are below minimum qualify for supplements.	Must be residents, EU nationals or recognized refugees; some provinces require Austrian nationality.	Income-tested allowance maintains minimum level of pension.	6.7	0.2	Supplements for minimum pension level in all schemes. Social assistance for those without coverage under earnings-related pension.
Belgium	General assistance, guaranteed income for old, minimum pension.	All citizens in need, age >18 qualify for general assistance. Older people (women age 60, men age 65) who cannot maintain minimum standard of living eligible for guaranteed income scheme.	General assistance for those registered; some restrictions on foreigners. Guaranteed income for Belgian or EU citizens plus residents of 5 years before claim or 10 years during lifetime.	Minimum pension of 9,253.11 euros/year for a single person fully insured. Means-tested allowance of 7,022.70 euros/year for a single person.	n.a.	0.7	n.a.
Bulgaria	Social pension.	n.a.	n.a.	Flat rate of 44 leva/ month.	n.a.	n.a.	n.a.

Table 11.8. (continued)

Country	General	Eligibility	Nationality/ residency requirements	Benefits	Percent share of elderly (65+)[i]	Social assistance expenditure as % of GDP	Comments
Cyprus	Social pension.	Those 65+ and not entitled to pension or similar payment from other sources. Lump sum payment to those aged 68 who do not meet contribution conditions for pension.	20 years of residency after age 40 or 35 years after age 18.	Lump sum payment of 15% of total earnings. Social pension is 133.63 pounds/month.	n.a.	n.a.	n.a.
Czech Republic	Minimum pension.	n.a.	n.a.	2,080 koruny/month.	0.2	n.a.	n.a.
Denmark	Noncontributory supplementary pensions scheme.	People with low pensions rights. Payable at age 67.	Residents of Denmark. EU citizens and recognized refugees given temporary help for 3 years until they become residents.	Income tested supplement of 4,406 kroner/month.	n.a.	1.4	n.a.
Estonia	n.a.	n.a.	n.a.	n.a.	2.6	n.a.	n.a.
Finland	Living allowance.	Those who have no other source of income; minimum age 18.	Residents registered by municipality.	n.a.	n.a.	1.1	n.a.

Country	Program	Eligibility	Coverage	Benefit		%	Comments
France	General assistance, benefits for elderly plus supplements to guarantee minimum income, minimum pension.	People ineligible for other benefits and age > 25. Benefits for elderly for people aged 65+ with low pension income or no pension.	French and EU nationals.	Minimum pension calculated at 50%, not less than 6,307.62 euros/year. Coverage for 150 quarters. Minimum reduction depends on length of coverage.	n.a.	2.0	n.a.
Germany	General assistance, basic security benefit.	Those with insufficient income to meet needs. Security benefits for those 65+ (even if not eligible for old age pension) and those 18+ with permanent reduction in earnings capacity (not eligible if held responsible for own situation).	Residents. Restrictions for non-Germans including refugees.	General assistance is means tested. Basic security benefit includes payment for housing and health care.	n.a.	2.3	Includes supplementary benefits for old age.
Greece	Assistance to old and needy, minimum pension, dependent's supplements.	Older people aged 65+ without adequate social coverage and those in need with no social security coverage.	Citizens who are permanent residents; refugees and asylum seekers with permit to stay.	Minimum pension of 360 euros/month plus 26.99 euros for nonworking wife or dependent disabled husband and 17.98 euros for each child.	n.a.	0.1	Benefits to older people without medical care and minimum pension. Lump sum paid to economically weak.
Hungary	n.a.	n.a.	n.a.	n.a.	n.a.	n.a.	n.a.

Table 11.8. (continued)

Country	General	Eligibility	Nationality/residency requirements	Benefits	Percent share of elderly (65+)[i]	Social assistance expenditure as % of GDP	Comments
Ireland	Supplementary allowance, old age noncontributory pension.	Older people 66+ with limited means; people with exceptional needs.	Residents. Restrictions on refugees and asylum seekers.	Up to 134 euros/week depending on means test plus 88.5 euros for each adult dependent and euros 16.8 for each child.	8.7	5.1	n.a.
Italy	Social assistance, social pension, social allowance.	All living independently eligible for assistance. Social pension for those 65+. Older people not eligible for social pension receive social allowance (minimum pension).	Residence in municipality, legal residents of Italy, EU citizens.	Minimum pension is 392.69 euros/month. Social allowance is 3,775.83 euros/year. For those 70+ with income < 6,714 euros/year may receive up to 516.46 euros/month.	n.a.	1.3	Social allowance scheme replaced social pension in 1996. No new claimants for social pension since 1996.
Latvia	Minimum pension.	n.a.	n.a.	30 lats/month.	n.a.	n.a.	n.a.
Lithuania	Basic pension.	n.a.	n.a.	110% of poverty level.	n.a.	n.a.	n.a.
Luxembourg	Income support benefit, minimum pension.	All above age 30; minimum pension coverage for at least 20 years.	Resident for 10 out of last 20 years and registered with local authority.	n.a.	n.a.	0.5	n.a.
Malta	n.a.	n.a.	n.a.	n.a.	n.a.	n.a.	n.a.

Netherlands	General assistance, income tested supplementary allowance for old.	All above age 18.	Residents. Non-citizens covered only if special agreements exist.	Supplementary allowance reduced by 2% for each unexcused year of noncontribution.	n.a.	2.2	n.a.
Poland	Minimum pension.	n.a.	n.a.	Minimum pension is 530.26 zlotys/month.	n.a.	n.a.	n.a.
Portugal	Guaranteed minimum income, social pension, social supplement to pension.	Guaranteed income for those in economic need. Social pension for older people (65+) not covered by any other social security scheme. Social supplement to pensioners whose contributions insufficient to generate minimum pension.	Nationals and EU citizens; six month residency required for stateless persons and refugees.	Social pension is 138.27 euros/month.	n.a.	0.5	n.a.
Romania	n.a.	n.a.	n.a.	n.a.	n.a.	n.a.	n.a.
Slovak Republic	Minimum pension.	n.a.	n.a.	550 koruny/month	n.a.	n.a.	n.a.
Slovenia	n.a.	n.a.	n.a.	n.a.	n.a.	n.a.	n.a.
Spain	Minimum income scheme, social pension.	Minimum income scheme for low income working age households; social pension for those 65+ without insurance pension.	One year residency requirement for minimum income; 10 years residency including 2 years preceding claim for social pension.	Minimum pension is 385.50 euros/month (for those aged 65), reduced minimum pension for those <65.	1.6	1.1	n.a.

Table 11.8. (continued)

Country	General	Eligibility	Nationality/ residency requirements	Benefits	Percent share of elderly (65+)[1]	Social assistance expenditure as % of GDP	Comments
Sweden	Social welfare allowance, guarantee pension.	People with no other means of support; also serves as a supplement to people claiming social security benefits.	Residents.	n.a.	n.a.	1.2	n.a.
United Kingdom	Income support benefit.	All excluding unemployed. Income must be below certain level. Not payable if savings are over 8,000 pounds or if working more than 16 hours per week.	Residents only unless under EU regulations or refugee; restrictions apply depending on immigration status.	Depends on age, income, and circumstances; 92.15 pounds/week minus other income for a single person.	n.a.	4.2	Noncontributory means-tested social assistance.

Sources: Gillion et al. (2000); United States Social Security Adminstration (2002); ISSA (2003).

Note: n.a. = not applicable.

1. Social assistance recipients as a proportion of total aged population.

retirement age of, say, 67 (which is increased with a rise in life expectancy). Second, coordinating a minimum NDC pension with a social pension with regard to labor market incentives requires different eligibility criteria (such as some kind of means- or affluence-testing), different amounts, different eligibility ages, or some combination of these. Finally, eligibility for a social pension may have to be conditioned on higher ages (say 70 onward), but means-testing may be kept light, for example in the form of affluence-testing, which excludes people having access to other pension provisions and financial assets. How much national preferences such a social pension pillar would be able to exhibit without excessively inhibiting the incentive structure of a proposed Pan-European pension system is open for discussion and requires more research.

Concluding Remarks

This chapter examined why a more coordinated Pan-European pension system is needed and which potential structure could achieve this best. Both social and economic needs call for pension reform that is more radical and that cuts across member states. The economic needs are closely linked with the common economic area and currency. The suggested structure for the current and future EU member states is a multipillar system, with a NDC system at its core and supplementary funded pensions and social pensions at its wings. Such an approach would fulfill all generic and EU-specific demands on a Pan-European pension system, including the room for national preferences.

Besides the *why* of a Pan-European approach and *which* structure it may have, what remains to be sketched is *how* such a system reform could come about. One could imagine three main avenues.

The first would be an approach initiated and led by the EU Commission. This is possible but not likely. First, there is no intention by the member states to empower the Commission with such a reform request. Social policy continues to be seen as a national agenda item subject to the subsidiarity principle and hence not open for "centralization" by the Commission. Second, there are no visible efforts by the Commission to take such a lead, as the necessity for a more rapid and comprehensive reform does not seem to be seen. Last but not least, the recently introduced method of open coordination as a peer review process to accelerate reforms in the member countries has its merits, but is unlikely to lead to rapid national reforms—and even less to create a Pan-European reform vision.

The second approach would be a competitive approach across EU countries. One of the existing or reformed pension systems would gradually be adopted by other countries as they see advantages with regard to social and economic policy goals. This is also possible, and a bit more likely, but not sufficiently rapid. Even if carried out, the outcome might be suboptimal. First, the advantages of reformed systems emerge and get documented only with lapses of time, which may be measured in decades—and this may prove too late. Second, imitation of system reforms are and will be taking place (for example the inspiration of the Polish reform by the Latvian NDC reform, which in turn was inspired by the Swedish reform, or the possible introduction of individual accounts in Austria and Hungary, inspired by those reforms in the north). But imitation by other countries is likely to be restricted. Third, even if all countries were to follow a lead example under competitive pressure, this may not ensure sufficient consistency of approaches across countries to provide the needed mobility of the workforce in Europe. Last but not least, and "to the extent that social policy is meant to redress market failures or to implement solidarity transfers, competition among systems will not lead to efficient outcomes when the elements of the relevant equation span the borders of policymaking constituency."[44] By definition, collective action is needed to eliminate inefficient or unfair economic interactions; hence one can argue that bringing back competition at the inter-constituency level defeats both purposes.[45]

The third possibility is a cross-country approach led by governments. Issues of pension reform have started to be addressed by government officials, such as the Economic Policy Committee (EPC) of the European Union, which represents high-level officials from ministries of finance and economy of EU member countries.[46] EPC has, so far, been largely concerned with the fiscal consequences of aging. These concerns may be enhanced by the broader stability issues, including the need for cross-European labor mobility. To foster the points for a better-coordinated Pan-European pension system is quite likely the tasks of academics and research institutions, examined and supported by the EPC or similar core groups, and at some moment in the future espoused by a charismatic European politician as reform champion. Perhaps this will happen after the first main asymmetric shock hits Euroland.

Notes

1. This and the next section draw partly on Holzmann, MacKellar, and Rutkowski (2003).

2. For a similar list of nondemographic arguments for pension reform, see Bovenberg (2003).

3. Other projections by academics and national research institutes are typically less optimistic and predict a much larger increase in expenditure under current service scenarios. See, for example, Rother, Catenaro, and Schwab (2003).

4. See Karacadag, Sundararajan, and Elliot (2003).

5. See Beck, Levine, and Loayza (2000) and Levine (2003).

6. See Holzmann, MacKellar, and Rutkowski (2003).

7. See Mueller (2003).

8. See Natali and Rodes (2003).

9. To deal with the fiscal issues resulting from aging, various recent reforms propose adjustments in annual pension indexation. For example, the recent Rürup Commission Report for Germany led to adjusting pensions in line with the shifts in the ratio of contributors to retirees, and the recent Austrian reform envisages capping indexation by the amount the median voter receives. Balancing the fiscal accounts with reduced indexation instead of a lower initial pensions and price indexation thereafter is questionable for three main reasons: First, it introduces a high level of uncertainty for individuals, as the future real pension level cannot be determined, but once it is known the capacity to react may be nil. Second, in view of the unsettled issue of financing long-term care for the elderly, the financial needs of the elderly may increase but not be reduced. Last but not least, the reform is not credible, as politicians may not be able to withstand future pressures for changes in indexation.

10. See Holzmann, MacKellar, and Rutkowksi (2003).

11. See Holzmann, Hervé, and Demmel (1996).

12. See Blanchard and Katz (1992).

13. See Decressin and Fatàs (1993).

14. See Braunerhjelm et al. (2000).

15. See Esping-Andersen (2001).

16. See Nicoletti et al. (2001).

17. On the recent debate about the need to harmonize or not to harmonize labor market policies in euro countries, see Calmfors (1998).

18. See Holzmann and Hinz (2005).

19. See Barr (2000).

20. There are various estimates for the implicit debt of European pension systems (see Holzmann, Palacios, and Zviniene 2001), but a simple rule of thumb may be sufficient, according to which the level of implicit debt is roughly 20 to 30 times steady-state annual pension expenditure. The average level of EU spending is more than 10 percent of GDP.

21. See Lindbeck and Perrson (2003).

22. Few other papers so far outline the basic structure of a more coordinated European social policy, even less a pension system. One recent exception is Bertola et al. (2001), which proposes contingent insurance provisions with three core elements: a minimum contribution rate, a close contribution-benefit link, and no penalization when moving.

23. This study is not the first one that proposes an NDC-type structure for a Pan-European pension system. The idea has popped up in various papers and presentations (including by the author) and references include Feldstein (2001) and Gora (2003). Yet this study provides, perhaps, the most comprehensive treatment so far.

NDCs for low- and middle-income countries have found very little attention. For a first exploratory paper, see Lindeman, Robalino, and Rutkowski (2006).

24. What constitutes an ideal NDC system and how it fares compared with other benefit options (such as nonfinancial defined benefit or financial defined contribution schemes), or how it performs in reality and under political stress, is still very much open to discussion and constitute the very reason for the Sandhamn conference of September 28–30, 2003. For an attempt at defining an ideal NDC system, see Palmer (2006a).

25. The applied discount rate is the rate of aggregate wage growth that is below the (risk-adjusted) interest rate in a dynamically efficient economy. The latter applies to a fully funded DC system, which is considered actuarially fair. Unfunded DC systems—that is, NDC systems—come close but are only quasi-actuarial.

26. See Palmer (2006b) and Settergren and Mikula (2006).

27. The quasi-actuarially fair annuity is determined by remaining life expectancy and notional interest rate. If productivity growth is above (negative) population/labor force growth, the growth rate of aggregate wages is still positive. Hence keeping pension benefits constant instead of indexing with positive notional interest rate provides a little surplus for reserve building, and additional indexation once a steady-state reserve fund is reached.

28. See Palmer (2006a).

29. See Knell (2004).

30. See Valdés-Prieto (2000).

31. See Settergren and Mikula (2006).

32. See Palmer (2006b).

33. See Valdés-Prieto (2000) and Settergren and Mikula (2006).

34. See Legros (2006).

35. The second (bottom-up) approach may be cheaper for countries that increased contribution rates from low levels and have not undertaken a benefit-cutting reform.

36. For details on supplementary and complementary funded pension arrangements in Europe and beyond, see ISSA (2003a; 2003b).

37. See Lindbeck and Persson (2003).

38. See Ooghe, Schokkaert, and Flechet (2003).

39. Please watch out: In the European terminology *second pillar* refers to corporate pensions (whether mandated or voluntary) and *third pillar* to individual pensions (whether mandated or voluntary). In the Anglo-Saxon terminology (and beyond) used by the World Bank, the *second pillar* refers to mandated and funded pensions (whether corporate or indi-

vidual), and the *third pillar* to voluntary and funded provisions (whether corporate or individual). In this chapter the European terminology is used.

40. On this topic of severance payments and their reform, a conference was held in Laxenburg, near Vienna, on November 7 and 8, 2003. The conference was jointly organized by the World Bank, Washington, DC, and the Ludwig Boltzmann Institute for Economic Analysis, Vienna, and was hosted by the International Institute for Applied System Analyses, Luxembourg. For the many interesting papers visit www.worldbank.org/SP or http://members.vienna.at/libecon/boltzanalyse. The conference volume is scheduled to be published as Holzmann and Vodopivec (2005/6).

41. See IPE (2003).

42. See Lindbeck and Persson (2003).

43. Data for European OECD countries suggest that while poverty incidence tends to be the highest among those in the 65+ age group, the poverty incidence in this group fell most markedly between the mid-1980s and 1990s (and for the Czech Republic and Hungary, in the early to late 1990s). See Förster (2003).

44. See Bertola et al. (2001).

45. See Sinn (2003).

46. See, for example, EPC (2001).

References

Americans for Divorce Reform, Inc. 2003. *Divorce Statistics 2002*. http://www.divorcereform.org

Barr, N. 2000. "Reforming Pensions: Myths, Truths, and Policy Choices." IMF Working Paper WP/00/139, International Monetary Fund, Washington, DC.

Beck, T., R. Levine, and N. Loayza. 2000. "Finance and the Sources of Growth." *Journal of Financial Economics* 58 (1–2): 261–300.

Bertola, G., J. Jimeno, R. Marimon, and C. Pissarides. 2001. "EU Welfare Systems and Labor Markets: Diverse in the Past, Integrated in the Future?" In *Welfare and Employment in a United Europe*, ed. G. Bertola, T. Boeri, and G. Nicoletti, 23–122. Cambridge, Mass. and London: MIT Press.

Blanchard, J. O., and L. Katz. 1992. "Regional Evolutions." *Brookings Papers on Economic Activity* 1: 1–75.

Blommestein, H. 2000. "Ageing, Pension Reform, and Financial Market Implications in the OECD Area." Center for Research on Pensions and Welfare Policies.

Börsch-Supan, A. 1999. "Gesetzliche Alterssicherung Reformerfahrungen im Ausland. Ein systematischer Vergleich aus sechs Ländern." Deutsches Institut fur Altersvorsorge GmbH, Cologne.

Bovenberg, A. L. 2003. "Financing Retirement in the European Union." *International Tax and Public Finance* 10: 713–34.

Braunerhjelm, P., R. Faini, V. Norman, F. Ruane, and P. Seabright. 2000. *Integration and Regions of Europe: How the Right Policies Can Prevent Polarization*. London: Centre for Economic Policy Research.

Calmfors, L. 1998. "Macroeconomic Policy, Wage Setting and Employment: What Difference Does the EMU Make?" Institute for International Economic Studies, Seminar Paper 657, Stockholm.

Chłoń-Domińczak, A. 2003. "Evaluation of Reform Experiences in Eastern Europe." In International Federation of Pension Fund Administrators, ed., *Pension Reforms: Results and Challenges*, 145–237. Santiago, Chile.

Council of Europe. 2001. *Recent Demographic Developments in Europe 2001.* Strasbourg: Council of Europe.

Decressin, J., and A. Fatàs. 1993. "Regional Labor Market Dynamics in Europe and Implications for EMU." INSEAD, Paris.

Denmark Ministry of Social Affairs. 2002. "The Danish Social Policy." http://www.sm.dk.

EPC (Economic Policy Committee). 2001. "Budgetary Challenges Posed by Ageing Populations." Brussels, http://europa.eu.int/comm/economy_finance/epc_en.htm.

———. 2001. "Budgetary Challenges Posed by Ageing Populations: The Impact of Public Spending on Pensions, Health and Long-Term Care for the Elderly and Possible Indicators of Long-Term Financial Sustainability of Public Finances." EPC/ECFIN/655/01-EN final (October 24, 2001). European Union, Brussels.

———. 2003. "Key Structural Challenges in the Acceding Countries: The Integration of the Acceding Countries into the Community's Economic Policy Coordination Process." EPC/ECFIN/114/03 final (April 29, 2003). European Union, Brussels.

Esping-Andersen, G. 2001. "Comments." In *Welfare and Employment in a United Europe,* ed. G. Bertola, T. Boeri, and G. Nicoletti, 127–43. Cambridge, Mass., and London: MIT Press.

EU (European Union). 2003. *Eurostat Yearbook 2003.* Luxembourg: European Union. http://europa.eu.int/comm/eurostat.

Feldstein, M. 2001. "The Future of Social Security Pensions in Europe." NBER Working Paper Series WP 8487 (September), National Bureau of Economic Research, Harvard, Cambridge, Mass.

Förster, M. 2003. "Income Inequalities, Poverty and Effects of Social Transfer Policies in Traditional OECD Countries and Central Eastern Europe: Patterns, Trends and Driving Forces in the 1990s." Ph.D. thesis, chapter 4.3.3, University of Liège.

Gesellschaft für Versicherungswissen-schaft und -gestaltung e.V. 2003. "Proceedings of the 2002 Workshop on the Social Protection Systems of the Candidate Countries." Brussels. http://www.gvg-koeln.de/deutsch/projekte.html.

Gillion, C., J. Turner, C. Bailey, and D. Latulippe, ed. 2000. *Social Security Pensions: Development and Reform.* Geneva: International Labour Organization.

Gora, M. 2003. "The Quest for Modern Pension System." In *Structural Changes in Europe,* ed. G. Tumpel-Gugerell and P. Mooslechner. United Kingdom: Edward Elgar.

Holzmann, R. 2003. "A Provocative Note on Coverage in Public Pension Schemes." In *The Three Pillars of Wisdom? A Reader on Globalization, World Bank Pension Models and Welfare Society,* ed. A. Tausch, 85–99. Happaugue, NY: Nova Science.

Holzmann, R., Y. Hervé, and R. Demmel. 1996. "The Maastricht Fiscal Criteria: Required but Ineffective?" *Empirica* 23 (1): 25–58.

Holzmann, R., and R. Hinz. 2005. *Old-Age Income Support in the 21st Century: An International Perspective on Pension Systems and Reform.* Washington, DC: World Bank.

Holzmann, R., L. MacKellar, and M. Rutkowski. 2003. "Accelerating the European Reform Agenda: Need, Progress, and Conceptual Underpinnings." In *Pension Reform in Europe: Process and Progress,* Directions in Development Series, ed. R. Holzmann, M. Orenstein, and M. Rutkowski, 1–45. Washington, DC: World Bank.

Holzmann, R., and R. Münz. 2004. "Challenges and Opportunities of International Migration for the EU, its Member States, Neighboring Countries and Regions: A Policy Note." Institute for Future Studies, Stockholm.

Holzmann, R., R. Palacios, and A. Zviniene. 2001. "Reporting the Implicit Pension Debt in Middle and Low Income Countries." *Journal of Pension Management* 6 (4): 355–384.

Holzmann, R., and M. Vodopivec, ed. 2005/6. *Improving Severance Pay: An International Perspective.* Washington, DC: World Bank.

ILO (International Labour Organization). 2003. Laborsta: Economically Active Population Estimates and Projections 1950–2010. Geneva. http://laborsta.ilo.org.

IPE (Investment & Pension Europe). 2003. "European Directive Debate." September Issue, Supplement.

ISSA (International Social Security Association). 2003a. *Complementary and Private Pensions Throughout the World 2003*. Geneva: ISSA.

———. 2003b. "Trends in Social Security." International Social Security Association, Geneva.

ISSA and INPRS (International Social Security Association, International Network of Pension Regulators and Supervisors). 2003. *Complementary and Private Pensions 2003*. Geneva: ISSA and INPRS.

Karacadag, C., V. Sundararajan, and J. Elliot. 2003. "Managing Risk in Financial Market Development: The Role of Sequencing." IMF Working Paper No. 03/116, International Monetary Fund, Washington, DC.

Knell, M. 2004. "On the Design of Sustainable and Fair PAYG Pension Systems when Cohort Sizes Change." Vienna: Austrian National Bank.

Legros, F. 2006. "NDCs: A Comparison of the French and German Point Systems." In *Pension Reform: Issues and Prospects for Non-Financial Defined Contribution (NDC) Schemes*, ed. R. Holzmann and E. Palmer, chapter 10. Washington, DC: World Bank.

Levine, R. 2003. "Finance and Growth—Theory, Evidence, and Mechanism." University of Minnesota and National Bureau of Economic Research, Harvard, Cambridge, Mass.

Lindbeck, A., and M. Persson. 2003. "The Gains from Pension Reform." *Journal of Economic Literature* XLI (March): 74–112.

Lindeman, D., D. Robalino, and M. Rutkowski. 2006. "NDC Pension Schemes in Middle- and Low-Income Countries." In *Pension Reform: Issues and Prospects for Non-Financial Defined Contribution (NDC) Schemes*, ed. R. Holzmann and E. Palmer, chapter 12. Washington, DC: World Bank.

Luxembourg Income Study. 2003. Project Data Base, Luxembourg, http://www.lisproject.org/techdoc.htm.

Mueller, K. 2003. *Privatising Old-Age Security—Latin America and Eastern Europe Compared*. Cheltenham, UK and Northampton, Mass.: Edward Elgar.

Natali, D., and M. Rodes. 2003. "The 'New Politics' of the Bismarckian Welfare State: Pension Reforms in Continental Europe." European University Institute, Florence.

Nicoletti, G., R. Haffner, S. Nickell, S. Scarpetta, and G. Zoega. 2001. "European Integration, Liberalization, and Labor Market Performance." In G. Bertola, *Welfare and Employment in a United Europe*, ed. T. Boeri and G. Nicoletti, 147–235, Cambridge, Mass. and London: MIT Press.

Ooghe, E., E. Schokkaert, and J. Flechet. 2003. "The Incidence of Social Security Contributions: An Empirical Analysis." *Empirica* 30 (2): 81–106.

OECD (Organisation for Economic Co-operation and Development). 2000. *Institutional Investors Statistical Yearbook: 2000 Edition*. Paris: OECD.

———. 2002. "Fiscal Implications of Ageing: Projections of Age-Related Spending." Economics Department Working Paper 305, OECD, Paris.

———. 2003. *Transforming Disability into Ability: Policies to Promote Work and Income Security for Disabled People*. Paris: OECD.

———. 2003. OECD Statistics Portal, Paris, http://www.oecd.org/statsportal.

Palacios, R., and M. Pallares-Miralles. 2000. "International Patterns of Pension Provision." World Bank, Washington DC, with updates.

Palmer, E. 2000. "The Swedish Pension Reform Model: Framework and Issues." Social Protection Discussion Paper 0012, World Bank, Washington, DC.

————. 2006a. "What Is NDC?" In *Pension Reform: Issues and Prospects for Non-Financial Defined Contribution (NDC) Schemes*, ed. R. Holzmann and E. Palmer, chapter 2. Washington, DC: World Bank.

————. 2006b. "Conversion to NDCs—Issues and Models." In *Pension Reform: Issues and Prospects for Non-Financial Defined Contribution (NDC) Schemes*, ed. R. Holzmann and E. Palmer, chapter 9. Washington, DC: World Bank.

Rother, P. C., M. Catenaro, and G. Schwab. 2003. "Aging and Pensions in the Euro Area—Survey and Projection Results." Social Protection Discussion Paper 0307, World Bank, Washington, DC.

Settergren, O., and B. D. Mikula. 2006. "The Rate of Return of Pay-As-You-Go Pension Systems: A More Exact Loan-Consumption Model of Interest." In *Pension Reform: Issues and Prospects for Non-Financial Defined Contribution (NDC) Schemes*, ed. R. Holzmann and E. Palmer, chapter 7. Washington, DC: World Bank.

Sinn, H.-W. 2003. *The New Systems Competition*. Malden, Mass.: Blackwell.

Uebelmesser, S. 2003. "Harmonization of Old-Age Security within the European Union." CESifo Working Paper No. 1108, CESifo (Center for Economic Studies & Institut fuer Wirtschaftsforschung), Munich.

United Kingdom Office of National Statistics. 2001. "Marriage and Divorce Rates: EU Comparison 2001." http://www.statistics.gov.uk/STATBASE.

United Nations. 2001. *UN Demographic Yearbook 2001*. New York: United Nations.

————. 2002. *World Population Prospects: The 2002 Revision*. New York: United Nations.

United States Social Security Administration. 2002. "Social Security Programs throughout the World—Europe 2002." http://www.ssa.gov.

Valdés-Prieto, S. 2000. "The Financial Stability of Notional Account Pensions." *Scandinavian Journal of Economics* 102 (3): 395–417.

Vidal-Meliá, C., and I. Domínguez-Fabián. 2006. "The Spanish Pension System: Issues of Introducing NDCs." In *Pension Reform: Issues and Prospects for Non-Financial Defined Contribution (NDC) Schemes*, ed. R. Holzmann and E. Palmer, chapter 23. Washington, DC: World Bank.

Whitehouse, E. 2000. "Pension Reform, Financial Literacy and Public Information: A Case Study of the United Kingdom." Social Protection Discussion Paper 0004, The World Bank, Washington, DC.

————. 2001. "Pension Systems in 15 Countries Compared: The Value of Entitlements." Centre for Pensions and Superannuation, London.

Williamson, J., and M. Williams. 2003. "The Notional Defined Contribution Model: An Assessment of Strengths and Limitations of a New Approach to Old Age Security." World Paper 2003-18, Center for Retirement Research at Boston College, Boston.

World Bank. 2003a. "The Labor Market Performance of ECA Countries—Recent Developments." HDNSP Labor Market Unit, World Bank, Washington, DC.

————. 2003b. World Bank Labor Markets Dataset, Washington, DC.

————. 2003c. World Bank Pensions Dataset, Washington, DC.

A Magic All-European
Pension Reform Formula: Selective Comments

Bernd Marin*

ROBERT HOLZMANN HAS PROVIDED AN INTERESTING AND INNOVATIVE APPROACH to rapid and comprehensive pension reform in Europe. He shifts the debate beyond the conventional focus on fiscal affordability at the national level toward broader economic and social adjustment needs. And he proposes NDC as an "ideal" approach not just for dealing with a great variety of reform requirements but also for inducing pension harmonization across Europe while allowing for continuous country-specific preferences "and to lead to a political reform movement" toward NDC. This is a strong claim and he puts forward strong and sophisticated arguments in favor, some but not all of them convincing to me. The rationale for much wider domestic reform needs throughout Europe as well as for a move toward a more coordinated Pan-European pension reform are more persuasive than the proposals for its potential structure and transition strategy. While I share the central claim of the paper, which is new and sound, this occasionally is done so for other reasons—starting from other working hypotheses and then coming to other policy conclusions—than the ones put forward by the author, as in the case of atypical employment. At times, additional or other empirical evidence is suggested to strengthen the points, as with exemplifying pension barriers to mobility between the public and private sector. While NDC may be generally close to an "ideal" pension framework, whether the "ideal" NDC as proposed in the Holzmann design is truly "ideal" is still to be explored. Partly, parameters are not yet fully specified, partly risk reinforcement may be more probable than the risk diversification claimed for the Holzmann design of combining pillars. Furthermore, the guaranteed minimum social pension should rather not be conceptualized as a "zero pillar." Crucial dimensions such as disability pensions may be missed. One could rather underline the primacy of political and not just economic desirability, feasibility, and sustainability of NDC. And finally one would stress some of its underestimated comparative advantages, such as its functions of fairness standard, anticorruption device and, as a core component of any pension constitution, its differentiation of welfare trigger, as well as its superior risk management (Gora and Palmer 2003).

Robert Holzmann foresees an increased need, rather than a diminishing one, for rapid and comprehensive pension reform in both current European Union member-states and future accession countries, due to worsening budgetary pressures, socioeconomic changes, and the impact of globalization, all related to societal aging. But expenditure levels are less a reflection of population age structures and aging dynamics than the

* Bernd Marin is executive director of the European Centre for Social Welfare Policy and Research.

I wish to thank Michael Fuchs for skillful and valuable support, Silvia Fässler for good graphical assistance, and Robert Holzmann for critical rejoinders to my comments. All weaknesses and good suggestions untapped or ideas not yet elaborated are, of course, my responsibility.

public/private mix of provision, benefit generosity, and the actual retirement age, which is typically low due to disincentives to work. In the future, further increases in longevity, which are likely, together with even modest rises in fertility, which are still below the replacement level, will continue to make for rapid population aging and corresponding increasing old-age dependency ratios. Even if system dependency ratios deteriorate less than old-age dependency ratios, due to reforms and to increased labor force participation of women and middle-aged workers, pension expenditures will rise till around 2040. With reforms, the expenditure increase may be "only" 30 percent, as against the demographically required 70 percent, or a "rough doubling" of expenditures "in a no-reform scenario." Under all circumstances, "a further major increase in pension expenditure can be prevented only if major reforms take place."

While nobody may object to this reasoning and its conclusions, additional forms of empirical evidence supplied to support the cases in point are suggested. Holzmann offers data on public pension expenditure in terms of percent of GDP and projections of old-age dependency till 2050, depicting the great—and increasing—variety within European Union and accession countries. He takes the design flaws of most existing pension schemes for granted: not in need of further documentation. But as the main goal of his chapter is to argue in favor of a reformed NDC system to replace current defined benefit (DB) systems and to push toward a coordinated pension system in Europe, I would like to strengthen his case by providing supplementary calculations.

Deeds Defying Words—Reform Flaws Visible through NDC

The approximation offered in this discussion is a comparison of four smaller European countries. Two (Sweden and Poland) adopted NDC schemes when introducing benefit cuts to discourage early labor market exit; two (Austria and the Czech Republic) did not. One big country (Germany) with a reformed DB system holds an intermediate position. The evidence supplied shows quite clearly that all of them have moved in the right direction of increased benefit reductions for pre-retirement—but only NDC pension systems (by using the wage growth rate as notional interest rate) are "quasi-actuarially fair" and neutral to individual preferences. Existing DB arrangements, in contrast, actually continue to strongly subsidize early exit and to heavily penalize working longer (see figure 11.2).

In this way, the governmental rhetoric of praising delayed retirement is undercut by counter-productive measures in the political economy. Words are defied by deeds: only fools willing to sacrifice a painful amount of money—or unable to make the elementary calculation of tangible advantages—will *not* escape the Austrian and Czech labor market at their earliest possible opportunity and convenience. Figure 11.3 shows that benefit rules in these non-NDC systems are detrimental to declared public objectives. The distortion factor is at least 1:2 in Austria and the Czech Republic, and between a third and a half in Germany. In the smaller DB countries, regular voluntary early retirees (that is, not those persons experiencing ill health, disability, unemployment, or another disadvantage) are exempt from more than half of the actuarial losses to be incurred by them (in special categories up to 80 percent). Those working longer than expected, on the other hand, would lose much more than half and up to around six-sevenths (Czech Republic) of the savings generated to the insurance collective.

No surprise, therefore, to find hardly anybody working up until the legal retirement age in such a country and to find less than 3 percent of the working population working to the official working age of 65. Without NDC standards of actuarial neutrality and fairness, neither the amount of distortions and of hidden taxes for younger working generations, nor the fact, so puzzling to policy-makers, as to why their well-intended and supposedly

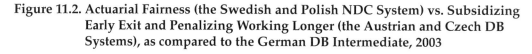

**Figure 11.2. Actuarial Fairness (the Swedish and Polish NDC System) vs. Subsidizing
Early Exit and Penalizing Working Longer (the Austrian and Czech DB
Systems), as compared to the German DB Intermediate, 2003**

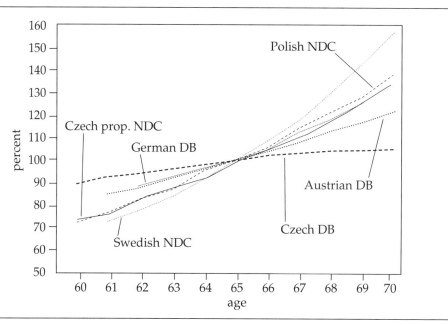

Source: Author.

"harsh" reform measures generate opposite effects than the ones intended, could be
explained. Recall the reasons for selecting those four smaller countries for paired comparisons. The Czech Republic has the single highest aging dynamics among the future EU-25
countries until 2050. Austria had confronted the single highest pension expenditures
worldwide already by 2003 and "as an extreme example, the pension-related deficit
amounts to almost 5 percent of GDP." Sweden ages more than a decade earlier than Austria, whereas Poland and the Czech Republic age almost two decades later—but much
more rapidly and drastically than Austria and Sweden.

The four countries, therefore, lend themselves to several paired comparisons. Although
all those overall tendencies can be seen from the tables provided by Robert Holzmann, I
have transformed data on population aging until 2050 into figures displaying the time
dimension in a comparative manner. They depict *"l'Europe a plusieurs vitesses"* of aging and
reform needs, lags, and peaks. Which country will reach its peak of collective aging when,
and how does this compare to European averages and sub-regional aging patterns? (See figures 11.4a, 11.4b, and 11.4c.) Which are the *avant-garde* countries and which are the laggards
hit latest by developments and therefore able to learn from the best, brightest and fastest?

Reform Needs Beyond Demography and Budgets

But "even if the budgetary and demographically induced pressures did not exist," Robert
Holzmann reasons, "there still would be a major need for most European countries to
reform their public pension systems to better align them with socioeconomic changes."
Holzmann cites three such changes—"increasing female labor force participation; high
divorce rates and changing family structures; and the rise in atypical employment"—and

Figure 11.3. Swedish NDC Actuarial Neutrality vs. Austrian DB, Amount of Labor-depressing Adverse Redistribution, 2003

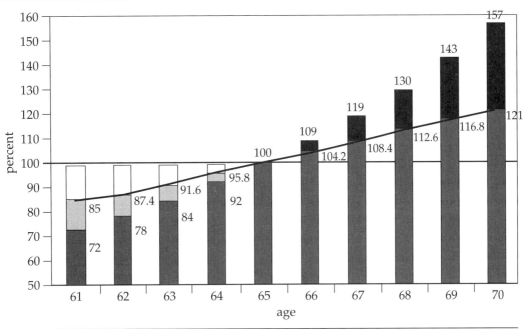

Source: Marin (2005); author's estimates.

Note: The line across the bars indicates the steepness of the bonus/malus function and its deviation from actuarial neutrality. The light gray difference indicates the amount of subsidies for early retirement, which, perversely, grows with ever earlier retirement in Austria (e.g. 15 percent cuts in Austria compared to 28 percent in Sweden when retiring at age 61). The black color shows the amount of taxing away collective benefits from late retirement (e.g. 12.6 percent instead of 30 percent increments when retiring at age 68, or 21 percent instead of 57 percent higher monthly payments when retiring at age 70). Thus, socially desirable behavior of retiring later is sanctioned or punished in Austria. Harmful early exit behavior, which is strongly supported in Austria but not in Sweden, has led to a striking difference in retirement behavior in the two countries (more than 97 percent of Austrians retire before age 65).

analyzes them. I once again agree with both the diagnosis and the remedies suggested, such as "the individualization of pension rights" to avoid benefit traps for women. But I sometimes do so for other reasons—starting from other working hypotheses and then arriving at other policy conclusions—than the ones put forward by the author.

The Atypically Employed as Winners in Non-NDC-Schemes?

Let me take Holzmann's assertion that "these atypically employed people do not fare well under some pension schemes, which are based on the full-employment fiction. . . . This situation calls for reform (and a stricter contribution-benefit relationship)." This is true, no doubt, as it is general enough—but, therefore, the opposite proposition is equally true, and probably even more frequently true: namely, the atypically employed often fare very well under current pension schemes, despite, or even because, these schemes are based on the fiction of full employment. Just one outstanding example are full-time pension entitlements for predominantly or long-term part-time employees. In table 11.9, I provide a truly

**Figure 11.4a. Europe Aging at Multiple Speeds, Lags and Peaks, 1995–2050:
Subregional Deviations from All-European Regional Averages (percent)**

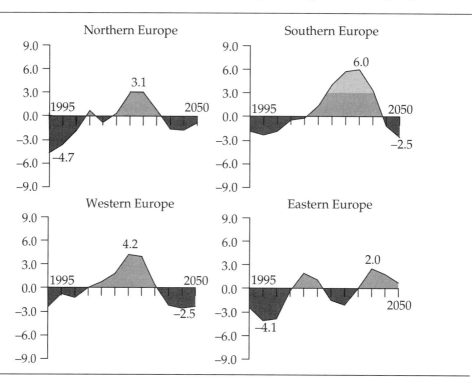

Source: Prinz and Lutz (1994a, 1994b).

Note: Y-axis values greater than zero are considered above average; those below zero are considered below average.

shocking example of "injustice" and "perverse redistribution" from long-term full-time workers without career development toward part-time employees with good careers (such as female academics). Despite much less than a lifetime working, these part-timers receive between around two and two and a half times higher a lifetime pension in real terms than the simple worker—with identical lifetime contributions.

Such inequities of equal contributions and highly different benefits (and vice versa) within the private market sector may become even more drastic across the private and the public sector boundaries (as will be seen soon), as long as "best years" pension formulas prevail. All systems without a lifetime calculation-base lend themselves to such erratic redistributions in all directions, including frequent perverse redistribution from low-income to wealthy people, which are more able to fiddle the system by superior knowledge and ease of more flexible and well-dosed, opportunistically adjusted labor supply. Vesting periods as entitlements thresholds and other devices may also make for similar advantages. They are often used by self-employed persons and their family members, part-time farmers, railway workers, civil servants, and other special corporatist interest groups, providing them with benefits far above of those of people with equal contributions—and even further above their own contributions.

Thus the "stricter contribution-benefit relationship" called for by the author (which, of course, I agree with), would actually make few people better and many people much worse off than they are today—for good reasons of fairness. This is because current distor-

Figure 11.4b. When the Aging Process Will Reach Its Peak: Average Annual Increase of the Population Above Age 60 in Three Scenarios, by European Subregions (percent)

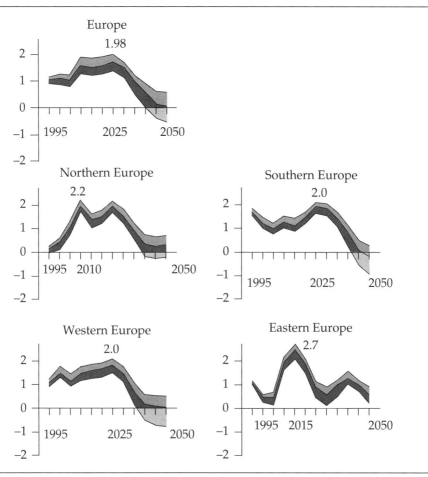

Source: Prinz and Lutz (1994a, 1994b).

tions from defined contribution standards are probably non-accidental, and well-structured by vested interests of atypical employees who typically stand to gain from existing pensions rules. Many "atypical" employees, in particular middle-class preferential part-timers, benefit from them at the expense of low-income people working long hours. In what one could call incomplete contributory Bismarckian insurance systems, DB pension awards are actually "based on the full-employment fiction." But—according to so my counter hypothesis to the one forwarded by Robert Holzmann and many other scholars—this may more often make for their upgrading closer to full-employment or to non-contributory guarantee pension standards. In contrast, their downscaling to a minimum contribution equivalent base—or to indirect pensions rights only, derived through marriage, widowhood and other family status dependencies—is less probable and frequent. And non-contributory systems generally take care of flex-workers through other provisions, moving their pension entitlements above their contribution base.

Figure 11.4c. When the Aging Process Will Reach Its Peak: Average Annual Increase of the Population Above Age 60 in Three Scenarios, by country (percent)

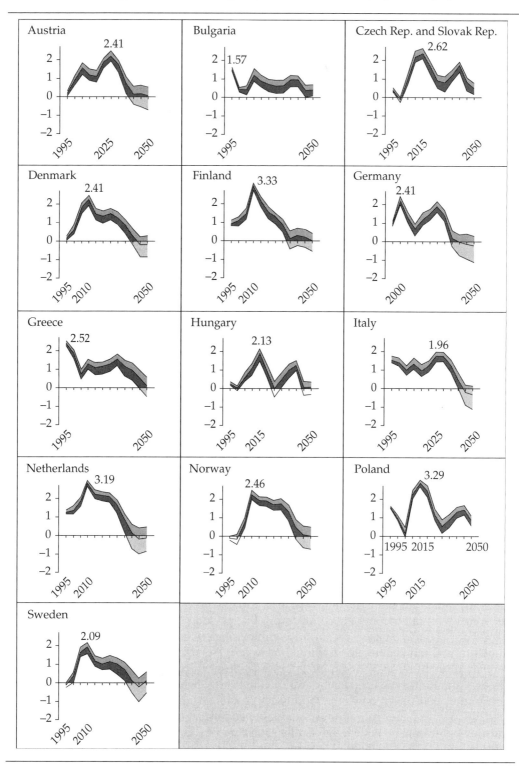

Source: Prinz and Lutz (1994a, 1994b).

Table 11.9. Same Lifetime Contributions, Highly Different Pension Entitlements for Atypically Employed Part-Timers and No-Career Regular Full-Time Employees, Austria, 2003 (euros)

	Part-timer, best years at start of career	Part-timer, best years at end of career	Full-time employee, constantly below average income
Lifetime contributions, indexed by:			
without any indexation, nominal	50,977	135,182	83,290
notional IRR median income	171,525	175,716	159,884
notional IRR covered wage sum	221,421	187,257	187,823
Nominal lifetime pension, residual life expectancy 24,25 years, calculated by:			
"best 15 years"	551,088	802,744	328,102
lifetime "40 years"	222,274	298,647	237,824
status quo: losses capped at 10%	**495,979**	**722,470**	**295,291**
median income 40 years	324,731	332,665	302,692
wage sum 40 years	419,195	354,516	355,587
Lifetime contributions, indexed by:			
without any indexation, nominal	54,026	135,182	91,743
notional IRR median income	**175,716**	**175,716**	**175,713**
notional IRR covered wage sum	225,944	187,257	207,383
Discounted lifetime pension, residual life expectancy 24, 25 years, discount 3% p.a., calculated by:			
"best 15 years"	399,206	581,504	261,166
lifetime "40 years"	166,111	216,339	190,026
status quo: losses capped at 10%	**359,285**	**523,354**	**235,050**
median income 40 years	**240,982**	**240,981**	**240,978**
wage sum 40 years	309,866	256,810	284,410
Lifetime contributions, indexed by:			
without any indexation, nominal	50,977	143,754	97,825
notional IRR median income	171,525	202,512	187,563
notional IRR covered wage sum	**221,421**	**221,423**	**221,418**
Discounted lifetime pension, residual life expectancy 24,25 years, discount 3% p.a., calculated by:			
"best 15 years"	399,206	581,504	278,102
lifetime "40 years"	161,015	242,015	202,774
status quo: losses capped at 10%	**359,285**	**523,354**	**250,292**
median income 40 years	235,234	277,730	257,228
wage sum 40 years	**303,663**	**303,666**	**303,659**

Source: Calculations by M. Fuchs, European Centre.

Note: The table shows how well atypically employed part-timers can do under current DB pension schemes compared to no-career regular full-time employees. The 9 boldfaced rows in the table indicate both the lifetime contributions indexed by notional IRR median income and notional IRR covered wage sum as well as the nominal and discounted lifetime pensions according to the "status quo: losses capped at 10%," an extended "best 15 plus a few years" combined with undervalued, "unfair" notional IRRs and crippling caps vs. a lifetime calculation base (40 years) with fair IRRs indexed by the median income or the wage sum. Whereas the first option (status quo after the 2003 reform) shows highly unequal (up to 1:2.4) pension entitlements with identical contributions, lifetime calculations with income or wage-sum-based notional IRRs display identical entitlements for identical contributions.

Other Non-Fiscal Reforms Needs Demanding NDC

Both the non-individualization of social rights to health insurance, social insurance, and pensions, as well as all existing deviations of current DB pension schemes from NDC standards of actuarial neutrality and fairness, are costly to society at large and increase public expenditures, Moreover, they tend to benefit those who are *not* most in need of support and targeted for special assistance, but those who are best able to seek the rents implicit in such incomplete arrangements, while taxing those outside the circle of the happy few privileged beneficiaries. NDC allows us to measure existing arrangements serving particular sectional interests at the expense of others against universalistic standards most broadly accepted as reasonable, equitable, and fair.

Another tendency requiring "changes in the way public programs operate, including in the area of pension provision" is increasing international market integration or globalization. It adds further non-fiscal reform needs to the already mentioned socioeconomic changes ignored by most countries that have introduced parametric reform packages during the last decade, exclusively addressed at balancing short- or mid-term fiscal requirements. But open economies will not do well in a globalizing world with social security and public pension systems that "limit if not eliminate" labor mobility between sectors, occupations, and countries. They will not reap the benefits of globalization with pension rules that impede the improvement of financial markets, including a development of portable liquid pension assets from fully funded pillars. And they will not do well with pension arrangements that block life-long learning indispensable for knowledge and skill formation, labor market flexibility, and prolonged activity in the workforce.

Socioeconomic changes, globalization, and societal aging require a reform approach "that must go beyond a parametric adjustment of existing schemes," Holzmann argues, "toward a more actuarial system structure that better links contributions and benefits, more individualization to handle professional and family mobility, and also some funding to allow more individual decision and choices." At this point of reasoning, Holzmann elegantly interweaves the view that more pension reform or "adjustments" are needed with his second core idea: that even with more pension reform, more European coordination is needed. He finally weaves it into the third core assumption or *leitmotiv*: namely, that NDC is "ideal" to make it happen, a cornerstone in the welfare architecture of a "Pan-European pension system."

The Claim for NDC as "Pan-European" Pension System

The most innovative aspect of Holzmann's study is his argument in favor of NDC as responding to "the need for a better coordinated pension system in an integrated Europe." His "Pan-European approach" is not the first, but probably the most encompassing, treatment so far of the proposition to design NDC-type institutions to promote the emergence of an all-European pension system. He rightly deplores the fact that "there is little understanding of and support for a Pan-European approach that should lead to a coordinated pension structure" and wonders why the Commission of the European Union (in contrast to other policy field) does little to overcome the perception of pensions as a strictly national agenda. Can European economic integration truly advance without at least some development toward an all-European pension reform approach?

Budget requirements under a Maastricht fiscal regime, and enhanced labor market flexibility, mobility, and labor supply in aging societies, all demand some convergence in the area of pensions, which crucially affects overall labor supply and employment levels and consumes up to half of all social expenditures. While migration and regional mobility will remain lower in Europe for a multitude of reasons, mobility is blocked not just across countries and regions, but also between sectors within countries and across professions within the same regions. In contrast to "other economically integrated areas under a common currency (such as Australia, Brazil, Canada, Switzerland, and the United States) . . . the European Union does not have a coordinated—even less a harmonized—pension system." While other states or provinces differ in many things "including income taxes or short-term social benefits . . . they have one thing in common—a public retirement income scheme across states." Even worse, European countries frequently have occupationally fragmented pension systems *within* the same countries, preventing mobility across professions and between the public and the private sector, even within nearby areas.

Barriers to Mobility

There is nothing to criticize or add to Holzmann's reasoning about barriers to mobility, except perhaps some empirical evidence illustrating the almost incredible extent of barriers to mobility between public and private sector. In a corporatist country like Austria, public sector civil servants receive on average 264 percent of the median retirement income in the private sector (European Centre 2004). Within the same education bracket, public sector workers get up to 44 percent higher lifetime income than private sector employees; the gap decreases as educational attainment increases (Synthesis 2003). Due to a more favorable pension formula, civil servants get around 50 percent higher return on their retirement income—or notional interest rate, in NDC language—for the very same contributions during active life (Marin and Prinz 1999).

To be even more specific: A female civil servant born in 1945 and retiring at age 56.5 in 2002 receives between 46 and 49 percent of her overall lifetime income as old-age pension. With primary education only, her lifetime income (1,926,190 euros) is more than double that of a private sector worker/employee (838,266 euros). Her retirement income (884,318 euros vs. 272,760 euros) is 3.24 times greater. With secondary education, the relationship of lifetime income is 2,408,151 euros, compared to 1,094,097 euros. The retirement income 1,175,108 euros vs. 370,124 euros, or 3.17 times higher (Synthesis 2003).

In many cases, more than 50 percent—or the greater part—of overall lifetime income comes in retirement! Net income of retired civil servants on the regional (*Länder*) or municipal level is rarely below 100 percent of their last (not their average) active income before retirement—and that is around 130 percent of average or calculation base active salary during their working life! In addition, the gap in retirement income between civil servants in the *Länder* or municipalities and that on the federal level in some of the regions may increase up to 43 percent over that of civil servants nationwide by the year 2025 (Marin and Fuchs 2003, table 3/B). And the minimal pension contribution varies up to around 10 times or 1,000 percent between different occupational groups for what may turn out to be the very same monthly retirement income entitlement (Marin and Prinz 1999; see also figure 11.5).

Under such circumstances, how could professional mobility ever take place, except in a unilateral direction toward the public sector? The most telling symptom in this context may be that even among academics, who profit least from these arrangements (and male academics hardly at all), more than 70 percent of university graduates seek public employment as civil servants. Correspondingly, the outflow rates from public sector functions with permanent status (*Pragmatisierung*) is virtually nil—except toward those ever more

Figure 11.5. Corporatist Pension Disharmonies: Cost of Minimum Contribution One Month of Retirement, Austria 2003

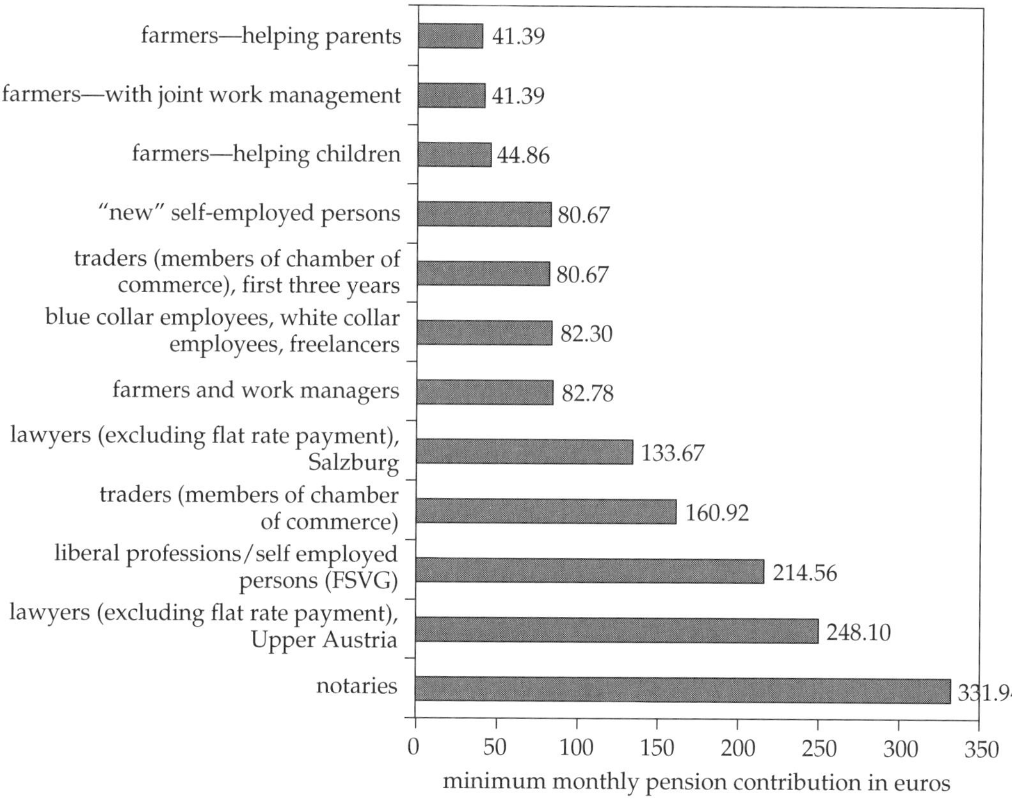

Category	minimum monthly pension contribution in euros
farmers—helping parents	41.39
farmers—with joint work management	41.39
farmers—helping children	44.86
"new" self-employed persons	80.67
traders (members of chamber of commerce), first three years	80.67
blue collar employees, white collar employees, freelancers	82.30
farmers and work managers	82.78
lawyers (excluding flat rate payment), Salzburg	133.67
traders (members of chamber of commerce)	160.92
liberal professions/self employed persons (FSVG)	214.56
lawyers (excluding flat rate payment), Upper Austria	248.10
notaries	331.94

Source: Hauptverband, AK department of statistics.

frequent cases of special early retirement arrangements in ever younger age cohorts down to 45 to 55 (*"Lehrermodell"* for all, *"Bundesbediensteten Sozialplangesetz," Berufsunfähigkeit-spensionen in "ausgeglieder-ten Einrichtungen"*). Despite annual decrements of 4 percent (capped at 20 percent)—calculated from a standard retirement age 5 years below that of the private sector—the absolute monthly retirement income usually is still far above of that of an average private sector employee working until the age of 65. It thus provides a frugal early retirement basic income over around 30 to 40 years of further life expectancy. In addition, varying by education but through all education attainment levels, the term of the pensions is several years longer in the public sector. Based on this generous basic income, pensioners may start a second career or undertake rather informal income-gathering activities, but rarely do, as entrepreneurship is neither promoted nor needed for a comfortable third age over decades: more than a quarter of a century on average.

The European Claims for NDC, Continued

Robert Holzmann checks the potential structure of a Pan-European pension system against the (primary and secondary) goals developed by him and his team at the World Bank

(Holzmann, Orenstein, and Rutkowski 2003). A good pension system should "provide adequate, affordable, sustainable, and robust old-age income, while seeking to implement welfare maximizing schemes in a manner appropriate to the individual country." In doing so, it should create economic growth and minimize negative impacts on labor markets and other areas. As "specific objectives of a Pan-European pension system," he also suggests the four criteria of "mobility, national preferences, solidarity, and feasible transition."

These ideal demands on a reformed and coordinated Pan-European pension system are then confronted with three main options for the "potential structures": "a basic pension plus a mandated fully funded pillar (Beveridge for all); an unfounded defined benefit system plus voluntary fully funded pensions (Bismarck for all); and a basic of noncontributory pillar plus an NDC pillar plus a voluntary (or mandated) funded pillar." Holzmann then discusses the main arguments in favor of each option and the difficulties in implementation, the choses the third as superior. The arguments are all in all convincing—apart from some reservations that I note below. NDC is designed as the crucial or first pillar, able to deal optimally with all system objectives and reform needs mentioned—from financial sustainability to all socioeconomic requirements, including divorce, survivorship, mobility across professions and frontiers, and transition issues across member-country groupings.

Holzmann considers coordination among the existing NDC countries, Italy, Latvia, Poland, and Sweden, which have adopted major differences in design and implementation elements, including transition rules, within the same overall NDC scheme. Germany and France are considered "quasi-NDC countries" most easy to transit. Other Bismarckian countries (Austria, Belgium, Czech Republic, Greece, Hungary, Portugal, Spain) may need more time and reform impetus. The greatest difficulty would be transitioning the European outliers with universalistic systems (Denmark, Ireland, the Netherlands, and the United Kingdom). Coordinated portability from/to other European systems may have to be achieved through buy-in options and transfers of the accumulated NDC amount.

In debating the transition issues in introducing such a potential structure of a Pan-European pension system, Robert Holzmann has no illusions, either about the speed or about the actors involved. "An approach initiated and led by the EU Commission" he considers "possible but not likely"; I would argue that is it impossible given the current interpretation of the subsidiarity principle with regard to pensions. This may also explain that "there are no visible efforts by the Commission to take such a lead," even if "the necessity for a more rapid and a more comprehensive reform" is seen. Also, the method of open coordination "is unlikely to lead to rapid national reforms—and even less to create a Pan-European reform vision." He does not expect a great deal from country competition as various countries adopt reformed pensions systems it is "again possible, and a bit more likely, but not sufficiently rapid. Even if carried out, the outcome might be sub-optimal." Apart from the great time lags in a copy-cat world where countries learn from one another through imitation, institutional transfers will probably remain restricted—and may themselves not yet "ensure sufficient consistency of approaches across countries to provide the needed mobility of the workforce in Europe."

Consequently, the only somewhat realistic perspective for Holzmann is a "cross-country approach led by governments," for instance, through the EU's Economic Policy Committee, should it take a broader view on aging issues. But the coalition to promote "a better coordinated, Pan-European pension system is quite likely the task of academics and research institutions, examined and supported by the EPC or similar core groups, and at some moment in the future espoused by a charismatic European politician as a reform champion. Perhaps this will happen after the first main asymmetric shock hits euroland."

I wish one could be more optimistic on that last point than the author. But perhaps Robert Holzmann's expectations already express the maximum feasible optimism in a Europe simultaneously growing together and drifting apart in many social policy areas, including pensions.

If "No System is Politically Foolproof," Not Even NDC, Is the "Ideal" NDC Truly "Ideal"?

Whether the very design of the "ideal NDC" in the Holzmann model—and the mix of pillars as such—is actually ideal must remain unanswered for the first and probably for the second query. The postulated mix of the model proposes the "structure of a (mandated) first pillar NDC plan, a (voluntary or mandated, if so desired) funded pillar with occupational and individual retirement plans, and a basic pillar of social/non-contributory pensions that provides minimum income support for the very vulnerable elderly." This, in my view, is preferable to the older World Bank perspective of suggesting a combination of mandatory DB-PAYG with a mandatory fully funded DC (corporate or individual) private pillar and a voluntary fully funded DC (corporate or individual) private pillar. But there are also disadvantages, such as potentially fewer synergies in risk spreading, as will be seen in the next section. And whether the better mix proposed now is the best or "ideal" one is not easy to prove. The first step would be to demonstrate the crucial first NDC pillar as optimally designed.

Generally, NDC may be close to an "ideal" pension framework, and thus the "basic structure of ideal NDC" as the core component of the overall combination is designed optimally almost by definition. But specifically, Robert Holzmann leaves actually open almost all parameters to be specified for an "ideal NDC." He neither specifies his choice of an ideal notional interest rate ("the discussion about the (most) appropriate . . . choice is far from over"), nor that of the remaining life expectancy, the indexation of benefits, the reserve fund to be created, or the amount of redistribution and the transition rules to new NDC benefits. Given the fact that all four European countries that have introduced NDC systems (Italy, Latvia, Poland, and Sweden) use different notional interest rates, different ways to determine the residual life expectancy, and different transition rules, some well-reasoned specificity in parameter choice for an "ideal" system would have been expected. But the only specific choice Holzmann makes is advocating a minimum eligibility age to a zero pillar pension that "may have to be conditioned on higher ages (say 70 onward)."

He carefully outlines the issues at stake with any one choice taken, and the non-trivial "technicalities" involved in opting, for instance, for aggregated wage growth rates or for per capita wage growth. The same applies to choices between cross-section life expectancies and estimated cohort expectancies, between price indexation and revaluation beyond price adjustments, or between a top-down and a bottom-up approach in transitioning from DB-PAYG to NDC. Holzmann weighs the pros and cons, the contexts, and follow-up problems of any single choice taken without opting for a preferred one. This is legitimate and academic prudence, but may be somewhat disappointing to readers expecting policy conclusions from a policy expert directing an intergovernmental economic and social policy institution. This even more so as we can see a risk of gradual erosion of NDC rules over time, from Latin America to Latvia. If *no* system is politically foolproof—not even NDC is a panacea, as Holzmann convincingly demonstrates—we may expect some more specific suggestions about how precisely to avoid choices that may turn out to be more foolish or less rational than intended.

Risk Reinforcement Instead of Risk Diversification by the Holzmann Design of the "Ideal" NDC-Mix?

As an "ideal" mix of pension systems around the core NDC pillar, Holzmann proposes combining this basic unfunded pillar with a supplementary funded scheme and with a social pension, unfunded as well. Whereas the crucial first NDC pillar and the social pension pillar or non-contributory pension (as a kind of fall-back device "for the elderly poor") are both PAYG and mandated, the funded pillar—the second or third—is now proposed to be voluntary. Still, it will have to play an important role in a future "more coordinated but not harmonized Pan-European pension system," where national "differences would still exist," but where "their mobility-reducing effects . . . can be limited with a strong (voluntary or mandated) funded pillar." Apart from facilitating "Pan-European mobility," the funded pillar is meant to allow further "consumption smoothing beyond NDC benefits" and "according to individual preferences" without distorting labor supply and saving decisions; "to support retirement flexibility in an aging society"; and to acheive "risk diversification."

Holzmann argues that "as funded and unfunded pillars have a different exposure to economic, demographic, and political risks, and as their rates of return are little correlated, diversifying pension benefits from two pillars is welfare enhancing." No doubt that it is welfare enhancing for globetrotting professionals like those assembled in Sandhamn: currently constrained by a conspicuous and hardly understandable lack of pension portability, great uncertainties about future entitlements, and significant retirement income losses from mobility. It thus, probably serves the great majority of internationally mobile experts at the Sandhamn conference very well. Actually, many of us, despite being specialists in international pension issues, cannot more than very vaguely if at all envisage the kind and amount of retirement income to be expected from a diversity of institutions in a variety of countries. Whether similar welfare gains from combining NDC with a funded DC pillar can be expected by broader middle classes and lower-income strata is still to be seen.

Again, Holzmann's argument holds in principle. But there usually is a much stronger complementarity of respective strengths and weaknesses between a traditional unfunded DB and a fully funded DC system (the previous World Bank priority mix) than between a funded DC and a formally "unfunded" but quasi-funded NDC scheme. As the last combination basically introduces the logic, structures, and processes of private funded DC schemes within public PAYGO systems, synergies of supplementing the other system get lost. By implication, at least two groups of persons may find themselves in more difficult situations than before. Both of them belong to the large section of the population losing through a "quasi-actuarially fair" NDC system because they before have unduly benefited from DB schemes far above their contribution base.

The first group is those in principle able to compensate for the expected losses in pension income. They may do so by investing significantly in a voluntary second or third pillar of a funded pension: for instance, by converting their severance payment claims into an old-age provision. But the new funded pillar is meant to be DC as well, simple in design (to avoid disappointing take-up rates such as with the German *Altersvermögensgesetz* or *Riester-Rente*), and voluntary: three design elements with which I agree. But being voluntary also implies that people free to choose may choose as well *not* to take care of their supplementary old-age provision—or not take care of it sufficiently.

Empirical evidence suggests that this is exactly what we have to expect, at least for some mid-term transition period. The majority of people are not fully aware of their "pension income gap." Those who are do only about a third of the savings they themselves consider necessary. The Sandhamn conference has provided additional evidence of incomplete information, lack of interest, severely limited rationality—and subjective preferences for DB schemes. Annika Sundén (chapter 13, this volume) shows that even for the comparatively well-informed participants in the Swedish system, less than half of them had looked at the benefit projection. They have less self-reported "good knowledge" in 2003 than they had in 2001 when NDC was started, and they show a relapse in most basic knowledge ("all years count") from 50 percent in the year 2000 to 38 percent in 2003. Low-income and younger participants are less likely to look at information at all. In the United States, workers generally lack knowledge about social security benefits, and those who depend most on them are least informed. In Michael Orszag's unpublished presentation to the Sandhamn conference, on which this book is based, he shows that people are generally more satisfied with quality of information in DB systems than in DC systems. Thus, combining two DC schemes will obviously reinforce subjective feelings of uncertainty and information deficiency.

As a consequence, even those who make provisions and voluntarily contribute to a funded DC scheme may at times find themselves with significant and unexpected real losses; and will always find themselves with the double uncertainty of two DC schemes and somewhat unpredictable annuities. Again, Mike Orszag has calculated the "loss in retirement income" in Europe and the United States from 2000 to 2003 as ranging from more than 15 to 25 percent for those who invested in half equity and from more than 40 to more than 50 percent for those who invested in all equity for the funded pillar. The index of all active funds in the Swedish PPM has gone down between the starting period in spring 2001 to 88 percent (spring 2002) and to 63 percent in spring 2003. The Swedish PPM is the Premium Pension system, with a contribution rate of 2.5 percent which accrues a capital-market-determined rate of return. The PPM complements the unfunded (first) pillar with a contribution rate of 16 percent in addition to a minimum "guarantee pension" which provides a basic safety net for those aged 65 and above. The corresponding share of Swedes opting for actively managing their premium pension capital has declined from 67 percent initially to over 14 percent last year to 8 percent in the first half of 2003, the third year of falling stock markets (Casey 2003).

While fluctuations of NDC and funded DC schemes may be independent from each other, co-variation of volatility and thus risk reinforcement cannot be excluded, either. There are many scenarios where risks accumulate or even interact instead of cancelling one another smoothly. For many people, not only getting much lower pension but getting much less predictable retirement income from more sources than before may be the most probable outcome. This may still be meaningful from an overall welfare perspective, but it certainly is in sharp contrast to the hyper-stability of DB final salary pension rights for, say, civil servants in many countries today. It will therefore inevitably be perceived as deterioration over time, even if the final result may be equal to or even better than the *status quo ante*. In Germany, for instance, the *Gesetzliche Rentenversicherung* plus 4 percent savings qua *Riester-Rente* may generate a higher gross replacement income with anything higher than the projected 4 percent annual rate of return on financial markets—nominally (Börsch-Supan and Wilke, 2003, figure 13).

But it will take time to find out what is actually going to happen—and how people actually perceive what is going to happen under uncertainty. Welfare and old-age security must not only be provided, they must also seen to be provided, to be accepted as "good enough," if not "best" a practice or "ideal" pension arrangement.

A Guaranteed Minimum Social Pension is Needed, Not a "Zero-Pillar"

This applies even more so to persons on a minimum social assistance or old-age provision for the elderly poor, who may have been fewer before reforms, or not so poor under a no-reform scenario. In OECD countries, old-age poverty fell for decades until about the mid-1990s, although it was still higher than average among the population above 65, and in particular the population over 75 (Förster 2004). Reforms will most probably reverse the past trend "of the increasing material well-being of the elderly population" and this turn-around has already been observed (Förster 2004). In an accession country like Hungary, for instance, around 150,000 more elderly poor in need of social assistance are expected as a consequence of reform, which is yet far from introducing an NDC scheme (see Marin, Stefanits, and Tarcali 2001).

Holzmann recognizes clearly that "having under the new structure a quasi-actuarial NDC system as first pillar and actuarial funded second and third pillars tends to increase the efficiency in the labor market but reduces the redistribution of income toward the poor" and therefore requires minimum benefits. "Income support for the very vulnerable elderly to prevent old-age poverty is part of the adequacy objectives of any pensions system.' Consequently, he unequivocally calls for "a strengthened social or non-contributory pension in EU member-countries" necessary to counter-balance increasing "vulnerability of the elderly as aging progresses. He argues that "with incomplete and perhaps falling coverage under earnings-related schemes, one can conjecture that poverty incidence will increase as the increase in life expectancy continues." Let us not forget that more than the increase in residual life expectancy, it was and is the increase in survival rates to pension age that determines the pension load. Those survival rates rose from around 15 percent at Bismarck times in the 1870s to over about two-thirds in the post-war period to 90 percent today. Again, who would not share both the diagnoses provided and the normative and policy conclusions drawn in accordance with "the solidarity objectives of the European Union"?

Two main questions remain. First, "how such a strengthened social pension pillar should be structured"? Second, as I added in my original comment on the Holzmann paper, "why should the guaranteed minimum social pension be conceptualized as—and initially even called—a 'zero-pillar'"? Holzmann's response to the second query was to fully accept the objection "and to do away with the, perhaps, questionable notion" but not "with the proposed concept." He thus changed "the language around the zero pillar" into "social pension pillar" or "non-contributory pension," which signals rather a tribute to political etiquette or correctness—and less a rethinking of the real implications of semantic choices.

Before returning to this issue, I accept that his answers to the first query, his own, are all specific enough and satisfying. He opts for a minimum pension under the NDC system in addition to a social pillar in order to "strengthen incentives for formal labor force participation." But he sees that this also requires eligibility restrictions "in order not to contradict the neutrality objective of the NDC structure with regard to the individual retirement decision." Again, I tend to partly agree with the philosophy as well as with the measures proposed. "For example, while allowing individuals to retire from the age of, say, 60 onward, it may have to be required to have a minimum accumulated notional amount equivalent to 100+ percent of the minimum pension or else the need to reach the standard retirement age of, say, 67 (which is increased with a rise in life expectancy). Second, coordinating a minimum NDC pension with a social pension with regard to labor market incentives requires different eligibility criteria (such as some kind of means or affluence testing of the social pillar), different amounts, or different eligibility ages—or some combination of these. Finally, eligibility for a social pension may have to be conditioned on higher ages (say 70 onward), but means-testing may be kept light . . ."

Still, Holzmann himself seems to be skeptic about the persuasiveness of his overall proposal: "How much national preferences such a social pension pillar would be able to exhibit . . . is open for discussion. . . ." This obviously needs more debate—and research. In this context, let me raise a few basic queries without having precise answers. Did not the very name of "zero pillar" originally disclose a preference for a residual conception of sheer poverty relief instead of a broader conception of welfare? Why not adopt the United Nations philosophy, as formulated from the time of the "Guiding Principles for Social Developmental Welfare Policies and Programmes in the Near Future" to the follow-up documents of the World Summit for Social Development (WSSD) 1995? Why not replace a concept of welfare as minority concern, program of poverty relief, and social control of those "living on welfare" by a more encompassing, comprehensive, and universal policy concern meant to "serve to raise the level of living of the widest possible sections of the population" (UN Guiding Principles; see European Centre 1993, pp. 212, 213 ff.)? Should guarantees regarding old-age pensions be restricted to protecting the marginal and vulnerable instead of more universal minimal standards of human well-being and social integration? Is protecting and compensating the most needy a sufficient complement to counting on self-help for all others, or may a strategy of enabling also require supporting those who generally take care of themselves—and assisting those who care for others?

Are no other forms of minimum income guarantees and non-contributory social rights qua redistribution conceivable, desirable, or even preferable? How does which kind of coverage of unemployment and periods of illness, disability, military service, and family-related time off, such as maternity leave or care leave, supplement insufficient earnings-related NDC claims to a decent minimum income guarantee? As they add up to several years, and frequently more than a decade of absenteeism from work during working life (Marin 2000), they may better assist consumption smoothing and provide more targeted, social policy goal-oriented support beyond poverty relief and to equal opportunities than a social pension. Generous cash contributions for non-contributory periods (related to unemployment, sickness, disability, military service, family-related time-off such as maternity leave, care leave, etc.) may supplement insufficient earnings-related NDC accumulations much better than unconditional basic social pensions, achieving a decent minimum benefit level and at the same time providing better incentives. This, at least, is my major hypothesis. Why should social pensions be means-tested and restricted to "the vulnerable elderly" and thus to the very margins of society, instead of being non-contributory universal grants available to specific categories of people, such as (working or lone) parents, caregivers, or the disabled?

In short: why, after all, should the social underpinning of NDC cum voluntary funded pillar be conceptualized as if it still were what it is not any longer called: namely, a "zero" pillar? Did "zero pillar" not imply unintentionally but tellingly that getting something for nothing (or at least for less than one's contribution equivalent) may end up with getting next to nothing ("zero") for something (a tax-financed primary social policy goal "pillar," withering away with other "national preferences")? Why not conceive the social safety net below the mix of mandated NDC and a supplementary voluntary funded scheme as a "grounding," a basic pension guarantee—as much a core component as the crucial NDC—and not as a "zero pillar," which may crack just when most needed? But I have to agree with Robert Holzmann's rejoinder in a personal communication to this critique that my "grandiose 'pension guarantee' sounds fine but is not fully thought through with regard incentives provided" and still "rather fluffy." Indeed, much more work needs to be done on the synchronization of minimum NDC pension, social pension, and the non-contributory supplements to regular earnings-related NDC schemes for social policy goals on work-, family- and health-related interruptions of working life—open to everybody in need and not just to the poor.

Disability Welfare: A Most Relevant Lacuna

One crucial aspect of the pension *problematique* in general, and of massive pre-retirement as probably its single most important determinant in particular, that is completely ignored in the Holzmann model is disability pensions. (For recent publications, see OECD 2003; Prinz 2003; Marin and Prinz 2003; and Marin, Prinz, and Queisser 2004). This is even more surprising in view of two trends: first, the uncontrollable spending dynamics on disability policies during the last few decades; and second, its foreseeable future aggravation. With coverage and replacement rates of monthly pension incomes probably falling, as well as with retirement age rising under earnings-related schemes, one can assume that the propensity to exit early from the labor market via disability pension claims may increase. But can an "ideal" Pan-European pension pillar mix formula even be conceived without some solution to one of the major causes of early retirement, if massive early retirement itself is one of the major causes of unsustainable pension dynamics today? In addition to fiscal unsustainability, in several European economies with high non-employment rates, disability pensions play a major role in depressing labor force participation.

Some facts and trends are puzzling indeed: How can invalidity pensions for the working age population significantly increase with improved health and higher disability-free life expectancy, compression and postponement of morbidity? How is a steep rise in incapacity rates in working age possible along with a simultaneous reduction of chronic and occupational diseases, accidents, and work injuries—and with less exposure to infectious and contagious diseases (some of which have virtually disappeared) and to dust and to hazardous substances such as asbestos and other carcinogens? How can disability pensions in working age rise with a decline in disability of population groups of higher risk such as the elderly beyond working age 65?

In Hungary, for instance, the majority of all new pensioners exit to retirement via invalidity (Marin, Stefanits, and Tarcali 2001, figure 2). In Austria, every second man retires during working age as disabled and the numbers climb to up to two out of three farmers or three out of four blue collar workers. For the age cohorts 55/56 years, invalidity pensions have increased by 555(!) percent in less than two decades. Despite many other avenues for early retirement, in the age group 60 to 64 years, 40 percent of males have an invalidity pension. For the OECD, the average is 23 percent. In the Netherlands, which has one of the world's most advanced medical and health care systems, almost 1 million persons of working age are on disability pension benefits; overall, invalidity recipiency rates have increased 86 percent between 1980 and 1997. In the United Kingdom, without any evidence of deterioration in health, government spending for sickness and disability has quadrupled over the past two decades, and 40 percent of working-age recipients of state benefits now claim sickness and disability compensation.

Correspondingly, the general slowing down of the rate of welfare expenditure expansion (social spending roughly doubled between 1960 and 1980 and has increased around 20 percent since) has affected disability pensions less than any other social expenditure. Extension of programs, number of beneficiaries, and amount of expenditures for disability have steadily increased for about 35 years, even if one controls for the changing age structure of societies. Periodic efforts at retrenchment (in the mid-1970s and 1990s) have succeeded in slowing down recipiency growth rates, but never the growth of beneficiaries as such; the stock of benefit recipients remained high, and the inflow rates much higher than outflow. As a consequence, even disability pension expenditures have begun to show reduced inflow rates: that is, continuing though slower expansion dynamics. But overall cost containment

Figure 11.6. Variation in Public Expenditure for Disability Related Programs (percentage of GDP)

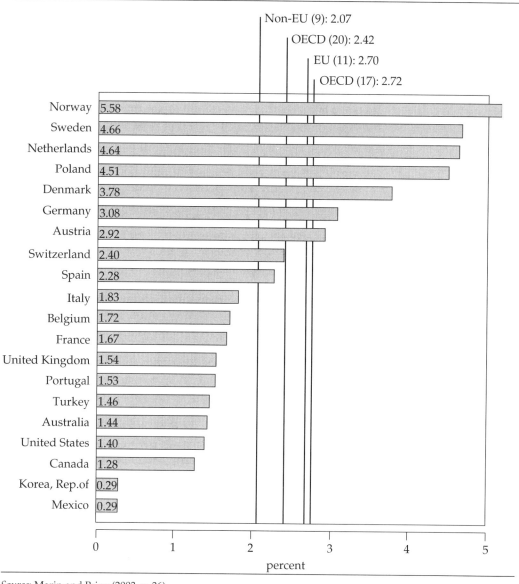

Source: Marin and Prinz (2003, p. 36).

Note: All disability-related programmes include broad disability benefits and employment-related programs for disabled people. OECD (17) excludes Republic of Korea, Mexico, and Turkey. The vertical lines in the graph indicate mean.

will be a core challenge in the years to come—more than in any other social policy field.

Expansion of disability pensions over the last decades has become uncontrollable (figure 11.6). Social expenditures on disability now total several times the social costs of unemployment, even under adverse conditions of very high unemployment rates. In 19 out of 20 OECD countries investigated, disability costs were significantly higher than the costs for unemployment. On average, they were more than double the costs (2.17 times). In Norway, they are up to 11.9 times the unemployment costs. Public expenditures go up to 5.58 percent of GDP, and are 2.72 in OECD-17 and 2.70 in EU-11 countries. Still, high costs do not guarantee good targeting. A recent OECD report (2003) shows that a clear majority of severely disabled people, most in need of support, are not awarded a disability benefit,

Figure 11.7. Disability Status of Disability Benefit Recipients

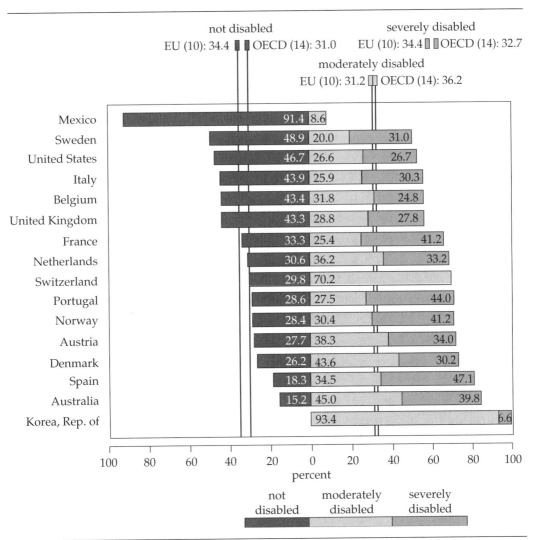

Source: Marin and Prinz (2003, p. 57).

Note: For Mexico and Switzerland, "severe" and "moderate" are one number. Mexico and Switzerland are excluded in the OECD average. The vertical lines in the graph indicate mean.

whereas more than 40 percent of disability pension recipients are self-declared non-disabled (figure 11.7). Scarce funds are thus wasted either on non-deserving persons, often neither poor nor needy, or on persons in need but deserving and being better helped by forms of support other than disability pensions. The European underemployment malaise seems to have shifted from mass unemployment to a massive non-employment, of which widespread invalidity has become a major current.

Above the age of 50, in particular, the relationship between unemployed and economically inactive persons, many of them on disability benefits, is now 1:8. During working age, Europeans are outside the labor force for between 10 years (men) and 22 years (women), of which the average person is likely to be unemployed or on job search for not more than two years. Thus unemployment (while still quite high) is becoming a minor problem as against overall non-employment. Whereas one-in-five adult men of working age is now outside the labor force and another one-in-ten-to-twelve is not working because of unemployment, male unemployed are less than a third of the male non-employed in Europe today. The proportion of women outside the labor force is six times greater than the proportion unemployed.

Obviously, invalidity pensions account for only one faction, though an important and growing one, of overall growing non-employment of adult Europeans of working age. And labor market hypotheses for explaining the rise of disability pensions are all the more plausible, as demographic explanations play no role for the working age population. All medical experts agree that there is no increase in the prevalence of invalidity and, therefore, no medical or epidemiological explanation for this steep increase in invalidity pensions and invalidity expenditures. Aarts, Burkhauser, and De Jong (1996) refer to a quantitative study of determinants of change in disability recipiency shares in the Netherlands in the 1980s (Aarts and de Jong 1992). They concluded that only a third of the variance in inflow into disability status is explained by medical factors. Two thirds is explained by non-medical determinants, above all benefit generosity and unemployment rates.

The Policy Shift Needed on Disability Pensions

Disability pensions seem to have become a kind of garbage can social welfare category. It probably will continue to depress labor force participation above the age of the median voter—around 45 years already, today. Thus it will contribute to aggravating fiscal pressures rather than to maintaining or restoring stability and long-term sustainable social policy. This *malaise* requires a paradigmatic turnaround in framing the social policy issue at stake. The very expansion of disability pensions cannot be seen any longer as a sign of more overall welfare and well-being of disabled people or "elderly" unemployed of middle age, but rather as an administrative incapacity to provide welfare and cater it well enough to the persons with impairments in need. In short, disability welfare extension is a potential welfare failure, rather than an unquestionable welfare and social policy success.

As with spending on unemployment, hospitals, prisons, and pharmaceuticals, more spending on sickness, accidents, work injuries, and disabilities or early retirement invalidity may signal less welfare for each disabled person and for society at large. Yet the failure of disability pension policies is not at all accidental but an inevitable byproduct, an unintended but unavoidable consequence, of a purposeful and successful social compensation policy. Compensation produces income security for persons with assumed health-related restrictions on earnings without a corresponding level of integration offers and activation demands. In all modern European welfare states, the main determinants of public spending are not revenue but entitlements to welfare benefits. But in contrast to transfers—for instance, for unemployment, social assistance programs, or even old-age pensions—spending on invalidity pensions and disability benefits cannot easily be changed and adapted even over mid-term periods. Disability pensions lend themselves to the temptation of political rent-seeking and manipulation, to using pre-retirement and invalidity pensions schemes for facilitating industrial restructuring or for hiding unemployment, for getting votes instead of making welfare schemes compatible with standards of fairness, competitive requirements, and long-term affordability. Disability pensions allow for trading short-term political popularity for long-term sustainability. Easier access to early retirement, broader coverage, more generous replacement income, more relaxed screening of eligibility and assessment of claims buy immediate satisfaction of interest groups and voters. The fiscal burdens of unfunded liabilities are shifted unto later generations of working populations, without easily discernible relationship with the goodies distributed in earlier periods (for this and the following, see de Jong 2003).

But in contrast to political leniency with respect to regular old-age security, thoughtless generosity regarding disability pensions changes the behavior not only of current invalidity beneficiaries; it also adversely affects the behavior of potential claimants: non-disabled employees, their employers, and social administrators, and all other interest groups as well. As with sickness and health insurance, moral hazard in disability welfare may become contagious, spreading over to others, demoralizing previously innocent bystanders watching what they may consider malingering at their own expense by free-riding recipients. They may possibly give in to the temptation to use incapacity schemes that are an easier and cheaper way to deploy surplus workforce than regular dismissals. Enterprises frequently find themselves in the paradoxical situation of complaining about a rise of non-wage labor costs, which they themselves have previously produced by abusing pre-retirement and invalidity pensions schemes to offload large proportions of middle-aged workers at public expense.

Currently, disability policies award many more people permanent pensions than they place in rehabilitation or employment programs, with much higher costs for social exclusion. They are not able to create employment through activating programs. Everywhere, they systematically exclude exactly those persons most in need for occupational reinsertion—those above 45 years of age where inflow rates are highest—from return to work programs, creating a great age-mismatch between disability inflow and vocational rehabilitation offer. Thus, they are completely writing off broad middle-aged cohorts of persons with partial impairments and whole generations of so called elderly workers that have gone through longer spells of unemployment. They invite massive claims for invalidity pensions and illness-related pre-retirement for ever younger cohorts and frequently even grant early retirement under false disability label. Large country differences are not even well documented, nor understood (figure 11.8).

Disability policies have led to a situation where invalidity expenditures and non-employment costs for disabled people within generally more healthy populations greatly exceed the expenditures for unemployment. These policies have led to an acceptance of widespread paid non-employment of employable persons with (partial) disabilities. They take it for granted that extremely low outflow rates for even partial disability tend to make invalidity benefits, once granted, a lifelong welfare dependency. They even tend to channel social problems of long-term unemployment, social assistance, and non-employment through the invalidity track, thus making disability a major entrapment for surplus labor populations. They thereby not just misallocate resources at a grand scale but misdirect and reduce energies and work capacities at large. They demoralize and misguide disabled and non-disabled citizens alike—to the extent these mismatches become widely visible and

Figure 11.8. Country Differences in Age-specific Inflow Rates (ratio of age-specific inflow rates over age group 35–44, 1999)

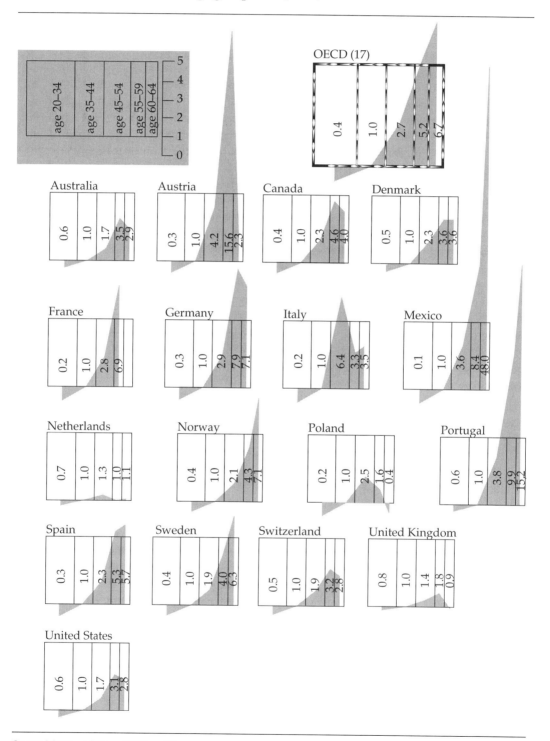

Source: Marin and Prinz (2003, p. 74).

Note: Data for Canada, France, Italy, and Spain cover contributory programs only rather than both programs.

publicly debated—corrupt norms of solidarity and reciprocity by inviting opportunistic behavior and widespread abuse of social rights, and threaten to undermine the legitimacy of welfare entitlements and pension arrangements altogether.

As a consequence, the radically ambiguous paradigm shift that has occurred during the last decades must be followed-up by a shift toward a more coherent employment-oriented equal opportunity model (OECD 2003; Marin, Prinz, and Queisser 2004). What is crucial is that the normalization and mainstreaming of disability inherent in the social model finally moves away from modeling disability benefits primarily according to a lifelong retirement pension scheme without return option, and move it instead more toward job search, job return, and other (re-)start or unemployment programs.

The Primacy of Political Desirability, Feasibility, and Sustainability of NDC: Its Underestimated Comparative Advantages

For all those reasons, introducing NDC as a core component within an overall Pan-European pension package or combination of multiple pillars should be argued both in political and economic terms. The mix Holzmann proposes has "an NDC model at its core and supplementary funded pensions and social pensions at its wings." It is a mix of mandatory and voluntary, of unfunded and funded, of public and private, occupational and individual retirement plans, of contributory earnings-related and non-contributory minimum income support. It will have to be argued convincingly—and that, in the last resort, is politically. When taking recourse to economic reasoning and formulated in its very framework, efficiency arguments are necessary, but not sufficient, whereas fairness and equity issues building on optimal efficiency are most important.

Policy conclusions follow this diagnosis. In order to win broader popular support for NDC schemes, their underestimated comparative advantages and *political assets* should be clearly presented.

- *NDC as a fairness standard, anti-corruption device, and promoter of pension literacy:* NDC sets broadly shared standards of fairness, as actuarial fairness may be the minimum common denominator, apart from and compatible with remaining ideological cleavages in matters of social justice. NDC thus makes explicit hidden or perverse redistributions, as well as implicit taxes for the benefit of special privileged sectional or particular interests, and discloses the true beneficiaries of pension arrangements and reform measures, as opposed to claimed beneficiaries. It makes people think in terms of lifetime contributions, lifetime incomes, annuities, and lifetime pension entitlements in relation to flexibly chosen retirement ages, as against monthly replacement rates to final or previous incomes. It induces thinking in terms of choices, trade-offs, and budget and other constraints, thereby living up to the requirements of modern pension systems, and generating pension literacy (against all well-known reasons for limited knowledge). It may unblock reforms and build political consensus on required adjustment options in situations where the current system is widely seen as unjust, but lack of credibility to continue with parametric reforms is difficult to overcome.
- *NDC as a functional differentiation of welfare trigger:* NDC allows for functionally differentiating old-age security from disability benefits, health or accident insurance, social assistance, unemployment benefits, survivor's income support, and other family policy measures such as child care credits, anti-poverty measures, and all minimum or basic income guarantees. While these and other social policy fields remain strongly interrelated, only functional differentiation and correspondingly separate

flows of resources permit transparent and politically defendable forms of redistribution. It also allows for autonomy and self-referentiality of the social security pensions system comparable to that of the central banks, the judiciary and court system, science and research, the market economy, and the political system. This system needs its own specialized language, vocabulary (translating all DB problems into NDC language), taxonomy, and framing. But finally, it makes for a "difference in philosophy, not just vocabulary" (Lindbeck 2003b). It is not an "autopilot" system (Monika Queisser, chapter 12, this volume), but helps safely navigate long distances (even with controlled naps or nodding off occasionally). And it eliminates the need for constant nerveracking, costly, and conflicting parametric reform maneuvers (for example, 35 since 1993 in Austria; 50 between 1963 and 1995 in Sweden).

- *NDC as better risk management:* As Gora and Palmer (2003) have shown convincingly, NDC is a superior form of risk management and risk diversification compared to all other pension paradigms. Of course, NDC faces the same macroeconomic and somewhat less demographic risks as all other systems. But compared to public defined benefit systems, it is much less exposed to political manipulation—and not at all subject to opportunistic behavior and moral hazard. It does not create overshooting expectations and no promises will ever be broken; it even depends less on good forecasts. And in contrast to financial defined contribution accounting systems, it is unexposed to financial market fluctuations. There are advantageous NDC features, but not all of them are inherent in NDC; rather, the tangible advantages are in political realities more than in design or superior formula. NDC is inevitably "underresearched" because of its newness, but it is not "oversold" (Diamond 2003) as long as it does not claim conceptual instead of practical and political superiority.

- *NDC as a core component of any pension constitution and autonomy:* NDC's comparative advantages in handling risk exposure—compared to DB-PAYG systems and financial DC systems—make NDC the single most powerful candidate for a core component of any pension mix and pension constitution. The "wings" making this rare bird fly best are still under construction and testing. But the NDC corpus as a PAYG lifetime saving scheme could help to turn an implicit and frequently heavily distorted generation compact into an explicit generation contract, providing fairness and equity within and between generations. It does not yet solve the transition legacy problem of how to handle overhang liabilities (which in Japan amounts to 95 percent of all excess liabilities; see Takayama, chapter 24, this volume) and how to share the legacy costs over generations. But in preventing future excess liabilities, NDC can help overcome system imbalances and correct a prevailing sense of opaqueness and injustice that so far have been the major obstacles to pension reform. It may still not yet be a magic Pan-European pension reform and coordination formula. But it may come close to an optimal device in that there are no better ones around. And trying to become the best workable pension arrangement, not only in Europe, may make NDC come close to the "ideal" self-binding mechanism claimed for by Robert Holzmann.

References

Aarts, L., and P. De Jong. 1992. *Economic Aspects of Disability Behavior,* Amsterdam, North Holland.

Aarts, B., and P. de Jong. 1996. *Curing the Dutch Disease. An International Perspective on Disability Policy Reform.* Aldershot, U.K.: Ashgate.

Barr, N. 2001. *The Welfare State as Piggy Bank.* Oxford and New York: Oxford University Press.

———. 2006. "Non-Financial Defined Contribution Pensions: Mapping the Terrain." In *Pension Reform: Issues and Prospects for Non-Financial Defined Contribution (NDC) Schemes,* ed. R. Holzmann and E. Palmer, chapter 4. Washington, DC: World Bank.

Börsch-Supan, A. H., and C. B. Wilke. 2003. "The German Pension System: How it Was, How it Will Be." Paper presented at the NDC Conference, Sandhamn, Sweden, September 28–30.

Casey, B. 2003. "Private Public Cooperation in Pensions" Paper presented at the E.I.S.S. conference on "Freedom of Choice in Social Security," Graz, September 25–27.

De Jong, P. 2003. "Disability and Disability Insurance." In *European Disability Pension Policies,* ed. C. Prinz, 77–106. Aldershot, U.K.: Ashgate.

Diamond, P. 2002. *Social Security Reform.* Oxford and New York: Oxford University Press.

———. 2003. Presentation at the NDC Conference, Sandhamn, Sweden, September 28–30.

Disney, R. 1999. "Notional Accounts as a Pension Reform Strategy." Social Protection Discussion Paper 9928, World Bank, Washington, DC.

European Centre. 1993. "Welfare in a Civil Society." Report for the Conference of European Ministers Responsible for Social Affairs—United Nations European Region.

———. 2004. "Pensionsharmonisierung oder-Disharmonisierung?" Handout, Press Conference, Presseclub Concordia, Vienna, January 8.

Fehr, E., and K. Schmidt. 1999. "A Theory of Fairness, Competition, and Cooperation." *Quarterly Journal of Economics* 114: 817–68.

Förster, M. F. 2004. "Increasing Well-Being Among the Elderly Population: Re-Writing the Story?" Vienna: European Centre.

———. 2006. "Income Inequalities, Poverty and Social Transfers—OECD and CEE." Aldershot, U.K.: Ashgate.

Góra, M., and E. Palmer. 2003. "Shifting Perspectives in Pensions." Warsaw / Uppsala. Unpublished paper.

Gruber, J., and D. Wise. 1999. *Social Security and Retirement Around the World.* Chicago: University of Chicago Press.

Holzmann, R., and J. E. Stiglitz. 2001. *New Ideas about Old Age Security. Towards Sustainable Pension Systems in the 21st Century.* Washington, DC: World Bank.

Holzmann, R., M. Orenstein, and M. Rutkowski. 2003. *Pension Reform in Europe: Process and Progress.* Washington, DC: World Bank.

Holzmann, R., and R. Hinz. 2005. *Old Age Income Support in the 21st Century: An International Perspective on Pension Systems and Reform.* Washington, DC: World Bank.

Lindbeck, A., and M. Persson. 2003a. "The Gains from Pension Reform." *Journal of Economic Literature* XLI (March): 74–112.

Lindbeck, A. 2003b. Presentation at the NDC Conference in Sandhamn, Sweden, September 28–30.

Marin, B. 2000. "Introducing Innovative Employment Initiatives." In *Innovative Employment Initiatives,* ed. Bernd Marin, D. Meulders, and D. J. Snower, 21–88. Aldershot, U.K.: Ashgate.

———. 2003. "Transforming Disability Welfare Policy: Completing a Paradigm Shift." In *European Disability Pension Policies,* ed. C. Prinz, 13–76. Aldershot, U.K.: Ashgate.

Marin, B., and M. Fuchs. 2003. "Pensionsharmonisierung in Kärnten." Expertise on behalf of the Kärtner Landesregierung, Vienna.

Marin, B., and C. Prinz. 1999. In *Pensionsreformen. Nachhaltiger Sozialumbau am Beispiel Österreichs,* 2nd edition, ed. B. Marin and C. Prinz. Frankfurt and New York: Campus.

———. 2003. *Facts and Figures on Disability Welfare. A Pictographic Portrait of an OECD Report.* Vienna: European Centre.

Marin, B., D. Meulders, and D. J. Snower. 2000. *Innovative Employment Initiatives*. Aldershot, U.K.: Ashgate.

Marin, B., H. Stefanits, and G. Tarcali. 2001. "Learning from the Partner Hungary: An Austro-European View." Paper presented at the International Institute for Applied Systems Analysis (IIASA)/World Bank Conference, "Learning from the Partners," April 5–7, Vienna.

Marin, B., C. Prinz, and M. Queisser. 2004. *Transforming Disability Welfare Policies. Towards Work and Equal Opportunities*. Aldershot, U.K.: Ashgate.

OECD (Organisation for Economic Co-operation and Development). 2003. *Transforming Disability into Ability. Policies to Promote Work and Income Security for Disabled People*. Paris: OECD.

Palmer, E. 2006. "Conversion to NDC—Issues and Models." In *Pension Reform: Issues and Prospects for Non-Financial Defined Contribution (NDC) Schemes*, ed. R. Holzmann and E. Palmer, chapter 9. Washington, DC: World Bank.

Prinz, C., ed. 2003. *European Disability Pension Policies. 11 Country Trends 1970–2002*. Aldershot, U.K.: Ashgate.

Prinz, C., and W. Lutz. 1994a. "Ältere Menschen in Europa. Demographische Perspektiven 1990–2050: Teil 1." *Journal für Sozialforschung* 34 (2): 197–220.

———. 1994b. "Ältere Menschen in Europa. Demographische Perspektiven 1990–2050: Teil 2." *Journal für Sozialforschung* 34 (3): 287–310.

Prinz, C., and B. Marin. 1999. *Pensionsreformen. Nachhaltiger Sozialumbau am Beispiel Österreichs*, 2nd edition. Frankfurt and New York: Campus.

Queisser, M. 2006. "Discussion of 'NDC Pension Schemes in Middle- and Low-Income Countries.'" In *Pension Reform: Issues and Prospects for Non-Financial Defined Contribution (NDC) Schemes*, ed. R. Holzmann and E. Palmer, chapter 12. Washington, DC: World Bank.

Synthesis. 2003. "Lebenseinkommen im öffentlichen und privaten Sektor. Ein Vergleich anhand ausgewählter Vergleichskarrieren." Expertise on behalf of the Bundesministerium für Wirtschaft und Arbeit, Vienna.

Chapter 12

NDC Pension Schemes in Middle- and Low-Income Countries

David Lindeman, David Robalino, and Michal Rutkowski*

THE NOTIONAL DEFINED CONTRIBUTION (NDC)[1] CONCEPT has been put forward as a paradigm shift to address fiscal, equity, and incentive problems with state pension regimes—mostly financed on a current disbursement or pay-as-you-go (PAYG) basis. Much of the policy discussion so far has been concerned with high-income countries such as Sweden and Italy. Little attention has been given to the question of whether NDC arrangements are desirable and viable in the case of middle- or even lower-income countries that are characterized by less stable macroeconomic environments, a narrow and volatile contributory base, and a more uneven income distribution; and often are in the midst of a demographic transition. This despite the fact that countries such as Brazil, China, the Kyrgyz Republic, Latvia, Mongolia, Poland, and Russia have introduced variants of the NDC concept.[2]

This chapter discusses the potential benefits of the NDC concept mostly in the context of middle- and low-income countries as well as the major constraints for implementation. Our scope, therefore, is what might loosely be called "non-OECD" countries. Clearly, the analysis of the costs and benefits of an NDC scheme should and will be very country specific. Here we focus on the general macroeconomic, demographic, and institutional variables that can affect the application and performance of the NDC concept.

The reminder of the chapter is organized in seven sections. The next section sets out a framework for subsequent discussions by introducing the NDC concept, outlining a typology of NDC variants and discussing differences and similarities with pure defined contributions (DC) and pure defined benefit (DB) schemes. In the following two sections, we discuss the potential primary benefits of the NDC concept in middle- and low-income countries in terms of reducing economic distortions (the third section) and improving financial sustainability of PAYG pension schemes (the fourth section). We identify key factors of design and initial conditions that are likely to influence the realization of these benefits. The rest of the chapter is concerned with implementation issues that need to receive particular attention in any country, including middle- and low-income countries: transi-

* David Lindeman has worked with the U.S. federal government, the World Bank, and the Organisation for Economic Co-operation and Development; David Robalino is a senior economist in the Middle East and North Africa Human Development Department of the World Bank; and Michal Rutkowski is a director in the Human Development Department in the Middle East and North Africa Region of the World Bank.

The authors would like to thank Anna-Marie Vilamovska for excellent assistance.

tion mechanisms and the integration of heterogeneous pension plans (the fifth section); redistribution and poverty (the sixth section); and institutional capacity (the seventh section). The last section concludes by outlining the advantages of NDC schemes over traditional DB schemes in middle and low income countries, even when the latter are well designed.

Description of the NDC Concept and Its Variations

We take the NDC concept to be the application of the structures and vocabulary from funded DC schemes (plans) to largely PAYG regimes. NDC attempts to internalize within the expectations of DB-PAYG pension participants all or some of the risks that are automatically borne by members in funded DC schemes.

In funded DC schemes, the sponsor (employer) and worker make contributions according to commitments set out in the pension contract, typically regulated by tax and labor laws. A member's retirement departure wealth is solely a function of past contributions plus interests on the investments of these contributions (at market prices). Absent illegal behavior, there is no future contingent liability on the "sponsor" (usually employers). Furthermore, at any moment the pension fund is "financially complete"—that is, liabilities by definition equal assets.[3] Accordingly, members, not the sponsor, bear investment risk and the consequences of increasing longevity.

Generally in an NDC scheme the pension at retirement is equal to the sum of past contributions revalorized by an exogenously defined factor, divided by a measure of life expectancy at retirement. The resulting pension itself can be indexed over time in a variety of ways. Formally the dynamics of the NDC pension are given by:

$$p_t = \frac{\left(\sum_{k=a}^{R} \beta.w_k.I_k\right)}{G_{A,R,r}} J_t; \ t \geq R,$$ (12.1)

where p_t is the pension at time t; β is the contribution rate; w_k is the imposable salary at time k; a is the time when the individual joins the social security system; R is the time of retirement; $G_{A,R,r}$ is the "g-factor" (annuity factor) at age A, in time R, given an interest rate r; I_k is the revalorization factor that affects contributions at preretirement time k; and J_t is the index that affects the pension at the time of retirement (R).

Choices regarding the parameters in equation 12.1 can define a large typology of NDC-type schemes. Among other possibilities, five examples are: (1) the "pure" wage-sum model, including annuities that move solely with wage-sum changes; (2) wage sum during accumulation, and annuities that are half price indexed and half tied to wage-sum changes (as in the Latvia variant); (3) a fiscally fully complete NDC model with smoothing for all contingencies along the lines of Swedish legislation; (4) average wage-indexed NDC accounts with participating annuities; and (5) government bonds that pay average wage growth (or other proxy of the sustainable implicit rate of return of the scheme), converted to participating annuities. These models differ in how they resolve the pervasive trade-off between solvency and predictability.

Whether Equation 12.1 can be formally considered a DC arrangement depends on whether I_k, J_t, and $G_{A,R,r}$ are set in a way that guarantees that at all times expected assets are equal to expected liabilities. As discussed in the fourth section, this is not always a simple matter. Among other difficulties, one technical trouble relates to the transformation of the notional capital (the numerator in equation 12.1) into the proper annuity. Hence, in many cases, NDC continues to be a DB arrangement in the sense that the "sponsor" (future generations) faces a contingent liability. A more adequate name for the scheme in this case would be "notional accounts."[4]

The fact is that the NDC mechanism used to compute the pension can internalize changes in life expectancies and some changes in the contributory base, thus reducing the risks faced by future payers (therefore reducing contingent liabilities) and increasing the risks faced by current workers (and even possibly retirees). Other benefits attributed to the NDC (or notional account) concept include improving incentives for work over retirement, overcoming adverse redistributive transfers within traditional DB schemes, improving transparency in the link between costs and benefits, facilitating issues of political economy related to parametric reforms, assisting in breaking PAYG reform deadlocks, and enabling the system to adjust automatically to changing circumstances.

Clearly, the same or similar outcomes can be achieved through a classic DB formula. Indeed, if lifetime salaries/wages are included in the calculation of the pension and these are adjusted (valorized) in the same way as contributions under the "incomplete" NDC formula, and if the index for pensions is also the same, then the DB formula gives:

$$p_t = \alpha . LOS_R . \frac{\left(\sum_{k=a}^{R} . w_k . I_k \right)}{LOS_R} J, \tag{12.2}$$

where α is the accrual rate and LOS_R is the length of service at retirement. We notice that equations 12.1 and 12.2 are mathematically equivalent as long as $\alpha = \beta / G_{A,R,r}$.

Basically, a DB formula where all wages are included in the calculation of the pension (indexed by an appropriate—that is, sustainable—rate), where the basic accrual rate is computed yearly on the basis of equation 12.2 and a reference minimum retirement age, and where there are actuarially neutral penalties (bonuses) for early (delayed) retirement (computed yearly) can generate the same outcomes, including the same individual behaviors, as the NDC formula.

Thus the key policy questions we address in this chapter are whether, in the case of low- and middle-income countries, it is feasible and desirable to move from a "flawed" DB formula toward a "good" DB or NDC formula (see box 12.1). What choices in terms of parameters (for example, which index for past wages or contributions) are preferable? Can the NDC concept be employed as a paradigm shift to facilitate the movement to a good DB formula, while simultaneously improving management, accounting, and reporting practices, which can also have a positive impact on individual behavior?

Incentives

It has been argued that by creating a stronger and more transparent link between contributions and benefits, the pension formula used in NDC-type schemes has the potential to reduce distortions in labor supply and saving decisions[5] associated with many traditional DB-PAYG formulas. This could be particularly relevant in the case of developing and transition economy countries where current DB-PAYG schemes often provide incentives for retirement over work, induce strategic manipulation of wages, and could be contributing to the informalization of the economy[6] while reducing savings rates.[7]

In this section, we analyze how individuals' behaviors regarding retirement, labor supply, and saving are likely to change as countries move from the typical ("flawed") DB-PAYG formula toward an NDC-type formula (see box 12.1).

Box 12.1. Gradations from "Flawed DB" to "Good DB" and NDC

1. Heterogeneous DB, characterized by various age/service qualification requirements by service, type of job, gender, usually use of final pay (or truncated wage histories, such as the best 20) in the calculation of the pension, accrual rates not linked to contribution rate and retirement age, no penalties for early retirement, and no automatic indexation of pensions.

2. Defined benefit, but adoption of lifetime valorized wages and possible use of linear (not actuarially neutral) adjustments for early retirement.

3. Same as the DB-2 formula but with retirement-age accrual rates (calculated on the basis of equation 12.2) fixed at entry and calculated on the basis of expected survival probabilities retirement age. This is equivalent to having a reference accrual rate linked to a reference retirement age and actuarially neutral penalties (bonuses) for early (delayed) retirement.

4. Same as the DB-3 formula, but with retirement age-dependent accrual rates that are computed on the basis of equation 12.2 when the individual retires. This is also equivalent to having a reference accrual rate linked to a reference retirement age, but computed yearly, and actuarially neutral penalties (bonuses) for early (delayed) retirement.

5. Change in formal expression to NDC vocabulary, possibly with additional measures: (a) "participating annuities," such that retirees share some of the risks associated with post-retirement longevity gains and periods of low real wage growth; and (b) a "balancing mechanism" to adjust promised (but not awarded) benefits to demographic or labor force trends.

As a practical matter, there are several options between DB-2 and DB-4 that reflect ad hoc legislative changes. For example, a country may decide to change the retirement age schedule but grandfather the previous schedule for work and credited service before the change was made.

Source: Authors.

Retirement Decisions

DB-PAYG pension formulas in developing countries often provide incentives for retirement over work. In most cases, the high prevalence of early retirement can be explained by low penalties and generous minimum pensions, which are awarded without an adequate minimum contributory period. Clearly, moving toward a "good" DB formula by setting penalties to actuarially neutral levels, reducing minimum pensions, and using adjusted lifetime wages (instead of final pay) can change the work/leisure choice considerably. Leaving these factors aside, however, there is still the question of whether moving toward an NDC-type formula provides incentive for delaying retirement beyond the minimum retirement age (which is often low relative to life expectancy, and politically "sticky").

There will be incentives to delay retirement if, under the new formula, the marginal utility of waiting (resulting from a higher pension and higher consumption) is higher than the marginal disutility (resulting from lower leisure). In the case of "flawed" DB formulas, switching to a DB-4 formula (or even DB-3) or to an NDC cognate will encourage delayed retirement and more work. This is because the marginal accrual in the DB-1 or DB-2 is linear (one more year equals one more percentage increment in the lifetime benefit), whereas in DB-4 or NDC the extra year of work both adds to one's lifetime benefit and it increases the benefit level based on the years of work before the minimum retirement ages (an upward slope in the price for delaying retirement).[8]

In simulations, we find that the NDC formula (or DB-4) can considerably delay retirement relative to the other DB formulas.[9] The difference between a DB formula with no adjustments for delayed retirement to the accrual rate and the NDC alternative is greater the higher the preferences for leisure and, as noted earlier, the higher the accrual rate in the DB formula (see the technical annex at the end of this chapter for a description of the model and the simulations).

Clearly, our results apply to rational-utility-maximizer agents. *Homo economicus* in real life might not display this type of behavior. Still, it is reasonable to assume that individuals will learn from their own and others experiences, as well as from the information provided by plan sponsors, that the ratio of the last pension to the last wage increases faster under an NDC formula than even a near-equivalent DB formula (DB-2 and DB-3 in box 12.1). Other things being equal, this is a good incentive to delay retirement. Moreover, even if retirement patterns do not change (that is, even if there are no gains in terms of labor supply), NDC-type formulas will guarantee that, regardless of age, all individuals are paid the same, presumably sustainable, rate of return.

Labor Demand and Supply Decisions

The informal sector in developing countries is often large, and a majority of these countries continue to struggle to reduce unemployment rates. It is argued that this is in part the result of rigidities in labor markets (downward rigidity in wages) and high taxes on labor.[10] Lower contribution rates to social security could increase the demand for labor and play a role in reducing the size of the informal sector. A DB formula that includes all benefits in the calculation of the pension could also contribute. The type of pension formula (good DB versus NDC) plays no clear role unless it affects workers' perceptions regarding the link between contributions (payroll tax) and the benefits. If the link is strong, then it would be easier for employers to shift the costs of higher taxes to the workers (as part of their compensation package). Gross wages in this case would be reduced and the demand for labor would be less affected.

From the supply side, the benefit formula can influence the probability of evading the public pension system (regardless of the level of the contribution rate),[11] since it affects the expectations about the rate of return that the system delivers. In many current ("flawed") DB schemes there are at least two factors that can contribute to evasion. First, rates of return tend to be considerably higher for individuals who strategically game the system by evading most of their lives and joining close to retirement. Second, in the absence of automatic stabilization mechanisms that adjust the parameters of the formula in response to changes in macroeconomic and demographic conditions, the dynamics of the pension system are vulnerable to political discretion and the vagaries of history. Individuals may thus harbor pessimistic expectations, also fueled by international experiences, about the capacity of the system to deliver on its promises. Hence, despite the fact that statutory rates of return in DB-PAYG schemes are often generous and unsustainable, implicit rates of return may be low and discourage enrollment. For the average employee, the nature of the benefit formula may also complicate the calculation of the rate of return on his/her savings.

Among the two reasons for evasion, the first could be dealt within the context of a DB-PAYG formula by introducing all wages in the calculation of the pension. The second reason has more to do with individuals' perceptions about the performance of the system and therefore it is less clear what the impact of moving to an NDC-type formula would be. There is some weak evidence from Latin America suggesting that, for a given level of the contribution rate, the probability of enrollment in the mandatory pension system is higher if part of the contribution is allocated to a DC scheme than if it is solely allocated to a DB scheme.[12] This could be because of better transparency (a clear link between contributions and benefits), ownership of the assets accumulated, and more trust in the financial sustainability of the system.

It is conceivable that the movement to an NDC system could generate similar signals, although individuals are not likely to feel the same degree of ownership about an "account" on a government register. Still, by better adapting to demographic and economic changes, the NDC scheme reduces the contingent liability of the government. As individuals are periodically informed of the status of their notional accounts and the financial position of the system, members may feel greater certainty that their contributions will produce a benefit.

Saving Decisions

The impact that the movement toward an NDC formula would have on individuals' savings would depend on the size of the mandate, the induced change in the expected rate of return, and the induced change in the retirement age.[13] There is no particular reason to expect individual savings to be higher or lower. Other things being equal, if expected rates of return are lower under the NDC formula, there would be incentives for developing other forms of savings. At the same time, however, if contributory periods are longer, savings rates should be expected to fall.

On balance, in our simulations we find that savings rates under the NDC formula appear to be lower than savings rates with DB-PAYG formulas without actuarial adjustments for delayed retirement. This is basically the result of longer careers. In line with theory, savings rates increase as the preference for leisure relative to consumption increases. Lower savings rates at the individual level, however, do not imply lower savings at the macro level, since higher government savings can compensate.

Financial Sustainability and Benefit Predictability

One of the features that make NDCs highly attractive for less-developed countries is their potential for constraining the growth of pension expenditure in often overly generous DB-PAYG schemes. Although in theory the parameters of these schemes (such as contribution rates, accrual rates, and retirement ages) could be periodically adjusted to adapt to changing macroeconomic and demographic conditions, in practice, usually as a result of social pressure and political discretion, this does not happen. Thus, the majority of DB-PAYG across Africa, the Middle East, and Asia are accumulating large unfunded liabilities. On the other hand, countries that introduced NDC, including Italy, Poland, and Sweden, show that such a reform, even if implemented over the long run, reduces future pension deficits. For instance, long-term projections[14] show that a shift to NDC keeps the pension expenditure level relatively unchanged in the long run (see table 12.1).

Table 12.1. Changes in Spending and Primary Balance in Countries with NDC Systems (percent of GDP)

Country	Total old-age spending 2000	Total old-age spending 2050	Change 2000–2050
Italy	14.2	13.9	–0.3
Poland[a]	10.8	8.3	–2.5
Sweden	9.2	10.8	1.6
OECD average	7.4	10.8	3.4

Source: Chłoń-Domińczak (2003).

a. Includes old-age spending and "early retirement" spending (including disability pensions for persons above 55 and preretirement benefits).

As discussed at the outset, in theory an NDC system can be designed in a way that internalizes not only changes in life expectancy but also expected changes (known demographic waves, structural adjustment) and unexpected changes (fluctuations in wages, unemployment and coverage resulting from economic cycles) in the contributory base. In this sense, the NDC scheme could reduce or even eliminate contingent liabilities, effectively transforming the DB-PAYG into a DC-PAYG.[15] Achieving this design, however, is not without complications and would necessarily imply less predictability in benefits, as these are adjusted to reflect changes in demographic and economic conditions. This may simply not be desirable or politically viable in most developing countries, particularly given less stable macroeconomic environments (for example, high variability in employment, coverage, and real wage growth rates) and usually in the midst of a demographic transition.

To assess the trade-offs between financial sustainability and predictability, we analyzed the impact that alternative NDC-type designs have on the dynamics of a representative middle- or low-income country's PAYG system. We focus on two aspects of the design: (1) the mechanism used to adjust or valorize contributions, and (2) the mechanism used to index pensions.[16] Our main objective was to understand how the various designs affect the dynamics of replacement rates as well as the balance of the system. For transparency, we focused only on a system that is "new" in the sense that there are no contributors prior to the start of the simulation. The implicit assumption is that the reform that introduces an NDC-style system "grandfathers" current plan members.[17] We analyzed two cases: a case with stable conditions regarding the growth rate of the average wage and labor force coverage rates, and a case where these two variables are subject to random shocks.

Under stable conditions, we found that both the NDC scheme with contributions and pensions indexed by the growth rate of the wage bill and the NDC with contributions indexed by the growth rate of the average wage and pensions indexed by prices converged to equilibrium. Long-term replacement rates were similar. Its steady states were mostly independent of the shocks affecting mortality rates, as the system adapted pensions to changes in these rates. Over the medium term, however, the wage-bill indexed NDC generated a larger deficit. This is because the wage-sum NDC had higher replacement rates in the medium term than the average wage NDC, resulting from fast growth in the wage bill during the first years of the scheme.

We also found that in the presence of uncertainty and volatility in the growth rate of wages and the coverage rate of the labor force, the NDC schemes with contributions linked to changes in the total wage sum displayed less stability than the other schemes. Although over the long run the wage-sum NDC converged to equilibrium (if we impose the existence of a steady state), in the medium term this policy variant generated both higher surpluses and higher deficits than the alternatives in our stochastic modeling. Indeed, it is well known that the standard Samuelson-Aaron conditions[18] for the financial sustainability of a PAYG system do not apply outside the steady state (that is, during the transition periods).[19] NDC schemes with contributions valorized by average wage growth displayed the best performance in terms of financial stability (though wage sum during accumulation and price indexing in the payment period was a second-best alternative).

In terms of the predictability of benefits, wage-sum NDCs were the least stable in replacement rates and other criteria. Similarly, indexation of pensions by the wage-sum changes generated fluctuations that are unlikely to be accepted by pensioners. The NDC that used average wage growth generated replacement rates that are as stable as those obtained with a traditional DB scheme—both because replacement rates are immune to the dynamics of the wage bill and because the growth rate of labor productivity was assumed to converge to a stationary process.

An important message from the analysis is that high volatility in wages and labor force coverage rates need not preclude low- and middle-income countries from adopting the NDC construct, provided that these countries carefully choose the indexes to valorize contributions and index benefits in payment. Pure wage sum is not advised. Instead, adjusting contributions by average wage growth rate seems always preferable, at least among the conditions for which we tested. First, the average wage alternative generated more stable replacement rates. Second, the wage-sum alternative did not outperform average wage, even when scenarios with persistent reductions in coverage rates are considered. This is largely because the average wage alternative never commits to high rates of return that lead to high pensions that become unaffordable once the dependency ratios increase.[20] We did not, however, consider wage-sum alternatives for low- and middle-income countries that use a smoothed wage bill index and/or impose a band, similar to exchange rate bands, where the index would be allowed to fluctuate (say between –5 percent and 5 percent). We also did not analyze the performance stabilization mechanisms à la Sweden. In conclusion, revalorization of contributions by the growth rate of the average wage and price indexation for pensions appears as a good compromise.

The results of our analysis also illustrate how NDC-type formulas can contribute to improve financial sustainability relative to the typical DB-PAYG. This said, none of the proposed arrangements is bullet proof. Appropriate reserves or buffer funds are required to handle unexpected demographic and economic shocks. In all cases contingent liabilities will persist.

Buffer Funds

In the case of DB-PAYG systems, a reserve fund of six months' to a year's worth of payments has become accepted practice for managing unexpected fluctuations in the covered wage bill. To the extent that such reserves are kept solely in government bonds, the functional equivalent is authority to borrow from the central budget in an equivalent amount.

Beyond this core agreement, opinions will differ on the size of reserves (*buffer funds*). Larger buffer funds, reaching the level of 20 to 30 percent of GDP, are invoked for several reasons. One reason is to smooth out known variations in demographics—for example, a baby boom, followed by a baby bust, followed by replacement fertility rates. The other reason is to manage unknown long-term demographic trends, such as a move from one birth rate pattern to another (for example, two plus to two minus children per woman). Such long-term trends can be mitigated by buffer funds. In addition, there is often the expectation, at least the hope, that the buffer fund, if well invested, will garner a rate of return that exceeds the PAYG return, thus softening the decline in the PAYG return.

Integrating Heterogeneous Pension Plans

Most developing countries with DB-PAYG have at least three separate regimes: civil servants, military personnel, and private sector workers. Countries such as Egypt and Tunisia have also public regimes for special categories of workers (for example, fisherman and agricultural workers). Occupational funds, usually linked to public companies, are also common (as, for example, in Iran and Morocco), not as complementary schemes to the public system, but as substitutes.

Integrating the various schemes is desirable to achieve economies of scale in management, improve financial sustainability, and facilitate labor mobility. The integration of the various regimes, however, has proven difficult. Beyond political resistance from managers and employees of the funds, the constraint to the merger is often technical, as contributions, benefits, and eligibility conditions vary considerably across funds. New rules can apply to new workers, but the transfer of employees in current schemes requires agreeing on a mechanism to value past contributions.

The shift in paradigm imposed by the NDC concept can facilitate the integration of heterogeneous schemes in low- and middle-income countries. Below we discuss the main lessons from international experiences in terms of the speed of transition, the mechanism used to give credit for past years, and the alternatives in terms of financing.

Speed of Transition

The fastest transition can be observed in Sweden, when relatively old people are covered fully by the new system. Such a solution was possible for several reasons. One of them is related to a good database of individual records dating from 1960 that allows for calculating notional accounts for cohorts born in 1938 and older. Second, as retirement age is not changed with the reform, the only change relates to the benefit formula. In contrast, the longest transition can be observed in Italy, where cohorts born prior to 1960 can stay in the old system. This means that pensions according to old regime in Italy will be paid until around 2030 or even later.

Latvia and Poland have more or less the same regulations, but in Latvia all contributors were covered by notional accounts when reform was introduced; in Poland, those born before 1949 remain in the old system. This can be explained by differences in both countries. One difference is that early retirement that has been deleted from public pension system in Poland but still kept for some occupations and women in Latvia; the other difference is the availability of employment records. In Latvia, those records were nonexistent, as inflation caused serious deterioration of salary levels in late 1980s and early 1990s. As a result, transition arrangements were introduced in Latvia where pension did not depend on salary level but only on the number of years of contributions.

In the case of developing countries with usually more favorable demographics, the transition to a new scheme could take place at a slower pace. Simulations in the case of Jordan and Iran, for instance, show that even if only new cohorts are enrolled in the NDC scheme, the financing gap of the current system could be virtually eliminated.[21] It also seems preferable to consider voluntary switching. Clearly, demographics is not the only factor to consider. Depending on the generosity of the system, the size of the financing gap, and the fiscal position of the government, more aggressive mechanisms could be considered.

Giving Credit for Past Service

In Sweden, because wage records existed and the pension reform did not violate any constitutional norm concerning acquired rights, the NDC could be projected backward, leading to a relatively quick truncation of the prior system. (It should also be noted that the old and new systems in Sweden have many similar design elements.) There are two other ways for transition to occur.

One way to make the transition is simply to keep the old pension regime in place with respect to years before the new scheme's introduction. This truncation strategy may require some "cleaning up" of the old regime, but it has the advantage of being clear and probably administratively the easiest of the different approaches. The other major way to make the transition is to recognize rights under the prior system and to translate those rights into "initial capital" in the NDC scheme.

Initial capital in NDC is similar to, and probably owes its origins to, the concept of recognition bonds used in Chile and other countries in introducing a DC fully funded system to convert acquired rights into a security in a funded individual account scheme. At least two types of initial capital conversions have been developed. Poland is an example of the first: there, acquired rights under the old system were converted to "initial capital" (or de facto recognition bond) based on salaries at the time of conversion. Poland generally uses a 10-best-years base to determine initial capital, but this is capped to minimize disparities and to keep aggregate cost in bounds.

So long as that initial capital is valorized (or indexed) by the growth rate (now the NDC "interest rate") existing under the prior scheme, the expected present values under the prior system are generally maintained. This option, however, is no small administrative matter and communication challenge. One of the key advantages of this approach is that it makes the work/leisure choice after the minimum retirement age apply to a larger amount of retirement wealth much sooner than a truncation strategy.

The second type of initial capital was pioneered in Latvia, where credible individual wage records before 1996 did not exist. In that country, service before 1996 was credited with an NDC rate of 20 percent. The contributions were then valued based on individuals' average wage histories for the four years 1996–9. This created substantial gains for those who had done well in the market economy and may have created a greater than intended legacy cost.

Clearly how initial capital is calculated can affect both rights and costs. In Russia, where individuals' pensions had been compressed, calculating initial capital became very problematic. If acquired rights were calculated without the ad hoc ceiling that compressed the top end of the statutory pension schedule, and then those rights were allowed to grow at the normal valorization factor, aggregate costs would blow up. Even deciding how to project the ceiling became difficult. Estonia, in a technically DB scheme that borders on NDC, avoided these issues by using national average wage for years before 1999. After 1998, individual wage histories are used, but only for new accruals.

Financing the Transition

In theory, the transition from a DB to an NDC system does not require any additional financing. As both of the schemes function on the PAYG basis, current contributions are still used to finance current expenditures. The difference between both systems lays in the way pension rights are accrued.

We have shown earlier that the NDC scheme would usually require a buffer fund as a stabilizing mechanism. In countries where the required level of the buffer fund is below reserves, the difference would need to be built out of contributions in the new NDC scheme. The reduction in the level of expenditures needed to pay for current beneficiaries may require transfers from the central budget. These transfers can be considered payments of part of the implicit debt accumulated by the "old" system.

Even countries such as Jordan, with reserves equivalent to 25 percent of GDP, out of which 60 percent are in liquid assets, the transition to the new scheme usually requires support from the general budget. In the Jordanian case, for instance, the military and civil servant pension funds (which do not have reserves) have been closed to new entrants. All the new employees in the public and private sector are joining the Social Security Corporation (initially designed for private sector workers). The unfunded liability of the closed civil servant and military pension funds, however, is being assumed by the central budget. Over the short run, as the flow of new contributions stops, cash expenditures will increase. Over the long run, however, important savings are being generated by this strategy.

In many, probably most, countries, the governance structure in public pension reserves or buffer funds has not been conducive to prudent investment policies. The shift to an NDC scheme could also be considered an opportunity to transfer the management of new cash surpluses to a different investment unit, which would operate under a different governance structure and adopt best practices in terms of accountability and financial risk management. Again in this case, new contributions would not be used to pay current pensions. These would need to be financed out of existing reserves in the "old" system and/or general revenues.

Poverty Prevention and NDC

As with any earnings-related scheme, it is a challenge to reconcile poverty prevention goals with transparency, uniform rates of return, and incentives to work longer. Many countries have saddled themselves with unrealistic minimum pension guarantees. For example, in Iran, the minimum pension has been set equal to the minimum wage, which in turn is equal to 66 percent of the average wage. This is high relative, for instance, to the case of Chile, where the minimum pension is set at 25 percent of the average wage. In OECD countries, minimum pension typically represents 20–25 percent of the average wage. In addition, eligibility conditions are often lax in the sense that individuals with short careers are eligible for the minimum pension. In many existing pension regimes, middle-income workers with short careers benefit from the pension at the expense of low-income workers with long careers.[22]

Any reform has to address what is a sustainable and affordable mandate for the public pension system and what is a realistic minimum benefit relative to a country's per capita income and absolute poverty measures. Countries where the marginal product of labor is so low as to generate wages that are close to the poverty line or below it, or equal to the minimum pension, in principle, should not be even consider contributory schemes. In fact, however, even countries such as Djibouti (US$800 per capita) or Yemen (US$400 per capita) have contributory schemes with an average covered wage above three times the poverty line. As discussed later, it is likely that when going down the ladder of countries classified by income per capita, the constraints of being able to implement an NDC (or a credible DB alternative) imposed by limited institutional capacities take hold and bind before constraints imposed by the level and distribution of income.

Once the mandate of the pension system has been defined, the objective is to achieve it efficiently and equitably. NDC or similar reforms can often improve current systems by homogenizing rates of return, reducing unfunded liabilities, and improving incentives. Indeed, adverse distributive transfers are pervasive in poorly designed DB schemes, which probably exist in greater number than well-designed DB regimes. First, it is common to observe high levels of heterogeneity in rates of return. Indeed, these rates of return depend on wage histories, life expectancies, and enrollment and retirement strategies. Usually, educated and healthy individuals generally have steeply growing wages and live longer, thus extracting higher rates of return. Other things being equal, individuals who game the system by evading most of their lives and joining close to retirement also obtain higher rates of return. Furthermore, heterogeneity is encouraged by multiple retirement rules and eligibility conditions (for example, lower retirement ages for high-risk professions, and various combinations of vesting periods and retirement ages). More importantly, the large unfunded liabilities that are being accumulated by the majority of funds imply a massive transfer of resources from future generations, including future low-income workers, to the current generations, including current high-income workers.

Critics of the NDC concept argue that improvements in efficiency and financial sustainability come at the expense of equity.[23] The fact is, however, that a good DB system or an NDC can achieve redistribution transparently and without generating negative incentives. Probably the most effective mechanism to do this is a complementary noncontributory pension that is reduced as the contributory pension increases. Elsewhere it is shown that special cases of this formulation are the flat pension (when the reduction factor is set equal to 0) and/or top-up minimum pension (when the reduction factor is set equal to 1).[24] The former, however, can be unnecessarily costly, while the latter introduces incentive problems. Countries try to strike a balance between transfer costs and incentives by having reduction factors apply to top-up minimums that fall between 0 and 1 or to claw back flat benefits among the affluent (termed *affluence testing*). Operational costs also can be reduced by using the tax system to impose any reductions, especially claw-backs among the affluent. An attractive aspect of the flat benefit approach is its simplicity and the fact that parameters such as the minimum vesting period, which can also discourage enrollment and contributions, could become redundant. Moreover, because the complementary pension is financed outside the contributory scheme, it may help reduce labor market distortions. An illustration of the mechanism is presented in figure 12.1.

The NDC concept is useful for developing retirement benefits. As with funded accounts, it is difficult to translate NDC accounts into disability and survivor benefits, both of which are necessary to prevent poverty.[25] Other mechanisms have to be developed for these other risks. In developing these mechanisms, care has to be taken not to make the total package too generous (for example, by allowing survivors to inherit NDC accounts without reference to collateral survivor benefits) or to make disability benefits more attractive than NDC annuities, especially for older workers. Integrating retirement and nonretirement benefits is a complex subject with many good and bad examples from existing practice, but this subject goes beyond the scope of this paper.

Demands in Terms of Institutional Capacity

NDC demands no less and—contrary to what is sometimes thought—no more than any thoroughgoing PAYG reform that depends ultimately on lifetime wage histories. In today's world that attention has to be paid to the following.

First, a set of administrative processes has to be put in place. These are processes that interact with employers, covered workers, and the self-employed as customers or clients, not as agents of the government to do its bidding. Second, thanks to information technology (IT), implementing such processes is less labor and paper intensive than before. IT, however, is a handmaiden, and should not be allowed to become the engine that drives the way processes are designed. In addition, decisions have to be made about (1) a unique identifier associated with each person's wage history and (2) how to interact with and use other government agencies, especially the tax authority, in collecting contributions.[26]

The most central administrative question revolves around the collection of data. The information that drives the regime must be credible. In some countries, monthly reporting is considered optimal if employers do not have payroll systems that can remember transient workers for very long (this is the case in Zambia, for example). In other countries, payroll systems are advanced, and annual reporting on workers, whether or not they are employed in the firm on the reporting date, is viable and probably cost-effective. Yet other countries prefer intrayear period reporting—inevitably quarterly—to help with compliance.

Information must also flow back to the workers if the reformed pension system is to have any solid incentive effect in linking benefits to contributions. NDC accounts, however, have to be translated into examples of probable annuity amounts, which requires heroic assumptions and lots of cautionary comments in the benefit statement (this is equally true in the close DB analogues).

Adequate time must be allowed to create a new system or do any substantial system overhaul. That includes internal processes, business processes with clients, and IT changes. If adequate time is not allowed for a careful understanding of what is now in

Figure 12.1. Implementing a Complementary Noncontributory Pension

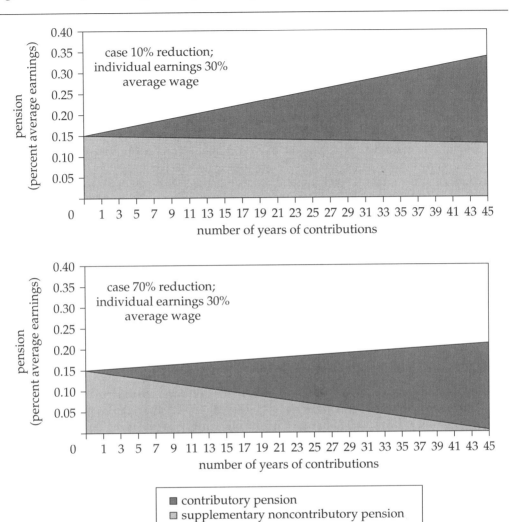

Source: Authors' calculations.

place as well as what is intended and also for careful pretesting, the agency (and the government of the day) may find itself in hole from which it is very hard to emerge. This institutional need is hard to reconcile with political imperatives and perceived moments of reform opportunity, but the pension reform landscape is replete with agencies climbing from such holes.

Systems that have large reserves or buffer funds—especially if they are invested in something other than government paper or very passively invested accordingly to a predetermined index—require another set of governance mechanisms, a topic that goes beyond this chapter. Suffice it to note, however, that nothing can be more destructive to a social insurance agency than to mire its top- and medium-level management in managing a portfolio. Not only can that be, and has been, corrupting in both blatant and subtle ways, it also distracts from the primary business at hand—collecting contributions (maybe via the tax authority); and collecting information, maintaining records, determining benefits, and dealing with customers.

If these relatively minimal conditions cannot be met, then two alternatives present themselves. One is to contract out to one or more private entities. The problem with this scenario is that a country that cannot run a contributory PAYG agency may not be able to credibly supervise nongovernment providers. In addition, this scenario probably makes sense only when there is both a mandatory funded tier as well as the NDC tier. Funded DC tiers in countries with low administrative capacity and/or probity are, if anything, more questionable than contributory PAYG schemes.

The second alternative is to put off having a standard contributory pension regime. After all, many now rich and cutting-edge countries started out with "basic benefits," which were simple citizens' pensions (for example, Sweden) or work-related flat benefits (for example, the United Kingdom). And when they had such minimal systems, they already were richer than today's lower-income countries and may have had more equal incomes than many of today's middle-income countries. In the case of low per capita countries, given the high current consumption needs of the population, the limited power of government to tax without serious compliance consequences probably is best directed to financing a very basic benefit. Limited fiscal capacity is generally correlated with limited administrative capacity.

Why an NDC Scheme Would Be Preferred to a DB Scheme in Middle- and Low-Income Countries

If "good" DB and standard NDC are very close substitutes, then why even bother with NDC? Why not just tinker with DB-PAYG to achieve best practice in terms of equity, incentives, and reasonable burden sharing across generations? A first answer is that if the DB formula is going to be modified to replicate the NDC formula (meaning that properly computed accrual rates are announced at the time of retirement), the DB formula loses its attraction of more predictability in benefits, and at that point the NDC formula is easier to implement and more transparent.

The second answer is found in pragmatic political economy. First, it may be easier to achieve reform objectives in different settings by adopting and using the DC vocabulary from the world of funded schemes than to push conventional DB-PAYG palliatives. This is particularly true in the instance of bounding liabilities to reflect increasing life expectancies in the payment period (internalizing longevity). Because NDC changes the paradigm (à la Kuhn) in which trade-offs are examined, it is extremely useful when it comes to analyzing and changing some of the nonfiscal aspects of many state-managed DB-PAYG regimes.[27]

Finally, an NDC system makes easier the tracking of its implicit liabilities (and the transfer of accrued rights between schemes). At the extreme, those liabilities can be made explicit if the contributions of the NDC system are invested in appropriately indexed government bonds[28] or wage-indexed bonds issued by the pension fund.[29] This improves transparency and provides incentives for a better management of fiscal policy. At the same time, this arrangement can allow, over the medium term, for a smooth transition to a fully funded scheme when those bonds can start to be traded.

As we have seen, most NDC regimes are unlikely to internalize all contingent liabilities. NDC benefits may be enhanced with imputations and minimum benefit top-ups financed from other revenue sources. And special unemployment benefits and age-related disability can become major sources of early retirement. Accordingly, governments cannot rely solely on capping the NDC contribution rate as the sole means of keeping mandatory retirement savings in bounds. But capping the contributions can help and, in so doing, can help develop a consensus and commitment for changes that are fiscally imperative and/or simply desirable for incentive and equity reasons. (Since retirement wealth is not easily translated into income flows, it must be admitted that there are countervailing challenges in communication.)

Having praised the potential virtues of NDC as a paradigm shift, we would be less than candid if we did not admit that both theory and experience teaches that the NDC concept can be misapplied just as much as the traditional DB concept has been. As discussed above and below, with the exception of Sweden, there are unresolved contingent liabilities in the NDC schemes of most countries, making them less than "DC" as that term is used in the world of privately funded pensions. But, if the DC model is further relaxed by not being rigorous about the "G factor"—the factor used for annuity conversion—it is not obvious that the outcome is superior to a cognate DB reform. (We mean rigorous in both reflecting the age at which someone retires and increases in cohort longevity.)[30] We say this because use of the term *NDC* may convince policy makers and the public into thinking more has been done than not. Indeed, some have argued that, without this G factor sine qua non, the NDC vocabulary has served only to harden benefit expectations that are not sustainable.

Annex 12A. Technical Notes

Characterizing Choices about Optimal Retirement Ages

We are interested in understanding how retirement decisions are affected by DB-PAYG formulas and NDC type formulas. The main difference between the two is that, while in the DB-PAYG case the accrual rate is constant when deciding to retire, it is effectively endogenous (depending on the retirement decision itself) in the case of the NDC formula.

We start by defining the expected utility derived from an individual retiring at time R, who will live at most until time L, and that it is assumed to depend *on* consumption and leisure:

$$E[U_R] = \sum_{t=R}^{L} \theta^t U\big(c_t(p_R), l_t\big) m_t, \tag{12A.1}$$

where U is the utility function (assumed to respect standard properties), c and l are respectively consumption and leisure, m_t is the probability of survival to time t, and p_R is the pension at retirement. An individual would be willing to delay retirement if the expected gains in utility from waiting, due to a higher pension and higher consumption, are higher than the expected losses in utility, due to lower leisure.

The present value of the marginal gain in expected utility at each future time t resulting from a change in the pension is given by:

$$\frac{dE[U_t]}{dp_R} = \theta^t m_t U_c\big(p_R, l_R\big) \frac{\partial c}{\partial p} \Delta p_R . \tag{12A.2}$$

The loss in utility for lower leisure today is given by:

$$\frac{dE[U_t]}{dl_R} = U_l\big(p_R, l_R\big) \Delta l_R . \tag{12A.3}$$

The question is under which benefit formula is the sum of future gains in utility (equation 12A.2) more likely to be higher than the loss in utility from waiting (equation 12A.3).

Let's first look at how the pension varies under each benefit formula. In the case of the NDC formula, the pension is given by:

$$p_R = \left(\sum_t \beta w_t I_t \lambda \right) G_R^{-1} , \tag{12A.4}$$

where β is the contribution rate, w_t is the wage at time t, and $I_t\lambda$ is the index that applies to contributions at time t. For generality and simplicity we assume that contributions are indexed by the growth rate of the average wage and that the growth rate of different individuals is always proportional to this growth rate. Hence, if λ is equal to 1, the individual has its wage growing exactly as the average wage. If λ is below (above) 1, the individual has its wages growing above (below) the average wage. Under these assumptions, the NDC formula can rewritten as:

$$p_R = w_R . S . \lambda . \beta . G_R^{-1}, \tag{12A.5}$$

where w_R is the wage at time R and S is the length of service at retirement. Then the change in pension resulting from contributing to the system an additional unit of time is simply given by:

$$\Delta p_R = \lambda \beta G_R^{-1} S \Delta w_R + \lambda \beta G_R^{-1} w_R - \lambda \beta w_R G_R^{-2} S \Delta G_R^{-1} = \alpha'(\lambda S \Delta w_r + w_R) - \alpha' w_r G_R^{-1} S \Delta G_R^{-1}, \tag{12A.6}$$

where $\alpha' = \beta G_R^{-1}$.

Assuming that wages in the DB-PAYG formula are indexed in the same way as contributions in the NDC formula, the pension can be written as:

$$p_R = w_R.S.\lambda.\alpha, \tag{12A.7}$$

where α is the accrual rate. Then the change in the pension resulting from an additional unit of time of contribution is simply given by:

$$\Delta p_R = \alpha(\lambda S \Delta w_r + w_R), \tag{12A.8}$$

The first observation is that if α and α' are equal—that is, if the accrual rate in the DB-PAYG is age-dependent, then the increase in pension resulting from an additional period of contributions will be higher under the NDC type formula. This is because in the second term of equation 12.6 ΔG_R^{-1} is negative (that is, the G factor decreases as the contribution period of the individual expands). Intuitively, the increase in the pension in the NDC scheme will be higher because the effective accrual rate will increase (as the G factor decreases). In fact, if α and α' are equal, it will be easier to meet the conditions for delaying retirement under the NDC formula than it would under the DC formula, because all the other terms in equations 12A.2 and 12A.3 would the same, except for Δp_R.

What happens if α and α' are different? It turns out that as α increases relative to α', the incentives to delay retirement diminish under the DB-PAYG formula. This is because the marginal utility of higher consumption resulting from a higher pension at time R (equation 12A.2) diminishes as the accrual rate increases. Certainly, Δp_R will increase, but it will increase less rapidly. To see this, we differentiate equation 12A.2 with respect to α (we assume that each extra unit of pension is translated into an extra unit of consumption).

$$\frac{dE[U_t]}{dp_R d\alpha} = \theta^t m_t U_{cc}(p_R, l_R) \frac{\partial p_R}{\delta \alpha} \Delta p_R + \theta^t m_t U_c(p_R, l_R) \frac{\partial \Delta p_R}{\partial \alpha}$$
$$= \theta^t m_t U_{cc}(p_R, l_R) w_R S \lambda.\alpha(\lambda S \Delta w_r + w_r) + \theta^t m_t U_c(p_R, l_R)(\lambda S \Delta w_r + w_r). \tag{12A.9}$$

For this expression to be positive—that is, for the marginal utility of a higher pension to increase as α increases—the following condition would need to hold:

$$w_R S \lambda.\alpha < -\frac{U_c(p_R, l_R)}{U_{cc}(p_R, l_R)}, \tag{12A.10}$$

which implies that the pension at time R is lower than the inverse of the growth rate of the marginal utility of consumption. This is unlikely.

The corollary is that if α is set low enough relative to α', incentives for delaying retirement under the DB-PAYG formula can be stronger than under the NDC formula.

Table 12A.1. Optimal Retirement, Savings, and Labor Supply Decisions under Alternative Benefit Formulas

Parameters

Contribution rate (percent)	14.5	14.5	14.5	14.5	14.5	14.5	20.0	20.0	20.0	20.0	20.0	20.0
Loss in informal sector (percent)	15	15	15	0	0	0	15	15	15	0	0	0
Preference for leisure	0.1	0.2	0.3	0.1	0.2	0.3	0.1	0.2	0.3	0.1	0.2	0.3

Optimal retirement ages

DB-PAYG last-salary (1%)	75	74	59	75	75	75	75	75	75	75	75	75
DB-PAYG last-salary (1.5%)	74	66	55	75	75	75	75	75	55	75	75	75
DB-PAYG full-career (1.5%)	75	74	56	75	75	75	75	75	59	75	75	75
NDC	75	75	69	75	75	75	75	75	69	75	75	75
DB-PAYG full-career ADA55 (0.94%)	75	75	63	75	75	75	75	75	75	75	75	75
DB-PAYG full-career ADA60 (1.04%)	75	75	61	75	75	75	75	75	59	75	75	75
DB-PAYG full-career ADA75 (2.38%)	73	62	55	75	75	75	72	55	55	75	75	57

Present value private savings (relative to initial wage)

DB-PAYG last salary (1%)	7.1	7.1	56.0	37.3	37.3	37.3	35.3	31.8	31.8	37.2	37.2	37.2
DB-PAYG last salary (1.5%)	0	13.0	43.9	37.3	37.3	37.3	35.3	31.8	38.5	37.2	37.2	37.2
DB-PAYG full-career (1.5%)	10.7	10.6	61.5	37.3	37.3	37.3	31.8	31.8	59.3	37.2	37.2	37.2
NDC	0	0	23.5	37.3	37.3	37.3	0	0	22.9	37.2	37.2	37.2
DB-PAYG full-career ADA55 (0.94%)	17.8	17.8	59.4	37.3	37.3	37.3	35.3	31.8	31.8	37.2	37.2	37.2
DB-PAYG full-career ADA60 (1.04%)	17.8	14.2	60.8	37.3	37.3	37.3	31.8	31.8	59.3	37.2	37.2	37.2
DB-PAYG full-career ADA75 (2.38%)	0	18.5	32.9	37.3	37.3	37.3	0	2.6	0	37.2	37.2	62.6

Average savings rate (percent noninvestment income)

DB-PAYG last salary (1%)	2.0	2.0	19.0	9.0	9.0	9.0	10.0	9.0	9.0	9.0	9.0	9.0
DB-PAYG last salary (1.5%)	0.0	4.0	16.0	9.0	9.0	9.0	10.0	9.0	15.0	9.0	9.0	9.0
DB-PAYG full-career (1.5%)	3.0	3.0	22.0	9.0	9.0	9.0	9.0	9.0	21.0	9.0	9.0	9.0
NDC	0.0	0.0	7.0	9.0	9.0	9.0	0.0	0.0	7.0	9.0	9.0	9.0
DB-PAYG full-career ADA55 (0.94%)	5.0	5.0	19.0	9.0	9.0	9.0	10.0	9.0	9.0	9.0	9.0	9.0
DB-PAYG full-career ADA60 (1.04%)	5.0	4.0	20.0	9.0	9.0	9.0	9.0	9.0	21.0	9.0	9.0	9.0
DB-PAYG full-career ADA75 (2.38%)	0.0	6.0	12.0	9.0	9.0	9.0	0.0	1.0	0.0	9.0	9.0	20.0

Share of time enrolled in public system (percent)

DB-PAYG last salary (1%)	100	100	100	0	0	0	0	0	0	0	0	0
DB-PAYG last salary (1.5%)	100	100	100	0	0	0	0	0	100	0	0	0
DB-PAYG full-career (1.5%)	100	100	100	0	0	0	0	0	67	0	0	0
NDC	100	100	100	0	0	0	33	33	33	0	0	0
DB-PAYG full-career ADA55 (0.94%)	100	100	100	0	0	0	0	0	0	0	0	0
DB-PAYG full-career ADA60 (1.04%)	100	100	100	0	0	0	0	0	67	0	0	0
DB-PAYG full-career ADA75 (2.38%)	100	100	100	0	0	0	33	100	100	0	0	33

Source: Authors' calculations.

Note: ADA55, ADA60, and ADA75 mean that the accrual rate is calculated on the basis of a retirement age of 55, 60, and 75 respectively. Accrual rates are in parenthesis. For the NDC system, and the DB system with all salaries included in the calculation of the pension, wages are revalorized by the growth rate of the average covered wage.

Dynamic Optimization Problem for Savings, Retirement, and Labor Supply Decisions

We assume that individuals solve the following optimization problem:

$$Max_{s_t, f_t, R_t} : E\left[U(c,l)\right] = \sum_{t=a}^{L} \rho \frac{\left(c_t^\beta l_t^{1-\beta}\right)^\tau}{1-\tau} m_t$$

s.t.:

$$c_t = \left(w_0(1+g)^t (1-f_t o_t)(1-T_j f_t) + k_{t-1} r_t\right) - s_t; \quad if \quad t \le R_t$$

$$c_t = p_t + k_{t-1} r_t - s_t; \quad if \quad t > R_t$$

$$p_t = \sum_{t=b_j}^{R_t} w_0 (1+g)^t (1+i_j)^{R_t - t} \alpha_j$$

$$k_t = k_{t-1} + s_t$$

$$k_L = 0, \tag{12A.11}$$

where the functions, variables, and parameters are as follows: E is the expectations operator, $U(.)$ is a constant absolute risk aversion utility function that depends on consumption (c) and leisure (l). We assume that individuals, when working, work full time either in the formal sector $(f = 1)$ or in the informal sector $(f = 0)$. Hence, extra leisure can be achieved only while retired. In the value function ρ is a discount factor, and m is the conditional probability of surviving to time $t + 1$ given that that the individual is alive at time t, R is the retirement age (endogenous), and a is the time when the individual starts working. In the consumption function, w_0 is the initial wage, g is the growth rate of this wage (assumed to be constant over time), o captures the costs of operating in the informal sector, T is the tax to the mandatory pension system, k is capital, r is the market interest rate, and s are savings. When the individual retires $(t > R)$, he or she receives a pension that depends on the type of pension scheme, j. This pension scheme is characterized by the parameters: b_j (the number of years included in the calculation of the pension), i_j (the factor used to index wages), and α_j (the accrual rate). Clearly, there is no close form solution to this optimization problem. Hence, we use numerical methods to approximate optimal choices regarding savings, retirement age, and labor supply.

The results are presented in table 12A.1. The name and value of the parameters that are kept fixed between simulations are summarized in table 12A.2.

Table 12A.2. Model Parameters

Parameter	Value
w_0	1
g	0.02
r	0.04
ρ	0.02
τ	1.3
a	20
L	120

Source: Authors.

Simulating the Dynamics of Alternative Pay-As-You-Go Systems

In our model, we fix the future dynamics of the labor force by age a and sex s $\{L_{a,s}\}_{t=1}^{200}$, the distribution of wages $\{w_{a,s}\}_{t=1}^{200}$, and retirement patterns $\{R_{a,s}\}_{t=1}^{200}$.

Nominal wages for each age are expressed as a fraction of a wage index I (our proxy for labor productivity), which responds to the following stochastic process:

$$\log I_t = \log I_{t-1} + \alpha_0 - \alpha_1 \exp(-\delta_1 t) + \mu_t; \quad u_t \sim N(0, \alpha_2 \exp(-\delta_u t)), \qquad (12A.12)$$

where α_0 is the steady state growth rate of the index; $\alpha_1 > 0$ is a short-term random distortion that holds the growth rate of labor productivity down, but that gradually fades away as development takes place; and μ is white noise with initial variance α_2 also assumed to fade away.

Similarly, coverage rates by age $\{c_{a,s}\}_{t=1}^{200}$ are assumed to evolve in proportion to the following index:

$$\log C_t = \log C_{t-1} + \beta_0 + v_t; \quad v_t \sim N(0, \beta_1 \exp(-\delta_v t)), \qquad (12A.13)$$

Finally, mortality rates are given by:

$$m_{a,s,t} = m_{a,s,t}^* \eta \quad \text{if} \quad t > t^*; \quad \eta \sim U[\eta_1, \eta_2], \qquad (12A.14)$$

where m^* are baseline mortality rate by age and sex and η is a random shock uniformly distributed between v_1 and v_2. These mortality rates affect steady state dependency ratios as well as the life expectancies used to compute G factors in the case of the NDC scheme.

Equations 12A.12 to 12A.14 and the fix distributions determine the dynamics of the average wage, the wage bill, total contributors, total pensioners, and ultimately the financial balance of the system.

The distribution of wages, coverage rates, retirement patterns, and baseline mortality rates come from real data for Jordan. The parameters used in the simulations for equations 12A.12 to 12A.14 have been chosen to generate a large set of paths for the exogenous variables of the system. Our main interest has been to explore the dynamic properties of the various schemes in cases where these paths are subject to high levels of uncertainty. The values for the various parameters are summarized in table 12A.3. The types of PAYG schemes considered are described in table 12A.4. Figures 12A.1 to 12A.4 summarize the results.

Table 12A.3. Parameters Used in the Dynamics Simulations

Parameter	Value
α_0	0.02
α_1	0.02
δ_1	0.025
α_2	0.03
δ_μ	0.025
β_0	0.0025
β_1	0.04
δ_v	0.02
t^*	50
η_1	0.50
η_2	1

Source: Authors.

Table 12A.4. Pension Schemes under Consideration

System	Indexation contributions	Indexation pensions
DB-PAYG with 1.5% accrual rate Pension computed on the basis of last two years of salary.	n.a.	Inflation
NDC 1	Wage bill	Wage bill
NDC 2	Wage bill	Inflation
NDC 3	Wage bill	Inflation (if real wage growth is positive); real wage (if real wage negative)
NDC 4	Average wage	Average wage
NDC 5	Average wage	Inflation
NDC 6	Average wage	Inflation (if real wage growth is positive); real wage (if real wage negative)

Source: Authors.

Note: n.a. = not applicable. In the Swedish system, pensions are indexed with the growth rate of the average wage. Generally speaking we have: $\dot{p} = \lambda \dot{w}$ where p is the pension, w is the average wage, and a dot over the variable denotes its growth rate. The factor λ is equal to one unless assets fall below liabilities and the stabilization mechanism is activated. In this case, $0 < \lambda < 1$. We observe that a system where pensions are indexed by prices when the average real wage grows and pensions are indexed with the average real wage when it falls, should in all cases generate lower pensions and therefore a more sustainable system without recurring to the complex calculation of λ.

Figure 12A.1. Illustration of the Dynamics of the Average Wage, the Wage Bill, and Coverage Rates

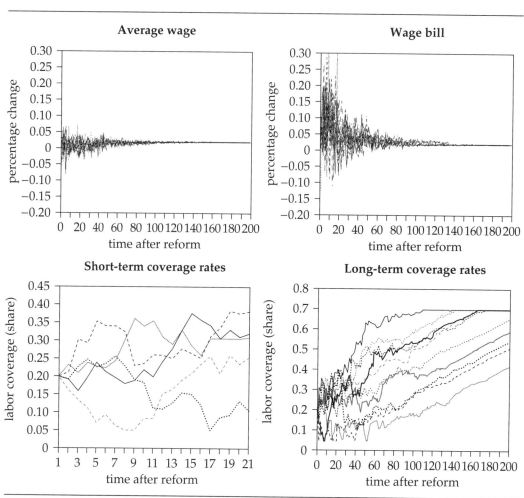

Source: Authors'calculations.

Figure 12A.2. Primary Balance and Last-Year Replacement Rates (Stable Environment)

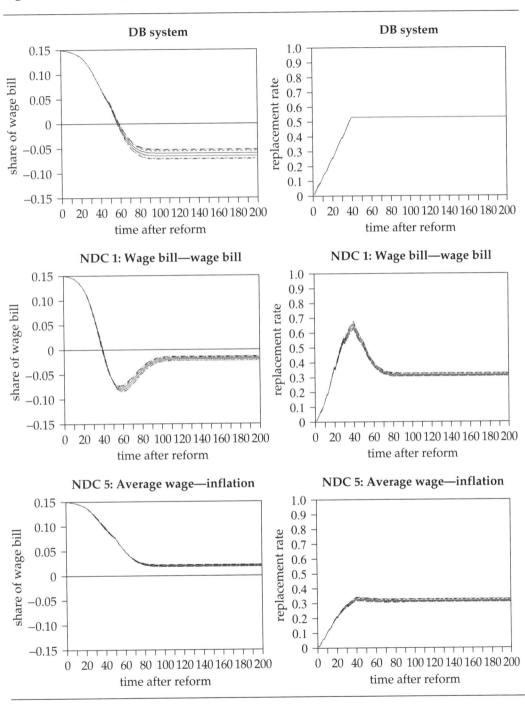

Source: Authors' calculations.

Figure 12A.3. Contributions Minus Expenditures (Volatility Environment)

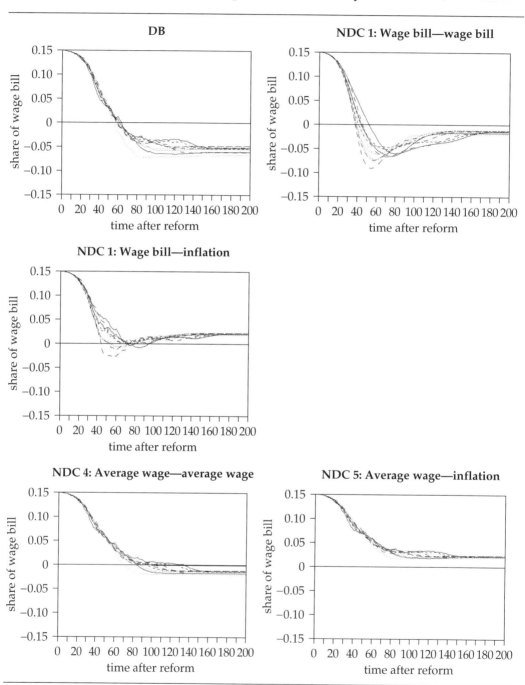

Source: Authors' calculations.

Figure 12A.4. Income Replacement at Age 60 (Volatile Environment)

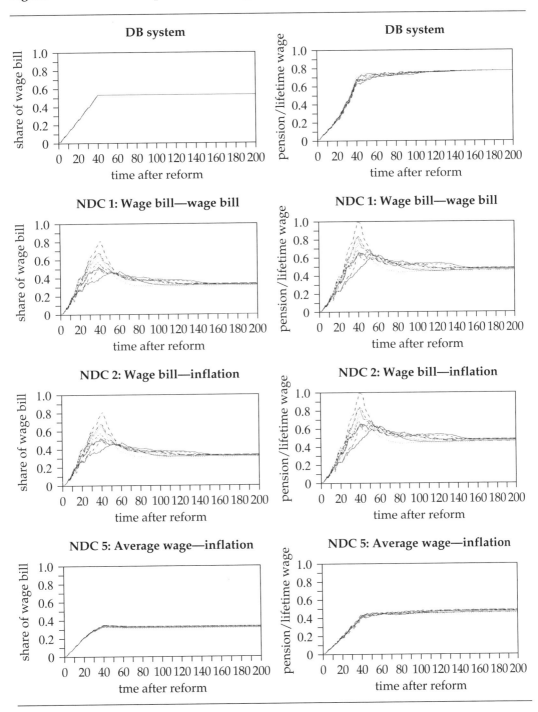

Notes

1. "Notional defined contribution" and "non-financial defined contribution" should be understood to have the same definition.

2. For some reviews, see Lindeman, Rutkowski, and Sluchynskyy (2001) and Chlon, Góra, and Rutkowski (1999).

3. In addition, most defined contribution (DC) arrangements do not redistribute across income classes. This, however, is not axiomatic. For example, Denmark has a small state-mandated funded DC tier that pays flat benefits financed by contributions proportional to earnings.

4. In funded pension schemes, similar hybrids exist. Cash-balance plans in the United States have the appearance of accumulation accounts, but investment returns are guaranteed, giving rise to a defined benefit promise. Australia has a similar scheme for national civil servants. In both instances, however, members bear "longevity risk" if and when converting the lump sum to an annuity or drawing it down overtime.

5. See Góra and Palmer (2001).

6. See Cowell (1985), Edwards and Cox-Edwards (2000), and Fiorito and Padrini (2001).

7. See Imrohoroglu, Imrohoroglu, and Joines (2000) for a review.

8. Under the DB-2 and DB-3 formulae, it is possible to conceive cases where the accrual rate is low enough relative to the contribution rate to provide more incentives to delay retirement than are provided by the NDC formula. Intuitively, this is because individuals in the small DB accrual world are less likely to have met their consumption target for retirement by the time they have reached the minimum retirement age. More technically, if the accrual rate is low enough, and therefore the marginal utility of additional consumption high enough, a DB formula with linear adjustments for delayed retirement to the replacement rate can generate more incentives to delay retirement than the NDC formula can generate. To put it differently, income effect may dominate the substitution effect if the overall wealth is low. Moreover, today there are DB schemes such as Morocco RCAR (Régime Collectif d'Assurance et de Retraite), where the accrual rate for individuals retiring after the minimum retirement age is adjusted by a factor that is above actuarially fair levels. Hence, the implicit rate of return paid by the system increases monotonically with the age of retirement.

9. The model used refers to rational agents with perfect information who make savings, labor supply, and retirement decisions in order to maximize intertemporal utility, which is assumed to depend on leisure and consumption.

10. See Edwards and Cox-Edwards (2000).

11. Evasion can be induced when contribution rates are "high." This is first because some individuals simply cannot afford the tax (for example, the long-term poor for whom joining the contributory system would be welfare decreasing). Second, this is because a mandate to save that is too large can also be welfare decreasing and encourage individuals to find alternative saving mechanisms. These problems, however, are not related to the type of benefit formula.

12. See Packard (2001).

13. See the technical annex at the end of this chapter.

14. See Chłoń-Domińczak (2003).

15. See Gora (2003).

16. For reference, we also look at the dynamics of a traditional DB-PAYG.

17. See the technical annex at the end of this chapter for a formal description of the model.

18. See Samuelson (1958).

19. See Robalino (forthcoming).

20. Clearly, fiscal completeness in this case would require recurrence to a buffer fund, probably coupled with some type of stabilization mechanism.

21. See World Bank (2003a; 2003b).

22. There are also cases when the contributory system plays simultaneously a social assistance function (for example, Algeria), thus reducing the value of the average pension.

23. See Williamson and Williams (2003).

24. See Robalino et al. (2005).

25. This difficulty applies not only to NDC but also to DB-PAYG schemes. One of the main criticisms of disability and survivorship pensions is that such benefits are not designed within an insurance framework. The systems are usually prone to abuse because of absent or lax certification criteria. Thus, disability benefits often substitute for unemployment insurance or more generous early retirement. Moreover, the way survivorship benefits are implemented tends to provide little incentive for survivor spouses to enter the labor market; in the case of death of the surviving spouse, surviving children can be left unprotected. Propositions that have been considered include outsourcing the provision of these benefits and having independent pension rights for both spouses with accumulated pension rights split after divorce or death. The move to an NDC scheme could allow for a more systemic reform of disability and survivorship pensions, whereby total costs for the "social insurance" package are not necessarily affected if leakages to people outside the normal ambit of social insurance protection are prevented. If the primary goal of NDC is forced savings solely for old age, then it is achieved by holding NDC accounts truncated by death or disability in abeyance until retirement and by imposing forfeiture on all accounts where the individual does not reach retirement.

26. This part of the chapter draws in part on Chłoń-Domińczak (2003).

27. See Rutkowski (2002).

28. See Robalino (forthcoming).

29. See Valdés-Prieto (forthcoming).

30. Cases in point are NDC reforms in the Kyrgyz Republic and Russia that explicitly manipulate the G coefficient to reflect current fiscal realities.

References

Bodie, Z., M. J. Clowes, and M. Clowes. 2003. *Worry-Free Investing*. Financial Times/Prentice Hall Books.

Buchanan, J. 1960. *Fiscal Theory and Political Economy*. Chapel Hill: University of North Carolina Press.

Chłoń-Domińczak, A. 2003. "Evaluation of the Notional Defined Contribution Option for the Reform of the Pension System in the Czech Republic." Washington, DC: World Bank Mimeo.

Chłoń, A., M. Góra, and M. Rutkowski. 1999. "Shaping Pension Reform in Poland: Security through Diversity." Social Protection Discussion Paper 9923, World Bank, Washington, DC.

Cowell, F. D. 1985. "Tax Evasion with Labor Income." *Journal of Public Economics*. 26 (1): 19–34.

Edwards S., and A. Cox-Edwards. 2000. "Economics Reforms and Labor Markets: Policy Issues and Lessons from Chile." NBER Working Paper 7646, National Bureau of Economic Research, Cambridge, Massachusetts.

Fiorito R., and F. Padrini. 2001. "Distortionary Taxation and Labor Market Performance." *Oxford Bulletin of Economics and Statistics* 63 (2): 126–42.

Gora, M. 2003. "Reintroducing Intergenerational Equilibrium: Key Concepts behind the New Polish Pension System," Warsaw School of Economics. Mimeo.

Góra, M., and E. Palmer. 2001. "Shifting Perspectives in Pension Reform." Warsaw-Stock-holm, Warsaw School of Economics. Mimeo.

Holzmann, R. 1997. "Pension Reform, Financial Market Development, and Economic Growth: Preliminary Evidence from Chile." *IMF Staff Papers* 44 (2): 149–78.

Imrohoroglu A., S. Imrohoroglu, and D. Joines. 2000. "Time Inconsistent Preferences and Social Security." Discussion Paper 136, Institute for Empirical Macroeconomics, Federal Reserve Bank of Minneapolis.

Lindeman, D., M. Rutkowski, and O. Sluchynskyy. 2001. "The Evolution of Pension Systems in Eastern Europe and Central Asia: Opportunities, Constraints, Dilemmas and Emerging Practices." *OECD Financial Market Trends* 80 (October): 79–130.

Merton, R. 1983. "On the Role of Social Security as a Means for Efficient Risk Sharing in an Economy Where Human Capital is Not Tradeable." In *Issues in Pension Economics*. ed. Z. Bodie and J. Shoven. Chicago: University of Chicago Press.

Robalino, D. Forthcoming. "Financial Stability in Earnings Related Pension Systems and the Role for Government Indexed Bonds." Policy Research Working Paper Series, World Bank, Washington, DC.

Robalino D., E. Whitehouse, A. Mataoanu, E. Sherwood, and O. Sluchinskyy. 2005. "Pensions in the Middle East and North Africa Region." Orientations in Development Series, World Bank, Washington, DC.

Packard, T. 2001. "Is there a Positive Effect from Privatizing Social Security? A Panel Analysis of Pension Reforms in Latin America." Unpublished Manuscript. Department of Economics, University of Oxford.

Rutkowski, M. 2002. "Pensions in Europe: Paradigmatic and Parametric Reforms in EU Accession Countries in the Context of EU Pension System Changes." *Journal of Transforming Economies and Societies (EMERGO)* 9 (1): 2–26.

Samuelson, P. 1958. "An Exact Consumption-Loan Model of Interest with or without the Social Contrivance of Money." *Journal of Political Economy* December: 219–34.

Smetters, K. 2002. "Controlling the Cost Minimum Benefit Guarantees in Public Pension Conversions." *Journal of Pension Economics and Finance* 1 (1).

Valdés-Prieto, S. "Pay-As-You-Go Securities." Forthcoming on Economic Policy (2005).

Williamson, J. B., and M. Williams. 2003. "The Notional Defined Contribution Model: an Assessment of the Strengths and Limitations of a New Approach to the Provision of Old Age Security." CRR WP 2003-18.

World Bank. 2003a. "Hashemite Kingdom of Jordan: Consolidating the Social Security Corporation as the National Pension System." April 2003. Report No. 25948, World Bank, Washington, DC.

———. 2003b. "Islamic Republic of Iran: The Pension System in Iran: Challenges and Opportunities." Report No. 25174.IR, World Bank, Washington, DC.

Discussion of "NDC Pension Schemes in Middle- and Low-Income Countries"

Monika Queisser*

In commenting on this very interesting and comprehensive paper, I would like to make three points about the applicability of notional defined contribution (NDC) schemes[1] in low- and very-low-income countries.

First, the relevance and usefulness of comparing existing—as the authors point out, "bad"—defined benefit schemes and NDC schemes in the context of low- and very-low-income countries is questionable. The more relevant alternative to a defined benefit scheme seems to be a noncontributory scheme rather than a defined benefit scheme, given that many of these countries' old people have spent most of their lives outside of the formal sector and often have to rely exclusively on family ties and informal support in old age. The chapter does mention the possibility of introducing basic pension or demogrant schemes, but it does so in passing. A more thorough discussion of the three options for this group of countries would have been beneficial and more relevant for practical policy purposes.

Second, if a decision has been made to have or maintain an earnings-related pension scheme in a low-income country, defined contribution schemes could indeed be a better solution than defined benefit schemes. Transferring more risk to the individual is preferable in a context where formal sectors are small and generous defined benefit systems are often subsidized by public transfers. Such transfers are financed predominantly out of indirect taxes. This means that many persons who do not benefit from the system in fact pay for coverage of a minority of formal sector workers. In this respect, a defined contribution system could reduce inequities and free government resources that could be used to finance social and health services for the excluded population.

The authors discuss the experience of provident funds, which exist in a number of low- and very-low-income countries in Africa and Asia. With the exception of some countries, such as Singapore and Malaysia, provident funds have been unable to provide retirement income security in most countries. Retirement savings have often been improperly invested and eroded by inflation. Administrative procedures, which are much easier in a provident fund than in a Swedish-style notional defined contribution scheme, were often inefficient and costly. Most observers would agree that the majority of pure funded defined contribution schemes in poor countries have failed. Now, are there good reasons to believe that defined contribution schemes would work better if there were no actual money to invest? I do not think so.

The experience with benefit management in these countries has not been encouraging. Annuitizing account balances and converting future pension payments into lump sums has caused enormous administrative and political problems. Many poor countries do not have reliable life tables and finding an appropriate discount rate valid in the long term is even more challenging than this already daunting task in the OECD context. Even if such a rate were found, it is very difficult to adjust pension or lump-sum benefits. Again, it is not obvious why these problems would not occur in a notional defined contribution scheme.

---

* Monika Queisser works on retirement systems and policies, disability, and other social protection issues in the Social Policy Division of the OECD.

My third comment is about rules. Successfully running NDC systems requires a fairly sophisticated set of rules. Even if one disregards administrative difficulties and data deficiencies that may prove obstacles to implementation, the question remains: How likely is it that rules would be kept and followed?

This problem is not restricted to middle- and lower-income countries. Changes of rules and regulations in pension systems are very frequent in OECD member countries. Even simple, well-defined rules are broken all the time for economic, financial, social, or political reasons.

Take the United Kingdom as an example. The basic state pension scheme provides a benefit that is indexed to prices. This is a comparatively simple rule on which the projections of the future burden of aging are based. In reality, however, the evolution of benefits has been different. Between April 1997 and April 2003, pensions increased by 24 percent while retail prices increased by 16 percent and average earnings by 29 percent. This is not meant to be a criticism of the United Kingdom for breaking the rules—these increases were necessary to prevent more pensioners from falling into old-age poverty. But it shows that it is very difficult to design and auto-pilot a pension system that is "sustainable" in the long term in all of its dimensions.

The U.K. pension system also shows that pension problems cannot be contained within a pension system and isolated from the overall social policy environment. The United Kingdom has had to introduce a whole range of additional, mostly means-tested, social policy measures in order to pick up the social problems of a financially sustainable system. The result is an extraordinarily complex structure of supplementary benefits and different credits that functions with a high degree of discretion of gatekeepers.

There are many more examples of pension rules made and subsequently broken to be found across OECD countries. Just recently Spain announced that the decision taken by the Toledo pact to move to lifetime averaging of earnings in the pension benefit formula was being postponed due to upcoming elections. In Germany, the social democratic government annulled the previous government's introduction of a demographic pension factor—only to realize that pension reforms toward a more sustainable system would not be possible without demographic adjustments. A modified factor will be reintroduced shortly.

The evidence seems to suggest that rules are there to be broken. Perhaps the Swiss approach is a more realistic one. Switzerland never believed in auto-piloting or even in the permanence of any pension arrangements. As a consequence, the system is being modified in a continuous series of revisions of the existing framework. The 11th revision of the social insurance scheme has just been completed, which means that the 12th revision is now being prepared—in a system that was started only in 1948. The population has gotten used to continuous reform and has come to accept that change is necessary, even if individual measures are hotly debated each time.

The introduction of notional defined contribution systems may or may not contradict the conviction that permanent change is necessary. Perhaps Sweden will show the rest of the world that auto-piloting is indeed possible. If it is not, or if it functions only in very specific country circumstances, the introduction of notional defined contribution schemes could actually be dangerous as it may convey a false sense of security and lead countries to sit back and rely on the auto-pilot without realizing that the system is about to crash.

Note

1. "Notional defined contribution" and "non-financial defined contribution" should be understood to have the same definition.

Discussion of "NDC Pension Schemes in Middle- and Low-Income Countries"

Elaine Fultz*

THE CHAPTER BY LINDEMAN, ROBALINO, AND RUTKOWSKI examines the potential for notional defined contribution (NDC) pension reform[1] to improve benefits and financing in low-income countries, but it contains limited analysis of the characteristics of these countries that might impinge on the success of such a reform. In particular, more needs to be said about issues of governance in low-income countries. In the transitional economies of Central and Eastern Europe, three typical features of governance not explored in the study might limit the success of this approach.

First, governments in transition may have less capacity to reach the kind of enduring consensus required to put an NDC system in place. Because defined contribution schemes operate on different principles than defined benefit schemes, the transition from one to the other will be a complex and time-consuming process. Governments in the transition countries of Central Europe tend to change rapidly, however, causing shifts in national policy. Between 1989 and 2000, for example, Latvia had five governments; Lithuania, Slovakia, and Slovenia had four; and the Czech Republic, Estonia, Hungary, and Poland had three. When the government changes, the new ruling coalition often tries to put its own distinctive mark on the pension system. If a major reform is not possible, the government may "tinker" with a newly passed reform, making mid-course adjustments. As has been explained in chapter 15 of this book (Palmer et al. 2006), Latvia has amended its NDC law nine times since its inception in the mid 1990s, introducing elements that change its form from pure NDC—for example, a mimimum benefit that varies according to years of work and a system for converting pension rights under the previous social insurance system to NDC capital that gave disproportionate weight to a few years of work, thus creating major winners and losers.

Second, transitional governments may be less able to set and maintain the needed contribution rate for an NDC scheme than more stable governments. Since NDC benefits are based on each individual's own pension contributions, the contribution rate must be set properly and maintained in order to ensure pension adequacy. However, many Central and Eastern European countries alter their contribution rates frequently, responding to forces that do not relate directly to pension adequacy—for example, public perceptions that the current rates are too high and impede international competitiveness. Two risks arise here: first, the risk that a government would adopt an NDC reform and then violate its key principle of a stable contribution rate, and second, the risk that the government would adhere to this principle but select a less than optimal rate initially and then be constrained from changing it.

A third possible mismatch relates to the heavy administrative and planning requirements of NDC versus the capacities of governments in transition. NDC poses extensive

---

* Elaine Fultz is the senior specialist in social security at the International Labor Organization, Subregional Office for Central and Eastern Europe, Budapest.

record-keeping requirements: each contribution made on behalf of each worker must be reported to, and recorded by, the pension agency. This is a major task even for high-income countries, few of which maintain this level of detail in pension contribution records. Governments in transition will find this a far greater challenge. As discussed previously, the Polish government experienced major problems in the recording of monthly contributions after the 1999 NDC reform, problems that initially paralyzed the pension system. Now, nearly five years later, it has a new record-keeping system up and running, but it still has not succeeded in recording a large backlog of contributions from the past. Nor, as we learned, has the Polish Social Insurance Institution (ZUS) yet been able to issue annual statements of contributions to scheme contributors.

In addition, because NDC operates on different principles than defined benefit (DB) schemes, there is a need for detailed planning of how the new pension scheme will interact with existing schemes for disability and survivorship. This makes an NDC reform more demanding in terms of planning than changes in the DB system with a similar thrust. In Poland, for example, problems of coordination exist between the NDC old-age scheme and disability pensions. Unless addressed, these will create horizontal inequities among workers with similar contribution records and put increasing financial pressures on the disability pension financing.

To sum up, a reform that works well under a steady, deliberative government with high levels of technical expertise cannot be expected to have the same effects in countries with less developed governmental capacities. Nor can a change of law alone be expected to circumvent weak governance. Rather, weaknesses in governance need to be dealt with as a prerequisite to major pension restructuring. A key challenge to those of us who offer policy advice to transitional governments is to gear our message to specific contexts and take governance into account. The risks of failing to do so are that a reform intended to impose new fiscal discipline may be too unwieldy and complex, ultimately producing greater difficulties for the pension system and those who count on it.

Note

1. "Notional defined contribution" and "non-financial defined contribution" should be understood to have the same definition.

Reference

Palmer, E., et al. 2006. "NDC Strategy in Latvia: Implementation and Prospects for the Future." In *Pension Reform: Issues and Prospects for Non-Financial Defined Contribution (NDC) Schemes*, ed. R. Holzmann and E. Palmer, chapter 15. Washington, DC: World Bank.

Chapter 13

How Much Do People Need to Know about Their Pensions and What Do They Know?

Annika Sundén*

PUBLIC AND OCCUPATIONAL PENSIONS ARE THE MAJOR SOURCES of income for most workers during retirement. How much income workers will have in retirement depends on a range of decisions—from how much to work and save to when to retire. In making sound decisions about retirement, savings, and portfolio allocation, adequate knowledge about the characteristics of pension plans is crucial.

Recent trends in pension reform around the world are likely to increase individuals' need for information about pension plans as well as their need for general financial literacy. Many countries are moving from defined benefit plans to defined contribution plans in both their public and private systems. Compared with defined benefit (DB) plans, defined contribution (DC) plans put more of the responsibility and risk in planning for retirement on individuals because these plans often require decisions about contributions, investment decisions, and withdrawal of funds at retirement. Furthermore, because of the increased financial pressures of aging populations, pension reforms often result in a reduction in replacement rates and hence increase the responsibility for individuals to save on their own for retirement.

Previous research has documented that individuals often have limited financial knowledge and know little about the characteristics of their public and occupational pension plans or how much to expect in retirement benefits. This could mean that many workers reach retirement with inadequate resources and as a consequence will need to postpone retirement or lower consumption in retirement. A possible reason for this lack of knowledge is that learning about pensions is difficult. The complexity involved makes the costs of collecting information appear greater than the benefits of understanding the plan. The retirement process is something individuals only go through once and they can therefore not learn from their mistakes. In addition, retirement is often viewed as something unpleasant and a cause for worry, which means that learning about pension systems and retirement can involve psychological costs. Furthermore, participants may not appreciate the benefits of collecting information because they expect that the public pension system will provide adequate benefits.

* Annika Sundén is a senior economist at the Swedish National Social Insurance Agency.

The views expressed herein are those of the author and not necessarily those of the National Social Insurance Board. I am grateful for valuable comments from John Ameriks, Edward Palmer, and participants at the Sandhamn conference.

The changing pension landscape and the widespread lack of knowledge about pensions have prompted policy makers and employers to provide more information about pension plans through information campaigns and financial education programs in the workplace.

The purpose of this chapter is to discuss the kind of information participants need to make decisions about their pensions and plans for retirement, and to review the literature dealing with how much people actually know about their pensions. The discussion will compare outcomes with respect to defined benefit, defined contribution, and notional defined contribution plans (NDC).[1] The chapter is organized as follows: The first section discusses the type of decisions workers need to make about their pension plans. The next section reviews the role of education and information to participants. The following section examines how much workers know about their pension plans and the effects of financial education. The chapter presents data on the information efforts undertaken in Sweden after the pension reform there and the effects on individuals' knowledge of the reformed pension system. A final section draws some conclusions.

Making Decisions about Pensions

Pensions are complex institutions. To make decisions about retirement and savings, individuals need information about the salient features—benefits, retirement age, and financing—of the pension plans they are covered by. Many pension schemes also require workers to make decisions about participation, level of contributions, investment allocations, and how they will withdraw funds at retirement.

Pension schemes differ on how much participants need to know and what type of information is accessible and easily understood. To discuss information needs, it is useful to classify pension schemes along two dimensions: how benefits and contributions are determined, and how the scheme is funded (table 13.1).

When considering how various pension characteristics affect information needs it is important to keep in mind that different plans involve different types of risks. For example, the level of future benefits will depend on a pension system's ability to meet its obligations. Pay-as-you-go (PAYG) and partially funded DB plans are sensitive to demographic change; many of these systems have projected financial deficits. The financial pressures can be remedied by reducing benefits or increasing contribution rates, but this could create uncertainty about the level of future retirement benefits. On the other hand, individuals who are covered by funded, DC schemes are subject to financial risks since benefit levels will depend on the rate of return in capital markets.

Table 13.1. Types of Pension Schemes

Pension Type	Funded	Unfunded: Pay-As-You-Go
Defined Benefit	Occupational schemes and employer-sponsored plans	Most public pension systems
Defined Contribution	Individual accounts in public pension schemes	NDC in Sweden, for example
	Employer-sponsored plans—for example, 401(k) plans in the United States	

Source: Author's compilation.

Benefits

Knowledge of the level of benefits and how this level varies with the choice of retirement age may be the most important piece of information for deciding when to retire and how much to save. Traditionally, public and private pension plans have been DB plans. In a DB plan, benefits are determined by some combination of earnings and years of service, and the benefit formula makes it easy to express benefits as a replacement rate—that is, how much of the final salary the pension benefit will replace. For example, a typical formula in an employer-sponsored pension plan in the United States is to replace 1.5 percent of final earnings for each year of service, so that a worker with 20 years would receive 30 percent of his or her final salary. The formula is straightforward, making it easy for a worker to estimate the expected benefit. It is also easy to compare the replacement rate with the advice often provided by financial planners about how much of preretirement earnings should be replaced to maintain living standards in retirement.

In other cases the formula is slightly more complicated. For example, in the earnings-related scheme in the previous Swedish public pension system, benefits replaced 60 percent of the average of a worker's 15 years with the highest earnings; or in the U.S. social security system, the benefit formula involves several tiers. In these cases, workers need to know which years' earnings count and how the level of earnings enters into the formula. But even with a more complicated benefit formula, it is straightforward for pension administrators to calculate replacement rates and communicate this information to beneficiaries.

In contrast, in a DC plan, benefits depend on the total amount contributed to the plan and the rate of return on those contributions. At retirement, the account balance is converted to an annuity or, in some cases, paid out as a lump sum. Because benefits are not defined but depend on contributions, it is difficult to express the expected benefit in terms of a replacement rate. It is also difficult to estimate benefits because they vary with the rate of return. Workers receive statements either quarterly or annually with information about the account balance; sometimes these statements provide information that translates the account balance into a monthly benefit. For example, in the Swedish NDC plan, workers receive an annual statement with information about the balance in their notional account as well as the expected monthly benefit. The expected benefit is calculated for three retirement ages—61, 65, and 70—and is based on an earnings projection that is an extrapolation of previous years' earnings. But it is still much more difficult to estimate benefits in a DC plan than in a DB plan.

The fact that earned pension rights are in the form of an account balance in financial defined contribution (FDC) and NDC plans could contribute to participants overestimating their expected pension benefits because of "wealth illusion." When people look at how much they have accumulated for retirement, they see a cash balance of, say, US$100,000, which (compared with a monthly benefit) looks like a lot of money. Nevertheless, it is not much when spread out over a retirement period of 15–20 years. The literature in psychology shows that people view lump sums differently than they do periodic payments: when a lump sum is compared with a monthly benefit, the lump sum looks like much more money than the monthly benefit even if they are worth the same in terms of present discounted value.[2]

How pension benefits are affected by job mobility is another important factor in estimating the expected benefit at retirement. The benefit formula in a DB plan often replaces earnings just prior to leaving, which means that a job change could reduce benefits. In a national scheme this is less of a problem because workers are covered by the same scheme regardless of where they work. But many employer-sponsored pension plans and occupational plans base benefits on earnings just prior to job termination. DC plans do not have this problem because the account balance is portable.

Finally, people often have coverage from public as well as occupational schemes. To get a full picture of the level of benefits at retirement, workers need information from all sources and this can sometimes be difficult to assemble.

Retirement Age

DB plans usually specify a normal retirement age at which workers are eligible for full benefits and an early retirement age at which workers can leave with actuarially reduced benefits. The benefit formula, combined with the specified retirement ages, means that DB plans usually provide information such as: benefits will be 60 percent of earnings if retirement is at age 65 and 42 percent if retirement is at age 60. Furthermore, the formula often provides strong incentives to retire at the specified ages.

In principle, this makes it easy for workers in DB plans to understand how much they will receive and at what age. In practice, however, this is not always the case. One problem is that it may be difficult to convey that the replacement rate at the early retirement date depends on the normal retirement age and that increasing the normal retirement age will affect benefits withdrawn early. For example, in the United States a large share of workers start withdrawing benefits as soon as possible at age 62. The normal retirement age was 65 until 2000, but has been gradually increased since then and will be 67 for people reaching age 62 in 2022. For someone who reaches age 62 in 2004, the normal retirement age is 65 and 10 months. The early retirement age will continue to be age 62. The gradual increase in the normal retirement age is equivalent to a benefit cut and those who continue retiring early will receive a lower monthly benefit.[3] So far, workers in the United States have not begun to withdraw benefits later, but it should be kept in mind that the normal retirement age has increased by only 10 months, so it will not be until workers born in the late 1950s and early 1960s reach retirement age that the full effect of the increase in retirement age will become clear.

DC plans need to specify a minimum retirement age, but they do not specify a normal retirement age and therefore do not have the same problems with early retirement incentives. But because of the difficulty in converting the account balance to a monthly benefit it may still be difficult to figure out how the benefit will vary with the choice of retirement age. Furthermore, in converting the benefit to an annuity, life expectancy matters. One innovation in the Swedish NDC scheme is that benefits are computed using life expectancy at retirement. This means that when the account balance is converted to a benefit, the annuity depends on the remaining life expectancy for the beneficiary's cohort. Thus, for a given retirement age, say 65, annual benefits will decrease as individuals live longer. To receive the same replacement rate, an individual has to work longer.

Financing in Non-Financial Pension Schemes

The financing and investment of pension funds affect participants' need for information and the kind of investment decisions they have to make. Most public pension schemes are funded on a PAYG basis and many countries face long-term financing deficits in their pension schemes. For a DB plan this means that benefits will either have to be reduced or contributions increased for the plan to meet its obligations. For example, the retirement age in the U.S. social security system is gradually increasing, and in recent years a discussion of social security reform has been on top of the political agenda. What matters for workers is to understand that benefits or contributions have to change to sustain the system and how this will affect their savings and retirement decisions.

In this context, the NDC plan is a special case. Increasing the contribution rate is not an option in response to financial shortfalls because it will automatically increase commitments in the future. Instead, the NDC system is designed so that pension commitments never exceed the system's capability to finance them with a fixed contribution rate. Thus participants' pension rights and benefits will be automatically adjusted.

Investment Decisions in Financial Pension Schemes

Some DB plans are either fully or partially funded. Contributions are placed in a trust fund and invested collectively, which means that workers do not need to make investment decisions and the investment risk is pooled among all participants.

DC plans can also manage funds collectively in a trust fund. Typically, however, individuals manage their own financial accounts and make decisions about investment allocation and changes in the allocation over time. Thus participants bear the entire risk of their investments. This requires knowledge about financial markets and how to balance risk and return, something that can be difficult.[4]

In sum, workers in general need to make few decisions in a DB plan. Benefits can be expressed as a replacement rate and the normal retirement age is often fixed. To estimate the replacement rate, workers may also need to know which years to count in the benefit formula. A risk in a DB plan is that benefits may be reduced in the future if the scheme cannot fulfill its obligations, but overall DB plans are fairly straightforward. DC plans, on the other hand, put more demands on participants to make decisions and thereby on pension administrators to find ways to communicate the features of the plan. With the exception of investment decisions, an NDC plan puts the same demands on participants as it puts in a regular DC plan.

Financial Education and Information to Participants

The changing pension landscape has prompted government agencies, firms, and pension administrators to engage in increased financial education and information efforts to participants. These campaigns often include improved information about the plans, more user-friendly account statements, and educational seminars aimed at teaching participants about investing and financial markets. This section will discuss information and education efforts in pension schemes with a focus on Sweden and the United States. These two countries are interesting because they illustrate information and financial education in view of the shift from DB to DC plans.

Pensions in the United States

In the United States, retirement income mainly comes from two sources: social security and employer-sponsored pension plans. The social security scheme is a DB plan, and in recent years the Social Security Administration (SSA) has increased its efforts in providing information to participants about their benefits. The main source of information about expected benefits is the SSA's annual earnings and benefit statement, which is sent to all participants. This statement provides information on a participant's earnings history and eligibility for benefits. It also provides a projection of the expected benefit based on the worker's earnings history at the early and normal retirement age. Previously, only workers approaching retirement automatically received these statements, but since the late 1990s, all workers receive annual earnings and benefit statements. Furthermore, the SSA provides a calculator on its Web site where individuals can estimate their own benefits based on their earnings and assumptions about future wage growth.

In addition to social security, about 50 percent of U.S. workers are covered by employer-sponsored pension plans, and employers play an increasingly important role in providing information and education about pensions in the United States. Employers' interest in providing education to employees can to a large extent be explained by the shift from DB plans to DC plans, and in particular the dramatic growth in 401(k) plans. The 401(k) plan is an employer-sponsored DC plan that has become increasingly popular. Today, it is the fastest growing occupational plan in the United States. The defining characteristics of 401(k) plans are that they are voluntary and workers have to make decisions about participation, contributions, investment allocation, and withdrawal of funds at retirement. Employers are interested in encouraging participation in 401(k) plans in order to pass nondiscrimination testing, and information and education are important tools for this purpose. According to a survey from the mid-1990s, almost 90 percent of all large firms with occupational pensions offered some kind of financial education, and most had added the programs after 1990.[5] The information usually consists of booklets that describe the company's retirement plan, information about financial markets, and the basics about investing as well as offering seminars on retirement saving.

Pensions in Sweden

Pension reform in Sweden transformed the public pension system from a DB scheme to a combination of notional and FDC (called Premium Pension in Sweden) schemes. The reform completely changed the structure of the pension scheme, and information to participants became a crucial component in implementing the reform. A broad information campaign was launched in the fall of 1998. The campaign included a detailed brochure that described the new pension system; public service announcements on radio, television, and in newspapers; seminars that discussed the reformed pension system; and a Web site. However, the cornerstone of communication with participants is the "orange envelope." The orange envelope contains the annual account statement for the notional and FDC schemes. In addition to the orange envelope, a Web site also provides a calculator that individuals can use to estimate their benefits given their account balances and assumptions about future earnings and retirement age.

The first orange envelope was sent out in 1999 and included information on participants' entire earnings histories and projections of expected benefits. In the years since, the NDC account statement includes information on the account balance, pension credits earned during the year, and the indexation of the account balance—that is, the rate of return. The orange envelope also includes account information on the Premium Pension. In addition to providing information about expected benefits, the orange envelope summarizes how the reformed pension system works and promotes the main message that lifetime earnings determine benefits.

Since the introduction of the orange envelope, the National Social Insurance Board has conducted an annual survey to investigate how participants use the orange envelope and how well it helps communicate information about the pension system.[6] Table 13.2 presents information on the extent to which participants read the materials from the 2003 survey. The results show that in 2003, almost everyone knew that they had received the envelope, and among all respondents two-thirds opened and read the contents. This is less than in earlier years: when the first orange envelope was sent out in 1999, 75 percent of all respondents opened and read the materials, and in 2000 more than 80 percent read at least part of the information.

Only about 10 percent of respondents looked at all of the information in the envelope. The results do not reveal any major differences between demographic groups, although women tend to read the materials to a larger extent than men.

Table 13.2. The Orange Envelope, 2003

Survey respondents	Know that they received envelope (%)[a]	Opened and read at least part of the contents (%)[a]	Read all the contents (%)[a]	Among those who opened and read at least part of the contents	
				Looked at benefit projection (%)	Examined increase in NDC benefit (%)
All	86	67	9	68	56
Gender					
Men	84	65	11	72	62
Women	88	70	8	63	51
Age					
18–29	82	65	4	41	47
30–45	87	66	6	73	55
46–62	89	72	16	81	64
Education					
Less than high school	82	62	12	69	58
High school	87	69	8	60	52
College	87	69	9	79	64
Household income (Swedish kronor)					
< SKr 160	85	62	6	56	57
161–200	88	71	11	63	50
201–300	84	71	8	77	60
>300	87	71	11	79	63
Work status					
Working	88	68	9	74	59
Student	75	60	2	37	47
Retired	85	66	21	50	49
Other	83	72	14	68	52
Working					
Blue-collar workers	87	66	10	69	59
White-collar workers	89	72	8	77	56
Self-employed	92	64	10	77	75

Source: Swedish National Social Insurance Board (2003).

a. Among all respondents.

To help participants translate their account balances to benefits at retirement, the orange envelope provides a benefit projection. The benefit projection calculates the expected annual benefit at three different retirement ages. Because it is difficult for participants to make these kinds of calculations on their own in a DC plan, this information is clearly important to assess whether retirement benefits will be adequate. The results show that, *among those who read the materials*, about two-thirds looked at the benefit projection. This means that, overall, less than half of all participants look at the benefit projection. Not surprisingly, older participants read the contents of the orange envelope to a greater extent than younger participants. The data also show that low-income individuals are less likely to examine the materials. In general, participants do not compare the information in the orange envelope from one year to the next. Only 27 percent answered that they had compared this year's information with last year's (not shown).

In addition to public pension benefits, almost all workers in Sweden receive benefits from one of four occupational pension plans, and these plans also provided information and education in connection with the pension reform. Furthermore, three of the four schemes changed from DB plans to DC plans in connection with the reform. As a result, all workers except white-collar workers in the private sector now have individual financial accounts in their occupational schemes. Occupational schemes have become increasingly important for overall retirement income in Sweden, and middle-income workers in particular are dependent on these benefits. To make decisions about saving and retirement, workers need information on all sources combined. Currently, individuals have to put together the information from the different sources themselves to get the full picture. However, an initiative is underway in Sweden that creates a Web site where workers will get information on their earned rights and projected benefits from all sources.

To summarize, the data show that although almost everyone knows that they have received information on their public pension, only about two-thirds have looked at some of the information.

How Much Individuals Know about Their Pension Plans and the Effects of Financial Education

How much do individuals know about their pension plans and to what extent do education efforts increase their ability to make decisions with regard to their pensions? Several studies have examined these issues, using mostly data from the United States. This section considers evidence from the United States and Sweden in greater detail.

Evidence from the United States

In an early study, Bernheim (1988) studied the accuracy of knowledge of expected social security benefits in a sample of U.S. workers close to retirement. The results indicated that workers formed expectations using only part of the information available to them and that their expectations about future benefits would have been more accurate had they used all available information. More recently, Gustman and Steinmeier (2001; 2004) used data on workers approaching retirement age and compared workers' reports on their expected social security benefits with the benefits calculated from their social security earnings record. Overall, their results suggest that workers are misinformed about their expected benefits—only half of respondents reported that they know what their benefits will be. Older workers are better informed than younger workers, and women are less likely than men to know their benefits. In general, the results indicated that those who depend most on social security are least informed. Similar to Bernheim's study, the Gustman and Steinmeier studies found that workers who have requested earnings and benefit statements from SSA have better knowledge about their social security benefits. However, because those who are most interested in learning about their benefits also are more likely to be those that request a statement, it is difficult to draw any conclusion about the effect of the benefit statement on knowledge from this result.

In an annual survey of retirement confidence conducted by the Employee Benefit Research Institute, individuals are asked several questions about their planning for retirement. The most recent survey is from 2003 and confirms the findings that individuals are not well informed about their social security benefits. An important change in the U.S. social security system is the scheduled increase in the retirement age. The increase in retirement the age is equal to a benefit cut, but only 16 percent of respondents in the survey were aware that the normal retirement age had been raised and could correctly give the age at which they would be eligible for benefits. One-fourth of respondents do not know the earliest age when they can start collecting benefits, and about half expect to be eligible earlier than they actually will be.

Researchers have also examined how much workers know about their employer-sponsored pension plans by comparing workers' reports on the characteristics of their plans with information from plan providers.[7] The results show that although knowledge has improved somewhat over time, many participants still lack knowledge about important parts of their plans, such as ages of eligibility for early and normal retirement benefits and the effects on benefits of postponing retirement past the early retirement age.

Most workers in the cited studies were covered by DB plans. The results of the studies indicated that workers lack information on characteristics that are fairly straightforward to understand, such as when they are eligible for benefits. This is a worrisome result in view of the shift in pension options provided from DB to DC plans, which often require workers to manage their own accounts. This is the case in 401(k) plans in the United States and in the Premium Pension in the Swedish system. When U.S. workers are asked about their 401(k) plans, they often report that pension plans are too complicated and difficult to understand.[8] Bernheim (1998) used survey data on financial planning collected by financial institutions and found evidence that people's knowledge about finances and investing in general is limited.

Does Financial Education Help?

Does financial education contribute to increased understanding of pension plans? To address this issue, researchers have examined the effects of employer-based informational programs in the United States. The conclusion that emerges is that teaching workers about their pension plans has had some positive effects, although the magnitude of these effects is difficult to measure. It is also important to remember that to fully evaluate the effects of employer education it is necessary to compare the benefits to the costs of providing education. Currently, no study has undertaken a cost-benefit analysis of pension education programs.

Several studies that have examined the effects of financial education have looked at what happens to participation and contributions in 401(k) plans. The results indicate that financial education has some positive effects. Clark and Schieber (1998) found that financial literacy played an important role in increasing the probability of participating in a 401(k) plan. Another study confirmed that employees who used the information materials had higher participation rates than employees who did not.[9] A survey of employers likewise found that workers who participated in retirement planning seminars had higher participation rates and that the largest educational gains were among not highly compensated employees.[10] On the other hand, the effect on contribution levels was small.

Researchers have also attempted to assess the effects of financial education on the investment decisions in FDC plans. Using data on individuals approaching retirement, Muller (2002) found no general effect of attending a seminar on investment decisions, but found that workers who were risk averse tended to adjust their portfolios in response to the seminar. Two recent studies examine the link between financial education and setting and achieving retirement savings goals.[11] The results show that workers who participated in a financial education seminar adjusted their retirement goals in response to the information in the seminar about the level of income needed in retirement. In many cases, adjusting goals meant increasing the expected retirement age.

Far from all employees attend financial education seminars or read the materials, something that was clear from the Swedish data on recipients of the orange envelope. This is of concern if those who do not take part also are nonsavers or those who rely most on pension income for their income security in old age. However, a recent study in the United States showed that peer effects can be an important factor in communicating information on pension plans. That is, even if some workers do not participate in financial education, the fact that their colleagues do and that they communicate the information could have a positive effect on the behavior of those who did not attend. This effect was demonstrated in a study by Duflo and Saez (2002), who examined the decision to participate in a 401(k) plan following education seminars. The authors undertook an experiment in which they offered a group of employees a monetary reward to attend an educational seminar. The reward tripled attendance, and 401(k) participation increased significantly among those who attended. Participation in the 401(k) plan also increased among employees who had not attended the seminar but who worked in the same departments as those who did— demonstrating the peer effect on participation decisions.

Experiences from Sweden

Similar to traditional DC plans, both the NDC-component and the Premium Pension in Sweden place increased responsibility on individuals to plan for retirement. A goal of the information and education efforts that were launched in 1998 was to build up knowledge about the system by 2001. To evaluate the effects of the information materials on knowledge about the new system, the same survey that asked about how the orange envelope had been used also investigated individuals' knowledge about the reform.

The survey indicates that almost everyone—93 percent of respondents—knows that the system has been reformed. In the survey, respondents were asked to rate how they perceived their knowledge about the system. The results are shown in figure 13.1. In 2003, less than 40 percent of respondents report that they have good understanding of what the reformed system entails, a slight decrease since 2001. About half report that they have some understanding of the new system, but that they view their knowledge as poor. The share of participants who report that they do not understand the new system at all has decreased from about 30 percent in 1998 to 13 percent in 2003. Not surprisingly, older participants are more likely than younger participants to report that they have good knowledge of the system. More men than women view themselves as being knowledgeable, and formal education appears to be positively correlated with knowledge about the pension system (not shown).

It is interesting to note that a larger share among those who report that they have good knowledge have read the information in the orange envelope as well as looked at the forecast of expected benefits, the change in the NDC account balance, and the Premium Pension account balance.

Benefits in the Swedish pension system are based on lifetime earnings—that is, all years with contributions count. As discussed above, it is inherently difficult to estimate expected benefits in DC plans. To make decisions about how much to work and save, it is therefore important to understand how benefits are determined and how it has changed compared with the previous public system. Therefore, one of the main messages of the information communicated to participants was that all years of work count toward pension benefits. To determine whether participants had understood this principle, the survey included a question about how benefits are determined. The results show that in 2000, half of respondents correctly answered that lifetime earnings determine benefits, but that share had decreased to 38 percent in 2003. Among those who view themselves as having good knowledge about the system, 50 percent knew that lifetime earnings determine benefits.

To further gauge participants' knowledge about the reformed system, the survey asked respondents if they could name the three components of the new system—the NDC, the

Figure 13.1. Self-Reported Knowledge about the Swedish Pension System

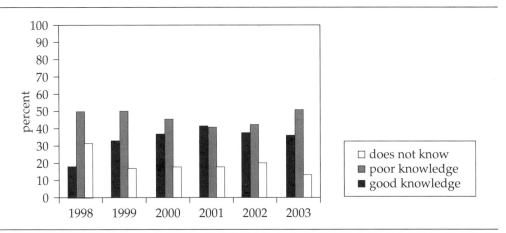

Source: Surveys taken by the Swedish National Social Insurance Board.

Premium Pension, and the guarantee benefit. This information may not be necessary to make decisions about, for example, when to retire, but still provides an indication about how well participants understand the system. Table 13.3 presents information on the share of participants who know how benefits are determined and the share that could name the NDC component and the Premium Pension component.

The results show that participants are more likely to know about the financial account component (the Premium Pension) than they are to know about the NDC component. This is not surprising in view of the enormous attention the Premium Pension received in connection with the initial investment choices in 2000, and the subsequent fall in the stock market. But the fact that participants seem to be more aware of the Premium Pension could mean that they view it as more important for overall retirement income than the NDC component and do not realize that it is only a small share of the total, although the orange envelope has provided this information on an annual basis.

Overall, men are somewhat more likely than women to have knowledge about the pension system. Income and education are also important determinants of knowledge: participants in the highest income class and with college degrees have better knowledge of the system than participants with low incomes and fewer years of education. The result confirms findings from the United States—the participants who are most dependent on the system often are those who have the least knowledge about it.

Another measure of financial literacy could be previous experience with saving for retirement. About half of the respondents in the Swedish survey had bought private pension insurance, an indication that they have spent at least some time thinking about retirement. Having a private pension appears to improve self-reported knowledge about the public pension system somewhat: about 50 percent report that they have poor knowledge of the system, compared with 60 percent among those without such insurance. Actual knowledge, measured by correctly indicating that lifetime earnings affect benefits, appears to be similar in the two groups. Only 40 percent of those with private pension insurance knew the correct calculation period. However, those with pension insurance are more likely to look at the forecast of expected benefits, and a larger share reports that they have enough knowledge to manage their Premium Pension account.

Table 13.3. Knowledge of Participants about the Swedish Pension System, 2003

Participants	Know which earnings are used to calculate benefits (%)	Know the name of the NDC component (%)	Know the name of the financial account component (%)
All participants	38	8	12
Gender			
Men	40	8	14
Women	36	8	9
Age			
18–29	37	8	10
30–45	36	6	11
46–62	43	10	14
Education			
Less than high school	31	4	6
High school	36	7	10
College	46	12	19
Household income (Swedish kronor)			
<SKr 160	31	7	9
161–200	40	9	8
201–300	39	8	14
>300	42	10	15
Work status			
Working	42	9	13
Student	34	4	9
Retired	16	8	7
Other	28	10	11
Working			
Blue-collar workers	38	8	10
White-collar workers	47	9	13
Self-employed	34	9	19

Source: Swedish National Social Insurance Board (2003).

An innovation in the NDC plan is that benefits are determined by life expectancy, so that for a given retirement age annual benefits will be lower as life expectancy increases. The system also allows for a flexible retirement age, and benefits can be withdrawn starting at age 61. The survey did not ask directly about the connections to life expectancy, but asked respondents if they think that benefits depend on the retirement age. Almost all participants were aware that annual benefits depend on the retirement age.

The results above indicated that individuals may have more knowledge about and interest in the Premium Pension than the NDC component. The orange envelope provides information on the change in the account balance for the NDC account as well as for the Premium Pension account. In 2003, 56 percent of participants had looked at how the NDC account balance had changed since the previous year; 74 percent had looked at the change in the account balance in the Premium Pension. It is also interesting to note that more than half of participants report that they do not have enough knowledge to manage their Premium Pension account. In particular, respondents answer that they would like to have more information on how the system works and how one should think about making investment decisions.

To assess whether the information materials have improved participants' knowledge, data are needed on to what extent participants read the materials. Table 13.2 indicated that two-thirds of participants had opened the orange envelope and more than half of respondents found the materials easy to understand. Still, less than 40 percent understand that lifetime earnings determine benefits, one of the most important characteristics of the pension system.

The question is whether more information is needed to help participants navigate the new system. In 2003, about 60 percent of respondents reported that they would like more information (figure 13.2). Although the share is down from 70 percent during the first years of the reform, it is still a significant share. Also, participants appear to trust the information they receive. In 2003, 72 percent reported that they feel confident about the information they received in the orange envelope.

In sum, the results from the information and education initiative in Sweden indicate only limited success in increasing knowledge about the new system so far. It is important to remember that the system has been in effect for less than five years. However, many participants are still unaware of the key principles of how benefits are determined, and the notion that the financial account component (the Premium Pension) is more important for retirement income than the NDC benefit seems to be widespread. At the same time, participants also report that they need more information. The question is what to do? A useful first step would be to find out what participants are missing in the information they currently are receiving. Given the amount of information currently available, more information is probably not the solution. Instead, alternative ways of presenting it to participants should be considered. It may also be helpful to consider policies to increase financial literacy in the overall population. One such policy could be to introduce financial education in the high school curriculum. Results from such programs in the United States have shown some positive long-term effects (Bernheim, Garrett, and Maki 1997).

Figure 13.2. Share of Participants Needing Additional Information

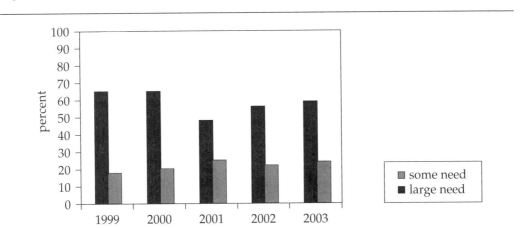

Source: Surveys taken by the Swedish National Social Insurance Board.

How Does Insufficient Knowledge Affect Participants' Decisions?

The discussion in this chapter has shown that individuals have limited knowledge about their pension plans. This is true for DB as well as for DC plans. The life-cycle model provides a theoretical framework for analyzing the allocation of time and resources over the lifetime, but it assumes that individuals understand institutions and financial markets. Insufficient information or knowledge about pensions can lead to individuals making decisions that have a negative impact on their retirement incomes. The result could be that individuals reach retirement with too little savings and have to postpone retirement or reduce their consumption.

Several studies have examined how insufficient knowledge and planning affect savings and retirement outcomes. In a series of studies, Lusardi (2002, 2003) examined workers approaching retirement and concluded that individuals who had thought less about retirement and not planned for it had lower savings. She argues that the lack of financial literacy plays an important role in explaining the low savings rate in the United States. This finding is supported by Ameriks, Caplin, and Leahy (2002), who used data on individuals working in higher education and found that those who had planned less had also saved less.

Another way researchers have looked at the adequacy of savings is to examine what happens to consumption at retirement. Although consumption is expected to be lower in retirement due to declining expenses, several studies indicate that consumption falls more than anticipated at retirement.[12] Furthermore, the drop in consumption is larger for households who have less generous private pension and social security benefits. One explanation for the unexpected fall in consumption at retirement is that workers have overestimated their benefits or not known how much the benefit would be. Studies have also shown that how much participants know about their pension benefits affects retirement outcomes.[13] For example, workers who underestimated their benefits were less likely to retire early than those who overestimated their benefits.

The experience with 401(k) plans in the United States provides further evidence that workers have insufficient information or find decisions about pensions too difficult and that this affects outcomes. Workers eligible for 401(k) plans have to make many decisions about plans: to participate, how much to contribute, how to invest the funds, and how to withdraw the money at retirement. Studies on participant behavior in 401(k) plans show that workers make mistakes at every step of the way: about one-fourth of eligible workers do not participate, less than 10 percent contribute the maximum, a majority of workers have not diversified their investments and rarely change allocations as they age, and many fail to annuitize their accounts at retirement.[14]

Conclusion

The pension landscape around the world is changing. Public and private pension systems are moving away from DB schemes toward DC schemes, and because of the increased financial pressures of aging populations, pension reforms often result in a reduction in replacement rates. This puts an increased responsibility on participants to understand how their pension plans and financial markets work, and to save for retirement on their own.

Both public and occupational pension schemes devote considerable effort to providing information to participants. Results from studies on the effects of educational programs show some positive results, but it is clear that a large share of participants do not know the details about their pension schemes and that this has negative effects on savings and retirement decisions.

Making decisions about any type of pension is difficult. The shift toward DC schemes has increased participants' need to learn about their pensions. The level of complexity of the schemes implies that the costs associated with understanding the pension scheme could appear greater than the benefits, even if information is available. Furthermore, the retirement process is something individuals only go through once, so they do not have the benefit of learning by doing. For many individuals, retirement is seen as something unpleasant and a cause for worry, which means that thinking and planning for retirement can also involve psychological costs. Workers may also fail to learn more about their public and private pensions because they expect that public pension system will provide adequate benefits. This may be particularly true for workers at the lower end of the income distribution because social security systems tend to be progressive.

As a result of the high costs of learning about pensions, workers often procrastinate about savings and retirement decisions. This chapter has shown that information and education leading to improved financial literacy clearly is important, but perhaps equally important is to design pension plans that make it easy for participants to make decisions.

Notes

1. "Notional defined contribution" and "non-financial defined contribution" should be understood to have the same definition.

2. See Fetherstonhaugh and Ross (1999).

3. In the United States, the replacement rate for an average worker retiring at age 65 will decrease from 41 percent in 2000 to 36 percent in 2030.

4. Participants often face a large number of investment options in DC plans. In the Swedish Premium Pension system, participants have more than 500 funds to choose from. In the United States, workers in large 401(k) plans on average have 38 different investment options.

5. See Bayer, Bernheim, and Scholz (1996).

6. The sample in the survey is 1,000 individuals; interviews are conducted by telephone.

7. See Mitchell (1988); Gustman and Steinmeier 1989, 2001, and 2004; and Starr-McCluer and Sundén (1999).

8. See Munnell and Sundén (2004).

9. See Bernheim and Garrett (1996).

10. See Bayer, Bernheim, and Scholz (1996).

11. See Clark and d'Ambrosio (2002) and Clark et al. (2003).

12. See Bernheim, Skinner, and Weinberg (2001) and Banks, Blundell, and Tanner (1998).

13. See Gustman and Steinmeier (2001, 2004) and Chan and Stevens (2003).

14. See Munnell and Sundén (2004).

References

Ameriks, J., A. Caplin, and J. Leahy. 2002. "Wealth Accumulation and the Propensity to Plan." NBER Working Paper 8920, National Bureau of Economic Research, Cambridge, Massachusetts.

Bayer, P. J., B. D. Bernheim, and J. K. Scholz. 1996. "The Effects of Financial Education in the Workplace: Evidence from a Survey of Employers." NBER Working Paper 5655, National Bureau of Economic Research, Cambridge, Massachusetts.

Banks, J., R. Blundell, and S. Tanner. 1998. "Is There a Retirement-Savings Puzzle?" *The American Economic Review* 88 (4): 769–88.

Bernheim, B. D. 1988. "Social Security Benefits: An Empirical Study of Expectations and Realizations." In *Issues in Contemporary Retirement*, ed. Rita Ricardo-Campbell and Edward P. Lazear, 312–45. Stanford: Hoover Institution Press.

———. 1998. "Financial Illiteracy, Education and Retirement Saving." In *Living with Defined Contribution Plans*, ed. O. Mitchell and S. Schieber, 38–68. Philadelphia: Pension Research Council and the University of Pennsylvania Press.

Bernheim, B. D., and D. M. Garrett. 1996. "The Determinants and Consequences of Financial Education in the Workplace: Evidence from a Survey of Households." NBER Working Paper 5667, National Bureau of Economic Research, Cambridge, Massachusetts.

Bernheim, B. D., D. M. Garrett, and D. M. Maki. 1997. "Education and Saving: The Long-Term Effects of High School Financial Curriculum Mandates." NBER Working Paper 5667, National Bureau of Economic Research, Cambridge, Massachusetts.

Bernheim, B. D., J. Skinner, and S. Weinberg. 2001. "What Accounts for the Variation in Retirement Wealth Among U.S. Households?" *The American Economic Review* 91 (4): 832–57.

Chan, S., and A. H. Stevens. 2003. "What You Don't Know Can't Help You: Pension Knowledge and Retirement Decision Making." NBER Working Paper 10185, National Bureau of Economic Research, Cambridge, Massachusetts.

Clark, R. L., and M. d'Ambrosio. 2002. "Saving for Retirement: The Role of Financial Education." TIAA-CREF Working Paper 4-070102-A, TIAA-CREF, New York.

Clark, R. L., M. d'Ambrosio, A. A. McDermed, and K. Sawant. 2003. "Managing Retirement Accounts: Gender Differences in Response to Financial Education." TIAA-CREF Working Paper 12-070103, TIAA-CREF, New York.

Clark, R. L., and S. J. Schieber. 1998. "Factors Affecting Participation Rates and Contribution Levels in 401(k) Plans." In *Living with Defined Contribution Plans*, ed. O. Mitchell and S. Schieber, 69–97. Philadelphia: Pension Research Council and the University of Pennsylvania Press.

Duflo, E., and E. Saez. 2002. "The Role of Information and Social Interactions in Retirement Plan Decisions." NBER Working Paper 8885, National Bureau of Economic Research, Cambridge, Massachusetts.

EBRI (Employee Benefit Research Institute). 2003. *The 2003 Retirement Confidence Survey.* Summary of Findings.

Fetherstonhaugh, D., and L. Ross. 1999. "Framing Effects and Income Flow Preferences." In *Behavioral Dimensions of Retirement Economics*, ed. Henry Aaron, 187–214. Washington, DC: Brookings Institution Press.

Gustman, A. L., and T. L. Steinmeier. 1989. "An Analysis of Pension Benefit Formulas, Pension Wealth and Incentives from Pensions." In *Research in Labor Economics*, ed. R. Ehrenberg, 53–106. Greenwich, CT and London: JAI Press.

———. 2001. "Imperfect Knowledge, Retirement, and Saving." NBER Working Paper 8406, National Bureau of Economic Research, Cambridge, Massachusetts.

———. 2004. "What People Don't Know About Their Pensions and Social Security: An Analysis Using Linked Data From the Health and Retirement Study." In *Public Policies and Private Pensions*, ed. W. Gale, J. Shoven and M. Warshawsky, 57–125. Washington, DC: Brookings Insititution.

Lusardi, A. 2002. "Preparing for Retirement: The Importance of Planning Costs." *National Tax Association Proceedings 2002*, 148–154.

———. 2003. "Planning and the Effectiveness of Retirement Seminars." Dartmouth College.

Mitchell, O. 1988. "Worker Knowledge of Pension Provisions." *Journal of Labor Economics* 6 (1): 28–39.

Muller, L. 2002. "Investment Choice in Defined Contribution Plans: The Effects of Retirement Education on Asset Allocation," Washington, DC: Social Security Administration.

Munnell, A. H., and A. Sundén. 2004. *Coming Up Short: The Challenge of 401(k) Plans*. Washington, DC: Brookings Institution Press.

Starr-McCluer, M., and A. Sundén. 1999. "Workers' Knowledge of their Pension Coverage: A Reevaluation." In *The Creation and Analysis of Linked Employer-Employee Data*, ed. J. Haltiwanger, J. L., J. R. Speltzer, J. Theeuwes, and K. Troske, 569–83. Amsterdam: North-Holland.

Discussion of "How Much Do People Need to Know about Their Pensions and What Do They Know?"

*John Ameriks**

As its title announces, this very interesting chapter by Annika Sundén sets out to compare individual needs for information about their pensions with what they report knowing. The issue of informational requirements is one that has not received a great deal of attention in the academic debate surrounding pension reforms, and I congratulate the author for a fine contribution on this important topic.

The chapter is motivated by the observation that the degree to which individuals are knowledgeable about their pension arrangements is important for a number of reasons. From the point of view of the individual, lack of knowledge of the features or provisions of a pension arrangement can inhibit the ability to plan. Thus, whether lack of familiarity is the result of uncertainty, complexity, or psychological barriers, "becoming informed" represents a real cost that individuals must bear to be able to plan for retirement, regardless of what type of pension they have. From the point of view of plan provider, whether a public or private entity, plan participants' ignorance of plan features or provisions may also be costly, inasmuch as unknown or misunderstood incentives are unlikely to be efficient incentives.

The author begins by reviewing needed information. There is not much to argue with here, as the chapter provides a comprehensive list of things people must know to estimate pension benefits. I agree with the author that "Knowledge of the level of benefits and how it varies with the choice of retirement age may be the most important piece of information for making decisions about when to retire and how much to save." Of course there are at least two ways to present this information to plan participants: one can report the expected future value of pension rights, expressed as a flow of income, or one can report the expected present value of pension rights, expressed as a stock of assets. This is the fundamental difference between defined benefit (DB) and defined contribution (DC) pension accounting.

The author argues in several places that DB accounting and the language of income replacement rates is "simpler" and more conducive to better retirement decision making. Yet it strikes me that a key issue here is that retirement planning is not done in a vacuum. If people spent every dollar or kroner they took home, and their only source of income in retirement were to be pension benefits, perhaps the argument would be more persuasive. Abstracting from issues around eligibility and uncertainty, in such a case DB accounting does seem "simpler." But most individuals in developed countries face a series of choices about saving and spending over the course of their preretirement years. It seems clear that good savings decisions though time require an accurate assessment of the accrued value of

---

* John Ameriks is a senior investment analyst at the Vanguard Group.

pension benefits through time, in terms that are consistent and comparable across assets and alternative opportunities for saving. For this purpose, it may be that DC accounting is "simpler" and more intuitive for decision-making.[1] Perhaps an ideal middle road, one seemingly built into the new NDC Swedish pension, is to present figures in both ways.

The chapter presents and analyzes a great deal of interesting new data regarding the Swedish public's understanding of their recently reformed public pension system. This type of information is unique and valuable to those of us struggling to understand how plan participants make financial decisions. From the point of view of someone who is used to seeing such surveys on the U.S. social security system or private pensions in the United States, the data on the Swedish public's familiarity with their new pension system is a bit stunning. More than 93 percent of the Swedish participants knew the pension system had been reformed, 86 percent recalled receiving the "orange envelopes," and more than two-thirds reported reading some of the material. In comparison, in the United States, only 50 percent claim to know their social security benefit, and only 16 percent knew the normal retirement age had changed. This appears to reveal a quite a remarkable difference in "knowledge."

Yet interpreting these answers is extremely difficult. It's not clear whether these data say more about the differences between Swedish citizens and U.S. citizens, about differences in knowledge, or about differences in pension systems. Even assuming that the responses have consistent meaning across national borders and pension systems, it's not clear what it means that most people have "read the materials." One thought might be that such reported knowledge metrics may indicate a level of comfort that citizens have with their pensions, but some more "unpacking" of these answers might be helpful.

Even if one accepts survey responses as valid knowledge metrics, there remains a difference between knowledge and wisdom (as the old saying goes). As the author points out, mountains of information are currently available to participants in all types of pension plans. Yet it is far from clear that this information has been useful in helping participants more effectively achieve their goals. Recent research is even starting to suggest the possibility that "information overload" (or choice overload) could be a problem rather than a solution (Sethi-Iyengar, Huberman, and Jiang 2004).

One statement with which I don't wish to let the author slip completely cleanly by is the assertion that "Studies on participant behavior in 401(k) plans show that workers make mistakes at every step of the way...." I will be among the first to admit that there are many ways in which individual choices in 401(k) plans and other situations appear difficult to reconcile with behavioral predictions arising from basic economic theories. But I think it is premature to conclude that "mistakes" are rampant. Certainly, ex-post outcomes in 401(k) plans may not be what some participants desired. This does not necessarily mean that mistakes were made, only that uncertainty exists. And uncertainty will still exist whether 401(k)s are used or not. Alternative systems may be able to provide a means to share risk to a larger extent—at the cost of less individual control and flexibility—and individual dissatisfaction with various aspects of such systems is well known.

I compare much of the debate about whether individuals will be able to finance retirement on their own in the face of informational and other hurdles with one of the great films (subjective measure) of 2003: *Finding Nemo*. In the film, Nemo is a cute little clownfish with inadequate knowledge (oops, I mean an undersized fin) and a protective father who "doesn't want anything to ever happen to him." Early on in the film, Nemo finds himself alone in a big dangerous ocean, and it's not at all clear that he'll ever be safely reunited with his father. I won't give away the ending, but suffice it to say that Nemo ends up getting lucky—several times.

Alternative approaches to dealing with widespread concerns over pensions and the adequacy of retirement saving seem to come down to one of three options: (1) providing information and allowing the chips to fall where they may, (2) putting constraints on flexibility in order to provide an "adequate" solution for all, or (3) finding a way to help people make reasonable choices without depriving them of their sense of control. A recent paper by Dick Thaler and Cass Sunstein (2003) lays out an interesting notion of "Paternalistic Liberalism" and offers a number of insights on how the latter may be achieved.

Clearly, much more work is needed to determine what types of information, and what methods of presentation, can be most helpful in enabling workers to make better financial decisions. A basic question that the author and her colleagues in Sweden may eventually be able to answer in future work is how actual saving or portfolio decisions of Swedes relate to an individual's familiarity with the new pension system. I look forward to the author's future work and her continued contributions on this important topic.

Note

1. Of course the unresolved issue with either method of accounting is strict comparability across sources. A US$10,000 per year pension at age 65 from a private employer may not have the same "expected value" as a US$10,000 per year pension at age 65 from the central government. Likewise, US$100,000 in assets in a DC pension that cannot be withdrawn may not have the same "present value" as US$100,000 in cash. Such differences reveal the existence of underlying complexities that neither a DB nor DC accounting system can simplify away.

References

Sethi-Iyengar, S., G. Huberman, and W. Jiang. 2004. "How Much Choice Is Too Much? Contributions to 401(K) Retirement Plans." In *Pension Design and Structure: New Lessons from Behavioral Finance*, ed. O. S. Mitchell and S. P. Utkus, 83–95. Oxford: Oxford University Press.

Thaler, R. H., and C. R. Sunstein. 2003. "Paternalistic Liberalism." *American Economic Review* 93 (2): 175–9.

Chapter 14

Lashed to the Mast?
The Politics of NDC Pension Reform

Sarah M. Brooks and R. Kent Weaver*

IN THE FINAL DECADES OF THE TWENTIETH CENTURY, governments around the world began to dramatically change the form and function of old-age pension systems. These reforms were generally motivated by a combination of population aging, slowing economic growth, and tightening budget constraints; together these led both to rising pension costs and to declining resources with which governments could finance old-age pension liabilities.[1]

Many governments responded to these pressures by revising the parameters of traditional defined benefit pay-as-you-go (PAYG) public pension systems with incremental changes to contribution or benefit rates, retirement age, or indexation rules to keep pension systems in line with changing economic and demographic trends and state fiscal capacity. Other governments, however, opted for more fundamental, structural revisions of the design and objectives of old-age pension systems through the creation of mandatory individual, financial defined contribution (FDC) pension schemes, wherein pension benefits are based on individual contributions to a (typically) privately managed pension fund, and the market return to capital on those funds. Throughout the 1990s, the ideas and technology behind funded pension schemes were disseminated broadly throughout the world. By the end of the decade, more than 20 countries, from South America to East Asia, Europe, and the Former Soviet Union had adopted funded, defined contribution pension schemes either as the dominant "pillar" in mandatory pension schemes, or as part of multipillar structural reforms.[2]

By the middle of the 1990s, however, a new model of structural pension reform—the non-financial (or notional) defined contribution (NDC) scheme—had also emerged.[3] The

---

* Sarah M. Brooks is assistant professor of political science at Ohio State University; R. Kent Weaver is professor of public policy and government at Georgetown University and a senior fellow in the Governance Studies Program at the Brookings Institution.

The research reported herein was partially funded pursuant to a grant from the U.S. Social Security Administration (SSA) funded as part of the Retirement Research Consortium at Boston College. The opinions and conclusions are solely those of the authors and should not be construed as representing the opinions or policy of the SSA or any agency of the federal government. The authors would like to thank Daniele Franco, Agneta Kruse, and Edward Palmer for extensive and helpful comments on an earlier draft of this chapter.

NDC approach was the key feature of a national pension reform in Sweden that was adopted as framework legislation in 1994 and as final legislation in 1998. Italy, Latvia, and Poland followed Sweden's lead.

NDC pensions combine the PAYG financing that is characteristic of traditional defined benefit (DB) schemes with the defined contribution (DC) structure of individual accounts. NDC schemes tie benefits closely to individual contribution history over an entire working life, but credit those contributions with a notional interest rate tied to wage growth or overall economic growth rather than providing a return on specific financial assets. Notional accounts contain no real capital that can be claimed at retirement as a lump sum or that can purchase an annuity in the private market. Instead, at the time of retirement, the government converts the notional account balance into an annuity on the basis of cohort life expectancy, and finances this benefit on a PAYG basis.

Although NDC pension schemes represent an important departure from both the incremental reforms of DB schemes and from individual account, prefunded DC models, many of the individual elements of the NDC scheme design that allow it to control costs are not new; they have been utilized on an ad hoc and often temporary basis in incremental reforms to PAYG-DB pension schemes. The originality of the NDC model lies primarily in combining those elements into a coherent package with a clear policy objective, and imbuing that package with presumed perpetuity.

A number of "good policy" arguments have been advanced for adopting NDC measures. First, proponents cite the enhanced "fairness" associated with the DC formula over DB schemes that base retirement benefits on the last salary or last few years' wages, which tend to redistribute implicitly toward high-income workers with steeper earnings profiles. NDC schemes make any redistribution more explicit by removing it from the main NDC pillar of the pension scheme and creating a separate scheme with the objective of reducing poverty. Second, supporters of NDC-based reforms argue that the tighter link between contributions and benefits signals to workers that it is important to work longer to secure an adequate pension, thus enhancing system financing along with individual responsibility and work effort. Third, NDC-based reforms ensure a long-term balance between pension contributions and payouts. Fourth, NDC reforms do not expose individuals to short- and medium-term fluctuations in market returns and annuity prices that may arise in FDC individual accounts. Fifth—and of particular importance to government finance ministries—NDC pension reforms may provide a fiscally attractive alternative to funding the transition to funded DC plans because they do not require government to finance benefits for a transitional generation as a country moves to a system of funded individual accounts.

A final potential advantage offered by NDC reform is the perception of permanency, and hence credibility, that it imparts to the social security system. By reducing the need for governments to intervene regularly to adjust pension system parameters, the "political risk" of policy change in response to political pressures associated with public pension systems is significantly reduced. Indeed, the repeated tinkering with rules of DB systems in many countries has made those systems much less of a "defined benefit" in practice than in theory, especially for future retirees whose benefits are most likely to be affected. The sense of ownership felt by workers who receive regular statements tracking their rising notional account balances reinforces this sense of permanency of the NDC scheme. The resulting sense of property rights may create a "lock-in" effect that deters politicians from intervening to arbitrarily reduce or confiscate the notional capital accumulated in the NDC accounts.

On the negative side, however, because NDC schemes accommodate increasing longevity completely through benefit reductions, stabilizing pension contribution rates will lead to gradual erosion of pension values as populations age if workers do not postpone their retirement.

This discussion of potential "lock in" and political risk suggests that political calculations as well as policy advantages and disadvantages may play a very important role in policy makers' calculations on NDC-based reforms. Indeed, the central working hypothesis in this chapter is that NDC-based pension systems offer important *political* advantages to politicians in an era when credit-claiming opportunities in pension policy are few and blame-avoiding incentives are strong. In particular, NDC-based systems:

- Provide a "clean hands" mechanism that lowers replacement rates as the system is phased in while allowing politicians to avoid blame.
- Obfuscate the degree of future retrenchment because it is not known in advance, but rather depends on future economic and demographic developments.
- Avoid having to repeatedly deal with pension retrenchment and refinancing in the future.

In short, the complexity and automaticity of the NDC scheme creates important opportunities to limit traceability and blame for benefit retrenchment: automatic adjustment mechanisms based on economic and demographic trends absolve politicians of responsibility for potential future benefit reductions. Like Ulysses in resisting the Sirens, governments may be able to "lash themselves to mast" of a fixed contribution rate and automatic adjustment mechanisms, resisting temptations to pay unsustainable benefits to current and future retirees.

The adoption of NDC schemes may also generate new political risks, however, because they accommodate increased liabilities (such as those from unanticipated longevity gains) or revenue shortfalls (for example, those due to wage decline) by reducing benefits. To the extent that benefit values for younger birth cohorts fall short of public expectations about the absolute and relative value of pensions, politicians may confront a powerful political backlash as populations age. This may in turn lead to a "loosening of the lashes" on contribution rates and automatic adjustments, to contributions to the system from the general government budget, and/or to pressure for enhanced "social protection" pensions outside the NDC pillar.

The spread of NDC-based pension reforms thus raises important questions both for social science theory and for pension policy making. From the perspective of social science theory, NDC-based pension reforms represent an important example of what Jon Elster has called "pre-commitment" or "self-binding" efforts to limit future options in a way that furthers their long-term interests. Indeed, Elster uses the Ulysses and the Sirens metaphor in much of his writing on precommitment (Elster 1979, 2000). NDC-based pension reforms can also be seen as a combination of several blame-avoiding strategies that allows politicians to reconcile their policy and political objectives by making politically risky decisions through what Kent Weaver (1986, 1988) has called "automatic government" mechanisms rather than by requiring politicians to make those decisions openly. Thus NDC systems do not represent a departure from the common practice in PAYG-DB pension systems of making hard-to-detect revisions, such as revisions to indexation rates, in order to achieve fiscal and policy goals.

Examining the adoption and implementation of NDC-based pension reforms provides an opportunity to examine how agenda-limiting precommitment mechanisms are adopted and how they operate in practice. Two questions are addressed in this study. First, are NDC-based reforms more likely to get on the agenda and win adoption in some countries than in others? If so, is it the characteristics of a country's current pension system, the political ideology of elites, or the characteristics of the political system—or some combination of these and other factors—that determines whether countries consider and adopt NDC-based reforms? Second, do NDC-based reforms actually succeed in de-politicizing painful and costly pension retrenchment decisions and limiting blame to incumbent politicians, or do they have a tendency to spark resistance that undercuts their intended effects?

In the first section of the chapter we briefly outline the characteristics of NDC pension systems, arguing that NDC pension schemes should be seen as a set of principles that may be more or less closely followed in practice. The second section develops a framework for analyzing why NDC pension systems have increasingly been on the agenda in recent years and discusses conditions that facilitate considering and adopting NDC-based reform, including the complex question of why there has been a stronger move toward adopting NDC in some countries and regions than others. The third section of the chapter examines implementation challenges that may arise in NDC systems as they are adopted and mature, as well as their political sustainability. The final section of the chapter assesses the prospects for a further spread of NDC pension systems. In short, the chapter asks whether and under what conditions adoption of NDC pensions is likely to be an effective means of allowing politicians to "lash themselves to the mast" of a stabilized contribution rate and depoliticize the process of pension retrenchment. This, in turn, plays into the broader question of whether NDC-based reforms are likely to play a major role in addressing the immense aging issue facing both developed and developing societies in coming decades.

How NDC Works

Although the NDC system represents a synthesis of the PAYG-DB and FDC systems, it differs from these in the way it apportions risk and reward, and in its likely political consequences. Although notional accounts share with FDC schemes a tight link between pension benefits and individual contributions, NDC systems are by design not advance funded.[4] As noted above, NDC schemes also differ markedly from FDC systems in their treatment of capital market risks. NDC systems diminish individuals' exposure to fluctuations in market rates of return and annuity prices associated with privately managed funded-DC schemes by using a notional interest rate. Workers in NDC schemes continue to be exposed to significant demographic risks, however, such as unanticipated gains in longevity during working life, and to sustained declines in fertility around the time of retirement. By shrinking the overall contribution base to the pension system, such trends would cause declines in pension benefits to maintain overall financial balance of the NDC system.[5] At the same time, the annual indexation of annuities to wage growth exposes retired workers to the risk of declines in benefits if wages and productivity fall.

NDC systems also differ from traditional DB schemes in important ways, as shown in the first and fourth columns of table 14,1, which show different gradations of DB and NDC pension schemes. But as the second and third columns of the table show, a number of "middle positions" between DB and NDC pension schemes are possible on many of these key elements of pension system design. Some elements associated with NDC pension systems, such as life expectancy adjustments, have been enacted as ad hoc reforms of existing DB pension systems (column 2). And NDC-based systems sometimes take a "weak" or "partial" form, with one or more provisions that make them less than fully self-sustaining or inclusive (column 3). Table 14.1 divides these elements of pension system structure into four categories: *structural features, coverage, time horizon,* and *exclusivity*.

Table 14.1. Non-financial Pension Provisions As a Continuum from Defined Benefit to Defined Contribution

Provision	Defined benefit	Middle position DB reforms	"Weak" or "Partial" NDC	"Strong" or "full" NDC
Structural features				
Funding	Entirely PAYG	May have some advanced funding, usually for liquidity purposes	Entirely PAYG	Reserves built up for large demographic cohorts, to hold transfers from general budget and for long-term system balance
Years of earnings and contributions incorporated in benefit rule	Can include anything from no work (but residency or nationality) requirement to specified years of contributions (including "best years" and "final salary" arrangements)	Replacement rate based on number of years that corresponds to the entire working life for typical worker	May include some nonfinanced credits for non-work activities	Full link between contributions and earnings
Life expectancy at retirement	No provision in benefit calculation	Inclusion of "demographic factor" in benefit calculation to fully or partially compensate for population aging	Infrequent or incomplete (for example, exclusion of postretirement) adjustment for increases in longevity; no automatic mechanism to correct for incomplete changes	Benefit levels adjust fully (including current retirees) and automatically for increases in longevity
Retirement age	Fixed standard retirement age (may include actuarial adjustments for earlier or later retirement; may be ad hoc increases in retirement age over time)	Flexible retirement age and/or automatic increases in retirement age to fully or partially compensate for longevity increases	Minimum age to claim benefit, but no standard retirement age. Inadequate adjustment for earlier or later retirement	Minimum age to claim benefit, but no standard retirement age. Partial retirement possible. Full actuarial adjustment for earlier or later and partial retirement

Table 14.1. (continued)

Provision	Defined benefit	Middle position DB reforms	"Weak" or "Partial" NDC	"Strong" or "full" NDC
Inflation and economic growth	Benefits adjusted for inflation and/or earnings increases, sometimes with ad hoc changes to restrain costs	Benefits adjusted for inflation and/or earnings increases; indexation rule incorporates brakes for poor economic performance and high inflation, which may or may not be followed in practice	Benefits adjusted with inflation and/or earnings. Incomplete brakes for poor economic performance and/or government makes ad hoc adjustments in brake to enhance electoral prospects	Benefits adjusted with the internal rate of return, which is tied fully to earnings growth
Financing	May include payroll taxes and/or general revenues; revenues adjusted to needs of PAYG system on automatic or ad hoc basis	Payroll taxes fixed "in theory" at maximum target level (for example, below 10 percent in Canada, 20 percent in Germany) but may be revised in practice	Payroll tax rate with part of contribution rate used to cover pension rights granted but not covered by individual's own contribution	Fixed payroll tax rate; all contributions paid give an NDC account value, and all noncontributory rights are financed externally (for example, with general revenues)
Redistribution across generations	First generations generally winners as in "Ponzi" scheme	May be restricted within DB tiers by lowering replacement rates and tying contribution rates to level needed to be self-sustaining over long term	Credits given to some cohorts for which no contributions were made; possible generational redistribution due to shifting labor market	Possible generational redistribution due to shifting labor market

Redistribution within generations	Permitted within DB tier, based on limited number of "high years" on which benefits are based, higher replacement rates for low earners, credits given for which no contributions have been made	May be restricted within DB tiers by increasing number of years on which benefits are based, replaced, eliminating or reducing replacement rate differentials and limiting credits for nonwage activity	Some credits given for activities for which no contributions were made	Barred within NDC tier unless financed by payments from government or others with respect to nonemployment activity. Exception: NDC implicitly redistributes from men to women and other population subgroups with longer life expectancy if single annuitization table is used
Coverage	No NDC coverage	Not applicable	Only some sectors (for example, private sector) are covered by NDC system	All workers in specified age cohorts are covered by NDC system
Time horizon	No coverage of NDC system	Later cohorts of workers covered by "quasi-NDC" reforms (for example, life-expectancy adjustments to benefits or retirement age)	Only some cohorts (for example, new labor market entrants or those under age 50) covered by NDC system	All employed workers, including those in labor force at time NDC introduced, covered by NDC system
Exclusivity	No NDC pension tier	Not applicable	NDC-based pension is only one of several public pension tiers	NDC is only public pension tier

Source: Compiled by authors.

Structural Features

A wide range of variation is possible on multiple dimensions of the structural features of pension systems (table 14.2). For example, while most non-financial DB pension schemes operate solely on a PAYG basis, the Swedish NDC scheme incorporates "buffer funds" that prefund some benefits and protect against small dips in contributions and demographic bulges in the population of retirees.[6] Indeed, proponents of NDC argue that buffer funds should in principle be included in an NDC scheme (see Palmer 2006a).

Table 14.2. The NDC Pension Continuum in Practice

Provision	Sweden (NDC initiator; full NDC)	Poland (full NDC)	Germany (middle position DB)
Structural features			
Advanced funding	PAYG plus buffer fund partially accumulated under old pension system	PAYG plus buffer fund (surplus in 1st pillar + privatization revenue + 1% temporary contribution)	PAYG with general revenues and "eco-tax" as well as payroll tax; small "sustainability reserve"
Life expectancy at retirement	Unisex, account balances and benefits adjusted both before and after retirement	Unisex, but calculated for life expectancy at the age of retirement	Benefits adjust for changes in system dependency ratio
Retirement age	Flexible, with NDC and FDC pensions drawable no earlier than age 61; partial withdrawal possible	minimum: 60 (women) 65 (men)	Normal retirement age of 65; incentives for early retirement being reduced
Inflation and economic growth	Account balances and benefits adjusted for wage growth (initial benefit is higher than actuarial amount and adjusted for wage growth minus 1.6%)	Accumulation is wage growth plus labor force growth; annuities indexed to consumer prices, unless real wages are falling, in which case they are uprated in line with nominal wages (that is, cut in real terms)	Benefits adjusted for wage growth
Payroll tax rate	Fixed at 16% for NDC tier and 2.5% for FDC tier	12.22% to NDC 7.3% to FDC	Government commitment to hold contribution rate to no higher than 20% through 2020 and 22% through 2030
Redistribution across generations	Eliminated once NDC system is fully phased in	Minimal, through minimum pension guarantee	Modest, through DB formula
Redistribution within generations	In pension annuity, from shorter-lived to longer-lived pensioners, and from men to women	In pension annuity, from shorter-lived to longer-lived pensioners, and from men to women	In pension annuity, from shorter-lived to longer-lived pensioners, and from men to women

Table 14.2. (continued)

Provision	*Sweden* *(NDC initiator; full NDC)*	*Poland (full NDC)*	*Germany* *(middle position DB)*
Coverage	Universal	Not universal; separate programs for farmers and uniformed services	Universal
Time horizon	Persons born 1938–1953 receive benefits partially in old system. Persons born 1954 and later receive benefits entirely in new system	New system mandatory for all born beginning in 1949; FDC mandatory for people born after December 31, 1968	Phases in beginning in 2005
Exclusivity	No. Combined with smaller FDC tier and inflation-indexed guarantee pension for those with low lifetime earnings	No. Combined with FDC system, plus tax-financed minimum pension supplement (for minimum 25 years' contributions) if NDC+FDC annuities are below minimum	No. Quasi-mandatory private pillar and "zero-pillar" added

Source: Information on Poland is from Góra and Rutkowski (2000) and Chłoń-Domińczak and Góra (2006); information on Germany is from Börsch-Supan and Wilke (2006); information on Sweden is from Sweden, National Social Insurance Board (2004).

With respect to population aging—and in particular rising life expectancy at retirement—PAYG-DB schemes generally do not provide for automatic adjustments to the changing demographic, social, and economic context in which the system is embedded. Thus, as populations age, the schemes may require periodic government intervention to adjust benefit levels or retirement ages. NDC schemes automatically accommodate changes in life expectancy by calculating annuities on the basis of individual accumulations and life expectancy at the time of retirement. But such measures can also be included in DB schemes to partially or fully adjust for population aging, for example the Kohl government's "demographic factor" enacted as part of a short-lived pension reform and the "sustainability factor" enacted by the Schröder government.[7] Similarly, public PAYG-DB schemes generally include a fixed standard retirement age, usually with some sort of adjustment (which varies greatly across countries in its actuarial accuracy) for earlier or later retirement. A number of countries have raised the standard age in recent years in response to population aging. The Swedish NDC scheme, on the other hand, has replaced the standard retirement age with flexible retirement age (pensions can be drawn no earlier than age 61), no upward age at which pension rights can be earned, and with the benefit based on the life expectancy of the retiree's birth cohort at the time of retirement. But NDC-like proposals have also been made for retirement age changes in public PAYG-DB, such as proposals in the United States that would raise the age for receipt of "full" social security entitlements as longevity increases.

Perhaps the most distinctive attribute of NDC pension systems is the fixing of a long-term contribution rate and the dependence of pension adjustments on the size of the wage base. With this "lashing to the mast" of contribution rates, future adjustments to keep pension systems sound must in theory be made on the benefit side. For DB pensions operated on PAYG basis, on the other hand, payroll tax contribution rates and benefit levels are usually adjusted on an ad hoc basis as current funding needs change. A number of countries also use general revenues or some other form of revenue (for example, the German eco-tax) to finance part of their PAYG-DB pension system costs. Given increased longevity in most countries and flagging employment growth in a number of countries, there has been strong upward pressure on DB pension contribution rates over the past 30 years.[8]

In response to this trend, many countries have in recent years tried to stabilize contribution rates to their DB pensions through a variety of mechanisms. In Canada, for example, the federal and provincial governments have pledged to keep payroll taxes under 10 percent in the long term; if benefit costs are projected to exceed that target within a specified projection period, a combination of benefit cuts and contribution rate increases is automatically triggered.[9] Germany, where pension contribution rates grew to over 20 percent of earnings in recent years, has also acted to try to stabilize contribution rates at no more than 20 percent through the year 2020 and 22 percent through 2030.[10] In the United States, congressional Republicans made it very clear at the time of the 1983 Social Security rescue package that they would tolerate no further increases in contribution rates, and there have been none.[11] In short, even without the explicit "lashing to the mast" of contribution rates associated with NDC pension reforms, public non-financial DB systems can and have undertaken a number of actions to stabilize contribution rates.

Non-financial DB and NDC pension systems also differ significantly in their potential for intergenerational redistribution. DB pensions typically offer a much higher rate of return on contributions to the first generations in the program, when the ratio of contributors to beneficiaries is much higher than in later generations (especially as longevity increases). NDC pensions, on the other hand, are intended to restrict intergenerational redistribution. However, several PAYG-DB pension schemes, notably in Canada and the United States, have also moved to restrict intergenerational redistribution by making very long term projections of contribution rates and benefit costs and developing contribution rates and benefit levels that are intended to be stable over that projection period with the support of reserve funds.[12]

In principle, NDC schemes treat all contributions to the system the same way in terms of accruing credits (with adjustments for wage or—as in Italy—GDP growth over time): only actual contributions accrue credits, and all credits result in equal payouts (actuarially adjusted for life expectancy at retirement). If credits are granted for other reasons, they must be accompanied by financing from general tax revenues, or the financial equilibrium of the system will be jeopardized. Even NDC systems may contain some elements of intragenerational redistribution in payout, however, notably in the use of gender-neutral annuitization tables that do not reflect real gender differences in life expectancy.

Many PAYG-DB schemes include more complex patterns of intragenerational redistribution. Some countries, notably the United States, offer higher replacement rates for the first dollars of earnings, effectively offering a higher replacement rate for low earners. Many PAYG-DB schemes also base benefits on a contributor's highest or final number of earnings years (for example, the highest three, fifteen, or twenty years). To the extent that the benefit formula is based on final salary or only the latest years' earnings, it privileges workers with a steeper career-earnings profile. Such workers are typically the most affluent and better educated in society. In recent years, public PAYG-DB pension systems in many countries have been altered to limit redistribution within generations in some ways, for example by lengthening the number of contribution years used in calculating pension entitlements or by flattening replacement rate differentials across earnings levels. But there has also been a widespread expansion in noncontributory credits given for caregiving in a number of countries.

The use by NDC schemes of a benefit formula based on contributions over the entire career both diminishes the degree of *regressive* redistribution caused by final salary benefit formulas and at the same time eliminates the possibility for *progressive* redistribution of pension benefits. The overall progressivity of an NDC-based retirement income system thus depends critically on the existence of mechanisms within or outside the NDC component to progressively reapportion risk and benefits to those who are the least well off. This can be done in either of two ways. First, contributions can be made for individuals that increase their benefit entitlement. In Sweden, for example, contributions are made into the system for periods spent in providing childcare, military service, unemployment, sickness and disability covered by public social insurance, and for compensated parental leave and higher education. The money to finance these credits is transferred from the general budget to the NDC reserve fund on a yearly basis. Partial NDC reforms have imputed credits without financing them immediately, but these elements require a future tax-based transfer burden to make the system sustainable. Second, changes may be made in other tiers of the retirement income system that add or "reinvent" existing redistributive elements, such as by topping-up benefits to a minimally guaranteed level. To date, all countries introducing NDC schemes have constructed a minimum benefit guarantee financed from general revenues. Indeed, without an adjustment of other pension tiers to ease the transition to NDC, the distributional change resulting from a change to NDC is likely to impose such heavy costs on some groups that its chances of winning adoption and being sustained are substantially reduced.

Time Horizon

Pension reforms can also be distinguished by their phase-in periods. The U.S. increase of retirement age from 65 to 67, for example, is being phased in over almost 40 years from the time it was enacted to the time it will be fully in effect. To date, countries implementing NDC reforms also show great differences in the time horizon over which they phase in their reforms. NDC reforms can be applied to rights acquired under the previous system, if adequate contribution records exist.[13] In the Swedish reform legislated between 1994 and 1998, for example, all workers born after 1953 are entirely in the new system; earlier cohorts born between 1937 and 1953 are partially in the new system. In Italy, on the other hand, only new entrants to the labor market will have their benefits fully calculated under the new NDC rules. A longer phase-in period is likely to weaken opposition from the most attentive publics—the elderly and the near-elderly—but it also lessens near-term budgetary savings from reform.

Coverage

Countries can also differ in the degree to which the NDC system will apply to all members of the workforce when it is fully phased in. Excluding key sectors (for example, the military, or, as in Poland, farmers) from a shift to NDC may help governments manage the politics of reform, although doing so clearly raises questions of equitable treatment. It will also mean that career changes into a sector covered by NDC can entail losing benefit privileges in the sector from which workers migrate.

Exclusivity

Most countries have multipillar pension systems. Thus even when an NDC system is fully phased in, it may not be the sole, or even the largest, source of public pension income. The 1994 pension reform in Sweden, for example, created a multipillar pension scheme in which the average wage worker could expect to receive a retirement pension from an NDC account and a mandatory individual financial DC account. There is also a *garantipension* financed from general revenues for low-wage workers and workers with interrupted earnings histories, which tops up their accumulated pension accounts to a socially acceptable minimum. The NDC tier is dominant, however—financed by a 16 percent payroll contribution, compared with a contribution of 2.5 percent of covered wages into financial (that is, funded) individual accounts. The Polish government similarly adopted a mixed NDC and funded-DC scheme, wherein 15 percent of covered wages are credited to the first (NDC) pillar and indexed with a notional interest rate equal to growth in the covered wage bill. Nine percent of covered wages are transferred to the funded scheme in Poland, and invested according to market principles.[14] The Latvian pension reform also combines an NDC pillar with a financial DC scheme. The NDC pillar was financed with contributions of 20 percent of covered wages from the outset. The individual financial account scheme, which came into force in 2001, initially received 2 percent of covered wages, while contributions to the NDC component decreased to 18 percent. Following a transition schedule specified in the law, the split will be 10 percent and 10 percent by 2010.[15]

Overall, the preceding discussion suggests that a political analysis of NDC pension systems must recognize that the boundaries between and NDC and non-financial DB pensions are fuzzy rather than sharp. Not only have certain elements of NDC, such as life-expectancy adjustments, been used since the mid-1990s on an ad hoc basis in incremental DB reforms, but also countries such as Italy have adopted partial NDC reforms in ways that may be unstable in the medium or long terms. In the case of Italy, for example, the government imputes contributions to notional accounts for some groups higher than those that are actually made. At the same time, the Italian system does not have automatic stabilizers, nor does it automatically take into account pre- or postretirement increases in longevity. Finally, Italy has established an inflexible rate of return on accumulated contributions, raising questions about the medium- to long-term stability of the system.[16] If incomplete adoption of NDC is possible, so too, presumably, is an incomplete dismantling: thus an analysis of NDC politics must also include an assessment of the risks of an ad hoc unraveling of NDC reforms.

Despite the tighter link between contributions and benefits, NDC schemes may nonetheless bear the heavy imprint of political values, objectives, and concessions to powerful domestic political groups. Governments may intervene in the accumulation phase of the NDC system, for instance, to credit socially valued activities that are not rewarded by markets, such as the provision of credits for child rearing, education, and military service. At the same time, powerful groups such as the military or specific industrial sectors may claim privileges within the NDC framework to the extent that governments credit notional accounts for workers in these sectors to finance special benefits such as early retirement.[17] The use of unisex mortality tables likewise represents a political decision to redistribute from men to women. At the same time, NDC systems usually redistribute credits of workers who die before retirement to other workers within the same cohort, rather than to the workers' surviving family members. This redistribution of credits represents a political judgment in which the claim of survivors within the family is weighed against those of workers within the cohort, to whom such credits are apportioned.

The Politics of NDC Innovation, Diffusion, and Adoption

The discussion above suggests some important general propositions about the politics of adopting NDC-focused pension reforms. First, it suggests that although NDC-based reforms have some features that may be politically attractive for reelection oriented politicians—in particular, such reforms enhance the capacity for politicians to distance themselves from long-term benefit and eligibility cuts—they are not without political drawbacks as well.

Second, it suggests that the attitudes of important actors in pension reform politics—notably finance ministries, trade unions, and groups representing retirees—are likely to be heavily influenced by what else is in the pension reform package, particularly by what protections are afforded to the aged through the provision of income-tested pensions or supplemental DC pensions to compensate for any losses, and who is expected to pay for the costs for those parts of the reform package.

Third, this analysis suggests that proponents of an NDC-based reform may be able to affect the political prospects for reform through specific design features in the reform. In particular, the pace of transition strongly influences the degree and visibility of the material and distributive effects of NDC reforms, and thus the political viability of these measures. If a reform is phased in quickly, the terms of the new scheme are not only more costly and transparent, they are also at greater risk of political backlash. Other features of NDC program design that are likely to affect a proposal's political prospects include the specific provisions of other pension tiers and how they compensate any losers from the shift to NDC (for example, the creation of new income-tested pensions), as well as which groups (for example, civil servants or the military), if any, are excluded from this shift. There may also be significant battles over whether and how much to provide credits for non-wage-related benefits within an NDC pension scheme, as well as over the question of who should pay for those credits.

Finally, the politics of NDC adoption and rejection is likely to be a moving target. How politicians perceive and react to NDC proposals is likely to evolve over time as the concept is diffused more broadly among technocratic elites and as experience with implementing NDC-based pension regimes grows.

This very general overview of the calculus of key actors does not take us very far, however, toward understanding why NDC pension reforms are likely to get on the government's agenda and win adoption in some countries and not in others, let alone whether an NDC-based reform will be sustained once it has been adopted. To understand these cross-national variations and how they are likely to evolve over time it is important first to introduce contextual factors that vary across countries, notably the severity of the challenges that extant pension systems face, the weight of various social actors, and the barriers that a political system imposes to instituting major reforms. Second, it is important to take a process-oriented approach, distinguishing between the forces that are critical at different stages of NDC politics: (1) initial development of the NDC idea and its first application, (2) diffusion of the concept to the agendas of other countries, (3) adoption or rejection of the NDC idea once it is on a government's agenda in a specific country, and (4) sustaining an NDC reform once it is in place. Third, it is important to examine whether NDC is adopted fully or partially—that is, to examine the structural features, coverage, time horizon, and exclusivity of NDC-based schemes in particular countries. Thus we can imagine a continuum of outcomes ranging from early "full" adoption of NDC-based reform to partial and/or later adoption, to consideration and rejection of NDC-based reforms, or to the issue never even making it onto the agenda, as shown in table 14.3. (Of course, countries may shift over time between categories.) Since the NDC "innovation" is now well developed, we will focus on the diffusion of NDC-based reforms and their full or partial adoption or rejection.[18] Sustaining implementation of NDC-based reforms will be considered in the next section of the chapter.

Table 14.3. Potential Relationships between Structural Variables and NDC Choice

Constraints on NDC adoption and diffusion	Innovation	Early "full" adoption	Partial and/or nonexclusive adoption	Later adoption	Consideration but rejection	Never reaches agenda
Economic/ demographic constraints						
Aging pressure	+ Very strong demographic aging pressures	+ Very strong demographic aging pressures	+ Strong demographic aging pressures	+ Moderate but increasing demographic aging pressures	+ Moderate demographic aging pressures	+ Weak demographic aging pressures
Fiscal pressure	+ Very high budget deficits and debt/GDP ratio	+ High budget deficits and debt/GDP ratio	+ Funded DC likely to play relatively larger role than NDC in multitier system where budget deficits and debt/GDP ratio are low	+ Moderate but increasing budget deficits and debt/GDP ratio	+ Declining budget pressure and debt/GDP ratio	+ Low budget deficits and debt/GDP ratio
Payroll tax rates	+ Very high payroll tax rates	+ Very high payroll tax rates	+ High payroll tax rates	+ High or rising payroll tax rates		– Low payroll tax rates or no payroll tax
Ideational forces						
Strength of domestic forces favoring market-based pension reform	+ Political forces favoring state-focused public pension system are strong	– Funded DC rather than NDC more likely to be adopted where ideologically conservative forces are very strong	+ Funded DC likely to play relatively larger role than NDC in multitier system where ideologically conservative forces are fairly strong	+ Parties favoring continued state focus in public pension system gain strength after period of stalemate		+ Funded DC rather than NDC more likely to be adopted where ideologically conservative forces are very strong

Participation in regional networks where NDC ideas common	Not applicable	+ Participation in regional networks with earlier adopters; elites view earlier adopters as peer countries	+ Participation in regional networks with earlier adopters; elites view earlier adopters as peer countries	+ Country does not participate in regional networks including early adopters = Regional network effect should dissipate as NDC ideas are fully diffused internationally		+ Country is outside regional networks of early NDC adopters = Regional network effect should dissipate as NDC ideas are fully diffused internationally
Interaction with international financial institutions and other supranational organizations	Not applicable	+ Supranational institutions: (1) press for pension expenditure reductions and (2) introduce and support NDC-based reforms	+ Supranational institutions: (1) press for pension expenditure reductions and (2) introduce and support NDC-based reforms	+ Supranational institutions press for pension expenditure cuts and support NDC-based reforms, but have limited bargaining leverage	+ Supranational institutions press for pension expenditure cuts and support NDC-based reforms, but have limited bargaining leverage	+ Low contact with IFIs − IFIs support FDC-based reforms only
Policy feedbacks						
Strong earnings-related pension tier	+ Strong earnings-related component in pension system + High replacement rates	+ Strong earnings-related component in pension system + High replacement rates	+ Mix of redistribution and earnings-related principles in current public pension system		− Flat-rate benefit in current public pension scheme	+ Prior adoption of FDC reform + Flat-rate benefit in current DB
Replacement rates	+ High replacement rates	+ High replacement rates	+ High replacement rates	+ Medium replacement rates		+ Low replacement rates
Payroll tax records	+ Complete payroll tax records	+ Complete payroll tax records	+ Complete or improving payroll tax records	+ Incomplete but improving payroll tax records	− Incomplete payroll tax records	− Incomplete or nonexistent payroll tax records

Table 14.3. (continued)

Constraints on NDC adoption and diffusion	Innovation	Early "full" adoption	Partial and/or nonexclusive adoption	Later adoption	Consideration but rejection	Never reaches agenda
Political/partisan constraints						
Multiple veto points in political system	– Multiple veto points in political system	– Multiple veto points in political system	+ Multiple veto points in political system	+ Multiple veto points in political system	+ Multiple veto points in political system	
Availability of cartelizing mechanisms	+ Strong political mechanisms available to overcome interest group opposition to losses resulting from NDC-based reform	+ Strong political mechanisms available to overcome interest group opposition to losses resulting from NDC-based reform	+ Moderately strong political mechanisms available to overcome interest group opposition to losses resulting from NDC-based reform	+ Moderately strong political mechanisms available to overcome interest group opposition to losses resulting from NDC-based reform	+ Weak political mechanisms available to overcome interest group opposition to losses resulting from NDC-based reform	+ Weak or nonexistent political mechanisms available to overcome interest group opposition to losses resulting from NDC-based reform

Source: Compiled by authors.

Note: + condition makes it more likely that country will be in this category; – condition makes it less likely that country will be in this category; = condition that is likely to become less important as NDC innovation is diffused; blank cells indicate no hypothesized relationship between this condition and outcome category.

Agenda Setting and Adoption

A critical component of any policy reform process is formulating the policy problem in such a way that the issue achieves agenda status. To Kingdon (1995), policy proposals are likely to reach and remain on a government's agenda only if they appear to be broadly congruent with the values of policy makers and the public, as well as politically feasible, affordable, and likely to make some improvement in a perceived policy problem. Of course, successful coupling of these dimensions is typically the work of a skilled policy entrepreneur. To Orenstein (2000), such "proposal actors" are critical in establishing the "intellectual agenda" of a reform. In addition to putting reform on the political agenda, proposal actors introduce new policy innovations and delimit the feasible range of policy outcomes for the country.[19] Examining structural pension reforms in Eastern Europe and Central Asia, Orenstein found that where there are fewer, and more like-minded, proposal actors, the possibility for adopting an ambitious structural reform was greatly enhanced. Importantly, however, while incorporating a broader range of interests in the early stages of reform (such as where disparate interest groups and government ministries advance reform proposals) tends to diminish the magnitude and pace of reform, to the extent that broad agreement (or "buy-in") is achieved during the agenda-setting phase, both the implementation and the longer-term prospects for sustainability are enhanced.[20] Accordingly, we examine in the next sections the key factors shaping whether and to what extent countries move toward NDC pension reform. These include (1) whether the *problem* or challenge of structural pension reform is brought onto the national agenda and how the problem is defined by key actors, (2) whether the specific *policy alternative* of NDC pension reform is one of the options considered by policy makers, and (3) how *policy feedbacks* from existing pension regimes as well as (4) the structure of *political institutions* shape both the alternatives considered and the prospects for NDC adoption.

In examining the first factor, we look at the extent to which governments are pressed to reform state pension schemes by varying degrees of demographic change, budgetary constraints, and macroeconomic pressures. Second, we discuss how exposure to, and hence adoption of, NDC ideas are influenced by the strength of various domestic ideological groupings as well as countries' interaction with supranational institutions such as the European Union and the World Bank. In looking at the third factor, we examine how feedbacks from prior policy choices may make considering and adopting NDC-based reforms more or less likely, such as by shaping how the problem and its feasible solutions are perceived, and by influencing the political coalitions that have developed around current policies. Last, we examine how the structure of political institutions and political competition affect both the political advantages and costs associated with NDC systems, and hence the likely barriers to policy change.[21]

Table 14.3 outlines hypothesized relationships between specific variables and several possible outcomes (for example, first innovation with NDC, early adoption, partial adoption, consideration and rejection of NDC, NDC never reaching agenda), while table 14.4 develops an informal "scorecard" of the relationship between causes and outcomes. Specifically, the table highlights the hypothesized relationship between our key variables and the outcomes achieved by several countries with respect to NDC reform (for example, with Sweden as innovator, Italy as a partial adopter of NDC, Uruguay as a country that rejected NDC in favor of a mix of DB and DC, and the United States representing a country where NDC has not yet reached the agenda).

Economic-Demographic Pressures for System Change

The wave of structural pension reforms that began in the 1980s and swelled in the 1990s has been widely attributed to significant demographic and economic changes, which

Table 14.4. Country Characteristics and NDC Reform Outcomes

Country	Sweden	Italy	Germany	Uruguay	United States
Outcome	Full NDC system adopted	Partial NDC system adopted with long phase-in	Elements of NDC adopted, retracted, and readopted	Mixed DB-funded DC reform	NDC not on agenda
Economic/demographic constraints					
Aging pressure (% population 65+ in parentheses)	Very high (17.4%)	Very high (17.8%)	Very high (16.1%)	High (12.9%)	High (12.3%)
Fiscal pressure	Very strong in early 1990s	Very strong	Very strong	Very strong	Moderate
Payroll tax rates (total payroll tax rates in parentheses)	High (26.09%)	Very high (41.11%)	Very high (40.91%)	Very high (35.5%)	Moderate (22.7%)
Ideational forces					
Strength of domestic forces favoring market-based pension reform	Weak	Weak	Fairly weak	Weak	Strong
Interaction with IFIs and other supranational organizations	No	No interaction with IFIs, but European Union pressure to reduce pension spending	No interaction with IFIs, but European Union pressure to reduce pension spending	Yes, with Inter-American Development Bank, which presented NDC option in 1992.	No
Participation in regional networks where NDC ideas are common	Became hub of network	Yes	Yes	No	No
Policy feedbacks					
Strong earnings-related pension tier	Yes	Yes	Yes	Yes	Yes
Replacement rates	Very high	Very high	Very high	High	Moderate
Complete payroll tax records	Yes	Yes	Yes	No	Yes
Political/partisan constraints					
Multiple veto points in political system?	Weak	Strong	Weak	Strong	Strong
Mechanisms for overcoming policy gridlock?	Strong	Mixed	Declining	Weak	Weak

Source: For data on aging and payroll tax rates: U.S. Social Security Administration, *Social Security Programs Throughout the World,* most recent editions.

raised the specter (and reality) of wide deficits in social security budgets and tighter pressures on overall government spending. These developments have clearly had a major impact on pension reform agendas.

Aging populations are a critical source of pressure for change in pension schemes. Most countries operate their pension systems on a PAYG basis, even where there is a dedicated payroll tax for pensions. Falling birthrates and life expectancy increases mean that there are fewer workers to support each retiree—a trend that is only expected to increase in future years. Demographic challenges vary significantly across nations, however.[22] In general, we would expect that countries that have had a high percentage of their populations over age 65 for an extended period would be most likely to have exhausted incremental retrenchment and contribution reforms and be more likely to consider NDC and other sorts of fundamental pension restructuring initiatives. Consistent with this hypothesis, many of the early adopters of NDC (notably Sweden and Italy) are among the world's oldest societies.

Fiscal concerns also increased pressure for austerity in public pension systems. Rising government deficits and debt to GDP ratios are clearly likely to raise pressures for pension reform. But the effects of such a fiscal crunch are complex. Indeed, a quantitative study of 57 developed and developing countries has shown that countries with a high public debt to GDP ratio are *less* likely to privatize their pension programs (at least when pension liabilities are low or moderate), because they cannot afford the transitional costs associated with moving from a public PAYG to fully funded individual accounts.[23] For example, Pinheiro (2004, pp. 112, 134) argues that Brazil's rejection of privatization in the late 1990s stemmed in large part from the high transition costs implied by such a measure. A plausible hypothesis is that a shift to NDC is most likely to at least get on government's agenda where (1) a government faces severe fiscal pressure, *and* (2) a high debt to GDP ratio and/or current fiscal pressures inhibit a move to funded DC.

Strong concerns about economic competitiveness sparked in particular by high payroll tax rates may also increase interest in NDC-based reforms. Higher capital tax rates are also severely constrained as a revenue source.[24] NDC-based reforms offer the opportunity to "lash policy to the mast" of a permanently fixed pension payroll tax, while the exact implications of that change for individual beneficiaries is made contingent on future economic and demographic developments. In general, we would expect countries that already have very high payroll tax rates along with the prospect of rapidly aging populations to be most likely to consider NDC. Countries without a preexisting payroll tax structure, like New Zealand, would be likely to find the transition to NDC politically and administratively very difficult. The data in table 14.4 suggest that consideration of NDC-based reforms is associated with countries with high or very high overall payroll tax rates.

Overall, there does appear to be an association between strong demographic, fiscal, and payroll tax rate pressures and the likelihood that an NDC-based reform reaches a country's policy agenda. Nevertheless, it is probably most accurate to infer from existing evidence that economic and demographic pressures are helpful in explaining when pension reform *generally* achieves agenda status, and when the alternative of a radical shift toward privatized individual accounts is less plausible. Thus, although demographic and economic pressures may have some impact on which policy responses are considered, they are insufficient to explain when NDC-based reforms in particular, rather than some other type of restructuring measure, are seriously considered or adopted.

Ideational and International Forces

In order to understand how and when the particular policy innovation of NDC pension reform is likely to be adopted in a given country, we must examine the ideational and international forces shaping the "policy stream," or range of options that are included in and excluded from serious policy debate.[25] At least three types of forces are important to the flow of pension reform ideas.

First, the "intellectual agenda" is likely to be influenced in a given country by the strength of the domestic political base for conservative ideological critics of public PAYG pensions. Specifically, we expect that proposals for pension privatization are likely to dominate debates over pension restructuring in countries where both the overall ideological climate and the ideology of the governing political elites is suspicious of governmental action and has strong faith in market solutions to policy problems. NDC solutions, by contrast, are more likely to be on the agenda where pressures for pension restructuring are strong but the national (and governing political party or coalition) ideological climate is more favorable to government and less favorable to privatization and individual accounts. Intermediate outcomes (for example, greater or lesser roles for NDC and FDC in a multi-pillar system) may occur when forces are more evenly balanced in a political system. Such prolonged haggling can in fact be observed in negotiations between the Social Democrats and nonsocialist parties over the relative sizes of the NDC and "premium pension" (FDC individual account) tiers within the new Swedish pension system.[26]

In addition to domestic sources of pension reform ideas, the policy models that gain agenda status may be "cued" from a second source: archetypal policy models or practices to which policy makers are exposed through informal regional networks of specialized policy elites.[27] Beyond the cognitive ease of looking to relevant examples rather than "reinventing the wheel," competitive and status concerns have entered prominently in the adoption of structural pension reforms in the past decade.[28] In particular, government technocrats draw information about the viability of a policy model from the experiences of relevant or "peer" nations. Such countries may be those that share similar structural conditions and policy regimes, or they may be those with common demographic, economic, or political structures. At the same time, peer nations may be those with which policy elites interact on a regular basis through regional organizations such as the European Union and the OECD, which actively promote policy diffusion—and harmonization—across member nations.[29]

All of these factors suggest that, at least initially, the dissemination of policy models is likely to be heavily regionalized—and available evidence confirms this hypothesis.[30] Just as the Latin American nations looked more to the Chilean model than to pension reformers in other regions, early adoption of the NDC system has been concentrated in Europe, with Italy, Latvia, and Poland among the early adopters, while recent German reforms contain elements of NDC, and NDC-inspired reforms are being considered in the Czech Republic and Norway. The effect of such regional networks as diffusion mechanisms may weaken over time, however, as NDC ideas become broadly disseminated through professional networks of pension experts.

A third source of ideas and pressures for specific courses of pension reform transcends regional networks; examples are "supranational" institutions such as the European Union (for member countries) and international financial institutions such as the World Bank and International Monetary Fund. Scholars have long attributed a central role to international organizations in shaping domestic policy processes around the world through the diffusion of norms and ideas.[31] We expect (1) that some form of structural pension reform is more likely to get on the agenda when a supranational institution sets deficit and debt reduction targets for participation in its programs, as in the case of the European Union; (2) that NDC in particular is more likely to get on a government's agenda when a government participates in institution-sponsored networks where NDC ideas are active; and (3) that governments are more likely to adopt an NDC-based reform when they anticipate that a shift to NDC will aid them in obtaining loan approval or another desired outcome from the institution.

Supranational institutions may influence a country's pension policy choice in several distinct ways, such as through loan conditionality (granting a loan is made contingent upon adoption of a specified policy), or by encouraging "anticipated reaction" (a country may adopt reforms that it thinks will win favorable action from the supranational institution). Alternatively, national policy elites may use perceived or alleged threats of negative actions by the supranational institution to win support for a policy change from reluctant domestic actors—in effect, making the international institution a "strategic scapegoat" in the reform process.[32] Supranational institutions also may act simply as agents of knowledge transfer for "best practices" from other countries. And last, such institutions may serve as a means of harmonization, encouraging member countries to develop common practices to lower regulatory barriers to labor and capital mobility.

Several of these channels can be seen in the pension austerity measures taken in European Union member countries. Perhaps most important, in countries such as Italy pension retrenchment was seen as necessary to meet the 3 percent of GDP target set for government deficit as a condition for entry into the European Monetary Union.[33] However, these actions by national policy makers largely took the form of "anticipated reactions" and strategic choices designed to win the acquiescence of domestic opponents of painful pension reforms.[34] The European Union has also set other requirements (for example, requiring gender neutrality in retirement ages) that have an impact on austerity policy choices and led indirectly to modest policy harmonization.

Moreover, the European Union has not even attempted to harmonize most aspects of the disparate pension systems of its member countries, and where it has tried to harmonize policies directly, notably in the area of supplemental pensions, it has had little success. Although some analysts have argued that NDC-based reforms could serve as a vehicle for pension harmonization in the European Union,[35] the European Commission itself has not endorsed such an approach. The absence of harmonization pressure within the European Union helps to explain the absence of overall policy convergence on NDC or any other single model for pension restructuring in Western Europe.

Despite the importance of the European Union among advanced industrial nations, few institutions have rivaled the global influence of the World Bank in disseminating the ideas and technology of multipillar pension reform. The World Bank's 1994 report *Averting the Old Age Crisis* brought unprecedented international attention to the issue of old-age pension reform, fundamentally transforming the way that policy makers conceptualized the issues and solutions to the challenges of old-age income reform. More concretely, the World Bank provided a knowledge base, resources to build institutional and technological capacity, financial support, and in some cases political cover (acting as "bad cop" to domestic politicians' "good cop") for governments to adopt some form of privately managed funded pension schemes.[36] Indeed, there is little doubt that the World Bank played a powerful role in promoting the adoption of structural DC pension reforms by disseminating policy ideas and technology to government technocrats. Moreover, by associating the shift from DB to DC (both financial and notional) structures with an array of micro- and macroeconomic benefits, World Bank actors generated strong attraction to DC pension reforms among finance ministry and central bank policy makers in disparate corners of the world.[37]

While the International Labor Organization (ILO) and International Social Security Association (ISSA) disseminated ideas in competition with the ideas of the World Bank, the Bank enjoyed important resource advantages over the ILO and ISSA, dedicating vastly greater human and financial resources to the research and dissemination of ideas and policy models based on the DC mechanisms.[38] Indeed, following the publication of its 1994 report, the World Bank social protection group launched a multiyear dissemination project, holding workshops and training seminars around the world. It likewise fostered cross-national policy sharing through a series of annual summer workshops that became a clearinghouse for pension reform ideas, bringing together academics, social security experts, and policy makers from around the world to build connections and share ideas about pension reform.

The World Bank has over the past five years shown a growing awareness of the shortcomings of FDC pensions in Latin America and elsewhere,[39] and has promoted the discussion of a wide range of pension reform models—in particular NDC-based reforms—rather than a single focus on FDC schemes. Indeed, the participation of social security experts from Sweden in these summer workshops opened up the NDC reform ideas to policy makers from far outside the original networks through which these ideas were carried in Europe. More generally, existing research provides little evidence to suggest that the loan conditionality has been the primary means through which international financial institutions have promoted social policy changes, including pension privatization or NDC-based reforms.[40] The predominant role of international financial institutions in influencing NDC and other pension reforms is in the agenda-setting process, by transmitting policy ideas and reform models through technocratic networks, rather than by coercing client governments to adopt specific reforms.

Policy Feedbacks

Once in place, public pension systems have a profound effect on subsequent battles over pension reform. The existing pension system defines not only the winners and losers of structural reform initiatives, but it also delimits the range and intensity of issues over which beneficiaries of the status quo will fight. The structure and performance of the current pension system affects several important aspects of policy choice, including public expectations about the "proper" role of the government and the "fair" level of redistribution in social security; the magnitude of vested interests in the status quo—that is, who stands to gain and lose and how much; and the cost structure and implicit pension debt associated with the current policy as well as the transitional cost of moving from an unfunded to a funded system. In short, policy feedbacks powerfully shape the agenda-setting process, making pension regime change heavily "path dependent."[41] Three policy parameters are *prima facie* likely to be conducive to both consideration and adoption of an NDC-based pension reform: (1) a strong earnings-related component to the pension system, (2) high implicit pension debt associated with generous replacement rates in a DB scheme, and (3) the existence of complete payroll tax records that allow compilation of lifetime earnings records for calculating benefits under an NDC scheme.[42]

First, NDC reforms are more likely where the existing system employs an earnings-related benefit structure (as in a Bismarckian social insurance model), because such a regime encourages public perceptions that a fair pension scheme should allow benefits to bear some relation to contributions. If the contribution-benefit linkage is widely perceived to work poorly (for example, by delivering benefits in a distorted or unfair fashion), however, or if public confidence in the capacity of the public PAYG-DB system to pay benefits in the near and medium term has been very badly shaken, public support for tightening the link between benefits and contributions may be more easily cultivated.

The structure of the old pension system also creates important financial constraints on reform options. As noted above, if payroll taxes are already high to finance a public DB scheme, market pressures to increase flexibility and lower nonwage costs leave little room to increase contributions to social security. Adding to the constraints of high payroll taxes and well-organized constituents is the heavy implicit pension debt associated with high replacement rates in most traditional DB pension schemes.[43] A large implicit pension debt makes the transition cost of a shift toward prefunding (for example, by diverting payroll contributions to individual accounts) very high. This transitional cost can in theory be financed through increased taxes, spending cuts, or issuing new debt, but political and financial constraints may place these options out of reach for many governments.

In Bismarckian countries with a very large public earnings–related pension tier, pressures to reduce pension costs and reduce rather than just stabilize pension contribution rates have been especially severe. Bismarckian countries are likely to begin with incremental retrenchment and refinancing measures, but as these have been exhausted, several have turned toward more fundamental restructuring reforms to reduce current and future costs. Because the public PAYG tier was already so large, however, proposals for a mandatory occupational or personal pension individual account tier had to adapt or be "crowded out" by the double payment problem. When expanded mandatory or quasi-mandatory individual account tiers have been adopted in these countries, notably in Sweden and Germany, it has been as a relatively small supplement to a still very large public pension tier that faced severe affordability problems. As table 14.4 suggests, NDC-focused pension reforms initially emerged in countries such as Sweden and Italy that offered generous Bismarckian pensions, for it is in these countries that current and future pension-funding problems were most severe, and where the double payment problem made a DC-based alternative less feasible. In what can be called "Bismarckian Lite" countries—Canada and the United States—pension replacement rates and financing burdens are relatively modest. These countries are likely to be able to maintain their current pension structures with incremental measures for some years into the future, and NDC-based reforms have not reached the agenda.

A third policy feedback that might be expected to make consideration and adoption of NDC-based reforms more likely is the existence of complete payroll records that allow retrospective calculation of lifetime earnings to establish NDC "account balances." In practice, however, this does not appear to be the case. Countries in Eastern and Central Europe that do not have adequate retrospective wage records have developed alternative mechanisms to credit initial capital in NDC accounts.[44]

Political System Characteristics

Specific characteristics of national political environments may also affect both the agenda-setting process—that is, whether a particular reform idea develops an institutional carrier that perceives political and policy advantages to a specific pension reform proposal—and the prospects for adoption once that proposal is on the agenda.

Understanding the development and diffusion of NDC-based pension reforms must begin with recognition of the opportunities and costs that these reforms impose for key actors in society. Within government, both elected politicians and finance ministries (or the equivalent ministries charged with budgetary and overall economic management) are likely to be involved in pension reform initiatives in most countries—frequently supplanting the social or labor ministries with direct responsibility for running pension programs.[45]

Elected politicians are driven by the powerful desire to avoid blame for costly policy adjustments.[46] Altering public pension systems is especially risky, because even small but well-publicized losses among retirees or those retiring in the near future are especially likely to provoke opposition from the affected group. Moreover, in many countries, the elderly are disproportionately likely to vote. For state leaders pressed by demographic and economic change to diminish long-term state pension liabilities, NDC reforms represent a possible way to reduce pension expenditures and commitments while avoiding blame for doing so.[47] In the short term, citizens (and politicians) who are unfamiliar with actuarial principles may be confounded by the NDC scheme. The contingency of future pension benefits on demographic and economic trends also makes it difficult for citizens to predict ex ante the precise material implication of NDC shifts. Although this uncertainty could limit initial opposition to NDC, it might also foster exaggerated fears that increase opposition to a shift to NDC. Of course, voters might prefer the type of uncertainty associated with adopting NDC—cuts in benefits are likely to occur in the future, but they will be rule-based and likely to avoid complete system collapse—to the even greater uncertainty associated with future ad hoc cuts in current pension schemes that are highly likely to occur but uncertain in their timing, magnitude, and targeting. But voters are likely to underestimate the likelihood of ad hoc cuts and may exaggerate the magnitude of cutbacks that are known to be automatic but unknown in magnitude.

In the longer term, NDC schemes release politicians from responsibility for benefit reductions as demographic and economic profiles change. By adjusting benefits automatically to life expectancy, not only do governments avoid the need to make such changes, but they can escape responsibility for the benefit reductions triggered by the demographic and economic trends, since these lie beyond the immediate command of government. NDC reform thus offers the appeal of a meaningful structural reform from which politicians can walk away with "clean hands."[48]

Finance ministry officials have likewise played an important role in the adoption of structural pension reforms. Their attitude toward, and activism in promoting, NDC-based pension reforms is likely to be conditioned by several factors. First, the importance of finance ministries is enhanced where fiscal pressures have been a primary motivator for pension reforms, and also in countries facing strong international financial constraints, either from foreign investors, international financial institutions, or supranational organizations such as the European Union. In Poland, for example, Góra and Rutkowski (2000) argue that finance ministry officials' demands for macroeconomic discipline in 1991 became an important force moving the country toward structural pension reform. NDC reforms thus become attractive to finance ministry officials to the extent that budgetary pressures from unfunded DB schemes collide with medium-term constraints on government's ability to finance a privately funded-DC reform. In Brazil, although finance ministry officials favored a structural pension reform in early 1999, central bank officials strongly resisted a mixed DB and funded-DC pension reform on account of the effect of such a reform's transition cost on short-term macroeconomic performance, which had come under intense international pressure following a currency crisis.[49]

However, the attitude of finance ministry officials toward NDC pension reform may also be heavily influenced by the overall design of the pension reform package: if, for example, the tighter link between contributions and benefits is accompanied by a requirement that greatly increased general government revenues be used for nonemployment credits (for example, for the care of young children) and for an expanded noncontributory pensions for low earners, then such officials are likely to balk.

Political institutions may also affect the prospects for adoption of NDC proposals once they are on the agenda. First, substantial literature suggests that multiple veto points in the policy adoption process can lower both the probability of any change from the policy status quo[50] and the scope of any change that is adopted.[51] Passing significant pension restructuring reforms should be particularly difficult in countries with large, multiparty governments where government leaders need to build majorities across parties occupying a broad range of ideological positions.[52] But institutional fragmentation is likely to be less of a barrier in a shift to NDC than in an FDC-focused reform, because the latter is likely to impose greater costs, risks, and redistribution. Indeed, Italy, Latvia, Poland, and Sweden are all proportional representation systems in which a large number of parties held seats in the legislature at the time that an NDC or NDC-oriented reform was passed.[53] In each of these countries, such reforms were adopted following intense negotiations across a diverse set of parties.

Beyond the compromises embodied within the structure of the NDC scheme, each country also combined distinct pillars of the revised social security system in a way that satisfied demands of diverse coalition partners and organized interests while working within the financial and political constraints posed by the old pension system. Although such broad negotiations may diminish the magnitude and pace of reform, they may have a positive, longer-term consequence. Indeed, Orenstein (2000) finds that although countries with more "veto actors" adopted less radical pension reform, compromises made in the coalition-building process dramatically enhanced the subsequent level of support for and compliance with the pension reform in the implementation phase.

When faced with political institutions that spread power broadly, governments have employed a variety of ad hoc mechanisms that can overcome these potential stumbling blocks. Such mechanisms range from technocratic governments with decree powers in Italy to informal cross-party agreements in Germany and formal multiparty working groups in Sweden.[54] Clearly the availability of a multiparty working group—which in turn reflected a longer history of cross-party political cooperation—was particularly important in facilitating the Swedish NDC reform. On the other hand, inability to work across parties has clearly paralyzed Social Security reforms in the United States in the post-1983 period.

Ultimately, the design of political institutions—whether concentrating power or spreading it broadly across parties and actors in government—obliges reformers to make important trade-offs in the pension reform process. Indeed, although evidence to support a systematic relationship between the concentration of political power and the depth of reform achieved remains mixed, it is clear that in the end, strategic political actors play a powerful role in bringing the issue of pension reform to the policy agenda, and mediating the competing tensions of building a broad coalition to ensure the permanency of the reform while preserving the main policy initiatives sought in the reform process.

Policy Design

The discussion to this point has emphasized features of the political and social context in which NDC-based pension reforms may reach the policy agenda and win adoption. But the chances of success in adopting reform may also depend on the exact provisions of an NDC reform package—notably who is covered by it, how quickly it is phased in, which groups are afforded special protections, and how much protection is provided by other pension tiers. For example, seniors' organizations and unions dominated by older workers are more likely to oppose a shift to NDC the faster it is phased in, because faster implementation will have a greater impact on their current membership. It is no accident that pension reform initiatives of all kinds generally "grandfather" current retirees and provide generous transition rules protecting older workers from most cutbacks.

NDC schemes offer reforming governments—especially those in fragmented, multiparty political systems—a way to resolve the diverse objectives of coalition partners from opposing ends of the ideological spectrum, and thus may facilitate the creation of legislative majorities behind this significant structural reform. For governments pressed by demographic and economic changes to reduce long-term state pension liabilities (in an unfunded DB pension system), the tighter link between contributions and benefits in the DC mechanism presents a key means to achieve this objective. Yet, unlike funded DC schemes, the creation of a large NDC component to mandatory pension systems will not alienate parties that are either skeptical about the privately managed pension schemes or that view a central role for the state in the pension system as the *sine qua non* of social security. By retaining the PAYG financing structure, and moreover by permitting legislative control over the notional interest rate, NDC reforms may conciliate the demands of parties seeking to protect bureaucratic jobs and the central role for the state in the collection and allocation of benefits. Furthermore, the aspects of NDC reforms that permit the government either to deliver privileges to constituencies such as the uniformed services, or to reward socially valued activities such as child-rearing, higher education, or military service, provides a variety of bargaining tools with which the government can propitiate interest groups or parties that oppose the NDC reform. If reformers are able to tailor NDC-inspired reforms to fit local policy and local political and social conditions, they may be able to move their countries from nonadoption to at least partial adoption of NDC reforms.

Evaluating Determinants and Explaining Patterns of Reform

The diffusion of NDC-based pension reform is clearly a complex, multicausal process. Even the long list of potential influences on adoption or rejection of NDC reform outlined in table 14.3 does not exhaust the list of plausible causal variables influencing the spread of NDC-based reforms.[55] Moreover, the patterns shown in table 14.4 do not reveal simple one-to-one relationships between specific independent variables and particular outcomes: causal effects are more aptly characterized as probabilistic and interactive rather than as individually necessary or sufficient.

Sweden's role as NDC innovator illustrates these patterns. Sweden's serious aging problem as well as a financial crisis and resistance to higher payroll taxes helped put pension reform on the Swedish agenda in the early 1990s, as similar economic and demographic constraints did in many other countries. High technocratic capacity and a fairly even balance (and change in control of government) between Social Democratic and nonsocialist forces, as well as the more idiosyncratic factors of a strong technocratic orientation in the working group planning the pension reform and the exclusion of "social partners" from a direct role in negotiations[56] all help to explain why Sweden was the first to adopt framework legislation for NDC-based reform. But Sweden's relatively open political system, and in particular, grassroots opposition within Sweden's powerful blue-collar labor confederation and the Social Democratic party explain why it took another four years for final legislation to be adopted rather than achieving a quick adoption.

Clearly both regional networks and supranational institutions were important in explaining the diffusion of NDC-based reforms beyond its origins in Sweden to other relatively early innovators such as Latvia and Poland. Both Swedish experts and the World Bank played particularly important roles in spreading these ideas. But as Orenstein (2003, p. 174) suggests, theories that focus on the diffusion of ideas through regional networks are not very helpful in understanding when, where, and how NDC-based reforms will be altered to fit local conditions by lengthening transition periods, excluding specific groups from the reform, or deciding on the relative size of an NDC-based tier within a multipillar pension system. To answer these questions, approaches that focus on policy feedbacks, societal interests, and political conditions are needed.

Policy feedbacks play a particularly important role in advanced industrial countries. Among these countries, NDC-based reforms have spread primarily among countries where Bismarckian social insurance principles of earnings replacement in the public pension system are deeply ingrained rather than those where a flat-rate system (New Zealand) or a mixed public-private system (Switzerland, the United Kingdom) is in place. Younger and less generous Bismarckian Lite pension systems (Canada and the United States) are also less likely to see NDC-based reforms on the agenda, at least in the near future.

Policy feedback effects are less clear in the developing and transitional economies of Central and Eastern Europe, however, where NDC-based reforms have been enacted even in the absence of adequate wage records and a strongly earnings-related precursor system. In these countries, regional and supranational influences appear to be more important. And in Africa and East Asia, where public pension coverage rates are generally much lower, NDC-based reforms have barely made a ripple. These patterns of regionally uneven policy feedback effects are likely to change over time: as NDC-based reforms become fully diffused over the next decade or so among pension policy experts worldwide, regional network biases and supranational institution effects in adoption of NDC-based reform may weaken in developing and transitional economies.

Implementation Challenges

Adopting NDC-based pension reforms can be an important mechanism for restraining pension costs and generating a closer link between individuals' contributions and benefits, as has been discussed above. But adoption of reform is only half of the battle. As Eric Patashnik (2003) has shown, major policy reforms are subject to erosion or reversal once they are enacted. Developing constituencies who have a stake in the new policy are particularly important to sustaining policy innovation.

In the case of NDC-based pension reforms, erosion is probably a greater risk than outright reversal. Indeed, erosion of NDC-based reforms may be attractive to governments because it offers short-term political gains (or avoids short-term political costs), while the effects of those actions on the sustainability of the system may not be immediately obvious. As table 14.5 suggests, this erosion could occur in any of the key attributes that define an NDC-based pension system. For example, governments might choose to impute contributions or rights that have not actually been financed, either for all contributors (as in Italy) or for certain groups (for example, caregivers or university students). In countries where the government has chosen to finance all noncontributory benefits (for example, for caregivers) from the general budget, there may be a temptation to simply impute those credits during periods of fiscal stress. Statistical agencies could also be pressured not to make projections that trigger politically unpopular benefit changes—for example, projections of increased longevity or low long-term economic growth. Although this may not be a problem in countries where statistical agencies are well-established, highly professionalized, and enjoy a high degree of independence, status, and deference, it could certainly be a problem in some developing and transitional countries where none of these things are true. Governments may also be tempted to use NDC contributions to pay some of the costs for pension tiers outside the NDC system that maintain benefit adequacy for selected segments of the elderly population as NDC is phased in, rather than using them to build a buffer fund.

Because NDC systems are not completely different from existing DB pensions, but there are in fact "partial" NDC positions (as shown in the fourth column in table 14.1), the big

Table 14.5. Potential Erosion in NDC Pension Systems

Provision	Strong or full NDC	Erosion possibilities	Conditions facilitating erosion
Advanced funding	PAYG with inclusion of buffer funds in benefit calculations	Government transfers funds from buffer funds to general treasury	Government experiences fiscal crisis
Life expectancy at retirement	Future benefit levels adjust automatically for increases in longevity	Government freezes annuitization tables	Weak rules in place on regularity and automaticity of life-expectancy adjustments Weak autonomy of statistical agencies
Retirement age	No standard retirement age with full actuarial adjustment for earlier or later and partial retirement	Higher nonactuarial benefits reestablished for workers who have reached a specified age or number of years in employment	Strong unions; pensions become electoral issue
Inflation and economic growth	Benefits tied fully to economic growth	Government continues inflation adjustments in annuities and account balances when economy is shrinking (for example, through cap on "brake" mechanism)	Economic recession and/or decline in labor force
Payroll tax rate	Fixed payroll tax rate	Increase in payroll tax	NDC tier experiences cash-flow crisis resulting from demographic "bulge"
		Decrease in payroll tax rate	Government seeks economic stimulus during recession
Redistribution across generations	Barred within NDC tier	Transition rules made more generous after initial NDC implementation	Transition rules in place create highly visible disparities between adjacent cohorts of retirees

Redistribution within generations	Barred within NDC tier unless financed by payments from government or others with respect to nonemployment activity. Exception: NDC implicitly redistributes from men to women and other population subgroups with longer life expectancy if single annuitization table is used	Government imputes NDC credits for nonemployment activity rather than actually making contributions	Government experiences fiscal crisis
Coverage	All workers in specified age cohorts are covered by NDC system	Favored groups win exclusion from NDC reform after initial inclusion	Favored groups have strong leverage in political system (for example, public sector unions or military)
Time horizon	All employed workers, including those in labor force at time NDC introduced, covered by NDC system	Time horizon for phase-in of NDC pension extended	Transition rules in place create highly visible disparities between adjacent cohorts of retirees
Exclusivity	NDC is only public pension tier	New means-tested tier or minimum guarantee created or existing one expanded after implementation of NDC	Income inequality or poverty among the elderly increase after implementation of NDC system (may also be pressures for expanding pension guarantee outside NDC tier if pension guarantee is not automatically adjusted for wage growth)

Source: Authors.

challenge of policy makers in NDC systems is likely to be to hold the line against reforms that move from "complete" NDC provisions to middle positions (for example, retaining brakes, but with a cap; temporary increases in contribution rates; infusions of general revenue to keep real benefits from falling; imputing contributions that are purely notional rather than real; and moving from universal coverage of NDC to exclusion of privileged categories of workers). The 1995 Latvian pension reform, for example, went into effect immediately, reducing benefits for a significant portion of workers retiring in 1996 while generating vast disparities in pension benefits.[57] The Latvian transition rules, however, were poorly designed and in some cases unfair for persons without work or work in the informal sector.[58] This created a popular backlash and placed intense pressure on politicians to revisit the pension reform law in October 1997 and March 1998, when a series of measures were adopted that provided a more generous transition rule for computing initial capital based on old-system records and contribution records during the turbulent 1990s. In practice, this enhanced the generosity of benefits and reinstated some degree of redistribution to the system to compensate for the economic turbulence of the 1990s. In addition, politicians in Latvia voted an extra indexation of benefits for all pensioners in 1997 and 1998, reflecting an effective pensioners lobby.[59] In Poland, changes made in 1999 moved new hires in the uniformed services out of the NDC pension system back into a more generous DB system enjoyed by current employees in the uniformed services.[60]

Several factors may lead to the erosion of NDC-based pension reforms. Most generally, the political party or coalition that instituted the reform may lose power to another political grouping that is hostile to the reform—that may indeed have used opposition to the reform as a key plank in their electoral campaign. Table 14.5 suggests several conditions that may also lead to the erosion of specific components of an NDC-based reform. As noted above, a government fiscal crisis is particularly likely to erode a government's commitment to make actual contributions in recognition of nonemployment activities (for example, childcare years and unemployment spells). A short-term cash flow crunch as a result of a demographic "bulge" may tempt governments to raise payroll taxes rather than injecting general revenues, even though doing so increases the long-term liabilities of the system. Unrest among the military or a strike threat from public transit workers may lead to their return to a more generous DB system. A decline in the overall labor force and wage bill may leave a government unwilling to cut annuity benefits for retirees and account balances for current workers. In short, as with decisions on adopting a public pension system, economic, demographic, and societal factors are likely to affect policy implementation and final outcomes.

Having an NDC-based system in place does shift the bargaining leverage in favor of those who want to put greater financial discipline in the pension system, because preventing the system's erosion requires them merely to block changes proposed by politicians or groups catering to short-term constituency interests rather than adopting new policies. This advantage is likely to be important (1) in political systems where the governing party or coalition has sufficient agenda control to keep reform-eroding proposals off the agenda, and (2) in systems with multiple veto points, where supermajorities are usually needed to move from the default position. But where agenda control is weak and where veto points are fewer and weaker, temptations for politicians to loosen the lashes will remain strong.

The most essential element to sustaining a complete NDC model once it has been adopted is likely to be the maintenance of a broad multiparty agreement in government that NDC is the right thing to do, and broad public understanding of and support for the reform. So far, this agreement within the government appears to be holding in Sweden, the home of the NDC idea. However, public opinion surveys suggest that even after several years of multimedia public information campaigns, most Swedish citizens lack basic knowledge of the fundamental precepts (and even the name) of the NDC scheme. As Sundén (2006) argues, because DC systems make it difficult for individuals to anticipate their retirement benefits, it is important for citizens to have a clear understanding of how benefits are determined under the new system and how the new system differs from the former DB scheme if they are to make informed decisions on how much to work and save. From a political standpoint, moreover, improving public information about NDC reforms and their implications for long-term benefits may be a crucial factor in avoiding the backlash experienced in Latvia in 1996 when pension benefits diverged radically from public expectations.

Whether the Swedish experience of broad political consensus sustaining an NDC-based pension system can be repeated in countries where traditions of interparty cooperation are weaker, trade unions are less cooperative, and politicians have stronger incentives to respond to independently organized groups of seniors remains to be seen. Although the public information campaign carried out by the Social Insurance Board in Sweden likewise represents a model for many countries, evidence that a majority of Swedes lack basic knowledge of the NDC component of the pension system, and that a majority also perceive that they have significant information needs, should serve as an important warning to politicians about the risk of public backlash in the future if citizens overestimate their old-age income protection and fail to save adequately.[61] Moreover, if such information problems exist in small, affluent, and highly educated nations such as Sweden, successful public information campaigns will likely be even more difficult in the developing and transitional countries.

Prospects and Potential Problems

NDC pension reforms are likely to be an important part of pension reformers' toolkits in the years ahead. For technocrats, NDC packages combine conceptual elegance and the promise of fiscal discipline that is seen to be lacking in most DB pension plans. For politicians, NDC plans combine an aura of fairness (in relating contributions to benefits) that can be explained to voters, as well as the prospect that those politicians will in the future be spared from dealing with politically painful benefit cutbacks and payroll tax increases. The "automaticity" of NDC is likely to give it continuing appeal to blame-avoiding politicians, especially in countries with social insurance–based systems and moderate debt to GDP ratios. This automaticity also makes NDC appealing to international financial institutions seeking to promote sustainable fiscal policies.

A political analysis of NDC-based reforms suggests that there is a central contradiction in the political appeal of NDC-based reforms, however; technocrats are attracted to NDC because in its "complete" form it sends clear signals to workers on the need to work longer and the need to save for retirement in order to obtain an adequate pension. The problem is that transparency on these issues may kill prospects for NDC-based reform, since workers are likely to object to making these changes, especially older workers who have limited time to adjust and blue-collar workers for whom working longer may be more difficult or even impossible. Politicians, on the other hand, are likely to be attracted to NDC for precisely this reason: it can hide the magnitude of future recipient losses vis-à-vis the policy status quo because (1) from the perspective of the "average" citizen, NDC benefit determinations are more opaque than DB plans—although the former may also be less exposed to future political risk; and (2) future cutbacks are contingent on future economic and demographic developments. There are strong incentives for politicians *not* to be clear about the likely effects of an NDC-based reform on individual workers if they hope to succeed in adopting and sustaining that reform. But this in turn may undercut many of the hoped-for effects of NDC-based reforms on retirement and savings behavior, and the political sustainability of the NDC reform itself.

Overall, the analysis in this chapter suggests that NDC is no panacea. Six issues in particular are important in considering the prospects for NDC-based reforms. First, there are limitations to the applicability of NDC systems. For countries with the weakest states, lacking the administrative capacity to collect and maintain adequate contribution records on a consistent basis, NDC systems are not likely to be workable. At a minimum, the phase-in period in such countries will have to be very long to develop such a capacity. Moreover, in countries where public pensions have not historically had a close link to earnings (for example, countries with a flat-rate pension), a shift to an NDC is likely to impose substantial losses for some recipients. Again, a long lead time is likely to be necessary to lessen political opposition to such a shift. In countries where NDC reforms are applied retrospectively, conflicts over transition rules for crediting past contributions are likely to be intense, and subject to multiple revisions to respond to the grievances of particular constituencies.

Second, there is a danger that adoptions of incomplete and flawed NDC pension plans, as in Italy, may lull politicians into a false sense of complacency, letting them think that they have "solved" their long-term pension problems when they have not. As both politicians and constituencies become more familiar with the dynamics of NDC pensions, the probability grows rather than shrinks that compromises will be built into reform packages that undercut their effectiveness and sustainability. Like a photocopy of a photocopy of a photocopy that still bears the original image in a perceptible but fuzzy way, future NDC pension regimes in some countries may be called NDC, and have many of their elements, but lack fiscal and political sustainability.

Third, adoption of NDC-based pension reforms are no panacea for providing political cover for long-term pension retrenchment. It still requires that politicians refrain from the politically easy course of demanding more generous pension benefits for visible groups of constituents, and that they refrain from going along when other politicians make those demands. It also requires that politicians refrain from political interference with buffer funds where they exist. There is no such thing as a "manipulation-proof reform"—pension or otherwise—although some political institutions and policy structures may be more resistant to political risk than others.

Fourth, although the novelty of NDC schemes and the contingency of future benefits on economic and demographic factors afford politicians a unique opportunity to rationalize state pensions without confronting strong opposition ex ante, these factors also enhance the need for effective political management of information and guidance of public expectations as to the value of future pension benefits. The Swedish strategy of providing workers with annual statements showing the evolution of notional account balances is emblematic of good public information and expectations management. Campaigns such as these diminish the risk that the government will face a political backlash if benefits under the NDC scheme diverge widely from public expectations.

A fifth potential shortcoming of NDC-based pension reform flows directly from the periodic information about balances in individual notional accounts that in theory should be provided to participants in an NDC system. As Daniele Franco pointed out in comments on an earlier draft of this chapter: when NDC is enacted in a flawed or incomplete manner that is likely to require further changes in the future, this information can in fact make those further reforms politically much more difficult. Notional account balance statements give workers a much greater sense of "property rights" in the balances in those accounts by making them much more visible. If a future reform, for example, were to eliminate pension rights for contributions that were credited but not actually made, the balances in the accounts would shrink. A major public uproar would likely result over politicians "stealing" their money—a politician's worst nightmare. Similarly, if expected increases in longevity are not included in statements regularly, irregular adjustments could lead to sudden drops in the benefit flow expected from account balances when they are included. Such changes would lead both to a decline in confidence in the pension system and to political problems for politicians.

Finally, while the stabilization of contribution rates remains an important concern, it should be emphasized that NDC pension systems transfer significant new risks to individuals, notably the risk of lower benefits due to poor macroeconomic performance and the risk of being unable to find appropriate (or any) work at an advanced age if workers are expected to stay employed longer to maintain a replacement rate similar to that enjoyed by current retirees.[62] The risk of poverty in old age remains a significant policy risk, especially in many developing and transitional nations, and may increase under NDC-based systems over the equivalent risk in what for many countries is the most likely alternative: continued ad hoc adjustments in underfinanced DB schemes. In particular, the reluctance of politicians to make unpopular adjustments to the parameters of pension systems may raise the longer-term risk that the cost of increasing longevity will be borne primarily in the value of pension benefits, which may erode pensions below a socially accepted level.[63] Thus the political advantages of NDC reforms in allowing politicians to avoid blame for costly benefit reductions may also give rise to a longer-term social cost if old-age pensions fail to provide sufficient protection against the risk of poverty in aging societies. This risk may be especially high in political systems with multiple veto points where the policy default position is privileged.

Thus it is important for governments to balance the goals of stabilizing or reducing payroll taxes with other political and social objectives in designing overall pension reforms. In the Latvian case, for instance, the authors of the *Latvia Human Development Report 2000/2001* observe that "[t]he average Latvian pension still remains considerably below the value of the minimum goods and services basket, although the difference between these two indicators is steadily diminishing."[64] Despite the increase in pension values, cost-saving measures passed in 1999 were expected to significantly decrease pension values in 2000 and 2001, more than half of which were already at the minimum value, due to early problems in the design of the transitional rules.[65] In Latin America also, given that a large portion of pensions granted are at the minimum level, efforts to control costs through benefit reduction alone should take into consideration issues of adequacy and poverty reduction when considering how to accommodate demographic change. In these cases, raising the retirement age and promoting higher individual savings may offer alternative mechanisms for enhancing the financial stability of public pension schemes without drastically lowering benefits.

Increasing the link between pension contributions and benefits will also almost certainly require supplementation of NDC benefits with "social pensions" if they are to provide adequate minimum benefits. This is true in both rich and poor countries, but it is especially true in less-developed countries and transitional economies. Social pensions complementing an NDC-based tier can be structured in several ways: as a universal pension received by all, or as a pension that is tested against income, against income and assets, or (as in Sweden), against only other pension income. It can also be financed in a variety of ways, notably through a separate payroll tax or general revenues.

Our overall conclusion is thus unsurprising but critical: NDC-based reforms are likely to work best in countries that have the political capacity to achieve and sustain a broad political agreement and the administrative capacity to produce independent forecasts of economic and demographic trends and complete and accurate records of earnings, as well as ensuring compliance and adequate understanding on the part of employers and employees. They are less likely to work well where those capacities are lacking. NDC should not, therefore, be thought of as a simple way to avoid the political dilemmas of pension politics by securely lashing politicians to the mast of an automatically adjusting pension system. Neither the mast nor the lashings are that strong, and the sirens' call remains very powerful in many countries. Moreover, a shift from DB to NDC-based pensions, although it does lower financial risks over an FDC system and may lower political risks over those in a financially unsustainable DB scheme, is nevertheless likely to increase workers' fears and uncertainty about their future pension incomes and create new employability risks for older workers.

Thus, although NDC-based reforms can be an important part of the pension reform repertoire for both domestically based politicians and expert groups and for transnational actors (including international financial institutions), there is no substitute for a careful analysis of a country's political and social environment and administrative capacity to determine how such a reform is likely to work on the ground. NDC at best is likely to be the least undesirable of many imperfect alternatives in achieving pension reforms that balance fiscal sustainability, benefit adequacy, and fairness within and across generations.

Notes

1. See, for example, Pierson (1998, 2001).

2. See, for example, Brooks (2002) and Madrid (2003).

3. "Notional defined contribution" and "non-financial defined contribution" should be understood to have the same definition.

4. See Palmer (2006a).

5. See Palmer and Góra (2004). While Palmer and Góra (2004) emphasize the financial stability of NDC pension schemes, Kruse (2002) argues that there remains a possibility of financial instability in NDC systems unless there is an automatic balancing mechanism (as in Sweden).

6. In this respect, the Swedish NDC scheme follows the practice of the prereform Swedish earnings-related pension. But buffer funds are by no means unique to Sweden, or to NDC systems. A number of other countries faced with deteriorating demographic situations have developed such funds in their defined benefit pension programs, including the United States, Canada, and (more recently) New Zealand. See Iglesias and Palacios (2001); Palacios (2002); Weaver (2004).

7. See Börsch-Supan and Wilke (2006).

8. Blöndal and Scarpetta (1997, pp. 17–18), in a survey of 18 OECD countries, found that pension contribution rates rose from an average of 9.3 percent in 1967 to 16.5 percent in 1995; the average contribution rate was 1.88 times its 1967 level in 1995.

9. A finding of a future deficit in the CPP's triennial review process sets in motion a process under which Ministers from Ottawa and the provinces are supposed to agree on any needed changes to keep the plan viable; if they do not agree, contribution rates will increase automatically to meet half of the anticipated deficiency (phased in over three years), and indexation of the CPP will be frozen for the next three years unless cabinet ministers agree to override these procedures. See Slater and Robson (1999, pp. 6–7).

10. See Gern (2002, p. 457).

11. See Light (1995).

12. The United States invests its reserve fund only in federal securities, however, while the Canada Pension Plan and Quebec Pension Plan invest in a broader range of financial instruments. See Weaver (2004).

13. Indeed, the absence of adequate contribution records in Brazil was a crucial obstacle to the creation of an NDC pension reform in that country. See Pinheiro and Viera (2000).

14. See Góra and Rutkowski (2000).

15. See Fox and Palmer (1999) and Palmer et al. (2006).

16. See Franco and Sartor (2006).

17. The Polish government is easing out certain early retirement privileges by financing "bridge pensions" for uniformed services, wherein the government makes additional contributions to finance a pension paid from early retirement age to the normal retirement age established under the 1997 reform law. See Góra and Rutkowski (2000).

18. A substantial literature on policy diffusion in a variety of sectors among the states within the United States suggests that innovating states—those who first design and implement a reform—are found predominantly among relatively wealthy states with high technocratic capacity and slack resources (see the discussion in Orenstein 2003). The fact that NDC was pioneered in Sweden, a wealthy country with strong technocratic capacity in the pension sector, is consistent with this line of argument.

19. See Orenstein (2000, pp. 12–13).

20. See Orenstein (2000).

21. Tavits (2003) in a review of Estonian pension reforms, categorizes causal variables affecting diffusion of innovation into three categories: internal determinants, external pressures, and lesson-drawing. In Tavits's categories, economic/demographic, policy feedbacks, partisan/political constraints, and societal constraints would all fit within the category of internal determinants, while ideational forces would be divided into Tavits's internal (strength of conservative forces), external and lesson-drawing (supranational institutions), and lesson-drawing (regional networks) categories.

22. See Kinsella and Velkoff (2001) and European Union, Economic Policy Committee (2001).

23. See Brooks (2002, pp. 513–5).

24. See Swank and Steinmo (2002), Swank (1998), and Garrett (1998).

25. See Kingdon (1995).

26. See Lundberg (2003).

27. See Bennett (1991), Haas (1992), and Most and Starr (1980).

28. Prominent research suggests that individuals are, in essence, "cognitive misers" who, due to their finite information-processing abilities, look to cues, heuristics, or information shortcuts to make decisions more tractable (see Tversky and Kahneman [1974], Kahneman, Slovic, and Tversky [1982]). Brooks (2005) has argued that competitiveness and status concerns were significant influences in the adoption of private pension reforms in developing countries seeking to attract foreign investment, while Hering (2004) has examined the role of such pressures in European nations seeking accession to the European Union.

29. See Hering (2004).

30. See Brooks (2005) and Madrid (2003).

31. See Keohane and Nye (1974), Finnemore (1993), Krasner (1982,1985); see also Nelson (2004) and Weyland (2004).

32. See Vreeland (1999).

33. See Schludi (2002).

34. See Franco and Sartor (2006).

35. See Holzmann (2006).

36. Brooks (1998) found that in Argentina, to gain leverage over domestic opponents to an FDC pension reform proposal, President Menem *requested* that the IMF place a condition in its Letter of Intent of its March 1992 Extended Fund Facility Agreement requiring the Argentine government to pass a structural pension reform by January, 1993. For the role of international financial institutions as strategic scapegoats, see also Vreeland (1999).

37. For the attraction argument, see Brooks (2005). Among the transition countries, Bulgaria, Hungary, and Latvia received considerable technical and financial support from the World Bank through conditional loans, but only Latvia adopted the NDC model. Nevertheless, the attraction to DC structures among Eastern European and Central Asian countries is striking, with FDC reforms adopted in Estonia, Kazakhstan, Lithuania, and (in addition to NDC) in Poland, while NDC was adopted with the later addition of an FDC tier in Latvia. Whether these governments chose financial or notional DC schemes may be understood to have been shaped by a combination of financing constraints, explained above, and political dynamics, discussed below.

38. See Brooks (2005) and Orenstein (2003).

39. See in particular Gill, Packard, and Yermo (2004).

40. See Brooks (2004a) and Hunter and Brown (2000). In Uruguay, loan conditionality also was not a relevant means of policy diffusion. The Inter-American Development Bank (IDB) played a more important role in transferring ideas and technology of pension reform than in promoting any specific policy model. The research that led up to the (eventually rejected) 1992 NDC reform proposal in Uruguay was financed by a loan from the IDB and based on technical advice from a team of Latin American pension experts, including a Brazilian scholar who later participated in the design of the 1999 pension reform in Brazil that contains some elements similar to NDC.

41. See Pierson (1994, 2000).

42. Although sufficient, the existence of complete payroll tax records is unlikely to be a necessary condition.

43. See James (1998).

44. See Palmer (2006b), Chłoń-Domińczak and Góra (2006), and Palmer et al. (2006).

45. See Orenstein (2000).

46. See Pierson and Weaver (1993).

47. Early evidence suggests that the adoption and diffusion of NDC and FDC pension reform models differ systematically in this respect, with governments being more likely to adopt NDC reforms where political institutions share power broadly across parties represented in government, and thus allow reformers to avoid direct blame for costs that become apparent after adoption (Brooks 2004b).

48. The need to "walk away with clean hands" is one problem that concerns more than simply pragmatic considerations of the likely backlash that elected politicians might incur. It reaches to a core dilemma of public ethics that suggests that in order to do the "right thing," politicians at times must do what citizens would otherwise oppose, such as automatic reductions in pension benefits when pension system revenue declines. For the meta-ethical discussion of the politics of "dirty hands," see Walzer (1973) and Parrish (2002).

49. See Brooks (2004a, p. 75).

50. See Immergut (1992) and Tsebelis (1999).

51. Other aspects of political institutions may also affect capacity for policy change. For example, countries that have relatively short electoral cycles may find it particularly difficult to make changes that impose visible losses on retirees and those approaching retirement. See the discussions in Pal and Weaver (2003) and Bonoli (2000).

52. See for example Immergut (1992), Kay (1998), and Brooks (2002). The advantages of concentrated power and minimal veto points may, however, be at least partially offset by the concentration of accountability in political systems: because voters know that it is the governing party that is imposing losses, governing parties may be reluctant to undertake initiatives that are very likely to incur retribution at the next election (Pierson and Weaver 1993). Because future losses may be obscured ex ante in NDC reforms, accountability concerns may be partly allayed. Moreover, even governing parties with very strong formal powers may refrain from enacting policies that are likely to be reversed by a later government.

53. Italy adoped a mixed-member majoritarian (MMM) electoral system in 1993. The new electoral system "did not reduce party fragmentation, but it did provide powerful incentives for parties to enter into pre-electoral coalitions." (D'Alimonte 2001, p. 323).

54. See Schludi (2002, chapter 9).

55. For example, in an analysis of the determinants of differences between pension reform in Estonia and Latvia, Tavits (2003) argues that a record of successful domestically initiated economic reform outside the pension sector in Estonia gave Estonian political elites greater confidence that they could successfully design and implement a homegrown pension reform, while a weaker Latvian record in this regard made them more inclined to borrow heavily from the Swedish NDC model. An extension of this argument would be that in countries where previous policy borrowing from supranational organizations or through regional networks in other sectors has been judged by political elites to be successful, they may be inclined to do it again in the pension sector.

56. See Lundberg (2003) and Lindbom (2001).

57. Bite and Zagorskis (2003, p. 41) report that pensions calculated in January 1997 ranged from as low as 8 lats to over 1,000 lats, which was "shocking to the society" that was accustomed to the traditional equalizing role of social security. In fact, no one actually received such a low pension due to the system's guarantee rule. The high pensions were not the result of NDC rules, but to a generous conversion of special privileges acquired under the old system, such as for Latvians forced into exile in Siberia for a large part of their lives. See Palmer et al. (2006).

58. See Palmer et al. (2006).

59. See Palmer et al. (2006).

60. See Chłoń-Domińczak and Góra (2006).

61. See Sundén (2006).

62. See Scherman (2003).

63. Diamond argues that while this diminishes the risk of excessive legislative intervention, the solvency promoted by automatic benefit reductions may enhance the risk that governments intervene too *infrequently* to balance the demographic adjustment to the contribution formula as well; see Diamond (2000, p. 86).

64. See Bite and Zagorskis (2003, p. 63).

65. See Bite and Zagorskis (2003, p. 64).

References

Bennett, C. J. 1991. "What Is Policy Convergence and What Causes It?" *British Journal of Political Science* 21 (April): 215–33.

Bite, I., and V. Zagorskis. 2003. Latvia Country Study, Study on the Social Protection Systems in the 13 Applicant Countries, carried out for the Commission by GVG, http://europa.eu.int/comm/employment_social/index_en.htm.

Blöndal, S., and S. Scarpetta. 1997. "Early Retirement in OECD Countries: The Role of Social Security Systems," *OECD Economic Studies* 29: 7–53.

Bonoli, G. 2000. *The Politics of Pension Reform.* Cambridge: Cambridge University Press.

Börsch-Supan, A., and C. B. Wilke. 2006. "The German Public Pension System: How It Will Become an NDC System Look-Alike." In *Pension Reform: Issues and Prospects for Non-Financial Defined Contribution (NDC) Schemes,* ed. R. Holzmann and E. Palmer, chapter 22. Washington, DC: World Bank.

Brooks, S. 1998. "Political Dynamics of Pension Reform in Argentina." Paper presented at the International Meeting of the Latin American Studies Association, Chicago, Illinois, September 25.

———. 2002. "Social Protection and Economic Integration: The Politics of Pension Reform in an Era of Capital Mobility," *Comparative Political Studies* 35 (5): 491–523.

———. 2004a. "International Financial Institutions and the Diffusion of Foreign Models for Social Security Reform in Latin America." *Learning from Foreign Models in Latin American Policy Reform,* ed. K. Weyland, 53–80. Washington, DC: Woodrow Wilson Center Press and Johns Hopkins University Press.

———. 2004b. "A Competing Risks Model of Structural Pension Reform," Paper presented at the annual meeting of the American Political Science Association, Chicago, Illinois, September 2–5.

———. 2005. "Interdependent and Domestic Sources of Policy Change: The Diffusion of Pension Privatization around the World." *International Studies Quarterly* 49 (2): 273–94.

Chłoń-Domińczak, A., and M. Góra. 2006. "The NDC System in Poland: Assessment after Five Years." In *Pension Reform: Issues and Prospects for Non-Financial Defined Contribution (NDC) Schemes,* ed. R. Holzmann and E. Palmer, chapter 16. Washington, DC: World Bank.

D'Alimonte, R. 2001. "Mixed Electoral Rules, Partisan Realignment, and Party System Change in Italy." In *Mixed-Member Electoral Systems: The Best of Both Worlds?* ed. M. Soberg Shugart and M. P. Wattenberg, 323–50. New York: Oxford University Press.

Diamond, P. 2000. *Social Security Reform.* Oxford: Oxford University Press.

Elster, J. 1979. *Ulysses and the Sirens.* Cambridge, U.K.: Cambridge University Press.

———. 2000. *Ulysses Unbound: Studies in Rationality, Precommitment, and Constraints.* Cambridge, U.K.: Cambridge University Press.

European Union, Economic Policy Committee. 2001. *Budgetary Challenges Posed by Ageing Populations.* Brussels: EPC/ECFIN/655-EN-fin, October 24.

Finnemore, M. 1993. "International Organizations as Teachers of Norms." *International Organization* 47 (4): 565–99.

Fox, L., and E. Palmer. 1999. "Latvian Pension Reform." Social Protection Discussion Paper No. 9922, World Bank, Washington, DC.

Franco, D., and N. Sartor. 2006. "NDC in Italy: Unsatisfactory Present, Uncertain Future." In *Pension Reform: Issues and Prospects for Non-Financial Defined Contribution (NDC) Schemes,* ed. R. Holzmann and E. Palmer, chapter 18. Washington, DC: World Bank.

Garrett, G.. 1998. *Partisan Politics in the Global Economy.* Cambridge, U.K.: Cambridge University Press.

Gern, K.-J. 2002. "Recent Developments in Old Age Pension Systems: An International Overview." In *Social Security Pension Reform in Europe,* ed. M. Feldstein and H. Siebert, 439–78. Chicago: University of Chicago Press.

Gill, I. S., T. Packard, and J. Yermo. 2004. *Keeping the Promise of Old Age Income Security in Latin America: A Regional Study of Social Security Reform.* Washington, DC: World Bank.

Góra, M., and M. Rutkowski. 2000. "The Quest for Pension Reform: Poland's Security through Diversity." Working Paper 286, Washington, DC, World Bank.

Haas, P. M.1992. "Introduction: Epistemic Communities and International Policy Coordination." *International Organization* 46 (1): 1–35.

Hering, M. 2004. "Rough Transition: Institutional Change in Germany's 'Frozen' Welfare State." Ph.D. dissertation, Johns Hopkins University, Baltimore.

Holzmann, R. 2006. "Toward a Coordinated Pension System in Europe: Rationale and Potential Structure." In *Pension Reform: Issues and Prospects for Non-Financial Defined Contribution (NDC) Schemes*, ed. R. Holzmann and E. Palmer, chapter 11. Washington, DC: World Bank.

Hunter, W., and D. S. Brown. 2000. "World Bank Directives, Domestic Interests, and the Politics of Human Capital Investment in Latin America." *Comparative Political Studies* 33 (1): 113–43.

Iglesias, A., and R. J. Palacios. 2001. "Managing Public Pension Reserves: Evidence from the International Experience." In *New Ideas About Old Age Security*, ed. R. Holzmann and R. Stiglitz, 213–53. Washington, DC: World Bank.

Immergut, E. 1992. "The Rules of the Game: The Logic of Health Policy-Making in France, Switzerland and Sweden." In *Structuring Politics: Historical Institutionalism in Comparative Perspective*, ed. K. Thelen and S. Steinmo, 57–89. New York: Cambridge University Press.

James, E. 1998. "The Political Economy of Social Security Reform: A Cross-Country Review." *Annals of Public and Cooperative Economics* 69 (4).

Kahneman, D., P. Slovic, and A. Tversky. 1982. *Judgment under Uncertainty: Heuristics and Biases*. New York: Cambridge University Press.

Kay, S. 1998. "Politics and Social Security Reform in the Southern Cone and Brazil." Ph.D. dissertation, Department of Political Science, University of California, Los Angeles.

Keohane, R. O., and J. Nye. 1974. "Transgovernmental Relations and International Organizations." *World Politics* 27 (1): 39–62.

Kingdon, J. 1995. *Agendas, Alternatives, and Public Policies*, second edition. New York: HarperCollins.

Kinsella, K., and V. A. Velkoff. 2001. *An Aging World: 2001*. U.S. Census Bureau, Series P95/01-1. Washington, DC: U.S. Government Printing Office.

Krasner, S. 1985. *Structural Conflict: The Third World Against Global Liberalism*. Berkeley, CA: University of California Press.

Krasner, S. 1982. *International Regimes*. Ithaca, NY: Cornell University Press.

Kruse, A. 2002. "Ageing Populations and Intergenerational Risk-Sharing in PAYG Pension Schemes." Working Paper 18, Department of Economics, Lund University, Sweden. Available at www.nek.lu.se/publications.

Light, P. 1995. *Still Artful Work: The Continuing Politics of Social Security Reform*, New York: McGraw-Hill.

Lindbom, A. 2001. "De borgerliga partierna och pensionsreformen." In *Hur blev den stora kompromissn mojlig. Politiken bakom den svenska pensionsreformen*, ed. Joakim Palme, 50–87. Stockholm: Pensionsforum.

Lundberg, U. 2003. *Juvelen I kronan: Social demokraterna och den allmänna pensionen*. Stockholm: Hjalmarson and Högberg.

Madrid, R. 2003. *Retiring the State: The Politics of Pension Privatization in Latin America and Beyond*. Stanford: Stanford University Press.

Most, B. A., and H. Starr. 1980. "Diffusion, Reinforcement, Geopolitics, and the Spread of War." *The American Political Science Review* 74(4): 932–46.

Nelson, J. M. 2004. "External Models, International Influence, and the Politics of Social Sector Reforms."In *Learning from Foreign Models in Latin American Policy Reform*, ed. K. Weyland, 35–52. Washington, DC: Woodrow Wilson Center Press and Johns Hopkins University Press.

Orenstein, M. A. 2000. "How Politics and Institutions Affect Pension Reform in Three Postcommunist Countries." Policy Research Working Paper 2310, World Bank, Washington, DC.

———. 2003. "Mapping the Diffusion of Pension Innovation." In *Pension Reform in Europe: Process and Progress*, ed. Robert Holzmann, Mitchell Orenstein, and Michal Rutkowski, 171–93. Washington, DC: World Bank.

Pal, L., and R. K. Weaver. 2003. *The Government Taketh Away: The Politics of Pain in the United States and Canada*. Washington, DC: Georgetown University Press.

Palacios, R. J. 2002. "Managing Public Pension Reserves Part II: Lessons from Five Recent OECD Initiatives." Social Protection Discussion Paper 0219, World Bank, Washington, DC.

Palmer, E. 2006a. "What Is NDC?" In *Pension Reform: Issues and Prospects for Non-Financial Defined Contribution (NDC) Schemes*, ed. R. Holzmann and E. Palmer, chapter 2. Washington, DC: World Bank.

Palmer, E. 2006b. "Conversion to NDCs—Issues and Models." In *Pension Reform: Issues and Prospects for Non-Financial Defined Contribution (NDC) Schemes*, ed. R. Holzmann and E. Palmer, chapter 9. Washington, DC: World Bank.

Palmer, E., and M. Góra. 2004. "Shifting Perspectives in Pensions." Discussion Paper 1369, Institute for Labor Studies, Bonn.

Palmer, E., S. Stabina, I. Svensson, and I. Vanovska. 2006. "NDC Strategy in Latvia: Implementation and Prospects for the Future." In *Pension Reform: Issues and Prospects for Non-Financial Defined Contribution (NDC) Schemes*, ed. R. Holzmann and E. Palmer, chapter 15. Washington, DC: World Bank.

Parrish, J. M. 2002. *From Dirty Hands to the Invisible Hand: Paradoxes of Political Ethics*. Ph.D. Dissertation, Department of Government, Harvard University.

Patashnik, E. 2003. "After the Public Interest Prevails: The Political Sustainability of Policy Reform." *Governance* (16) 2: 203–34.

Pierson, P. D. 1994. *Dismantling the Welfare State*. Cambridge: Cambridge University Press.

———. 1998. "Irresistible Forces, Immovable Objects: Post-Industrial Welfare States Confronting Permanent Austerity." *Journal of European Public Policy* 5 (4): 539–60.

———. 2000. "Increasing Returns, Path Dependence, and the Study of Politics." *American Political Science Review* 94 (2): 251–67.

———. 2001. *The New Politics of the Welfare State*. Oxford: Oxford University Press.

Pierson, P. D., and R. K. Weaver. 1993. "Imposing Losses in Pension Policy." In *Do Institutions Matter?* ed. R. Kent Weaver and Bert A. Rockman, 110–50. Washington, DC: The Brookings Institution.

Pinheiro, V., and S. Viera. 2000. "Reforma previsional en Brasil: La nueva regla para el cálculo de los beneficios." Serie Financiamiento del Desarrolo No. 97, CEPAL, Santiago de Chile.

Pinheiro, V. 2004. "The Politics of Social Security Reform in Brazil." In *Learning from Foreign Models in Latin American Policy Reform*, ed. Kurt Weyland, 110–38. Washington, DC: Woodrow Wilson Center Press and Johns Hopkins University Press.

Scherman, K.G. 2003. "Old Age Security in Sweden, Quo Vadis?" Paper delivered at the Forschungsnetzwerkes Alterssichung, Erfurt, December 4–5.

Schludi, M. 2002. "The Reform of Bismarckian Pension Systems." Ph.D. dissertation, Humbold University, Berlin.

Slater, D. W., and W. B. P. Robson. 1999. *Building a Stronger Pillar: The Changing Shape of the Canada Pension Plan*. Toronto: C.D. Howe Research Institute.

Sundén, A. 2006. "How Much Do People Need to Know about Their Pensions and What Do They Know?" In *Pension Reform: Issues and Prospects for Non-Financial Defined Contribution (NDC) Schemes*, ed. R. Holzmann and E. Palmer, chapter 13. Washington, DC: World Bank.

Swank, D. 1998. "Funding the Welfare State: Globalization and the Taxation of Business in Advanced Market Economies" *Political Studies* 46 (4): 671–92.

Swank, D., and S. Steinmo. 2002. "The New Political Economy of Taxation in Advanced Capitalist Democracies." *American Journal of Political Science* 46 (3): 477–89.

Sweden, National Social Insurance Board. 2004. *The Swedish Pension System Annual Report 2003*, Stockholm: Riksförsäkringsverket (National Social Insurance Board).

Tavits, M. 2003. "Policy Learning and Uncertainty: The Case of Pension Reform in Estonia and Latvia." *Policy Studies Journal* 31 (4): 643–60.

Tsebelis, G. 1999. "Veto Players and Law Production in Parliamentary Democracies: An Empirical Analysis." *American Political Science Review* 93 (3): 591–608.

Tversky, A., and D. Kahneman. 1974. "Judgement Under Uncertainty: Heuristics and Biases." *Science* 185: 1124–31.

Vreeland, J. 1999. "The IMF: Lender of Last Resort or Scapegoat?" Midwest Political Science Association Annual Meeting, Chicago, IL, April 15–17.

Walzer, M. 1973. "Political Action: The Problem of Dirty Hands." *Philosophy and Public Affairs* 2 (2): 160–80.

Weaver, R. K. 1986. "The Politics of Blame Avoidance." *Journal of Public Policy* 6 (4): 371–98.

———. 1988. *Automatic Government: The Politics of Indexation*. Washington, DC: The Brookings Institution.

———. 2004. "Whose Money Is It Anyway? Governance and Social Investment in Collective Investment Funds." In *Rethinking the Welfare State: The Political Economy of Pension Reform*, ed. M. Rein and W. Schmähl, 294–316. Cheltenham: Edward Elgar.

Weyland, K. 2004. "Conclusion: Lessons About Learning in Latin American Policy Reform." In *Learning from Foreign Models in Latin American Policy Reform*, ed. K. Weyland, 241–83. Washington, DC: Woodrow Wilson Center Press and Johns Hopkins University Press.

Discussion of "Lashed to the Mast?
The Politics of NDC Pension Reform"

Daniele Franco*

THE CHAPTER BY SARAH BROOKS AND KENT WEAVER PROVIDES a broad overview of the economic and political factors underlying the introduction of NDC pensions. The analysis is based on an extensive survey of policy developments at the country level and of the relevant economic literature.

I share most of the views and the conclusions of the authors. I will focus my comments on three aspects that may require some integration of the analysis of the authors.

First, the authors note that the shift from a traditional defined benefit (DB) system to a non-financial defined contribution (NDC) system can diminish the visibility of benefit cuts: the NDC system is a new system, it is complex. As the authors note, it can even appear opaque. Benefits are contingent on several possible events. This may imply, in particular, that the introduction of the NDC system can determine benefits cuts that are not noticed by citizens.

These considerations are surely reasonable, although they do not apply to the case of Italy, where the reform was not exploited to cut future spending. However, this lack of visibility may disappear once the NDC system is introduced. In fact, the NDC framework makes the pay-as-you-go (PAYG) liabilities more explicit than they were before: each citizen is informed about her or his pension wealth. Therefore, NDC liabilities can be perceived as a harder form of public debt than the non-explicitly specified liabilities of more traditional PAYG schemes.

This development is probably not problematic if the parameters of the system are sustainable and if corrective mechanisms keep the system in balance, which is basically the case in Sweden. It may be problematic, however, if the design of the system is incomplete or the system involves spending and revenue levels that may not be sustainable in an open economy. This is probably the case in Italy.

Defaulting the PAYG debt via further pension reforms becomes more visible and politically more difficult because individuals are more aware of their pension wealth than in a traditional PAYG scheme. Moreover, financial markets can perceive a higher default risk. This higher risk may be particularly problematic for emerging market economies in which a relatively small public debt can sometimes be difficult to manage. These considerations may suggest some additional caution in advocating the introduction of NDC systems in these countries: revenue levels should be clearly sustainable and corrective mechanisms should be very effective.

* Daniele Franco is director of the Public Finance Division in the Research Department of the Bank of Italy.

The opinions expressed are those of the author and do not involve the responsibility of the Banca d'Italia.

Second, the chapter examines the economic and political factors underlying the introduction of NDC systems in some countries. Some of the authors' preliminary conclusions do not seem convincing.

The authors attribute a role to international economic institutions in spreading NDC systems. There is no evidence in the cases of Italy and Sweden that these institutions did have a role. Surely the European Commission did not advocate the introduction of NDC pension systems. The role of regional networks should also not be overestimated. Italy and Sweden were not influenced by neighboring countries. The introduction of the NDC system in Brazil does not seem to have been influenced by the debate that has taken place in Uruguay. Rather, the Brazilian discussion was initiated following contacts with Swedish reformers.

Some caution is also warranted in drawing general conclusions about the role of economic factors and political factors. As to the role of overall budgetary conditions, Sweden, for instance, introduced the NDC system in a period in which its public finances did not face serious immediate fiscal problems. However, when the Swedish reform was formulated and legislated in 1992–1994, the impact of the recession of the early 1990s was still vivid. In Sweden, the recession had been substantially more severe than in the rest of Europe. Sweden was confronted with a serious crisis in the financial market and there was considerable discussion about long-term structural problems that would give rise to increasing debt, the most apparent structural issue being the pension system. The Swedish pension system reformers benefited greatly from this general feeling of crisis among politicians, institutional players, and the average person on the street.

In Italy, the NDC system was introduced in a period characterized by continuous efforts to reduce the budget deficit. However, given the long transition phase envisaged for the introduction of the NDC system in Italy, the reform was not expected to contribute to fiscal consolidation over the short to medium term. Moreover, even in the long term it may not reduce pension spending more than under the previous set of pension rules.

As to the role of new-liberal ideologies, in Italy the NDC system was introduced by a center-left government. In Sweden it was implemented by a Social Democratic government—following the consensus between conservatives, liberals, and social democrats reached in 1994; all the parties supported the reform as it went through parliament in June 1994.

In sum, we do not yet have systematic indications concerning the factors underlying the introduction of NDC regimes in some countries and not in others. There are just too few available case studies.

Third, the authors stress that one of the greatest advantages of NDC pensions is the perception of permanency that they provide. The system is designed to last forever. But they also note that there is "no such thing as a manipulation-proof reform" and they suggest that there is a risk of erosion of NDC rules.

This discussion may remind us of the debate about fiscal rules and discretionary fiscal policy. Fiscal rules are said to make policies more time consistent and to reduce the room for short-term political exploitation of fiscal policy. Basically, one does not trust governments to always take the best discretionary decisions.

However, the evidence on the effectiveness of fiscal rules at the national level is very much mixed.[1] Democracies keep changing fiscal rules for a variety of reasons. Basically, governments and parliaments feel entitled to change whatever was decided previously.

So, even if pension schemes are well designed and corrective mechanisms keep them in balance, we cannot expect too much in terms of the long-term durability of pension rules. This should not discourage pension experts from trying to improve the design of schemes, but it should remind them that pension schemes are also a tool in the political debate.

Note

1. See Kopits and Symansky (1998) and Banca d'Italia (2001).

References

Banca d'Italia, ed. 2001. *Fiscal Rules*. Rome, Banca d'Italia.

Kopits, G., and S. Symansky. 1998. "Fiscal Policy Rules." IMF Occasional Paper 162, International Monetary Fund, Washington, DC.

Discussion of "Lashed to the Mast?
The Politics of NDC Pension Reform"

*Agneta Kruse**

SWEDEN WAS THE FIRST COUNTRY TO ADOPT A PENSION SYSTEM designed as a notional defined contribution system, that is, an unfunded (pay-as-you-go) defined contribution system, what has become known as a non-financial defined contribution (NDC). The old system, a defined benefit, price-indexed pay-as-you-go system, turned out to be both unsustainable and unfair. However, according to public choice theory—at least in its crudest form (majority rule/median voter)—a reform such as the Swedish one should not be possible. And still, there it is! I discuss this contradiction in Kruse (2003) without reaching any definite explanation or conclusion. So, it is a pleasure for me to comment on Sarah Brooks and Kent Weaver's chapter, in which they tackle the problem from a different angle.

The focus of their chapter is on reasons for adopting such a scheme and whether, once adopted, the politicians will be "lashed to the mast." As a background, the chapter starts with a lengthy and informative description of different ways of organizing pension systems with a focus on an NDC system. The description emphasizes that it is possible to choose a system that is not a clear-cut NDC. They point out that many systems currently in use mix features from NDB (defined benefit) and NDC systems. This is an important observation and points to the fact that all reforms are path dependent; thus actual systems turn out to be mixtures. In an informative table, the NDC pension provisions are presented as a continuum. The categories presented are then used to fit in countries with different reforms. The description is ambitious as it tries to cover all possible combinations of features.

The authors want to discuss pros and cons of an NDC system in order to pin down the reasons that politicians should choose such a system. For such a purpose the description occasionally becomes confusing as it is sometimes unclear about whether it is an NDC system that is being described or some specific features of an NDC system in a certain country. It is unclear whether the merits or drawbacks of NDC depend on NDC per se or the particular design (mixture) chosen in a specific country.

Brooks and Weaver maintain that pension reforms are as easy to do in defined benefit (DB) systems as in an NDC system. This might be true, and there is a list of reforms done in DB systems. However, also true is that even today there is a lack of insight among workers and pensioners (voters) in many countries that have DB systems about what reforms are needed in order to get a sustainable system. The investigation by Boeri, Börsch-Supan, and Tabellini (2001) is witness to this lack, and last but not least the strikes last year in France and the mass demonstrations in Spain. More important, though, is that even if there are a lot of (limited) reforms, the question is whether that is such a good thing. Brooks and Weaver do not discuss the uncertainty these reforms bring about or the

---

* Agneta Kruse is senior lecturer at the Department of Economics, Lund University.

increased planning problems it causes to people trying to maximize their lifetime utility. The merits of a stable system as a risk-reducing device are obvious, but this is not mentioned by Brooks and Weaver. This omission is probably the reason why they conclude that everything that can be achieved in an NDC system can also be achieved in a DB system.

In the description of different reform options, one aspect of the difference between a DB system and a defined contribution (DC) system is missing in Brooks and Weaver's chapter. When it comes to risk sharing between generations in the face of demographic and economic changes, there are important differences between the systems. In DB systems, all adaptation is borne by the working generation. NDC systems with their fixed contribution rates and growth index make co-living generations share the burden of lean years and the fruits of good years (see Kruse [2002] and references therein for a discussion of risk sharing between generations). Brooks and Weaver do discuss how the two systems differ when it comes to intergenerational distribution. They describe the intergenerational distribution in the following way: in a DC system ". . . benefits adjusts automatically to return financial balance to the system." In a DB system, the benefit rate is fixed as a social objective according to Brooks and Weaver. I have no objections to this. However, what is not stressed in the chapter is that when the benefits are reduced in a DC system, it is caused by bad economic times and low growth. In such a situation, the working part of the population also gets a reduction in consumption possibilities. In a DB system, this decrease will be magnified by increases in the contribution rate. As the focus of the chapter is on the benefit side of the system, it is rather hidden that in a DB system the bill is passed on to the younger generation, sometimes even to generations not yet born, let alone not having a vote in a democratic process. Having such a strong focus on the benefit side also means that the important life-cycle aspects of a pension system are missed.

When it comes to intragenerational redistribution, Brooks and Weaver find that DB systems have a "more complex pattern of redistribution." Somehow it is often taken for granted that this means redistribution in favor of low-income groups. This seems to be the case in the U.S. system. However, very often it turns out to go in the opposite direction. In DB systems the benefit often depends on the last year's wage or an average of the last X (X = 3, 5, or 10) years' wages, transferring resources from flat career, blue-collar worker to white-collar worker in career jobs. This is true in many European countries, it was true in the old Swedish system, and this is why a DC system where such "perverse" redistribution does not take place may win political support.

The analysis would be improved with a life cycle approach to pension systems. With such an approach the fact that everybody will eventually become a pensioner is evident; also evident is that the aim of a pension system is to help the individual even out income and consumption possibilities over the life cycle (plus risk sharing within and between generations). The chapter gives the impression that a reform is of interest only to the elderly and not to the younger generations who are still in active ages. The life cycle approach brings forward the individual's planning problem and considers how a pension system handles risk. There are different kinds of risk—economic, demographic, and political[1]—affecting the rate of return the system gives. How these risks are met differ with the design of the chosen system. These risks can never be totally eliminated, but they are heavily reduced in an NDC system.

However, the individual, the insured person, does not exist in the Brooks and Weaver chapter. Instead the focus is on public bodies. These are used as variables in the section on political viability of reforms. Although I miss the perspective of the individual, I find this perspective innovative and interesting.

A main conclusion from the description seems to be that whatever is achievable in an NDC system is also achievable in an NDB system. If I understand it correctly, the only reason for choosing an NDC system is that the politicians than can get rid of the responsibility for retrenching the benefits.

Political Viability of an NDC Reform

The questions here are why the NDC gets on the agenda in some countries and not in others, and why, once on the agenda, NDC is adopted in some countries but not in others. Case studies for Brazil, Italy, Sweden, and Uruguay are used to highlight the questions.

The first question—why reform gets on the agenda—is sort of an odd question in the Swedish case. The NDC system was actually *invented* in Sweden. On the agenda was what to do about an unsustainable system with perverse redistribution (from low-income, blue-collar workers to high-income, white-collar workers). The reform was preceded by a number of investigations by parliamentary committees. Slowly an awareness of the necessity of a reform arose. In scrutinizing the problems, a reform proposal took form, a design that years later (in 1997) came to be named NDC. Of course there have now and then been discussions and proposals in specific areas that mimics parts of the NDC system, but not a coherent proposal like the Swedish one. The description in the chapter gives the impression that there is a basket of ready-made reform options from which one can be drawn.

Be that as it may, in order to answer the questions a great number of interesting hypotheses are presented. The first hypothesis is that NDC is more likely to be introduced in a country the more that country's population has aged. The second hypothesis is that NDC is most likely in countries with severe governmental fiscal pressure and a high public debt in relation to GDP. A third one is that NDC is most likely in countries where the payroll taxes are so high that *they limit economic and political sustainability* (my italics).[2] Also, the strength of various domestic ideological groups, plus the interaction with supranational institutions such as the European Union and the World Bank, are assumed to be influential. The hypotheses are presented and summarized in a table. The authors then proceed and give examples from countries and reforms where specific factors seem to have been at hand. The analytical approach chosen is a difficult one, as the examples often open up possibilities of counterexamples. For example, the description of the World Bank's efforts to convince countries of the advantages of NDC must build on a misunderstanding. The 1994 World Bank publication *Averting the Old Age Crisis* did not advocate a NDC system. On the contrary, it took quite a few years to convince people at the World Bank (if this was ever done!) of the merits of a NDC system.

So far the chapter gives only tentative answers to the hypotheses posed. A problem is, however, that the authors do not indicate what a more systematic analysis would look like. A full-fledged formal testing of the hypotheses is probably beyond the scope of the chapter. As the variables listed are quantifiable, a step in the right direction would be to have them presented for a large number of countries. A table showing population structure plus projections, public debt in relation to GDP, and perhaps also the level of payroll taxes and whether the country has adopted a pension reform and if so what kind of reform, would give a good opportunity to judge the relevance of the hypotheses.

For an economist it seems odd that, when discussing the politics of pension reforms, voters are nonexistent. There is a very rich literature discussing the possibilities of pension reforms in democracies with majority voting, showing among other things how the result differs with the assumptions made. The literature contains both theoretical analysis (Browning [1975], Sjoblom [1985], and Verbon [1993] are but a few examples) and empirical studies (see Breyer and Craig [1997], Tabellini [2000], and Galasso and Profeta [2002]). One conclusion is that the age structure among voters is important, indeed significant, in explaining pension systems and reforms. However, the results from these studies do not seem to be consistent with Brooks and Weaver's discussion.

An important aspect of public pay-as-you go pension systems is that they are a social contract between generations—an implicit one, but still a contract. The generation voting for the system and introducing it hopes that coming, yet unborn, generations will fulfil the contract. The problem is that unborn generations do not have a vote in a democracy. This is one of the reasons it is so difficult to keep a pay-as-you-go DB system on an optimal level and also why a DC system (be it notional or funded) may do the trick. In Brooks and Weaver's description it is taken for granted that the aim of adopting a NDC system is to reduce benefits and retrench the system, not to make the system robust, able to sustain in bad as well as in good times. In comparing NDC with reforms in DB systems, Brooks and Weaver say that introducing NDC is politically advantageous as the politicians can hide the retrenchment. Such a statement needs to be substantiated. Also, there is no explanation of why a politician would like to retrench the system. Why not just let the snowball keep growing and let coming generations (not having the right to vote, thus not being able to throw a politician out of office) inherit the debt? This is the intriguing question I would like to get answered. Also, here it would not be out of place to remind the readers about Disney's (1996) ironic comments about one of the British reforms in the 1980s. According to Disney, the indexation (in a DB system) was changed in such a complicated way that "no one" realized what the effects on benefits would be!

An aspect not discussed is to what extent the short time period since the first NDC system was introduced hampers the possibility of drawing conclusions. In the discussion about the diffusion of ideas, Brooks and Weaver bring forward the importance of networking for adopting a system like NDC, or the possible contagious effect of a neighborhood with an NDC system. Brooks and Weaver try to highlight the influence of these kinds of factors and it would be interesting to see these factors explored even further. There is a vast literature, perhaps mostly by economic historians such as D. North and N. Rosenberg, about the rise, spread, and development of different institutions. In most cases it does not seem to be a very speedy process. Probably there are neither enough cases, nor enough time that has elapsed, to make it possible to reject or accept this hypothesis about NDC systems.

In the chapter, a large number of hypotheses is presented and discussed in the light of examples from different countries. It is, however, difficult to judge the value of the isolated examples given as the examples sometimes seem to be chosen in a rather unsystematic way. In any event, as the article contains such a great number of possible explanations, it is a plentiful source to use for future researchers wanting to perform a more formalized analysis.

Notes

1. I define *political risk* as a decrease in the rate of return that individuals (think they) have been promised, a decrease caused by politically decided changes in the system. The ultimate risk in a pay-as-you-go system is of course that coming generations refuse to accept the social contract—that is, it turns out that you belong to the terminal generation. In this chapter there is a totally different definition of *political risk*: it is defined there as the risk that the politician will not be reelected.

2. These "limits" are highly dependent on a country's history and culture. I doubt such limits are possible to establish in an objective way. Thus, it will be hard (impossible?) to accept or reject that hypothesis.

References

Boeri, T., A. Börsch-Supan, and G. Tabellini. 2001. "Would You Like to Shrink the Welfare State? The Opinions of European Citizens." *Economic Policy* 16 (32): 7–50.

Breyer, F., and B. Craig. 1997. "Voting on Social Security: Evidence from OECD Countries." *European Journal of Political Economy* 13: 705–24.

Browning, E. 1975. "Why the Social Insurance Budget is too Large in a Democracy." *Economic Inquiry* 13: 373–88.

Disney, R. 1996. "Can We Afford to Grow Older?" Cambridge, MA: MIT Press.

Galasso, V., and P. Profeta. 2002. "The Political Economy of Social Security: A Survey." *European Journal of Political Economy* 18: 1–29.

Kruse, A. 2002. "Ageing Populations and Intergenerational Risk-Sharing in PAYG pension Schemes." WP 2002:18, Department of Economics, Lund University. www.nek.lu.se/publications.

———. 2003. "Svenska pensionsreformer under 1900-talet. Ett "Public Choice-perspektiv." [Swedish Pension Reforms during the 20th Century: A Public Choice Perspective.] In *25 år i täten. En vänbok till Per Gunnar Edebalk*. ed. L. Harrysson, O. Mallander, and J. Petersson Socialhögskolan, 83–98. Lund, Sweden: Lund University.

Sjoblom, K. 1985. "Voting for Social Security." *Public Choice* 45: 225–40.

Tabellini, G. 2000. "A Positive Theory of Social Security." *Scandinavian Journal of Economics* 102 (3): 123–35.

Verbon, H. 1993. "Public Pensions. The Role of Public Choice and Expectations." *Journal of Population Economics* 6: 523–45.

World Bank. 1994. *Averting the Old Age Crisis*. Washington, DC: World Bank.

PART III

LESSONS FROM COUNTRIES WITH NON-FINANCIAL DEFINED CONTRIBUTION SCHEMES

Chapter 15

NDC Strategy in Latvia: Implementation and Prospects for the Future

Edward Palmer, Sandra Stabiņa, Ingemar Svensson, and Inta Vanovska*

INSPIRED BY THE REFORM LEGISLATION PASSED IN SWEDEN IN 1994, Latvia formulated and passed its own NDC legislation in 1995. In doing so, Latvia became the first country in Central and Eastern Europe to legislate an NDC reform. With the implementation of its reform in January 1996, it was the first country to make a complete transition to NDC for the entire working population. This study tells the story of how the Latvian pension reform evolved, discusses problems encountered along the road of its implementation, assesses its results, and discusses the main lessons to be learned from the Latvian experience.

The reform set a contribution rate of 20 percent for non-financial defined contribution[1] (notional) accounts from 1996 and for notional accounts and financial accounts together from July 2001, with a planned gradual transition to a 50-50 split of the 20 percent contribution rate between non-financial (NDC) and financial defined contribution (FDC) pension schemes by 2010. The cost of old age pensions at the time of the reform was well over 20 percent; since a contribution rate of only 20 percent gives total pension rights to current workers, contributions above this level are viewed as a tax. The tax covers the transition from the old to the new regime and also finances a minimum guarantee.

All of the main bolts of the Latvian Pension reform were in place in 2001 with the introduction of the individual financial account scheme. The reform promises stability in the face of demographic and economic fluctuations and manages a broad range of possible economic and demographic scenarios—or risks—that the country may have to face. It provides an adequate average pension level for career workers and guarantees an acceptable minimum pension standard. The reform path was bumpy, however. The conversion to NDC in 1996 brought a number of transition issues that had to be resolved; some of these issues had to be revisited in the period immediately following the initial reform legislation. The most important conversion issues involved the questions of how to value rights acquired under the old regime and how to introduce the system in an economic environment characterized by structural upheaval as the country was just beginning the process of transition from a command to a market economy.

---

* Edward Palmer is at the Swedish Social Insurance Agency and the University of Uppsala; Ingemar Svensson is at the Swedish Social Insurance Agency; and Sandra Stabiņa and Inta Vanovska are at the Ministry of Welfare of Latvia.

The model used for calculations in this study is the official model used by the Latvian government for the analysis of medium- and long-term pension policy.

Setting a reasonable minimum pension age for the new system was a major systemic issue in Latvia, but also a political one. With the actuarial character of NDC and FDC it became important to set a high enough pension age so that persons leaving the labor force at the minimum age would receive an adequate pension. However, in accordance with the rules in the old regime, workers—especially women—were used to receiving a benefit at a young age: 55 years old for women and 60 for men. For this reason, raising the pension age was a sensitive political issue. A third important issue was how to phase out widespread special privileges—dating from the pretransition period—for listed groups of persons below the prereform minimum pension ages of 55 for women and 60 for men. The final major issue, which was also a topic of discussion during many years after 1996, was that of phasing in the mandatory financial account scheme, given the alternative goals of reducing the contribution rate and phasing in wage indexation of pension benefits.

How these issues were dealt with and the loose ends that still remain at the time of this writing are among the topics of this study. We begin with a brief overview of the economic environment prevailing as the government began to consider the reform and review the reasons for why reform was necessary. The following section summarizes the reform legislation. Then we devote separate sections to discussing the transition issues and transition process during the initial years, and to discussing the design of the overall reform, including the phasing in of the FDC scheme, and the issue of long-term financial stability. The final section addresses the questions of political sustainability and popular acceptance.

The Early Transition Years and Picture Prior to the 1996 Reform

After gaining independence in 1990, Latvia moved with determination toward establishing a market economy and democratic institutions. As in other transition countries, this process led to a collapse in the economy. At its worst, in 1992, prices skyrocketed by 900 percent. Latvia responded with resolve to the transition challenge, and by 1993 the currency was stabilized and structural reforms were under way, trade was open, and prices were largely deregulated. Nevertheless, in the initial years of the transition, 1990–94, GDP fell by more than 40 percent.

As the bottom fell out of the economy, enterprises produced articles no longer marketable. One of the harsh but necessary tasks of the transition was to dissolve unproductive enterprises and privatize enterprises that had some market value in the new economy. This process of necessary structural change led to disrupted working careers for a large percentage of the Latvian population. By 1995, only a few large enterprises remained to be fully privatized. Latvia had become a nascent market economy, but, as it looked in 1995, at a high price. In 1995, as the pension reform was being formulated, there was still no sign that the economy would rebound into sustained growth, unemployment was high, and many of those who did have work did not have fulltime employment.

As pension expenditures were largely fixed, the 40 percent fall in GDP and the wage base meant that the ratio of pension expenditures to GDP went from 5.5 in 1985 to around 10.5 percent in the mid-1990s.[2] This was precisely when a relative increase in budget expenditures was most difficult to afford. Expenditures of a little more than 10 percent of GDP on old age pensions may not seem alarming gauged by Western European standards; however, at the time, given all the other demands on dwindling public revenues and the difficulties people had in just making ends meet for the day, this was high. Per capita income had fallen dramatically and poverty was widespread. In addition, pensioners were generally no worse off than families with children, and persons in the rural areas were struggling because of the collapse of the farming infrastructure.[3]

From 1991 to 1995, the number of persons for whom contributions were being paid declined by almost 50 percent, and, by the end of 1995, there were about 1.5 persons receiving a pension per contributor.[4] So, the point of departure for the reform was that there were too many people receiving benefits and too few paying contributions. The first problem—the large number of pensioners—was created by the especially low pension age of 55 for women and an extensive list of occupations and circumstances that entitled people to benefits as early as age 40. The rules were inherited from the old Soviet system, in which there was a proclivity to use pensions—promises of remuneration in the future—not only to compensate for harsh or dangerous working conditions (rather than to improve them) but also to provide special privileges for persons in, for example, the police, military, and judiciary occupations; to reward mothers giving birth to a large number of children; and so on. By the 1990s, there was a long list of occupations and circumstances for which there were special pension privileges, since this was a way to negotiate relative income advantages under the old regime.

The second problem—too few contributors—was, first, in part simply the other side of the early retirement coin. But it was also exacerbated by unfavorable demography. In addition, it was a manifestation of the informal economy that had blossomed in the transition. Deals were made between employers and employees where minimum wages were declared for revenue collection purposes, and remuneration above this was paid under the table. For those who worked where the opportunity to avoid paying contributions was present and wages were low, evasion—or making a payment based on a minimum wage—appeared to be a rational form of behavior. Those penalized by this state of affairs were persons "within" the system, those who had little or no opportunity to evade paying social insurance contributions—for example, employees in large companies and civil servants.

Most importantly there was no link between contributions and benefits in the old pension formula, and no actuarial adjustment for postponed retirement. For all of these reasons, the Latvian pension system was in crisis when the reform concept was formulated in 1995. In sum, the rules of the old defined benefit system were not appropriate for a market setting and an aging population. The old system had created—and would continue to create—too many pensioners and too few contributors. Moreover, there were weak incentives to pay contributions and no incentives to postpone collecting pension benefits past the minimum pension age. Foremost on the agenda of policy makers was an increase in the minimum pension age, and thereafter a change in the benefit formulas leading to a combination of universal, mandatory non-financial and financial pension schemes based on lifetime accounts and life expectancy, with a direct link between contributions and benefits.

The Latvian Reform

The Latvian reform of the statutory old-age pension system, formulated and legislated in 1995, consists of two components. A non-financial defined contribution (NDC) component was implemented on January 1, 1996; since July 1, 2001, a financial defined contribution (FDC) component has also been part of the new system. In the first component, individuals have notional individual accounts, whereas in the second they have individual financial accounts. There is also a general and a temporary transition guarantee in the form of a minimum pension for persons who reach the minimum pension age. This is financed by revenues outside the overall contribution rate of 20 percent for the NDC and FDC schemes, together. As has already been mentioned, during the transition, the total cost of paying benefits granted under the old system and covering the introduction of the FDC scheme is over 20 percent, with the excess being regarded as a tax to finance the transition.

The transition from defined benefit scheme(s) to defined contribution schemes introduced the principle that the present value of an individual's benefit is equal to the present value of his or her contributions, and the systemic restriction that the present value of total assets in the system must be at least equal the present value of total liabilities. The latter condition is fulfilled automatically in an FDC scheme, and is fulfilled in the NDC scheme given that the rate of return on credited accounts is not greater than that necessary to fulfill this condition.[5] Here we describe in greater detail how the two schemes are set up.

The NDC Component of the Reform

The NDC scheme covers all persons living and working in Latvia from age 15, including the self-employed and farmers. Rights acquired in the old scheme were converted to NDC capital beginning January 1, 1996, and persons retiring in 1996 and after have retired according to the new rules, with NDC capital computed with a transition formula (described in detail below). The details of the conversion to NDC are discussed below. The contribution rate on earnings noted on individual accounts was set at 20 percent from January 1, 1996.

Accumulated notional pension capital is determined by contributions, paid on all earnings up to a ceiling (in 2004 about 10 times the average wage), and during a whole working life. As long as one works, one pays contributions and these are noted on individual accounts. A benefit can be claimed at any time from the minimum pension age (see below), and it is possible to combine work with an NDC annuity after reaching the minimum pension age. The principle behind this is that it provides an opportunity and support for gradual withdrawal from the labor force.

Noncontributory rights in conjunction with childcare and military service are financed with transfers from the state general budget. Rights in the old-age pension system derived during periods covered by social insurance for unemployment, compensated sickness absence of employees and the self-employed, work injury, and disability are financed by transfers from the other accounts in the overall social insurance budget to pension accounts.[6]

The "rate of return" on notional capital is set equal to the growth of contributions, that is, the contribution wage sum. This arrangement has two features worth pointing out. The first is that the rate of return earned during the accumulation period will reflect not only the growth of productivity and the wage rate, but also the effect of changes in fertility, the net migration of working age persons, and the gradual transition from the informal to the formal economy. Productivity and wage growth can be expected to be high in Latvia in the coming two decades, whereas fertility is expected to remain low. What's more, well-educated and well-trained younger persons are expected to leave Latvia to seek better labor market prospects abroad. Finally, with time, market formality will increase, providing a broader contribution base.

Fertility dropped to around 1.2 children per woman in the mid-1990s and has remained more or less at this level up to the time of this writing, in 2005. Demographers do not believe that the fertility rate will reach the level of 2.1 or higher needed to reproduce the population in the coming two decades—even in the most optimistic of scenarios.[7] For the birth rate to once again become so high, it is important for younger Latvians to feel that they have achieved a sufficient level of economic and job market security, and that they can look forward to a living standard sufficient to support larger families. Furthermore, transfers to parents will compete for some time to come with transfers to children within the family.

In the 1990s, the shadow economy was estimated to account for 30 to 35 percent of total national production. There are two sources of underreporting of income. One is that some workers just don't report earnings at all for some hours worked to the tax authority, which is a labor component—and has an effect similar to having a smaller labor force. The other is the practice of not reporting a full salary, but, for example, reporting a salary close to the minimum wage. This is a per capita wage component that has the same effect as a lower wage per capita. Both components of informality are expected to improve over the coming decades as the economy evolves into an overt market economy. As this happens, these gains will also be reflected in the overall scale of the system, and the long-term ability of the system to finance better benefits. In sum, the gradual transition from the informal to the formal market economy will contribute to formal growth in contributions and constitute a separate component of the rate of return on current NDC accounts of workers and pensions, the latter through the partial real indexation formula of the Latvian system (see below).

To date the real average annual rate of growth of the covered wage sum has been 6.7 percent, with annual growth of (covered) per capita real wages of 5.5 percent on average from 1997 through 2003. The real rate of return on individual notional accounts was, thus, 6.7 percent during 1997–2003. The number of contributors grew by 1.1 percent during the same period. The rate of inflation was about 3.6 percent. The nominal rate of return on capital was, hence, 10.5 percent. The key parameters for NDC pensions for the period 1997–2003 are summarized in table 15.1.

The growth in the number of contributors at an average annual rate of 1.1 percent is particularly noteworthy. This is consistent with the idea that the introduction of NDC (and FDC) is at least neutral in terms of promoting formality, and also supports the idea that it can have a positive effect. However, it is difficult to separate this effect from an overall effect of successful transition from dishevel to a formal market setting. These processes go hand in hand. At the least, the introduction of NDC in 1996 provided a logical framework for a system moving in the direction of formality.

What turned out to be important for the rate of return in the NDC scheme in the first decade of its existence was the high rate of growth of real wages per capita at an annual average of 5.5 percent—in spite of the negative repercussion of the "Russian Crisis" of 1998. Overall, growth in contributors and real wages provided an overall real rate of return of 6.7 percent for NDC accounts. As table 15.2 indicates, the percentage of economically active persons contributing increased dramatically from 1997 through 2003. Again, this was probably a general effect of the realization of the transition, but it was also encouraged by a social insurance system where benefits are tightly linked to individual contributions, a major message propagated to the public since the pension reform came in 1996. The positive effect generated by the growth of contributors will continue as long as the positive impact of increasing formality surpasses the negative impact of a declining population—according to present demographic projections the labor force will decrease at a rate of a half percent per year or more (see below). The scales are likely to be tipped

Table 15.1. Overview of Some Key Economic Indicators for NDC Pensions

1. Real per capita wage growth, average 1997–2003	5.5%
2. Growth of contributors, average 1997–2003	1.1%
3. Growth of real wage sum, average 1997–2003	6.7%
4. Rate of inflation, average 1997–2003	3.6%
5. Career years for newly granted benefits in 2003 (1996)	31 (30)
6. Unisex life expectancy at age 60 in 2002 (1996)	18.66 (17.88)

Source: Ministry of Welfare of Latvia (2003).

Table 15.2. Key Demographic Pension Ratios

Ratio	1997	2003
(1) Ratio of working-age population (20–59) to population age 60 +	2.70	2.45
(2) Ratio of persons in employment to population age 60 + excluding job seekers	2.05	1.96
(3) Ratio of contributors to economically active persons	0.81	0.93
(4) Ratio of contributors to population age 60 +	1.96	2.04
(5) Ratio of contributors to old age pensioners	1.86	2.15
(6) Ratio of contributors to old age and disability pensioners	1.57	1.86

Source: Ministry of Welfare of Latvia. Prepared for this study.

toward a net negative process, which can be expected at latest around 2020, but quite possibly earlier given the rapid pace in the increase in formality since 1997.

The rate of growth of real per capita wages is also likely to subside well before the 2030s. Hence workers around 30–35 and older around the year 2000 will be the recipients of this growth when they become pensioners. Younger birth cohorts, on the other hand, are covered increasingly by the FDC scheme and will rely much more on this scheme rather than on NDC for their future benefits. Also, as calculations presented in a separate section in this study indicate, the introduction of an NDC reserve fund is essential to maintain financial balance in the coming 40 years. Latvia does not have the Swedish automatic balancing mechanism. If it were to be introduced in Latvia it would most likely reduce NDC commitments even further than in the calculations presented in this study for the most pessimistic scenarios—those where fertility, net immigration, mortality, and real per capita wage growth all move *against* the system. On the other hand, such a balancing mechanism would not be needed in practice to maintain a ratio of assets to liabilities greater than unity—financial balance—in scenarios with "non-pessimistic" economic and demographic outcomes.

Generally speaking, the NDC scheme can also afford indexation of *benefits* with the rate of growth of the contribution base. This was not possible to implement in practice, however. In the beginning of the reform in 1996, it was only possible to price-index (all) benefits. Then the stock of pensioners consisted almost solely of persons whose benefits had been determined under the old rules, including the special rights giving benefits from age 40. Largely because of this generosity in granting pension benefits, but also because of the fall of GDP during the early 1990s, pension costs at the time of the reform were already too high. Pensioners will increasingly become NDC pensioners and eventually the system can move toward including indexation based on real growth.

It is also important to note that the historical demographics of Latvia also work in favor of NDC system implementation, since large cohorts born in the 1980s will be entering the labor force in the period 2000–10. However, this also means that internal financial equilibrium in the system requires demographic reserves. In sum, it will be possible to move gradually in the direction of full wage indexation, but a course should be set out that also takes the need for reserves into consideration. The Ministry of Welfare has recently performed calculations[8] similar to those presented below in this study that show how this path could be taken. In fact, in principle, the Latvian NDC scheme is "overfinanced" given the counterfactual of possible full-fledged NDC indexation for NDC pensioners.

The introduction of the FDC scheme in 2001 was given priority over full indexation of NDC benefits, as both were not affordable in parallel during the initial years. Until 2002 the indexation of benefits was based solely on the consumer price index. In 2002–3, pensions with small amounts were indexed on the basis of both the change in the Consumer Price Index and 25 percent of the real growth of contribution wage sum. From 2004 until 2006, small pensions (that is, pensions not exceeding three "social benefits"[9] or 105 lats in 2004) will receive 50 percent real indexation—in addition to inflation adjustment. According to the current pension law in 2006–10, all pensions with an amount not exceeding five "social benefits" will receive 25 percent real indexation and after that the real growth component will be increased to 50 percent for all pensioners.

The annual pension (P) at retirement in the Latvian NDC pension scheme is calculated as $P = K/G$, where K is the accumulated life-time notional pension capital at retirement and G is cohort unisex life expectancy at retirement. G values are calculated from projected cohort life tables.[10] Assumptions for the projections are prepared and analyzed by an official committee of Latvian demographic experts, including the experts from the Statistical Bureau. A report from mortality experts is discussed and approved in the committee and delivered to the Ministry of Welfare. The initial set of cohort projections were determined by examining mortality trends in countries with much lower mortality rates than Latvia and then judging probable paths of convergence of Latvian mortality to "better practice." The value of G is set annually, by the Ministry of Welfare for retirement ages between 40 and 80,[11] in accordance with the recommendation of the committee. In 2004, the G value for retirement at ages 60, 65, and 70 were 19.7, 15.67, and 12.46, respectively. According to the present projection, the G value at age 65 is expected to increase by about 2 years during the coming 30 years.

The long-term projections of mortality should change only gradually as new evidence becomes available. More importantly, even large changes in current period mortality rates will have no effect on the G values of future retirees, as long as the projected long-term mortality trend is not revised. There were two arguments in favor of using cohort projections for Latvia. The first is a general, not country-specific argument: Compared with using recent historical cross-sectional data, cohort trend-based projections are expected to come close to the actual development of future mortality, and should minimize the gap between the ex ante mortality rate used to compute the annuity at retirement and the ex post outcome, viewed when participants have deceased some time in the future.

The second argument in favor of cohort projections is relevant for many transition countries. If the G values had been based on a procedure involving recent current history, this would have led to undesirable fluctuations in G values from one year to the next. As figure 15.1 shows, there have been very large and rapid changes in mortality rates in Latvia since the mid-1980s. Between 1985 and 1987, Gorbachev's antialcohol campaign led to a sharp rise in life expectancy for men, but this was followed by a relapse in the late 1980s. The situation then deteriorated even more during the break-up of the Soviet Union and the transition period to the market economy in the 1990s.

Between 1987 and 1994, unisex life expectancy at birth fell by five years. In the high ages, which are directly relevant for G-value calculation, there was an extreme increase in mortality during the early and mid-1990s, probably as a consequence of the economic hardship and disruption in health care created by the transition. These changes were not seen as relevant for younger cohorts claiming an annuity after 1996. On top of this, in 1996 life expectancy at birth increased by 3.2 years for males and 2.5 years for females (see figure 15.1) based on period life tables—that is, data representing current mortality rates. It would not have been reasonable to construct longevity projections on the basis of these short-term historic down and upturns. Hence, for this reason too cohort projections were preferable.

In sum, the method used to determine the rate of return on NDC capital balances during the accumulation phase, along with the forward-looking cohort mortality estimate

Figure 15.1. Life Expectancy at Birth in Latvia

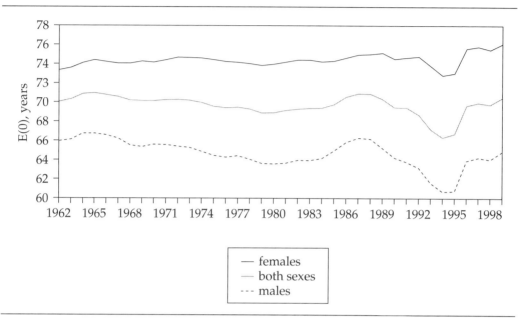

Source: Krumins (2000).

used in the calculation of the annuity, contribute to creating long-term financial stability. The data needed to create an NDC financial balance along the lines created in Sweden are still not available. Among other things, in the initial years of the reform initial capital was computed and registered only for persons claiming benefits. The process of registering transition notional capital for *all*, which involves individuals turning in their workbooks from the Soviet times to the Social Insurance Administration and subsequent checks of authenticity, is not expected to be completed until 2007, at the earliest. Until this is done, it is possible to provide only rough estimates of total NDC liabilities. Once completed, however, it will be possible for Latvia to implement the balance sheet approach developed and adopted in Sweden.[12] Whether or not this will be done is a new policy issue. In principle, this would be desirable to ensure that system assets are always at least as great as liabilities. In practice, ceteris paribus, as long as there is substantially less than full wage indexation of benefits the system will run a surplus. Hence, given the present design of the system, it is highly unlikely that a brake would be needed in the nearest decades. We return to the issue of future financial stability, given the present legislation, in a separate section below.

The FDC Component of the Overall Latvian Reform

The FDC scheme is mandatory for persons born after July 1, 1971—that is, persons under the age of 30 on July 2001, when the FDC scheme started operating. Participation is voluntary for persons who at the time of introduction were at that moment in the age group 30–49 (born between July 2, 1951, and July 1, 1971), with no limiting date on the time at which people can opt into the FDC scheme. According to the current legislation, the contribution rate for participants in the FDC scheme will abide by the following schedule:

from 2 percent in years 2001–6 to 4 percent in 2007, 8 percent in 2008, 9 percent in 2009, and 10 percent from 2010. Their NDC contribution rate is reduced by the same schedule as the increase in the FDC rate.

Voluntary participation in the FDC scheme was very low in the beginning. However, by the end of 2003, the participation rate of volunteers had increased sharply: to 28 percent from 8 percent at the end of 2002, as private asset managers took over the management of individual accounts and marketed the system.[13] At retirement, participants in the FDC scheme can choose between contracting an annuity on the market and transferring their accumulated financial funds to the NDC reserve fund,[14] allowing them to receive an NDC benefit based on the sum of their NDC and FDC capital. This is a unique feature of the Latvian FDC system. The FDC scheme is expected to be fully mandatory around 2035, when cohorts of voluntary participants will no longer be in the work force.

To conclude, as the FDC contribution rate increases, the NDC rate decreases commensurately for participants in the FDC scheme. The implications of the transition for the financial development of the overall system are discussed in a separate section below.

The Pension Age and Special Rights

Two major reform issues were the low pension age and the widespread use of special rights. How these were dealt with is the topic of this section.

The reform concept, passed in 1994, called for an increase in the minimum age for retirement. This established a pension age of 60 for both men and women, which meant increasing the pension age of women from 55 to 60. Later the minimum age was raised to 62 for both men and women. The increase followed a gradual schedule, increasing at the rate of a half year per year. The retirement age became 62 for men already in 2003, but it will not reach 62 for women until 2008. Note that in 2002 life expectancy at age 60 was over 15 years for men and almost 22 years for women, suggesting that even a minimum age of 62 is low. Certainly, the issue of the minimum pension age will have to be revisited within the coming decade or so.

In the reform legislation of 1995 there are specific paragraphs detailing how special rights—for example, those for workers working under hazardous conditions who had a right to a pension at age 40—are to be phased out. This was accomplished by valuing and converting acquired rights in the old regime into NDC capital. The process of phasing out special rights inherited from the old regime went smoothly politically, perhaps because the conversion was perceived as fair, and perhaps because it was seen as fair for everyone to move into the new system on an equal status. On the other hand, as we will discuss in the next section, a new group of special rights was nevertheless legislated after the 1996 reform for persons who were still working once they had passed the full benefit age in the old DB scheme. These turned out to be so blatantly unfair that it is unlikely that this will occur again.

Latvians retiring in 2003 had participated 31 years in the labor force, which can be compared with a unisex average of around 35 years for the Western European Union countries in the mid-1990s.[15] More importantly, it is also much lower than it was in Latvia at the time of the reform in 1995, when the average number of covered years was 36 years—for the entire stock of pensioners. In 2003 the average for the stock had dropped to 33, however, reflecting the drop in years of newly retired persons during the second half of the 1990s. The number of covered years for a person receiving a newly granted benefit was only 30 in 1996, with an increase to 31 by 2003. The drop in years of lifetime labor force participation is probably a temporary effect of the difficult years of the transition,[16] when it became particularly difficult for older workers to move into new jobs, and this provided clear justification for a transition guarantee for older workers (see below).[17]

Open Issues

Among the open issues in the Latvian pension reform is the issue of what to do with inheritance capital of persons who die *before* reaching the pension age in both the NDC and FDC schemes. NDC inheritance capital generated by deaths of contributors prior to retirement provides an extra source of finance. Presently in Latvia, it is used to finance the PAYG survivor benefits, which under the new law applies mostly to surviving parents with children under the age of 18 (or up to 24 if they are full-time students). According to the present legislation for the FDC scheme, inheritance capital arising in the FDC scheme is transferred to the social insurance budget, also to finance a mandatory survivor benefit. However, with the present construction of the survivor benefit rules, the benefit is overfinanced from these sources.

There are several possible candidates for use of "non–ear-marked" inheritance capital. First, the existing survivor benefit could be improved, which *de facto* means improving the income status of women (as survivors` pensions are granted for children). This would require a change in the legislation. Second, it could be used to create a better noncontributory childcare credit for women (and men if spouses so choose) to be paid into the NDC and FDC accounts. Third, these gains could be distributed to all surviving participants in each cohort at the minimum pension age in proportion to their share in the total notional capital of the cohort.[18] Fourth, it could be used to cover unfinanced commitments, such as the transition guarantee and, even more generally, the overall cost of transition to the new system—both of which are to be financed without increasing the present contribution rate. Implicitly, the latter is the option chosen today, more by default than conscious political design.

Conversion of Rights Acquired under the Old System to NDC Capital

At the time of the reform, it was estimated that only 65 to 70 percent of earnings were being reported.[19] In fact, for many years in the 1990s, the remaining state-owned enterprises were among the most avid sinners. The transition rules of the new pension law were created with an emphasis on quickly reducing underreporting of earnings and evasion, and thus reducing labor market distortions created by evasion. More generally, the practice of keeping "two books" was widespread; in fact, no one was penalized directly as long as benefits were not directly related to contributions. Instead, those who were really penalized were those who actually paid full contributions, since by paying for the entire system costs they were subsidizing workers who had the opportunity to evade. A goal of the reform was to introduce the NDC scheme quickly, in the hope that the link between contributions and benefits would discourage underreporting and evasion—and in any event tip the "fairness" scales more in favor of those who paid their contributions.

Acquired rights under the old system were to be converted into notional *initial capital* following the logic of the NDC principle. Accordingly, initial capital was based on the individual's covered wage after 1996, and service years acquired prior to 1996. Acquired "special rights" were valued and converted into initial capital. The general formula in the 1996 legislation for initial capital is: IC = individual covered earnings × individual service years × 0.20.

The original rule used to determine the individual's covered wage was: the average covered wage for *all* participants in 1995 for persons retiring in 1996; the individual's own average covered wage in 1996 for retirees in 1997; the individual's own average covered wage in 1996–7 for retirees in 1998; the individual's own average covered wage in 1996–8 for retirees in 1999; and the individual's average covered wage in 1996–9 for persons claiming a benefit in 2000 and later.

The choice to use the individual's *own* wage after 1995 as the basis for conversion of pre-reform service years to initial capital was aimed at creating a strong incentive to report income and penalize evasion.[20] This method had its drawbacks, however. The timing and length of the period used to compute this wage proved to be a problem for persons who genuinely had a poor footing in the labor market during the designated conversion period of 1996–99.[21] This meant that persons with similar working histories before 1996 could receive very different pensions based on their employment status after 1995, which could easily be claimed to be unfair particularly to older workers with the vast majority of their years in the old system. On the other hand, in judging this result it is important to keep in mind that there was a dispersion of earnings even before the transition, when most service years were accumulated, and at least to some extent, the distribution of posttransition individual earnings in the initial decade reflected the distribution of pretransition individual earnings. For this reason, the use of a universal average-wage rule would also have been unfair to persons with pre-1996 above average earnings careers.

Given the conversion rule chosen, another conversion problem was that some employees did not have a complete contribution record during 1996–99, either because the employer had defaulted, or because they chose themselves to work informally. In principle, contributions of bankrupt employers should have been covered by the state as a part of the bankruptcy process, even in a transition setting,[22] which is the usual practice in the European Union and other countries outside the transition block. This did not happen in Latvia. Whether persons working under informal circumstances after 1996, who had service records (and rights) under the old regime but consciously defaulted under the new regime, were treated unfairly has no clear-cut answer. It could be argued both ways. However, for some it just was not easy to find regular employment in this phase of the transition, and for this reason the employment-related transition rule for computing the value of capital to be taken forward from the old system could give a poor pension.[23]

Because exclusion from the labor force in the first years after the reform—in spite of a long prereform contribution record—was one of the reasons some initial pensions were too low, there was a need to provide a transition guarantee, and for this reason additional rules were adopted for computing initial capital. These rules were adopted in parliament in 1996 and were applied in 1997–99, and then again from 2002 to 2010, following a new revision of the law. The transition-guarantee rule applies to persons with at least 30 years of service. According to the guarantee, initial capital is based on the best of either the individual's earnings according to the main law, or an amount based on the average wage for all participants in the years 1996–99.[24] For all others, initial capital is computed as the best of either the computation using the individual's own earnings or an amount based on 40 percent of the average covered wage, which is approximately the minimum wage. Hence, in practice, the *minimum* guaranteed amount of initial capital based on service years prior to 1996 is that which corresponds to the minimum wage. As time passes, the importance of initial capital will decline, and total notional capital will depend more and more on actual individual earnings and contributions, and less on pre-1996 service years and the transition rule.

In sum, the labor market was in such a state of disarray during the transition that the conversion rule in the original law proved to be unfair for persons with long work careers but who were genuinely excluded from the labor market during the latter half of the 1990s. For this reason, a separate guarantee rule was introduced—in spite of the existence of a general guaranteed minimum pension—that covered rights earned prior to the transition and introduction of the reform. The design of the special guarantee was nevertheless influenced by the goal of minimizing an overly generous transition rule that would continue to reward underreporting and evasion, an ever-present problem throughout the transition.

Individual Benefits the First Decade after Reform

How did the reform affect newly granted benefits during its first years? This question can be answered by examining what has happened with the factors that determine an NDC benefit: life expectancy, the average wage, the rate of return applied to accounts, and the number of covered years of new retirees. Increasing real wages and a positive rate of return on accounts mean the yearly increments to NDC capital of younger birth cohorts will exceed those for older birth cohorts. If the average number of covered years remains constant, then development of benefits will depend on the development of unisex life expectancy and the average age at which people choose to retire.

We have already seen (table 15.1) that average wage growth was 5.5 percent for all workers, and that the rate of return on NDC accounts was even higher—6.6 percent—in the period 1997–2003 because of positive growth in the number of persons contributing. This suggests that wage and contribution growth have had a strong positive effect on new benefits. Since 1996, the unisex life expectancy factor at age 60 has increased from 18.25, applied for pension calculation in 1996 to 19.17 in 2004. In 1997, the number of covered years for a newly retired person was 30 years, while in 2003 it was 31. The average age of a new retiree for men in 1997 was 59.8 and for women 55.7 and in 2003 it was respectively 61.1 and 57.7, respectively. Hence, all the factors except life expectancy worked in the direction of increasing the average real value of a newly granted annuity. In fact, the real growth factor was especially strong.

Surprisingly, viewed in 2003, the average value of a pension granted in 1996 and each succeeding year thereafter was about the same, with the notable exception of 1999 for men and 1999 and 2000 for women. There are several reasons why the average benefit remained so stable and, together, these disguised the "pure" effect of the introduction of the NDC scheme. One is that early retirement with an actuarially reduced benefit is possible until 2008. Hence, in spite of the increase in the pension age, people could leave the labor force earlier during the initial years, albeit with an actuarially reduced benefit. In practice, this was what many—especially many women—did.

Probably the most important reason why a trend increase in the average real benefit level of new cohorts of pensioners is not observable is that parliament granted extra indexation of benefits in 1996–99, with especially large changes in 1997 and 1998.[25] The overall effect of these extra indexations was to bring benefits granted earlier up to about the level of newly granted benefits.

In 1999, the level of an average pension granted was raised by yet another ad hoc measure, this time the introduction of a new special right. Working pensioners whose benefits had been granted under the old law were allowed to recalculate their benefits using the new NDC formula, if they had worked at least three years from 1996. This procedure was passed by parliament in response to a powerful interest lobby (those who benefited were older professional workers), in spite of the Ministry of Welfare's objections.

In 1995, when the reform was being considered, the ratio of an average newly granted benefit to an average wage was around 44 percent at age 55 for women, and 46 percent at age 60 for men.[26] In 2003, an average newly granted benefit was 67 lats and an average wage was 172 lats in the same year. This gives a ratio of average newly granted benefit to a gross average wage of 39 percent. At the same time pensions (below 100 lats) are not taxed, while wages have an average tax of 25 percent. The ratio of an average newly granted benefit to an average after-tax wage is thus about 49 percent. Overall, the effect of the life expectancy factor and the decline in the number of average covered years during the initial transition decade have tended to reduce the level of newly granted benefits. With a more stable economic environment and increase in the minimum pension age, the number of covered years will increase.

Summing up, a low number of covered years on average together with a pronounced tendency for people to avail an option to retire before the minimum pension age until July 2005 contributed to holding down the average size of newly granted pensions in the initial years. In addition, extra indexations raised the benefit levels of the pre- and early post-reform pensioners to a level close to newly granted benefits in the following years. NDC accounts have grown with the rapid increase in the per capita wage, but the average replacement rate is nevertheless slightly lower than immediately prior to the reform, largely because of the low number of covered years. It is reasonable to believe that the number of years of coverage will once again return to a higher level—the average number of covered years was around 35 for the whole stock of pensioners at the time the reform was being formulated in 1995. Both longer careers with covered earnings and adaptation to the new higher retirement age will contribute to higher pensions in the future.

The Long-Term Financial Picture

The primary goal of the 1996 Latvian pension reform was to create an adequate benefit for career workers through a system that links benefits to contributions within the framework of a system that is financially stable in the long run. This was the reasoning behind the choice of a combination of NDC and an FDC.[27] The introduction of NDC and FDC also provides a framework for minimizing labor-market distortions and creating savings, while in the long run this new framework can contribute to higher economic growth and prosperity for all. In this section we analyze the long-term financial picture for this choice. We begin by discussing demographic and economic scenarios for the coming half century, and then show how the financial development of the new pension system is affected by more extreme assumptions about economic growth, fertility, morality, and net immigration.

The Demographic and Economic Setting

The future development of fertility, mortality, and net migration are all extremely uncertain in any country. Latvia is no exception. Latvia experienced a baby boom in the 1980s, but since the beginning of the transition the fertility rate has been persistently low. In 2003, the period fertility rate was only 1.2 children per woman, far below the 2.1 required to maintain a stable population. In addition, there is considerable uncertainty regarding the effect of EU membership on net migration. In the medium term, there is no doubt that many Latvians, particularly younger and better-educated ones, will seek economic opportunities outside Latvia. Both the strength and duration of this effect of the transition is difficult to judge, however. Furthermore, there is considerable room for mortality to drop dramatically in the coming decades if diets, smoking, and living habits in general become healthier, and as modern medical technology becomes more accessible and affordable.[28]

The question addressed here is how financially resilient the new Latvian system is in the face of extreme demographic and, hence, demographically generated economic pressure. In order to examine the resilience of the reform to various constellations of parameters, a number of scenarios—some with very extreme economic and demographic assumptions—are examined. The baseline scenario assumes an increase in fertility from the 2003 level of 1.2 to 1.5 in 2015, and then to 1.7 for the remainder of the period examined. An even more optimistic scenario, with period fertility reaching 1.8 in 2015 and then increasing and maintaining a level of 2.0—assuming optimistically that economic prosperity will increase the propensity to have children—is also examined. The baseline scenario assumes net migration from Latvia through 2010. Thereafter, net migration is zero. Two other scenarios for net migration include positive and negative net immigration flows after 2010.

Two mortality scenarios are examined. In the baseline scenario, survival of men from age 60 increases from 15.1 in 2002 to 18.1 years in 2050, and for women from 21.8 in 2002 to 23.5 years in 2050. A set of more dramatic changes is also examined, with an increase in survival for men age 60 to 23.3 in year 2050 and for women age 60 to 28.1. This more dramatic change assumes more than an 8-year increase in longevity for men and more than a 6-year increase for women. This would put Latvians on a level closer to their Scandinavian neighbors.

As figures 15.2 through 15.4 show, in the baseline demography the total Latvian population declines from about 2.3 million persons in 2003 to 1.5 million persons in year 2075, which assumes that the present net migration out of the country stops by 2010. In the scenario with the continued net migration of younger persons out of the country, the population falls to less than 1.3 million persons in 2075. The yearly rate of decline in the population is 0.57 per year in the baseline, where net emigration stops in 2010, and 0.76 per year in the pessimistic scenario, where it continues. The "pessimistic" scenario embodies, thus, high migration and low fertility—and reduces the population dramatically.

Figure 15.2. The Latvian Population

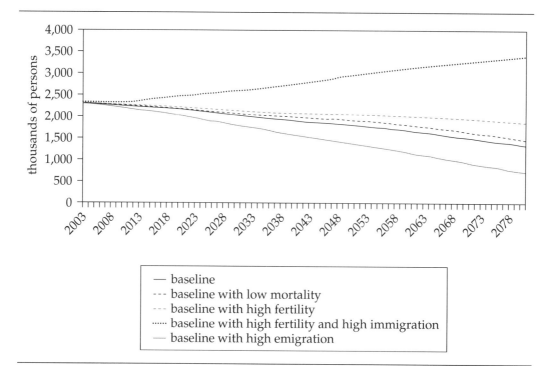

Source: Authors' calculations using the Latvian Ministry of Welfare's Technical Model.

Of course various combinations of the fertility rate and net migration can give similar demographic results. Given these demographic assumptions, the baseline scenario yields an even more dramatic fall in the working-age population from a high of about 1.2 million persons around the year 2015 to only about 0.6 million persons in the year 2075. This is not an entirely unrealistic scenario, since it involves a considerable improvement in fertility, even though the improvement falls far short of that needed to reproduce the population. In addition, the assumption that net migration from the country will cease is a strong assumption. The pessimistic scenario with continued net emigration after 2010 is even more dramatic, leaving only 0.4 million working-age persons year 2075. Logically, the tendency for Latvians to leave the country could be counterbalanced by immigration—probably from Russia and other countries with a language similar to Russian, since there are already many Russian-speaking residents in Latvia, which would make it easy to assimilate these immigrants.

The system dependency ratio deteriorates in the baseline scenario to around 1.1–1.2 workers per old-age pensioner by around 2055, where it becomes relatively stable. In the high-emigration scenario—combined with the high survival scenario—the system dependency ratio becomes even worse, with less than one worker per old-age pensioner. These scenarios include an assumed retirement age of 62 beginning for men born 1944 and women born 1948 and from 63 beginning with birth cohorts born 1967. Obviously, a higher de facto retirement age would increase the labor force and improve the dependency ratio a little, albeit without changing the fundamental picture.

In the baseline scenario, real per capita wage growth is around 4 percent until about 2015, when it decreases progressively toward 3 percent in 2023 and continues to fall to 2

Figure 15.3. Economically Active Population (age 15 up to the minimum pension age)

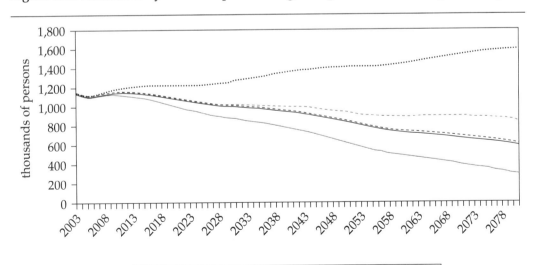

Source: Authors' calculations using the Latvian Ministry of Welfare's Technical Model.

Figure 15.4. System Dependency Ratio

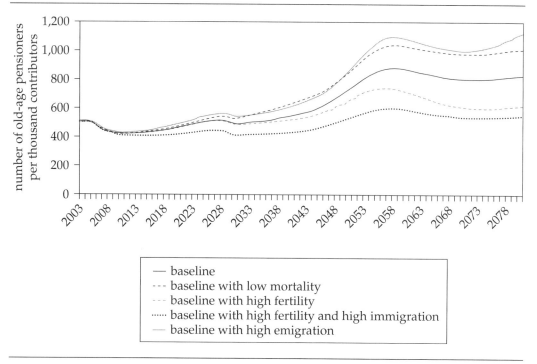

Source: Authors' calculations using the Latvian Ministry of Welfare's Technical Model.

percent by 2030, where it remains thereafter. The more optimistic growth scenario entails real growth of around 5 percent until about 2020 when it drops first to 4 percent, where it remains through 2045, and then to 3 percent for the remainder of the period. The pessimistic growth scenario drops to below 3 percent already in 2013 and reaches 1.2 percent in 2020, where it remains throughout. This pessimistic growth scenario is far from the annual combined growth rate of the real wage rate and formal labor force of 6.6 percent actually achieved by Latvia in 1997–2003. In fact, even the optimistic scenario involves a lower growth rate than that accomplished during this period.

In sum, the demographic picture is extremely uncertain. An improvement in the fertility rate from 1.2 to 1.7, as in the baseline scenario, still leads to a decline in the working-age population by half, and a yearly average rate of decline in the work force of over a half a percent! If Latvia is to grow, then the fertility rate must reach at least 2.1, and/or net migration into the country must be positive. Unfortunately, at present all signs point toward a continued net flow of people out of the country. Obviously, the minimum pension age will have to be increased even more in the future, but this cannot provide much relief. The conclusion is that Latvia is headed toward a ratio of around one worker per pensioner. The question is, then, how does the reformed pension system handle this?

Long-Term Financial Development of the Pension System

The aim of the Latvian NDC scheme is to create a stable contribution rate over the long run, but, at present, without automatic balancing as there is in Sweden.[29] At the same time, Latvia is gradually phasing in the FDC scheme through 2010. This means that NDC commitments will have been created that have no explicit future financing, since the overall contribution rate of 20 percent needed to finance past NDC commitments is to be shared between the declining NDC and increasing FDC components. In other words, the process of phasing in the FDC scheme is accompanied by the creation of an explicit tax, which will be needed to finance NDC commitments already granted that cannot be financed by the lower future NDC contribution rate, until a new equilibrium is reached when all the NDC liabilities are based on a contribution rate of 10 percent.

This section of the study uses the Social Insurance and Pension Model developed at the Ministry of Welfare to analyze the question of how well the Latvian pension reform does in maintaining financial stability over the coming 75 years, given Latvia's policy choices. In addition, the long-term stability of the NDC scheme in the absence of the introduction of the FDC scheme is illustrated. Finally, a long-term contribution rate of 6 percent to the FDC scheme is also considered to illustrate the difference in the tax burden between this scale and the 10 percent scale for the FDC scheme in the legislation.

Figure 15.5 illustrates the transition process given the current legislation. Note that it takes until around 2040 before the last persons with benefits acquired under the pre-1996 legislation have died, primarily due to the low pension age of women (55) and the opportunities for early retirement from age 40 possible under special rights in the old system. What's more, until around 2065, the bulk of pensioners are persons whose pensions were at least partially determined by pre-1996 work careers, and it takes until around 2075 for the NDC scheme to reach maturity in the sense that all pensioners were new labor force entrants from the implementation of the reform in 1996.

A Hypothetical Reform without the FDC Component

We begin by asking how the NDC scheme would have performed financially in the future, without the gradual transition from NDC to FDC. To this end a set of scenarios has been

Figure 15.5. Number of Old-Age Pensioners with Grants under the Old Law, Transition, and New Law

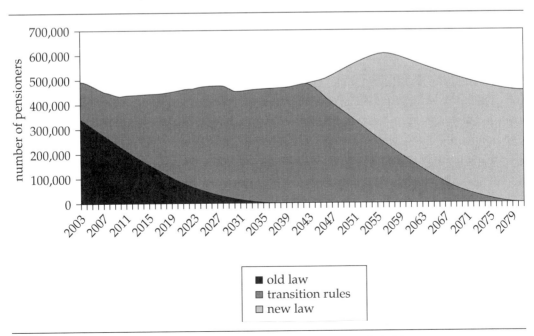

Source: Authors' calculations using the Latvian Ministry of Welfare's Technical Model.

run in which the NDC scheme is the only pension scheme in the future. This is accomplished by continuing to allocate those contributions that would otherwise have gone to
the FDC scheme to the NDC scheme, giving, thus, an overall NDC contribution rate of 20
percent forever. Indexation follows the legislation until 2011. This means that there is real
indexation of benefits of 50 percent for small pensions since 2004 and 50 percent indexation for everybody from 2011.

Figures 15.6–15.8 show the results for the various scenarios, assuming only an NDC
scheme. The system builds up a surplus in all but one of the scenarios through 2035–40. In
fact, in the baseline scenario there is a surplus past 2045. The surplus would ideally be held
in a reserve fund, earn a financial rate of return at least equivalent to the rate granted on
accounts of workers up until this time, when it is needed to finance the pensions of the
baby boomers from the 1980s, in 2045–65.

One of the scenarios that does not appear to quite achieve equilibrium by 2080—
although it is not far from it, given reserves built up prior to 2040—is the scenario where
the working-age population declines from 1.2 million persons in around 2015 to 0.4 million in 2080, which is a harsh scenario for any country. Nevertheless, the financial deficit is
relatively modest given the nature of the shock.[30] In the other difficult scenario, the decline
in the working-age population is "only" from 1.2 to 0.6 million persons—a decline at a rate
of 0.6 percent per year, but with a rate of growth of real wages per capita steadily declining
to a long-term rate of 1.2 percent—giving overall contribution base growth of about 0.6
percent. In this case, the full indexation of old-law commitments together with high indexation of newer transition NDC commitments in the initial decades creates a drain on
reserves during the first 40 years.

Figure 15.6. Old-Age Pension Expenditures As a Percent of the Contribution Base

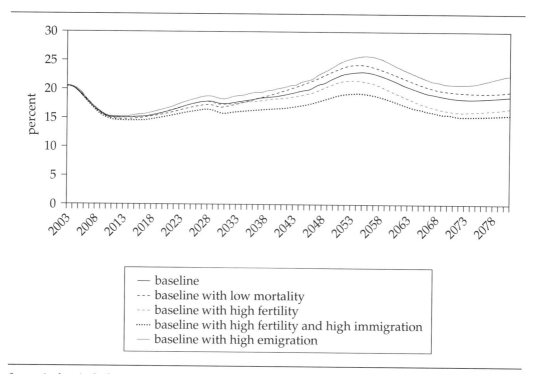

Source: Authors' calculations using the Latvian Ministry of Welfare's Technical Model.

Figure 15.7. Old-Age Pension Expenditures As a Percent of the Contribution Base

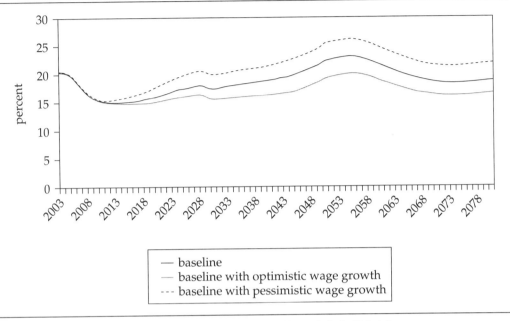

Source: Authors' calculations using the Latvian Ministry of Welfare's Technical Model.

Figure 15.8. Total Social Insurance Expenditures As a Percent of the Contribution Rate

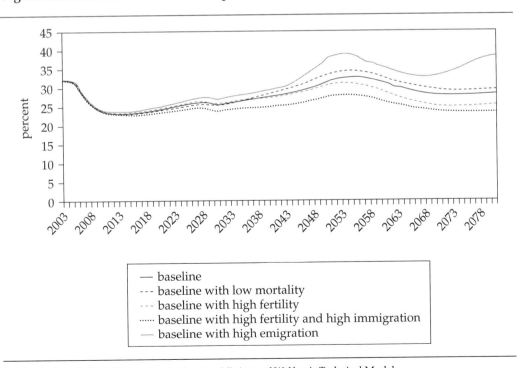

Source: Authors' calculations using the Latvian Ministry of Welfare's Technical Model.

The financial analysis based on the contribution rates on earnings in figures 15.7 and 15.8 does not include the financing of pension rights acquired during insured periods of sickness, disability, and unemployment. Since there is no reserve fund to hold these, they are a part of the general surplus in the overall social insurance budget. Once there is a reserve fund, these monies would be transferred to the fund and held there until they are needed to finance commitments to old-age pensioners. For this reason, a complete analysis of the financial picture really requires a look at the surplus or deficit in the overall social insurance budget. This is done in figure 15.8.[31]

With the present contribution rate of 33 percent it is clear that, with a reserve fund to hold the accumulated surpluses until around 2040, the system will be in balance. The overall scenario that leads to a long-term financial deficit is the one with high emigration, with a drop in the working-age population from 1.2 million to 0.4 million persons over only a half century. In this hypothetical case, a higher contribution rate would be needed to sustain the overall system. A higher overall contribution rate for the social insurance system is also needed because of the imbalance in the other systems, in part as a result of the generous indexation of disability benefits, in line with current legislation.

Financial Development of the System with NDC and FDC

The actual legislation includes the FDC scheme with a scheduled gradual increase in the FDC contribution rate to 10 percent and a commensurate decrease in the NDC rate also to 10 percent in 2010. What does this mean for financial stability? Figures 15.9 and 15.10 show both this scenario, which is legislated, and an additional scenario where the increase in the contribution rate to the FDC scheme stops at 6 percent and the final NDC contribution rate is 14 percent.

The first conclusion is that with the scheduled increase to 10 percent, the overall system will require a higher contribution rate than the present 33 percent, at least until the scheme matures in around 70 years (figure 15.9). Of course, if the Latvian government follows the schedule, this additional cost could be financed through general tax revenues. On the other hand, the government has the option of restricting the scale of the FDC scheme. The alternative, which stops with an FDC contribution rate of 6 percent (figure 15.10), is easily financed within the present contribution rate of 33 percent, given that reserves are accumulated to around 2035, with, once again, the exception being the scenario where the working-age population declines from 1.2 to 0.4 million persons because of emigration.

The overall system costs less for the transition generation with NDC alone than it costs in the combined scenario with NDC and FDC. This is a gross rather than a net cost, however. Why? First, the transition generation is likely to get a higher long-run rate of return out of the FDC scheme. Second, it is likely that the FDC scheme will contribute to net national savings and yield higher economic growth, assuming this saving would have been crowded out by a more comprehensive NDC scheme. Third, the FDC scheme will help "force" financial market deepening, which will provide an additional stimulus to economic growth.

Figure 15.11 shows the financial outcome for the baseline case. This outcome reflects the fact that NDC commitments from the past, when the NDC rate was higher than 10 percent as well as remaining old-law commitments, must still be paid but with a lower NDC contribution rate, until the transition has been completed and everyone has NDC and FDC commitments based on 10 percent each. This creates a tax. However, in the case where the FDC scheme has a maximum contribution rate of 6 percent, this tax is covered within the 33 percent overall contribution rate. The tax is higher with an FDC contribution rate of 10 percent. The overall costs are actually highest after about 2045–65.

Figure 15.9. Total Social Insurance Costs As a Percent of the Contribution Base (FDC with a 10% contribution rate from 2010)

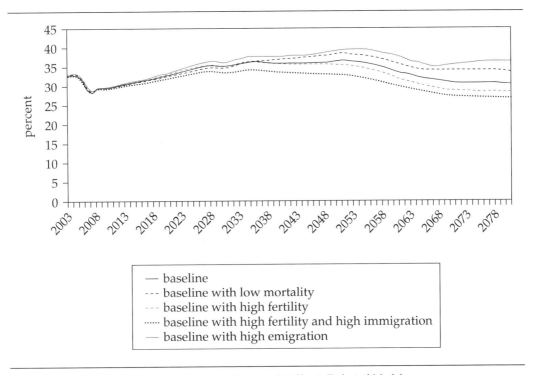

Source: Authors' calculations using the Latvian Ministry of Welfare's Technical Model.

Note: Costs of covering expenditures on all benefits and payments to the FDC scheme.

The tax associated with introducing the FDC scheme has a counterpart in financial savings, however, as we have just noted. Figure 15.12 shows that the funds accumulated through the FDC scheme can become considerable. These savings will undoubtedly help to develop the domestic financial market and provide domestic liquidity for financing domestic investments. If a large part of the FDC portfolio is invested abroad, however, this provides a mixed portfolio for pensioners, with a smaller component based on the development of Latvia's demography and future productivity than would have been the case with pure NDC (or some other pay-as-you-go scheme). In the long term this more balanced portfolio will be to the advantage of both workers and pensioners. In addition, in the long run, the introduction of the FDC scheme reduces the overall debt passed on to future generations—but this takes up to three-quarters of a century to accomplish.

The model used in this calculation exercise assumes no direct link between these increased savings and economic growth, either through fixed investments or through the deepening of the financial market. As we have already noted, real growth could be greater in the combined FDC-NDC scenario embodied in the legislation than in a pure NDC scenario without an FDC scheme, ceteris paribus. The disadvantage of the introduction of the FDC scheme is that it occurs at the expense of higher indexation of benefits, until transition equilibrium is reached after a half century. This can be counterbalanced, however, if the FDC scheme delivers higher growth and a higher overall rate of return for pensioners

Figure 15.10. Total Social Insurance Costs As a Percent of the Contribution Base (FDC with a 6% contribution rate from 2008)

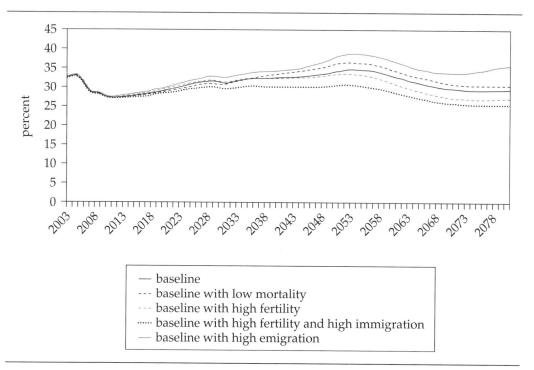

Source: Authors' calculations using the Latvian Ministry of Welfare's Technical Model.

Note: Costs of covering expenditures on all benefits and payments to the FDC scheme.

with a large part of their pension coming from this scheme. Finally, for pensioners not covered by the FDC scheme, indexation will nevertheless be higher with higher overall growth, even though indexation of benefits is not 100 percent linked to real growth.

Political Sustainability and Popular Support

The principles of the multipillar pension system have found a strong political footing in Latvia since 1996, and there is no doubt that this system will be maintained. This notwithstanding, the law on state pensions was amended 10 times during the first eight years. Some of the amendments involved the extra indexations granted through 1999 and the new amendment granting special rights to working pensioners whose pensions had been granted under the old law discussed above. Finally, after 1996, a series of changes were made in the law to create better transition rules and a transition guarantee for older workers retiring prior to 2010. The latter could have been avoided if better transition rules had been created from the outset, which is an important lesson from the Latvian experience.

The challenge for the future will be to safeguard the expected growth of the cash surplus in the pension budget, as it will be needed to cover future liabilities. As the pension amounts are still low, there will be pressure put on the government from old-age pensioners (21 percent of population) to increase pension levels, disregarding the principles of the system. These principles include the need for a reserve to cover commitments already

Figure 15.11. Total Social Insurance Costs As a Percent of the Contribution Base

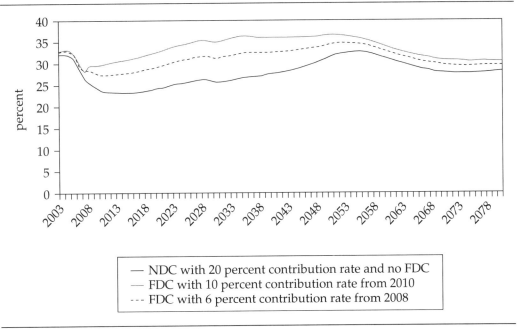

Source: Authors' calculations using the Latvian Ministry of Welfare's Technical Model.

Note: Costs of covering expenditures on all benefits including financing the FDC scheme.

Figure 15.12. Total Assets of the FDC Pension Scheme As a Percent of GDP

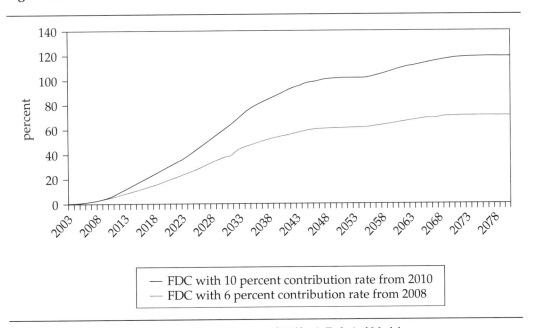

Source: Authors' calculations using the Latvian Ministry of Welfare's Technical Model.

made and that will have to be honored in the future. Therefore, as has already been noted, the introduction of the reserve fund for the NDC scheme remained as a first priority of pension policy still in 2005.

Latvians in general support the NDC and FDC schemes. In 2003, when individual portfolio choices became possible, the FDC scheme won popular support because of the advertising of fund managers. People appear to favor that the scheme is privately run and offers a degree of choice. The important message here is that the government must continue with its information for both the components of the reform, and that this should be supported by frequent opinion polls that can indicate the direction and content for future information campaigns. It will be important to continually remind people of the principles of the new reform so that they can make informed decisions. This will require a more regular information from the government and the pension administration.

Summary and Final Remarks

In sum, the Latvian NDC reform, implemented with a full conversion from old-system rights to NDC capital in 1996, has withstood the test of time. After 10 years, the system has proven to be politically robust, surviving numerous changes in governments and several national elections from 1996 through 2004. A major reason for the general acceptance of the system is a general acceptance of the underlying principles.

The most difficult challenge in the initial years was finding the right balance between a guarantee for older workers retiring according to the new rules and the aim of curbing widespread underreporting of income to the insurance (and tax) system. The initial set of rules could not discriminate between persons with long careers in the old system who had become genuine victims of the general labor-market havoc of the 1990s and those who consciously withheld information about income in order to avoid paying contributions. The latter occurred both on an individual and an employer basis. The Ministry of Welfare devised a guarantee rule for the transition that aimed at treating the first group fairly, which generated additional short-term political support for the reform.

Noteworthy is that the parliament's amendment of the legislation in 1998 creating extremely high and unfair benefits for a small group of persons who had retired according to the old law prior to the 1996 reform, but who were still working after the reform, was not accepted favorably by the public once the result was generally known.

The NDC scheme has generated a substantial return to participants since its introduction. From 1997 through 2003, the real rate of return on notional accounts was 6.7 percent per annum, driven by real per capita wage growth of 5.5 percent per annum. In addition, the number of covered workers increased at a rate of 1.1 percent per year in the initial years of the NDC scheme, 1997–2003, and there was a strong increase in the number of economically active persons paying contributions between 1997 and 2003. This increase in formality is certainly attributable to the overall success of the Latvian transformation from a command to a formal market economy, but it also supports the contention that direct contribution-based benefit schemes, such as NDC, provide an incentive to formally declare earnings and pay contributions in order to become participants in public benefit schemes.

Pensions were price indexed, but ad hoc indexations during the 1990s raised the value of previously granted benefits so that they were more or less on a par with newly granted NDC benefits in later years. These measures served to share the economic rewards of better times with pensioners who had received their benefits prior to 1999, but at the same time suggested that politicians could still intervene with ad hoc measures outside the long-term framework set out for the reform. On the other hand, no ad hoc changes in benefits have occurred since 1999. This provides solid evidence of political stability.

The calculations presented in this study show that the Latvian pension system is financially stable in the face of extremely unfavorable economic and demographic conditions, including a long-run proclivity to exit the labor force at (on average) age 63, that is somewhat past the minimum age of 62 to be in force for both genders by 2007. Of course, more favorable scenarios create less pressure. In addition, Latvian politicians will probably find themselves motivated to increase the minimum pension age by even more as improved living habits and better health care yield considerable improvements in longevity in the period covered by this study—to 2075.

The analysis illustrates the fact that Latvia needs to create a reserve fund to save an expected surplus associated largely with persons born in the 1980s in order to cover their NDC pensions beginning around 2040–45. On its own, the NDC scheme displays financial balance in the long run, but the introduction of the FDC scheme creates "uncovered rights"—that is, NDC account values built up with a contribution rate higher than that pertaining when benefits are to be paid out. These benefits are nevertheless covered within the framework of an existing overall contribution rate of 33 percent, if the FDC scheme is scaled down to a final contribution rate of 6 percent.

As the legislation stands, the Latvian pension reform is financially stable in the face of potential, extreme demographic challenges. This study shows that this would have been especially true in a hypothetical situation with only an NDC reform—that is, without the phasing in of the FDC reform during 2001–10. The study shows that if the planned increase to a contribution rate of 10 percent for the FDC scheme and decrease to 10 percent for the NDC scheme is carried out, tax revenues above the present contribution rate will be needed around 2045–65. The FDC scheme, assuming that the 10 percent contribution rate becomes effective, constitutes considerable forced savings within the mandated insurance system, which will be registered as private savings in the national income accounts. This will be counterbalanced, ceteris paribus, by a decline in public savings as new tax money is channeled into the overall social insurance budget to cover the social insurance deficit implicit in the calculations presented here, which will be needed to fulfill commitments to the large cohorts born in the 1980s. In other words, the reserves built up in the NDC scheme during the period prior to 2045 will be insufficient to cover all commitments within the limits of a fixed contribution rate. This means that even generations of workers 2045 and later will still be paying for the transition to FDC. Whether this is reasonable depends on the value one gives to introducing such a large-scale mandatory FDC scheme.

The logic of introducing the FDC scheme on a significant scale is clear, as is discussed in the text of this study. The first reason is to diversify the pension portfolios of Latvians. The demographic future for Latvia seen through today's glasses is bleak, with low fertility, improving mortality, and a high risk for net migration from the country to other EU countries. By 2075, the population and labor force may be half today's size and older. Latvia seems to be on a course with an annual rate of decline in the labor force of 0.5–0.7 percent. The negative effect of population growth will be counterbalanced by an increase in the degree of formality up to around 2015 or so and an increase in the retirement age. Also, in the long run, the real rate of growth of per capita wages is bound to slow down to around 2 percent as Latvia's productivity and wage structures converge with those of the rest of Europe.

From this perspective, it seems reasonable for Latvia's (or any other country's) mandatory pension portfolio to consist of a combination of FDC assets invested largely abroad, presumably in high-growth areas, and NDC assets determined by the growth of the home economy. The latter also serves to provide a part of the overall pay-as-you-go financed minimum pension for future Latvian workers.

Finally, the study points out several outstanding technical NDC issues. One is that no explicit decision has been taken on what to do with the surplus inheritance gains. Another, once again, is that there is currently no NDC reserve fund. Among other things, this fund is needed to hold money transferred to the NDC scheme for noncontributory rights and rights granted in conjunction with insured periods of sickness, disability, and unemployment. In addition, also in line with the NDC principle, a portion of contributions paid by the cohort from the 1980s, due to their large size, will need to be funded. These demographically driven reserves will rise for the coming more than three decades, but eventually they will be needed to finance the pensions of larger retiring cohorts. Last, until it has actually occurred, the full transition to an FDC contribution rate of 10 percent in 2010 remains an open issue, and is part of the tradeoff in the overall set of options for coming years.

Notes

1. This study follows the framework for viewing pension systems developed in Góra and Palmer (2004). Pension systems are seen as being non-financial or financial (fully funded) and as following either defined contribution or defined benefit rules. This gives rise to four categories of pension schemes: financial defined benefit (FDB), financial defined contribution (FDC), non-financial defined benefit (NDB), and non-financial defined contribution (NDC). Therefore it is argued that that non-financial defined contribution is a more appropriate description than "notional" defined contribution for NDC.

2. See Fox and Palmer (1999).

3. See Gassmann's (2000) analysis of poverty in Latvia during this period.

4. See Fox and Palmer (1999).

5. The theoretical framework for NDC is discussed in Palmer's "What Is NDC?" (2006).

6. In order to do this properly, a reserve fund has to be set up, but Latvia has still not done this. The problem in delaying this is clear: it creates a tax burden on future workers to eventually pay for these nonfinanced rights. The delay in implementing this procedure can be explained by the financial constraints of the transition years, when from 1998 through 2001 the overall social insurance budget was in deficit. From 2002, there was an overall surplus, but the debt accumulated from previous years still remained, and the government is committed to transferring surplus money to the central budget until the debt has been paid off. Projections show that the accumulated deficit will be fully covered by 2006. After that, the introduction of a reserve fund will become a political priority.

7. Current official demographic projections are discussed in depth in the Ministry of Welfare's report, *The State Social Insurance System in Latvia* (2003).

8. *The State Social Insurance System in Latvia: Financial Analysis* (2003).

9. The *social benefit* is the amount to which a person who has never been able to work due to some form of physical or mental impairment is entitled.

10. See Krumins (2000 and 2003).

11. In the initial years after the reform in 1996, it was possible for persons with acquired special rights under the old system to claim a benefit as early as at the age of 40, which is why values are calculated from this age. As a part of the transition legislation, all special rights earned under the old system are phased out over time.

12. Settergren (2001) and the *Swedish Pension System Annual Report 2001.*

13. Money was managed by the state treasury during the first year and a half.

14. This fund still needs to be created, as has already been pointed out. However, there is some time left until the first FDC annuities can be claimed on a large scale in 2014.

15. See Palmer (1999).

16. See Vanovska (2004),

17. The Labor Force Survey shows that participation among older workers actually increased slightly from 1996. Employment was spread out over a large number of individuals who only had sporadic employment, however. A large percentage of workers did not have employment—or at least did not have contributions paid for them by employers—all months of the year according to the contribution records of the State Social Insurance Agency. Also, in the early years of the transition, 1991–96, the agricultural and industrial sectors more or less collapsed, creating a large number of persons without employment.

18. This is the method employed in Sweden's NDC scheme.

19. See Fox and Palmer (1999).

20. An alternative—the use of the overall average wage for all contributors for everyone—would have favored low-income earners and penalized high-income earners, and in this sense would also have been unfair. Unfortunately, some people were in a position to gain from these transition rules by negotiating with their employers to declare higher wages during this short period.

21. See Vanovska (2004).

22. There is of course the question of whether such a policy would encourage employers to withhold payments. This is at least a theoretical risk, especially with small employers. On the other hand, individuals should not have to bear the cost in terms of lost pension rights because their employer has gone out of business, which they usually cannot influence by their own individual behavior.

23. See Vanovska (2004).

24. Note, however that this guarantee also covers persons who consciously evaded paying full contribution payments, which is an inadvertent consequence of having such a rule.

25. Together, extra indexations during 1996–9 increased old-law pensions by about 24 percentage points and NDC pensions by about 11 percentage points. From 2000, the indexation procedure was revised and put again on the track of the backward approach.

26. See Fox and Palmer (1999).

27. See Vanovska (2004).

28.The demographic prospects of Latvia are discussed in greater depth in *The State Social Insurance System in Latvia: Financial Analysis* (2003).

29. As has already been discussed, the size of the future debt will not be known until a long-term project of registering all service years earned prior to 1996 is completed. These data are needed to calculate initial capital, in order to calculate the scale of the NDC debt to create a balance between NDC assets and liabilities.

30. The general problem is that with a constantly declining labor force, the adjustment mechanism is one period behind—or more if the index used to compute the rate of return on NDC accounts is based on a moving average of past values—with a slowly cumulating effect (Palmer 1999).

31. Note that even disability benefits are also contribution wage-indexed with 50 percent from 2004, which creates symmetry with the old-age system, but which to date has not been discussed as a policy measure. Wage indexation is a method of indexation that could be justified in a system with a tight entrance, but which would have the undesirable disadvantage of providing extra incentive to enter disability for older workers.

References

Fox, L., and E. Palmer. 1999. "Latvian Pension Reform." Social Protection Discussion Paper 9922, World Bank, Washington, DC.

Gassmann, F. 2000. "Who and Where Are the Poor in Latvia?" Ph.D. dissertation at the University of Maastricht, Department of Economics.

Góra, M., and E. Palmer. 2004. "Shifting Perspectives in Pensions." Institute for Study of Labor (IZA), Discussion Paper 1369, Bonn, Germany.

Krumins, J. 2000. *Life Expectancy Trends, Methodology and Construction of Life Tables to Be Used in the Computations of Latvian G-Values.* Report to the Ministry of Welfare. Riga: Ministry of Welfare of Latvia.

———. 2003. *Life Expectancy Trends and Projections: Latvia.* Report to the Ministry of Welfare. Riga: Ministry of Welfare of Latvia.

Labor Force Survey. Riga: National Bureau of Statistics.

Ministry of Welfare of Latvia. 2003. *The State Social Insurance System in Latvia. Financial Analysis.* Riga: Ministry of Welfare of Latvia.

Palmer, E. 1999. "Individual Decisions and Aggregate Stability in a NDC PAYG Account Scheme." http://www.rfv.se/english.

———. 2006. "What Is NDC?" In *Pension Reform: Issues and Prospects for Non-Financial Defined Contribution (NDC) Schemes,* ed. R. Holzmann and E. Palmer, chapter 2. Washington, DC: World Bank.

Swedish National Social Insurance Board. 2001. *The Swedish Pension System Annual Report 2001.* Stockholm: Swedish National Social Insurance Board.

Settergren, O. 2001. "The Automatic Balancing Mechanism of the Swedish Pension System: A Non-Technical Introduction." *Wirtschaftspolitische Blätter* 4 (2001): 339–49.

Vanovska, I. 2004. "Pension Reform in Latvia: Achievements and Challenges," *Reforming Public Pensions. Sharing the Experiences of Transition and OECD Countries.* Paris, OECD.

Chapter 16

The NDC System in Poland: Assessment after Five Years

*Agnieszka Chłoń-Domińczak and Marek Góra**

THE NEW POLISH PENSION SYSTEM, WHICH WAS INTRODUCED under the banner of "Security through Diversity," started on January 1, 1999. It replaced all previous legislation on old-age pensions for the majority of the working population.[1] The implementation of any pension reform is a long process, and this is true of the new Polish pension system. In 2004, it was still difficult to draw lessons from the system implementation, as no pensions will be paid until 2009. However, although the general design of the system has remained unchanged, some elements remain debated in Poland. There are also some lessons from the implementation that can be drawn from the administrative perspective.

In this chapter we present the design of the NDC system in Poland in the context of the framework of the entire pension system implemented in 1999. We also present an assessment of the early Polish experiences with implementation as well as the current debate on the future of the NDC pension system in Poland.

The chapter is structured as follows. In the first section we present an overview of the new pension system in Poland. In the second section we present transition aspects, which are related to the specific design of the Polish pension system. In the third section we examine the system design from both a microeconomic and a macroeconomic perspective. The fourth section focuses on the implementation experiences. The final section summarizes the discussion and draws conclusions.

Key Features of the New Polish Pension System

Designing the new system from scratch provided the unique opportunity to create a system that can be neutral or at least close to neutral vis-à-vis economic growth and irrespective of population aging.[2] It also allowed for the design of a simple and transparent system

* Agnieszka Chłoń-Domińczak is deputy minister in the Ministry of Social Policy in Poland. In 1997–99 she was a core member of the team preparing and implementing the pension reform in Poland. Marek Góra is a professor at the Warsaw School of Economics. He and Michal Rutkowski were authors of the pension reform concept in Poland.

The authors would like to thank Edward Palmer and the participants of the Sandhamn Conference for their comments on the earlier version of this chapter and Tomasz Mazur, actuary of the Social Insurance Institution, for providing help on the projections presented here.

that avoids the complications inherent in a system that has been reformed through ad hoc changes.

On January 1, 1999, the previous Bismarckian pension system based on a social tax was terminated and a new system, entirely based on individual accounts of two types, was introduced. The account types are:

- Non-financial defined contribution (NDC): individual accounts based on government quasi-bonds (an idea similar to Buchanan bonds) not traded in financial markets, and yielding a rate of return that equals the wage sum growth (GDP growth in the long run).[3]
- Financial defined contribution (FDC): individual accounts based on instruments traded in financial markets.[4]

It should be strongly stressed that both accounts are annuitized at the same moment and play exactly the same role within social security. The sole role of the pension system is to provide the working generations with an efficient method of income allocation over their life cycles. In particular, there is no such element in the system as a "basic state pension." Social redistribution exists, but it has been moved out of the pension system. The minimum pension guarantee (the topping-up difference between an individual's pension and the minimum pension level defined in the legislation) is financed from the general taxes.

The social security contribution that existed prior to reform has been split so that the portion that goes to old-age pension is a separate contribution. The contribution rate on wages is divided into 12.22 percent that goes to the NDC scheme and 7.3 percent that goes to the FDC scheme. The tax regime has been exempt-exempt-tax (EET), which means that old-age pension contributions are tax exempt, similarly income from pension savings investment, while future pensions will be taxed. This applies for both NDC and FDC.[5] Contributions for old-age pensions are paid half by employee and half by employer.[6]

From the macroeconomic perspective, the retirement age does not play any active role in balancing the revenue and expenditure sides of the new system, though it can provide some liquidity gains in the short run. But retirement age is still important from the point of view of social policy and labor supply. For these reasons, there is a minimum retirement age of 60 for women and 65 for men in the new pension system.[7]

The pension system is a method of sharing GDP between generations. The key feature of the NDC system is the stabilization of the share of GDP being transferred to the entire retired generation (GDP^R). Technical (demographic) reserves are created in the system in order to smooth fluctuations that inevitably influence the system's revenue and expenditure side.

From the perspective of an individual, the new system is a method of life-cycle income allocation.[8] Within this system, old-age pension contributions are based on a fixed percent of individual earnings that create account values. The account balances in the NDC system earn a rate of return based on the growth of the sum of paid contributions. At the time of retirement, the accumulated account values are annuitized. Annuities are calculated on the basis of accumulated capital and life expectancy at the age of retirement.

Pillar terminology is often used in the area of pensions, but there can be with some confusion about definitions, as they depend on who is doing the classification.[9] This terminology is sometimes used in Poland, especially for public communication. However, the metaphor of pillars fits the Polish case only partially. If we use this terminology we should say there is no "first pillar" at all in the system. The "second pillar" consists of two types of individual accounts (two accounts per participant: one NDC account and one FDC

Table 16.1. Alternative Approaches to Pension Reform

Typical three-pillar reform	*Polish "Security through Diversity"*
• Rationalized old system (redistribution; anonymous participation): the first pillar • New part of the system based on financial individual accounts run by private asset managers: the second pillar • Contribution split between the old and the new system • Promotion of various forms of additional savings: the third pillar	• Splitting social security into old-age and non–old-age benefits • Termination of the old-age part of the old system • Creation of entirely new old-age part of the system (individual accounts of two types) • Contribution split between two accounts • First account: non-financial; rate of return determined by GDP growth; publicly run (possible privatization) • Second account: financial; rate of return determined in financial markets; privately run • Annuitization of account values (both accounts) • Promotion of various forms of additional savings

Source: Góra (2003).

account) that have the same objective (income allocation) but use different ways of generating the rate of return (the NDC through real economy and the FDC through financial markets). Table 16.1 presents a comparison of key features of the three-pillar approach and the Polish approach.

It should be stressed that the idea of implementing a completely new system was rather radical, in that it put a complete end to the old system for the vast majority of the population. Attempts to introduce numerous minor modifications into pension systems can erode public trust and even create social unrest about the future of the system more than a complete paradigmatic reform. This certainly proved to be the case for Poland. First, during the entire reform process, the reform concept was communicated to the social partners and the media, and their voices were carefully listened to. Second, the reform did not affect the oldest working cohorts, who would retire shortly after the reform. Third, the reform followed a ruling of the constitutional tribunal against additional unexpected changes in the pension system. Finally, the long-term projections were presented and explained, showing long-term threats faced by the old pension system (which was actually bankrupt). As a result, in Poland there was no significant public criticism of the new system.

Transition from DB to DC: Some Practical Aspects

Beginning January 1, 1999, the entirely new system replaced the old one for all people born after December 31, 1948. Participation in the new system was not subject to individual choice. The new system automatically covered the entire group of people born after that date. There was no switching.[10] However, a group of participants (those who were born before January 1, 1969) chose one of two versions of the new system—either NDC plus FDC or only NDC. Their choices were taken in the period until December 31, 1999. Table 16.2 provides a summary of the procedure.[11]

Table 16.2. Introduction of the New System (age groups)

New system (people born after December 31, 1948)		Old system (people born before January 1, 1949)
People born after December 31, 1968	*People born before January 1, 1969*	
Automatically covered by the new system; OA contribution *automatically* split between two accounts (NDC+FDC)	*Automatically* covered by the new system; OA contribution either split between two accounts *or* paid into one account ([NDC+FDC] or NDC)	Stay in the old system (*no possibility* of participating in the new one); *no accounts*

Source: Authors' analysis based on the law on the social security system.

The introduction of a new pension system from scratch required establishing the transition from the Bismarckian pay-as-you-go (PAYG) defined benefit to individual accounts (the combined NDC and FDC system). A special procedure was designed to transform pension rights into account values. Everybody who began participation before January 1, 1999, received on their NDC account an amount called "initial capital." This procedure can be interpreted as retiring the entire population born after December 31, 1948, according to the old rules on December 31, 1998. After sending all participants to this hypothetical "retirement," the old system was terminated. After January 1, 1999, everyone participated in their chosen option of the new system.

Rights acquired under the old system were then converted into initial capital in the new system. Initial capital is calculated to deliver the same pension benefit as the old system formula (adjusted for age and contribution years), if everyone had retired on the last day of the old system. There is no differentiation of initial capital between those who split their contributions between two accounts those who have only one account.[12]

The conversion of accrued rights under the old system into initial capital under the new system allows for gradual transition from the one system to the other without complex and time-consuming re-creation of hypothetical pension account values. The reformers decided to follow this path for several reasons. First, there were no individual data that could be used to retrieve the value of contributions paid before the reform. In the old pension system, the Social Insurance Institution (ZUS) received individual information only upon retirement. Because most of the individual records prior to 1980 were destroyed, this method of converting old-system rights into initial capital provided a way to deal with initial notional account status.

Second, recalculating the accrued rights to the initial capital allows smoothing the transition from the old to the new systems, keeping the incentives to work longer intact. Projections show that replacement rates in the pension system will gradually decrease as the initial capital portion of the notional account decreases.

Third, this procedure gave neither incentives nor disincentives to participate solely in the NDC scheme or in both the NDC and FDC schemes in the new system, as workers received exactly the same pension rights, regardless their choice.

The formula used to calculate initial capital follows the old system's formula,

$$P_0 = 24\%W\rho + (1.3\% \ T + 0.7\% \ N)B, \tag{16.1}$$

where:

P_0 = monthly accrued pension at the end of 1999,

T = total years of contributions,

N = other eligible years (unemployment, military service, parental leave etc.),

B = individual assessment base,

W = average, gross, economywide monthly wage in second quarter of 1998, and

ρ = adjustment factor (specific to the initial capital) equal to

$$\min\left(\sqrt{\frac{A_i-18}{A_r-18}\cdot\frac{C_i}{C_r}},1\right),$$

where

A_i = individual's age at the end of 1998,

A_r = retirement age (60 for women and 65 for men),

C_i = total eligible years at the end of 1998 (= Min[$(T + N)$; $(4/3\ T)$]), and

C_r = required eligible years (20 for women and 25 for men).

The individual assessment base equalled to the average individual monthly earnings over a period of 10 consecutive years of earnings after 1980 indexed for wage inflation, as follows:

- The pay in a chosen year is compared to the average, economywide wage for that year, and
- The resulting ratio, capped at 250 percent, is multiplied by the indexed figure for economywide earnings, to derive the assessment base for the averaging process.

Figure 16.1 shows an estimated value of the hypothetical pension taken for the initial capital calculation. For older workers, the value of hypothetical pension increases.

Figure 16.1. Value of Hypothetical Pension for the Initial Capital Calculation

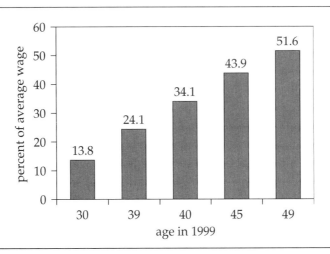

Source: Authors' calculations.

Note: Calculated for average male wage earner who started working at age 25.

The formula for the initial capital (K_0) calculation can be defined as:

$$K_0 = P_0 \cdot G_{62}^{1998}.$$

The life expectancy (*G*-value) used for the calculation of initial capital was based on uni-sex life tables and used age of 62 for both men and women. In 1998, the life expectancy for a 62-year-old was 209 months; this value was used for the calculation. If *G*-values for 60 and 65 were used to calculate the initial capital, women with identical work history would receive 30 percent higher initial capital.

This choice of the *G*-value has implications for the future pension size. The contribution of the initial capital to the NDC pension (P_0^r) will be:

$$P_0^r = \frac{K_0^r}{G_{age}^r} = P_0 \cdot \prod_{i=1999}^{r} (1+n_i) \cdot \frac{G_{62}^{1998}}{G_{age}^r}, \qquad (16.2)$$

where

n_i = notional rate of return in year i,

r = year of retirement, and

G_{age}^r = life expectancy at retirement age and retirement year.

This shows that the value of the future pension will depend on the return yielded from 1999 until the year of retirement and the relation between the life expectancy of a retiring person and the *G*-value used for the initial capital calculation. In the case of the latter factor, as a result of the increasing life expectancies, the value of the denominator will be increasing. In addition, if the difference in retirement age of men and women remains— that is, women would retire at age 60 and men at 65—women will have relatively lower pension resulting from the initial capital.

The legislation gave a period of five years, until the end of 2003, to calculate the initial capital for all contributors in the new pension system. This time was needed for some 10 million workers covered by the new pension system to collect necessary information for the initial capital calculation. Despite this time, the calculation of the initial capital was not completed—less than half of eligible workers filed their documents in ZUS. It is now envisaged that the entire process should take until 2006.

Implementation of the New Pension System

In this section we focus on the outcomes from the implementation of the new pension system, from both macroeconomic and microeconomic perspectives. However, the current projections differ to some extent from those in 1998, mainly because of the development of the macroeconomic situation in Poland in recent years. Thus, we also present a short summary of the developments after 1999.

Demographic, Macroeconomic, and Pension System Developments after 1999

One of the most important reasons for the introduction of the new pension system in Poland was the aging of the population. From 1999, the aging process deepened. In particular, fertility rates fell dramatically, while life expectancies increased. In addition, the 2002 census results show that the Polish population was smaller than projected (mainly because of previously underestimated emigration flows). One of the signs of the aging of the population was the increasing life expectancies of persons at retirement age. In the period

Table 16.3. Changes in Life Expectancy of Persons at Retirement Age, 1995–2002

Life expectancy	Year							
	1995	1996	1997	1998	1999	2000	2001	2002
women age 60	20.52	19.69	19.98	20.21	20.31	20.68	20.97	21.31
men age 60	15.84	15.93	16.13	16.38	16.29	16.72	17.03	17.19
women age 65	16.55	15.77	16.03	16.26	16.34	16.68	16.93	17.25
men age 65	12.88	12.93	13.13	13.37	13.28	13.63	13.92	14.05

Source: GUS lifetables (1996–2003).

between 1998 and 2002, the life expectancy for both men and women at 60 and 65 increased by almost a year. If this process continues at the same pace, in 10 years the average time that retirees receive an old-age benefit will be more than 2 years longer than currently (table 16.3).

In 1998, when the Polish pension reform was implemented, the Polish economy was growing at a very fast pace. After 1999, the Polish economy started to slow down and only in 2003 showed signs of economic recovery. In particular, the employment level decreased: in 1999 there were 14.5 million persons working in Poland, and in 2002 there were only 13.7 million. Also the real growth of wages was quite small. The economic growth and the wage increase picked up in 2003, but growth of employment did not follow.

This drop in employment affected the financing of the pension system. Contribution revenues decreased, resulting in high deficits in the pension system. At the same time, the public finances were deteriorating and the public debt reached about half of GDP. This resulted in an increasing social security subsidy, which led some politicians to question the long-term principles of the pension reform, given the short-term problems with the state budget deficit.

From 1999 to 2002, the total number of covered workers (both under new and old pension systems) fell gradually from 13.27 million to 12.76 million, an almost 4 percent decrease (shown in table 16.4). Currently it is not possible to monitor the number of active

Table 16.4. Number of Covered Workers, 1998–2002 (thousands of persons)

Year	Total	Old system	New system: NDC	New system: FDC + NDC	Registered members in the FDC scheme[a]
1998	12,737	12,737			
1999	13,271	1,993	3,684	7,594	8,694
2000	13,060	1,749	3,570	7,741	9,973
2001	12,851	1,731	3,375	7,745	10,637
2002	12,761	1,608	3,300	7,853	10,990

Source: Authors' estimates based on Social Budget Model (The Gdansk Institute for Market Economics 2004).

a. The number of persons registered in the FDC scheme is based on the supervision (KNUiFE) registry. The difference between estimated number of covered workers and persons registered in the FDC scheme results from the accumulation of fluctuations in the workforce and covered persons. The number of registered members represents all those persons who at any point of time paid contribution and even some who actually never contributed. The number of persons with NDC and FDC accounts is based on the estimates on the number of workers who contributed to the pension system in a given year.

covered workers under new and old pension systems precisely. The only figure than can be observed is the number of persons that joined open pension funds—in 2002, almost 11 million persons were open pension fund members. The number of those who are in the NDC and FDC system is based on estimates, which are confirmed also by the fact that monthly ZUS transfers some 8 million contributions to the FDC accounts.

Moreover, over past the few years, the growth of real wages was lower than real GDP growth, a factor that also contributes to the lower amount of contribution revenues. The reduction in revenues was particularly strong in 2002, when not only real but also nominal contribution revenues dropped. Table 16.5 presents the collected contribution revenue to the social security system (including NDC, FDC and non–old age contributions) and the estimated covered wage bill relative to GDP, which has been falling since 1998.

As a result, the overall financial situation of the Social Insurance Fund (FUS) worsened. The level of state budget subsidies to FUS relative to GDP increased, which is shown in figure 16.2. It should be noted that, contrary to the actual outcome, the projections made in 1998 assumed a reduction of state budget subsidies in the years following the pension reform.

These developments, though not a result of the implementation of the NDC and FDC system, had some implications for the implementation. First, the notional rate of return has been relatively low, reflecting the decrease of the covered wage bill shown above. Second, the planned size of technical reserves (the Demographic Reserve Fund, or FRD) was reduced by the government. Initially, the FRD was expected to receive a transfer representing one percentage point of the wage bill annually from 2001 to 2008. However, the government decided that this flow should be reduced to 0.1 percentage point in 2001 and 2002 and then increased by 0.05 percentage points annually until 2008. As a result, the planned transfer of 1 percent of GDP to the FRD has not materialized and the balance of the FRD at the end of 2003 was only 0.6 percent of GDP.

Also, according to the revised projections of the pension system, it is highly unlikely that the system would generate financial surpluses prior to 2010, which was expected when the pension reform was introduced.

Table 16.5. The Collected Contribution Revenue and Covered Wage Bill As a percent of GDP

Year	Collected contribution revenues[a] (as percent of GDP)	Estimated covered wage bill (wages plus contributions)[b] (as percent of GDP)
1998	11.35	36.56
1999	10.79	36.27
2000	10.26	34.48
2001	10.47	35.20
2002	10.07	33.85

Source: Chłoń-Domińczak (2004).

Note: The estimates include contributions paid by employees and self-employed, as the latter could not be separated from the total contribution revenue.

a. The collected contribution revenue covers all contributions paid for social security purposes (including old-age and non–old age); b. The covered wage bill includes all wages and contribution paid by employers to social security institution. This information is fully comparable in time.

Figure 16.2. State Budget Subsidies to Social Insurance Fund

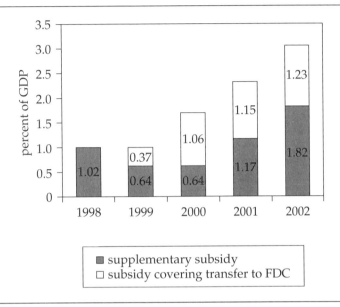

Source: Authors' calculations based on ZUS and GUS data.

Microeconomic Effects of the Polish Pension Reform

Looking at the microeconomic effects of the pension reform, two issues need to be taken into account. First, the old pension system was in actuarial deficit—promised benefits were higher than revenues in the long run. Introducing the NDC system and keeping constant contribution rates means that the level of benefits relative to wages should decrease. This effect was strengthened by imposing an implicit tax of 25 percent on the NDC interest rate, reducing its size below neutrality, so that it was set at the consumer price index (CPI), increased by 75 percent of the covered real wage fund growth. This tax was levied in 2004, when the parliament increased indexation of notional accounts to full covered wage fund growth.

Second, the NDC pension formula, which is actuarially neutral, creates significant differences in the size of pension for people retiring at different ages—and, as already mentioned, retirement ages for men and women are different in the Polish pension system. If such a difference remains in the future, pensions of men and women will differ significantly.

INDIVIDUAL PENSIONS IN THE NEW SYSTEM: POLITICAL DEBATE AND POSSIBLE CHANGES

Simulations of individual pensions in the new system show that under current conditions, a woman who started to work in 1999 at age 25 and who retires at age 60 can expect a benefit (sum of NDC and FCD benefits) that represents around 40 percent of her final income, while a man who retires at age 65 can expect a pension representing almost 60 percent of his final income (table 16.6). In the case of older workers, the expected value of their benefits measured in relation to their final wage is higher. This reflects the impact of initial capital on future pensions.

Based on the projections of future pensions and replacement rates, the Polish government proposed two changes to the pension system. The first one was to increase the rate of return on NDC accounts to 100 percent of covered wage fund growth, measured by the growth of the contribution sum. As a result, future pensions should increase. However, as shown in table 16.6, the increase is higher when retirement age is 65 and relatively smaller for persons retiring at the age of 60.

Because of the discrepancy of benefit amounts due to men and women, the Polish government was reconsidering the equalization of retirement ages of men and women at 65 years. A proposal to equalize retirement ages for men and women was included in the package for public finance reform in October 2003—presented in the Green Book "Rationalisation of Social Expenditure in Poland." All proposals presented in the Green Book were subject to discussion with experts, social partners, and NGOs. The initial proposal included a gradual increase of the retirement age of women, to begin in 2009 (that is, from the year when the first pensions from the new system are paid) and to be completed by 2018.

The discussion on equalizing the retirement age in Poland is quite difficult. The society in general is in favor of an earlier retirement age for women. The results of public opinion polls conducted at the end of 2003 show that 51 percent of the society prefers the existing solution (retirement at age 60 for women and at 65 for men). On the other hand, more than one-third favors solutions that lead to a flexible retirement age between 62 and 65. The vast majority (85 percent) of persons surveyed did not approve of the proposal for equalizing retirement ages at the age of 65, while only 5 to 10 percent supported it. However, almost 35 percent of women would agree to work longer if it would mean a higher future pension.[13]

In February 2004, the government, following the consultation process, recommended preparing for the change that would equalize retirement ages of men and women by 2023 and, at the same time, introduced the possibility of drawing a partial pension starting at the age of 62. At the end of February 2004, the proposal was presented to trade unions, employers' organizations, and NGOs for consultations. Despite the objections of the social

Table 16.6. Simulations of Replacement Rates for Different Cohorts, both Men and Women, Depending on Retirement Age and Taxation of NDC Returns (percent of final wage)

Age in 1999	Notional rate of return 75 percent of wage bill growth		Notional rate of return 100 percent of wage bill growth	
	retirement at age 60	retirement at age 65	retirement at age 60	retirement at age 65
25	42.7%	59.5%	45.9%	64.5%
30	46.1%	62.3%	50.8%	69.2%
35	47.7%	63.3%	52.7%	70.8%
40	49.4%	64.6%	54.4%	72.1%
45	51.6%	66.4%	56.1%	73.5%
49	53.8%	68.3%	57.4%	74.6%

Source: Authors' calculations.

Note: Simulations for average wage earner starting work at the age 25 and assuming average real wage growth of 3 percent per annum, average funded tier rate of return of 4 percent per annum and up-front fee on funded system at 5 percent, and also assuming constant employment level (that is, average wage growth = wage bill growth) and constant life expectancies. Replacement rate is calculated net of social security contributions.

partners, a draft law was submitted to the parliament in April 2004. In May 2004, the new Belka government withdrew from this proposal.

Both of the proposed changes should lead to an increase in the future replacement rates of pensioners. The idea of increasing the NDC rate of return, however, would also result in an overall increase of the level of expenditure, though the long-run macroeconomic balance of the pension system is maintained.

The discussions in Poland show that, though initially designing the pension system was based on the economic principles leading to reaching macroeconomic stability, with time some elements are being revisited—both from an economic and from a political perspective. In sum, the pension system is still a subject of political debate.

INDIVIDUAL PENSIONS IN THE NEW SYSTEM: THE IMPACT OF DEMOGRAPHIC CHANGES

The simulations presented above assume constant life expectancies at the level of 2002. Further increases in life expectancy will have an impact on future pensions. Figure 16.3 shows the results of the simulation of the replacement rates in the case of a person retiring at age 65 under the scenario when life expectancy at age 65 increases by a quarter of the year each year (that is, linearly following past years' trend). Not surprisingly, the "demographic price" is highest for youngest cohorts—in the scenario for those aged 25 in 1999, the pension size might be lower by more than one-third than it would be in the scenario with constant mortality.

Figure 16.3. Change in Pension Value Because of Increases in Life Expectancy

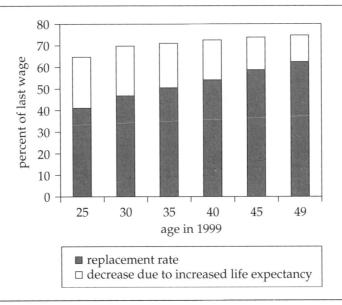

Source: Authors' calculations.

Note: Simulations are for an average wage earner starting work at age 25 and retiring at age 65, and assuming average real wage growth of 3 percent per annum, an NDC rate of return equal to 100 percent of wage bill growth, an FDC rate of return of 4 percent per annum, and an up-front fee on the funded system of 5 percent, and also assuming a constant employment level (that is, average wage growth = wage bill growth), assuming increases in life expectancy of one-quarter of a year each year. Replacement rate is calculated net of social security contributions.

This simulation shows how strongly changes in mortality and longer lives on retirement affect the pension system. Under traditional DB schemes, adjustment to mortality changes is subject to political decision on changing some of the parameters of the pension formula, otherwise increases in contribution rate are necessary.

Under DC schemes, this shows that in the future people's working lives need to be extended in order to offset the demographic improvements. Seen in this light, retirement ages should become a topic for discussion in Poland.

Macroeconomic Effects of the Polish Pension Reform

The implementation of the new system means an ex ante adjustment of the flow of its future expenditure. This produces very strong macroeconomic effects. Almost 500 billion euros (in 2000 prices) is the value of debt that will not be avoided until 2050 because of implementing the new old-age pension system.[14] Table 16.7 provides demographic dependency ratio projections for selected OECD countries, and pension expenditures and primary surpluses needed to keep debts at their 2000 levels. In comparison with the projections made for other countries, the Polish case looks really very strong. The lack of a large part of the pension debt—and hence the absence of a need to finance its servicing—will give a great deal of freedom to both the public and private sector to achieve various goals contributing to the country's development.

Two conclusions on the Polish case can be drawn from the projections provided in table 16.7. First, the demographic situation (measured by the dependency ratio) will change from relatively good at present to one of the worst in the OECD in 2050. Second, at the same time—because of the implementation of the new system—old-age pension expenditure will substantially drop from its current rate as one of the highest to one of the lowest in the OECD area in 2050. Calculations provided in the table did not take into account the change in the NDC account indexation made in 2004. As a result of this change, the overall pension expenditure will be slightly higher than the provided projections.

Table 16.7. Projected Effects in Poland Compared with Projections in Selected OECD Countries

| Country | Dependency ratio | | | Pension expenditure (percent GDP) | | | Required primary surplus (percent GDP) | |
	2000	2050	Change	2000	2050	Change	Debt constant	Debt reduced
France	27.2	50.8	23.6	12.1	15.8	3.7	5.9	6.6
Germany	26.6	53.2	26.6	11.8	16.9	5.1	4.3	4.7
Italy	28.8	66.8	38.0	14.2	13.9	−0.3	4.9	5.9
Poland	**20.4**	**55.2**	**34.8**	**10.8**	**8.3**	**−2.5**	**−1.0**	**−1.0**
Spain	27.1	65.7	38.6	9.4	17.4	8.0	4.8	5.2
Sweden	29.4	46.3	16.9	9.2	10.8	1.6	1.0	1.1
United Kingdom	26.6	45.3	18.7	4.3	3.6	−0.7	0.8	1.2
United States	21.7	37.9	16.2	4.4	6.2	1.8	2.7	3.2
OECD (average)	23.8	49.9	26.1	7.4	10.6	3.2	—	—

Source: Dang, Antolin, and Oxley (2001).

Note: — = not applicable. If only pension expenditure is taken into account, then the required surplus needed in the case of Poland is even more favorable (−2.8 percent of GDP). A negative primary surplus means the debt will not explode even if a country runs a deficit.

The shift to the NDC system in Poland allows for controlling total pension liabilities. In the traditional DB system, measuring the implicit pension debt depends on the methodology that can be used. In the NDC system, the total value of pension accounts is equal to the value of pension liabilities, in a way similar to the total assets accumulated in the FDC scheme. Keeping future pension liabilities under control is important because of the accelerated aging that is expected in Poland.[15]

A more detailed future outlook of the macroeconomic performance of the NDC system can be drawn from long-term projections prepared by in the Social Insurance Institution (ZUS). The ZUS is obliged to prepare annual projections of the long-term revenue and expenditure for old-age pensions. The aim of the projections is to prepare the strategy for managing the Demographic Reserve Fund. The first projection was published in 2003, the second in 2004. The projection, accompanied by the opinion of the independent actuary, is submitted to the Council of Ministers. In this chapter we present the results of the 2004 projection.[16]

The demographic forecast used for this projection shows that the number of people of postproductive age is likely to double within the next half of the century. In addition, the number of persons of productive age is going to decrease by one-third. The demographic dependency ratio is going to increase by half (table 16.8).

To test the sensitivity to the assumptions, the results were calculated under three different macroeconomic scenarios: *baseline*, *pessimistic* (in the sense of a harder burden put on the social security system), and *optimistic*, shown in table 16.9.

Table 16.8. Demographic Assumptions (baseline scenario)

Population cohort	2002 census	Projection 2010	2020	2030	2040	2050
Total population (millions)	38.2	39.0	39.4	38.5	36.8	35.0
men (millions)	18.5	18.9	19.1	18.7	17.9	17.0
women (millions)	19.7	20.1	20.2	19.8	19.0	18.0
Life expectancy from birth						
men	70.3	72.0	74.2	75.6	77.0	78.5
women	78.4	79.4	80.7	81.9	83.2	84.7
Life expectancy						
65-year-old man	14.3	14.7	15.4	16.1	17.0	17.9
60-year-old woman	22.1	22.7	23.6	24.5	25.6	26.8
Preproductive age (million persons)	8.9	7.4	7.7	6.9	5.8	5.6
men (0–17) (millions)	4.5	3.8	3.9	3.6	3.0	2.9
women (0–17) (millions)	4.3	3.5	3.7	3.4	2.8	2.7
Productive age (millions)	23.6	25.2	23.3	22.1	20.8	17.8
men (18–64) (millions)	12.1	13.2	12.4	11.7	11.2	9.7
women (18–59) (millions)	11.5	12.0	10.9	10.4	9.5	8.1
Postproductive age (millions)	5.7	6.4	8.4	9.5	10.3	11.6
men (65 and more) (millions)	1.8	2.0	2.8	3.4	3.7	4.4
Women (60 and more) (millions)	3.9	4.4	5.6	6.0	6.6	7.2
Demographic dependency ratio	0.62	0.55	0.69	0.74	0.78	0.97

Source: Mazur (2004).

Table 16.9. Macroeconomic Assumptions

	2002	2010	2020	2030	2040	2050
CPI (rate)	1.9%	2.0%	2.0%	2.0%	2.0%	2.0%
Real GDP growth	1.4%	5.0%	5.0%	4.0%	3.0%	2.1%
Unemployment rate						
Baseline	20.1%	14.8%	10.0%	7.1%	6.4%	6.0%
Pessimistic	20.1%	19.2%	12.2%	10.0%	10.0%	10.0%
Optimistic	20.1%	12.2%	7.8%	6.0%	5.1%	4.5%
Real net wage growth						
Baseline	1.53%	2.0%	1.5%	1.0%	1.0%	1.0%
Pessimistic	1.53%	1.0%	1.0%	0.5%	0.5%	0.5%
Optimistic	1.53%	2.5%	2.5%	2.5%	2.0%	2.0%

Source: Mazur (2004).

The results of the projection for all scenarios are presented in table 16.10. These include revenues, expenditures, and one-year balance of the old-age scheme (including both old and the NDC systems) measured in relation to the GDP, as well as number of covered workers (again both under new and old systems), number of pensioners (old and new systems together), and resulting system dependency ratio.

More detailed results of the baseline scenario are presented below. Figure 16.4 shows projections of the reciprocal dependency rates. Because of the aging of the Polish population, between 2002 and 2050 the ratio of the number of people in the productive age (18–59/64) to the number of people in the postproductive age (60+/65+) is expected to decrease from the level above 4 to around 1.5. These developments, however, will not be initially reflected in the system dependency rates. The relation of the number of workers to the number of old-age pensioners is expected to increase until 2014. The projected increase is caused by a projected rise in the number of insured (discussed below), as well as by a reduction in the number of old-age pensioners that will occur as a result of eliminating early retirement options. In the second decade of the century, the trend will reverse, following the demographic developments.

Taking into account all pensions (disability and survivor pensions as well as old-age pensions), the system dependency rate follows a similar pattern. By the end of the projection period (2050), the system dependency rates and the demographic dependency rate are likely to converge.

The projected development of dependency rates follows the projected changes in the number of pensioners and insured. The number of pensioners is expected to increase until the end of 2006 (when the retirement under the old system expires). Between 2007 and 2012, the number of old-age pensioners will be decreasing, as there will be very little inflow of new old-age pensioners—most of those retiring under the old system are going to retire at an early age before the end of 2006, and the pensioners in the new system can retire only from 2009 (women) and 2013 (men), when they reach retirement age. After 2012, the number of old-age pensioners will increase, following the aging process. According to the projection results, the number of other pensioners (disability and survivor) is also going to increase, but not that significantly (see figure 16.5).

The stock of pensioners distinguished by their participation in the old or new pension system is presented in figure 16.6. During the next couple of decades, the majority of the old-age pensioners will be receiving pensions under the old system regulations. After

Table 16.10. Projection's Results

Scenarios	2002	2010	2020	2030	2040	2050
Baseline						
Revenues*	9.2%	8.2%	6.0%	4.1%	3.1%	2.3%
of which contributions*	8.7%	8.0%	5.9%	4.1%	3.1%	2.3%
Expenditures*	12.7%	9.9%	7.3%	5.0%	3.6%	2.7%
One-year balance*	−3.5%	−1.7%	−1.3%	−0.9%	−0.5%	−0.4%
Covered workers (million)	12.9	14.9	15.5	15.2	14.3	12.6
Pensioners (old-age and other pensions) (million)	7.5	7.1	7.9	8.5	8.9	9.5
System dependency ratio	0.58	0.48	0.51	0.56	0.62	0.75
Pessimistic						
Revenues*	9.2%	7.3%	5.1%	3.2%	2.3%	1.7%
of which contributions*	8.7%	7.1%	5.0%	3.2%	2.3%	1.7%
Expenditures*	12.7%	9.7%	6.9%	4.6%	3.3%	2.4%
One-year balance*	−3.5%	−2.4%	−1.8%	−1.4%	−1.0%	−0.9%
Covered workers (million)	12.9	14.2	15.2	14.8	13.9	12.2
Pensioners (old-age and other pensions) (million)	7.5	7.1	8.0	8.7	9.6	10.4
System dependency ratio	0.58	0.50	0.53	0.59	0.69	0.85
Optimistic						
Revenues*	9.2%	8.7%	6.8%	5.3%	4.4%	3.6%
of which contributions*	8.7%	8.4%	6.8%	5.2%	4.3%	3.6%
Expenditures*	12.7%	9.9%	7.5%	5.5%	4.3%	3.4%
One-year balance*	−3.5%	−1.3%	−0.7%	−0.2%	0.1%	0.2%
Covered workers (million)	12.9	15.2	15.9	15.4	14.5	12.7
Pensioners (old-age and other pensions) (million)	7.5	7.1	7.8	8.4	8.8	9.3
System dependency ratio	0.58	0.47	0.49	0.54	0.61	0.73

Source: Mazur (2004).

Note: An asterisk denotes percent of GDP.

2020, the share of new system pensioners will be increasing; by 2050, almost all pensioners will be drawing pensions under the new pension system (though some of them will be drawing only from an NDC account).

The development in the number of covered workers is presented in figure 16.7. Following the demographic trends and projected changes on the labor market as well as increases in retirement age, the number of covered workers is expected to increase over the course of the next decade. Afterward, because of the aging process, the number of covered workers will decrease. In time, the difference between the number of people who have two accounts (NDC and FDC) and total number of covered workers will diminish. According to the projection, by 2025 the vast majority of covered workers will participate fully in the new combined system.

Figure 16.4. Demographic and System Dependency Rates, 2002–50

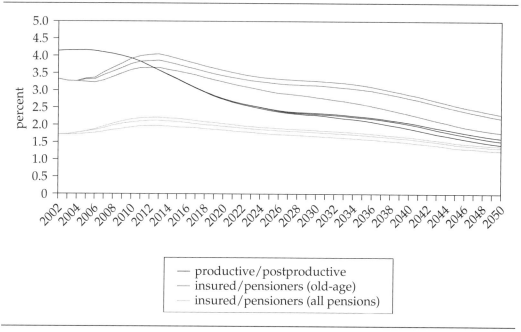

Source: Mazur (2004).

Note: These projections are for three various demographic scenarios: baseline, higher fertility, and lower mortality.

Figure 16.5. Number of Pensioners, 2002–50

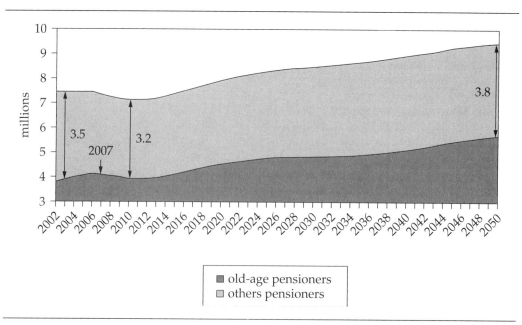

Source: Mazur (2004).

Figure 16.6. Pensioners Distinguished by Participation in the Old or New System, 2002–50

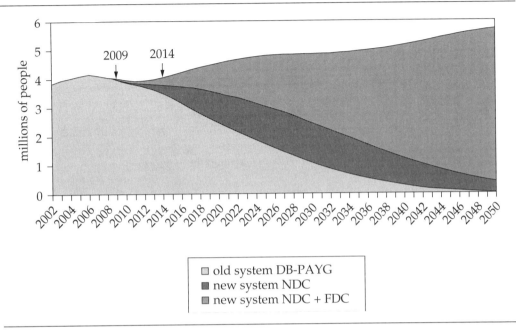

Source: Mazur (2004).

Figure 16.7. Covered Workers: Total and Those with NDC and FDC Accounts, 2002–50

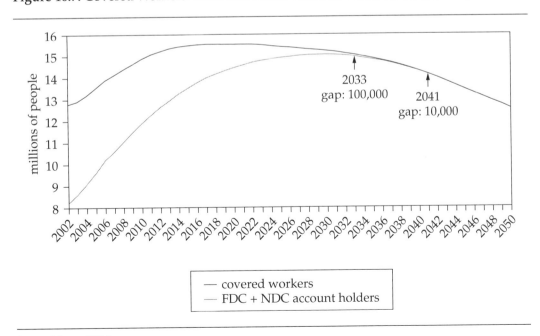

Source: Mazur (2004).

Figure 16.8. Non-Financial Scheme Contribution Revenues (Old System and NDC), 2002–50 (% of covered wage bill)

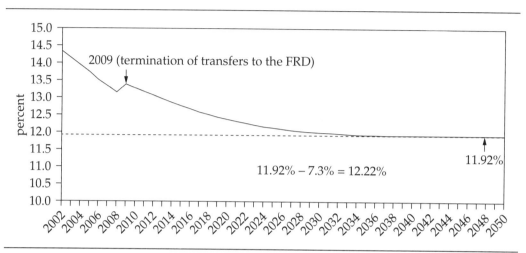

Source: Mazur (2004).

Figure 16.8 presents the projected value of contribution revenues to the non-financial part of the pension system expressed in relation to the covered wage bill. The projection also takes into account the collection rate. At the beginning of the projection, as not all covered workers have FDC accounts, the contribution revenues to the non-financial scheme are higher. In time, when the share of covered workers with FDC accounts increases, the contribution revenues will reach 11.92 percent (reflecting the contribution rate for NDC account adjusted for projected collection level).

According to the projection, the expenditures of the pension system will be decreasing sharply after 2006, reflecting the reduction in the number of pensioners (figure 16.9). After 2014, expenditures will increase slightly, following demographic developments and the increase in the number of old-age pensioners from the post-war baby boom generation. In the 2020s, the expenditures will go down again, as most of the pensioners retiring at that time will have part of their pension paid already from the FDC account. Under the baseline macroeconomic assumptions, the system's deficit should gradually reduce and it should reach a surplus at the end of the projection period (in 2049).

Early Experiences with Implementation

Management of the pension system is an issue that needs careful consideration when designing the system. However, management of the system should not be confused with the system itself. Implementing the new pension system was a complex task, and the number of institutions involved in the day-to-day operations of the pension system and their responsibilities increased. Box 16.1 summarizes the most important key Polish institutions in the reform and their tasks under the new pension system.

The introduction of individual accounts is a technological and operational challenge. In individualized pension systems there are many processes that need to be recorded. The most important is the collection and assignment of the payments. All other processes (registration, transfers, and so on) support the main process. However, these supportive

Figure 16.9. Pension System Revenue and Expenditure, 2002–50 (% of covered wage bill)

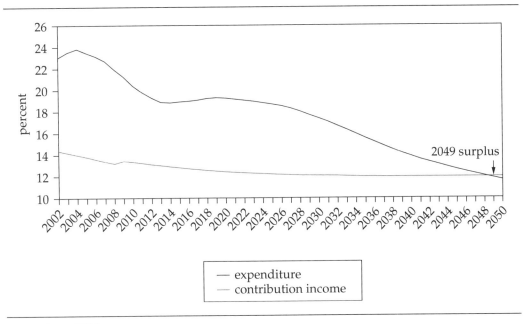

Source: Mazur (2004).

Note: Expenditure of the pension system covers both the old pension system and the NDC pensions.

processes still have to meet quality standards to ensure the proper assignment of payments. Thus sufficient time should be allowed between completing the legislation and implementing the pension system. An NDC system is very demanding for social security administrators, as individual accounts need to be kept for all insured people, not only for pensioners.

Establishing and running individual accounts requires sophisticated information systems. The quality of the systems depends on the quality of inputs provided by employers and the social security administration. Later on, particular elements of the system need to be serviced by various institutions.

The old age pension scheme itself requires relatively simple information. It can be run using only four pieces of information:

- For whom the contribution has been paid (identification of employee and employer),
- How much has been paid (amount),
- When the contribution was paid (date), and
- Wage base (control variable).

The pension reform in Poland was implemented very quickly, without sufficient time to prepare for managing the new system. As a result, adapting to the new administrative requirements that were imposed by the new pension system was initially chaotic, leading to many implementation problems. Delays in implementing the IT system as well as new reporting requirements for employers created a lot of room for possible errors.

In order to establish individual accounts, all individuals and employers had to be properly identified. All documents related to social security contribution payments had to

---

Box 16.1. Tasks and Managing Institutions

Registration and other initial procedures	ZUS, employers
Collection of contributions	ZUS
Transfer of contributions to OA individual accounts and NOA parts of social security	ZUS
Running NDC accounts	ZUS
Running FDC accounts	PTE (private)
Providing NDC annuities	ZUS
Providing FDC annuities	Annuity companies (private)[a]

Source: Authors' analysis.

Note: ZUS = Social Insurance Institution; PTE = pension fund society (asset manager)

a. This element of the institutional structure serving the pension system still needs more legislation.

---

include appropriate ID numbers. As determined during the prereform preparation, the existing ID numbers in Poland fulfilled the most important requirements:

- They are unique (that is, no two individuals or employers can have the same number), and
- They are common (that is, all individuals and employers have such ID numbers).

However, upon implementation it turned out that there were many problems with identifying both individual workers and employers. First, problems resulted from wrong information provided in registration documents. Second, banks were introducing errors in the transfer documents, so many of the identification numbers were incorrect. Finally, it turned out that some of the employers with regional networks were misusing their tax identification numbers by using them also for social security purposes. Specifically, all regional branches were using the same number, though they represented different payers. As a result, contributions could not be properly assigned.

During the initial phase of implementation, the majority of the new social security documents were sent to ZUS in paper form. The software supporting electronic processing was not fully developed. However, with time the quality of the software improved. Also, the law was amended to require the majority of employers to send information electronically. As a result, the quality of the information improved significantly.

Between September 2001 and December 2003, the overall accuracy of the information increased from 71.14 percent to 98.09 percent. The largest improvement in the accuracy of the information has been observed in two fields: (1) the identification of employees and (2) formal control (including such elements as amount of contributions due for each type of risk from employees and employers, and type of employment contract). It has to be noted that much of this improvement is a result of increased control of documents, which was accommodated by a 20 percent increase in the number of employees at ZUS between 1999 and 2003 (from 40,000 to 48,000 employees).

In 2003, ZUS straightened out all individual accounts and was able to send individual reports on contributions paid in 2002. The reports were sent at the end of the year 2003 and the beginning of 2004. This is a big step toward full individualization of contribution payments. However, there is still not full information on individual accounts, which can be distributed only after reconciliation of contributions paid between 1999 and 2001. This means that insured workers still do not receive their annual account statements.

The new system financing is based on accrual accounting. The Social Security Institution, prior to the start of the new system, did not use accrual accounting and individualized contribution. Implementing these elements, combined with the delays in implementing the IT system, created the delays in the full establishment of the NDC accounts for workers. Information technology implementation has been the curse of more than one new public policy initiative.

Conclusions

The new pension system in Poland reshaped the traditional perception of how the pension system can provide people with social security. As a result, Poland belongs to a small group of countries that are prepared for one of the most difficult challenges of our time— the aging of the population.

In the future, expenditure on old-age pensions will not only stop increasing, but also the overall expenditure will fall in relation to GDP. This will leave more resources available for development, which, in turn, will contribute to stronger growth and the increase of living standards for both the working and the retired generations.

The example of the new Polish pension system in the NDC framework is interesting for yet another reason. This type of system contributes to labor mobility, which is particularly needed in Europe. Free movement of labor cannot be achieved if moving from one country to another affects expected retirement income. As such, aiming at pension system neutrality will be more and more important for European integration.

Finally, the system allows pension liabilities to be monitored. This is particularly important, as public liabilities play an important role in the perception of the shape of the public finances. Introducing pension reform in Poland helped to reduce the level of the implicit pension debt, creating additional room for economic growth.

As far as administrative implementation goes, the lessons from the Polish experience teach us that one should never underestimate the technology and complexity of transactions in the individualized system. Efforts directed toward resolving these issues can save time and money in the future. On the other hand, delaying implementation of pension reform is also a risk. First, the window of political opportunity can be closed; second, the longer the implementation of a neutral pension system is delayed, the higher the pension debt to be paid back in the future will be.

Notes

1. The new system covered workers born after 1948—that is, persons less than 50 years old when the reform was introduced.

2. For more extended descriptions of the pension system in Poland see Góra (2003c); Chłoń-Domińczak (2002); Chłoń, Góra, and Rutkowski (1999); and Góra and Rutkowski (1998).

3. Until recently there was a 25 percent tax on returns yielded on account values in NDC accounts; this tax was removed in 2004.

4. There are no tax on returns on FDC accounts at the moment.

5. In order to avoid reduction of the net wages, all wages were grossed-up from 1999, adding the amount equal to the contribution due from the employee to the wage.

6. Before, only employers paid the contribution. The non–old age part of the contribution amounts to 17.07 percent of wage.

7. The initial reform project set retirement age at 62 for both men and women. For political reasons this was not accepted in 1998. In 2004, the government presented a draft law to

the parliament that proposed to equalize the retirement age at 65 for men and women by 2023; after public discussion, the government withdrew the proposal.

8. See Góra and Palmer (2004).

9. For instance, the "second pillar" can be a part of the universal system (World Bank terminology) or it can refer to occupational (partial) schemes (terminology used in many countries).

10. Offering people the opportunity to take decisions is usually well received. However, the idea of a universal system means not only universal coverage but also universal rules. Choice is to some extent an illusion in a mandatory system. Choice is appropriate for voluntary partial programs, not for mandatory universal ones.

11. Farmers are covered by a special pension scheme, heavily subsidized by the state budget. The so-called uniform services (army and police) were covered by the new universal system, but that concerned only those who started their service after December 31, 1998, while the rest of this group stayed with their special pension scheme. The current government decided to move all military workers back to the old system. This provides a dangerous precedence that should by no means be followed in the future.

12. This was not the case, for example in Hungary, where acquired rights were reduced for those who decided to switch to a funded pillar.

13. Results of surveys conducted in October and December of 2003 on the representative sample of Poles aged 15 and over.

14. For details on projections, see Chłoń-Domińczak (2002).

15. In 1999, the estimated value of the accrued pension liabilities represented some 120 percent of GDP, of which two-thirds belonged to persons covered by the new pension system. Between 1999 and 2002, the estimated value of contributions accumulated in the NDC was equal to some 21 percent of GDP, while the value of the pension assets in the FDC at the end of 2002 was around 4 percent of GDP.

16. The methodology of the model is described in Mazur (2004).

References

Barr, N. 2002. "Reforming Pensions: Myths, Truths, and Policy Choices," *International Social Security Review* 55 (2): 3–36.

Chłoń-Domińczak, A. 2004. "The Collection of Pension Contributions in Poland." In *Collection of Pension Contributions: Trends, Issues, and Problems in Central and Eastern Europe,* ed. E. Fultz, T. Stanownik, 155–96. Budapest: ILO.

———. 2002. "The Polish Pension Reform of 1999." In *Pension Reform in Central and Eastern Europe, Volume 1, Restructuring with Privatization: Case Studies of Hungary and Poland,* ed. E. Fultz, 98–205. Budapest: ILO.

Chłoń, A. M. Góra, and M. Rutkowski. 1999. "Shaping Pension Reform in Poland: Security through Diversity." Social Protection Discussion Paper 9923, *Pension Reform Primer Series*, World Bank, Washington, DC.

Dang, T., T. P. Antolin, and H. Oxley. 2001. "Fiscal Implications of Ageing: Projections of Age-Related Spending." Economics Department Working Paper 305, OECD, Paris.

The Gdansk Institute for Market Economics. 2004. Social Budget Model, The Gdansk Institute for Market Economics, Warsaw.

Góra, M. 2001. "Polish Approach to Pension Reform." *Private Pension Systems*, No. 3: 227–46. Paris, OECD.

———. 2003a. *The Pension System.* Polskie Wydawnictwo Ekonomiczne (PWE): Warsaw.

————. 2003b. "The Quest for a Modern Pension System." In *Structural Challenges for Europe*, ed. G. Tumpel-Gugerell and P. Mooslechner, 217–30. Cheltenham: Edward Elgar.

————. 2003c. "Reintroducing Intergenerational Equilibrium: Key Concepts behind the New Polish Pension System." Working Paper 574, William Davidson Institute, Ann Arbor.

Góra, M., and E. Palmer. 2004. "Shifting Perspectives in Pensions." IZA Discussion Paper No. 1369, Bonn.

Góra, M., and M. Rutkowski. 1998, "The Quest for Pension Reform: Poland's Security through Diversity." Social Protection Discussion Paper 9815, *Pension Reform Primer Series*, World Bank, Washington, DC.

GUS (Central Statistical Office for Poland). Life tables for years 1995–2002, published in 1996–2003.

Holzmann, R., M. Orenstein, and M. Rutkowski. 2003. *Pension Reform in Europe: Process and Progress.* Washington, DC: The World Bank.

Mazur, T. 2004. "Long-Term Social Security Actuarial Projections in Poland: Model Description." A note prepared for the attention of the Ageing Working Group of the Economic Policy Committee, Warsaw.

Palmer, E. 2002. "Swedish Pension Reform—How Did It Evolve and What Does It Mean for the Future?" In *Coping with the Pension Crisis: Where Does Europe Stand?* ed. M. Feldstein and H. Siebert. Chicago: University of Chicago Press.

Chapter 17

The NDC Reform in Sweden:
The 1994 Legislation to the Present

Bo Könberg, Edward Palmer, and Annika Sundén*

THE SWEDISH PENSION REFORM DATES BACK TO THE SUMMER OF 1992 when the Parliamentary Working Group on Pensions published a "sketch" containing almost all the essential elements of the reform. The working group was formed at the end of 1991 as the new nonsocialist government took office, following the publication, debate, and official comments on a parliamentary pension commission's final report on the problems of the old pension system that was published in 1990. The reform itself was passed by a large majority—around 85 percent—of parliament in June 1994. The 1994 parliamentary decision was much more than a decision "in principle": all the main components of the reform were set out here except automatic balancing, which was developed after 1994. Implementation began in 1995, and moved forward in stages. This chapter discusses how the Swedish reform came about, what it is, its public image, and remaining issues.

Overview of the 1994 Reform

The 1994 legislation transformed Sweden's public pension scheme from a pay-as-you-go (PAYG) defined benefit (DB) system into a defined contribution (DC) system that combined notional or non-financial defined contribution scheme (NDC)[1] and a financial defined contribution (FDC) scheme.[2] The public NDC and FDC schemes are mandatory for all persons working in Sweden and cover earnings up to a ceiling. The total contribution rate is 18.5 percent, with 16 percent going to NDC accounts and 2.5 percent going to FDC accounts. The public benefits are supplemented under the ceiling—which as a part of the reform is indexed to wage growth—by quasi-mandatory occupational benefits for over 90 percent of employees, and involves an additional contribution rate of around 3.5 percent, but with some variation between schemes. These schemes also provide coverage up to a higher ceiling for all white-collar workers.[3]

Occupational benefits supplementing pensions up to the ceiling in the public system were also transformed into FDC plans, as a result of the reform of the public system, with

---

* Bo Könberg is governor of the county of Sörmland, Sweden and a member of the Implementation Group for the Swedish Pension Reform. Edward Palmer is professor of social insurance economics at Uppsala University and head of the Division for Research at the Swedish Social Insurance Agency. Annika Sundén is a senior economist at the Swedish Social Insurance Agency.

the exception—to date—of the plan for private white-collar employees. As a result, new rights earned in schemes for civil servants and other public sector workers are now being fully funded. With the transformation of the occupational schemes, most employees in Sweden now have a mixed pension portfolio, with a contribution rate of 16 percent for the NDC scheme and an additional some 6 percent for the public and occupational FDC schemes together. In the public and occupational schemes, employees can choose their own investments (in the former) and individual account managers (in the latter).

In Sweden, as in most countries up until the 1990s, the public PAYG old-age, survivors, and disability schemes were all part of the same package. In addition, noncontributory rights were implicitly a part of the old DB schemes. As a part of the Swedish reform, the public old-age scheme was separated from the PAYG disability and survivor schemes, which were moved over to the general budget. This enabled the old-age scheme to become a financially autonomous contribution based scheme. All noncontributory benefits, such as childcare rights and the minimum guarantee, were made explicitly. These benefits are noncontributory and thereby financed out of general tax revenues. Money is transferred to the NDC scheme and directly to private individual accounts in the FDC scheme.

Implementation took some time, first, because one party to the agreement—the Social Democrat Party—needed additional time to discuss the reform in 1995–96, and second, because many practical legislative issues had to be resolved. All the old legislation had to be replaced by new legislation, and related legislation had to be identified and adjusted. Income tax legislation had to be adjusted because the reform also abolished the special deduction for pensioners, putting all pension income on an equal basis with individual earnings. In addition, it was decided to use the pension reform as an opportunity to replace the National Social Insurance Board's outdated computer technology, and politicians were not willing to risk the potential repercussions of errors in either the legislation or hastily implemented computer technology.

One of the most arduous components of the reform in terms of writing new legislation was the decision to transform the combined flat rate benefit and a special tax deduction for pensioners into a taxed guarantee benefit—which meant coordinating taxation rules, both for persons not covered and persons covered by the new system. In addition, the legislation for the means-tested housing allowance for low-income pensioners had to be rewritten accordingly. Legislation was written and passed in parliament mainly in 1997–98.

The new pension system went into full effect in 1999. In January and February 1999, all participants received their first NDC and FDC account statements. Calculations of future individual pensions according to the new rules were made from the year 1995 for persons born 1938 or later. A transition rule means that individuals born between 1938 and 1953 will receive part of their pension from the new system—for example, half of the total pension for persons born in 1944 is calculated according to the new rules. For those born in 1954 the whole pension is calculated according to the new rules.

The FDC scheme started in practice in 1995, as contributions were paid and deposited in a blocked account held at the national debt office, earning a bond rate of return. The contributions were not distributed individually until all individual accounts were ready in January 1999, however.[4] Individual investment choices in the FDC scheme were made for the first time in 2000.[5] The first benefits determined according to the reform legislation (NDC and FDC) were paid out in 2001.[6]

The aim of this chapter is to provide an overview of pension reform in Sweden and describe how the Swedish NDC system works. The next section discusses the reasons for the 1994 reform. The following section discusses the reform process. The chapter then describes how the system works and the following section discusses whether the pension reform will achieve its goals. Conclusions are drawn in a final section.

The Need for Reform

The prereform public pension system in Sweden combined a flat-rate universal benefit, the *folkpension* (*FP*), with an earnings-related benefit (*allmänna tilläggspension* or *ATP*). The ATP system had been introduced in 1960 after what may have been the toughest political fight in modern Swedish history.[7] Benefits in the ATP system were based on an individual's 15 years of highest earnings, required 30 years of covered earnings for a full pension, and replaced 60 percent of average earnings—based on the highest 15 years—up to a ceiling. Individuals with no or very low ATP benefits received an additional benefit, the pension supplement, which was about 50 percent of the FP benefit, and, if they qualified for it, also a quasi-means-tested housing allowance.

An FP benefit of 1.5 times the flat rate plus the housing benefit were usually just enough to bring a pensioner's income up to and slightly above the minimum standard of living based on consumption needs. This idea has been retained after the reform, but the FP component, the pension supplement, and favorable tax rules have been replaced by a *minimum pension guarantee* plus the housing allowance. (See Palmer 2000 for a more extensive discussion of the minimum pension guarantee.) Pension rights, benefits, and the ceiling in the old system were indexed to the Consumer Price Index.

The FP and ATP benefits were financed primarily through payroll taxes levied on the employer. The system was PAYG with partial funding. In the prereform system, old-age, disability, and survivor (widows and children) pensions were all a part of the same system. The FP was financed by a contribution rate of about 6 percent *plus* the equivalent of an additional 2 percent contribution rate financed from general revenues. The ATP benefits were financed by a 13 percent contribution rate at the time of the reform in the mid-1990s. This was not enough to cover expenditures, however, and additional funds had to be drawn from the returns on the large reserve funds to cover remaining costs.

The cost of the old-age pension system *alone* in the old system corresponded to a contribution rate of about 20 percent in 1995, of which a little more than 17.6 percent was the cost of the pure earnings-related component and about 2.2 percent the cost of the non–earnings-related supplements.[8] The total cost of around 20 percent also became a kind of benchmark for the new system, which has an earnings-related component of 18.5 percent (the NDC is 16 percent and the FDC is 2.5 percent) and non–earnings-related supplements financed through general revenues.[9] An additional constraint on the new system in the political process was the fact that more than 90 percent of Swedish employees were also covered by negotiated quasi-mandatory private schemes associated with their occupation or branch.[10]

When the ATP system was introduced in 1960, the contribution rate was set so that the system would build up a surplus.[11] The surplus was funded in a set of buffer funds (the AP funds in the ATP system), and at the time of the reform the net assets in the buffer funds were equal to approximately five years of benefit payments. As it turned out, these funds were crucial in helping to phase in the NDC scheme, as the Swedish baby boomers were to become pensioners beginning around 2010. Without these funds, and given the demographic picture, the Swedish NDC scheme would have faced a growing financial deficit soon after its outset.[12]

The prereform pension system had several problems:

- *The development of costs was inversely related to economic growth.* Pension benefits and rights were indexed to prices rather than wages. The absence of a link between benefits and the real wage growth of the working population made the system sensitive to changes in productivity growth. The absence of a link to the labor force meant that the system was exposed to the risk of a declining labor force. Lower real growth of the contribution base, regardless of the cause, created higher costs.

- *No response to demographic change.* As in most of the world, Sweden's population is aging. Sweden's mortality rate is among the lowest in the world and is expected to continue to improve dramatically over coming decades. At the time of the reform, the share of individuals 65 years and older in the population was expected to be 20 percent in 2025, an increase by almost 25 percent since the turn of the century.[13]

- *The principle of earnings-related benefits was weak and becoming weaker.* To begin with, the link between contributions and benefits was weak because of the FP and ATP benefit formulas. The situation became even worse through reforms during the period up to the middle of the 1980s, however. Only earnings up to a ceiling counted toward pension rights, and the ceiling, which was high compared with an average wage when introduced in 1960, had not changed in real terms since then. Because the ceiling was indexed to consumer prices, more than 30 years of real wage growth since the introduction of the ATP scheme in 1960 meant that successively larger proportions of the population earned wages above the ceiling, eroding the ATP system as a source for income replacement. This process would continue indefinitely and was soon to become a serious problem for the large group of blue-collar workers with average full-time wages approaching the ceiling, and with no organized compensation above the ceiling.

- *Perverse redistribution.* The connection between contributions and benefits was weak. Contributions were paid on all earnings from age 16 until retirement, while benefits were based only on the 15 years with highest earnings. Thus the formula redistributed income from those with long working lives and a flat life-cycle income (typically low-income workers) to those with shorter work histories and rising earnings profiles (typically high-income workers).[14] In fact, studies showed that blue-collar workers, with relatively flat earnings profiles and long working careers (contribution years), and especially blue-collar women, were the losers in the old system.[15]

- *Labor market distortions.* The combination of the benefit formula and the fact that contributions were paid on all earnings meant that reducing labor force participation did not necessarily translate into lower pension benefits.

- *Weak incentives to save.* A PAYG system may reduce national savings, although this is an empirical question. Studies for Sweden suggest that the ATP pension system indeed had a negative effect on the personal savings rate.[16]

In sum, there were many reasons for reform. The driving force was nevertheless the threat that the prereform system would be unaffordable in the future. In addition, the vulnerability of relative costs to changes in the contribution base was emphasized in the short-term perspective as Sweden went into a deep recession from the autumn/fall of 1992. By 1994, the contribution base had fallen by 10 percent, and the contribution rate needed to finance old-age pensions had increased accordingly. As will be discussed below, these recessionary years emphasized the overall need for structural reform of systems— including the welfare system.

The Reform Process

In 1984, the government had already appointed a commission to study the pension system. The commission completed its report in 1990, and concluded that the Swedish pension system was bound to run into serious financial difficulties at latest around 2020. The report discussed indexing the system to economic growth and increasing the normal retirement age as well as the number of years required for a full pension as solutions to the long-term financial deficit.

In the end, the politicians in the commission could not agree on a reform proposal.[17] The commission's report nevertheless revealed all the weaknesses and problems of the old system. During the late 1980s, public trust in the pension system had begun to erode and the view that the system would not be able to meet its promises started to become widespread, in particular among young entrants into the workforce.[18]

The public review process for the pension commission's final report—a usual process in Sweden where organizations, government agencies, and representatives in the field from universities are requested to express their opinions about a government commission report—was extended past the elections in the fall of 1991. In the elections, the Social Democratic government was defeated and replaced by a four-party center-right government. Pension reform became a top priority for the new government, and a parliamentary group with representatives of all seven parties then in the parliament was appointed.

This group, the Working Group on Pensions, was organized along rather unconventional lines for a Swedish national commission. It was chaired by the minister for health and social insurance,[19] and included high-ranking members of the parties represented in parliament.[20] However, membership was confined to the parliamentary political parties. No representatives of labor, employer, or pensioner organizations were included.[21]

The success of the group would depend on the members' willingness to share the *direction* for reform. It was important that the group be comprised of individuals with leading positions in their parties who could bring with them the trust that leadership entails. The group, including a group of experts, also had to be small and, maybe most important of all, everyone in the group had to participate in the discussions, as opposed to the "typical" commission where representatives of various interest groups often participate as observers whose main purpose is to defend the their group's specific interests.

At the outset, the seven political parties in the working group had considerably different views on what reform should entail. To begin with, the ATP system was viewed as the cornerstone of Social-Democratic welfare policy, "the jewel in the crown" as it was often stated, and the party was strongly opposed to introducing financial accounts in the public system. The second largest party, the Conservatives, argued to reduce the scope of the public scheme and introduce privatized individual financial accounts. The Liberal Party was also in favor of introducing financial accounts, and, generally, favored strengthening the link between benefits and contributions. The Center Party supported financial individual accounts but had long advocated a flat-rate pension benefit. The latter view was also to some extent shared by the Christian Democratic Party. The group also included representatives of a right-wing populist party and of the Left Party, although these two parties were soon to reveal that they did not share the goal of the other five parties to create a new pension system, based on a shared set of principles—albeit for very different reasons.

The terms of reference for the group were extremely short: the pension system should be financially sustainable, the link between contributions and benefits should be strengthened, and the pension system should encourage private saving. The group began by reviewing the problems of the prereform pension system. They decided not to argue their political convictions during this initial phase but instead to listen and talk to the country's leading pension experts. Only after this preliminary stage did the discussions between the representatives from the parties begin in earnest.

The analysis of the pension system showed that the problems were severe—the projections indicated that with a future real wage growth of 1.5 percent, increasing longevity, and unchanged contribution rates, the buffer funds would be exhausted sometime between 2010 and 2015. In order to maintain financial stability, total contribution rates would have to be increased to about 24 percent by 2015 (from slightly under 20 percent at the time of the reform and continue to increase thereafter). In fact, projections showed that the system would be sustainable only at future real wage growth of at least 2 percent or more and then only because an increasing share of workers would have a portion of their earnings above the ceiling (Ministry of Health and Social Affairs 1994a). The latter would be a gradual process, moving the system further and further away from the goal of creating a stronger link between benefits and contributions, and in an ad hoc manner. Maintaining the status quo would only increase individual uncertainty about the future framework of the public system.

Because of the increasing financial burden and eroding public trust in the existing public system, the group rejected the alternative of making piecemeal changes along the lines suggested by the previous pension commission. Their conclusion was that such changes would be only a temporary fix, implying continued uncertainty about the system—one important objective was to propose a system that was robust and stable in the face of changes in political majorities—and that a fundamental reform of the system was necessary.

The government's goal was to propose a reform that had broad parliamentary support, and the Working Group on Pensions faced strong pressures to find a political compromise. The question of financial individual accounts was not in focus in the group's early discussion because it was viewed as too controversial and would have to be negotiated if and when an agreement was in sight.

One of the main points in the terms of reference for the working group was that the system should have a strong link between contributions and benefits. Following rather short discussions, the group agreed that the principle that "every *krona* counts" should apply. Thus, without much struggle, the group had decided that the *life income principle* should govern the system, and, consequently, that the system would be a defined contribution scheme and also that benefits should be based on life expectancy. They also agreed that the overall public system would continue to be based mainly on the PAYG principle.[22] Furthermore, there was agreement that earned pension rights should be indexed to wages instead of prices, while pension benefits could continue to be price indexed (this later was changed—see below). There was also agreement that the benefit reflect mortality changes and that the retirement age should be flexible. Thereby—in retrospect—the NDC system had its political birth with the working group's publication of the sketch in the late summer of 1992.

The principles behind the reform and a more detailed outline of what a pension system following these principles would look like were presented in the sketch. The report also included a discussion of replacing part of the PAYG system with a financial individual accounts component, but mentioned explicitly that this was an issue on which the group had not agreed.[23]

The group continued its work and reached a five-party agreement in January 1994. This proposal was passed in parliament in June of 1994. The reform was supported by more than 85 percent of parliament, with members representing the five parties supporting the reform. The reform still maintains about this level of parliamentary support. Two parties, the Left Party, which was represented in the working group, and the Green Party, which at the time had too few votes to be in parliament, but which since then has been in parliament, still opposed the reform a decade later. However, those two parties differ considerably in their critique of the reform. The former wanted only minor revisions in the old ATP system, and still maintains this position; the latter supports a flat-rate system.

The 1994 proposal differed in some respects from the 1992 sketch. In the legislation passed in 1994, both earned pension rights and benefits were to be indexed with wage growth. However, the calculation of the initial annual pension would be accomplished by computing an annuity with a presumed real rate of return of 1.6 percent, and then adjusting yearly indexation for deviations from this rate. The system would have no upper limit on the accumulation period: Individuals should be able to earn pension rights as long as they worked and paid contributions. In the political discussions in the autumn of 1993, the group eventually agreed that the mandatory pension system should also include a financial individual account component, which in the original agreement was given a contribution rate of 2 percent. This rate was later increased to 2.5 percent (under the Social Democratic government that replaced the center-right coalition in the autumn of 1994).

Between 1994 and 1998, an implementation group consisting of representatives of those political parties from the working group that supported the reform, and assisted by experts, was appointed to create legislation and resolve remaining issues. (This implementation group still exists.) Implementation came to a standstill in 1995. The reform proposal met serious opposition within the Social Democratic Party when some of the local labor unions began to speak out against it. The leadership of the Social Democratic Party resolved this by calling a "time out" of about two years, during which reform proponents within the party could discuss and debate with the opposition. With this impasse, little happened until 1997 when the Social Democratic Party again was fully on board, and lawyers began to draw up the final legislation. The implementation group presented the final legislation in the spring of 1998, and it was passed by parliament in June 1998.

As the implementation group was working on finalizing the legislation, the National Social Insurance Board worked on an overall business plan, including construction of a Web site for individuals to obtain individual information and perform their own personal calculations, and training of local office staff. A three-year information campaign was designed and launched, and a new IT platform and technology were constructed. Finally, in mid-1998, the PPM (*Premiumpensionsmyndighet*), the public clearinghouse for the new FDC scheme, was created.

How Does the New Swedish Pension System Work?

In the new public pension system, the earnings-related scheme consists of two components: the nonfinancial (notional) defined contribution scheme (NDC) and the premium pension (FDC) scheme. The contribution rate is 18.5 percent of earnings: 16 percent is credited to toward the notional account and 2.5 percent is contributed to the FDC scheme, called the "premium pension" in Sweden. Contributions are intended to be split equally between employees and employers, and contributions to the two schemes are paid on earnings up to the ceiling.[24]

Individuals earn pension rights from labor income and income from unemployment, sickness, disability, and other social insurance programs, as well as from years at home taking care of children, time in military service, and in education.[25] Note that the latter noncontributory rights and rights earned during periods covered by other forms of social insurance are financed with general tax revenues. For individuals with no or low earnings-related benefits, the system will provide a guaranteed benefit to ensure a minimum standard of living in retirement. The guaranteed benefit is means-tested against public pension rights and supplements the NDC and FDC benefits, for those who qualify. It is financed by general tax revenues. It is payable from age 65 and it provides a benefit of approximately 30 percent of the wage of an average worker. Currently, approximately 30 percent of new retirees collect at least some pension income from the guaranteed benefit. The benefit is indexed to prices, and with real wage growth, the share of the guaranteed benefit in total retirement income will decrease over time.

The NDC Component

The main part of the new pension system is the NDC component. The basic idea of a PAYG system based on defined contributions, NDC, is the same as in a conventional financial defined contribution (FDC) scheme. Contributions are recorded on individual accounts and the account values represent individuals' claims on future pension benefits. But contrary to an FDC scheme, annual contributions are used to finance current pension benefit obligations as in any PAYG system. Hence, the individual accounts are nonfinancial or notional.

Individual account balances grow with annual contributions and the rate of return on the account. The rate of return in the Swedish NDC scheme is determined by the per capita wage growth. Initially, the policy makers considered using the change in the contribution wage sum (total wage growth) as the measure of the rate of return, since this reflects changes in contributors (labor supply) and, as it is the relevant measure of the system's contribution base and financial capacity, it would come closer to achieving the goal of system financial stability. However, a competing political goal of the reform was to ensure that earned pension rights and benefits followed the growth in living standards for the working population and that individuals' relative income had the same effect on their pension income irrespective of when they earned it during their lifetime. It was decided that this goal is best achieved by tying the rate of return on per capita wage growth.

The disadvantage with an index based on wage growth per capita, however, is that when the workforce decreases, benefits and pension rights will grow faster than the contribution base from which benefits are paid. To ensure financial stability, an automatic mechanism that temporarily abandons indexation by average wage growth if the stability of the system is threatened has been introduced. This is discussed further below.

The retirement age benefits can be drawn at any time from age 61. (In the previous legislation the early retirement age was 60). At retirement, annual benefits are calculated by dividing the balance in the notional account by an annuity divisor. The divisor is determined by average life expectancy at retirement for a given cohort at age 65 and an imputed real rate of return of 1.6 percent (an "expected" long-term real growth rate of the economy assumed by the policy makers).[26]

Since the annual pension benefit is equal to the net present value of benefits using a real rate of return of 1.6 percent, the initial benefit at retirement is higher than it would have been if instead benefits had been adjusted annually for per capita wage. The reason for this construction was to provide a relatively high initial benefit rather than having a high benefit at the end of life. The alternative would of course have given an increasing benefit profile from a lower initial level. The method also provided a smooth transition from the ATP system that was price indexed.[27] The divisor is the same for men and women. It is fixed at age 65 for a given birth cohort. No adjustments are made for changes in life expectancy after age 65.

Benefits are adjusted each year for inflation. Since the initial benefit calculation already includes an implicit real rate of return (1.6 percent), pension benefits are also wage indexed, but only with the difference between the "advance return" of 1.6 percent and the *actual* outcome for per capita real wages. For example, if real per capita wage growth is 2 percent and consumer prices change by 1 percent, benefits will be adjusted by 1.4 percent. On the other hand, if real wage growth falls below the norm, benefits will be adjusted by less than inflation. Over an average worker's lifetime this type of indexation gives the same result as regular wage indexation.[28]

Financial Stability

One of the most important objectives of the pension reform was to design a financially stable system that would remain stable when faced with adverse demographic and economic developments. However, the system is still a PAYG system; the government has to cover its pension liability through annual contributions. Increasing the contribution rate is of course possible, but is not a viable option in the NDC framework for permanently solving an imbalance since it automatically increases liabilities. Therefore, the automatic balancing mechanism and the buffer funds are crucial for securing the system's financial stability.

AUTOMATIC BALANCING

Five features in the design of the system could introduce financial instability. The first is the indexation of benefits to the average wage chosen rather than to the growth in the wage sum. If the labor force (and contributors) declines, this creates instability since the wage rate and, hence, the rate of return accredited to the accounts, will grow faster than the contribution wage base. The second is the use of cross-section estimates of cohort life expectancy based on the actual outcome in the immediate past in the annuity calculations, rather than on either a cohort projection or a rate that is allowed to change with changing life expectancy as it becomes known.[29] Third, funded reserves must generate a financial rate of return at least as high as the rate of return accredited accounts.[30] Fourth, the system's financial balance is a function of work earnings and payment profiles. Finally, since in practice indexation is on the basis of historical data, the system will lag behind an instantaneous index.

In order to deal with these sources of financial instability, an automatic balancing mechanism has been introduced in the Swedish NDC system.[31] When the automatic balancing mechanism is applied, per capita wage indexation will temporarily be abandoned and the indexation will be reduced to bring the system back in balance. As indicated by its name, the mechanism works automatically and does not require any political decisions. An important aspect of the pension reform was that the pension system should be autonomous from discretionary changes and the risk of manipulation for political gain should be minimized.

The automatic balancing mechanism is based on a financial balance sheet constructed specifically for the NDC system. The balance sheet makes it possible to produce a measure that summarizes the financial stability, the balance ratio. The balance ratio that relates the pension system's assets to its liabilities and is defined as follows:

Balance Ratio = (Capitalized Value of Contributions + Buffer Funds) / Pension Liability

The assets consist of the capitalized value of contributions and the current value of the buffer funds. The capitalized value of contributions is equal to the pension liability that the annual contributions could finance in the long run. It is derived by multiplying annual contributions by the turnover duration, which is the expected average time between when a contribution is made to the system and when the benefit based on that contribution is paid out.[32] The current turnover duration is about 32.5 years.[33] The pension liability is the current vested liability.[34] A balance ratio of one means that the NDC system is in financial balance—that is, assets and liabilities are equal. If the balance ratio is below one, the system is in imbalance and liabilities exceed assets. If the balance ratio exceeds one, the system has an accumulated surplus. Table 17.1 shows the financial balance of the NDC for the period 2001–4.

The change in the balance ratio is due both to technical changes and also to the very positive indexation of the pension rights and outgoing pensions that have been the result of the fairly good increase in real wages. The increase has been some 3 percent in real value. During the former system, the ATP-system, no such change occurred.

The automatic balance mechanism is activated as soon as the balance ratio falls below one and the indexation of earned pension rights and current benefits are reduced accordingly. Balancing will continue as long as the balance ratio is less than one.[35]

Currently, the automatic balance mechanism is applied only in the event that system liabilities exceed assets. However, it is possible that the system builds up a permanent surplus under certain economic and demographic conditions. For this reason the policy makers in the implementation group have agreed that if the surplus becomes "so large that the risk for a future deficit is negligible," the unnecessary reserves should be distributed to the participants. The question is of course what is meant by "so large that the risk for a future deficit is negligible." A government inquiry has examined the level of the balance ratio at which a distribution can be made without threatening the system's financial stability and has proposed that the level shall be set to 1.10.[36]

THE BUFFER FUNDS

The buffer funds are important in their own right as an integral component of the NDC scheme, but in the Swedish reform the already-existing funds also played an important role in the implementation of the new pension system. In the short term, the funds alleviate the pressures from the demographic hangover of the old system.

As mentioned above, two programs (the disability pension and survivor pension) that previously were integrated with the old-age pension system and financed through payroll taxes are now detached from the old-age system and, in addition, are financed through general tax revenues. This freed a portion of the existing employer payroll taxes for the new contribution-based old-age pension system. The short-term total cost to the general budget of the commitments created through the reform was greater than the contribution of general tax revenues to financing the pension commitments prior to the reform. To help offset the increased financial burden on the general budget, money was transferred from the buffer funds in 1999, 2000, and 2001 to the general budget. The amount was equal to a one-time transfer of about one-third of the total assets in the funds.[37] An additional and final transfer from the buffer funds to the general budget was discussed during the spring of 2004, but the decision was postponed, possibly for a couple of years.

Table 17.1. Assets and Liabilities NDC 2001–4 (Swedish kronor, billions)

	2004	*2003*	*2002*	*2001*
Contribution asset	5,607	5,465	5,293	5,085
Buffer funds	646	577	488	565
Total assets	6,253	6,042	5,780	5,650
Pension liability	6,244	5,984	5,729	5,432
Assets – Liabilities	9	58	52	218
Balance ratio	1,0014	1,0097	1,0090	1,0402

Source: Social Insurance Agency (2005).

Note: 1 US dollar = 7.5 Swedish kronor.

In the long run, the buffer funds are needed to cover projected deficits in the financing of benefits when the large 1940s cohorts start to retire. Thus, although the pension reform creates a pension system that is financially stable in the long run, it was important that money had been funded before the economic strains to help finance the benefits of these cohorts. Note that had the NDC scheme been implemented around 1960, just prior to the entrance of these large birth cohorts into the labor force, the NDC rules themselves would have created an NDC demographic fund. For this reason, it was fortunate that Sweden had such a high degree of funding in its PAYG system prior to the reform. In fact, an explicit goal of the legislation setting up the ATP scheme introduced in 1960 was to create a demographic reserve, and this was honored right up until the reform in the mid-1990s.

Given the importance of the buffer funds for the financial stability of the system, the governance and investment rules of the funds have been reassessed. Prior to the pension reform agreement in 1997–98, the buffer funds had been criticized for sacrificing returns in order to achieve political goals, in particular for subsidizing government and the mortgage market with artificially low interest rates. The new investment rules require that investments are made on risk and return considerations and economically targeted investments are not allowed. The guidelines also allow a larger share to be invested in equities (up to 70 percent of the portfolio) and international assets (up to 40 percent of the portfolio can be exposed to currency risk).

Transition

The transition to the new system will be implemented over 16 years.[38] The first to participate in the new system are persons born in 1938, and they will receive one-fifth of their benefit from the new system and four-fifths from the old system. Each cohort will then increase its participation in the new system with 1/20 so that, as mentioned, those born in 1944 will receive half of their benefit from the new system and half from the old system. Those born in 1954 and later will participate only in the new system.[39] Benefits will not be paid completely from the new system until persons born 1937 and earlier have reached the age of around 100 around the year 2040. Nevertheless, the implementation of the new rules can be considered to be fast, especially when compared with pension reforms in other countries, since all the rights acquired by persons born 1938 and later—almost the entire workforce at the time of the reform—were converted in part or fully into NDC rights.

Individual Financial Accounts: The Premium Pension

In addition to contributions to the NDC, 2.5 percent of earnings will be contributed to a mandatory funded individual account. One of the main motives behind the introduction of funded individual accounts was to help increase savings in Sweden.[40] The financial account component is a carve-out: of the 18.5 percent total contribution rate, 2.5 percentage points are allocated to individual financial accounts in the FDC scheme. A new government agency, the *Premiumpensionsmyndigheten* (Premium Pension Agency, or PPM), was established to administer the FDC scheme and will act as a clearinghouse. The PPM will also be the sole provider of annuities. The investments in the accounts are self-directed, and participants can choose up to five funds from among domestic and international funds registered (in 2004).[41] Any fund that is licensed to do business in Sweden is allowed to participate in the system, as long as they fulfill certain criteria established by the PPM. Since the inception of the program, the number of participating funds has increased from about 450 to roughly 700 funds.[42] For individuals who do not make a choice, a default fund managed by the government has been set up. The default option is mainly invested in global equities. In 2004, this fund held around 65 percent of its assets in global equities and 17 percent in Swedish equities (the remainder is mostly invested in interest-earning assets).

Contributions (and fund switches) are transferred to the individual by the PPM in lump sums in daily transactions. As a result, the fund companies receive only aggregate figures and do not know who the individual participants are. The first individual investment choices in the premium pension scheme took place in 2000. Roughly two-thirds of participants made an investment decision at that time, and the assets for the remaining one-third were invested in the default fund. Among those who decided how to allocate their funds, almost 75 percent invested in equity funds and on average chose 3.4 funds.[43] The participant is free to claim an annuity at any time after age 61, independently from or in conjunction with claiming (a partial or whole) NDC annuity. Annuitization is mandatory and the account balance at retirement is, subject to individual choice, converted to either a fixed or variable annuity.

Information Needs

The NDC reform increases the need for information about the system, and it also places additional requirements on the availability of high-quality statistics. High quality is important from the perspectives both of managing the system through automatic balancing and of the individual who needs to be informed about the status of his or her account to make private decisions about saving.

From the perspective of a well-functioning system, a well-developed infrastructure is crucial for administering an account-based system. Furthermore, for transparency and for the construction of a financial balance sheet, high-quality data are needed to compute reliable estimates of the system's assets and liabilities.

The need for information for participants has also increased (Sundén 2006). The reform completely changed the principles and structure of the pension system and the shift to a defined contribution plan put increased responsibility on individuals. Therefore, information for participants was a crucial component in the implementation of the reform. In 1998, the year before the new system went into effect, a broad three-year information campaign was launched to educate participants about the new system. The campaign included a detailed brochure that described the new pension system; a series of public television programs; public service announcements on radio, television, and in newspapers; seminars open to the public that discussed the new pension system; and a Web site. During the campaign, participants also received their first annual account statement for the pension scheme, the "orange envelope," together with a brochure explaining the system. The orange envelope is sent out annually and includes account information and a projection of benefits for the NDC as well as the premium pension, for the hypothetical retirement ages of 61, 65, and 67—although participants can continue to postpone claiming a benefit to any age after 61.

Following this initial campaign, the orange envelope has been the primary source of information to participants about the pension scheme. In addition to providing information about expected benefits, the orange envelope summarizes how the new pension system works and promotes the main message that lifetime earnings determine benefits. For the FDC component, the PPM also sends out annual information on fund choices, investment risk and fees, and the agency has its own Web site where participants can review and manage their accounts.

Will the Reform Achieve Its Goals?

One of the most important objectives of the reform was to design a pension system that would be financially stable over time, even when faced with adverse demographic and economic developments. Other important goals were to provide increased work incentives and give participants the possibility of controlling some of their pension funds. Will the reform achieve its goals, and what are the challenges for the future?

Financial Stability

The Swedish reform has introduced several features to ensure financial stability. However, the system is still a PAYG system; the government has to cover its pension liability through annual contributions. Because the contribution rate in an NDC scheme is fixed by the design of the system, the system maintains long-term stability through the rate of return accredited to the accounts—which determines benefits in the future. This means that the system shifts the risk of financing benefits from future generations to current generations.[44]

Furthermore, the automatic balancing mechanism adjusts the indexation of benefits immediately when the system is in financial imbalance. Activation of this mechanism does not distinguish between financial imbalances caused by temporary downturns and those caused by more serious economic and demographic developments, however. Thus it is possible to trigger the balancing mechanism unnecessarily. In terms of benefit levels, the effects of such an event will be small, but it could have repercussions on the political stability of the system. When the automatic balancing mechanism was introduced, it was often described as an "emergency brake" that would be used only rarely and only in situations when the system was in crisis. Thus, if automatic balancing occurs, there is a clear risk that this will signal to the public that the system is in crisis and that their benefits are threatened, even if the present value of benefits have increased in real value over time due to steady indexation commensurate with the real per capita wage growth in the economy. The challenge is to modify this image of the automatic balancing, and instead characterize the mechanism as a component of the indexation of earned pension rights and benefits. In general, benefits will grow with average earnings but the return can vary the same way the rate of return on financial capital varies.

Fairness and Redistribution

The new system creates a close link between contributions and benefits. However, for workers in the lower part (presently approximately the lower one-third) of the wage distribution, this link is blurred because of the offset between the benefit from the NDC and the guaranteed pension. For these individuals, additional work does not (necessarily) increase pension benefits (one-for-one). The choice of retirement age is also less flexible for the group who are dependent on the guaranteed pension, since it is payable only from age 65. But a high guaranteed pension was important to ensure sufficient income security for individuals with no or low earnings.

Choosing to index the system with the change in average wages supplemented by an automatic balancing mechanism has implications for the distribution of benefits between cohorts. The activation of the automatic balancing mechanism reduces the indexation of account values of workers and current benefits of pensioners by the same amount. Participants in the beginning of their careers have longer horizons in which to recoup the loss in benefits compared with retirees who already have started to collect their benefits. The expected size of this type redistribution has not yet been fully examined, but some cohorts are likely to bear a larger share of the burden of adjustment.

Incentives to Work

In order to provide stronger work incentives, the retirement age in the new pension is flexible and the increase in benefits from an additional year's work is actuarially fair. For most, the effect of retiring at 66 instead of at 65 will be an increase of the monthly pensions of some 9 percent, and the effect of retiring at 67 instead of 65 results in an increase of almost 20 percent. The system does not have an age limit for covered earnings: participants earn pension credits for as long as they work. For example, a worker could start collecting benefits and then return to work and continue earning pension credits after any age. However, collective labor market agreements and the unwillingness of employers make it difficult for workers to continue working past age 67.

Most workers in Sweden exit the labor market earlier than age 67, normally with either private occupational early retirement or public disability benefit—the average retirement age is approximately 62 (National Social Insurance Board 2000). Several of the occupational schemes provide early retirement incentives, and sickness and disability insurance is frequently used as a path to retirement (Palme and Svensson 1999). However, as the working capacity of older workers—and the demand for their services—improves and life expectancy continues to increase, the relationship between the pension system and labor legislation must be revisited. Also, given that disability insurance is available for those whose work capacity is seriously reduced, both the minimum pension age and the minimum age for claiming the guarantee should be adjusted with increasing life expectancy.

Conclusion

The Swedish pension reform gave NDC an institutional context by 1992, although without the label "NDC" at the outset. The reform as it came to be implemented was already specified in legislation in 1994. What came later in terms of developing the concept further was the methodology behind automatic balancing. The overriding political goal of the reform was to create broad political support for the reform, with the support of parties both on the right and left of the political spectrum. The reform was successful in this respect, gaining around 85 percent of the votes in parliament.

However, following the passage of legislation in 1994, it proved necessary to devote additional time for public debate—in spite of the open public discussion of proposals between the summer of 1992, when the initial reform sketch was presented, and the presentation of a legislative package in February 1994 by the working group. Implementation was gradual, because of the arduous work of changing a large amount of legislation and the goal of implementing new computer technology into the administration of the system.

The first lesson from the reform is that—in spite of the extensive period of debate in the initial years and an expensive information campaign that ran over three years (1998–2000)—the level of the population's knowledge about the reform is still too low, ten years after the passage of the first legislation. The need to reduce information to essential messages has become clearer now than it was in the initial years of implementation. The three most essential messages are, first, that all the years one works and contributes are important in determining the size of a pension. The second is that with increasing longevity, people will have to work longer to receive a given replacement rate. There is some evidence that these two messages have begun to take hold.

The third message is that the NDC rate of return should be expected to fluctuate and, although it should generally be expected to be positive, it can even be negative under some circumstances. This is similar to the financial rate of return, but variation in the rate of return on the NDC accounts will be much more modest. What the NDC pension system can afford to pay is determined by the internal rate of return, which in an economy with positive economic growth will be positive in the long run.

With regard to the possibilities of introducing NDC in other countries, mimicking exactly the Swedish NDC reform, it is important to keep in mind that the transition to the new system was easier because Sweden had already accumulated large reserves in the old system to meet the demographic burden of the postwar baby boomers. Similarly, the present reserve fund will help to provide payments when the next boomer generation retires—the children of the postwar boomers. Calculations show that this will stress finances in the 2040s, and this will be taken into consideration in solving the remaining problem of "balancing"—a method of determining when reserves are large enough to allow them to be distributed to the then-living participants. What still needs to be studied are the implications of the construction of the balancing mechanism for intergenerational distribution of resources.

It is not possible to form a view of the new system without taking into account the fact that over 90 percent of the wage earners in Sweden also participate in one of the occupational pension schemes, which probably will give at least a 10 percent in replacement rate. This also means that an average Swede pays some 22 percent of his or her income in order to receive pension benefits. On top of this come the costs (financed through general tax revenues) of the guaranteed pension; the pension rights for those who receive unemployment, sickness, and disability insurance; and also noncontributory rights for newly born children under four years. Altogether, the system should give adequate pension benefits for the vast majority of persons living and working in Sweden during a normal working career. What's more, the system is now transparent—all commitments are accounted for in the balance sheet—*and* financially sustainable.

Finally, it is important what we do with our pension systems, but it is even more important what our pension systems do with us. On top of giving good pensions, systems must be designed so that they include the incentives to do what is good for society's general welfare, such as working and saving. In our definite opinion, the new Swedish model includes such positive incentives.

Notes

1. "Notional defined contribution" and "non-financial defined contribution" should be understood to have the same definition.

2. We use the terminology introduced in Góra and Palmer (2004). NDC and FDC are both individual account schemes based on defined contribution (DC), the difference being the determinant(s) of the rate of return and the presence of funding in FDC.

3. See Palmer and Wadensjö (2004) for a discussion of public pension reform and occupational pensions.

4. An example of the tasks that needed to be accomplished was the establishment of child rights retroactively from 1960, with three alternative rules. This involved combining information from a large number of sources, covering almost 40 years.

5. Implementation was delayed a year due to a procurement problem with the international supplier contracted to deliver the IT system.

6. The reform brought not only new legislation, it also brought a complete renewal of the National Social Insurance Board's information technology.

7. The introduction of the ATP system required one referendum, one extra-parliamentary election, and finally a decision with one vote majority—and that by one abstaining vote!

8. Ministry of Health and Social Affairs (1994b, p. 74).

9. It is noteworthy that the major "unexpected" cost since the reform was proposed is the cost of financing rights accrued under the disability scheme, which together with dis-

ability take up, have skyrocketed. These figures can be found in the pension system's annual report (National Social Insurance Board 2003).

10. There are four major occupational schemes: one for blue-collar workers in the private sector, one for white-collar workers in the private sector, one for local government workers, and one for central government workers. With the exception of the scheme for white-collar private workers, these schemes were converted into DC schemes up to the ceiling in the mandatory system following the announcement of the reform of the public system in 1994. See Palmer and Wadensjö (2004) for a discussion of how this has affected overall benefits.

11. The reasons for building up a buffer fund were to create a demographic buffer and offset an expected decrease in savings following the introduction of a universal earnings-related benefit.

12. Such deficits would have implied either identifying and financing the "tax" with an amount of money labeled a tax, or waiting for the "balancing mechanism," to be described below, to balance assets and liabilities.

13. See Palmer (2002).

14. See Ståhlberg (1990).

15. See Ståhlberg (1988).

16. See Markowksi and Palmer (1979) and Ståhlberg (1988).

17. A proposal to increase the 30/15 rule in the ATP system to 40/20 was withdrawn in response to a public protest from the white-collar workers' central union, whose members benefited by the short 30-year full-benefit qualification period and even shorter 15-year period for calculating a benefit. The only legislation proposed by the commission and passed by parliament was replacement of the benefits for widows with a temporary survivor's benefit for either surviving spouse.

18. See Palmer (2002).

19. Bo Könberg, coauthor of this chapter, was then the Minister for Health and Social Insurance.

20. The Social Democrats were represented by the outgoing Minister for Social Affairs and the outgoing Under-Secretary of State.

21. Although the labor market parties were not included in the group, a "reference group" consisting of the unions was continuously briefed on the progress of the group.

22. Although the group had different opinions on the fundamental question of whether PAYG systems or funded systems were preferable, there was general agreement that the reform could not convert the entire PAYG system to a fully funded system because of the transition costs from an almost mature PAYG system.

23. See Working Group on Pensions (1992).

24. The ceiling is approximately 1.5 times the average wage.

25. Credits for child rearing are earned for all years until a child is four years old, and although both men and women are entitled to claim them, in practice women by and large claim the benefit.

26. Another decision of the reformers was that pre- and postreform pensioners should have the same indexation of benefits. Since the difference between the norm and the actual (average) rate of change in the per capita wage would constitute real indexation of benefits even for prereform pensioners, it was important to set the norm at what was calculated to be an affordable level. However, an additional consideration was to restrict the level of the norm to one that was reasonably achievable in practice, since benefits would have to be adjusted downward for real growth under the norm—which in practice could be politically sensitive.

27. See Palmer (2002).

28. See Palmer (2002).

29. With continuously increasing longevity, the latter involves continually adjusting annual pension benefits downward. Compared with a fixed annuity, this is much less appealing.

30. The reserves are necessary to fund the benefits of relatively large birth cohorts. The postwar baby boomers, and their children, and so on are examples.

31. See Settergren (2001) and Settergren and Mikula (2006).

32. The inverse of the turnover duration is the discount rate of the flow of contributions.

33. See Social Insurance Agency (2005).

34. The calculation of the balance ratio involves only current values and no projections are employed for assets and liabilities. Traditional projections of the financial status of the pension system are presented in an appendix to the annual report of the pension system.

35. To smooth out the effects of temporary downturns, a three-year moving average is used in the calculation of the balance ratio.

36. See Swedish Government Official Reports Series.

37. At the time of the reform, the funds could cover more than five years of benefit payments; currently, after the transfers, but also after taking into consideration the funds' yields during the period, assets in the buffer funds were some 3.7 times annual benefit payments at the end of 2003.

38. The transition period was originally 20 years, but it was shortened because the reform was delayed.

39. Although individuals born from 1938 to 1954 will get increasingly more of their pension benefits from the new system, their decisions about labor supply (these cohorts would normally have had already been in the work force for 20 years or more, with a 30-year rule for coverage in the old system) and savings were made under the old regime. For this reason, the pension rights for the transition cohorts earned in the old system until 1994 are guaranteed in the event their benefits with the new rules are lower. However, practically all will do better under the new rules.

40. The introduction of individual accounts will only increase savings if it constitutes new savings. It is likely that there will be an offset between pension and nonpension savings. For example, see Gale (1999) for an overview.

41. Contributions to the funded pillar are invested in low-risk government bonds until individual pension rights have been established. This occurs when employer and employee tax statements have been reconciled, which takes an average of 18 months.

42. Funds that wish to participate must sign a contract with the PPM. The contract governs the fee structure for the fund (see Palmer 2000 for a description and discussion of how fees are determined) and reporting requirements, which among other things must occur daily and electronically.

43. See Sundén (2004).

44. See Palmer (2002).

References

Eriksen, T., and E. Palmer. 1994. "The Deterioration of the Swedish Pension Model." In *Beveridge and Social Security: An International Retrospective*, ed. J. Hills, J. Ditch, and H. Glennerster, 203–19. Oxford: Clarendon Press.

Gale, W. 1999. "The Impact of Pensions and 401(k) Plans on Saving: A Critical Assessment of the State of the Literature." Paper prepared for Brookings, Stanford Institute for Economic Policy Research, and TIAA-CREF Institute conference, "ERISA after Twenty-Five Years," Washington, DC, September 17.

Góra, M., and Palmer, E. 2004. "Shifting Perspectives in Pensions." IZA Discussion Paper Series No 1369, October 2004.

Markowksi, A. and E. Palmer. 1979. "Social Insurance and Saving in Sweden." In *Social Security Versus Private Saving in Post-Industrial Democracies*, ed. G. von Furstenberg. Cambridge, Mass.: Ballinger.

Ministry of Health and Social Affairs. 1994a. *Reformerat Pensionssystem* [A New Pension System]. Sweden's Official Publications SOU 1994:21. Stockholm: Allmänna Förlaget.

————. 1994b. *Reformerat Pensionssystem* [A New Pension System: Financial and Individual Effects]. Sweden's Official Publications SOU 1994:21. Stockholm: Allmänna Förlaget.

National Social Insurance Board. 2000. *Social Insurance in Sweden 2000.* Stockholm: National Social Insurance Board.

Palme, M., and I. Svensson. 1999. "Social Security, Occupational Pensions and Retirement in Sweden." In *Social Security and Retirement Around the World*, ed. J. Gruber and D. Wise, 355–402. Chicago: University of Chicago Press.

Palmer, E. 2000. "The Swedish Pension Reform Model: Framework and Issues." Pension Reform Primer, Social Protection Paper No 0012, The World Bank, Washington, DC.

————. 2002. "Swedish Pension Reform: Its Past and Its Future." In *Social Security Pension Reform in Europe*, ed. M. Feldstein and H. Siebert, 171–205. Chicago: University of Chicago Press.

Palmer E., and E. Wadensjö. 2004. "Public Pension Reform and Contractual Agreements in Sweden—Future Directions." In *The Political Economy of Pension Reform*, ed. M. Rein and W. Schmäll. London: Edward Elgar Publishing.

Settergren, O. 2001. "The Automatic Balancing Mechanism of the Swedish Pension System," *Wirtshaftspolitische Blätter* 4: 339–49.

Settergren, O., and B. D. Mikula. 2006. "The Rate of Return of Pay-As-You-Go Pension Systems: A More Exact Consumption-Loan Model of Interest." In *Pension Reform: Issues and Prospects for Non-Financial Defined Contribution (NDC) Schemes*, ed. R. Holzmann and E. Palmer, chapter 7. Washington, DC: World Bank.

Social Insurance Agency. 2005. *The Swedish Pension System Annual Report 2004.* Stockholm: Social Insurance Agency.

Ståhlberg, A.-C. 1988. *Pensionssystemets inverkan på hushållsparande* [The effect of the pension system on household savings]. Spardelegationen. Stockholm: Allmänna förlaget.

————. 1990. *ATP-systemet från fördelningspolitisk synpunkt, expertrapport till Pensionsberedningen* [Distributional aspects of ATP, expert report to the Pension Commission], SOU 1990: 78. Stockholm: Allmänna förlaget.

Sundén A. 2004. "How Do Individual Accounts Work in the Swedish Pension System?" *Issue in Brief*, No. 22, August 2004, Center for Retirement Research, Boston College.

————. 2006. "How Much Do People Need to Know about Their Pensions and What Do They Know?" In *Pension Reform: Issues and Prospects for Non-Financial Defined Contribution (NDC) Schemes*, ed. R. Holzmann and E. Palmer, chapter 13. Washington, DC: World Bank.

Swedish Government Official Reports Series (SOU). 2004. Utdelning av överskott i inkomstpensionssystemet [Distribution of Surpluses in the Swedish Notional Defined Contribution Plan], SOU 2004:105, Stockholm: Swedish Government Offical Reports.

Working Group on Pensions. 1992. *En Promemoria av Pensionsarbetsgruppen* [A Proposal of the Working Group on Pensions]. Ministry of Health and Social Affairs 89. Stockholm: Nordstedts.

Chapter 18

NDCs in Italy: Unsatisfactory Present, Uncertain Future

Daniele Franco and Nicola Sartor*

REFORM OF THE PENSION SYSTEM IS AT THE CORE OF THE EFFORT to ensure fiscal consolidation and long-term fiscal sustainability in Italy. Pension spending is proportionally higher than in any other Western industrial country (15.5 percent of GDP in 2002) and the fertility rate is the lowest (1.2 children per woman of childbearing age). The ratio of the population aged 65 and over to the population aged 15 to 64 is expected to increase from 26.6 percent in 2000 to 37.2 percent in 2020 and 60.1 percent in 2040;[1] it will be among the highest in the world. Pension reform is an important component of any policy aimed at improving the functioning of the labor market, particularly at increasing the present low participation rate. Since pensions account for 70 percent of total social spending, pension reform is also a precondition for improving public support for nonelderly groups and additional spending on long-term care.

The reform process began in 1992 when about a quarter of prospective public sector pension liabilities were canceled. A second major reform was introduced in 1995. This latter reform, which has many similarities to the reform process undertaken in Sweden in 1994, introduced NDC in the pay-as-you-go (PAYG) pension pillar. According to this second reform, pensions are determined on a defined contribution basis, and notionally accumulated contributions will be transformed into an annuity at retirement.

Further minor reforms were introduced in the years immediately following 1995. Significant changes were legislated in 2004. Some changes question the underlying philosophy of the 1995 reform. This continuous debate contrasts with the rule stability required for the proper functioning of an NDC scheme.

This chapter examines the achievements and the main problems of the 1995 pension reform. Among the achievements are improvements in the incentive structure—in particular, the greater incentive to postpone retirement—and the introduction of some self-equilibrating mechanisms. Among the problems are the slow transition to the new regime, the expected increase in the ratio of pension expenditure to GDP, the social unsustainability of

* Daniele Franco is with the Banca d'Italia, Research Department, in Rome. The views expressed in this chapter do not represent the Banca d'Italia. Nicola Sartor is with the Università di Verona, Dipartimento di Diritto dell'Economia, in Verona (Italy).

The issues dealt with in the chapter are also examined in Franco (2002a, 2002b) and Sartor (2001). The authors are grateful to Edward Palmer for useful comments on the preliminary version of the study. The usual disclaimer applies.

some features of the system, and flaws in the design of the self-equilibrating mechanisms. The chapter also examines the process that led to the fast introduction of the reform, and the consequences of the lack of an extensive open debate about its implications. Finally, it considers the future of NDC in Italy.

The next section briefly outlines the reforms introduced up to 1995. The following section describes the 1995 reform, which introduced NDC in Italy. The next two sections, respectively, examine the impact of the reforms on individuals and on overall long-term spending. The chapter then highlights the vulnerability of the new pension rules to economic and demographic shocks. The following section points to the possible lack of microeconomic effects. The chapter next surveys the proposals for further reforms, and then considers the future of NDC in Italy. The final section draws some conclusions.

The Reform Process up to 1995

The issue of pension reform has been extensively discussed since the late 1970s,[2] but no major action was taken till the early 1990s when changes became extremely urgent.

The Need for Reform

Three main factors called for a reform.[3] First, pension expenditure, which had increased from 5.0 percent of GDP in 1960 to 14.9 percent in 1992, was expected to increase further and get close to 25 percent of GDP by 2030. The contribution rate needed to cover benefits of private sector employees was set to increase from 44 percent in 1995 to 60 percent in 2025. The pension formula, the eligibility conditions, and the indexation rules granted rates of return that were considerably higher than the rate of growth of the social security tax base.[4] Pension spending contributed largely to the overall imbalance of Italian public finances.[5]

Second, there were labor market reasons. Provisions allowing for seniority pensions— that is, the possibility of receiving a full benefit irrespective of age with 35 years of contributions (20 to 25 years in the public sector)—tended to foster early retirement and informal employment arrangements to avoid paying contributions. Similar effects were exerted by the rules limiting the possibility of receiving pension and labor income at the same time. The lack of an actuarial correlation between the size of the pension benefit and the age of retirement was an incentive for the earliest possible retirement. In other words, there was a high implicit tax on continuing to work.[6] This situation was reflected in the low employment rates of older men and women.[7] In addition, the segmentation of the overall pension system into several separate pension schemes, each one operating with its own rules, hampered the mobility of workers both between and within the public and private sectors.

Finally, there were equity reasons for reform. The rate of return on contributions was extremely uneven.[8] The reference period for calculating pensionable earnings worked in favor of those whose earnings had risen most rapidly toward the end of their careers. In particular, public sector employees and the self-employed had very advantageous rules.[9] Inflation rates affected the relative value of retirement benefits both at award and after. Although the increase in outlays was accompanied by a sharp improvement in the economic conditions of the elderly and of pension beneficiaries in general,[10] it also constrained the resources available for other social policies.

The 1992 Reform

The first main reform came in 1992 under the pressure of an exchange rate crisis and the urgent need to curb the deficit.[11] It was a parametric reform that introduced several changes, which had been extensively discussed over the previous years (see table 18.1).[12] The retirement age for old-age benefits was raised (over a 10-year period) from 55 to 60 for women and from 60 to 65 for men in private employment. The reference period for calculating pensionable earnings was lengthened from 5 to 10 years; for younger workers it was extended to the whole working life.[13] The minimum number of contributing years for entitlement to an old-age pension was raised from 15 to 20. The reference index for the indexation of pension benefits was changed from wages to prices. The minimum number of years of contributions required for public sector employees to be entitled to a seniority pension was gradually raised to 35, a threshold previously applied to private sector workers only.[14]

The reform implemented in 1992 substantially changed the outlook for pension expenditure. At least a quarter of net pension liabilities were canceled. According to Beltrametti (1996), total outstanding liabilities were reduced from 389 percent to 278 percent of GDP.[15] Rostagno (1996) estimates that the liabilities of the scheme for private sector employees were reduced by 27 percent.

The reform also started a gradual harmonization of pension rules and, by relating the pension levels of younger workers to lifetime contributions, strengthened the link between contributions and benefits. However, it did not tackle the issue of seniority pensions for private sector workers. This aspect substantially reduced the impact on the effective retirement age of the increase in the age limit for old-age pensions. Moreover, the exclusion of individuals with at least 15 years of contributions from changes in the pension formula determines a long transition period and an uneven distribution of the reform burden.

By breaking the deadlock of Italian pension policy and immediately restraining expenditure increases, the parametric reform of 1992 set the conditions for better planned and more systematic changes.

The 1995 Pension Reform

In spite of the 1992 reform, expenditure prospects still remained rather worrying. In 1995, both the National Social Security Institute (INPS) and the Ministero del Tesoro released projections that were more worrying than those carried out in the two previous years.[16] These expenditure forecasts and the high level of contribution rates that would be needed to finance spending pointed to the need for a major new reform. This came in 1995. The reform determined a shift from a defined benefit to a defined contribution system in which the notional accumulated contributions on individual accounts are transformed into an annuity at retirement.[17]

The new reform aimed at stabilizing the incidence of pension expenditure on GDP, at reducing distortions in the labor market, and at making the system fairer.[18] A tighter link of pensions to individual contributions was instrumental in achieving the latter objectives. It was expected that contributions would have been more clearly perceived as individual savings, thereby reducing the distortionary effect of labor income taxation. Evasion was expected to be reduced by the contribution-based formula combined with the reduction in the minimum service requirement for old-age pensions.[19] The 1995 reform aimed at equalizing the yields of the contributions paid by all workers of the same sex and the same pension cohort (that is, those who begin to work and retire in the same years). It removed the favorable treatment previously granted to workers with dynamic careers. Under the new rules, which apply to all categories of workers, individual pension wealth would depend on contributions made on lifetime earnings.

Table 18.1 summarizes the main features of the reform, which are that:

1. Old-age pensions are related to the contributions paid over the whole working life (capitalized at a five-year moving average of GDP growth) and to the age of the individual, at retirement. Each worker holds a notional social security account. On retirement the pension is determined by multiplying the balance of the account by an age-related conversion coefficient. Benefits will continue to be provided on a totally PAYG basis.

2. Contributions are proportional to earnings. However, the rate at which contributions are imputed to the notional accounts (33 percent for employees and 20 percent for the self-employed) is higher than the rate actually paid by individuals (which were initially 32 percent and 15 percent, and are now respectively 32.7 percent and about 17 percent; the latter rate will gradually increase to 19 percent).

3. The formula used to calculate the initial pension award is the following:

$$P_t = \beta c W_l \sum_{k=1}^{a}(1+w)^{k-l}(1+g)^{a-k}$$

where β is the conversion coefficient; c is the contribution rate; W_1 is the entry wage; a is the number of years of contribution; w is the average annual rise in the earnings of each worker over his/her entire career; and g is the average rate of increase in real GDP. The conversion coefficients, which are determined on the basis of average life expectancy—including the probability of paying benefits to survivors—and a 1.5 percent rate of return on accumulated contributions, range from 4.7 percent (for those retiring at 57 years of age) and 6.1 percent (for those retiring at 65 years of age).

4. Conversion coefficients are to be revised every 10 years on the basis of changes in life expectancy and a comparison of the rates of growth of GDP and earnings assessed for social security contributions.

5. Individuals can choose their retirement age between 57 and 65 years, provided the pension is at least 1.2 times higher than the welfare benefit for elderly citizens. Seniority pensions are abolished for individuals covered by the new regime. However, this change is purely notional, as a pension granted to a 57 years old person can hardly be labeled an old-age benefit.

6. The minimum number of years of contributions required for an old-age pension is reduced to 5. The guaranteed minimum pension level is abolished. Welfare pensions for elderly citizens are to be reformed.

7. Survivors' benefits are retained, but they are reduced by up to 50 percent depending on the spouse's other incomes. The reduction does not apply to families with children who are minors, students, or disabled.

8. Pension benefits are adjusted yearly to changes in price levels, measured by the consumer price index.[20]

The rapid introduction of NDC represents a striking development in Italian pension policy. Over a short period, Italy introduced new rules aimed at improving the incentive structure of the pension system, simplifying its complex redistributive effects, and automatically adjusting benefits to demographic and economic trends. However, a number of problems remain open: the transition to the new regime is extremely slow, pension expenditure will continue to increase faster than GDP for some time to come, and the self-equilibrating mechanisms are partial and slow. As a result, both the microeconomic benefits and the macroeconomic sustainability of the new rules are far from granted.

Table 18.1. Mandatory Public Pension Scheme for Employees[a]

Main Features	Before 1992		1992 Reform		1995 Reform
	Private sector	General government	Private sector	General government[b]	Everyone
Old age Age:	men: 60 years women: 55 years	everyone: 65 years[c]	men: 65 years women: 60 years	everyone: 65 years	57 years of age and 5 years of contributions[d] OR age 65+, OR 40+ years of contribution
Minimum contribution:	15 years	15 years	20 years		
Eligibility requirements for: Seniority	35 years of contribution	20 years of contribution[e]	35 years of contribution		Abolished
Survivors	5 years of contribution	5 years of contribution	5 years of contribution		5 years of contribution
Earnings for computing pension benefits	Average of last 5 years	Final year[f]	Average lifetime earnings	Average lifetime earnings	Average lifetime earnings
Ceiling	N.A.[g]	N.A.[g]	N.A.[g]	N.A.[g]	68,000 euros per year
Replacement rate	2% per year[h]	2.33–1.80% per year[l]	2% per year[h]	2% per year[h]	Negatively related to expected life, applied to 33% of the present value of lifetime contributions compounded at the nominal GDP growth rate
Floor	4,150 euros per year[j]	N.A.	4,150 euros per year[j]	N.A.	N.A.
Pension benefit indexed to:	Nominal wages[k]	Nominal wages[k]	Retail prices[k]	Retail prices[k]	Retail prices[k]

Source: Sartor 2001.

a. As far as the 1992 and 1995 reforms are concerned, the table highlights the rules applicable to workers with less than 18 years of contribution in 1995.
b. Central government employees. Other public employees are subject to different eligibility rules, specified in footnotes.
c. Reduced to 60 years for blue-collar women and for all employees of local bodies.
d. Provided that the pension benefit exceeds the "social benefit" by at least 20 percent. For 1996, the social benefit amounts to € 3,200.
e. The eligibility condition is reduced to 15 years of contribution for married women, women with children, and military personnel.
f. Base salary is increased by 18 percent as a one-off compensation for the exclusion of parts of the effective salary.
g. The replacement rate is reduced on wages exceeding a certain threshold.
h. The rate is progressively reduced to 0.9 for earnings exceeding € 27,650 per year.
i. Applicable respectively to the first 15 and to the remaining years of contribution. For employees of local bodies (to whom footnote e is not relevant), the rate applied to the first 15 years is increased to 2.50 percent.
j. Entitlement to the floor is conditional upon holding other incomes not exceeding twice the floor.
k. The indexation coefficient is progressively reduced from 100 percent to 75 percent for pension benefits exceeding twice the floor.

Further changes were introduced in the pension system in 2004. The eligibility conditions for seniority pensions will tighten as of 2008. The minimum retirement age in the new NDC system will be 65 years for men and 60 for women. These measures are not expected to modify the long-term expenditure outlook.

The Overall Impact of Reforms on Individuals

The reforms introduced in the pension system in the 1990s substantially contributed to changing the outlook for Italian public finances.[21] To analyze the long-run effects of the reform, it is useful to split the upward pressure on pension expenditure into its main components. In each point in time, pension expenditure depends on: (1) entitlement rules; (2) the demographic structure; (3) labor market performance; and (4) the macroeconomic scenario.

Figure 18.1 and table 18.2 summarize the main effects in the change of entitlements.[22] Under a stationary population (for example, a population the age structure of which is determined by survival rates only), comparison between the situation before the 1992

Figure 18.1. Effective Equilibrium Contributory Rates (legislated transition)
 r = 3.0%; g = 1.5%

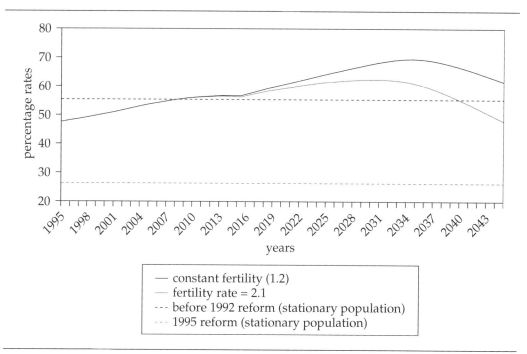

Source: Sartor 2001.

a. Contributory rates are expressed as a percentage of gross salary and computed on the basis of a 1.5 percent long-term increase of productivity and a 3.0 percent real interest rate.
b. Constant number of newborns. The relative dimension of cohort is therefore determined by survival rates.
c. The demographic scenario assumes a 10 years increase in the total fertility rate from the current value (1.2) to 1.8.
d. Average effective seniority observed in the 1993 surveys carried out by the Bank of Italy.
e. As for state employees, effective average seniority is taken from Pandimiglio (1990).

Table 18.2. Equilibrium Contributory Rates for Employees[a]

	Pay As You Go				
	Stationary population[b]			Effective demographic structure	
				1995	2040[c]
Pensions to survivors	Overall	Private sector	State	Overall	
Before 1992 Reform					
Minimum seniority					
No	59.4	53.5	87.3	50.9	88.3
Yes	60.9		52.2	90.6	
Average[d] seniority					
No	52.5	49.4	58.1	45.2	84.9
Yes	54.1		46.6	87.4	
Average[e] seniority					
No	53.8	49.4	68.2	46.2	84.4
Yes	55.4		47.6	87.0	
1995 Reform					
Minimum seniority					
No	25.2			21.8	39.3
Yes	26.3			22.8	40.8

Notes:

a. As a percentage of gross salary, on the basis of a 1.5 % long-term increase of productivity and a 3.0% real interest rate.
b. Constant number of newborns. The relative dimension of cohort is therefore determined by survival rates.
c. The demographic scenario assumes a 10 years increase in the total fertility rate from the current value (1.2) to 1.8.
d. Average effective seniority observed in the 1993 surveys carried out by the Bank of Italy.
e. As for state employees, effective average seniority taken from Pandimiglio (1990).

Source: Sartor (2001).

reform and after the 1995 reform shows that the contribution rate required to finance expenditures has been more than halved (from the 54 to 61 percent range to between 25 and 26 percent).

Table 18.3 reports three sets of indexes of pension incidence calculated for representative workers: the first summarizes the incidence of the years after retirement in the lifetime of an individual and the other two refer to the amount of pension benefits. The indexes refer to the conditions that a member of a cohort born in the base year will experience during his or her lifetime, and are therefore independent of the current population structure. Indexes related to benefits are normalized to the average wage paid in the base year to a representative member of the group.

It can be noted that the time spent in retirement is reduced for all categories. As expected, the reduction is largest for public employees, because in the past they were entitled to a special early retirement scheme. The reduction is very small for a non-university-graduate man employed in the private sector. The reduction of time in retirement is much greater when assessed relative to the working period, as the reform decreases the numerator and increases the denominator. Time spent in retirement is reduced by 23 percent if compared with a whole adult life, and by 38 percent if compared with years of work. Most importantly, the degree of dispersion across groups is substantially reduced,

Table 18.3. Selected Indicators of the Italian Mandatory Pension Scheme for Employees Old-Age and Seniority Pensions for Employees—Average Seniority

| | Frequency | | | | Average effective pension at 60[c] | | Net present values | | | |
| | Retirement during lifetime[a] | | Retirement over work[b] | | | | Pension[d] | | Lifetime earnings[d] | |
	Before 1992 reform	1995 reform	Before 1992 reform	1995 reform	Before 1992 reform	1995 reform	Before 1992 reform	1995 reform	Before 1992 reform	1995 reform
Private sector										
Men										
nongraduates	0.33	0.35	0.49	0.52	2.57	1.58	2.93	1.66	20.01	18.50
university graduates	0.35	0.33	0.64	0.57	3.47	1.65	7.02	2.91	35.39	32.76
Women										
nongraduates	0.43	0.40	0.77	0.66	1.96	1.33	2.61	1.45	15.07	14.42
university graduates	0.43	0.38	0.86	0.71	1.95	1.19	4.22	2.02	21.67	20.58
General government[e]										
Men										
nongraduates	0.49	0.34	1.01	0.53	1.34	1.30	3.06	1.51	16.62	17.92
university graduates	0.47	0.33	1.13	0.59	1.70	1.28	5.05	1.99	21.43	23.14
Women										
nongraduates	0.53	0.39	1.23	0.68	1.91	1.29	4.68	1.67	17.49	17.56
university graduates	0.54	0.38	1.46	0.73	1.65	1.33	4.68	1.94	17.48	19.41
Overall[d]	0.41	0.37	0.72	0.59	2.16	1.43	3.23	1.63	18.09	17.44
Mean absolute deviation	0.06	0.07	0.34	0.14	0.62	0.29	1.54	0.48	5.60	5.23

Notes:
a. Ratio of cumulative retirement frequencies to the cumulated survival rates between age 18 and age 90+.
b. Ratio of cumulative retirement frequencies to cumulative employment frequencies.
c. As a ratio to the average salary earned in the base year by a male employed in the same sector with seniority lower than 5 years.
d. Based on mortality rates observed in the base year and a 3% real interest rate. Also see footnote (c).
e. Average seniority at early retirement based on data reported by Pandimiglio (1990).

Source: Sartor 2001.

as the mean absolute deviation decreases from 0.75 to 0.14, thus increasing the neutrality of the mandatory pension scheme vis-à-vis labor force allocative decisions. The reduction in dispersion (between 50 and 70 percent) primarily reflects the abolition of the preferential treatment (minimum seniority requirement) previously awarded to public employees (see endnote 14) and can be interpreted as a quantitative indicator of the improvement in overall equity.

The reforms determine a large reduction in per capita benefits. This point is illustrated by the last two sets of indexes in table 18.3, referring respectively to the average pension benefit at the age of 60[23] and the net present base-year-value of incomes. Under the baseline scenario, the average pension earned at the age of 60 is reduced by 34 percent, of which 14 percentage points are due to the longer time horizon for determining earnings for computing benefits (from the final 5 years and the final year, respectively, for private and public sector employees under the old rules, to the entire working life for both categories under the new rules). The reduction in benefits reaches 50 percent if the lifetime stream of pension benefits is taken into account. The reason for this further reduction is twofold. First, fewer years, on average, will be spent in retirement (the *frequency effect*); second, the 1992 reform has abolished the indexation of pension benefits to productivity growth. Although in terms of net present value the greatest reduction is suffered by public employees (because of the above-mentioned frequency effect), their average effective pension at the age of 60 is not significantly decreased because the effect on benefits accompanying the lengthening of the working period offsets the reduction in the replacement rate.

As far as lifetime income from earnings and pension benefits are concerned, individuals will be marginally affected (the reduction for the representative member of the cohort is equal to 4 percent), as the increase in labor earnings caused by lengthening the minimum contributory period almost offsets the decrease in pension benefits. This overall result subsumes different outcomes for the two sectors: public sector workers will experience an increase in net present base-year-values of earnings, while private sector workers will suffer a reduction. The above results stress the importance of separating welfare effects from income effects when assessing pension reforms. Although the reform may be welfare reducing for all the cohorts who will have to spend a longer period in work, income effects are sometimes positive and, when negative, are quantitatively minor.

Overall, the 1992 and 1995 reforms have significantly modified the size and features of pension entitlements. The new pension system, when reaching maturity, will be characterized as follows: (1) the degree of horizontal equity of the system will be significantly increased; (2) the reduction of pension spending will be mainly achieved by lengthening the working period, thus avoiding significant cuts in individuals lifetime earnings; (3) if the demographic outlook were not so gloomy, the contribution rates needed to balance contribution revenues and expenditures would be far below current legal rates and long-run financial sustainability would have been achieved.

The Long-Term Outlook of Overall Spending Remains Problematic

Expenditure Trends

Despite the relevant cut of entitlements, the contributory rate at which the system reaches equilibrium is bound to increase above the initial level irrespective of the demographic scenario (figure 18.1). This largely depends on the demographic outlook and, to only a minor extent, to the slow transition to the new rules. According to generational accounting estimates,[24] the reforms decreased the intertemporal balance gap (that is, the amount of future implicit overall government liabilities) from 106 percent to 58 percent of outstanding public debt. Full fiscal sustainability would require a 9.7-point increase in overall taxation (or an expenditure cut of a similar magnitude). With a faster and more equitable transition based on a pro-rata criterion, the increase in overall taxation would be 1.7 percentage points lower (8.0 percent instead of 9.7 percent).

When analyzing the long-term outlook, the role of the slow transition is minor when compared with the effects of the demographic scenario and the overall delay in changing entitlements. Even if the new rules were applied to all workers, a progressive deterioration of the financial equilibrium would derive from the slow but continuous change of the age structure of the Italian population.[25] The relative importance of the demographic scenario and the overall delay in reforming the system can be quantified with reference to the following two counterfactual scenarios: (1) if the population size and structure remained constant through time, the intertemporal balance gap would be negative (net future implicit assets would be equal to 64 percent of outstanding public debt) and fiscal equilibrium would allow a tax cut (or an expenditure increase) equal to 5.0 percentage points even under the legislated slow transition; (2) if the pension reforms were already mature in 1995 (which would require that they had been introduced four decades earlier), the intertemporal balance gap would still be negative, although its size would be smaller than under the previous hypothesis (net public assets would be equal to 46 percent). In this latter case, fiscal equilibrium would allow a tax cut equal to 3.7 percentage points.

As for the transition, workers with at least 18 years of contributions in 1995 will receive a pension computed on the basis of the rules applying before the 1992 reform. Those with fewer than 18 years of contributions in 1992 will be subject to a pro rata regime: the 1995 reform will apply only to the contributions paid after 1995.[26] Only individuals beginning to work after 1995 will receive a pension fully computed on the basis of the new rules. Moreover, only these individuals will be subject to the new eligibility conditions, in particular the abolition of the seniority pension and the introduction of the 57–65 age bracket for old-age pensions. For those exempted by the changes, the incentive to retire early will even be increased by the expectations that retirement conditions might be tightened in the future.[27] This implies that, in spite of the increase in the age limit for old-age pensions, the effective retirement age is likely to remain unaffected for the next 15 years.[28] According to the estimates based on intergenerational accounting,[29] the deviation from a general pro-rata rule represents a windfall gain the magnitude of which varies according to individual characteristics and reaches a maximum of a 40 percent increase in net lifetime transfers (that is, pension benefits net of contributions) for cohorts aged 45 in 1995.

Several other studies, some of them prepared by official bodies,[30] point to the need for further tightening of the pension rules. Ministero del Tesoro (2002) estimates that the ratio of pension expenditure to GDP of the main public schemes will rise from 13.8 percent of GDP in 2001 to 16.0 percent in 2033. Subsequently, even though the ratio of pensioners to workers is forecast to rise sharply, expenditure is expected stabilize in relation to GDP for some years and to significantly decline thereafter (to 13.6 percent in 2050).[31]

These expenditure trends imply either larger transfers from general taxation or a further increase in social security contribution rates, which are already higher than in the other leading industrial countries.[32] Both these solutions appear problematic in a context of growing mobility of tax bases, which accentuates the distortionary effects produced by taxation in the markets for goods and factors of production.

In the end, the further expansion of pension expenditures may mean that primary nonpension expenditure will have to be substantially squeezed. This may be quite difficult in a situation in which increased labor market flexibility requires a strengthening of the social security net to cope with the higher probability of frequent unemployment spells.

Unsustainable Spending Cuts?

Further concern stems from the composition of the expenditure cuts introduced by the 1992 and 1995 reforms. As noted earlier, the NDC pension formula provides greater incentives to postpone retirement. A lengthening of the working period would avoid significant cuts in individual pension levels; some workers retiring late would even receive higher pensions than under the previous retirement rules (although the net present value of lifetime pension benefits would be lower than under the old system); overall lifetime income could even increase (see table 18.3). The actual average retirement age, which will determine the average future pension level, will depend both on the decisions of the individuals and the conditions of the labor market. There is a risk that the average retirement age will not increase significantly.

The official pension expenditure projections seem to take the view that this risk exists. According to Ministero del Tesoro (2002), the ratio between the pensions paid by the main pension funds and the total number of persons in work will rise from about 87 percent in 2000 to 90 percent in 2015, 110 percent in 2030, and 125 percent in 2050. The ratio of the average pension to per capita GDP will increase from 15.7 percent to 16.1 percent in 2015 and then decline to 14.3 percent in 2030 and 11 percent in 2050. These projections assume that pensions will remain indexed exclusively to prices and that the conversion coefficients used to relate new pensions to the contribution record of each individual will be revised every 10 years on the basis of demographic trends. In these forecasts the plan for bringing the pension system back into balance relies primarily on reducing the average pension, and limiting the number of beneficiaries plays a relatively modest role.

This composition of expenditure cuts depends on several factors. First, in spite of the increase in longevity, individuals will still be allowed to obtain a pension at 57.[33] The actuarial reduction of benefits will provide individuals with a greater incentive to delay retirement than under previous rules, but the conversion coefficients embody a discount rate that may still provide an incentive to quit the labor market[34] or may not discourage individuals from claiming a poor, actuarially reduced, pension at an early age.[35]

Second, indexation to prices implies that the income of each pensioner declines over time in comparison with the income of workers and younger pensioners.[36] This effect ("vintage pensions") is particularly important if individuals are allowed to retire rather early. The problem is particularly acute for relatively small pensions. In the long run, if indexed only to prices, these pensions would provide income on the borderline of poverty. However, a full or a partial indexation to increases in real wages would have required a reduction in the replacement rate at retirement.[37] If individuals are not fully aware of the long-term implications of price indexation on the relative purchasing power of their pensions, this solution may induce them to anticipate retirement with respect to a situation in which pensions are lower at retirement but are wage-indexed thereafter.

Finally, the current wage structure, which puts a strong premium on seniority, may prevent the labor market from accommodating an increase in labor supply by elderly individuals.

The decisions to allow retirement at 57 and to rely on price indexation may also depend on the desire to facilitate the introduction of the reform by shifting difficult problems into the future. The same consideration applies to the decision to have revisions of conversion coefficients at 10-year intervals, starting from 2005. This solution is going to produce large differences in the treatment of contiguous generations of pensioners, which may be politically problematic.

Overall, the solutions adopted in 1995 may create political pressure for discretionary increases of pensions in real terms,[38] which would not be sustainable. In the end, there may be a need to rely increasingly on solutions that tighten the eligibility conditions for retirement and to remove obstacles limiting the work activity of elderly workers.

Vulnerability to Shocks Is Still Large

At the individual level, the system—by mimicking the logic of a fully funded scheme—is based on a close link between contributions and benefits. As such, it poses no major problems from a horizontal equity perspective. However, financial problems may arise at the macro level, as the system, being pure PAYG, remains vulnerable to demographic and economic shocks.[39] Stability of the equilibrium contributory rate therefore requires either the presence of built-in stabilizers, such as those incorporated into the Swedish system since 2001,[40] or periodic ad hoc adjustments to the changed scenario. The difficult and lengthy process that all parliamentary democracies face when cutting entitlements suggests the former solution. In the case of NDC, the traditional political difficulties may be fostered by psychological difficulties arising from the (wrong) perception by contributors that the pension system as a whole is always in balance, insofar as individual benefits are linked to past individual contributions. If this misperception is in place, it will be hard to convince public opinion that benefits have to be reduced because of an unexpectedly unfavorable macroeconomic or demographic scenario.

The Italian system has no automatic stabilizers. In particular, the indexation of pension is exogenous. There is only a general proviso that requires a reassessment of parameters every 10 years to take any change in the demographic scenario into account. Moreover, the law does not indicate any precise methodology, or formula, for changing the parameters.

As for the sources of fluctuation, the switch from wage to price indexation of benefits has been a move toward disequilibrium. If on one hand price indexation determines a gradual decrease of expenditures, on the other it increases the sensitivity of the equilibrium contributory rate to productivity increases. Sartor (2001, table 10), by considering productivity growth rates between 0 and 4 percent, estimates that under a stable population, the mean absolute deviation of the equilibrium contributory rate has almost doubled (from 3.8 to 7.0) because of the indexation switch. The reason is quite simple: as contributions are a function of the wage bill, wage indexation of benefits makes expenditure move with revenues, thus stabilizing the equilibrium rate.

Increases in life expectancy would reduce new pension benefits via the conversion coefficients. However, it takes a long time before the impact of increases in life expectancy on the number of pensions is fully offset by the reduction in the average amount paid to each pensioner. This depends on the fact that reductions in mortality rates that take place after a pension is awarded do not affect its level. The 10-year interval between revisions in coefficients increases further the adjustment lag.[41] The system is also vulnerable to reductions in birth rates, which do not affect the amount of accumulated contributions and the pensions already awarded. A lasting decline in the ratio to GDP of earnings assessed for social security contributions can affect new pension benefits via the conversion coefficients. As in the case of changes in life expectancy, financial equilibrium would lag far behind.

In the end, given the incompleteness of the corrective mechanisms, adverse demographic and economic events can determine cash deficits that can be avoided only by ad hoc cuts in pensions and changes in the pension formula, just as in traditional PAYG systems. As is well known, with an NDC scheme, increases in contribution rates would only have temporary effects, since they would translate into higher benefits.[42] Moreover, the conversion coefficients have been computed without taking part of the expenditure for disability and survivors' pensions into consideration. More specifically, it has not been considered that disabled workers will receive benefits in excess of those awarded on the basis of their contributions. Gronchi (1998) tentatively estimates that this expenditure may represent 2 percentage points of earnings. Pensions paid to survivors of deceased workers have also been disregarded. These benefits have been implicitly considered welfare benefits to be financed by the government budget.[43]

The predetermination of the rate of return on accumulated contributions (1.5 percent) introduces some further inflexibility in the system.[44] It reduces the capacity to absorb shocks and, given the decline in the population of working age, it may generate persistent imbalances if productivity does not increase fast.

Is the Reform Providing the Expected Microeconomic Effects?

The strengthening of actuarial principles in social security systems has been advocated to limit some of the negative effects of the systems on labor market and employment.[45] Contributions are often loosely related to benefits, so that they are largely regarded as a tax; expenditure controls frequently rely on administrative constraints rather than on built-in incentives; redistribution and insurance features are frequently mixed; and insurance schemes are utilized for inappropriate distribution objectives. The strengthening of the contributions-benefits link increases the incentive to work and, more specifically, to stay on in regular jobs (since benefits would depend on work record), to delay retirement, and to move from benefits to work. In the case of pension schemes, this may imply increasing the role of funding (where the contributions-benefits link is typically very strong), or shifting PAYG schemes from defined benefits systems (which base pensions on earnings in final period of work) to defined contribution systems (which base pensions on contributions paid over whole working life). Since 1995, Italy has taken both routes.

Table 18.4 illustrates the incentive effect of the reform on a private sector, married worker by considering the effect of postponing retirement by one year on: (1) the replacement rate, (2) the accrual rate on notional contributions (for example, the percentage change in social security wealth), and (3) the implicit overall net tax rate on potential earnings. Data from 1995 refer to the situation that would prevail when the system has reached maturity, thus ignoring the long transitional period. Substantial progress has been made with reference to the situation prevailing before 1992. Despite the overall cut in the replacement rate, the marginal tax rate has been greatly reduced (for a 57-year-old worker, from 25.7 percent to 4.4 percent). The 1995 scheme, however, still incorporates minor disincentives to work. The accrual rate is always negative (ranging from –0.4 percent at the age of 60 to –4.6 percent at 65) and the marginal tax rate is always positive. As for the latter, its value is small in the 57–61 age range (from 4.4 percent to 6.3 percent), but increases thereafter, reaching a peak of 43.2 percent at the age of 65; after this age there is no further increase in the actuarial adjustment factor to the NDC conversion coefficient.

Moreover, an actuarially-based pension system such as that introduced in Italy in 1995 cannot be expected to automatically deliver the expected labor market benefits. As long as citizens do not understand how NDC works, it is unlikely that they will consider contributions to be like investments in pension funds. The link between contributions and benefits should be transparent, easy to grasp, and perceived as stable by citizens. Workers should be informed about their benefit entitlements (for example, accrued pension rights).

Finally, welfare benefits should be separated from insurance benefits, and funded out of general revenues. Governments should make an effort to explain the new rules to citizens.

Table 18.4. Incentive to Postpone Retirement by One Year

Last year of work (age)	Replacement % rate		Accrual % rate		Marginal % tax rate	
	1992	Post 1995	1992	Post 1995	1992	Post 1995
55	63.8	n.a.	−1.4	−1.9	16.9	14.9
56	65.6	n.a.	−1.8	−2.2	22.7	18.1
57	67.4	46.3	−2.0	−0.5	25.7	4.4
58	69.2	48.2	−2.3	−0.8	29.0	6.3
59	71.0	50.2	−2.5	−0.8	31.8	6.8
60	72.9	52.3	−2.7	−0.4	35.2	3.7
61	75.1	54.7	−3.0	−0.7	38.8	6.3
62	77.0	57.0	−3.2	−1.3	41.7	11.4
63	78.8	59.3	−3.5	−1.7	45.0	15.9
64	80.9	62.2	−3.8	−2.2	49.0	20.2
65	80.9	62.8	−5.8	−4.6	74.6	43.2

Source: Brugiavini 1998.

Note: n.a. = not applicable.

To sum up, several factors may reduce the impact of the rules introduced in Italy in 1995 on the behavior of individuals:

1. An important component of the workforce is not affected by the reform.
2. There is a gap between the effective contribution rate and the (higher) imputed rate used in the computation of benefits.
3. As there is public awareness that long-term financial equilibrium has not yet been reached, young workers may expect that further changes will be introduced and therefore may have the perception that the return to their contributions is uncertain.[46]
4. Governments have not undertaken any extensive effort to explain the functioning of NDC; only recently have individuals been receiving a statement of their contributory account presenting their future pension entitlements.
5. There is some lack of clarity about the way the system works. No official document has explained the working of the new system; the formula underlying the conversion coefficients has not been officially published;[47] and the methodology envisaged for the revision of the coefficients has not been specified.

Any effort to fully implement the NDC system in Italy and reap its microeconomic benefits would require progress on all these fronts. In particular, it would require significant reforms bringing to an end the continuous debate on the need for further changes in legislation. This in turn requires full hedging of the system against macroeconomic and demographic shocks. It would also require an extensive public debate about the benefits of the system and the way it works.

Policy Options: A Long Menu

Several proposals for further reforms have been formulated in recent years. They can be classified in three broad categories: (1) implementing the changes envisaged by the 1995 reform earlier than planned, (2) tightening the steady state eligibility rules established by the 1995 reform, and (3) accelerating the development of the funded pillar.

1. Speeding the 1995 reform. The transition to the new regime can be accelerated by the extension to all workers of the formula introduced in 1995 and by the elimination of de facto seniority pensions.[48] These proposals are technically simple, since they do not call into question the architecture of the pension system. However, they are politically sensitive, since they immediately affect a large number of older workers.

2. Tightening the steady state eligibility rules. Several modifications of the 1995 regime have been contemplated in the large number of studies that have recently examined the reform.[49] The extensive ex post analysis of the reform is in stark contrast to the lack of preparatory work. Among the main proposals are:

- A reduction of current coefficients and a shift in the old-age retirement bracket (for example, from 57–65 years to 62–70 years)[50]
- A steeper curve of conversion coefficients, providing an incentive to postpone retirement[51]
- More frequent revisions of the conversion coefficients and an increase in the number of factors considered in the revision of the coefficients, to broaden the range of shocks taken into consideration
- The indexation of contributions to the rate of growth of wages rather than to the rate of growth of GDP
- A reduction in the pensions awarded at retirement associated with the introduction of an adjustment to real GDP growth or real earnings dynamics that takes into account the demographic and economic changes[52]
- A separation of the contributory rates for the old-age pension from those for disability and survivors' pensions. In the case of the survivors' pensions, one can also consider offering different insurance options to the individual.

These changes would increase the effective retirement age and shift the focus of expenditure control from the reduction of replacement ratios to the reduction of the ratio of pensioners to workers.[53] They would remove any implicit tax on continuing work and take the negative externalities of retirement on public accounts into consideration. The margins for this policy action are very large: in 2000, the average retirement age was about 58 years for private sector workers and 60 for public sector workers; in 1998 about 25 percent of pension expenditure was paid to individuals below 65 years.[54]

The modifications considered above would ensure the financial equilibrium of the pension system. In conjunction with a greater role of funded schemes, they would also allow a reduction of the PAYG contribution rate while still guaranteeing high replacement rates to workers with long contributory periods.

3. Accelerating the development of the funded pillar. Several recent studies[55] have considered the transition from the current situation, in which the overall contributory rate is about 40 percent (33 percent for the PAYG scheme plus at least 7 percent for the severance-pay funds or the supplementary schemes), to a situation in which the PAYG contribution rate is 23 to 25 percent and the supplementary funds have a contribution rate of 7 to 10 percent. The simulations show that even under prudent assumptions about the returns of funded schemes, the PAYG and supplementary pensions would altogether guarantee relatively high replacement rates to individuals retiring at 65. However, they show that there is a tradeoff between the benefits of a larger share of funding and the budgetary cost of the transition. For this reason, several studies suggest reducing PAYG contributions for new entrants in the labor market only. The government would have to finance a deficit that would peak after 40 years at about 2 percent of GDP. The budgetary cost of the transition would be substantially reduced if the payroll tax reduction induced positive effects on labor productivity and employment.[56]

In conclusion, there is considerable consensus among pension experts that a comprehensive package including a faster implementation of the 1995 reform, some parametric changes in the pension regime established by that reform, and an acceleration of the development of funded schemes would avoid the expected rise of the pension expenditure to GDP ratio and reduce the negative effects of the systems on the labor market and employment. The acceleration of the implementation of the 1995 reform would provide some budgetary margins for a gradual reduction of the contributions to the PAYG system, which could be implemented in parallel with the development of funded schemes. Pension reforms could be supplemented by reforms in the labor market, such as changes in the age profile of wages, more training for elderly workers, and more flexibility in work arrangements.[57]

The optimal mix of PAYG pensions and funded pensions remains open to discussion. However, high present contribution rates and budgetary constraints limit the speed of the transition to funding. It is likely that the Italian pension system will remain for a long time predominantly based on PAYG criteria.

The Future of NDC in Italy

A reflection about the future of notional funding in Italy requires an analysis of the factors underlying its introduction in 1995 and of the current critical aspects.

An Excessively Fast Introduction

The actuarial approach underlying the 1995 reform represents a structural break in Italian pension policy making, since in previous decades actuarial considerations did not have any significant role.[58] The change is quite remarkable, since most of the potential benefits and distributive effects of the new defined contribution system could have been achieved by adapting the old defined benefit system.[59] The break came without an extensive debate about the usefulness of defined contributions and NDC, so it cannot be claimed that it reflected a change in the policy views of policy makers, experts, and the general public. The philosophy of NDC is actually still widely misunderstood in Italy.

The introduction of a new pension formula is sometimes used to make cuts in benefits more acceptable than explicit changes in the old pension parameters.[60] However, this does not apply to the 1995 reform, which—despite the introduction of a completely new formula—did not reduce future pension spending with respect to the 1992 reform.

The introduction of a new pension formula could have also have been an opportunity to explicitly signal the change in the incentive structure. However, in the absence of a relevant effort to explain the changes to the general public, this justification of the reform does not seem convincing.

It is likely that political considerations were the main factors underlying the introduction of this reform. The reform was introduced after a short preparation period following the fall of the center-right government, which had tried to introduce a parametric reform in the second half of 1994. The new government was committed to introducing a pension reform: NDC, joined with a generous transitory phase, provided the chance of introducing a significant reform without modifying the pension entitlements of elderly workers, who are overrepresented within trade unions and in parliament. For trade unions, the reform may also have represented a solution that allowed the preservation of the PAYG system and reduced the regressive redistribution in favor of workers with rising earnings.

Although the new Italian system shares several elements with the Swedish system, the political process that led to the 1995 reform is in stark contrast with the Swedish experience. Legislation was passed a few weeks after the bill was discussed within the cabinet.[61] The new pension regime was introduced without the publication of a report outlining the different options and examining in detail their implications for the labor market and the future economic situation of pensioners. Although the lack of adequate preliminary work was understandable in the aftermath of 1992 exchange-rate crisis, it was less so in later years, when the focus shifted from expenditure control to a wider range of objectives. Gronchi and Aprile (1998) relate some deficiencies of the 1995 reform to the swiftness of its introduction, which prevented the analyses and discussions necessary to fully understand its implications.[62]

The sudden introduction of the reform also prevented an adequate analysis of its financial implications. The effects of the reform on expenditure trends were examined in a report released by the treasury budget office in June 1995.[63] According to this report, the reform would have reduced pension expenditure. The equilibrium contribution rate of the private employees' pension scheme rate was forecast to be slightly lower than in the pre-reform scenario.[64] The incidence of spending on GDP was expected to decline from 7.3 percent in 1995 to 6.3 percent in 2010, then rise to 7.0 percent in 2030. Similar results were derived for the self-employed schemes. Surprisingly, however, these results were significantly modified in the next report released by the same body, which set out a markedly worse baseline scenario.[65] In that second report, spending for private employees' pensions was projected to rise from 8.3 percent of GDP in 1995 to 8.4 percent in 2010 and to 9.8 percent in 2030. Total spending by all the main pension schemes was projected to rise from 13.6 percent to 14.1 percent and to 16.0 percent, respectively. From a technical point of view, the changes in the estimates largely depended on the models used for projecting the reference population.

The lack of preparatory work and the above-mentioned political considerations also shaped the design of the reform. First of all, the reform avoided showing cuts on replacement rates at retirement. The conversion coefficients were computed assuming a rate of return of 1.5 percent after retirement on accumulated contributions. Expenditure control was essentially achieved, albeit not evidently, via price indexation. As already mentioned, over a long retirement period this solution may lead to pressures for discretionary increases of benefits.[66] The reform also postponed the first revision of conversion coefficients until 2005, and envisaged an extremely long and complex transitory arrangements that substantially exempted a large portion of Italian workers from notional funding. Altogether, these decisions contributed to shifting political tensions far into the future.

Even more surprisingly, the formula used in computing the conversion coefficients has never been published. This contributes to making the future revision of coefficients more problematic.

The fact that the philosophy of NDC was not fully understood by policy makers shows in some solutions adopted in 1995 and in the following years. Some exceptions were introduced in the actuarial approach underlying the 1995 reform: the gaps between actual and imputed contribution rates introduced in 1995 are in stark contrast with the NDC approach. The situation did not improve in the following years: the new pension reform project submitted to parliament in December 2001 envisaged a reduction by 3 to 5 points of the contribution rate to be paid by employers for new entrants in the labor market, but without any change in pension benefits. In 2004, as already mentioned, the minimum age of retirement for men in the new NDC system has been raised to 65 years without changes in the conversion coefficients. This implies disregarding one of the main aspects of the 1995 reform: that of allowing some flexibility in the choice of retirement age within an actuarial regime. Finally, the first revision of conversion coefficients, which is expected to be significant in view of the increase in life expectancy, is not likely to take place in 2005 as envisaged in the 1995 reform.

In the end, Italy has an NDC system that is not yet perceived by the policy makers and the general public as fully operational, that cannot yet provide its expected microeconomic benefits, and that requires sizeable adjustments of rules and parameters to remain sustainable. Moreover, so far no significant effort has been made to inform each citizen about his or her own notional fund. The revolution of notional funding is still largely unfinished.

The Need to Make a Clear-Cut Choice

As to the future, it would be advisable to either fully implement the NDC system or explicitly move to other solutions.

The first solution would require the introduction of procedures and parameters ensuring the sustainability of the NDC system. In particular, it would require the changes considered in the section on policy options: the reduction of current coefficients; a shift in old-age retirement bracket; more frequent revisions of the conversion coefficients and an increase in the factors considered in the revisions; the indexation of contributions to the rate of growth of wages; the use of indexation procedures to preserve the balance of the system; and the separation of old-age, disability, and survivors' pensions. Extensive efforts to explain the functioning of the NDC system to citizens would also be required.

The benefits of NDC systems in terms of allocative efficiency have been mentioned above. Moreover, NDC can increase the transparency in redistribution and can allow the introduction of self-equilibrating mechanisms. Notional accounts may also allow the integration of pensions and other social protection schemes, thereby giving citizens some flexibility in managing their social security wealth.[67]

However, some factors may favor adopting other solutions in Italy.

First, one may doubt the optimality of coupling a PAYG defined contribution system and a large funded defined contribution system, while leaving redistribution to a third welfare pillar. If contribution rates to PAYG pensions are significantly scaled down and benefits are accordingly reduced as considered in the studies mentioned in the section on policy options, the level of many pensions would be close to the minimum income guaranteed to all citizens. The incentive effects of the link between contributions and benefits would be somewhat weakened. To limit this effect, it would be necessary to raise the minimum age—which is currently 65—for qualifying for a minimum welfare pension. This solution might be socially unacceptable.

Second, PAYG pension rights are not usually embodied in formal contracts. The government can modify both the timing and the amount of the payment. Although failure to repay financial liabilities may give rise to legal claims and political reactions, the repudiation of PAYG pension liabilities may raise only the latter. The introduction of NDC reduces the possibility of defaulting pension rights and introducing further pension reforms. Although this aspect of NDC reforms can in principle be positive because of the greater certainty of individuals, it is highly problematic in the Italian case. The size of the pension liabilities resulting from the choice of the NDC parameters in 1995, combined with the dramatic demographic trends, is such that it is highly unlikely that the corrections can take place in a single step.[68]

Although these factors mostly apply to Italy, one can also question whether in a fast evolving economic and demographic situation, which may require substantial continuous changes in the rate of return on contributions to ensure the sustainability of the system, the microeconomic benefits expected from strengthening the contribution-benefit link can actually be achieved.[69] Individuals may consider that the returns on their contributions are anyway rather uncertain. A more traditional PAYG scheme would, at least, appear to provide greater certainty to individuals concerning their replacement ratio.

However, the choice between either approach may primarily depend on political considerations. In the end, whatever solution allows the formation of a political consensus for further reforms that postpone retirement, avoid increases in spending, and conclude the lengthy reform process may be preferred.

Conclusions

The reforms introduced in the 1990s significantly changed the outlook for the Italian pension system. Prospective expenditure growth has been contained. The harmonization of the different schemes is well under way. The incentives for early retirement have been reduced.

The reform process is not yet completed. Significant parametric changes in the pension regime established in 1995 are necessary in order to avoid further increases in the equilibrium contributory rate. The rules applying in the transition may have to be tightened to reduce spending in the medium term. An increase in the effective retirement age is necessary to shift the focus of expenditure control from the reduction of replacement ratios to the reduction of the ratio of pensioners to workers.

But there is also a need for a decision concerning the general framework of the Italian pension system. NDC has been introduced but has not been fully implemented. Some recent reforms are not consistent with the underlying philosophy of an NDC plan. This situation risks giving Italy the problematic aspects of NDC systems (complexity, explicit pension liabilities) without its benefits (microeconomic effects, self-equilibrating mechanisms).

Both policy makers and experts seem unwilling to reopen the debate on the grand design of the system. This probably is because of a certain reform-fatigue, which suggests that focusing on a more concrete step-by-step approach would be more effective. However, without some explicit decisions, the emerging NDC scheme is likely to evolve incrementally in a different regime.

This chapter argues that either NDC must be fully implemented—including the introduction of procedures and parameters ensuring its sustainability and including extensive efforts to explain its functioning to citizens—or it would be advisable to move to another solution, along the lines of a more traditional PAYG system. The latter system could retain some features of NDC systems, such as reference to the lifetime work record and retirement flexibility on actuarial basis.

Whatever the decision concerning the future design of the pension system, it would be highly advisable that it be the result of an open debate and an extensive analysis.

Notes

1. See Ministero del Lavoro (2002).
2. See Morcaldo (1977) and Ministero del Tesoro (1981).
3. See Banca d'Italia (1991) and Franco and Frasca (1992).
4. See Ministero del Tesoro (1994) and Padoa Schioppa Kostoris (1995).
5. See Franco et al. (1994).
6. Brugiavini (1998) estimates that the net tax rate on postponing the retirement age by one year monotonically increases from 25.7 percent at the age of 57 to 74.6 percent at the age of 65.
7. In 1990, only 32 percent of individuals 55 to 64 years old were employed. In 1995, this percentage was down to 27 percent and was far below the percentages recorded in most other Western countries.
8. See Gronchi and Aprile (1998).
9. See Castellino (1996) and Peracchi and Rossi (1998).

10. The poverty rate for households headed by individuals older than 65 had steadily declined over the 1970s and 1980s (Cannari and Franco 1990). These trends continued in the following years (Cannari and Franco 1999; Baldacci and Inglese 1999).

11. See Franco (1993), Vitaletti (1993), and Ferrera and Gualmini (1999).

12. Moreover, in order to immediately restrain public expenditure, the adjustment of pensions to price dynamics was temporarily limited and the disbursement of new seniority pensions was curtailed.

13. Past earnings were revalued at a rate equal to the rise in the cost of living plus 1 percentage point per year.

14. Seniority pensions allowed workers to retire at any age provided they had a minimum contributory period, which was 35 years in the private sector and 20–25 years in the public sector (with a minimum as low as 16 years for certain categories).

15. These estimates refer to the present value of pensions to be paid in the future on the basis of accrued rights to pensioners and existing workers, net of the contributions that the latter will pay under current rules.

16. In spite of the 1992 reform, INPS expected the equilibrium contribution rate for private sector employees to remain stable at its 1995 level (49 percent) (the projections are reported in Senate of Italy 1995). According to Ministero del Tesoro (1996), this rate would decline from 47 percent in 1995 to 42 percent in 2010 and then increase to 46 percent in 2030. The equilibrium contribution rates of the schemes for the self-employed workers were also revised upward.

17. As is well known, a similar reform was discussed in Sweden in 1994 and introduced in the following years. For a comparison, see Gronchi and Nisticò (2003).

18. See Aprile, Fassina, and Pace (1996), Banca d'Italia (1995), Castellino (1995), Padoa Schioppa Kostoris (1995), Peracchi and Rossi (1998), Rostagno (1996) and Saraceno (1995).

19. The eligibility requirement set by the 1992 reform (of 20 years of contributions) encouraged evasion by those workers who expected they would never reach the minimum service requirement.

20. The 1995 reform also provided for the partial indexation to real wage growth of pension up to 10 million lire per year (about 5,000 euros). The provision is to be applied from 2009, with both a ceiling and procedures still to be indicated.

21. The 1995 reform did not contribute to the reduction of expenditures in the long term. Rostagno (1996) estimates that this reform increased the liabilities of the private sector employees pension scheme by 4 to 9 percent of GDP depending on the rate of growth of GDP (the higher GDP growth, the greater the increase in liabilities, since—contrary to contributions of the pre-1995 regime—contributions are adjusted to GDP growth).

22. See Sartor (2001).

23. The table refers to the ratio of the average effective pension at the age of 60 to the initial wage rather than to the more traditional replacement rate (the ratio of pension benefit to the last salary). This is because the former ratio provides a common basis for assessing the characteristics of two pension regimes characterized, inter alia, by different contributory periods for retirement.

24. See Cardarelli and Sartor (2000).

25. The continuous aging of the Italian population is mainly the result of Italy's very low fertility rate and, to a minor extent, its increase in life expectancy. The Italian fertility rate has been below replacement since 1977; since 1993 it has been below the 1.3 threshold (considered by U.N. demographers a critical threshold); it reached its minimum value of 1.18 in 1995.

26. The pensions paid to individuals in the pro rata regime will be computed on the basis of two components: the pre-1995 contributions and the contributions paid from 1995 onward.

27. See Porta and Saraceno (1997).

28. The sharp difference in the treatment of workers who in 1992 and 1995 had small differences in contributory records also raises an equity problem (Commissione ministeriale per la valutazione 2001).

29. See Sartor (2001).

30. The budgetary effects of the 1995 reform and of the measures introduced in the following years have been examined in Commissione ministeriale per la valutazione (2001). The overall expenditure cuts were broadly in line with the early estimates.

31. According to INPS (1998) projections, the equilibrium contribution rate of the private sector employees' pension fund will rise from 45 percent in 2000 to 47.8 percent in 2010 and 48.5 percent in 2025. The corresponding rate of the artisans' pension scheme is projected to increase from 21.3 percent to 28.2 percent and then to 30 percent, and that of the shopkeepers' pension scheme from 18.5 to 25.4 percent and then to 33.9 percent.

32. See Commissione ministeriale per la valutazione (2001).

33. The decision taken in 2004 to increase the minimum retirement age to 65 years for men and to 60 years for women would evidently reduce the number of pensions and increase the average pension. However, the abolition of any flexibility for men combined with the preservation of the conversion coefficients introduced in 1995 does not seem an optimal and sustainable solution.

34. See Brugiavini (1998).

35. See Palmer (1999).

36. See Aprile, Fassina, and Pace (1996).

37. See Banca d'Italia (1995), Castellino and Fornero (1997), and Giarda (1998). This solution would have been in contrast with the government's objective of ensuring that individuals retiring at 62 after 37 years of service would get the same replacement rate that they accrued before the reform.

38. See Peracchi and Rossi (1998) and D'Amato and Galasso (2001). The Ministero del Tesoro (2000) estimates that if pensions were adjusted to increases in real wages from 2005 onward, the ratio of pension expenditure to GDP would be 2 percentage points higher than in the baseline scenario in 2015 and more than 3 points higher in 2030.

39. See Aprile, Fassino, and Pace (1996), Rostagno (1996), Hamann (1997), Gronchi and Aprile (1998), and Sartor (2001).

40. See Settergren (2001).

41. Baldacci and Tuzi (1999) estimate that the new mortality ratios would already imply a 1 percent cut in the benefits paid to those retiring at 57 and a 3 percent cut for those retiring at 65. Caselli et al. (2003), on the basis of the 1997 life tables, point to cuts respectively of 2.5 percent and 3.7 percent for the same age groups. They estimate that the mortality rates considered in the baseline demographic scenario of the National Statistical Office imply a reduction of 8.9 percent for those retiring at 57 and a 11.8 percent for those retiring at 65.

42. The need for a built-in equilibrating mechanism operating via the indexation of pensions was highlighted in a study carried out at the end of 1994 for the main parliamentary group supporting the reform (Aprile, Fassina, and Pace 1996). For instance, the study advocated the introduction of a coefficient offsetting the effects of changes in working-age population.

43. The usefulness of the solution of considering survivor benefits to be welfare benefits payable by the government is questionable, since providing a guaranteed minimum pension to disabled workers and survivors may be considered a component of social insurance, particularly as the contribution rates are relatively high (Giarda 1998).

44. See Gronchi and Aprile (1998), Giarda (1998), and Nicoletti-Altimari and Rostagno (1999).

45. See Orszag and Snower (1999).

46. This perception has been reinforced by some measures taken in recent years to curtail pension expenditure.

47. See Gronchi (1997).

48. See Giarda (1998), Ferraresi and Fornero (2000), and Fornero and Castellino (2001). The changes introduced in 2004 move in this direction.

49. See Commissione per l'analisi delle compatibilità macroeconomiche della spesa sociale (1997), Giarda (1998), Gronchi (1997 and 1998), Gronchi and Aprile (1998), Hamann (1997), Padoa Schioppa Kostoris (1996), Peracchi and Rossi (1998), Angrisani et al. (2001), Fornero and Castellino (2001), Sartor (2001), and Franco and Marè (2002).

50. It has also been suggested that (1) effective contribution rates should be equal to the rates taken into account to determine the accumulated contributions, (2) disability and survivor's pensions should be fully financed out of the contribution rate, and (3) any residual restriction to the cumulability of pension and labor income should be abolished. The abolition of the retirement bracket for men decided in 2004 is not an optimal solution: it reduces the flexibility allowed to individuals without significantly curtailing spending.

51. Brugiavini and Peracchi (2003) show that there are significant margins to increase the incentive to postpone retirement. They estimate that a hypothetical regime characterized by a 6 percent increase of benefits per year of delayed retirement (which they define as actuarial adjustment) would generate a sizeable increase in employment rates compared with the 1995 reform regime, especially after age 60.

52. This solution would reduce the political pressure for discretionary increases of pension in real terms stemming from sizeable disparities among pensioners depending on the year of retirement. It would also introduce a second built-in equilibrating mechanism in the system: adjustments in the conversion coefficients would offset the effects of changes in life expectancy, and the indexation mechanism would take cyclical aspects and birthrate changes into account. These devices, which were considered in the preparatory work for the reform (see Aprile, Fassina, and Pace 1996), would make the pensioners share the burden or take advantage respectively of negative and positive shocks. See also Giarda (1998) and Gronchi (1998).

53. This strategy is in line with the policy response to population aging advocated by the European Commission and the Organisation for Economic Co-operation and Development (OECD), which is centered on increasing the average number of years individuals spend active in the labor force and on guaranteeing adequate income to pensioners. See European Commission (2002) and Visco (1999).

54. See ISTAT (2000).

55. See Castellino and Fornero (1997), Brambilla and Leoni (1998), Brugiavini and Peracchi (1999), Forni and Giordano (2001), and Fornero and Castellino (2001). See also Amato and Marè (2001) and Messori and Scaffidi (1999).

56. Modigliani and Ceprini (1998) take a different approach and suggest a gradual transition to a fully funded system. The funded scheme would operate on defined benefits criteria with the government guaranteeing a minimum rate of return on assets and benefiting from returns above this minimum.

57. See Marano and Sestito (2004).

58. See Castellino (1996).

59. See Cichon (1999). The equalization of yields on contributions and the strengthening of the link between contribution and benefits could have been achieved by applying the same pension formula to all categories, computing pensions on the basis of lifetime earnings and introducing an actuarial discount of benefits in relation to the age of retirement.

Gronchi and Nisticò (2003) point to the different implications of the defined benefit and the defined contribution solutions.

60. See Pizzuti (1998).

61. Giarda (1998) notes that the complex technicalities of the NDC system had to be understood and implemented into legislation in about two months.

62. See also Aprile, Fassina, and Pace (1996).

63. See Ragioneria Generale dello Stato (1996a).

64. The contribution rate was estimated to be 40.2 percent rather than 42.2 percent in 2010 and 44.8 percent rather than 46.2 percent in 2030. The estimates are based on a scenario in which GDP and total wage growth rate were 2 percent and the conversion rate was revised every 10 years. The expenditure projections for the self-employed schemes were examined in Ragioneria Generale dello Stato (1996b).

65. See Ragioneria Generale dello Stato (1996c).

66. Pizzuti (1998) remarks that this decision, which relies on the shortsightedness of individuals, is in stark contrast with one of the main roles of public action in retirement provision: that of compensating for this shortsightedness.

67. See Fölster (1999) and Orszag and Snower (1999).

68. As it is put by Boskin (1982): "I would not wish to have the current rules and regulations of the social insurance program cemented into a unified capital account of the government as if we had issued explicit long-term contractual debt obligations, that is, I do not want to enshrine pay-as-you-go financing of these programs and government activities at current projected levels" (p. 300).

69. See the more general point made in Tamburi (1999) about the need for periodic adjustments of pension provision.

References

Amato, G., and M. Marè. 2001. *Le pensioni – Il pilastro mancante*. Bologna: Il Mulino.

Angrisani, M., G. De Filippi, M. Marè, A. Pedone, G. Pennisi, and S. Zecchini. 2001. *Le pensioni: guida a una riforma*, Roma, Ideazione Editrice, September.

Aprile, R., S. Fassina, and D. Pace. 1996. "Equilibrio ed equità in un sistema a ripartizione: un'ipotesi di riforma." In *Pensioni e risanamento della finanza pubblica*, ed. F. Padoa Schioppa Kostoris, 273–324. Bologna: Il Mulino.

Baldacci, E., and L. Inglese. 1999. Le caratteristiche socio-economiche dei pensionati in Italia. Analisi della distribuzione dei redditi da pensione, Riunione Scientifica Gruppo MURST, Messina, November 22–23.

Baldacci, E. and D. Tuzi. 1999. "Gli effetti delle riforme degli anni '90 sull'evoluzione della spesa per pensioni." XI Riunione Scientifica della Società di Economia Pubblica, Pavia, October 8–9.

Banca d'Italia. 1991. "The Pension System: Reasons for Reform." *Economic Bulletin* 13 (October): 68–70.

Banca d'Italia. 1995. "The 1995 Pension Reform." *Economic Bulletin* 21 (October): 65–79.

Beltrametti, L. 1996. *Il debito pensionistico in Italia*. Bologna: Il Mulino.

Boskin, M. J. 1982. "Federal Government Deficits: Some Myths and Realities." *American Economic Review, Paper and Proceedings* 72 (2): 296–303.

Brambilla, A., and S. Leoni. 1998. "Primi passi verso il riequilibrio tra previdenza pubblica di base e complementare." *Economia italiana* (3): 625–53.

Brugiavini, A. 1998. "Social Security and Retirement in Italy." In *Social Security and Retirement around the World*, ed. J. Gruber and D. A. Wise, 181–238, Chicago: University of Chicago Press.

Brugiavini, A., and F. Peracchi. 1999. "Reforming Italian social security: Should we switch from PAYG to fully funded?" Paper prepared for the 6th Conference "Le nuove frontiere della politica economica" IGIER, June 7, 1999, Rome.

———. 2003. "Social Security Wealth and Retirement Decisions in Italy." *Labour* 17 (Special Issue): 79–114.

Cannari, L., and D. Franco. 1990. "Sistema pensionistico e distribuzione dei redditi." *Contributi all'analisi economica* 6, Banca d'Italia.

———. 1999. "Poverty Among Children in Italy: Dimensions, Characteristics, Policies." Paper prepared for the conference "Child Well-Being in Rich and Transition Countries." September 30–October 2, Luxembourg.

Cardarelli, R., and N. Sartor. 2000. "Generational Accounts for Italy." In *Fiscal Sustainability*, ed. Banca d'Italia, 501–57. Rome: Banca d'Italia.

Caselli, G., F. Peracchi, E. Barbi, and M. R. Lippi. 2003. "Differential Mortality and the Design of the Italian Pension System of Public Pensions." *Labour* 17 (Special Issue): 45–78.

Castellino, O. 1995. "La previdenza sociale dalla riforma Amato alla riforma Dini." *Rivista Internazionale di Scienze Sociali*, 103 (3): 457–72.

———. 1996. "La redistribuzione tra ed entro generazioni nel sistema previdenziale italiano." In *Pensioni e risanamento della finanza pubblica*, ed. F. Padoa Schioppa Kostoris, 59–146, Bologna: Il Mulino.

Castellino, O., and E. Fornero. 1997. "Privatizzare la previdenza sociale? Condizioni, modalità e limiti." *Politica Economica* 13 (1): 3–25.

Cichon, M. 1999. "Notional Defined-Contribution Schemes: Old Wine in New Bottles?" *International Social Security Review* 52 (4): 87–105.

Commissione per l'analisi delle compatibilità macroeconomiche della spesa sociale. 1997. "Relazione Finale." *Lavoro Informazione*, XVI (7).

Commissione ministeriale per la valutazione degli effetti della legge n. 335/95 e successivi provvedimenti. 2001. *Relazione finale*, Ministero del Lavoro e delle Politiche Sociali, Roma.

D'Amato, M., and V. Galasso. 2001. "È la riforma Dini politicamente sostenibile?" Paper presented at the Conference "Le nuove frontiere della politica economica 2001 – Pensioni: davvero una verifica?" IGIER, September 20, Rome.

European Commission. 2002. *Joint Report by the Commission and Council on Adequate and Sustainable Pensions*. Brussels.

Ferrera, M., and E. Gualmini. 1999. "Rescue from Without? Italian Social Policies 1970–1999 and the Challenges of Internationalisation." Working Paper 13, European University Institute, Florence.

Ferraresi, P. M., and E. Fornero. 2000. "Costi e distorsioni della transizione previdenziale ed effetti correttivi di alcune proposte di riforma." *Politica Economica* 16 (1): 3–48.

Fölster, S. 1999. "Social Insurance Based on Personal Savings Accounts: A Possible Reform Strategy for the Overburdened Welfare State." In *The Welfare State in Europe*, ed. M. Buti, D. Franco, and L. Pench, 99–115. Cheltenham, UK: Edward Elgar.

Fornero, E., and O. Castellino, eds. 2001. *La riforma del sistema previdenziale italiano: Opzioni e proposte.* Torino: Rapporto CeRP.

Forni, L., and R. Giordano. 2001. "Funding a PAYG System: The Case of Italy." *Fiscal Studies*, 22 (4): 487–526.

Franco, D. 1993. "Il sistema pensionistico fra provvedimenti di emergenza e riforme di struttura." In *La finanza pubblica italiana: Rapporto 1993*, ed. L. Bernardi, 105–40. Milano: Franco Angeli.

———. 2002a. "Italy: A Never-Ending Pension Reform." In *Coping with the Pension Crisis – Where Does Europe Stand?*, ed. M. Feldstein and H. Siebert, 211–61. Chicago and London: Chicago University Press.

———. 2002b. "Italy: The Search for a Sustainable PAYG System." In *Taste of Pie: Searching for Better Pension Provisions in Developed Countries*, ed N. Takayama, 137–83. Tokyo, Maruzen Co.

Franco, D., and F. Frasca. 1992. "Public Pensions in an Ageing Society: The Case of Italy." In *The Future of Pensions in the European Community*, ed. J. Mortensen, 69–95. London: CEPS, Brassey's.

Franco, D., J. Gokhale, L. Guiso, L. Kotlikoff, and N. Sartor. 1994. "Generational Accounting: The Case of Italy." In *Saving and the Accumulation of Wealth*, ed. A. Ando, L. Guiso, and I. Visco, 128–60, Cambridge: Cambridge University Press.

Franco, D., and M. Marè. 2002. "Le pensioni: l'economia e la politica delle riforme." *Rivista di Politica Economica* 92 (VII-VIII): 197–276. XCII.

Giarda, P. 1998. "La revisione del sistema pensionistico nel 1997: come avrebbe potuto essere." *Economia Politica* 15 (2): 267–94.

Gronchi, S. 1997. "Un'ipotesi di correzione e completamento della riforma delle pensioni del 1995." *Studi e Note di Economia*, (2): 7-40.

———. 1998. "La sostenibilità delle nuove forme previdenziali ovvero il sistema pensionistico tra riforme fatte e da fare." *Economia Politica* 15 (2): 295–316.

Gronchi, S., and R. Aprile. 1998. "The 1995 Pension Reform: Equity, Sustainability and Indexation." *Labour* 12 (1): 67–100.

Gronchi, S., and S. Nisticò. 2003. "Sistemi a ripartizione equi e sostenibili: medelli teorici e realizzazioni pratiche." CNEL-Documenti, N. 27.

Hamann, A. J. 1997. "The Reform of the Pension System in Italy." IMF Working Paper WP/97/18, IMF, Washington, DC.

INPS (Istituto Nazionale per la Previdenza Sociale). 1998. *Modello previsionale 1998*. Roma.

ISTAT (Istituto Nazionale di Statistica). 2000. *I beneficiari delle prestazioni pensionistiche – Anno 1998,* Roma.

Marano, A., and P. Sestito. 2004. "Older Workers and Pensioners: The Challenge of Ageing on the Italian Public Pension System and Labour Market." CERP Working Paper 32/04, CERP, Torino.

Messori, M., and A. Scaffidi. 1999. "Lo sviluppo dei fondi pensione 'chiusi': il possibile ruolo del TFR e del regime fiscale." Mimeo, MEFOP, Roma.

Ministero del Lavoro e delle Politiche Sociali. 2002. *Rapporto sulle strategie nazionali per i futuri sistemi pensionistici – Italia*. Roma.

Ministero del Tesoro. 1981. *La spesa previdenziale e i suoi effetti sulla finanza pubblica. - Relazione della Commissione di studio istituita dal Ministro del Tesoro*, Istituto Poligrafico e Zecca dello Stato, Roma.

———. 1994. "I rendimenti impliciti della previdenza obbligatoria: un'analisi delle iniquità del sistema." *Conti pubblici e congiuntura economica*, No. 2.

———. 1996."Il progetto di riforma del sistema pensionistico pubblico presentato dal governo: le tendenze di medio-lungo periodo del FPLD." *Conti pubblici e congiuntura economica*, No. 2.

———. 2000. "Medium and Long-Term Trends of the Italian Pension System Year-2000 Update of the Projections Based on the RGS Model." *Quaderno* 2.

———. 2002. *Le tendenze di medio-lungo periodo del sistema pensionistico obbligatorio – Le previsioni del Dipartimento della Ragioneria Generale dello Stato aggiornate a maggio 2002 utilizzando le nuove basi assicurative dell'INPS*. December.

Modigliani, F., and M. Ceprini. 1998. "Social Security Reform: A Proposal for Italy." *Review of Economic Conditions in Italy*, 2: 177–201.

Morcaldo, G. 1977. "Analisi della struttura dei trattamenti pensionistici e della sua evoluzione." *Contributi alla ricerca economica*, 7, Banca d'Italia.

Nicoletti-Altimari, S., and M. Rostagno. 1999. "The *Dis*-Advantages of Tying One's Hands—Yield Rate Flexibility in Unfunded Pension Systems." Paper presented at the conference on "Le nuove frontiere della politica economica." IGIER, Rome, June 7.

Orszag, J. M., and D. J. Snower. 1999. "Expanding the Welfare System: A Proposal for Reform." In *The Welfare State in Europe*, ed. M. Buti, D. Franco, and L. Pench. Cheltenham: Edward Elgar.

Padoa Schioppa Kostoris, F. 1995. "A proposito dei tassi di rendimento interno per i neopensionati italiani: 1995–2001." In *Le pensioni difficili*, ed. O. Castellino, 143–64. Bologna: Il Mulino.

———. 1996. "La riforma italiana delle pensioni anzianità e vecchiaia del 1995 e gli effetti di finanza pubblica." In *Pensioni e risanamento della finanza pubblica*, ed. F. Padoa Schioppa Kostoris, 399–480. Bologna: Il Mulino.

Palmer, E. 1999. "Exit from the Labor Force for Older Workers: Can the NDC Pension System Help?" *The Geneva Papers on Risk and Insurance* 24 (4): 461–72.

Peracchi, F., and N. Rossi. 1998. "Nonostante tutto, è una riforma." In *La costituzione fiscale*, ed. F. Giavazzi, A. Penati, and G. Tabellini, 149–272. Bologna: Il Mulino.

Pizzuti, F. R. 1998. "Pension Reform and Economic Policy Constraints in Italy." *Labour* 12 (1): 45–66.

Porta, P., and P. Saraceno. 1997. "The Mandatory Pension System in Italy: Country Report of the Phare-Ace." *Contributi di Ricerca IRS* (Istituto per la Ricerca Sociale), 37.

Ragioneria Generale dello Stato. 1996a. "Il progetto di riforma del sistema pensionistico pubblico presentato dal governo: le tendenze di medio-lungo periodo del FPLD." *Conti Pubblici e Congiuntura Economica* 6 (2): 117–32.

———. 1996b. "Il progetto di riforma del sistema pensionistico pubblico presentato dal governo: le tendenze di medio-lungo periodo del Fondo Artigiani e Commercianti." *Conti Pubblici e Congiuntura Economica*, 6 (2): 133–52.

———. 1996c. "Tendenze demografiche e spesa pensionistica: alcuni possibili scenari." Quaderno Monografico N. 9, *Conti Pubblici e Congiuntura Economica.*

Rostagno, M. 1996. "Il percorso della riforma: 1992–1995. Nuovi indicatori di consistenza e sostenibilità per il FPLD." In *Pensioni e risanamento della finanza pubblica*, ed. F. Padoa Schioppa Kostoris, 325–98. Bologna: Il Mulino.

Saraceno, P. 1995. *Vecchie e nuove pensioni: la proposta Dini*, IRS (Istituto per la Ricerca Sociale), Contributi di Ricerca, 34, Milano.

Sartor, N. 2001. "The Long-Run Effects of the Italian Pension Reforms." *International Tax and Public Finance* 8 (1): 83–111.

Senate of Italy. 1995. "Crisi del sistema previdenziale italiano e confini tra pubblico e privato." *Incontri di studio a Palazzo Giustiniani*, No. 8.

Settergren, O. 2001. "The Automatic Balance Mechanism of the Swedish Pension System." Mimeo, National Social Insurance Board, Stockholm, http://www.rfv.se/english/publi/index.htm.

Tamburi, G. 1999. "Motivation, Purpose and Processes in Pension Reform." *International Social Security Review* 52 (3): 15–44.

Visco, I. 2000. "Welfare Systems, Ageing and Work: An OECD Perspective." *Quarterly Review* 53 (212): 3–29.

Vitaletti, G. 1993. "Apparenza e realtà degli effetti dei provvedimenti di riforma pensionistica." *Economia Pubblica* 23 (11): 491–99.

Chapter 19

Implementing the NDC Theoretical Model: A Comparison of Italy and Sweden

*Sandro Gronchi and Sergio Nisticò**

IN THE COURSE OF THE LAST CENTURY, MOST OF THE INDUSTRIAL COUNTRIES adopted public pay-as-you-go (PAYG) pension systems; after World War II, a period of rapid economic and population growth created the conditions for award formulae and methods of indexation that brought retirement benefits ever closer to final salary and also yearly adjusted to the earnings growth of active workers. Subsequently, those conditions of rapid economic and population growth vanished. The sharp economic slowdown of the 1970s was accompanied by the harbingers of a population aging that is expected to be accentuated drastically in the coming decades. However, the downward rigidity of benefits has prevented pegging the growth of expenditure to the reduced growth of available resources. In some countries such a difference in growth rates has already caused the emergence of disequilibria. Italy stands out from the others: 30 to 35 percent of its pension expenditure is financed from the state budget and half of its public debt has been generated by this expenditure.

Some scholars hold that the unbalance has to be warded off by a courageous process of liberation from the "trap" of pay-as-you-go to arrive ultimately, if after a lengthy and costly transitional phase, at the safe haven of funded public retirement systems[1] or private ones.[2] Others question the curative powers of funding,[3] while still others call for facing the demographic emergency by simply revising the parameters to make the traditional award and indexation rules less generous.[4] The debate on the "virtues and vices" of the two types of pension plan and their ability to weather demographic cycles has not yet produced a victor, although the recent difficulties of the financial markets appear to have temporarily clipped the wings of the most ardent advocates of funding. In the absence of reliable theo-

* Sandro Gronchi is a full professor of economics at La Sapienza University of Rome. He is at present seconded to the School of Economics and Finance, the researching and training unit of the Italian Ministry for Economy. Sergio Nisticò is a professor of economics at the University of Cassino.

For invaluable comments and collaboration, the authors thank Onorato Castellino, Giulio De Capraris, Richard Disney, Elsa Fornero, Fosco Giovannoni, Mario Intorcia, Agneta Kruse, Beniamino Lapadula, Raimondo Manca, Marcello Messori, and Ole Settergren. Our special thanks go to Gudrun Ehnsson of the Swedish National Social Insurance Board, for patiently supplying the statistical-actuarial data, the laws and regulations, and the explanations that made possible the in-depth study of major aspects of the Swedish pension reform.

retical bases, there is growing support for the compromise proposal of mixed systems to diversify working people's retirement portfolios, a position long advocated by the World Bank, among others.[5]

The range of possible plans has recently been extended by a sort of "genetic innovation" that has inspired the Italian and Latvian reforms that went into effect in 1996 and those of Sweden and Poland, in effect since 1998 and 1999 respectively. Retaining the PAYG financial architecture, meaning that current pension expenditure is still financed by current contribution revenues, the new scheme switches over to the award formula and indexation rule typical of funded, defined contribution systems. This is why Italians call it the *contributions-based* scheme. Internationally, different terms are used to label the new plan: *notionally funded*, *notional accounts*, *notional defined contribution*, or simply the acronym *NDC*.[6]

The present work aims to provide a detailed comparative analysis of the Italian and Swedish NDC reforms as produced independently within their respective national confines, in the absence of any opportunity for fruitful interchange between Swedish and Italian experts, or even trade unions or political leaders.[7] The comparison will be made in the light of a preliminary theoretical inquiry, which will better allow us to assess the main differences separating the two reforms.

The NDC Scheme

In most PAYG defined benefit schemes, newly granted benefits are the product of three factors: the number of years of contributions, a percentage called the *accrual rate*, and a conventional salary called *pensionable earnings*—the mean of the earnings obtained over the final years of work, revalued at a given rate. Although in some countries the mean is calculated over a certain number of "top" earnings years rather than the last ones, award formulae are still dominated by "last earnings rules."[8] As to indexation, pension benefits have traditionally grown with wages, while the recent strains that adverse demography has exerted on PAYG systems have induced most countries to adopt less generous rules.[9]

In defined benefit schemes that exhibit financial equilibrium—that is, that year by year levy a tax rate equal to the ratio between pension expenditure and wage bill—paid in contributions are implicitly remunerated with a rate of return equal to the growth rate of the wage bill itself. This is a well-known theorem[10] that rigorously holds when wage and population growth as well as mortality rates are constant through time.[11]

It is important to emphasize that the return referred to in the theorem is a "generational" one—that on the indistinct aggregate of contributions paid by a cohort as a whole—while the "individual" returns on the contributions paid by each member will differ significantly from one another. It has been shown that earnings-based schemes are inherently unfair in that they reward early retirement and careers with fast rising wages.[12]

The principal purpose of the NDC scheme is precisely to preclude differences in individual returns, so as to guarantee *actuarial fairness*. On the other hand, the scheme is also intended to ensure *sustainability* of the PAYG pension systems—that is, to adjust automatically to demographic shocks and so avoid the delays inevitably faced by unpopular policies that have either to reduce benefits or to increase tax rates.

A Broad Definition

The NDC scheme conceives the PAYG system as a "virtual bank." Every individual has a savings account in which the contributions are "deposited" up to retirement and from which the yearly pension benefits are "withdrawn" afterward.

For the purpose of taking into account the incongruities of the Italian reform discussed below, it is helpful to accept a broad definition of contribution-based schemes that admits the partial heterogeneousness of the rates of return that the virtual bank credits to the personal accounts. Specifically, these schemes should be allowed to remunerate pensioners' accounts at one rate (for instance, the yield on short-term government paper) and active workers' accounts at another (say, the yield on long-term government bonds). In any case, the *deposit-exhaustion constraint* must be satisfied; that is, the money withdrawn must equal the money deposited including the interest accrued. In other words, the account balance must be zero after the last annual benefit has been withdrawn.

Assuming for simplicity that time is discrete, the deposit-exhaustion constraint takes the form of the following equivalence between the future value of contributions deposited up to retirement and the present value of pension benefits that will be withdrawn from then on:

$$a \cdot \sum_{i=1}^{n} w_i \cdot \prod_{j=i+1}^{n+1} \left(1+\pi_j^L\right) = p \cdot \left(1 + \sum_{i=n+2}^{n+m} \prod_{j=n+2}^{i} \frac{1+\sigma_j}{1+\pi_j^R}\right), \tag{19.1}$$

where n denotes the duration of working life, a the contribution rate, w_i the wage earned in ith year, p the first annual benefit, π_j^L and π_j^R the value taken in jth year by the returns chosen to credit the account balances of workers and pensioners respectively, σ_j the value taken in jth year by the rate chosen to index pension benefits, and m the life expectancy at retirement.

From equation 9.1 it follows that:

$$p = \left[a \cdot \sum_{i=1}^{n} w_i \cdot \prod_{j=i+1}^{n+1} \left(1+\pi_j^L\right) \right] \cdot h \tag{19.2}$$

where

$$h = \left(1 + \sum_{i=n+2}^{n+m} \prod_{j=n+2}^{i} \frac{1+\sigma_j}{1+\pi_j^R} \right)^{-1}. \tag{19.3}$$

Adopting Italian terminology, hereafter h will be called *conversion rate* and the term in square brackets on the right-hand side of equation 19.2 will be *notional capital* accrued at retirement.[13]

When the first annual benefit must be granted according to equation 19.2, the notional capital is known in that it can be calculated from the worker's wage history and the time series of the past values taken by the rate of return for active workers, π^L. Calculating the conversion rate would instead require knowledge of the future values that will be taken in the next $m - 1$ years by both the indexation rate σ (for instance, inflation or the average wage growth) and the rate of return for pensioners, π^R.

Calculating h becomes possible if one forgoes the idea of choosing σ independently from π^R. One can elect one of two options. Under one, adopted by the Italian reform, the policy maker chooses the indexation rate, which is therefore the exogenous variable, and allows the annual rates of return to pensioners to be endogenously determined by the formula

$$\pi_j^R = (1+\sigma_j) \cdot (1+\delta) - 1 \quad \forall j, \tag{19.4}$$

where δ is also set by the policy maker. Notice that δ is the amount by which π^R will deviate from σ in each year, which explains why it is called *deviation rate* in this study. Substituting equation 19.4 into 19.3, h reduces to the following function of only two independent variables, δ and m:

$$h(\delta,m)=\left[\sum_{i=1}^{m}(1+\delta)^{1-i}\right]^{-1}.$$ (19.5)

Under the second option, which was taken by the Swedish reform, the policy maker sets exogenously the rate of return to pensioners, letting the annual indexation rates be endogenously determined by the formula

$$\sigma_j=\frac{1+\pi_j^R}{1+\delta}-1.$$ (19.6)

Algebraically, formula 19.6 is simply the inverse of 19.4. Therefore, substituting it into equation 19.3, one again gets equation 19.5.

Formula 19.5 shows that the conversion rate is an increasing function of the deviation rate. It is important to note that choosing high values of δ to have more generous initial pension awards will have effects that differ depending on whether the policy maker opts for the endogenous return to pensioners (19.4) or for the endogenous indexation (19.6). If the former, the rate of return to pensioners will be higher; if the latter, the indexation rate will be lower. Under option 19.6 there is thus a trade-off between the initial pension award and indexation, while δ is the "lever" to resolve it.

Formula 19.5 also shows that for any given value of the deviation rate δ, the conversion rate is decreasing with respect to life expectancy, so that (gender given) it increases with age at retirement and (age given) is higher for men.

The Canonical Scheme

The definition of the NDC scheme set out above is broad enough to cover both the Italian and the Swedish reforms as well as the canonical scheme discussed here. The comparative discussion of the three is deferred to the following section.

The canonical scheme is characterized first of all by the option expressed in equation 19.6, which takes the rate of return to pensioners as exogenous, and, within that option, by the further choice

$$\pi_j^R=(1+\alpha_j)\cdot(1+\lambda_j)-1 \ \forall j,$$ (19.7)

where α and λ denote respectively the growth rates of wages and employment so that the right-hand expression is the growth rate of the wage bill in year j. Second, the canonical scheme is characterized by the following condition:

$$\pi_j^R=\pi_j^L \ \forall j,$$ (19.8)

which precludes different treatment of workers and retirees, thus ensuring *spatial* or *horizontal* uniformity of returns.

In a steady state—that is, under the assumption that α and λ are constant through time—uniformity takes on a "temporal" or "vertical" dimension as well, in that the rate of return the virtual bank accords in each year to all account holders is the same overall rate it accords to each of them throughout all years. Therefore, in steady state the scheme precludes different overall returns to individuals that assume different behaviors and/or belong to different cohorts.

In a less restrictive context—a semisteady state where the rate λ is constant while the rate α is allowed to vary—it can be proved that the canonical scheme is sustainable in that it generates a pension expenditure equal to revenue generated by the preset contribution rate.[14] That is why the growth rate of the wage bill is referred to below as the *sustainable return*.

In the presence of variable employment growth rates, the canonical scheme cannot ensure equilibrium year by year. Nevertheless, temporary surpluses or deficits that result from an increase or decrease in λ are progressively absorbed.[15] Therefore, the NDC scheme is endowed with a powerful "automatic pilot" that, in the presence of recurrent shocks of opposite sign due to business cycles, ensures equilibrium as a trend. In the event of a stable reduction in λ that occurs because of a long-run demographic depression, the pilot immediately takes countermeasures to curb expenditures, avoiding the usually protracted waiting period necessary before governments resign themselves to bearing the electoral cost of parametric reforms and unions assume the responsibility of agreeing to such changes. As this prompt intervention takes the two-fold form of slower indexation of existing pensions and reduction of the notional capitals being formed (thus containing future pensions that will be awarded to present workers), the sacrifice is correctly imposed on all generations in being.[16]

The Italian and Swedish NDC Reforms

Neither the Italian nor the Swedish pension reform of the 1990s adopted the canonical scheme set out in in the previous section. Nevertheless, they both fit the broad definition given in this chapter. The two schemes are discussed below.

The Crucial Differences

A first difference, quite radical, concerns the choice between the option expressed by equation 19.4 and that expressed by equation 19.6. Italy opted for equation 19.4, with indexation solely to inflation, so that the real return to pensioners each year will be equal to the value chosen for the deviation rate δ. Sweden opted for equation 19.6, giving pensioners a return equal to the increase in the average wage and thus each year letting indexation be equal to the average wage growth net of δ.

A second important difference concerns the rate of return to active workers. In Sweden it is identical to the rate of return of pensioners (nominal wage growth); in Italy it is equal to nominal GDP growth. It follows that Sweden has perfectly achieved spatial fairness, in that year by year the same return is credited to workers and pensioners, while Italy has not achieved this fairness.

These choices carry implications for sustainability. As a consequence of the contraction of the work force presaged by demographic projections, in the decades to come, the increase in average wage will tend to exceed the sustainable rate indicated by the wage bill growth rate. Accordingly, in 2001 the Swedish parliament acted to remedy this problem, introducing an ingenious balance mechanism that went into effect in 2003.[17]

In Italy, sustainability is not ensured, because neither the return to workers nor the return to pensioners is equal to the sustainable return. The return to workers (the GDP growth rate) can be equal to the wage bill growth rate only if the distributive shares in GDP remain constant. For the return to pensioners, only by a fluke could the warranted rate of δ percentage points in real terms match the sustainable rate.

Other Implementation Features

There are other, equally important features characterizing the two NDC reforms. The most significant are those involving values chosen for the deviation rate δ, retirement age, survivor's benefits, differentiation of conversion rates by gender, the contribution rate, the updating of the conversion rates, disability pensions, administrative costs, the fragmentation of the pension system, and the diversification of the workers' retirement portfolio *via* a parallel funded scheme. Discussion of all these features will provide the occasion for an overview of the options and flexibilities offered by NDC pension schemes.

THE VALUES FOR δ

A modest difference between the two NDC schemes concerns the value of the deviation rate δ for calculating the conversion rates under equation 19.5 Italy took δ = 1.5 percent, Sweden δ = 1.6 percent. These values are both fairly high in order to provide replacement rates comparable to those in being prior to the reforms.

As a consequence of the different choice between option 19.4 and option 19.6, discussed above, the high values chosen for δ will have quite different effects in the two countries. First of all, the Swedish NDC scheme is open to a "social" threat deriving from negative real indexation that will occur any time the real return (real wage growth possibly adjusted by the balance mechanism) is lower than 1.6 percent. If such reductions in the purchasing power of pensions will not be politically viable, unsustainability problems will arise. Italy precluded negative real indexation but offered to pensioners a nominal return equal to inflation plus 1.5 percent, a choice which, as noted above, jeopardizes both horizontal fairness and sustainability.

In addition, both the Italian and the Swedish schemes are open to another kind of social threat to sustainability. This threat derives from the excessive divergence between the rise in newly granted pensions (which should tend to parallel real wages growth) and the indexation of old ones. In Sweden, the differential is 1.6 percentage points, so that the pensions first paid in any given year have purchasing power 1.6 percent greater than those initiated in the previous year, 17 percent greater than those initiated 10 years earlier, 37 percent greater than those started 20 years earlier, and 61 percent greater than 30-year-old pensions. Such pronounced disparities may prove to be socially intolerable, resulting in periodic equalizations of the longest-standing pensions. In Italy, these equalizations threaten to create analogous or even more severe problems, because pensions are indexed only to prices and because ordinarily real wages rise by more than 1.6 percent.[18]

There is an important difference, however, between Italian and Swedish "vintage pensions" deriving from the choice the two countries made between options 19.4 and 19.6. Italy's small, long-standing pensions will be perceived by public opinion as the product of an unfair indexation rule that politicians have arbitrarily chosen and that they should redress (for instance by raising indexation to wages), whereas in Sweden the endogenous indexation rule should make people understand that vintage pensions are the price retirees have to pay for higher replacement rates. This trade-off could be understood even better if, at retirement, workers could opt for stronger indexation in exchange for a lower conversion rate. This could deter them from complaining about not having done it afterward.[19]

RETIREMENT AGE

When the reformed Italian pension system is fully phased in,[20] workers will ordinarily be allowed to retire between the ages of 57 and 65. However, provision is also made for employees to agree with their employer to continue working beyond the normal retirement age. Consequently, conversion rates should have been defined for all ages from 57 up. As this was not done, and conversion rates are specified only for the normal retirement ages, there will be quite a technical problem in determining the benefits for those retiring after 65. Should these benefits be unfairly determined on the basis of the 65-year-old conversion rate? And should the pensions for categories such as university teachers and magistrates, whose mandatory retirement age is traditionally after 65, be determined on the same basis?

No such neglect is to be found in the Swedish system. Retirement is ordinarily envisaged between 61 and 67 but, as in Italy, can be deferred with no upper limit (employees must have the employer's consent).[21] Thus the conversion rates have been calculated for all foreseeable retirement ages.[22] Since the age range is broad indeed, the conversion rates are highly differentiated. The rate for someone retiring at 80 is nearly two-and-half times as high as the rate for a retiree at 61.

Actually, the Swedish reform allows for a "partial retirement" that essentially does away with the very notion of standard retirement ages. For starting at age 61, part of the individual's notional capital can be converted into a pension while he or she continues to work.[23] The contributions paid by these "worker-pensioners" augment the residual notional capital that at full retirement will be converted into a supplement to the pension.

The free choice of retirement age, in some way preserved by both the Italian and the Swedish reforms, is a "value" that the NDC schemes can allow for. Those who choose to retire earlier actually self-finance their choice by accepting a lower conversion rate. However, the system can undergo temporary unbalances when sudden changes of the individuals' behaviors take place that determine large alterations of the average age at retirement. Clearly, the broader the range of the allowed retirement ages is, the higher the risk of temporary unbalances.[24] In Sweden, the risk might be attenuated by the possibility of partial retirement that allows for smooth changes of behavior.

SURVIVOR'S BENEFITS

In the area of survivor's benefits, the reforms of both countries retained the preexisting rules. Sweden has retained a 1990 law that had abolished the survivor's pension, to which only women had been entitled previously. Italy kept the survivor's entitlement, for which both men and women are eligible, to 60 percent of the deceased spouse's pension.[25]

Excluding survivor's benefits implies that the cost of welfare benefits for needy survivors must be defrayed by the state. The cost may be substantial in a country (such as Italy) where women's labor market participation is low.

At the same time, however, the concession of survivor's benefits raises some major questions. First, the conversion rates are significantly lower than the rates that can be granted when pensions are not paid to survivors, because the second term in equation 19.1 must be augmented by the weight of the continuation of the pension payment to the survivor. So, in order to keep the income replacement rate from being too low, appreciably higher contribution rates are required. Second, it must be decided whether the conversion rates are differentiated only according to the age at retirement or also according to marital status and possibly also spouse's age.

Note that the latter option must take into account the social acceptability (or lack thereof) of the idea that one individual should get a smaller pension than another "just" because he or she has a spouse, or a spouse who is younger. However, this reluctance could be attenuated if pensioners could choose freely between conversion rates (hence pension awards) "on one head" or "on two heads."[26]

Also note that the former option (differentiation by age) produces a significant redistribution in favor of married persons, especially those with younger spouses. It also poses practical problems, because calculating conversion rates requires detailed information that national statistics do not generally furnish, such as the probability of a deceased pensioner's leaving a spouse and the difference in age between direct beneficiary and spouse. Both of these data may vary with the age of the deceased pensioner, so data would have to be collected for all possible ages.

Under the time pressure on the reform process stemming from the general political situation in Italy,[27] consideration of the two options (together with the various questions of fairness and calculation raised by each) could not be exhaustive and the decision was taken to differentiate conversion rates only by age at retirement. Most statistical information was not available, so that a rather serious lack of data surrounded the Italian decision.[28] Nor was the National Statistical Institute ever assigned to collect the data needed for proper calculation of the conversion rates. Thus the first decennial review of the system intended to produce the conversion rates that will go in effect starting from 2006[29] will face exactly the same lack of information.

Finally, Italy makes the survivor's benefit available also in the cases of workers dying before retirement age. The pension going to the surviving spouse is 60 percent of the "virtual" pension that the deceased worker would have been entitled to. Similar to calculating disability allowances (see the discussion of disability below), such a virtual pension is calculated by means of a "quasi-contributions-based formula." In fact, it is calculated by multiplying the notional capital accrued to the deceased by the conversion rate corresponding to 57 years of age (whatever the actual age of the survivor).

The Swedish system, not recognizing survivor's benefits to pensioners' spouses, does not accord them to worker's spouses either. When a worker predeceases a spouse, the surviving spouse is assisted by a welfare institute entirely separate from the pension system, while the deceased worker's notional capital is distributed to the members of his or her cohort in the form of a contingent rise in the rate of return.

Notice that the Swedish choice ensures financial stability, whereas the Italian way of transforming the balance of the predeceased worker's account into a survivor's benefit does not.

DIFFERENTIATION OF CONVERSION RATES BY GENDER

Differing on survivor's benefits, the Italian and Swedish schemes are united in excluding differentiation of conversion rates according to gender. As life expectancy for men and women is fairly different, this approach tends to reward women.[30] In Italy the premium is appreciably attenuated by the presence of survivor's benefit. In particular, it is attenuated by the following two factors:

- Women are much less likely to leave a surviving spouse than men, and
- Male survivors are less long-lived than female survivors.

Both of these factors are further accentuated since the husband is generally older than the wife, so that male workers might actually be getting a premium if survivor's benefits were not significantly lower than the direct pension of the deceased (60 percent).

Unisex conversion rates should be based on parameters (mortality tables and the other statistics necessitated if survivor's benefits are available) that are neutral—that is, derived from mixed populations of both sexes. The Swedish calculations use precisely this rigorous technique, while the Italian conversion rates are an average of rates calculated separately for men and women.

THE UPDATING OF THE CONVERSION RATES

Three main issues should be taken into account by the mechanisms that regulate the updating of the conversion rates. First of all, system sustainability requires that the conversion rates be continuously updated according to mortality rates.[31] Second, the system must safeguard workers' right to choose their retirement age on the basis of stable conversion rates. In other words, the decision to postpone retirement in order to be entitled to a larger pension must not be neutralized (even in part) by the subsequent lowering of the conversion rates (due to updating). Third, the system must prevent a different updating of conversion rates for workers in the same cohort who elect to retire at different ages. This would be an unacceptable intragenerational unfairness, tantamount to positing different life expectancies to different workers born in the same year.

The Swedish reform has sought to reconcile these three needs by devising a procedure for assigning conversion rates by cohort, as follows.

- At the start of the year (say, 2002) before that in which a cohort first reaches the minimum retirement age of 61 (2003 for those born in 1942), the workers in this cohort are informed of the conversion rates for ages 61 to 64. These rates are based on the life expectancy tables referring to the last five years (1997–2001). They have temporary validity in that they are used to calculate the provisional pension benefit, up to age 65, of the workers in this cohort retiring over the next four years (2003–6).
- At the start of the year (2006) before that in which the cohort turns 65 (2007), the conversion rates for all ages from 65 up are announced, calculated according to the life expectancy tables referring to the last five years (2001–5).
- In the year (2007) when the cohort turns 65, the provisional pensions of workers already retired (having elected to retire between the ages of 61 and 64) are definitively recalculated on the basis of the new conversion rate for 65-year-olds and their notional capital that remains after the deduction of the benefits received and the addition of the returns credited to the balance since retirement.

In practical terms, full conversion rate stability, and hence full retirement planning, is ensured only from age 65. Retiring earlier is not prohibited, but those who elect to do so must accept the uncertainty implicit in the fact that at 65 their imputed life expectancy will be the same as the life expectancy that will be assigned to contemporaries who elected to continue working.

Unfortunately, the Italian procedures for revising the conversion rates do not satisfy any of the three needs—for continuous updating according to mortality rates, for safeguarding workers' right to choose retirement age based on stable conversion rates, and for preventing the attribution of different life expectancies to individuals belonging to the same cohort—set out above. First of all, the Italian procedures do not effectively contain disequilibria, because revision takes place only every 10 years. The rates in effect from 1996 will not be updated until 2006. Second, the intragenerational inequities cited above are not avoided, because the new rates apply to all workers (regardless of cohort) retiring over the subsequent decade. For example, someone born in 1962 and retiring at 64 in 2026 will be assumed to have a longer life expectancy (at birth) than someone belonging to the same cohort who retires at 63 in 2025. And finally, not all cohorts can plan their retirement on the basis of stable conversion rates. Indeed, as the range of retirement ages spans 9 years (57–65) while coefficients are updated every 10 years, full planning is assured to only two of every ten cohorts: the first to reach retirement age after each revision. This uncertainty is aggravated by the fact that there is no provision for the new conversion rates to be announced before the old ones expire. Fears of the worst could thus trigger massive retirement on the eve of every revision.

To conclude, let us mention the different nature of the decision-making process whereby the conversion rates are revised. In Italy, the process is political, involving parliament and business and labor organizations and ending with a joint decision taken by the minister for social policy and the minister for the economy and finance. In Sweden, the revision is performed in a strictly technical *forum*, namely the statistical-actuarial bureaus of the National Social Insurance Board, based on life expectancy tables prepared by the national statistical institute.

CONTRIBUTIONS

Italy has an overall contribution rate for payroll employees of 32.7 percent. Formally, 27 percent of this amount is charged to workers and 73 percent to employers. In Sweden, the overall rate is 14.884 percent, 40 percent of which charged to workers and 60 percent to employers.[32]

For the self-employed, when fully phased in the Italian system will have a contribution rate of 19 percent.[33] In Sweden, since 1998 the self-employed have paid contributions equal to those of payroll employees (including the employers' quota).

It should be noted that in Italy the rate actually paid, called the *financing rate*, is different from the rate used to determine the notional capital, which is a conventional "award rate" equal to 33 percent for payroll employees and 20 percent for self-employed workers.

The difference between the two rates amounts to a creeping transfer of the cost to general tax revenue, further undermining not only the self-sufficiency of the system but also its fairness. In fact, one can prove that such a difference rewards early retirement and careers marked by steeper earnings increases.[34]

Sweden's enormously lower contribution rate, by comparison with the Italian award rate, is only partly reflected in income replacement rates, thanks to two factors:

- The higher Swedish retirement age, which permits more generous conversion rates and larger notional capitals because of the additional years of contribution and the returns on them; and
- For the same retirement age in both countries, the Swedish conversion rates are higher, owing to the absence of survivor's benefits and the slightly higher value of δ (1.6 instead of 1.5 percent).

Finally, both countries have limited the social security earnings base by exempting income above a given ceiling from the tax.[35]

DISABILITY

In the area of disability risk, again the two countries have responded differently. In Sweden the social security system provides disability allowances through a program totally separate from retirement provisions. The disability program is financed by contributions charged to firms alone. The arrangements are as follows.

- Disability allowance is treated like wages, in that it is subject to pension contributions. More precisely, the program that finances the disability allowance also pays the employer's portion of the old-age pension fee, while the beneficiary pays the portion levied on employees. The overall contribution goes to augment the beneficiary's notional capital, in addition to any contributions paid in connection with work (payroll or self-employed) that the beneficiary may continue or undertake notwithstanding the disability.
- The beneficiary receives the disability allowance up to retirement age, and in any case not beyond 65, when it is replaced by the old-age pension, calculated ordinarily on the basis of the notional capital accumulated up to that point (as a result of total contributions paid, both before and after the disabling event).[36]
- Consistent with this, no allowance is paid when the disability occurs after age 65.

The Swedish arrangement is rational. The disability program does not weigh on the old-age pension system because it is financed by a different contribution, while inclusion of the allowances in the tax base for the old-age system gives the latter the resources to finance the retirement benefits of the disabled.

Italy's reformed pension system retains the old "mixed" formula, paying retirement benefits and also covering disability risk. More restrictive eligibility requirements have been in effect since 1984, but disability allowances nevertheless still account for a significant part of total system spending.

The NDC reform of old-age pensions would have required a quite separate disability program in the style of the Swedish; alternatively, specific procedures should have been identified allowing full financing of disability pensions out of total contributions paid to a mixed system. As we can see, this was not the case:[37]

- The Italian disability allowance is equal to the notional capital at the time of disability multiplied by the conversion rate used to calculate the pension award of a 57-year-old retiree.[38]
- The allowance is paid up to age 57,[39] when it gives way to the old-age pension calculated on the basis of the notional capital accrued at that time thanks to contributions paid previous to disability or also afterward, if the disabled worker continues work activity.
- Consistent with this, as in Sweden, no allowance is paid when the disability occurs after the lowest pensionable age (57) has been reached.

It is evident that there is no correspondence between the disability allowance (received up to age 57) and contributions paid prior to disabling event because these go entirely to determine the old-age pension. To remedy these faults, disability allowance should be financed through a "set-aside rate"—a portion of the total contribution that must not count toward the old-age pension. Further, the formula used to calculate the disability allowance appears to be meaningless; a better formula should not consider the disabled worker's contribution history.

Administrative Costs

NDC schemes have two ways of covering administrative costs. One option is for the costs to be financed by a set-aside quota of the contribution rate along the lines of that envisaged in the discussion on contributions above to finance disability allowances. The other option subtracts administrative costs from the return credited to workers and pensioners.[40]

Sweden took the second option.[41] Italy simply ignored the problem, so that administrative costs will increase the deficit implied by the shortcomings discussed so far.

The Fragmentation of the Pension System

Even when the long-run equilibrium of the whole pension system is ensured by correct NDC rules, fragmentation of the whole into different occupational funds may generate fairly serious financial problems owing to the diversification of the growth rates of categories.[42]

This is precisely the case in Italy, where NDC reform has not coincided with unification of the pension system, which remains divided into a number of different funds. Most private sector employees are covered by the Employee Pension Fund, but some categories have funds of their own. Among these are mass transit workers, telephone workers, public and private electricity workers, clergymen, civil aviation flight personnel, show business workers, professional athletes, and others.[43] The same applies to public employees (central government, local government, health system, and so on) and the self-employed (shopkeepers, craftsmen, farmers, lawyers, notaries, doctors, pharmacists, journalists, and so on). Most of these category funds operate under the two major public retirement institutions, one for the private sector and the other for the public sector of the economy. Only a few are actually independent funds, and even these are subject to central government oversight. The NDC reform was not automatically extended to these independent plans, which have a fairly small number of members, mostly professionals.

In Sweden, the reformed system is strictly unified. Truth to tell, there does exist an unexpected form of fragmentation. At the time of the 1998 reform, the existing public PAYG system had substantial assets equal to four times the system's outlay in 2001,[44] accumulated thanks to large surpluses that the system has continued to run.[45] To optimize the management and maximize the return on these assets, they were divided into four parts and assigned to four different, competing funds with broad freedom on portfolio choices.[46] Each fund receives one-fourth of the contribution revenue and pays out one-fourth of pension benefits. Revenue and expenditure being equally distributed among the funds, assets (initially equal) will increase more (or decrease less) in the fund that achieves the highest yield. At the end of 2001, the "best" fund had 1.2 percent more assets than the "worst."

DIVERSIFICATION OF THE SOCIAL SECURITY PORTFOLIO

The intellectual battle between advocates of PAYG and of funding being undecided, many countries are opting for mixed compulsory systems under which workers' retirement portfolios can be diversified. Sweden is one such. The 1998 reform flanked the compulsory, PAYG pillar with an advanced, funded pillar financed by compulsory contributions equal to 2.326 percent of earnings. In the case of payroll employees, 60 percent of the contributions are paid by the firm and 40 percent by the worker.[47] Unlike the first pillar, which is state guaranteed and unified, the second is mainly private and fragmented in a multitude of open funds in genuine competition with one another (there were 571 pension funds in 2001). Competition is guaranteed principally by the workers' right to transfer from one fund to another at no cost and without delay.[48] To permit risk diversification, workers may distribute both accrued capital and new contributions among different funds (a maximum of five).

Relations between workers and the private pension funds are conducted by means of a public agency, the Premium Pension Authority (PPA), which has five main objectives:

- Provide standardized, certified information on the performance of the competing funds, allowing workers to make informed choices;
- Centralize the collection of contributions and the transfers of retirement savings between funds, thus reducing the administrative costs, which are defrayed by workers in the form of lower net yields;
- Guarantee anonymity—that is, keep the funds from knowing the names of their members, thus preventing costly forms of publicity and promotion (addressed to nonmembers), which would reduce net yields;
- Act as annuity provider while the funds keep the money left after each annual installment; and
- At the worker's request, start administering the capital accrued at retirement and guarantee a constant 3 percent nominal yield.[49]

This second pillar also comprises a "residual" public pension fund into which are channeled the contributions of workers who, for one reason or another, fail to choose one of the authorized private funds.[50]

The private pension funds already existing in 1998 were relegated to the third pillar. Most of these funds, which arose spontaneously out of collective bargaining in the 1970s, are occupational, and cover between 80 and 90 percent of workers. Contributions (tax-exempt) to the third pillar are at rates ranging from 2.5 percent to 4.5 percent.[51]

In Italy, at present no true compulsory funded retirement plans are in effect. However, there are compulsory severance pay funds. Tax-exempt contributions are fairly large (about 7 percent of wages). The funds are set aside by the employers (who pay the contributions "to themselves") while the workers are credited with a return of three-fourths of the inflation rate plus 1.5 percentage points. When the employment relation is terminated, for whatever reason, the firm pays the accrued credit to the worker as a lump sum.

This anomalous second pillar provides firms with low-cost funds[52] and enables them to obviate, at least in part, the credit rationing to which smaller firms especially are subject.

A 1993 law allows transformation of severance pay funds into funded pension plans through collective bargaining. Under the law, this tax-exempt contribution (generated by the transformation of the severance pay funds) can be supplemented by additional contributions from employer and employees of up to nearly 14 percent of wages (subject to an annual ceiling of just over €5,000). If this opportunity were fully exploited, tax-exempt retirement savings would total more than 50 percent of wages (32.7 percent for the first pillar, 7 percent + 14 percent for the second).

So far, the voluntary conversion of severance pay funds has involved 10 percent of private sector employees and has generally been partial—that is, only a part of the firms' contribution to these internal funds have been channeled into external pension funds.[53] The reason for this relative lack of interest is not only the cost to firms, but also workers' affection for an established scheme that provides a semi-guaranteed (albeit low) yield and, allowing the payment of a lump sum whenever an employment relation is terminated, is particularly helpful in case of unemployment or when moving to a new job in another part of the country. Workers have two additional reasons for reluctance to give up the severance pay scheme: first, today's low interest rates; and second, the high income replacement rates of the first pillar, due not only (in the short-to-medium run) to the extreme gradualness with which the NDC reform is being phased in[54] but also (in the long run) to the generous benefits that the new formula can still provide (even for those retiring relatively young), thanks to a contribution rate that, at more than twice Sweden's, is unparalleled in the rest of the world.

The Transition

Any time pension rules are changed, the problem of safeguarding the claims accrued under the old rules arises.[55] Sweden and Italy adopted quite different criteria in facing this question.

Sweden chose:

- No protection (no preservation of old entitlements) for workers born after 1953—that is, those not yet 45 in 1998, when the reform was passed;
- Full safeguards (no application of the new award formula) for workers born before 1938—that is, those already at retirement age (61 or more) in 1998;
- Partial application of the new rules for workers born from 1938 through 1953, giving them 5 percent of the earnings-based pension that they would have been entitled to in the absence of the reform for each year of age above 44 in 1998. For example, those born in 1950, who turned 48 in 1998, will receive a portion of the earnings-based pension calculated as follows: 5 percent · (48 – 44) = 20 percent.

These standards give outcomes set forth in detail in columns 2 and 5 of table 19.1. Note that these safeguards apply even to persons who had not begun to work at all before the reform was enacted.

Italy opted for a criterion based on contribution seniority rather than age, with these rules:

- Full protection (no application of the new award formula) for "senior" workers who, at the time of the reform, had already paid contributions for at least 18 years;
- *Pro rata* protection for "junior" workers, who are entitled, for each year of contribution prior to the reform, to a portion of the earnings-based pension they would have been entitled to under the old system equal to the reciprocal of their total contribution seniority upon retirement.

The lesser severity of the Italian transition is shown first of all by the fact that it totally exempted 40 percent of existing workers from the new contributions-based formula, compared with 7 percent in Sweden. Given the different criteria taken (age and seniority), no specific comparison is possible without assumptions concerning age at the start of the career and the duration of work activity, so as to convert seniority into age or vice versa. Supposing the start of work in one's 24th year and a career of 40 years (ending at age 63), the Italian rules would produce the outcomes "by age" set forth in columns (3) and (6) of table 19.1. These confirm the much greater swiftness of the Swedish transition.

In terms of fairness, Italy's manner of protecting acquired entitlements is unsatisfactory for two reasons.

- There is an unacceptable gap between the oldest "junior" workers (with 17 contribution years and thus aged 41 on our posited career pattern) and the youngest "senior"

Table 19.1. Protection of Prereform Entitlements in Sweden and Italy

Age at reform (1)	Percentage of earnings based pension preserved		Age at reform (4)	Percentage of earnings based pension preserved	
	in Sweden (2)	in Italy (3)		in Sweden (5)	in Italy (6)
24	0	2.5	43	0	100
25	0	5.0	44	0	100
26	0	7.5	45	5	100
27	0	10.0	46	10	100
28	0	12.5	47	15	100
29	0	15.0	48	20	100
30	0	17.5	49	25	100
31	0	20.0	50	30	100
32	0	22.5	51	35	100
33	0	25.0	52	40	100
34	0	27.5	53	45	100
35	0	30.0	54	50	100
36	0	32.5	55	55	100
37	0	35.0	56	60	100
38	0	37.5	57	65	100
39	0	40.0	58	70	100
40	0	42.5	59	75	100
41	0	45.0	60	80	100
42	0	100.0	over 60	100	100

Source: Authors' calculations.

workers (18 years seniority and aged 42); the former get 45 percent protection, the latter 100 percent.

- Two junior workers with the same prereform seniority get disparate protection depending on how many years they work after the reform. If two workers with 10 years of contributions at the time of reform continue working for 10 and 30 years respectively, the first has 50 percent protection ($10 \times 1/[10 + 10]$) but the second gets only 25 percent ($10 \times 1/[10 + 30]$) . To apply the seniority principle fairly, it would have been necessary to emulate the way in which Sweden applied the age principle, providing that for every year of seniority at the time of the reform a certain portion of the pension would be awarded under the old formula, regardless of one's seniority at retirement. For example, putting such a portion at 3 percent, the two junior workers hypothesized just now would both enjoy 30 percent protection (both would get 30 percent of their earnings-based pension).

The two countries also constructed the NDC portion of the total benefit in different ways. In Sweden, this portion is a percentage of the total NDC pension generated by contributions paid both before and after the reform. The portion is the complement of 100 of the percentages given in columns (2) and (5) of table 19.1 In Italy, such workers get only the NDC pension generated by contributions paid after the reform (not a portion of the total NDC pension generated by the contributions paid both before and after).

Finally, Italy excluded application of the new retirement age range (57–65 for both men and women) to all current workers, who continue to be subject to the old retirement ages of 65 for men and 60 for women. However, there is the possibility of early retirement with at least 35 years of contributions at a minimum age that is diversified by occupational category and extended gradually, though it does not apply to all workers until 2006 (at age 57).[56] Sweden extended the retirement age immediately (to a range of 61–67) for all current workers from the prior age of 65 for both men and women.

On indexation, Sweden did not hesitate to extend the new rate for the contributions-based pensions (the rate of return less 1.6 percentage points) to the pensions awarded according to the old rules (until then indexed to prices), or to be awarded during the transition. The overriding concern, in fact, was to avoid the coexistence of two different indexation regimes.

In Italy, the same concern presumably played a role in making the diametrically opposite choice—namely to extend the existing price indexation to the contributions-based pensions. It is a pity that the correct indexation of NDC pensions, which would have ensured sustainability and fairness, was permanently sacrificed to a medium-term necessity.

Conclusions

The comparative examination of the Italian and Swedish NDC reforms shows the former's fragility. The main conceptual defect of the NDC scheme Italian-style remains the refusal to make the rate of indexation of pensions endogenous, which rate should result from the difference between the sustainable return (albeit as proxied by GDP growth) and the value of 1.5 percent assigned to deviation δ in calculating the conversion rates. The fundamental objectives of fairness and sustainability are jeopardized.

The many other shortcomings and inconsistencies discussed in this chapter testify to the weak NDC culture that accompanied both the approval and the subsequent management of the reform in Italy. The intensive debate that stirred the passions of scholars, politicians, and trade unionists for years, which enabled Swedish society as a whole to understand and come to agree with the economic and ethical bases of the new scheme and enabled Swedish parliament to pass a consistent and rational reform, was lacking in Italy. The same process has prompted Swedish lawmakers to introduce further refinements. One of these is the balance mechanism, a statistical-actuarial method to correct the return that better ensures the trend sustainability of the NDC scheme, effectively overcoming not only the problems created by the choice of the average wage growth rather than of wage bill growth, but also other causes of temporary disequilibrium.[57]

None of the governments in power in Italy since 1996 has worked to consolidate the NDC reform and remedy the errors due to the hastiness—which has been a source of complaint not only by the authors of the present paper[58]—with which it was drafted in 1995. The theoretical and conceptual complexity of the matter should have suggested the appointment of committees of experts who could properly bridge the gap between the theoretical foundations of the NDC scheme and the countless details that implementation would inevitably bring. By doing so it would have been possible to recoup, at least after the fact, the crucial work of analysis and study that Sweden scrupulously performed beforehand.

Possibly, this study could provide a preliminary agenda for some emerging policy maker interested in providing the country with a fair and sustainable pension scheme.

Notes

1. See Modigliani, Ceprini, and Muralidhar (1999).
2. See Feldstein (1998).
3. See Orszag and Stiglitz (2001).
4. See Chand and Jaeger (1996).
5. See World Bank (1994).
6. The idea was developed independently in the early 1990s in Italy and in Sweden. In Italy, the contributions-based scheme has been proposed by Gronchi with the aim of remedying the unfair redistribution typical of the earnings-based formulae and to ensure sustainability for the pay-as-you-go scheme. A different version was put forward by Niccoli with the alternative aim of awarding the forced savings accrued to social security with the same return earned by savings directed toward financial markets. In particular, see Niccoli (1992), Italian Ministry of Treasury (1994) of which Gronchi (1993) is the first draft while Gronchi (1995b) is a revised version, Gronchi (1994a, b), Niccoli (1994) and Gronchi (1995a). The attention of the Italian parliament was drawn to the new ideas in 1994 when a detailed contributions-based plan was produced by the Democratic Party of the Left. One year later, the same ideas were resumed by the draft bill that the Dini Cabinet brought before parliament and that was approved by a large majority of votes.

In Sweden, the new plan, already outlined in the works of Bröms (1990), Olsson and Schubert (1991), Persson (1991), and Ackerby (1992), gradually took shape in the expert committees mandated to develop reform proposals based on the principles of sustainability and correspondence between contributions and pension entitlements. In particular, see *En Promoria av Pensionsarbetsgruppen* (1992), *Reformerat pensionssystem: Bakgrund, principer och skiss* (1992), Palmer and Sherman (1993), *Reformerat pensionssystem: Betänkande av pensionsarbetsgruppen* (1994), and *Reformerat pensionssystem: Kostnader och individeffekter* (1994).

It must be pointed out that this Italian and Swedish literature of the early 1990s seems to be unaware of the anticipations to be found in two important works of the late 1960s, rediscovered in Gronchi (1998) and Valdés-Prieto (2000), one of which is by J. Buchanan and the other by O. Castellino. In the scheme proposed by Buchanan (1968), all income earners are requested to purchase "social insurance bonds" whose return is set equal to the higher of the rate of growth in GNP and the rate of interest on U.S. treasury bonds. It is interesting to note that the aim of the author was to secure workers with more generous benefits than those granted by the earnings-based scheme. Castellino (1969) thoroughly analyzed the properties of a sort of a contributions-based pay-as-you-go second pillar where the return is set equal to the growth of the average wage. Neither of these articles gained sufficient attention within the international literature or could inspire any economic policy choice. On the other hand, those proposals were formulated in abstract terms without tackling the many complex details (discussed for instance in this work) that one inevitably faces when building a real contributions-based scheme. Valdés-Prieto (2000) recalls that an old-age contributions-based scheme was also proposed by Boskin, Kotlikoff, and Shoven (1988) within a more comprehensive social security model entirely based on personal accounts.

7. There is no evidence for the suggestion hinted at in Franco (2002, p. 221), according to which the echo of the discussion going on in Sweden would have inspired the Italian reform.

8. See Disney (1999).

9. In Italy, the "all" earnings rule was substituted for the "last five" earnings rule in 1992. At the same time the price indexation rule was substituted for the wage indexation.

10. See Samuelson (1958), Aaron (1966), and, in Italian, De Finetti (1956). Note that in Samuelson (1958) the theorem is not explicitly proved in a defined benefit context, and that in Aaron (1966) the award formula is not properly related to earnings, in that the first annual benefit is equal to the average wage of active workers. A proof of the theorem is given in Gronchi and Nisticò (2004) within a clear-cut defined benefit framework that also realistically allows for different retirement ages and career patterns.

11. Actually, some other conditions are needed for the theorem to hold. See Gronchi and Nisticò (2004, Appendix A.1).

12. See Gronchi (1993), Italian Ministry of Treasury (1994) and Gronchi (1995b) for an empirical analysis of unfairness characterizing the Italian earnings-based scheme prior to the 1996 NDC reform. These papers showed the existence of other sources of inequalities in individual returns besides those stemming from the differences in retirement age and in earnings growth. Moreover, they showed that the Italian decision in 1992 to calculate the pensionable earnings as an average of all annual earnings attenuated but did not eliminate the disparity in individual rates of return.

13. In Swedish practice, the pension award is obtained by dividing the left-hand side of equation 19.1, which is called *account balance*, by the reciprocal of h, called *annuitization divisor* (Settergren 2002, p. 61).

14. The proof of this sustainability is given in Gronchi and Nisticò (2004) for the realistic context referred to in note 10.

15. See Gronchi and Nisticò (2004). Valdés-Prieto (2000, pp. 407–8) wrongly maintains that an increase in λ generates temporary deficits.

16. The theoretical foundations of the canonical scheme are better discussed in Gronchi and Nisticò (2004). Among the various issues there discussed, one is worth summarizing, namely the critical examination of the idea—expressed, for instance, by Chicon (1999)—that extending pensionable earnings to the whole career is a quick way of attaining the purpose of the contributions-based scheme while avoiding the announcement of falsely innovative reforms. Actually, this thesis can be easily refuted. To understand why, let us recall that the traditional earnings-related formula for the first annual benefit is

$$p = n \cdot k \cdot \frac{\sum_{i=n-r+1}^{n} w_i \cdot \prod_{j=i+1}^{n+1}(1+\gamma_j)}{r} \ ,$$

where k is the accrual rate, r the number of years of salary used to calculate pensionable earnings, and γ the revaluation rate. In fact, for $r = n$ the above equation becomes

$$p = k \cdot \sum_{i=1}^{n} w_i \cdot \prod_{j=i+1}^{n+1}(1+\gamma_j),$$

from which it readily follows that

$$p = \left[a \cdot \sum_{i=1}^{n} w_i \cdot \prod_{j=i+1}^{n+1}(1+\gamma_j)\right] \cdot \frac{k}{a}.$$

Therefore, the earnings-based pension can be rearranged to display formal analogies with that of the canonical NDC scheme, as it too can be expressed as the product of a notional capital and a conversion rate. In other words, the canonical NDC scheme can be disguised under DB dresses. It suffices to choose special values of the parameters involved in the award formula. In particular, one should set γ equal to the growth rate of the wage bill, differentiate the accrual rate by age according to the equation $k = h(\delta, m) \cdot a$ and select indexation according to equation 19.6. However, the camouflage could not last. How would the bizarre indexation rule be justified? Or how could one justify the circumstance that, for a given mortality, the contribution rates could not be altered without at the same time altering the accrual rate? Or, even, that whenever mortality decreases, the accrual rates will be diminished?

17. See Settergren (2001a, 2003).

18. In the last 30 years, real wages in Italy have risen at an average annual rate of 2 percent (ISTAT 2002).

19. The unrestricted choice of δ could generate adverse selection. That is, it could encourage those who know they have lower-than-average life expectancy to choose higher δ. Even so, this is a circumscribed phenomenon that will result in much less severe disequilibria than the mass equalizations needed to adjust very low vintage pensions. Adverse selection can produce greater disequilibria where, as in Italy, survivor's benefits are provided for but the conversion rates are not differentiated according to the presence and age of the spouse (see the section on survivor's benefits).

20. See the section on the transition.

21. See Settergren (2002, p. 48).

22. The rates have been announced for all ages from 61 to 80 and may be calculated for still older ages "on request."

23. The pensionable quotas allowed are one-fourth, two-fourths, and three-fourths. See Palmer (2000) and Settergren (2001b).

24. On this matter, see Gronchi (1996), Beltrametti and Bonatti (1996), and Bosi (1997).

25. Actually, this entitlement is attenuated in that entitlement to the full percentage is means-tested. In addition to the spouse's benefit, there may be entitlements for minor children, up to a ceiling of 100 percent of the deceased's pension.

26. For the purpose, among other things, of not discriminating against common law couples, the second person could also be freely chosen.

27. See note 58 below.

28. See Gronchi (1998). Other informational shortcomings stemmed from the choice of making the survivor's benefit variable according to the survivor's other income (see note 25). This choice was made without sufficient awareness of the great difficulties that it would entail for the calculation of the conversion rates.

29. See the discussion on updating conversion rates.

30. See Kruse (2002).

31. Even continuous updating does not guarantee the perfect balance of the system. In the presence of "backward-looking" conversion rates, given steadily lengthening life expectancies, deficits cannot be avoided. On the other hand, surpluses would be generated if conversion rates were of the forward-looking type (see Valdés-Prieto 2000).

32. The 14.884 percent tax that finances the compulsory pay-as-you-go scheme is supplemented by 2.326 percent that goes to the funded scheme (also compulsory) discussed in the section on diversification of the social security portfolio. The total tax rate is thus 17.21 percent. Official sources cite a rate of 18.5 percent. The difference depends on the tax base, which for the higher rate is unusually equal to the wage net of the worker's social security contribution (Settergren 2002, p. 33).

33. This common value will be reached gradually. For instance, in 2003, the contribution rate is 16.8 percent for craftsmen and 17.19 percent for traders.

34. See Gronchi (1996, 1998) and Gronchi and Nisticò (2004). The "disorder" is aggravated by the fact that in Italy (under a rule not abrogated by the 1995 reform) earnings above a certain ceiling are subject to a financing rate that is 0.7 percentage points higher than the award rate. The same additional rate is levied on the earnings of self-employed above a certain ceiling (different from that of employees).

35. Swedish firms pay contributions also on earnings above the ceiling. But these contributions are a true tax on firms, as they are paid to the state and not to the social security system. They do not form part of the notional capital.

36. Legislative changes affecting some of these provisions are under way. For more details see Palmer (2000, Appendix 2).

37. See Gronchi (1996b, 1997).

38. Notice that if the disabled person continues to work, the disability allowance is diminished according to his earnings. Moreover, the Italian legislation considers a more generous and permanent disability allowance, which is granted to those seriously disabled. Though life expectancy of the beneficiaries is generally very short, these allowances constitute quite a heavy burden for the system, given that they are extended to the survivors.

39. Actually, the reform does not set any age ceiling. The age of 57 is obtained by extrapolating earlier rules for the automatic transformation of the disability allowance into an old-age pension at retirement age (or earlier, in case of early retirement). The disability allowance is granted at first for a three-year period and becomes definitive after two renewals.

40. For pensioners, the decrease in the rate of return would take the form of a lower indexation rate.

41. Actually, Sweden elected to exempt pensioners from defraying these costs, avoiding reduction in their indexation.

42. See Gronchi (1996b).

43. Actually, the first three groups have now been switched into the Employee Pension Fund, albeit with separate accounts.

44. See Settergren (2001b, p. 4).

45. Contribution revenues in 2001 exceeded pension outlays by about 10 percent (Settergren 2002, p. 15). The 1998 reform was not enacted to counter a present deficit but to prevent the emergence of one after 2010, when the baby boomers will begin to retire (Palmer 2002, p. 173).

46. The relative absence of portfolio constraints is shown by the fact that, overall, 48 percent of the four funds' portfolio consists of foreign securities. Of these foreign investments, 73 percent consist of shares (Settergren 2002, p. 27).

47. See note 32.

48. The law provides that the worker's transfer order be executed within 24 hours (Palmer 2000, p. 33).

49. This option is taken by those individuals who want to avoid further risk after retirement. Their money is invested at low risk and returns possibly exceeding 3 percent cannot be claimed though they can be awarded at PPA's discretion. To avoid adverse selection, the single allowed adjustment rule is zero indexation (implying fixed annual installments).

50. For a more detailed description of the second pillar, see Palmer (2000, pp. 30–42), and Premium Pension Authority (2001).

51. For a more detailed description of the third pillar, see Palmer (2000, pp. 4, 8–9), and (2002, pp. 180–2).

52. Assuming an inflation rate of 2.5 percent, the finance provided by the severance pay fund costs 0.875 percent in real terms.

53. By law, conversion cannot be partial for workers hired after April 28, 1993.

54. See the section on transition.

55. On the fairness effects of tax changes, see Feldstein (1976a, b). For a different viewpoint see Graetz (1985) and Kaplow (1986). For a specific analysis of social security changes, see Giovannoni (2000) and Nardini (2001).

56. In 2005, the lower age limit is 56 for blue-collar workers and 57 for white-collar workers. According to a 2004 law, starting from 2008, the minimum age for early retirement will be 60 for all workers.

57. Such causes are discussed in Gronchi and Nisticò (2004).

58. Professor Giarda, who was undersecretary for the economy and as such among the most authoritative drafters of the reform, writes: "Almost everyone involved in the preparation of the measure—both in government and in the unions—had to master the complex technicalities of the contributions-based scheme and translate them into legal norms in scarcely two months. The defined-contributions method had a rigorous high priest in Professor Sandro Gronchi. His acolytes—including myself—in those spring months of 1995 were not always up to his standards." Moreover, "The strict time limits for the drafting of the measure resulted in unsatisfactory determination of several fundamental parameters in the award formula. The result, in practice, was a violation of the conditions for long-term financial equilibrium and of some rules of fairness" (Giarda 1998, p. 275). On the same wavelength, Professor Salvati, one of the most authoritative economists of the Italian left sitting in parliament, commented as follows on the agreement between government and unions that opened the way to the reform: "Let me merely say that up until a year ago the contributions-based scheme was discussed in circles scarcely broader than academia, and now we find it as the calculation criterion upon which the entire public pension system will converge" (Salvati 1995).

References

Aaron, H. 1966. "The Social Insurance Paradox." *Canadian Journal of Economics and Political Science*, 32 (3, August): 371–74.

Ackerby, S. 1992. *Pensionsfrågan*, bilaga 12 [*The Pensions Issue*, supplement 12] till SOU 1992: 12, Finansdepartementet, Stockholm.

Beltrametti, L., and L. Bonatti. 1996. "Sulla Possibile Indeterminatezza della Dinamica dell'Aliquota di Equilibrio di un Sistema Pensionistico." "[On the Possible Indeterminacy of the Dynamics of the Equilibrium Tax Rate in a Pension System]." *Politica Economica* 12 (2): 229–43.

Bosi, P. 1997. "Sul Controllo Dinamico di un Sistema Pensionistico a Ripartizione di Tipo Contributivo." "[On the Dynamic Control of a Pay-as-You-Go Contributive Pension System]." Mimeo presented at the IX Annual Meeting of the Italian Society of Public Economics. Published in *Per l'economia italiana, Scritti in onore di Nino Andreatta*, ed. C. D'Adda, 211–46 (2002). Bologna:Il Mulino.

Boskin, M., L. Kotlikoff, and J. Shoven. 1988. "Personal Security Accounts: A Proposal for Fundamental Social Security Reform." In *Social Security and Private Pensions*, ed. S. Wachter, 179–208. Lexington: Lexington Books.

Bröms, J. 1990. *Ur askan av ATP* [*Out of the Ashes of the Pension System*]. Stockholm: SACO.

Buchanan, J. 1968. "Social Insurance in a Growing Economy: A Proposal for Radical Reform." *National Tax Journal* 21 (4): 386–95.

Castellino, O. 1969. "Un Sistema di Pensioni per la Vecchiaia Commisurate ai Versamenti Contributivi Effettuati e alla Dinamica dei Redditi Medi da Lavoro." "[A System of Old Age Pensions to be Awarded in Proportion to Contributions and to the Average Wage Growth]." *Giornale degli Economisti e Annali di Economia* 28 (1–2): 1–23.

Chand, S. K., and A. Jaeger. 1996. "Aging Populations and Public Pension Schemes." Occasional Paper 147, International Monetary Fund, Washington, DC.

Chicon, M. 1999. "Notional Defined-Contribution Schemes: Old Wine in New Bottles?" *International Social Security Review* 52 (4): 87–105.

De Finetti, B. 1956. "Sviluppo della Popolazione e Sicurezza Sociale." "[Population Growth and Social Security]." *Atti del Convegno di Studi su I Problemi Attuariali e Statistici della Sicurezza Sociale*. Ordine Nazionale degli Attuari, Roma.

Disney, R. 1999. "Notional Accounts as a Pension Reform Strategy: An Evaluation." *Pension Reform Primer Series*, Social Protection Discussion Paper 9928. www1.worldbank.org/sp.

En Promoria av Pensionsarbetsgruppen. 1992. [*A Proposal of the Working Group on Pensions*]. Socialdepartementet. Ds 1992:89. Stockholm: Norstedts.

Feldstein, M. 1976a. "Compensation in Tax Reform." *National Tax Journal* 29 (2): 123–30.

———. 1976b. "On the Theory of Tax Reform." *Journal of Public Economics* 6 (1–2): 77–104.

———. 1998. *Privatizing Social Security*. Chicago: University of Chicago Press.

Franco, D. 2002. "Italy: A Never-Ending Pension Reform." In *Social Security Pension Reform in Europe*, ed. M. Feldstein and H. Siebert, 211–61. Chicago: University of Chicago Press.

Giarda, P. 1998. "La Revisione del Sistema Pensionistico nel 1997: Come Avrebbe Potuto Essere." "[The 1997 Revision of the Pension System: How It Could Have Been]." *Economia Politica: Rivista di Teoria e Analisi* 15 (2): 267–94.

Giovannoni, F. 2000. "La Riforma Previdenziale. Analisi Economica del Mutamento Normativo dal Punto di Vista dell'Equità." "[Social Security Reform: An Economic Analysis of Legal Transition from the Viewpoint of Fairness]." *Studi e Note di Economia* 1: 145–68.

Graetz, M. 1985. "Retroactivity Revisited." *Harvard Law Review* 98 (8): 1820–41.

Gronchi, S. 1993. "I Rendimenti Impliciti della Previdenza Obbligatoria." "[Social Security Implicit Rates of Return]." Mimeo presented at the Wokshop on "La Riforma della Previdenza Pubblica," Fondazione Cespe, serie azzurra: incontri istruttori, n.13.

———. 1994a. "Sostenibilità ed Equità del Sistema Previdenziale Italiano." "[Fairness and Sustainability of the Italian Social Security]." In *Le pensioni difficili: la previdenza sociale in Italia tra crisi e riforma* ed. O. Castellino. Bologna: Il Mulino, 1995.

———. 1994b. "Nuove Regole per il Sistema Pensionistico in Italia." "[New Rules for the Italian Pension System]." *Parole chiave*, 6: 145–56.

———. 1995a. "Sostenibilità ed Equità del Sistema Pensionistico Italiano." "[Fairness and Sustainability of the Italian Pension System]." *Economia Politica: Rivista di Teoria e Analisi* 12 (1): 3–21.

————. 1995b. "I Rendimenti Impliciti della Previdenza Obbligatoria: un'Analisi delle Iniquità del Sistema." "[Social Security Implicit Rates of Return: an Analysis of System's Unfairness]." *Economia Italiana* 1: 41–93.

————. 1996. "Sostenibilitá Finanziaria e Indicizzazione: un Commento alla Riforma del Sistema Pensionistico." *Economia Italiana* 1: 115–56.

————. 1997. "Un' Ipotesi di Correzione e Completamento della Riforma delle Pensioni del 1995." Ministero del Tesoro, Commissione Tecnica per la Spesa Pubblica, nota 10.

————. 1998. "La Sostenibilità delle Nuove Forme Previdenziali ovvero il Sistema Pensionistico tra Riforme Fatte e da Fare." "[Sustainability of the New Social Security: What Has Been Done and What More Has to Be Done]." *Economia Politica: Rivista di Teoria e Analisi* 15 (2): 295–316.

Gronchi, S., and S. Nisticò. 2004. "Theoretical Foundations of Pay-As-You-Go Defined-Contribution Pension Schemes." Mimeo presented at the Conference *Economic Growth and Distribution: On the Nature and Causes of the Wealth of Nations*, Lucca, Italy.

ISTAT. 2002. *Conti Economici Nazionali Annuali [Annual National Economic Accounts]*. Roma: Istituto Nazionale di Statistica.

Italian Ministry of Treasury. 1994. "I Rendimenti Impliciti della Previdenza Obbligatoria." "[Implicit Returns within Social Security]." *Conti Pubblici e Congiuntura Economica*, n.2/94.

Kaplow, L. 1986. "An Economic Analysis of Legal Transitions." *Harvard Law Review* 99 (3): 509–617.

Kruse, A. 2002. "Notional Defined-Contribution Pension System. The Effects of the Swedish Design on Efficiency and Distribution." Paper presented at the 53rd International Atlantic Economic Conference, March 12–17, Paris, France.

Modigliani, F., M. Ceprini, and A. Muralidhar. 1999. "A Solution to the Social Security Crisis From an MIT Team." Sloane Working Paper 4051, Massachusetts Institute of Technology, Cambridge, MA.

Nardini, F. 2001. "Should All Promises Be Kept? Pension Reform and Accrued Rights." Mimeo presented at the 5th International Congress on Insurance: Mathematics & Economics, State College PE, July 23–25.

Niccoli, A. 1992. "Un Approccio di Equilibrio Finanziario di Lungo Periodo ai Problemi di un Sistema Pensionistico a Ripartizione [Long-Term Financial Stability of a Pay-As-You-Go Pension System]." *Moneta e Credito* 45 (177): 23–47.

————. 1994. "Sistema Pensionistico Italiano, Sistema Finanziario e Capitalizzazione Senza Riserve." "[The Italian Pension System, The Financial System and Notional Funding]." In *Le Pensioni Difficili: la Previdenza Sociale in Italia tra Crisi e Riforma*, ed O. Castellino. Bologna: Il Mulino, 1995.

Olsson, H., and G. Schubert. 1991. *Det framtida pensionssystemet [The Future Pension System]*, ESO, Ds 1991:27, Stockholm.

Orszag, P., and J. Stiglitz. 2001. "Rethinking Pension Reform: Ten Myths about Social Security Systems." In *New Ideas about Old Age Security*, ed. R. Holzmann and J. Stiglitz, 17–56. Washington, DC: World Bank.

Palmer, E. 2000. "The Swedish Pension Reform Model: Framework and Issues." Social Protection Discussion Paper 0012. www1.worldbank.org/sp.

————. 2002. "Swedish Pension Reform: How Did It Evolve and What Does It Mean for the Future?" In *Social Security Pension Reform in Europe*, ed. M. Feldstein and H. Siebert, 171–210. Chicago: University of Chicago Press.

Palmer, E., and K. G. Sherman. 1993. *En ny socialförsäkrin [A New Social Insurance]*. Stockholm: National Social Insurance Board, RFV.

Persson, M. 1991. "Vad är det för fel på ATP-systemet?" "[What Is Wrong with the Pension System?]" *Ekonomisk Debatt* 19 (3): 205–18, Stockholm.

Premium Pension Authority. 2001. "Information and News on Your Premium Pension." *PPM Nyheter*, 3.

Reformerat pensionssystem: Bakgrund, principer och skiss. 1992. [*The Pension Reform: Background. Principles and Draft*] Sweden's Official Publications 1992, Stockholm: Norstedts.

Reformerat pensionssystem: Betänkande av pensionsarbetsgruppen. 1994. [*The Pension Reform: Proposal of the Working Group on Pensions*] Sweden's Official Publications 1994 n.20, Stockholm: Norstedts.

Reformerat pensionssystem: Kostnader och individeffekter. 1994. [*The Pension Reform: The Financial Consequences for Individuals*] Sweden's Official Publications 1994 n. 21, Stockholm: Norstedts.

Salvati, M. 1995. "Sotto l'euforia i dubbi." "[The Fear Behind Euphoria]." *Corriere della sera*, May 10.

Samuelson, P. 1958. "An Exact Consumption Loan Model of Interest with or without the Social Contrivance of Money." *Journal of Political Economy* 68 (6): 467–82.

Settergren, O. 2001a. "The Automatic Balance Mechanism of the Swedish Pension System: A Non-Technical Introduction." *Wirtschaftspolitische Blätter*, n. 4: 239–49.

———. 2001b. "Two Thousand Five Hundred Words on the Swedish Pension Reform." Stockholm: The National Social Insurance Board, RFV.

———, ed. 2002. *The Swedish Pension System. Annual Report 2001.* Stockholm: The National Social Insurance Board, RFV.

———. 2003. "Financial and Inter-generational Balance? An Introduction to how the Swedish Pension System Manages Conflicting Ambitions." *Scandinavian Insurance Quarterly* (2): 99–114.

Valdés-Prieto, S. 2000. "The Financial Stability of Notional Account Pensions." *The Scandinavian Journal of Economics* 102 (3): 395–417.

World Bank. 1994. *Averting the Old Age Crisis: Policies to Protect the Old and Promote Growth.* New York: Oxford University Press.

PART IV

THE POTENTIAL OF NON-FINANCIAL DEFINED CONTRIBUTION SCHEMES IN OTHER COUNTRIES' REFORMS

Chapter 20

Investigating the Introduction of NDCs in Austria

Bernhard Felderer, Reinhard Koman, and Ulrich Schuh*

AUSTRIA, LIKE A NUMBER OF OTHER ORGANISATION FOR ECONOMIC CO-OPERATION AND DEVELOPMENT (OECD) MEMBER STATES, faces the challenge of ensuring the long-term financial stability of the public pension system. In recent years the reform of the Austrian pension system has become a dominant issue in the political and public debate. Despite the fact that the Austrian government has implemented a number of far-reaching modifications of the pension system in the last decade, a comprehensive and persuasive reform is still out. This chapter addresses the issue of the long-term financial stability of the Austrian pension system by demonstrating the impact of different scenarios on expenditures, revenues, and replacement rates of the public pay-as-you-go (PAYG) pension system for the period 2000 to 2050. In addition, we describe the effects of the introduction of a multipillar system with a notional defined contribution (NDC) pillar.[1]

We proceed as follows: the next section gives an overview on the provisions of the Austrian pension system prior to the most recent 2003/04 pension reform, provides some indications for the need to reform, and summarizes the most recent debate on pension reform in Austria. The following section describes the effects of a multipillar reform with notional accounts. We undertake projections for the Austrian pension insurance system and simulations of pension reform using the World Bank's Pension Reform Options Simulation Toolkit (PROST). We explain the required inputs and the assumptions underlying the different scenarios, and present the results that were obtained from the simulations with PROST. For the different labor force scenarios, the key results for a multipillar system with notional accounts are confronted with the results for the current monopillar system. The final section concludes.

Retirement Income Provision and Pension Reform in Austria

The Austrian public PAYG pension system consists of different schemes for employees; farmers; self-employed persons in commerce, trade, and industry; and some groups of

_____

* Bernhard Felderer is professor of economics in Cologne, Germany, and director of the Institute for Advanced Studies in Vienna; he may be reached at felderer@ihs.ac.at. Reinhard Koman holds a Ph.D. in economics and is currently working as an economist at the Institute for Advanced Studies in Vienna; he may be reached at koman@ihs.ac.at. Ulrich Schuh is the head of the Department of Economics and Finance at the Institute for Advanced Studies; he may be reached at schuh@ihs.ac.at.

Helpful comments by Robert Holzmann, Yvonne Sin, Asta Zviniene, Hans Stefanits, Michaela Mayer-Schulz, Karl Grillitsch, and Reinhard Haydn are gratefully acknowledged.

freelance professionals. Civil servants have their own retirement schemes, which are funded by their contributions and their respective public employers.

The Austrian Pension System Prior to the Recent Reform Process

The Austrian public pension system is mandatory for every worker except a small group of self-employed persons and those with very low earnings. Hence, coverage by the public pension system is very high: approximately 93 percent of the labor force is covered by the public pension system. The public pension schemes also provide disability and survivor benefits.[2]

The Austrian pension system is financed mainly by the contributions of the insured, supplemented by transfers from other systems (for example, unemployment insurance and the family burden equalization fund) and a federal contribution that essentially covers the gap between revenues and expenditures. The pension insurance contribution for employees is 22.8 percent of the contributory wage, which is the part of the pay below the upper earnings threshold, of which 10.25 percent is paid by the employee and 12.55 by the employer. The contribution rate has more than doubled since 1956, when it was 10 percent. The contribution rates for self-employed persons in commerce, industry, and trade and for farmers are currently 15 and 14.5 percent, respectively. When the public pension system was extended to farmers and other self-employed workers, contributions were fixed at a rate similar to the employees' contribution rate, with the government taking over a "fictitious employer share." Some groups of freelance professionals pay 20 percent.

The statutory retirement age for a standard old-age pension is 60 for women and 65 for men. Persons are entitled to an old-age pension if they have accumulated at least 15 years of contribution. In 1992, it was decided to raise women's statutory retirement age gradually until it is the same as it is for men. This adaptation will start in 2024 and finally be implemented by 2033. Five years earlier, between 2019 and 2028, the age limits for early retirement will be similarly harmonized. The age limits for early retirement due to long insurance coverage have been increased in recent years from 55 and 60 to 56.5 and 61.5 for women and men, respectively.

The current basis of pension assessment is derived from the average salary during the highest-paying 15 years of contribution. Earnings in each year are revalued to the year in which the individual retires by a series of revaluation factors. The actual pension level is derived from the assessment basis by applying a replacement rate, which is calculated from increments credited for each year of contribution to the system. Currently, for each year of contribution, 2 percentage points, so-called *increment* points, are credited. The maximum replacement rate at the statutory retirement age is 80 percent of the assessment base, which is consequently achieved after 40 years of contribution. There does exist a bonus for later retirement and a penalty for retirement before the statutory retirement age. The deduction for retiring earlier is currently set at 3 percentage points per year, with 10.5 percentage points and 15 percent of the replacement rate as upper limits. The bonus per year is now 4 percent of the assessment basis. This bonus, however, is subject to the maximum replacement rate, 80 percent plus 2 percentage points per year after the statutory retirement age, with 90 percent as upper limit.

The Austrian pension system has no provision for a minimum pension. However, a means-tested support for low-income persons is incorporated in the system by way of equalization supplements awarded to all those who have a general claim for pension payments and fall below the minimum income level. The means test takes into account the family income. The minimum income for nonmarried pensioners is approximately equal to half the median net income from active work earned by dependent employees.

The annual adjustment of existing pension claims is based on the principle that the average pension and the average wage, both net of social contributions, should increase at the same rate. This makes sure that an increase in pension contributions would not only increase the burden on wage incomes but would also reduce net pensions. The adjustment formula also takes into account structural changes in pensions due to relatively high first-time pensions and relatively low benefits for persons leaving the pension schemes, leading to an "automatic" increase of the average pension: the annual adjustment factor and this "structural effect," approximately 1.5 percent per year, should add up to a net pension increase equal to the net wage increase. This principle of net indexation of pension increases curbs the growth of pension expenditures. This concept, however, makes any reductions in pension benefits for new pensioners ineffective with respect to overall pension expenditures: any reductions in average expenditures per new pensioner are automatically compensated for by increased benefits for existing pensioners.

In addition to old-age pensions, the Austrian pension insurance provides benefits to survivors and disability pensions to invalids. A disability pension may be claimed on the condition that a certain amount of insurance years has been accumulated, always provided that the claimant is an invalid. The required number of insurance years depends on the claimant's age. Persons are in any case entitled to a disability pension if they have accumulated 15 years of contribution. The definition of *invalidity* varies depending on the type of work. If invalidity is due to an accident at work or an occupational disease, no minimum number of insurance years is required. The pension of a widow or a widower is 60 percent of the deceased spouse's (actual or hypothetical) pension entitlement in all cases where the survivor receives only this benefit and has no other income. In all other cases, the percentage depends on the income gap between spouses during their active working lives; the minimum was 40 percent until the recent reform and is now 0 percent. Orphans are entitled to an orphans' pension until they have completed their eighteenth year of age, provided that the deceased parent has accumulated sufficient insurance years for a disability pension. The age limit is extended when the orphan is still in school, at university, in occupational training or incapacitated for work.

Overall public expenditures for all kinds of pension benefits are relatively high in Austria. In 2000, public pension expenditures amounted to 14.5 percent of GDP, which was the highest value for all OECD countries. This figure has to be seen alongside the practically nonexistent funded pillar of the Austrian pension system. Nonpublic forms of social protection continue to be less important than they are in other Western countries, and funded schemes are quantitatively insignificant.[3]

The Need for Reform

Like any PAYG pension system, the Austrian public pension scheme is strongly affected by demographic trends. For decades, the Austrian pension system took advantage of the favorable relationship between contributors and retired persons. Since the middle of the 1980s, the constraints for the fiscal balance of the system became apparent, leading to a sequence of reform attempts.

The official demographic projections of the Austrian Statistical Office, Statistics Austria, for the period 2000–50, used in the calculations below, point to a rather uncomfortable development.[4] The main variant of the projections assumes an increase in the fertility rate from 1.34 per women to 1.5, and assumes that this stays constant thereafter. It is projected that life expectancy will rise during the projection period by about 6 years to 82 and 87 years for men and women, respectively. Net immigration is assumed to follow the recent trends and is projected to increase from about 17,000 persons to 24,000 persons in the year 2050.

The assumptions described above imply that total population is projected to increase slightly until 2030, showing some decline afterward. It is expected that, until the year 2050, total population will increase by 100,000 persons to 8.1 million people. According to this projection, the period 2000 to 2050 will be characterized by a rather dramatic change in the age structure of the Austrian population. In the year 2000, the share of persons aged less than 15 years amounted to 16.7 percent of total population. The corresponding share of people with age above 60 was 20.7 percent. Until 2050, the share of young persons will decline to 13.2 percent, whereas the share of people aged above 60 will increase to 35 percent. The ratio of persons aged 60 and above with respect to persons aged 15 to 60 will climb from 33 percent in the year 2000 to 67 percent in 2050. The average age increases from 39.6 to 47.1.

The demographic trends imply a considerable deterioration of the conditions for the fiscal stability of the Austrian pension system. With a view to permanently monitoring the statutory pension insurance system, a committee was established—the Committee on Long-Term Pension Sustainability—which has the task of preparing long-term scenarios on the development of the statutory pension insurance system in three-year intervals. The first report was presented in the year 2002.

The committee presented different scenarios resulting from different assumptions on the demographic development (that is, using different variants of the official projections of Statistics Austria described above) as well as the development of labor participation and productivity. All scenarios were developed on the basis of the legislation in force in the year 2002.

In addition to the demographic development, the fiscal balance of the pension system is determined primarily by labor force participation. In this respect, the labor force participation of the age group 55–65 is of crucial importance. Higher labor force participation of this age group implies both higher contributions and a reduction of expenditures because of later retirement.

Three different scenarios for labor force participation have been used in the projections. The initial reference value for the labor force participation rate is 67 percent in the year 2000. All three scenarios assume an increase of labor force participation on the basis of the main demographic variant of Statistics Austria. The increase in the labor force participation rate is assumed to be driven mainly by higher participation of women and persons aged above 55. Until 2050, it is assumed that the participation rate increases to 72 percent (low scenario), 76 percent (medium scenario), and 84 percent (high scenario), respectively. Labor force participation of persons aged between 55 and 65 increases from 26 percent in 2000 to 43 percent, 53 percent, and 74 percent for the different scenarios in 2050.

In the year 2000, the total expenditure of the general private sector pension scheme expressed as a share of GDP was about 10.5 percent.[5] In all scenarios this ratio increases steadily but slowly until the year 2015, with an acceleration of the increase in the period 2015–2040, and a slight decline afterward. Under the main demographic variant, the expenditure-to-GDP ratio increases to 15.6 percent (low participation scenario), 13.4 percent (medium scenario) and 11.5 percent (high scenario) in the year 2050.

Another figure that reveals the fiscal burden of the pension system is the implicit contribution rate. This is the contribution rate that would be necessary to finance the pension insurance completely from contributions of insured persons, so that no additional transfers from the general government budget would be required. At present, the implicit contribution rate is 31.3 percent. According to the projections of the committee, this rate would rise to maximum values of 44.4 percent (low scenario), 40.7 percent (medium scenario), and 36.7 percent (high scenario).

Based on a generational accounting exercise, Keuschnigg et al. (2000a, b, 2002), Koman et al. (2000), and Koman, Keuschnigg, and Lüth (2002) provide data about the intergenerational incidence of recent fiscal and pension reforms and their effect on long-term fiscal sustainability. The authors calculated the actuarial implicit debt[6] of the isolated general private pension scheme for the year 2000—that is, the present value of the excess of projected pension expenditures, including means-tested equalization supplement—over projected pension insurance contributions.

According to the legal situation in 2000, the implicit debt of the general private pension scheme amounted to approximately 200 percent of GDP. In their analysis the authors also demonstrated the measures needed to dispose of the debt of the pension system. The drastic consolidation requirements following from this idea illustrate the still alarming dimensions of the sustainability gap in the pension system: a consolidation exclusively financed by an increase of pension contributions would have to more than triple contributions (an increase of 217.6 percent) if it were to be limited to future generations—that is, to cohorts born after 1995. Even if the increase in contributions were to be extended to all (current and future) generations, it would have to amount to an increase of approximately 70 percent. If, on the other hand, the consolidation were to be financed exclusively by spending cuts, it would mean an immediate reduction of pension expenditure by around 40 percent. It should be noted in this context, however, that a not-too-small part of the sustainability gap of the Austrian pension system is due to non-insurance-related benefit entitlements, particularly because insurance periods during which insured persons pay no contributions—such as periods of unemployment, sickness, maternity leave, or military service—increase pension claim.

The results described above reveal the existence of a huge fiscal imbalance in the Austrian pension system. This is caused not only by demographics trends, but also by low labor force participation rates of the elderly, particularly after the early retirement age—a rather distinctive feature of the Austrian pension system is the large share of early retirement pensions. To eliminate fiscal imbalance and to restore long-run solvency, it seems inevitable that the labor force participation of the elderly and the effective retirement age will have to be raised considerably. A key question is to what extent can the very low participation rates of the elderly be attributed to current incentive effects of the public pension system.

Based on the method portrayed in Gruber and Wise (1999), Hofer and Koman (2001) provide an overview of the interaction between social security and retirement behavior in Austria and present the results of a series of simulations aimed at assessing the retirement incentives generated by the pension system. Austria has labor force participation rates at older ages that are among the lowest in similarly developed countries; participation rates have been falling dramatically in the postwar period and this process has even accelerated since the 1970s, particularly among men over age 55. Between the ages of 60 and 65, only about 10 percent of the population is in the labor force.

To some extent, the sharp drop in labor force participation among the elderly must be attributed to major disincentives of the Austrian pension system; on closer examination, this system turns out to provide significant incentives to retire early. Hofer and Koman quantify these incentives by computing measures of social security wealth and of the implicit tax rates on continued work generated by the current system. The tax on continued work becomes quite large after the early retirement age; the implicit tax on additional work is particularly high, even before the early retirement age, for workers who are entitled to claim disability pensions or equalization supplements.

Figure 20.1 summarizes labor force participation data and retirement incentives for Austria and the 11 countries covered by Gruber and Wise, presenting a scatter plot of the unused labor capacity and the tax force to retire. The *unused labor capacity* is defined as the unweighted average of the proportion of men not working in the age groups between 55

Figure 20.1. Unused Capacity versus Tax Force to Retire

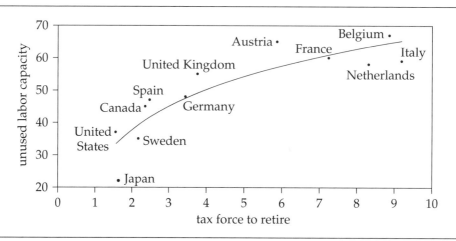

Source: Gruber and Wise 1999, Hofer and Koman (2001).

and 65; the *tax force to retire*, an indicator intended to summarize the country-specific incentives for early retirement, is calculated as the sum of the implicit tax rates on continued work beginning with the earliest possible retirement age.[7] The measures for the tax force to retire range from values close to 10 (Italy, Belgium) to values only slightly higher than 1.5 (the United States, Japan). The tax force to retire calculated for Austria amounts to 5.88, which is close to the top rates in the sample, although it is still below the very top. As already documented by Gruber and Wise, the international comparison of labor market and retirement behavior shows a strong correlation between the tax on continued work and labor force participation; the solid line in the figure is a regression curve based on the regression of unused capacity on the logarithm of the tax force. About 80 percent of the variation in unused capacity can be explained by the tax force to retire. Austria has the second highest unused capacity in the sample, 65 percent (according to 1997/98 micro-census data), which is exceeded only by the Belgian value (67 percent).

Pension Reform in Austria: Recent Reforms, Current Debate, and Reform Perspectives

As mentioned above, since the mid-1980s the Austrian pension system has been the object of a sequence of reform attempts aiming at financial sustainability. However, the results presented in the previous section indicate that the fundamental underlying problems of the system have not been addressed adequately.

In the year 2000, the new Austrian government emphasized the will to reform the Austrian pension system in its working program. A pension reform commission was appointed to discuss the long-run perspectives of the Austrian pension system. The reform commission has initiated a lively discussion on the direction of future reforms of the system and a number of proposals have been submitted.

Another significant step in the reform process marked the most recent pension reform enacted in 2003 and 2004, which was to a considerable extent influenced by the discussions of the pension reform commission.

Following Holzmann and Heitzmann (2002), proposals for reforming pension systems may be classified into two categories: *parametric reforms* adhere to the existing provisions of the PAYG pension system and tend to adjust the main parameters of the system (that is, contribution rates, retirement age, and replacement rates). Historical and most recent reforms of the Austrian pension system belong to this type of reform approach. The pension reform of the year 2000 raised the early retirement age by 1.5 years to 56.5 for women and 61.5 years for men, raised the deductions and bonuses for retiring before and after the statutory retirement age, and abolished the early retirement scheme that allowed retirement because of reduced working capacity. The most recent 2003 pension reform, which became effective with the beginning of the year 2004, will lead to a gradual abolition of early retirement due to long insurance periods until the year 2017. There will remain, however, some exemptions from this reform for blue-collar workers, depending on their age. The increments awarded for each year of contribution, which determine the replacement rate, are gradually lowered from 2 to 1.78 in 2009. This implies that the maximum replacement rate of 80 percent will be attained only with 45 years of contribution. The number of years included in the assessment basis will be gradually extended from currently 15 years to 40 years in the year 2028. In order to cushion the immediate effects of the reform, an upper limit of benefit reductions vis-à-vis the 2003 legal situation of 10 percent was introduced.

A significant number of Austrian pension experts still advocate the parametric approach to reform the pension system. Proponents of this approach argue that the main factors determining the financial sustainability of the system are beyond the domain of the provisions of the pension system. Consequently, efforts to safeguard the long-term solvency of the system should concentrate on the main exogenous factors, which are, according to this view, economic growth and labor market performance.

This view does not, of course, imply that this group of experts regards reforms of the pension system as unnecessary. An overwhelming majority of Austrian experts is in favor of harmonizing the currently rather diverse provisions of the pension schemes for different occupational groups, a situation that is considered not only to be in conflict with intragenerational fairness, but also to hamper labor market flexibility. There is also a broad consensus that there is a need to develop a consistent and transparent scheme for the currently very complex and unsystematic way in which the financing of the pension system is organized. This applies in particular for the current financing of fictitious insurance periods (such as child care, unemployment, sickness, and military service). Finally, the majority of Austrian pension experts endorses the extension of the assessment period to the whole working career.

Parametric reforms, however, are unlikely to put pension systems on a long-run, stable financial footing. For politicians facing the option of setting the parameters of a PAYG pension system at a level that safeguards long-term fiscal stability, a problem of time inconsistency arises.[6] Following this argument, it seems more promising to undertake a comprehensive reform effort with clear and transparent rules. Whereas most effects of "fundamental reforms" could also be generated through parametric reforms, such a fundamental reform approach would have the advantage that politicians are able to convince the public of the necessity and fairness of the reform. A *fundamental reform* approach has been advocated by an increasing number of Austrian experts, particularly by Prinz and Marin (1999), Holzmann (2000b), Gauss (2000), and the Institute for Advanced Studies (Buczolich et al. 2001). What these proposals have in common is that they are based on a notionally defined contribution (NDC) approach, as it has already been implemented in a number of countries.[9] It is argued by all experts that a complete switch to a fully funded system is not realistic for Austria, as it would require immediate financing of the accrued-to-date liabilities of the current PAYG system. It is proposed, however, that the current PAYG system is reorganized by introducing individual pension accounts where all contributions to the pension system are recorded, and pension benefits would be calculated on the basis of the contributions accumulated during the whole working career. These proposals imply the harmonization of the currently diverse occupational pension schemes. Central to these proposals is the idea that individuals will become convinced through this introduction of individual accounts that they will acquire tangible claims on future benefits by contributing to the system.

This group of reform approaches explicitly aims to build a pension system that is equipped to sustain long-term changes in external conditions such as changes in fertility, mortality, productivity, or employment. Individual accounts would provide an exact description of the sources and the level of individual benefit claims. One of the most attractive aspects of these proposals is that they are able to contribute to a solution of the problems associated with the low actual retirement age: individuals can choose their optimal retirement age on the basis of their benefit levels, which depend strictly on contributions. Thus any adverse effects on labor markets are avoided. Financial stability of the system under this reform is basically introduced by using the growth rate of the contribution base as the relevant effective internal interest rate. A buffer fund shall help to smooth the expected long-term changes of fertility.

Another important issue is the development of a funded pillar of the Austrian pension system. As mentioned above, funded pension schemes are practically nonexistent in Austria. In June 2002, the Austrian parliament adopted a government bill reforming the Austrian severance pay system. The reform aimed at improving the efficiency of the severance payment scheme. Among other goals, it was the intention of the Austrian government that the new scheme should form the basis of the underdeveloped second pillar of the Austrian pension system. However, the contribution rate to this scheme is set only to 1.53 percent of gross wages, and contributors may withdraw assets before retirement.[10]

Another school of thought[11] has emerged that intends to mirror the benefit levels of the old system in the new pension accounts system by adapting the internal interest rates so as to reproduce, approximately, the current replacement rates. Such a benefit-defined pension accounts system, however, would not yet solve the problem of fiscal imbalance.

An important issue in these reform proposals is also the time horizon for the transition into the new system. Most experts are in favor of a rather slow and smooth transition to the new system of pension accounts. The proposal of the Institute for Advanced Studies, however, explicitly proposed to switch to the new system immediately and to refrain from any transition periods. Long transition periods would make the overall pension system even more opaque and would only be fostering distrust in the system.

In 2004, the Austrian government finally decided to introduce a "harmonized" system of benefit-defined pension accounts beginning January 1, 2005. This new pension system basically extends the 2003 reform for private sector employees to all other occupational schemes, including the civil servants' scheme. The new pension law applies to all persons aged 50 years and less.

A Multipillar Reform Model with Notional Accounts

The following section presents, for a time horizon up to 2050, projections for the current Austrian pension insurance system and simulations of a multipillar pension reform with notional accounts, using the World Bank's Pension Reform Options Simulation Toolkit (PROST).

The underlying demographic trends are based on the main variant population projection of Statistics Austria as described above. We consider five labor force participation scenarios, one based on the status-quo participation rates, one on the legal situation in 2000—taking into account the 2000 reform legislation and also including, between 2019 and 2033, the implementation of the already enacted increase in the female statutory and early retirement age up to the age limits applicable to men—and the low, medium, and high labor force participation scenarios specified by the Committee on Long-Term Pension Sustainability appointed by the Austrian government (see above).[12]

The main exercise here is to link the five labor force participation scenarios with four policy scenarios—one scenario assuming that the current system remains in force and three reform scenarios. The initial reform measure is the move from the current notional defined benefit (NDB) scheme to a unified NDC scheme at the beginning of 2005, involving a complete switch of all active contributors, the harmonization of contribution rates, a full recognition of accrued rights, and a full protection of pensions already in payment. We compare the replacement rates of the newly retired and the financial flows—contributions, expenditure, and current balance—under those two regimes. As the switch to a defined contribution scheme implies the reduction of the internal PAYG rate of return to a sustainable level and thereby leads to a reduction in the replacement rate (at a given retirement age), we also investigate the effects of a second, mandated fully funded pillar on the total replacement rate, evaluated under two additional policy scenarios: contribution rates to the funded pillar of 5 percent and 10 percent, respectively.

The civil servants' pension schemes (for which sufficient data are often not available) are not included in the simulations. We also assume that the current size of the civil servant force, measured by the age- and gender-specific shares in total population, remains at its current level. Thus, employment effects of any labor force expansion will affect only the private sector.

Objectives and structure of the next subsections are as follows: the next subsection introduces the input data determining the demographic structure of the pension system, age, and gender-specific information on contributors, beneficiaries, and length of service at retirement. It then describes how these data were generated and checked for consistency. The next subsections give a short overview of the underlying macroeconomic trends, the benefit calculation in PROST, and the trend in non-pensions-related expenditure. The fifth subsection deals in more detail with the multipillar reform specifications and the final subsection presents the results of the simulations. Additional details about the simulations can be found in the annex.

Contributors, Beneficiaries, and Length of Service

The labor force scenario determines the age- and gender-specific numbers of contributors. *Nominal contributors* account for all those to whom pension rights are accruing in a particular year. Not all of those people are actually employed and do actually contribute to the pension system. Some are, as described above, exempt and receive contribution credit for periods of nonemployment, as when they are recipients of unemployment benefits, sickness benefits, or maternity allowance, or are military servants or persons serving in alternative civilian service. Finally, up to four years per child are credited as periods of child-raising. To get the number of *effective contributors*, who actually pay pension contributions, PROST simulations require input of age- and gender-specific exemption rates. We apply the age- and gender-specific exemption rates of 2000 for the whole time period until 2050.

Data on contributors have to be consistent with age- and gender-specific input data on old-age pensioners and disabled persons—that is, with the number of eventual retirees in the cohort and the length of service they claim at retirement. Data on length of service at retirement are used, in the case of old-age benefits, in the PROST benefit formula, as described below. PROST adjusts input data on the number of old-age pensioners in order to ensure that the total length of service accrued by a cohort is equal to the total length of service claimed by the cohort at retirement. To avoid an adjustment of retirees beyond what would be consistent with the underlying scenario, input data for the length of service were derived from given data on contributors and retirees for each cohort by a separate procedure. Further details can be found in the annex.

The starting point of the simulations and the base case is the *status-quo scenario,* in which the age- and gender-specific shares of nominal contributors in the population remain constant at the year 2000 level. Flows of old-age pensioners and disabled persons over the simulation horizon are principally based on the flows, as a percentage of the age- and gender-specific population, observed at the beginning of the simulation horizon. These flows were then adapted in such a way that, over the whole simulation horizon, the stock of pensioners and disabled persons has, as a share of the age- and gender-specific population, a peak that is consistent with the peak in the nominal contributors. Finally, the age and gender profile of the average length of service at retirement was derived from the data on contributors and retirees. Input data on length of service by age and gender in 2000 are based on a random sample provided by the Austrian ministry of social affairs and generations.

The *scenario 2000 legal situation* takes into account the increase of the early retirement age from 60 to 61.5 for men and from 55 to 56.5 for women between 2000 and 2003 and, between 2019 and 2033, the increase in the female statutory and early retirement age up to the age limits applicable to men (65 and 61.5, respectively). People who would have retired under the base case and are now denied that possibility were to some extent assumed to claim disability; we used the available pension entry data, as far as the 2000 reform is concerned, and assumed, as far as the harmonization of retirement ages is concerned, a share of 10 percent in the case of men and a share of 30 percent in the case of women. This leads, after the harmonization process, to a gender convergence in the age-specific population shares of disabled persons. The rest of those prevented from retiring were not completely assumed to enter the labor force and become nominal contributors: a significant number of new retirees at the early retirement age are moving from out of the labor force into retirement and are therefore not likely to enter the labor force simply because this age limit is raised. Finally, again the age-and-gender profile of the average length of service at retirement was derived from the data on contributors and retirees.

In the remaining scenarios—*the low, the medium, and the high participation scenario* specified by the Committee on Long-Term Pension Sustainability—the labor force increases are translated into additional numbers of nominal contributors. We take into account, however, that these additional contributors will not necessarily imply a one-to-one reduction in the stock of pension recipients; some of them will be mobilized from out of the labor force. Furthermore, the substantial increases of female participation rates will also lead to additional pension claims of women who would not have satisfied the minimum contribution requirement and would not have qualified for a pension in the base case. Again, length-of-service data were derived from the data on contributors and retirees.

The number of recipients of survivor and orphan benefits is taken from the recent long-term report of the committee. They do not depend on the labor force participation scenario.

Macroeconomic Trends

The annual rate of labor productivity growth is set at 1.8 percent, the average value in recent years. Real wage growth is linked to productivity growth, which implies that the wage income share in GDP remains at its level at the beginning of the simulation horizon and GDP growth equals wage sum growth. We also maintain current age and income profiles and current income differentials between men and women. Finally, we maintain the age- and gender-specific unemployment rates of 2000 for the whole time period until 2050. The real interest rate is set at 3 percent, and the long-term inflation forecast at 1.7 percent.

Pension Benefits

PROST offers the opportunity to provide input for the average survivor and the average orphan replacement rates, which are defined as the average survivor benefit and the average orphan benefit as ratios of the average covered earnings, for the base year, the end year, and any year in between. We take into account the 2000 pension reform. In Austria, survivor benefits depend on the relative lifetime incomes of spouses. Until 2000, the pension of a widow or a widower was, depending on the income gap between spouses during their active working lives, 40 to 60 percent of the deceased spouse's (actual or hypothetical) pension entitlement. The 2000 reform abolished the 40 percent floor. If the assessment basis of the surviving spouse is more than 2.5 times higher than that of the deceased, that spouse's pension is now 0. We take account of the reduction of the average survivor replacement rate in 2001 due to this reform. Furthermore, because increasing participation rates of women lead to additional and higher pension claims on their own behalf and reduce income gaps between spouses, we adjust the average survivor replacement rate according to the increase in women's own pension claims.

For new old-age pensioners and new disabled persons, replacement rates in the base year, the end year, and any year in between, again in terms of the average covered earnings, can even be specified by age and gender. Data on the average new old-age pension and the average disability benefit in 2000 by age and gender are available from a sample provided by the Austrian ministry of social affairs and generations. We use these data for the simulation of disability benefits and take into account the fact that the average disabled person's replacement rate will also be determined by people who would have been old-age pensioners under the base case, but who claim disability in one of the other scenarios.

For old-age benefits, PROST offers also the use of a benefit formula that automatically, year by year, calculates old-age pension benefits, based on given input data on required years of service, length of service at retirement, the incremental replacement rate, the maximum replacement rate, actuarial deductions for early retirement, the assessment period, indexation of earnings included in the assessment base, and minimum benefits.[13] Finally, the Austrian system of pension indexation had to be implemented into the simulation by iteration.

Other Expenditures

Non-pensions-related expenditures are assumed to grow in line with GDP—that is, other pension fund expenses as a percent of GDP remain at the level observed at the beginning of the simulation horizon, which is 0.9 percent.

Multipillar Reform Specifications

The multipillar reform specifications required for the simulation comprise important assumptions about the NDC and the fully funded pillar. As mentioned above, all contributors, without any exemption, are assumed to be transferred to the new system at the beginning of 2005, the assumed time of reform. Pensions already in payment are 100 percent protected and pension rights accumulated by those not yet retired are fully recognized and translated into notional initial capital. The pension entrants of the reform year receive the replacement rate promised under the old law, and accrued rights of still-active contributors are calculated as a pro rata proportion of the pension that could have been expected under the old law, depending on the number of working years spent in the old system. The PAYG contribution rates are harmonized at the current level in the blue- and white-collar workers' scheme, 22.8 percent of gross wage income, which yields a harmonized rate of about 20.25 percent if the contribution base is grossed up by the part of the contribution paid by the employer (12.55 percent). Furthermore, we introduce a pensioner contribution rate of 2.3 percent on pension payments.[14] As the notional interest rate we choose the growth rate of the covered wage bill, which incorporates changes in the number of contributors and most closely corresponds to changes in revenue. For annuitization we use unisex mortality tables. Pension benefits (also pensions from the old system) are indexed for inflation, and the inflation rate is also the annuitization interest rate—that is, the only interest being paid on the balance postretirement is what has been specified as indexation. The reform is assumed to decrease or increase PAYG benefits to disabled persons, survivors, and orphans by the same proportion as PAYG old-age benefits. Finally, as in the NDB simulation, non-pensions-related expenditures grow in line with GDP.

The long-term nominal rate of return in the funded pillar is 4.75 percent (based on the interest and inflation forecast), which is a relatively modest assumption. For annuitization we use again unisex mortality tables, and annuities are indexed to inflation.

Results

Tables 20.1 through 20.5 present the main results of the simulations. The projected numbers of contributors and beneficiaries in the status quo labor force participation scenario show the crucial effect of the expected aging process on the demographic structure of the population. At the beginning of the simulation horizon, about 49.1 percent of men and about 39 percent of women are nominal contributors. Under the current participation rates, population aging would translate into a decline in the population share of contributors down to 40.5 percent and 31.9 percent, respectively. Pension recipients, on the other hand, rise considerably, from 17.2 to 30 percent of the population in the case of men and from 18.0 to 31 in the case of women. The increase of survivor benefits is less remarkable; orphan benefit recipients will be slightly reduced.

An increasing labor force participation, however, can have a powerful impact on the demographic structure of the pension system. Under the most optimistic participation scenario, the ratio of contributors in the male population could almost be held at the current level and the ratio of female contributors could even be raised close to the same level. Accordingly, the ratio of old-age and disability pensioners in the population would be at about 24 percent for both men and women, which is considerably lower than they would be in the worst case. This would imply, however, a substantial increase of the average retirement age, even above 65, the current statutory retirement age for men.

The tables also present, in terms of the economywide average contribution base, projected average replacement rates of new old-age pensioners in the current pension system and in a multipillar system over the simulation horizon to 2050, based on the different labor force participation scenarios. According to the base-case projection, replacement rates of new old-age pensioners in 2005 would be about 79 percent in the case of men and 47 percent in the case of women. Until 2050, the average replacement rate of newly retired men would remain roughly at the current level and female replacement rates would go slightly up, to 50.5 percent. In the 2000 legal situation scenario, the average replacement rate of male retirees would grow slightly above the current level and female replacement rates would increase to approximately 57 percent.

Under the same labor force participation scenario, a multipillar reform as described above would, until 2050, reduce replacement rates in the first pillar to about 41 percent of

Figure 20.2a. Replacement Rate, NDC Pillar

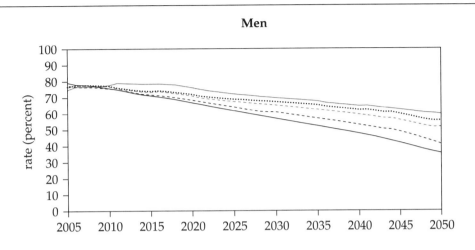

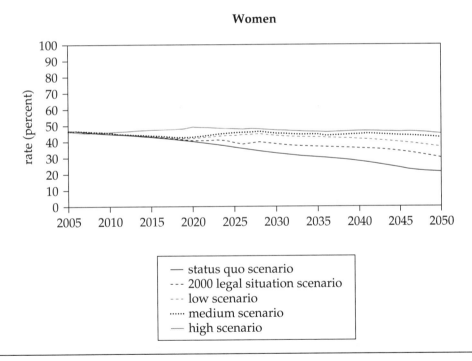

Source: Authors' calculations.

Note: 0 = status quo scenario; 2 = 2000 legal situation scenario; L = low scenario; M = medium scenario; H = high scenario.

Table 20.1. Status Quo Scenario

	2000	2005	2010	2015	2020	2025	2030	2035	2040	2045	2050
Men											
Nominal contributors	49.1%	48.5%	47.9%	47.0%	45.2%	43.2%	41.7%	41.1%	40.9%	40.7%	40.5%
Old age pensioners and disabled	17.2%	18.9%	20.5%	22.0%	23.9%	26.1%	28.0%	29.1%	29.6%	29.9%	30.0%
Survivors	1.0%	1.0%	1.1%	1.2%	1.3%	1.3%	1.4%	1.5%	1.5%	1.5%	1.5%
Average retirement age		60.8	60.7	60.7	60.6	60.7	61.0	61.1	60.9	60.9	60.9
Average length of service		38.5	38.9	38.6	38.8	38.6	38.1	37.8	38.0	38.0	37.9
Women											
Nominal contributors	39.0%	38.8%	38.6%	37.8%	36.2%	34.3%	33.1%	32.7%	32.4%	32.2%	31.9%
Old age pensioners and disabled	18.0%	19.8%	21.3%	23.0%	25.1%	27.3%	29.0%	29.8%	30.4%	30.8%	31.0%
Survivors	10.6%	10.7%	10.9%	11.1%	11.4%	11.9%	12.4%	12.8%	13.0%	13.1%	12.9%
Average retirement age		58.0	57.9	57.8	57.8	58.0	58.2	58.2	58.1	58.1	58.1
Average length of service		33.7	34.1	34.9	35.3	35.4	35.5	36.1	36.8	37.3	37.8
Orphans	0.6%	0.6%	0.6%	0.6%	0.6%	0.6%	0.6%	0.6%	0.6%	0.6%	0.6%
Average replacement rate of new male old age pensioners											
NDB (current scheme)		79.1%	79.4%	78.7%	78.6%	77.8%	77.5%	78.0%	78.8%	78.8%	78.4%
NDC		79.1%	75.6%	71.1%	66.7%	61.7%	56.8%	52.3%	47.6%	41.8%	35.4%
NDC + FF 5%		79.1%	77.2%	74.1%	71.3%	67.8%	64.5%	61.3%	58.0%	53.2%	47.5%
NDC + FF 10%		79.1%	78.7%	77.2%	75.9%	74.0%	72.1%	70.3%	68.4%	64.7%	59.6%

Average replacement rate of new female old age pensioners

NDB (current scheme)	46.8%	47.2%	48.2%	48.6%	48.0%	47.0%	47.8%	49.1%	49.8%	50.4%
NDC	46.8%	44.6%	42.8%	40.1%	36.5%	32.9%	30.5%	27.9%	23.9%	21.3%
NDC + FF 5%	46.8%	45.6%	44.7%	43.0%	40.4%	37.8%	36.4%	34.9%	31.6%	29.2%
NDC + FF 10%	46.8%	46.5%	46.6%	46.0%	44.3%	42.6%	42.4%	42.0%	39.3%	37.1%

NDB (current scheme) financial flows

Employer and employee contributions	7.4%	7.5%	7.5%	7.5%	7.5%	7.5%	7.5%	7.5%	7.4%	7.4%	7.4%
Total contributions	7.4%	7.5%	7.5%	7.5%	7.5%	7.5%	7.5%	7.5%	7.4%	7.4%	7.4%
Old age and disability pensions	8.2%	8.8%	9.6%	10.5%	12.0%	13.7%	15.2%	15.9%	16.2%	16.5%	16.7%
Survivor and orphan pensions	1.7%	1.6%	1.7%	1.7%	1.8%	2.0%	2.1%	2.1%	2.2%	2.2%	2.1%
Total expenditure	10.8%	11.4%	12.2%	13.2%	14.7%	16.6%	18.2%	19.0%	19.3%	19.6%	19.7%
Current balance	–3.4%	–3.9%	–4.7%	–5.7%	–7.3%	–9.1%	–10.7%	–11.5%	–11.9%	–12.2%	–12.3%

NDC financial flows

Employer and employee contributions	7.7%	7.7%	7.7%	7.7%	7.7%	7.7%	7.7%	7.6%	7.6%	7.6%
Total contributions	7.9%	7.9%	7.9%	8.0%	8.0%	8.0%	8.0%	8.0%	7.9%	7.9%
Old age and disability pensions	8.8%	9.4%	10.0%	11.0%	12.1%	12.7%	12.4%	11.8%	11.0%	10.1%
Survivor and orphan pensions	1.6%	1.6%	1.6%	1.7%	1.7%	1.7%	1.7%	1.6%	1.5%	1.3%
Total expenditure	11.4%	12.0%	12.6%	13.6%	14.8%	15.4%	15.1%	14.3%	13.4%	12.3%
Current balance	–3.5%	–4.0%	–4.7%	–5.6%	–6.8%	–7.4%	–7.1%	–6.4%	–5.5%	–4.4%

Source: Authors' calculations.

Note: Contributors and beneficiaries in percent of population; contributions and benefits as percent of GDP.

Table 20.2. 2000 Legal Situation Scenario

	2000	2005	2010	2015	2020	2025	2030	2035	2040	2045	2050
Men											
Nominal contributors	49.1%	48.9%	48.4%	47.4%	45.8%	43.9%	42.6%	42.0%	41.8%	41.6%	41.4%
Old age pensioners and disabled	17.2%	18.4%	19.9%	21.5%	23.2%	25.3%	26.8%	28.1%	28.6%	28.9%	29.0%
Survivors	1.0%	1.0%	1.1%	1.2%	1.3%	1.3%	1.4%	1.5%	1.5%	1.5%	1.5%
Average retirement age		61.9	61.8	61.9	61.8	62.0	62.7	62.8	62.8	63.0	62.8
Average length of service		37.6	38.6	38.4	39.0	39.0	38.4	38.3	38.8	38.8	39.4
Women											
Nominal contributors	39.0%	39.0%	38.8%	38.1%	36.9%	35.9%	35.2%	34.8%	34.6%	34.3%	34.1%
Old age pensioners and disabled	18.0%	19.5%	21.1%	22.7%	24.4%	25.5%	26.4%	27.5%	28.1%	28.5%	28.6%
Survivors	10.6%	10.7%	10.9%	11.1%	11.4%	11.9%	12.4%	12.8%	13.0%	13.1%	12.9%
Average retirement age		58.4	58.4	58.2	59.6	60.9	62.2	62.5	62.6	62.5	62.5
Average length of service		33.9	34.4	35.4	34.4	34.7	35.7	36.6	38.2	39.9	41.4
Orphans	0.6%	0.6%	0.6%	0.6%	0.6%	0.6%	0.6%	0.6%	0.6%	0.6%	0.6%
Average replacement rate of new male old age pensioners											
NDB (current scheme)		77.4%	78.9%	78.6%	79.3%	78.7%	78.7%	79.4%	80.8%	81.3%	81.3%
NDC		77.4%	75.5%	71.6%	68.3%	64.0%	60.7%	56.8%	52.9%	48.7%	41.0%
NDC + FF 5%		77.4%	77.0%	74.7%	73.0%	70.3%	68.7%	66.3%	63.8%	61.0%	53.9%
NDC + FF 10%		77.4%	78.5%	77.8%	77.7%	76.6%	76.6%	75.7%	74.6%	73.3%	66.7%

Average replacement rate of new female old age pensioners

NDB (current scheme)		46.6%	47.3%	48.5%	48.9%	49.7%	49.9%	49.7%	52.4%	54.8%	56.9%
NDC		46.6%	44.7%	43.0%	40.6%	39.4%	38.6%	36.9%	35.9%	34.0%	30.0%
NDC + FF 5%		46.6%	45.6%	44.9%	43.4%	43.2%	43.8%	43.3%	43.6%	43.1%	39.7%
NDC + FF 10%		46.6%	46.5%	46.8%	46.1%	47.1%	49.0%	49.7%	51.4%	52.1%	49.4%

NDB (current scheme) financial flows

Employer and employee contributions	7.4%	7.5%	7.5%	7.5%	7.5%	7.4%	7.5%	7.5%	7.5%	7.4%
Total contributions	7.4%	7.5%	7.5%	7.5%	7.5%	7.4%	7.5%	7.5%	7.5%	7.4%
Old age and disability pensions	8.2%	9.2%	10.2%	11.4%	12.5%	13.4%	14.3%	14.6%	14.8%	15.0%
Survivor and orphan pensions	1.7%	1.6%	1.6%	1.6%	1.7%	1.7%	1.7%	1.7%	1.6%	1.5%
Total expenditure	10.8%	11.8%	12.7%	14.0%	15.1%	16.0%	16.9%	17.2%	17.4%	17.4%
Current balance	–3.4%	–4.3%	–5.2%	–6.5%	–7.7%	–8.6%	–9.4%	–9.7%	–9.9%	–9.9%

NDC financial flows

Employer and employee contributions	7.7%	7.7%	7.7%	7.7%	7.7%	7.6%	7.7%	7.7%	7.7%	7.6%
Total contributions	7.9%	7.9%	8.0%	8.0%	8.0%	7.9%	8.0%	8.0%	7.9%	7.9%
Old age and disability pensions	8.5%	9.1%	9.7%	10.6%	11.4%	11.7%	11.9%	11.5%	11.1%	10.4%
Survivor and orphan pensions	1.6%	1.6%	1.5%	1.5%	1.5%	1.4%	1.5%	1.3%	1.2%	1.0%
Total expenditure	11.0%	11.6%	12.2%	13.0%	13.8%	14.1%	14.2%	13.8%	13.2%	12.4%
Current balance	–3.1%	–3.6%	–4.2%	–5.0%	–5.8%	–6.2%	–6.2%	–5.8%	–5.2%	–4.4%

Source: Authors' calculations.

Note: Contributors and beneficiaries in percent of population; contributions and benefits as percent of GDP.

Table 20.3. Low Labor Force Participation Scenario

	2000	2005	2010	2015	2020	2025	2030	2035	2040	2045	2050
Men											
Nominal contributors	49.1%	49.8%	49.5%	49.1%	48.1%	46.7%	45.3%	44.7%	44.5%	44.5%	44.5%
Old age pensioners and disabled	17.2%	18.2%	19.6%	20.7%	21.9%	23.6%	25.5%	26.8%	27.3%	27.6%	27.7%
Survivors	1.0%	1.0%	1.1%	1.2%	1.3%	1.3%	1.4%	1.5%	1.5%	1.5%	1.5%
Average retirement age		62.3	61.9	62.4	62.5	63.3	63.7	64.0	64.2	64.4	64.4
Average length of service		36.7	39.1	38.3	38.8	38.2	38.6	39.0	39.8	40.4	41.3
Women											
Nominal contributors	39.0%	40.3%	41.0%	40.7%	39.9%	39.1%	38.4%	38.2%	38.0%	38.0%	37.9%
Old age pensioners and disabled	18.0%	19.2%	20.3%	21.6%	23.1%	23.9%	25.3%	26.5%	27.3%	27.9%	28.4%
Survivors	10.6%	10.7%	10.9%	11.1%	11.4%	11.9%	12.4%	12.8%	13.0%	13.1%	12.9%
Average retirement age		58.4	57.9	58.7	61.3	63.0	64.5	64.9	64.9	64.8	64.9
Average length of service		33.8	35.2	35.1	33.4	36.0	37.8	38.6	39.6	40.9	41.9
Orphans	0.6%	0.6%	0.6%	0.6%	0.6%	0.6%	0.6%	0.6%	0.6%	0.6%	0.6%
Average replacement rate of new male old age pensioners											
NDB (current scheme)		76.4%	80.1%	79.5%	80.2%	79.3%	80.3%	81.9%	83.8%	85.5%	85.9%
NDC		76.4%	76.8%	73.2%	70.9%	67.4%	65.0%	62.2%	59.2%	55.7%	51.6%
NDC + FF 5%		76.4%	78.4%	76.5%	76.0%	74.1%	73.6%	72.4%	71.0%	69.1%	66.5%
NDC + FF 10%		76.4%	80.0%	79.8%	81.1%	80.8%	82.1%	82.5%	82.7%	82.4%	81.3%

Average replacement rate of new female old age pensioners

NDB (current scheme)	46.2%	47.9%	47.8%	48.1%	51.7%	53.3%	54.1%	55.8%	57.2%	57.9%
NDC	46.2%	45.5%	43.3%	41.9%	43.7%	43.8%	42.8%	41.6%	39.6%	36.6%
NDC + FF 5%	46.2%	46.6%	45.5%	44.9%	48.1%	49.5%	49.8%	50.0%	49.3%	47.2%
NDC + FF 10%	46.2%	47.6%	47.6%	48.0%	52.5%	55.2%	56.8%	58.3%	58.9%	57.8%
NDB (current scheme) financial flows										
Employer and employee contributions	7.4%	7.6%	7.6%	7.6%	7.6%	7.6%	7.6%	7.5%	7.5%	7.5%
Total contributions	7.4%	7.6%	7.6%	7.6%	7.6%	7.6%	7.6%	7.5%	7.5%	7.5%
Old age and disability pensions	8.2%	8.7%	9.3%	10.1%	10.9%	11.9%	12.7%	13.0%	13.2%	13.3%
Survivor and orphan pensions	1.7%	1.5%	1.5%	1.5%	1.5%	1.6%	1.5%	1.5%	1.4%	1.3%
Total expenditure	10.8%	11.1%	11.7%	12.5%	13.4%	14.4%	15.1%	15.4%	15.5%	15.6%
Current balance	-3.4%	-3.6%	-4.2%	-5.0%	-5.8%	-6.9%	-7.6%	-7.9%	-8.0%	-8.1%
NDC financial flows										
Employer and employee contributions	7.7%	7.8%	7.8%	7.8%	7.8%	7.8%	7.8%	7.7%	7.7%	7.7%
Total contributions	8.0%	8.0%	8.0%	8.0%	8.0%	8.1%	8.0%	8.0%	8.0%	8.0%
Old age and disability pensions	8.2%	8.6%	8.9%	9.5%	10.2%	10.9%	11.2%	11.1%	10.8%	10.3%
Survivor and orphan pensions	1.6%	1.5%	1.4%	1.4%	1.4%	1.4%	1.4%	1.3%	1.1%	1.0%
Total expenditure	10.7%	11.0%	11.3%	11.8%	12.5%	13.3%	13.6%	13.3%	12.9%	12.3%
Current balance	-2.8%	-3.0%	-3.3%	-3.8%	-4.5%	-5.2%	-5.5%	-5.3%	-4.9%	-4.3%

Source: Authors' calculations.

Note: Contributors and beneficiaries in percent of population; contributions and benefits as percent of GDP.

Table 20.4. Medium Labor Force Participation Scenario

	2000	2005	2010	2015	2020	2025	2030	2035	2040	2045	2050
Men											
Nominal contributors	49.1%	49.8%	49.5%	49.1%	48.2%	47.0%	46.1%	45.6%	45.6%	45.6%	45.7%
Old age pensioners and disabled	17.2%	18.2%	19.6%	20.7%	21.8%	23.3%	24.5%	25.9%	26.1%	26.4%	26.4%
Survivors	1.0%	1.0%	1.1%	1.2%	1.3%	1.3%	1.4%	1.5%	1.5%	1.5%	1.5%
Average retirement age		62.3	61.9	62.4	62.5	63.3	64.0	64.3	64.3	65.0	64.9
Average length of service		36.8	39.3	38.6	39.3	38.9	39.2	39.9	40.9	41.3	42.6
Women											
Nominal contributors	39.0%	40.4%	41.0%	41.1%	40.6%	39.9%	39.6%	39.7%	40.0%	40.2%	40.5%
Old age pensioners and disabled	18.0%	19.1%	20.3%	21.5%	22.6%	23.7%	24.6%	25.7%	25.9%	26.1%	26.3%
Survivors	10.6%	10.7%	10.9%	11.1%	11.4%	11.9%	12.4%	12.8%	13.0%	13.1%	12.9%
Average retirement age		58.5	58.0	58.8	60.9	63.1	63.9	64.9	65.7	66.1	66.4
Average length of service		33.7	35.1	35.0	34.1	36.9	39.5	40.6	41.2	42.7	44.2
Orphans	0.6%	0.6%	0.6%	0.6%	0.6%	0.6%	0.6%	0.6%	0.6%	0.6%	0.6%
Average replacement rate of new male old age pensioners											
NDB (current scheme)		76.6%	80.5%	80.1%	81.3%	80.9%	81.8%	83.7%	85.4%	86.2%	86.2%
NDC		76.6%	77.1%	73.8%	71.9%	68.8%	67.2%	65.2%	62.0%	59.6%	55.5%
NDC + FF 5%		76.6%	78.7%	77.1%	77.0%	75.6%	76.0%	75.7%	74.1%	73.5%	70.9%
NDC + FF 10%		76.6%	80.3%	80.3%	82.1%	82.5%	84.7%	86.2%	86.3%	87.4%	86.4%

Average replacement rate of new female old age pensioners

NDB (current scheme)	46.2%	46.2%	47.8%	48.0%	49.1%	53.5%	54.9%	55.0%	56.3%	58.0%	58.5%
NDC		46.2%	45.5%	43.6%	42.8%	45.5%	45.0%	44.5%	44.6%	43.8%	42.4%
NDC + FF 5%	46.2%	46.2%	46.5%	45.8%	45.9%	50.0%	50.9%	51.7%	53.4%	54.0%	54.0%
NDC + FF 10%	46.2%	46.2%	47.5%	47.9%	49.0%	54.5%	56.8%	59.0%	62.1%	64.2%	65.5%

NDB (current scheme) financial flows

Employer and employee contributions	7.4%	7.6%	7.6%	7.6%	7.6%	7.6%	7.5%	7.5%	7.5%	7.5%	7.5%
Total contributions	7.4%	7.6%	7.6%	7.6%	7.6%	7.6%	7.5%	7.5%	7.5%	7.5%	7.5%
Old age and disability pensions	8.2%	8.2%	8.7%	9.2%	9.9%	10.6%	11.2%	11.8%	11.9%	11.9%	11.9%
Survivor and orphan pensions	1.7%	1.6%	1.5%	1.5%	1.5%	1.5%	1.5%	1.4%	1.4%	1.3%	1.2%
Total expenditure	10.8%	10.7%	11.1%	11.6%	12.3%	13.1%	13.7%	14.2%	14.2%	14.1%	14.0%
Current balance	−3.4%	−3.1%	−3.6%	−4.1%	−4.7%	−5.5%	−6.1%	−6.7%	−6.7%	−6.6%	−6.5%

NDC financial flows

Employer and employee contributions	7.7%	7.7%	7.8%	7.8%	7.8%	7.8%	7.7%	7.7%	7.7%	7.7%	7.7%
Total contributions	8.0%	8.0%	8.0%	8.0%	8.0%	8.0%	8.0%	8.0%	8.0%	8.0%	7.9%
Old age and disability pensions	8.2%	8.2%	8.6%	8.9%	9.3%	9.9%	10.3%	10.6%	10.4%	10.1%	9.8%
Survivor and orphan pensions	1.6%	1.6%	1.5%	1.4%	1.4%	1.4%	1.4%	1.3%	1.2%	1.1%	1.0%
Total expenditure	10.7%	10.7%	11.0%	11.2%	11.6%	12.2%	12.6%	12.9%	12.5%	12.1%	11.6%
Current balance	−2.7%	−2.7%	−3.0%	−3.2%	−3.6%	−4.2%	−4.6%	−4.8%	−4.5%	−4.2%	−3.7%

Source: own calculations.

Note: Contributors and beneficiaries in percent of population; contributions and benefits as percent of GDP.

Table 20.5. High Labor Force Participation Scenario

	2000	2005	2010	2015	2020	2025	2030	2035	2040	2045	2050
Men											
Nominal contributors	49.1%	50.9%	52.0%	51.4%	50.6%	49.4%	48.2%	47.6%	47.7%	48.0%	48.2%
Old age pensioners and disabled	17.2%	17.3%	17.6%	18.8%	19.9%	21.5%	23.2%	24.5%	24.7%	24.7%	24.6%
Survivors	1.0%	1.0%	1.1%	1.2%	1.3%	1.3%	1.4%	1.5%	1.5%	1.5%	1.5%
Average retirement age		63.5	63.6	63.6	63.6	63.9	64.2	64.7	64.8	65.3	65.4
Average length of service		34.4	36.2	38.5	40.4	40.8	41.4	41.9	42.6	43.2	44.4
Women											
Nominal contributors	39.0%	41.5%	43.9%	44.7%	44.8%	44.5%	44.2%	44.3%	45.2%	46.2%	47.3%
Old age pensioners and disabled	18.0%	18.1%	18.0%	18.8%	19.5%	20.8%	22.0%	23.3%	23.6%	23.7%	23.9%
Survivors	10.6%	10.7%	10.9%	11.1%	11.4%	11.9%	12.4%	12.8%	13.0%	13.1%	12.9%
Average retirement age		59.0	61.1	62.0	64.6	64.8	65.2	65.6	66.3	66.4	66.4
Average length of service		34.5	33.2	35.2	36.9	38.2	39.9	41.4	42.6	44.4	46.1
Orphans	0.6%	0.6%	0.6%	0.6%	0.6%	0.6%	0.6%	0.6%	0.6%	0.6%	0.6%
Average replacement rate of new male old age pensioners											
NDB (current scheme)		74.7%	79.6%	83.4%	84.3%	83.0%	83.4%	84.5%	85.3%	86.2%	86.3%
NDC		74.7%	77.6%	78.4%	76.0%	72.1%	69.6%	67.6%	64.5%	62.2%	59.5%
NDC + FF 5%		74.7%	79.4%	82.0%	81.4%	79.2%	78.6%	78.6%	77.1%	76.5%	75.5%
NDC + FF 10%		74.7%	81.2%	85.6%	86.8%	86.4%	87.7%	89.5%	89.6%	90.7%	91.5%

Average replacement rate of new female old age pensioners

NDB (current scheme)	46.2%	46.8%	50.0%	53.0%	53.7%	54.5%	54.9%	56.3%	57.5%	58.0%
NDC	46.2%	45.7%	47.2%	49.2%	47.9%	47.1%	46.1%	46.6%	46.1%	44.8%
NDC + FF 5%	46.2%	46.9%	49.6%	52.9%	52.8%	53.3%	53.7%	55.6%	56.6%	56.7%
NDC + FF 10%	46.2%	48.2%	52.0%	56.5%	57.7%	59.5%	61.2%	64.7%	67.1%	68.6%
NDB (current scheme) financial flows										
Employer and employee contributions	7.4%	7.6%	7.6%	7.6%	7.6%	7.6%	7.6%	7.6%	7.6%	7.5%
Total contributions	7.4%	7.6%	7.6%	7.6%	7.6%	7.6%	7.6%	7.6%	7.6%	7.5%
Old age and disability pensions	8.2%	7.2%	7.6%	8.0%	8.7%	9.4%	9.9%	9.9%	9.8%	9.6%
Survivor and orphan pensions	1.7%	1.4%	1.4%	1.4%	1.4%	1.4%	1.3%	1.3%	1.2%	1.1%
Total expenditure	10.8%	9.6%	9.9%	10.3%	11.0%	11.7%	12.2%	12.1%	11.9%	11.6%
Current balance	−3.4%	−2.0%	−2.3%	−2.7%	−3.4%	−4.1%	−4.6%	−4.5%	−4.3%	−4.1%
NDC financial flows										
Employer and employee contributions	7.8%	7.8%	7.8%	7.8%	7.8%	7.8%	7.8%	7.8%	7.7%	7.7%
Total contributions	8.0%	8.0%	8.0%	8.0%	8.0%	8.1%	8.0%	8.0%	8.0%	7.9%
Old age and disability pensions	7.5%	7.0%	7.4%	7.9%	8.6%	9.3%	9.8%	9.4%	9.1%	8.7%
Survivor and orphan pensions	1.5%	1.4%	1.4%	1.4%	1.4%	1.4%	1.3%	1.2%	1.1%	1.0%
Total expenditure	10.0%	9.3%	9.8%	10.2%	11.0%	11.7%	12.0%	11.6%	11.1%	10.6%
Current balance	−2.0%	−1.3%	−1.7%	−2.2%	−2.9%	−3.6%	−4.0%	−3.6%	−3.1%	−2.7%

Source: Authors' calculations.

Note: Contributors and beneficiaries in percent of population; contributions and benefits as percent of GDP.

the economywide average contribution base in the case of newly retired men and about 30 percent in the case of female retirees (see also figure 20.2a). This figure shows only that the internal rate of return of the current system is far from sustainable. Increasing the labor force participation, however, would also increase the NDC replacement rates, because faster wage bill growth implies a higher notional rate of return and every extra year of work means that another year's contributions will be added to the notional capital stock and there will be a year's less pension for it to finance. Replacement rates of new male retirees in 2050 would be about 51.5 percent under the low participation scenario, 55.5 percent under the medium participation scenario, and 59.5 percent under the high participation scenario. Nevertheless, even under a very optimistic labor force participation scenario, a transformation of the current PAYG system into an NDC pillar would leave a certain gap to be filled. The projections for women are, because of the already enacted increase of the retirement age and the continuing trend of higher female labor force participation, a little more favorable: NDC replacement rates for women in 2050 would be 36.5 percent, 42.5 percent, or 45 percent under the low, medium and high scenarios, respectively. This means that under a very optimistic scenario a contribution defined PAYG pillar could maintain current female replacement rates.

To provide a sense of the total replacement rate possible with a multipillar model, we have to add the annuity supplied under the second pillar, however. What would be sufficient second pillar contribution rates if the overall multipillar replacement rates should be close to the current rates? Tables 20.1–20.5 also take into account, assuming different contribution rates, projected replacement rates in a fully funded pillar under the different participation scenarios (see also figure 20.2b). A contribution rate of 5 percent would, depending on the labor participation trend, yield a replacement rate of up to 16 percent for male and up to 12 percent for female contributors; a contribution rate of 10 percent would yield replacement rates between 24 and 32 percent and between 16 and 24 percent, respectively.

This means that, if the reform should approximately maintain current replacement rates of new male pensioners, a contribution rate of 5 percent would be the lower limit, even under the most optimistic scenario. A contribution rate of 10 percent would be sufficient even under the low participation scenario. A second pillar contribution rate of 10 percent would be sufficient to maintain replacement rates of new female retirees even under the 2000 legal situation scenario, and a contribution rate of 5 percent would be sufficient under the low scenario.

It should also be kept in mind that a reform along the lines outlined here would considerably improve actuarial fairness and thereby improve work incentives for the elderly, which means that a substantial increase of labor force participation is not unrealistic. We conclude that a contribution rate of 5 percent could already be a major step toward a sufficient second pillar retirement income, leaving still some reasonable room for the third, voluntary pension pillar.

The reform would also curb expenditure growth. Under the base-case scenario, overall expenditures of the PAYG system (equalization supplements included) would rise from 10.8 percent to 19.7 percent of GDP in 2050 (see also figure 20.3). Even if we take into account the 2000 legal situation, the expenditure-to-GDP ratio would rise up to 17.4 percent and the expenditure increase would still be substantial under the remaining scenarios, implying ratios of expenditure to GDP of 15.6 percent, 14 percent, and 11.6 percent, respectively. Overall, first pillar expenditure per GDP in a multipillar model would be significantly lower. In the worst-case scenario, the expenditure-to-GDP ratio would peak in 2030 at 15.4 percent; in the most optimistic scenario, the maximum expenditure-to-GDP ratio projected for the mid-2030s would be 12 percent. At the end of the simulation period,

Figure 20.2b Total Replacement Rate, NDC Pillar with Fully Funded Pillar (5 percent contribution rate)

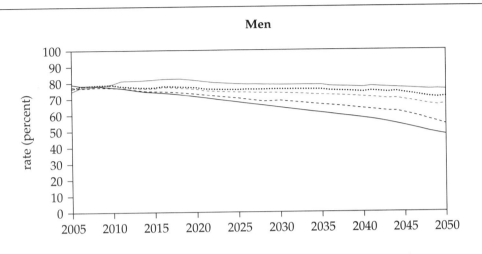

Men

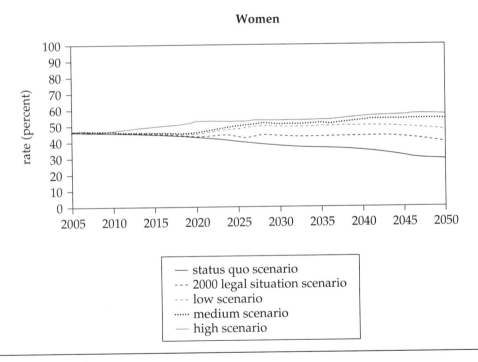

Women

— status quo scenario
--- 2000 legal situation scenario
--- low scenario
······ medium scenario
— high scenario

Source: Authors' calculations.

Note: 0 = status quo scenario; 2 = 2000 legal situation scenario; L = low scenario; M = medium scenario; H = high scenario.

Figure 20.3. Expenditure As percent of GDP, NDB versus NDC Pillar

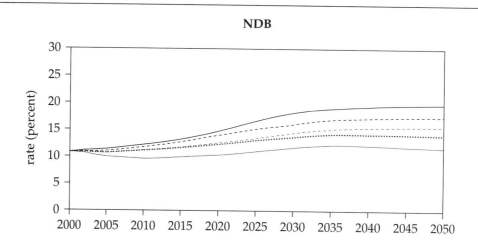

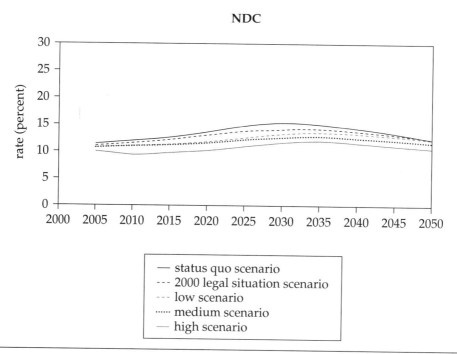

Source: Authors' calculations.

Note: 0 = status quo scenario; 2 = 2000 legal situation scenario; L = low scenario; M = medium scenario; H = high scenario.

total expenditure would in no scenario be above 12.5 percent of GDP; in the most optimistic scenario, expenditure per GDP would be roughly at the same level as in 2000, 10.6 percent.

These results would imply a significant reduction in the fiscal deficit of the pension system and a considerable relief for future federal budgets. The current balance in the mono-pillar system, defined here as total expenditure less pension contributions, would climb until 2050 from 3.5 up to 12.3 percent of GDP in the status quo scenario. Even in the more optimistic scenarios the increase would be substantial, leading to balance-to-GDP ratios of 9.9 percent in the 2000 legal situation scenario, 8.1 percent in the low participation scenario, and 6.5 percent in the medium scenario. Even in the worst case, the current balance of the NDC pillar would peak below 7.5 percent of GDP. In 2050, balance-to-GDP ratios would be below 3 percent in the most optimistic scenario, actually lower than in 2000, and in the remaining scenarios it would be between 3.75 and 4.5 percent.

Conclusions

The Austrian public pension system stands out for its nearly universal coverage of the Austrian population and its rather generous pension benefits. However, the Austrian system faces a number of challenges in the future. The heterogeneous pension provisions for different types of employees and the self-employed hamper labor mobility and erode the potential for strong economic growth. The actual incentives of the pension system have resulted in a situation where Austria exhibits an extraordinary low labor force participation rate of persons older than 55. The most important challenge, however, is to ensure the long-term financial stability of the public pension system. We have referred to existing studies that point to sizeable deficits of the public pension system in the future. As a consequence, the need for reform is acknowledged in the political and public debate and major steps have been undertaken by the Austrian government in recent years. However, a comprehensive and persuasive reform of the Austrian pension system is still out, even after the most recent reform efforts.

In this chapter we have used the World Bank's PROST model to calculate the development of key variables of the Austrian pension system under different labor force scenarios for the period 2000–50. The central assumptions adopted for the different scenarios are similar to those used by the Austrian Committee on Long-Term Pension Sustainability. In addition, a number of consistency checks have been conducted. Results have been calculated for different labor market scenarios for both the actual PAYG pension system as well as for our favored reform model, a model that implies an immediate switch to a multipillar pension system with an NDC pillar.

Our results verify the expected high fiscal burden that is inherent in the current Austrian pension system. We find that even in the most optimistic (and very implausible) labor market scenario, the deficit of the actual pension system would increase significantly until 2050.

The introduction of an NDC pension system would lead to a significant improvement of the fiscal balance of the Austrian pension system, particularly if labor market participation rates of the elderly would increase in the future. As we have pointed out, providing adequate incentives to postpone retirement is a necessary precondition for higher activity rates. In this respect an NDC scheme has to play an important role as it generates a close link between benefits and contributions.

Our results indicate, however, that overall multipillar contribution rates would have to be increased, even under rather optimistic labor market assumptions, if in the medium to long term replacement rates are to be kept at current levels. The introduction of a fully funded mandatory second pillar could play a prominent role in this respect. According to our calculations, additional contributions to this second pillar in the range of 5 to 10 percent of the contribution base are required to safeguard acceptable benefit levels for future pension recipients. We conclude that a contribution rate of 5 percent could already be a major step toward a sufficient second pillar retirement income, leaving still some reasonable room for the third, voluntary pension pillar.

Annex 20A. Assuring Consistency between Numbers of Pensioners and Length of Service

PROST assumes that all people who ever contributed to the pension system claim an old-age or disability pension before they reach the maximum age used in the simulation (95 in our case), unless they die. Contributors who do not satisfy a minimum contribution requirement and never qualify for a pension are consolidated into pensioners with a full pension—that is, contributors who do not satisfy a minimum contribution requirement are combined with those who qualify for a full pension, so that the number is a total of both. Based on this assumption, the total length of service accrued by a cohort has to equal to the total length of service claimed by the cohort at retirement. The equation below assumes that those who become disabled or die have accumulated the average cohort-specific length of service at that time. NC denotes the nominal contributors, NP denotes the new pensioners, ND denotes the newly disabled, CD denotes the contributors who died before retirement, los_rt denotes the average old-age pensioner's length of service at retirement, and los_av denotes the average accrued length of service among all the contributors in a cohort. All variables are indexed with age (a), with a_{work} being the youngest working age (14 in our case), time (t), and gender (g).

$$\sum_i NC(a_{work}+i,t+i,g) = \left(\begin{array}{l} \sum_i \left[ND(a_{work}+i,t+i,g)+CD(a_{work}+i,t+i,g) \right] \cdot los\_av(a_{work}+i,t+i,g)+ \\ \sum_i NP(a_{work}+i,t+i,g) \cdot los\_rt(a_{work}+i,t+i,g) \end{array} \right)$$

If the above equation does not hold for a cohort for which PROST has all the contribution and retirement data, it assumes that the user has made a mistake in the retirement data and adjusts the numbers of new old-age pensioners for that particular cohort.

This can lead, in a case where an unintended inconsistency between the length of service input data and the data on contributors is too great, to an adjustment of the input data on retirees that is beyond what the user would accept as part of the scenario he or she actually has in mind. To avoid an unintended major adjustment of this kind, input data for los_rt was derived from given data on contributors and retirees for each cohort by a separate procedure.

Notes

1. "Notional defined contribution" and "non-financial defined contribution" should be understood to have the same definition.

2. A detailed description of the Austrian system of retirement income provision and pension reforms in postwar Austria can be found in Hofmeister (1981), Hörndler and Wörister (1998), Koch and Thimann (1999), Wöss (2000), Hofer and Koman (2001), Part and Stefanits (2001), Holzmann and Heitzmann (2002), and Buczolich et al. (2003).

3. See Holzmann (2006).

4. See Hanika (2001).

5. In our analysis we refer to the general private sector pension schemes, which comprise schemes for dependent employees, self-employed, and farmers. We do not include the existing schemes for civil servants or special schemes such as those for notaries.

6. See Holzmann, Palacios, and Zviniene (2004) for alternative ways to calculate the implicit debt of a pension scheme.

7. The case of Austria is based on retirement due to disability at age 55, a very common pathway to retirement.

8. See Holzmann (2000a).

9. See, for example, Palmer (2000) for a description of the Swedish NDC system.

10. See Koman, Schuh, and Weber (forthcoming).

11. See Pagler, Stefanits, and Wirth (2001).

12. We do not take into account the measures of the 2003/04 reform that include the abolition of the early retirement option between 2004 and 2017.

13. Although, designed for worldwide use, this formula can hardly be perfectly suited for the benefit formula of an individual country, it seemed to us to be the preferable option, at least for technical reasons. Calculating old-age benefits by a separate calculation on the side and entering the results, such as the replacement rates for disabled persons, into the PROST pension input sheet would have absorbed additional space in an input sheet where there is already little space and would have required providing a less complete database on pension recipients, letting the program linearly interpolate to fill in the missing values. This, however, would have distorting effects that would overcompensate the benefits of a tailor-made pension formula.

14. The introduction of a pensioner contribution rate is primarily motivated by considerations of intergenerational fairness, given that pensions already in payment and accrued rights remain untouched by the reform. It can also be justified from a harmonization viewpoint, since retired civil servants already pay a contribution of 2.3 percent on their pension benefits.

References

Buczolich, G., B. Felderer, R. Koman, and U. Schuh. 2001. "Überlegungen zu einer Reform des österreichischen Pensionssystems." *Wirtschaftspolitische Blätter* 4 (2001): 378–83.

———. 2003. "Pension Reform in Austria." In *The Three Pillars of Wisdom? A Reader on Globalization, World Bank Pension Models and Welfare Society*, ed. A. Tausch, 201–22. New York: Nova Science Publishers, Inc.

Gauss, R. 2000. "Über die künftige Ausrichtung des österreichischen Pensionssystems." Mimeo, Vienna: Federal Ministry of Finance.

Gruber, J., and D. A. Wise. 1999. *Social Security and Retirement around the World*. Chicago and London: University of Chicago Press.

Hanika, A. 2001. "Bevölkerungsvorausschätzung 2001–2050 für Österreich und die Bundesländer." *Statistische Nachrichten* 9 (2001): 626–37.

Hörndler, M., and K. Wörister. 1998. "Altersversorgung." In *Soziales Österreich. Sicherungssysteme im Überblick*, ed. Bundesministerium für Arbeit, Gesundheit und Soziales, pp. 40–51. Vienna: Federal Ministry for Labour, Health and Social Affairs.

Hofer, H., and R. Koman. 2001. "Social Security and Retirement in Austria." Ludwig-Boltzmann-Institut zur Analyse wirtschaftspolitischer Aktivitäten, Research Memorandum no. 5/2001.

Hofmeister, H. 1981. "Ein Jahrhundert Sozialversicherung in Österreich." In *Schriftenreihe für Internationales und Vergleichendes Sozialrecht*, Band 6b, ed. P. Köhler and H. Zacher, 445–730, Berlin: Duncker und Humblot. Munich.

Holzmann, R. 1999. "On the Economic Benefits and Fiscal Requirements of Moving from Unfunded to Funded Pensions." In *The Welfare State in Europe: Challenges and Reforms*, ed. M. Buti, D. Franco, and L. R. Pench, 139–96. Cheltenham and Northampton: Edward Elgar.

———. 2000a. "The World Bank Approach to Pension Reform." *International Social Security Review* 53 (1): 11–34.

———. 2000b. "Skizze eines Pensionsreformkonzepts für Österreich." Mimeo, June 23, Harvard University.

———. 2006. "Toward a Coordinated Pension System in Europe: Rationale and Potential Structure." In *Pension Reform: Issues and Prospects for Non-Financial Defined Contribution (NDC) Schemes*, ed. R. Holzmann and E. Palmer, chapter 11. Washington, DC: World Bank.

Holzmann, R., and K. Heitzmann. 2002. "Die Reform der Alterssicherung in Österreich." In *Kompendium der österreichischen Finanzpolitik*, ed. E. Theurl, R. Sausgruber, and H. Winner, 507–42, Vienna: Springer Verlag.

Holzmann, R., R. Palacios, and A. Zviniene. 2004. "Implicit Pension Debt: Issues, Measurement and Scope in International Perspective." Social Protection Discussion Paper 0403, World Bank, Washington, DC.

Keuschnigg, C., M. Keuschnigg, R. Koman, E. Lüth, and B. Raffelhüschen. 2000a. "Restoring Generational Balance in Austria." In *Generational Accounting in Europe*, ed. European Commission, 149–61. European Economy No. 6 (2000).

———. 2000b. "Public Debt and Generational Balance in Austria." *Empirica* 27 (3): 225–52.

———. 2002. "Intergenerative Inzidenz der Österreichischen Finanzpolitik." In *Kompendium der österreichischen Finanzpolitik*, ed. E. Theurl, R. Sausgruber, and H. Winner, 263–95. Vienna: Springer Verlag.

Koch, M., and C. Thimann. 1999. "From Generosity to Sustainability: The Austrian Pension System and Options for its Reform." *Empirica* 26 (1): 21–38.

Koman, R., C. Keuschnigg, M. Keuschnigg, E. Lüth, and B. Raffelhüschen. 2000. "Intergeneratives Ungleichgewicht und Staatsverschuldung in Österreich." In *Österreich Neu. Herausforderungen nach der Wende*, ed. A. Payrleitner, 30–45. Vienna: Molden Verlag.

Koman, R., C. Keuschnigg, and E. Lüth. 2002. "Intergenerative Umverteilung, Pensionsreform und Budgetkonsolidierung in Österreich." In *Zukunftsperspektiven der Finanzierung öffentlicher Aufgaben*, ed. E. Theurl and E. Thöni, 209–47. Festschrift für Christian Smekal, Wien: Böhlau Verlag,.

Koman, R., U. Schuh, and A. Weber. Forthcoming. "The Austrian Severance Payments Reform." In *Mandated Severance Pay Programs: An International Perspective on Status, Concepts and Reforms*, ed. R. Holzmann and M. Vodopivec. Washington, DC: World Bank.

Kommission zur langfristigen Pensionssicherung. 2002. "Gutachten über die längerfristige Entwicklung der gesetzlichen Pensionsversicherung in den Jahren 2000 bis 2050." Vienna: Federal Ministry of Social Affairs and Gebnerations.

Pagler, F., H. Stefanits, and F. Wirth. 2001. "Vorschlag für ein leistungsorientiertes persönliches Pensionskonto." Mimeo, Vienna: Federal Ministry of Social Affairs and Generations.

Palmer, E. 2000. "The Swedish Pension Reform Model—Framework and Issues. World Bank's Pension Reform Primer." Social Protection Discussion Paper 0012, World Bank, Washington, DC.

Part, P., and H. Stefanits. 2001. "Austria: Public Pension Projections 2000–2050." Working Paper 7/2001, Federal Ministry of Finance, Vienna.

Prinz, C., and B. Marin. 1999. *Pensionsreformen—Nachhaltiger Sozialumbau am Beispiel Österreich*. Frankfurt and New York: Campus.

Wöss, J. 2000. "Gesetzliche Pensionsversicherung—Rückblick auf die letzten 30 Jahre." *Soziale Sicherheit* 12: 1000–9.

Chapter 21

The NDC Reform
in the Czech Republic

Agnieszka Chłoń-Domińczak and Marek Mora*

THE CZECH GOVERNMENT IS FACING THE NEED to reform its pension system. As projections show, the current system is not sustainable in the future and shifting to NDC was an option considered by the Czech government. This chapter analyzes the possibility of a shift to a notional defined contribution (NDC) system from the current defined benefit (DB) system in the Czech Republic. In particular, it aims to analyze the pros and cons of the implementation of such a scheme in the Czech Republic.

This chapter is structured as follows. First, it sheds light on the major challenges that the Czech pension scheme currently faces. Second, it summarizes main reform measures that have been adopted since 1990, including the most recent measures incorporated in the fiscal reform of 2003–4. Third, it develops arguments in favor of the introduction of the NDC system in the Czech Republic, and identifies those issues that can be problematic in a shift to NDC. The discussion is also illustrated by some financial simulations of the results of the implementation of the NDC in the Czech Republic. Finally, it offers conclusions regarding possible implementation of the NDC reform.

Main Challenges for the Czech Pension Scheme

The current Czech pension system is currently dominated by a state-run, mandatory, defined benefit pay-as-you-go (PAYG) pillar that provides old-age, disability, and survivor

* Agnieszka Chłoń-Domińczak is currently deputy minister of the Department for Economic Analyses and Forecasting in the Ministry of Social Policy in Poland; Marek Mora works at the European Commission, Directorate-General for Economic and Financial Affairs.

Revised conference version. The authors would like to thank Edward Palmer for his insightful comments to the first version of this paper, which contributed a lot to the final version.

The chapter includes findings of the report on the options for the NDC implementation in the Czech Republic, prepared by Agnieszka Chłoń-Domińczak for the Ministry of Labor and Social Affairs, the Czech Republic, at the request of the World Bank. The report benefited from comments from Jiří Kral and Jan Škorpík, Ministry of Labor and Social Affairs, the Czech Republic, and Hermann von Gersdorff from the World Bank.

The ideas expressed in this chapter should be attached only to the authors and they should not be understood as an official policy of the respective institutions for which they benefits. Old-age pensions account for about 70 percent of total pension expenditures. The PAYG pension benefits are financed by a pension contribution levied on the gross wage of employees and a part of the profits of the self-employed. The state subsidizes the PAYG scheme, either directly by financing gaps between revenues and expenditures, or indirectly by acknowledging noncontributory periods for the calculation of pensions (covered unemployment, higher education, military service, and maternity leave).

Like almost all pension schemes in Europe, the Czech pension scheme will face the problem of an aging population. Currently, fertility rates in the Czech Republic are very low. According to the United Nations (2005) the fertility rate in the Czech Republic between 2000 and 2005 was the fourth lowest in the world. In addition, average life expectancy is already increasing and projected to rise still further, which will lead to a growing number of pensioners. According to the projection of the Czech Statistical Office, the elderly dependency ratio—the share of population aged 65 or more in population to working age (15–64)—is projected to increase from 20 percent in 2004 to almost 40 percent in 2030. This will be caused both by a decrease in the working-age population (in the period between 2000 and 2030 by some 14 percent) and by an increase in the post-working-age population (by more than 60 percent in the same time period).

After 2030, the aging process will be even more advanced. The UN population projections show that among the European countries, the Czech Republic—together with Greece, Italy, and Spain—should have the highest share of people older than 65 years in the year 2050. More importantly, the demographic transition in the Czech Republic between 2000 and 2050 is expected to be extremely pronounced. According to Eurostat (2005), the elderly dependency ratio will almost triple between 2004 and 2050, reaching 54.8 percent, above the average of the European Union (52.8 percent). The change in the elderly dependency ratio is projected to be the second largest in the European Union (figure 21.1).

This negative demographic development will create pressure on the financial sustainability of the pension scheme. Since the late 1990s, the pension system has already been in

Figure 21.1. The Increase in the Elderly Dependency Ratio in EU Countries between 2004 and 2050

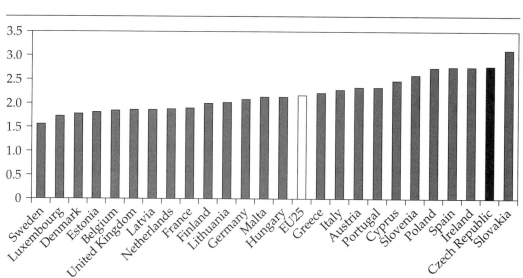

Source: Eurostat (2005).

Figure 21.2. Share of Economic Active Population[a]

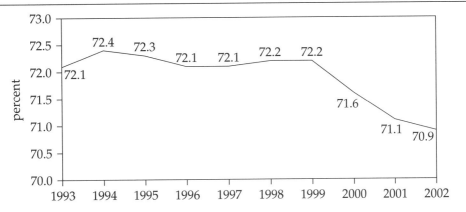

Source: Pre-Accession Economic Programme (2003).

a. Calculated as the ratio of the workforce (EU) between 15 and 64 years of age to the total number of people in this age category (based on average figures for the given year). The figures include everyone with permanent residence in the Czech Republic, regardless of his or her citizenship.

deficit for several years and, according to the IMF estimates, this deficit was projected to increase from 5 percent of GDP in 2025 to 11 percent of GDP in 2050.[1] In 2002, the Czech Ministry of Labor and Social Affairs estimated that—in order to finance the liabilities of the pension system—the contribution rate would have to rise to around 45 percent in 2030, almost twice the contribution rate of 26 percent.[2]

The PAYG pension system is also influenced by the recent developments of the labor market. On the one hand, the share of active labor force (calculated for the group 15–64 years old) has been declining, despite the fact that the number of people in the age category 15–64 years reached a record level of 7.2 million persons in 2002 (see figure 21.2). On the other hand, the rate of structural unemployment has been relatively high and still appears to be slightly rising. The registered unemployment rate has been increasing and, in 2004, reached its historical maximum of 10.2 percent.

The unfavorable development in the labor market can partly be explained as a consequence of pension policy itself as the Czech pension system creates serious distortions. The pension formula is a sum of a constant element, equal for all retirees, and a wage-dependent element. However, this second part of the old-age pension takes into account a fraction of wage in a regressive manner (the higher the wage, the smaller the percentage considered for the assessment base). This implies large intragenerational redistribution, as persons with lower earnings can expect benefits that are higher in relation to their wages than persons with higher earnings. An estimate of this redistributive effect of the pension formula is shown in figure 21.3.

This means that the marginal taxation of labor income is highly progressive, and at some point it reaches 100 percent. This feature of the pension scheme, combined with the structural problems in labor market, is a reason why people (especially those with low skills) often leave the labor market as soon as possible—mostly through early retirement. As a result, the actual exit age is much lower than the statutory age for an old-age pension. In 2002, the actual exit age was 56 years for women and 59 for men.

Figure 21.3. Replacement Rates by Earnings Level in the Czech PAYG System

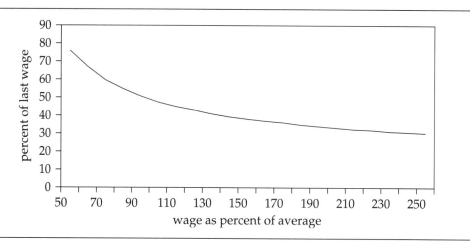

Source: Chłoń-Domińczak (2003).

Note: Calculated for a person retiring at 62, with 42 years of insurance (average wage = CZK 14 ,718, limits in the assessment base, as in 2002).

Changes in the Czech Pension System after 1990

Since 1990, when economic transition started, the Czech Republic has implemented a number of changes in its pension system. First, several parametric reforms of the PAYG scheme were introduced in the 1990s. Second, a fully funded pillar with a voluntary participation was introduced in 1994. Third, the public finance reform of 2003–4 introduced further parametric changes.

Parametric Changes of the PAYG Pillar

During the 1990s, the government succeeded in introducing a number of parametric changes in the PAYG scheme. Most important was the abolishment of special occupational pension rights, which occurred in two steps, partly in the period 1990–92, and then entirely in 1995. An overview of parametric changes in 1990s and in 2001 is given in table 21.1.

The Second Pillar

In addition to parametric reforms, a fully funded second pillar was introduced in 1994. The participation in this pillar is voluntary and contributions are paid on individual basis, but subsidized by the state budget.[3] There have been several legislative changes in this area as well. Those changes have mainly been aimed at increasing the security of deposits of participants. In 2003—10 years after the introduction—there were 12 private pension funds operating on the Czech pension insurance market. Despite the high number of contributing participants (more than half of those in the PAYG system, almost one-third of the total population), the accumulated pension capital in the second pillar is still very low. In 2003, it amounted to 3.3 percent of GDP.

Pension Reform Process after 2002

The fact that the first pillar of the Czech pension system is clearly financially unsustainable in the medium and long term and that it needs to be reformed has been generally acknowl-

Table 21.1. Parametric Reforms in the Czech PAYG Pension Scheme (1990–2002)

1990–92	• Elimination of some special pensions; with the exception of the self-employed whose pension contribution base is only 35% of their net income (compared with 100% of gross wage of employees)
1993	• Creation of an earmarked contribution rate for financing social policy (including pensions), as a part of the state budget • Creation of an explicit pension formula
1996	• A new law on pension insurance (several parametric changes aiming at reducing the fiscal burden and strengthening intragenerational equity), inter alia, gradual increase in the statutory retirement age by 2007—to 62 for men and to 57–61 for women, depending on the number of children; reduction in the contribution rate from 27.2% to 26% • A special account for pensions in the state budget (an asymmetric measure as contributions credited to this account can be spent only on pensions, whereas any loss must be covered by general taxes)
1997	• Tightening up the indexation rule; reduction in noncontributory periods
2001	• Tightening of early retirement provisions

Source: Authors' analysis.

edged not only by pension experts, but also by political leaders. Nevertheless, since 2001, the pension reform has been de facto stopped. The parliament refused to accept several reform proposals (for example, the creation of an independent social insurance agency) and the reform process was in a gridlock, awaiting an election in 2002.

The intensity of the debate on pension reform options increased after the election. Facing high deficits of public finances (6.8 percent of GDP in 2002 and 11.7 percent of GDP in 2003), the Czech government decided to reform its public finances. As pension expenditures constitute a major part of the overall spending of the state budget, the fiscal reform package as adopted in 2003 included more parametric changes in the PAYG system. The reform measures took effect in the beginning of 2004. They include:

- Significant cuts in noncontributory periods counted in pension rights for higher education
- Elimination of the possibility of early retirement with only a temporary benefit reduction
- Increase in the contribution base for self-employed persons (50 percent of net income compared with 35 percent previously)
- Commitment to limit the pension increase in the period 2004–6 only to the minimum indexation required by the law (increase in the Consumer Price Index plus 33 percent of real wage growth, considered over a two-year period)
- A further and gradual increase of the retirement age to 63 by 2008 for both men and women
- An increase in the pension contribution from 26 percent to 28 percent (the overall social security contribution was unchanged because the contribution to the employment policy was lowered by 2 percent at the same time)[4]

In 2003, the medium-term reform strategy of the Czech Ministry of Labor and Social Affairs was to reform the first pillar along NDC lines and possibly to extend the variety of the old-age savings instruments by introducing a second occupational pillar on a voluntary basis. The NDC reform was considered to be implemented by the year 2010.[5]

Why Is NDC Considered a Reform Option in the Czech Republic?

When thinking about reform options, it is worthwhile to analyze the dynamics behind pension "reform" performance in the Czech Republic since 1990. It has been generally acknowledged that medium- and long-term financial sustainability of a PAYG pension scheme can be achieved by parametric reforms. Although this is true technically, parametric reforms face several problems in practice. The major difficulty of this approach is that decisions about parametric reforms are often taken ad hoc and there is no clear reform path. This increases reform costs in economic terms because adjustments often take place among people shortly before retirement age or even among those already retired. It also creates a credibility problem that increases reform costs measured in terms of political resistance. People oppose reform proposals not because of the proposals themselves, but rather because of uncertainty about any further changes. This general mistrust is further aggravated by the fact that politicians have often misused parametric reforms to serve their political client groups. In the Czech Republic, the opposition to parametric reforms was shown when the trade unions fiercely opposed government proposals to cut some of the noncontributory periods and increase retirement age for women under the 2003 fiscal reform package.

When reforming their pension systems, many of the middle-income/transition countries have decided to follow the reform benchmark of the World Bank and implemented the three-pillar concept. The introduction of the fully funded pillar is often seen as a way to overcome the above-mentioned difficulties with parametric reforms. Among the new EU member states, this kind of radical reform was introduced in Estonia, Hungary, Latvia, Lithuania, Poland, and most recently in Slovakia (on January 1, 2005). The Czech Republic differs significantly from many other middle-income/transition countries in this respect. The main explanation of why the Czech Republic has followed a different path is linked to general scepticism about a mandatory fully funded pillar. This scepticism has a number of sources.

First, so far, the first PAYG pillar has still not faced any serious financial crisis and, despite all its shortcomings, it is considered to be a reliable and well-functioning part of the Czech pension system, and of the Czech state in general.

Second, there is a general scepticism among the Czech population and politicians about the functioning of capital markets. This scepticism has its specific reasons, which can be found in recent history. In the process of voucher privatization, high expectations were created that "ownership society" would be created in the Czech Republic after the majority of Czechs received shares in exchange for the privatization vouchers. However, after two waves of voucher privatization, many people saw the value of their shares disappear because of poor regulation of capital markets and because of underdeveloped corporate governance. There is also the concrete experience with the private pension funds operating within the Czech second pillar, whose performance has not been very convincing so far: the annual real net rate of return was on average only 0.7 percent over the period 1995–2003 (table 21.2).

Table 21.2. Real Net Rate of Return (RNRR) of the Czech Second Pillar
             (in percent per year)

	1995	1996	1997	1998	1999	2000	2001	2002	2003	Annual average
RNRR	0	0.2	0.3	−2.3	3.9	0.3	−0.6	1.7	3.1	0.7

Source: Data from the Ministry of Labor and Social Affairs (2002).

Third, awareness about the medium- and long-term financial development of the PAYG pension pillar arose mostly after 1995. On the one hand, this increase of awareness was linked to the paradigmatic shift in thinking about pensions that was to a large extent influenced by the publication of the World Bank report *Averting the Old-Age Crisis* in 1994. On the other hand, more in-depth insights were enabled because of a broader use of information technology, which made it possible to produce longer projections of the financial situation of the pension system. However, at that time the liberal-conservative governments had to deal with more immediate problems, such as the financial crisis in 1997. Since 1998, the Social Democratic government has not supported the introduction of a compulsory fully funded pension pillar for several reasons. One group of reasons is technical. Although the problems in Czech Republic's the first pillar are well recognized and acknowledged, there has been enduring scepticism about the economic benefits usually claimed to follow from the introduction of a second pillar (that it deals better with the aging population, and that it results in higher savings, less distortions in the labor markets, a deepening of capital markets, and higher economic growth).[6] On the contrary, political costs linked to intergenerational redistribution arising from the financing of transition from a PAYG to a fully funded system are almost sure (table 21.3). The ongoing discussion among pension experts about the uncertain economic effects of a shift toward a mandatory funded system also made it easier to oppose the radical pension reform for "ideological" reasons.

In sum, a combination of three factors explains why the NDC reform has begun to be considered as a reform option in the Czech Republic. First is the acknowledged unsustainability of current pension policy. Second is the lack of support for further parametric reforms of the existing system by the society. And third is the general scepticism at the political level about a mandatory fully funded pillar, based either on technical or on ideological reasons.

Advantages of Introducing the NDC Pillar

As economic and demographic conditions in the Czech Republic are likely to change significantly over the next decades, advantages from introducing the NDC pillar can be numerous. First, financial conditions of the pension system would improve, because of both its automatic adjustment mechanism and its almost zero transition costs. Second, NDC systems would also have a positive on labor supply and mobility. Third, NDC systems are more transparent than other systems, thus lowering the costs of necessary adjustment. And fourth, NDC reform could help form policy preferences about further reform steps.

Table 21.3. Costs and Benefits of the Switch from PAYG to Fully Funded Financing

Economic benefits	
higher rates of return	uncertain (risk adjustment, transition costs, administrative costs)
higher savings	uncertain
deepening of capital market	likely
elimination of labor market distortions	no (rather a shift from DB to DC)
higher economic growth	uncertain
better protection against aging	limited
Political costs	
intergenerational redistribution arising from the financing of transition	almost sure

Source: Authors' analysis.

Financial Stability and Its Automatic Adjustment to Demographic Trends

It is commonly believed that the greatest economic advantage of NDC systems is their high degree of financial stability, which stems from the built-in automatic stabilizers to changing economic and demographic conditions. Most importantly, in an NDC scheme the net present value of an individual's account value is always equal to the expected value of his or her entitlement for any given life expectancy. The notional interest and the annuity factor lead to adjustments in the pension level as economic and demographic conditions fluctuate. NDC schemes are thus much better equipped to adapt themselves to demographic shocks, whether they are well predicted or not.

The NDC critics correctly point out that the PAYG could still display short-term financial imbalances that result from time lags of built-in stabilizers. Moreover, they claim that long-term financial stability can be achieved in the traditional pay-as-you-go defined benefit (PAYG-DB) schemes as well, when proper repeated adjustments to the benefit formulae are carried out.[7] From an economic point of view, this critique is correct. From a political economy point of view, however, the NDC pension scheme is by far superior to the traditional pension schemes, just for its rule-oriented institutional characteristics. As already mentioned, the traditional parametric approach allows for discretionary measures, whereas the NDC rate of return is generated directly by economic and demographic factors and there is no administrative discretion involved other than what can be applied to fully funded schemes.[8]

No Transition Costs

Another important advantage from the point of financial stability is that the transition from a DB to an NDC system does not require any additional financing. As both of the schemes function on the PAYG basis, current contributions are still used to finance current expenditures. The implicit pension debt, which is often considered to be a major obstacle for the introduction of capital funding, should not increase because of the strict application of actuarial rules. The difference between DB and NDC systems lies in the way pension rights under each regime are accrued. Deficits can be observed in the short run, as the transition is a long-term process and pensions from the old system will still be paid to all those persons who were working when reform was introduced.

To minimize transition costs, implementing the NDC system should be accompanied by several measures. The required steps include:

- Limiting pensions' indexation to the statutory minimum (one-third of real wages growth)
- Faster increase of retirement ages for men and women
- Equalizing the retirement age of men and women and eliminating earlier retirement based on the number of children.

Labor Market Neutrality and Explicit Trade-Offs

Compared with the traditional DB systems, the NDC does not create distortions in the labor market. As the pension formula is based on actuarial adjustments, the marginal taxation should be close to zero. There are no built-in incentives for early retirement, and the individual chooses only between the replacement rate and the retirement age. By deferring retirement, the individual increases the value of the notional account, through additional contributions paid and additional interest accrued on the account. In addition, the expected period of receiving the benefit is shorter (due to lower remaining life expectancy at higher retirement age), which also contributes to higher pension benefit. As marginal taxation is close to zero, the NDC contributions can be perceived by workers as an individual savings scheme, not as an element of the tax wedge.[9] Moreover, the NDC system can also allow an individually designed gradual exit from the active labor force.

Table 21.4. Employment Rate in 2004

Employment rate	Total	Men	Women
Age group 15–64	64.2	72.3	56.0
Age group 55–64	42.7	57.2	29.4

Source: Eurostat (2005).

As a result, one could expect that the NDC scheme would raise the employment rates of the working-age population. In particular, it is important to increase the employability of the older workers and to increase female participation. The employment rates of the older workers in the Czech Republic are still far below the targets set by the European Union in the Lisbon Strategy.[10] Female employment rate is significantly below the men's level, particularly between the ages of 55 and 64 (see table 21.4).

An NDC pension scheme not only makes the trade-off between the level of pension benefit and the retirement age explicit, but, more importantly, retirement age is no longer a politically set variable, as this trade-off can be decided at the purely individual level. The only politically set variable is the minimum retirement age, which defines the earliest time that an individual can start receiving the benefit. The minimum retirement age should be high enough to avoid having too many people end up with a pension below the subsistence minimum, thus creating pressure on public finances. It should also reflect the process of aging, in particular changes in the longevity.

Figure 21.4 shows results of simulation, comparing values of the old-age benefit under the PAYG scheme as it was in 2002 with the values under the NDC scheme. In both cases it is

Figure 21.4. Simulation of NDC versus DB Pension in the Czech Republic (2004)

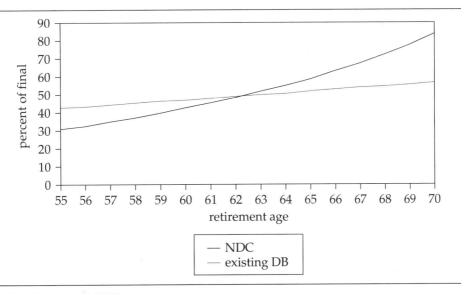

Source: Chłoń-Domińczak (2003).

Note: Assumed level of real wage growth and notional accounts indexation: 3 percent per year.

assumed that a person starts his or her career at the age of 20 and works until retirement age, earning an average wage. The comparison is based on the DB formula, and assumes that a person does not receive any reduction for early retirement or advancement for later retirement.

It should be noted that under the pension system as of 2002, early retirement (up to 2 years prior to reaching retirement age) was additionally punished:

- Pension was reduced by 1.3 percent of the calculation basis (the adjusted personal assessment basis, based on the average earnings 10 years before retirement) for each 90 days of earlier retirement but no longer than 2 years before the legal retirement age. This reduction was temporary, and was in force until the person reached retirement age.
- Pension was reduced by 0.9 percent of the calculation basis for each 90 days of earlier retirement but longer than 2 years and no longer than 3 years before the legal retirement age. This reduction was permanent.

There was also an "reward" for later retirement, equal to 1.5 percent of the calculation basis per each 90 days of working past the legal retirement age. This would change the presented figure slightly. However, as adjustments were still below actuarial neutrality, the majority of retirees decide to retire below legal retirement age.

Under the NDC system, it is assumed that contribution rate equals 20 percent of wages. Life expectancies are computed as the average value for men and women together, based on 2000 data. Replacement rates are calculated based on gross wages. Though based on relatively simplistic assumptions, the results of the simulation show that benefits expected under both systems are similar at the age of 62. In case of lower retirement age, benefits in the NDC system are smaller, but above age 62, the NDC system would offer higher pensions.

Therefore, a shift to an NDC scheme would increase incentives to postpone the decision to retire by introducing a more actuarially fair value for future pensions if the worker remains employed for longer.

Labor Mobility

Another reason why the NDC system should be introduced is that it would make it a lot easier to provide adequate pension coverage for workers who move from country to country. Despite the fact that current mobility of the work force is still low, it is likely to increase with the further integration of product and financial markets—especially in Europe. As pension coverage is going to become a major issue for mobile workers, the NDC approach seems to be particularly well suited to such an environment.

Transparency and Lower Adjustment Costs

In an NDC system, the present value of accounts for each individual is always known and everybody in the system is treated equally. This increased transparency is one of greatest advantages of NDC systems. Higher transparency lowers the adjustment costs of the pension schemes, both economic and political. First, transparency is important from the point of view of optimal intertemporal consumption smoothing. Members in NDC pension schemes are informed about their accumulated pension capital during their working careers. This allows them to make more informed choices about their individual savings and about the "correct" timing of retirement. In contrast, frequent and unpredictable adjustments of DB pensions are clearly suboptimal for individual decisions.

Second, the high degree of transparency of NDC schemes is important from the political economy point of view. The NDC formula does not include an income redistribution element, as it gives pension rights for contributions actually paid. For the same reason, everybody in the system is treated equally, which makes the concept more transparent for the population. The history of financial imbalances of pension schemes shows that they arose partly because of the lack of information about consequences of certain decisions and partly because of their conscious abuse by politicians. Thus, transparency in the NDC scheme substantially reduces the probability of risk that the pension schemes would either be changed with unintended consequences or intentionally misused.

The NDC System and the Formation of Reform Preferences

Institutional economics stipulates, on the one hand, that institutions are the result of the preferences of voters, and, on the other hand, that institutions might have a large impact on forming the preferences of voters. If preferences on pension policy are endogenous, we would argue that the NDC reform could be used as an institution for preference formation about future policy options.

As the study of Boeri, Börsch-Supan, and Tabellini (2001) shows, the level of information among individuals seems to be dependent not only on their individual characteristics (age, sex, income, and education), but also on institutional characteristics of the pension scheme, especially on the degree of individualization of the pension scheme that in turn affects the quality of information among its participants. Boeri, Börsch-Supan, and Tabellini (2001) claim that Germans, Italians, and to a lesser extent Frenchmen, are relatively better informed about (the cost of) their pension schemes than Spaniards. About three-quarters of respondents from Germany, Italy, and France expect that there will be pension reform, which will significantly reduce the level of public pensions; in Spain only 47 percent of respondents expected this (Boeri, Börsch-Supan, and Tabellini 2001, p. 25). One can interpret these results as a consequence of a long social-insurance (Bismarckian) tradition of German and French pension schemes (the so-called point system) and of the NDC pension reform in Italy. People are ready to accept cuts in their pensions if these are "fair." This "fairness" is in turn derived from the understanding about their accumulated individual pension rights. Also in Poland during the preparation of the 1999 pension reform, the majority of respondents in opinion polls preferred having a close link between contributions and benefits.[11]

Moreover, the study of Boeri, Börsch-Supan, and Tabellini (2001) indicates that the willingness of people to opt out from PAYG pension scheme and to bear the related transition burden is relatively low. In all four countries considered (Germany, France, Italy, Spain), only little more than 10 percent of the respondents are willing to opt out if that entails bearing the transition burden (pp. 31–32).

In other words, the NDC reform could enable people to learn about the real costs of their pension scheme and make it in this way easily comparable with its chief counterpart—the financial (or funded) DC scheme. This institutional gain is worth considering. On the one hand, costs to enter the NDC system are very low, in particular compared with the costs of radical financial pension reform. On the other hand, the NDC system does not create any additional obstacles for further reform options.

Main Risks of NDC Reform from the Czech Perspective

There are four main kinds of risk of NDC reform in the Czech Republic: risks to equity, to portfolio considerations, to the political economy, and to building administrative capacity.

Equity

First, the issue of equity can be considered from the point of view of welfare economics. If pensioners are assumed to be more risk-averse than workers (contributors), pensions should be subject to more modest adjustments than adjustments in contribution rates. In an NDC scheme, the contribution rate is fixed and the pension to a large extent depends on growth of the wage bill during the working time and on the expected wage-bill growth and on the life expectancy at the moment of retirement. This would imply a worsening compared with the original DB system. However, neither wage-bill growth nor life expectancy change abruptly. The transparent system allows workers to be informed about estimates of their future NDC pensions and make appropriate advanced adjustments in their consumption behavior.

Second, the issue of equity can be considered from the political economy point of view. The pension formula in the Czech Republic, in particular its flat-rate part and the regressive wage-dependent part, aims at redistributing from the rich to the poor. Persons with lower earnings can expect benefits that are higher in relation to their wages than persons with higher earnings. In addition, selected noncontributory periods are also counted for pension calculation. In contrast, the NDC system gives pension rights only for actually paid contributions. Persons who have paid the same amount of contributions and retire at the same age may expect similar pensions.[12] It thus appears that one of the most important elements of the NDC system is a reduction of intragenerational transfers. This consideration is, however, not straightforward.

On the one hand, redistribution under the DB systems might have several shortcomings. First, redistribution related to noncontributory periods is delayed in time, as costs of financing these periods are not paid when they occur, but only after a person retires. Thus, in the case of aging populations, it means that additional higher burden, related to financing of these periods, is put on the younger cohorts. Second, the direction of the redistribution may be disturbed by the method of calculating the assessment base. If it is based on the earnings history obtained from the end of a working career, people who tend to have higher earnings just before retirement age are "the winners." Thus it may happen that persons who have longer working careers but lower wage levels have lower pensions, even if they paid the same amount in contributions. Third, DB pension formulae are often perceived as unfair and lead to higher evasion on the part of those who could not benefit from additional contributions.

On the other hand, intragenerational redistribution in the NDC system is possible to avoid workers with low wages or interrupted work careers not receiving receive an adequate retirement income.

Countries with existing NDC schemes, such as Latvia, Poland, and Sweden, introduced the concept of minimum pension guarantee. Pensions from the NDC scheme are topped up to the statutory level of minimum benefit from the general revenue of the state budget. For those who need it, social assistance should be provided, based on a means test. This social assistance should, however, be separated from the social insurance pension system and be a part of the general social assistance scheme, financed by general taxes.

Figure 21.5 shows the results of simulations for the Czech Republic if the minimum pension level is set at 30 percent of the average wage (the contribution rate is equal to 20 percent). The simulation results show that persons earning below 60 percent of the average wage who started to work at age 20 and retired at age 62 would be eligible to minimum-pension guarantee (assuming a notional interest rate of 3 percent).

Another solution that can be applied is to introduce a flat benefit, financed from general revenue. The simulation in figure 21.6 shows the outcome of such a solution for persons with different wage levels. In the simulation it is assumed that the level of flat benefit is 25 percent of average wage and the contribution rate for NDC pension is 12 percent.

Comparison of replacement rates for both simulations is shown in figure 21.7. Compared with the minimum guarantee concept, the pension distribution is flatter, which influences the replacement rates. With the minimum pension guarantee, replacement rates are increased for low-income earners and remain unchanged for persons not covered by the guarantee, while in the case of the flat benefit, replacement rates fall continuously with income.

When choosing the appropriate option, long-term financial projections are necessary. In the aging environment, costs of the flat pensions increase with the increase of the depen-

Figure 21.5. Functioning of the Minimum Pension Guarantee

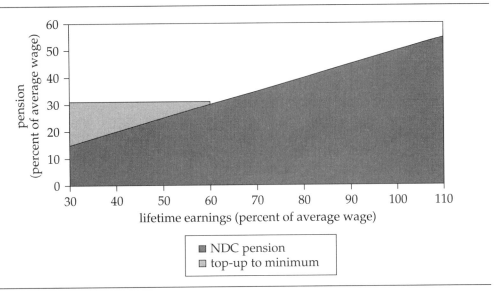

Source: Chłoń-Domińczak (2003).

Figure 21.6. An Alternative: Flat Benefit plus NDC Pension

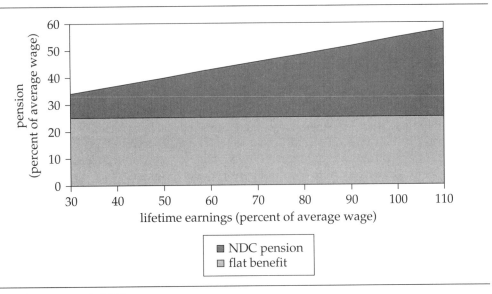

Source: Chłoń-Domińczak (2003).

Figure 21.7. Replacement Rates: Minimum Guarantee versus Flat Benefit

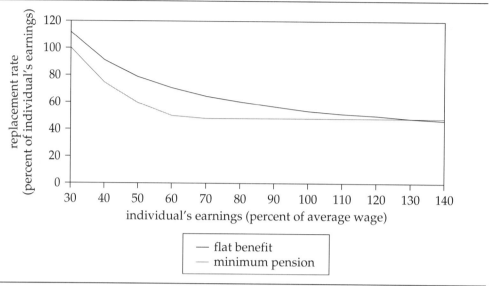

Source: Chłoń-Domińczak (2003).

dency rate. In the case of the topping-up option, as the level of subsidy from the state budget is smaller, the costs for the state budget also increase, but not to the same level.

This type of redistribution broadens the base for financing, not relating it only to the pension contribution as the one embedded in the DB pension system, which is socially more justified and less distortive for the labor market. As already discussed, to keep the costs of such guarantees reasonable, the minimum age to receive such a guarantee should be set relatively high and it should increase with the increase of life expectancies.

Portfolio Considerations

The NDC reform does not accommodate the portfolio advantages pointed out by the promoters of radical financial pension reform, namely that the two forms of pension financing (PAYG and capital funding) face different risks. The argument that NDC reform does not accommodate portfolio advantages requires at least two qualifying remarks. First, the question of to what extent both forms of pension financing really face different risks is disputable, especially as regards demography. And second, the composition of portfolio of assets used for financing consumption at the retirement stage should be left to individual choice. As Disney (2000) argues, the "voluntary" route of offering incentives to individuals to make private retirement savings arrangements as public commitments are cut back has proved to be a popular reform vehicle. NDC reform makes pension benefits for each individual dependent on his or her contributions and retirement age. If information about the approximate NDC pension is known in advance, the individual can complement NDC pensions with a long-term savings scheme of his or her choice (private pension insurance, life insurance, mortgage, and so on). To achieve this, various forms of long-term savings schemes should be given equal treatment by the government.

Political Economy

The major weakness of any pension reform is its political feasibility. NDC reforms contain basically only adjustments of current pension rights through changes in the rate of return on accounts and the life expectancy factor used in computing the annuity. In particular, in the NDC framework those adjustments are explicit and they cannot be compensated for by any promise of future benefits. This is a key contrast to radical financial pension reforms, which have always pointed out that short-term cuts in the PAYG state pillar would be more than compensated for by long-term benefits in the fully funded private pillar.

Another major political economy consideration under the NDC reform is that it does not have any natural advocates. Normally, radical financial pension reforms are supported by private financial institutions because they usually profit from them. This is, however, not the case with NDC reforms. It has been only recently that the World Bank, as the major intellectual institution in the field of pension reform, started promoting this reform option.

Building Administrative Capacity

A shift to the NDC system requires significant administrative preparations. Introducing individual accounts is a technological and operational challenge. Usually such a change requires recording money and information flows in the pension system. In the individualized pension systems, there are many processes. The most important is the collection and assignment of the payments. All other processes (registration, transfers, and so on) support the main process. However, they have to fulfill quality standards, to ensure proper assignment of payments. The NDC system is very demanding for social security administrators, as individual accounts need to be kept for all insured people. Thus sufficient time should be allowed between completing the legislation and implementing the pension system.

Introducing the NDC has several technical preconditions. These include:

- Building administrative capacity that also includes development of the IT system necessary to run individual accounts and preparing all actors—including bank and employers—for the new information requirements
- Separating social security from the state budget and building a demographic reserve fund as a stabilizer of the NDC system
- Assessing the quality of identification numbers necessary to have proper information for individual accounts.

Financial Simulations for the Future

In this section, some assessment of the costs for old-age pensions is presented.[13] The simulation is based on the demographic projection until 2030, prepared by the Central Statistical Office of the Czech Republic. However, as data on life expectancies were not available, the relevant values for the Polish population were used for the purpose of pension calculation.[14]

Other assumptions include:

- A wage growth of 3 percent annually
- A constant employment rates, based on 2002 data
- A real pension indexation at the level of 33 percent of real wage growth
- NDC assumptions:
  - The contribution rate for the NDC system is equal to 20 percent of the wage
  - The notional accounts indexation is equal to wage bill growth
  - The benefit formula is equal to the value of accumulated capital divided by life expectancy at retirement
  - The pension rights under the old regime are calculated as a percent of accrued pension rights at the end of 2003.

Figure 21.8 presents the results of simulation for the application of latter assumption on the calculation of the accrued pension rights. It is assumed that retirement age is equal to

Figure 21.8. Simulated Value of Old-Age Pension: The Role of Initial and NDC Pension for Transition Cohorts

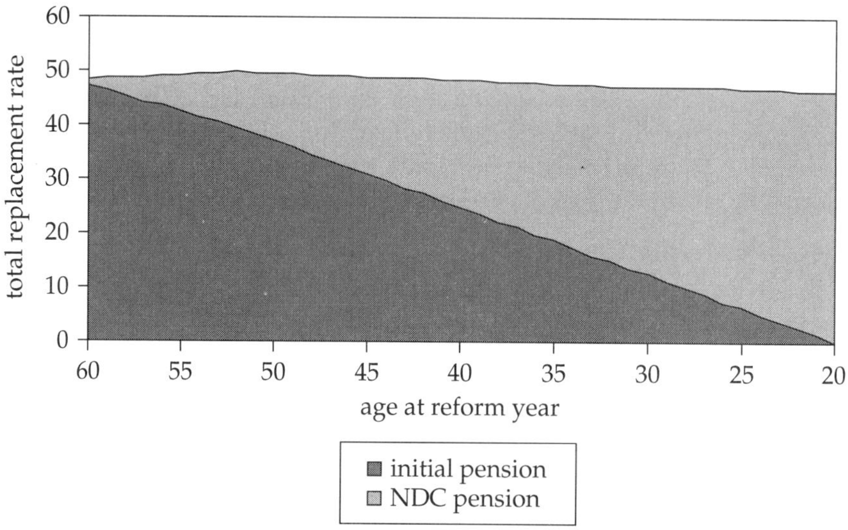

Source: Chłoń-Domińczak (2003).

62, the required insurance period is 25 years, individuals start work at the age of 20, and the person earns an average wage for the entire period. The role of the initial pension decreases for younger cohorts, but the total value of old-age pensions remains relatively stable. Such an approach leads to the equal treatment of all workers when calculating the pension rights, contrary to, for example, the Polish approach, where the initial capital is calculated by multiplying the accrued pension right by life expectancy at age 62. As a result, women who have a lower retirement age lose from the conversion of pension rights.[15] This assumption also has its drawback. Namely, when life expectancies increase, the value of the accrued pension rights remains unchanged. This may increase the future pension expenditure compared with the situation where all pension rights are adjusted to changes in the life expectancy.

Two retirement ages scenarios are calculated. The first one assumes that retirement ages are equalized to 63 by 2008 (the current reform scenario). However, to achieve this, given the current age structure of pensioners, in the period from 2005 to 2009 no women should actually retire, as most have already retired at a younger age. The second scenario assumes that current retirement ages are kept.

Increased Retirement Age Scenario

Assuming the increase of retirement ages, the relation between the number of workers and the number of old-age pensioners is expected to decrease compared with the current level, resulting in lowering the system dependency ratio (figure 21.9).

The average pension to average wage ratio is also expected to decline, since the indexation of benefits is close to the Consumer Price Index. The decline observed during the first years of the simulation is the result of small number of new pensioners. As a result, benefits are reduced because of the assumed indexation level (figure 21.10).

Figure 21.9. Employed and Pensioners: Increased Retirement Age Scenario

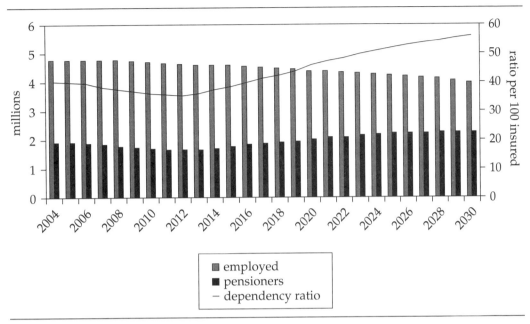

Source: Chłoń-Domińczak (2003).

Figure 21.10. Average Pension As a Percent of Average Wage: Increased Retirement Age Scenario

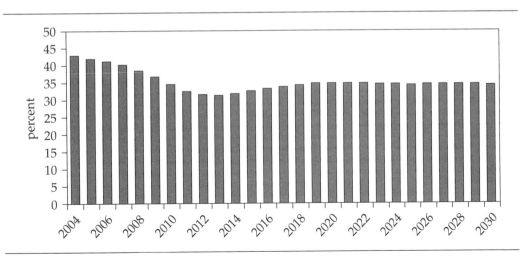

Source: Chłoń-Domińczak (2003).

Figure 21.11. Expenditures and Revenue of the Old-Age Pension System: Increased Retirement Scenario

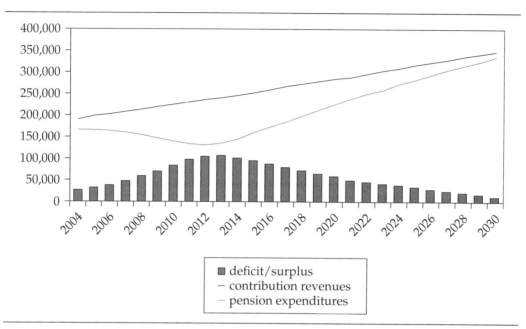

Source: Chłoń-Domińczak (2003).

Combining the two effects, total expenditure on pensions should decline and the system should generate surpluses, in particular between 2008 and 2020. After that date, as the aging of the population accelerates, the difference between revenues and expenditures is likely to diminish (figure 21.11).

Constant Retirement Age Scenario

Under the constant retirement age scenario, the situation looks different. First, the system dependency ratio is increasing throughout the entire simulation period (figure 21.12).

Second, as the inflow of new pensioners is not disturbed, the average pension to average wage level is decreasing, but at a much slower pace. However, at the end of the projection period, the average pension level is slightly lower than in the case of the increased retirement age. This is because of the actuarial pension formula that would result in lower pensions under current retirement ages (figure 21.13).

Finally, overall old-age pension expenditures are increasing above expected revenues from contributions, which shows a significant risk of insolvency of the pension system. This is mainly due to keeping low retirement ages, which results in both increased number of pensioners and a reduced number of workers contributing to the pension system in the future (figure 21.14).

The results of the simulations show that the implementation of the NDC alone is not sufficient to improve the financial situation of the old-age pension system. Other changes, such as increasing retirement age or lowering pension indexation level, are necessary.

Under the full reform scenario—including the shift to an NDC scheme, changes in the pension indexation, and rising retirement age—it is expected that in the next decades pension systems can generate some surpluses. This shows that there is some room for accumulating reserves for the next decades, when aging of the population is expected to be more advanced.

Figure 21.12. Employed and Pensioners: Constant Retirement Age Scenario

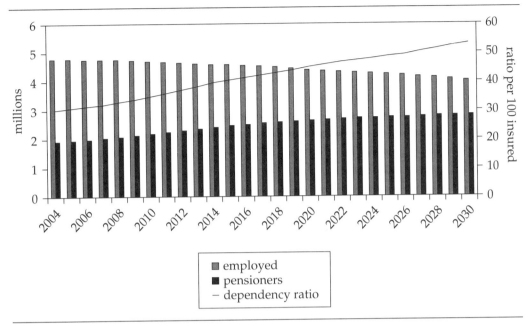

Source: Chłoń-Domińczak (2003).

Figure 21.13. Pensions As a Percent of Average Wage: Constant Retirement Age Scenario

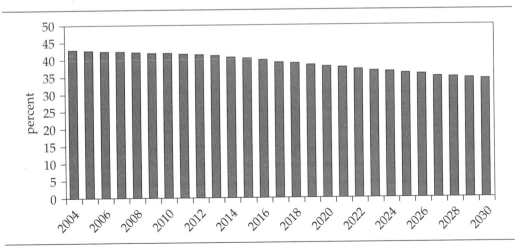

Source: Authors' calculations.

Figure 21.14. Expenditures and Revenues of the Old-Age Pension System: Constant Retirement Age Scenario

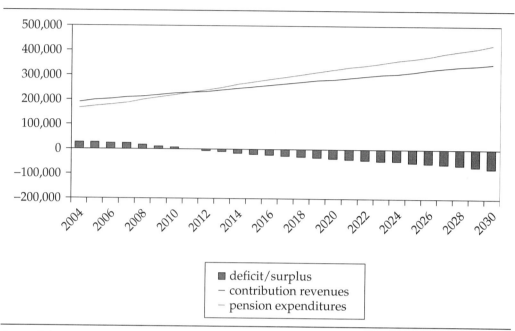

Source: Chłoń-Domińczak (2003).

Conclusions

Given the current prospects of the pension system in the Czech Republic, urgent steps are necessary to reform it. Demographic projections show that the number of working-age persons will be decreasing while the number of pensioners will be increasing. After several years of the PAYG pension system facing deficits, the fiscal reform package adopted in 2003 included parametric changes that safeguarded its fiscal sustainability for about the next 10 years. However, further actions are necessary to ensure long-term stability.

From this point of view, introducing an NDC scheme would link the system's liabilities to contribution revenues, thus making the pension system stable. NDC would also provide incentives to lengthen the working career and enhance transparency, which in turn may increase financial literacy and thus support the development of individual savings. Introducing an NDC scheme does not generate transition costs, as would be the case with a funded system, as both of the schemes function on the pay-as-you-go basis, where current contributions are still used to finance current expenditures. That also means that NDC scheme—when compared with the current DB system—would not create any extra transition costs for the introduction of a funded system later on. Moreover, the NDC system provides similar microlevel incentives to contribute, as benefits are closely tied to contributions.

Thus, it seems that such a reform option may be attractive. However, an NDC reform might have also some disadvantages. One of the criticized elements of the NDC system is the elimination of income redistribution and its failure to broaden a portfolio of assets to finance retirement. This criticism is not fully warranted. For instance, income redistribution can be maintained by establishing the minimum pension guarantee. Concerning port-folio of assets to finance consumption at retirement, the transparent NDC system enables people to make choices about their private savings. From the political point of view, a major weakness of an NDC system is that it does not offer any future benefits in exchange for the immediate cuts in real pensions and it does not have any natural advocates. An NDC reform would also require building administrative capacity.

Stylized simulations show that the shift to an NDC scheme—accompanied by changes in the pension indexation and rising retirement age—would be a viable reform option for the Czech Republic.

Notes

1. See Laursen (2000).
2. See Ministry of Labor and Social Affairs (2002).
3. Using the vocabulary of the World Bank, the Czech second pillar would be a third pillar.
4. This measure is questionable. On the one hand, it means an effective increase in the already very high contribution rate. On the other hand, it is a decrease in financial resources for the active labor market policy in a situation with rising rate of unemployment.
5. In the meantime, the range of preferred reform approaches became much wider. To analyze those approaches, the government decided in 2004 to set up an independent group of experts. Its main objective was to carry out calculations of pension reform pro-posals put forward by the political parties.
6. These sceptical points have also been raised by Barr (2000), Lindbeck and Persson (2003), Thompson (1998), and others.
7. The most outstanding critics of this reform approach are Disney (2000) and Valdés-Prieto (2000).
8. See Palmer (2002).
9. See Góra and Palmer (2004).
10. The Lisbon Strategy, adopted by European Union in 2000, is aimed at implementing actions that would enable the EU by 2010 to "become the most competitive and dynamic knowledge-based economy in the world capable of sustainable economic growth with more and better jobs and greater social cohesion." To achieve this, the employment rate in the EU area should reach the level of 70 percent, employment of women, 60 percent, and employment of older workers (aged 50–74) 50 percent.
11. See Chłoń (2000).
12. This could be observed for example in Poland, where in opinion polls 76 percent of people answered that they expect to have a direct link between contributions and benefits in the pension system (Chłoń 2000).
13. The simulation here is based on very limited information and, thus, it should be seen as indicating the general direction of the results. Further, more detailed, simulations are necessary when working on the actual proposal of the discussed pension reform.
14. The most comprehensive set of new simulations for the NDC reform and for other reforms options was presented in June 2005 by the Executive Team for Pension Reform. See www.reformaduchodu.cz.
15. See Chłoń-Domińczak (2002).

References

Barr, N. 2000. "Reforming Pensions: Myths, Truths, and Policy Choices." IMF Working Paper WP/00/139, IMF, Washington, DC.

Boeri, T., A. Börsch-Supan, and G. Tabellini. 2001. "Would You Like to Shrink the Welfare State? A Survey of European Citizens." *Economic Policy* (April): 9–50.

Chłoń, A. 2000. "Pension Reform and Public Information in Poland." SP Discussion Paper 0019, World Bank, Washington, DC.

Chłoń-Domińczak, A. 2002. "The Polish Pension Reform of 1999." In *Pension Reform in Central and Eastern Europe, Volume 1, Restructuring with Privatization: Case Studies of Hungary and Poland*, ed. E. Fultz, 95–205. Budapest: ILO.

———. 2003. "Evaluation of the Notional Defined Contribution Option for the Reform of the Pension System in the Czech Republic." Report prepared for the Czech Ministry of Labor and Social Affairs.

Disney, R. 2000. "Declining Public Pensions in an Era of Demographic Ageing: Will Private Provision Fill the Gap?" *European Economic Review* 44 (4-6): 957–73.

Eurostat. 2005. *Population projections 2004–2050*. Eurostat Press Release 48/2005.

Góra, M., and E. Palmer. 2004. "Shifting Perspectives in Pensions." IZA Discussion Paper 1369, Bonn.

Laursen, T. 2000. "Pension System Viability and Reform Alternatives in the Czech Republic." IMF Working Paper WP/00/16, IMF, Washington, DC.

Lasagabaster, E., R. Rocha, and P. Wiese. 2000. *Czech Pension System: Challenges and Reform Options*. Washington, DC: World Bank.

Lindbeck, A., and M. Persson. 2003. "The Gains from Pension Reform." *Journal of Economic Literature* XLI (March): 74–112.

Ministry of Labor and Social Affairs. 2002. *Social Insurance in the Czech Republic. Pension and Sickness Insurance*. Prague.

Palmer, E. 2002. "Swedish Pension Reform: How It Evolved and What Does It Mean for the Future?" In *Social Security Pension Reform in Europe*, ed. M. Feldstein and H. Siebert, 231–48. Chicago: University of Chicago Press.

Pre-Accession Economic Programme. 2003. Ministry of Finance of the Czech Republic.

Thompson, L. H. 1998. *Older and Wiser: The Economics of Public Pensions*. Washington, DC: The Urban Institute Press.

United Nations. 1998. *World Population Prospect: The 1998 Revision*. New York: UN Population Division.

———. 2005. *World Population Prospects: The 2004 Revision*. New York: UN Population Division.

Valdés-Prieto, S. 2000. "The Financial Stability of Notional Account Pensions." *Scandinavian Journal of Economics* 102 (3): 394–417.

World Bank. 1994. *Averting the Old Age Crisis: Policies to Protect the Old and Promote Growth*. New York: Oxford University Press.

Chapter 22

The German Public Pension System: How It Will Become an NDC System Look-Alike

Axel H. Börsch-Supan and Christina B. Wilke[*]

A Historical Perspective

The German pension system, designed by Bismarck almost 120 years ago, was the first formal pension system in the world. It has been very successful in providing a high and reliable level of retirement income in the past at reasonable contribution rates, and it became a model for many social security systems around the world. It has survived two major wars, the Great Depression, and, more recently, unification. It has been praised as one of the causes for social and political stability in Germany. Times have changed, however, and these days this system is under severe pressure from population aging and adverse incentive effects. This chapter addresses how this prototypical system emerged and where it will go.[1]

As opposed to other countries such as the United Kingdom and the Netherlands, which originally adopted a Beveridgian social security system that provided only a base pension, public pensions in Germany were from the start designed to extend the standard of living that was achieved during work life also to the time after retirement. Thus, public pensions are roughly proportional to labor income averaged over the entire life course and feature only few redistributive properties. The German pension system is therefore called "retirement insurance" rather than "social security" as in the United States, and workers used to understand their contributions as "insurance premia" rather than "taxes." The insurance character is strengthened by institutional separation: the German retirement insurance

[*] Axel Börsch-Supan is director of the Mannheim Research Institute for the Economics of Aging (MEA), professor for macroeconomics and public policy at the University of Mannheim, Germany, and is research associate at the National Bureau of Economic Research (NBER) in Cambridge, Massachusetts; Christina Benita Wilke is a research fellow in the area of social politics at the Mannheim Research Institute for the Economics of Aging (MEA).
The first version of this paper was commissioned by the Michigan Retirement Research Center (MRRC Working paper UM03-01). Additional financial support was provided by the National Institute on Aging (NIA) through the NBER, the German Science Foundation (DFG) through the Sonderforschungsbereich 504, the State of Baden-Württemberg, and the German Insurers Association (GDV). We are grateful for many helpful comments by Anette Reil-Held and the participants of the MRRC Conference on Improving Social Security Programs at the University of Maryland, September 13, 2003. All remaining errors are ours.

system is not part of the government budget but a separate entity. This entity is subsidized by the federal government. Rationale for this subsidy—which comes to about 30 percent of expenditures—are noninsurance benefits, such as benefits paid to German immigrants after opening the iron curtain. Any surplus, however, remains in the system. It is not transferable into a "unified budget" as in the United States.

The German retirement insurance started as a fully funded system with a mandatory retirement age of 70 years when male life expectancy at birth was less than 45 years (see table 22.1 for a timeline of the system). Today, life expectancy for men is more than 75 years, but average retirement age is less than 60, and even lower in the German Democratic Republic.[2] The system converted to a de facto pay-as-you-go (PAYG) system when most funds were invested in government bonds between the two world wars. After a long and arduous debate, the German Bundestag decided in 1957 to convert the system gradually to a PAYG scheme. The remainder of the capital stock was spent about 10 years later. Since then, the German system has been purely PAYG with a very small reserve fund lasting less than 14 days of expenditures in spring 2004.

A second historical reform took place in 1972. It made the German pension system one of the most generous of the world. The retirement behavior visible in current data is mainly influenced by the reform. The 1972 system is generous in two respects. First, the

Table 22.1. The German Public Pension System from Bismarck until Today

1889/1991	Introduction of capital funded disability pension Old-age pension for workers age 70 and older Employer and employee share contributions equally
1913	Retirement at age 65 (white-collar workers only)
1916	Decrease in retirement age for disability pensions from 70 to 65
1921–23	Inflationary compensation
1923	Retirement at age 65 (blue-collar workers)
1929	Retirement at age 60 for elderly unemployed (white-collar workers only)

1957	Conversion into PAYG system
	   Contribution related pension benefits
	   Safeguarding the standard of living in old age is main objective
	   Dynamic benefits: indexed to gross wages and salaries
	Normal retirement age 65
	Retirement at age 60 for elderly unemployed (blue-collar workers)
	Retirement for women at age 60

1968	Pure PAYG-system with minimum reserves for three months
1972	Public retirement insurance system open for all citizens (self-employed, housewives) Ex post payment of contributions becomes possible Flexible early retirement age for insured with a long service life (63) and disabled persons (60) New minimum pension mechanism
1977	Pension splitting option for divorced couples
1978	Minimum reserves are reduced to one month
1986	Benefits for child education (usually one year of service life) Equal treatment for men and women regarding survivor's pensions

Table 22.1. (continued)

1992	Integration of the German Democratic Republic Indexing of pensions to net instead of gross wages and salaries Step-wise increase of retirement ages for unemployed, disabled persons, and women Introduction of actuarial adjustments for early retirement Significant reduction in years of education counting toward service life Benefits for child education are raised to three years of service life
1998	Value-added tax is increased to stabilize contributions to the GRV Introduction of the demographic factor

1999	Introduction of demographic factor is revoked
	Early retirement options for women and unemployed are restricted
	   Early retirement only for the long-insured and with benefit adjustments
	   Exceptions for disabled persons
	Ecological tax is increased to stabilize contributions to the GRV

2001	Transition to multipillar pension system (Riester reform)
	   Reduction of first pillar pensions through modified gross indexation
	   Strengthening of capital funded second and third pillars by subsidies and tax relief
	Redefinition of "disability"
	Further allowances for child education
	   Higher value in terms of recorded years of service life
	   Additive recording of employment becomes possible
	   Bonus for part-time employment
	Reform of survivors pensions
	   Expansion of eligible income base
	   Reduction of survivor's pension benefits
	   Introduction of a child bonus
	   Optional pension splitting for married couples

2002	Minimum reserves are reduced to two weeks
2004	Introduction of a "sustainability" factor, effectively transforming the PAYG pillar into a quasi-NDC system

Source: Authors' compilation.

Note: GRV is the German public pension insurance.

system has a high replacement rate, generating net retirement incomes that are currently about 70 percent of preretirement net earnings for a worker with a 45-year earnings history and average lifetime earnings.[3] This is substantially higher than, for example, the corresponding U.S. net replacement rate of about 53 percent.[4] The high initial level of public pensions was exacerbated by indexation to gross wages. Second, the 1972 reform abolished the mandatory retirement age of 65 years for those with a long service life[5] in favor of a flexible choice during a "window of retirement" between age 63 and 65, with no actuarial adjustments. Adding to these very generous early retirement provisions were easy ways to claim disability benefits and low mandatory retirement ages for women and unemployed persons, further increasing the number of beneficiaries and extending the "window of retirement" to between 60 and 65.

It is no surprise that the German public pension system is the single largest item in the German social budget. In the year 2001, public pension expenditures amounted to some 200 billion euros, representing 21 percent of public spending and 11.8 percent of GDP. It is the second largest pension budget in the Organisation for Economic Co-operation and Development (OECD) countries, surpassed only by Italy (at 14.2 percent of GDP). It is more than 2.5 times as expensive as the U.S. social security system (which is 4.4 percent of GDP).[6]

The generosity of the German public pension system is considered a great social achievement, but negative incentive effects and population aging are threatening its very core. Although incentive effects are still arcane in the eyes of politicians and the electorate, population aging has become a "megatrend" in the popular debate. All industrialized countries are aging, but Germany—together with Italy and Japan—will experience a particularly dramatic change in the age structure of the population. The severity of the demographic transition has two causes: a quicker increase in life expectancy than elsewhere, partly because of the still relatively low level in the 1970s, and a more incisive baby boom/baby bust transition (than the United States, for example) to a very low fertility rate of 1.3 children per woman, only a bit higher than the rock-bottom fertility rate of 1.2 in Italy and Spain. Consequently, the ratio of elderly to working-age persons—the old-age dependency ratio—will increase steeply. According to the latest OECD projections, the share of elderly (aged 65 and above) will exceed a quarter of the population in 2030, and the German old-age dependency ratio will almost double, from 24.0 percent in 2000 to 43.3 percent in 2030[7] (see figure 22.1).

The increase in the dependency ratio has immediate consequences for a PAYG social insurance system because fewer workers have to finance the benefits of more recipients. The German social security contribution rate, which in 2003 was 19.5 percent of gross income, was projected at the end of the 1980s to exceed 40 percent of gross income at the peak of population aging in 2035 if the accustomed replacement rates and the indication of pensions to gross income were maintained.[8] This led to a major pension reform in 1992.

Figure 22.1. Development of the Economic Dependency Ratio

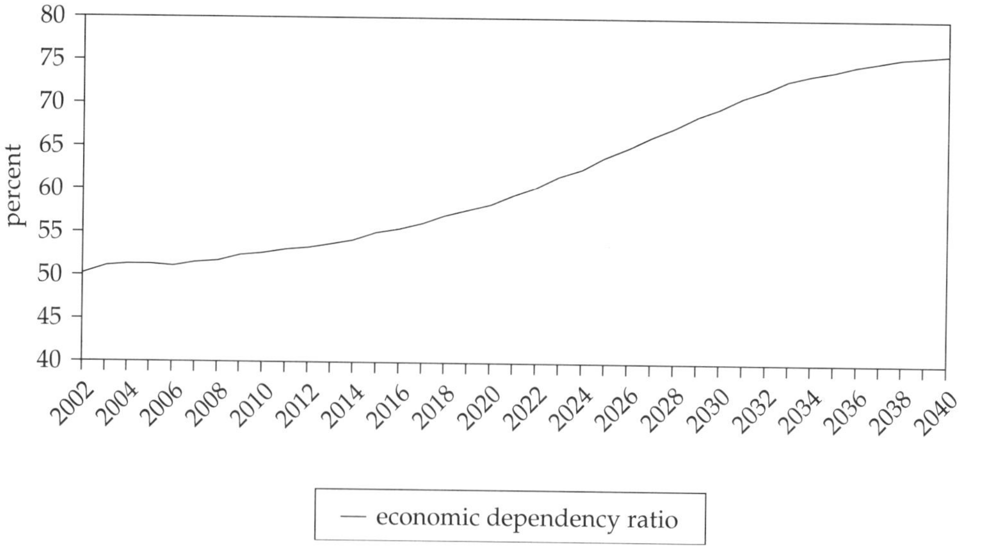

Source: Data supplied by the Rürup commission.

Note: Economic dependency ratio here is the number of equivalence pensioners to the number of equivalence contributors.

This reform abolished the indexation of pensions to gross wages in favor of net wages. While this is still more generous than indexation to the cost of living (such as in the United States), it was an important move away from the destabilizing feedback loop in which pensions increased when taxes and contributions heaved upward. In addition, the 1992 reform introduced adjustments of benefits to early retirement age and abolished the generous "window of retirement" for all but those who have long service lives. Benefit adjustments are, however, not fully actuarial. Changes in mandatory retirement ages are being introduced with a very long delay. First cohorts started experiencing these adjustments in 1997; the adjustments will be fully phased in by 2017.

It quickly became clear that the 1992 reform was too little and too late to put the German system on a stable and sustainable path. Another "parametric" reform introduced by the conservative government and due to become law in 1999, failed after the change in government in 1998. As a remarkable irony in politics, the social democratic secretary of labor, Walter Riester, successfully passed a major reform bill through parliament in 2001. This reform bade farewell to the pure PAYG system and introduced a multipillar pension system with a small but growing funded pillar. The new system will be fully phased in about 2050, but its main implications will be felt from 2011 onward.

Future reforms are likely.[9] None of the reforms so far has touched the normal retirement age, which is at age 65. This may come as a surprise, since in the light of a prolonged life span, increasing the active part of it appears to be a rather natural reform option, particularly since it simultaneously increases the number of contributors and decreases the number of beneficiaries and because age-specific morbidity rates appear to have shifted in line with mortality.[10] As noted before, average, median, and modal retirement age was about 60 years in 2002, the earliest eligibility age for old-age pensions and more than 5 years younger than the "normal" retirement age in Germany. In late fall of 2002, the government established a reform commission for the "Sustainability in Financing the Social Insurance Systems," popularly called the *Rürup commission*.[11] It delivered concrete proposals in August 2003. Most significantly, it transformed the PAYG pillar into a notional defined contribution (NDC) look-alike by introducing a sustainability factor into the benefit indexation formula and recommended an increase in the normal retirement age.[12] The new reform package was put into law in the spring of 2004.

This chapter describes the current reform process. It is structured as follows: the next two sections describe the institutional background for private sector and civil servants' pensions as they shaped the retirement behavior from 1972 until the end of the 1990s. The following three sections describe and assess the past and current reform process, culminating in the "Riester reform" of 2001 and continuing with the efforts of the Rürup commission. The final section concludes with the question of whether the 1992–2001 reforms and the current reform proposals will solve the problems of the German pension system. Although there is further work to be done to stabilize the German pension system, we are optimistic: substantial good work has been done, and we hope that some lessons can be drawn for other countries as well.

PART A: THE GERMAN PUBLIC PENSION SYSTEM—HOW IT WAS

The core of the German public pension system provides pensions to all private and public sector dependent employees, excluding civil servants and self-employed persons. We simply and somewhat loosely refer to this core system as "public pensions" or "private sector pensions" and describe it in the next subsection. In addition, civil servants—about 7 percent of the workforce—have their own PAYG system, which we describe in the following subsection. Self-employed persons—about 9 percent of the workforce—can participate in the public system (some trade associations make this mandatory; about two-thirds participate) or self-insure (about 3 percent of the labor force). We largely ignore their special status in our description.

Private Sector Pensions

The German *public retirement insurance* (*Gesetzliche Rentenversicherung*,or GRV) covers about 85 percent of the German workforce.[13] Most of these are private sector workers, but the GRV also includes those public sector workers who are not civil servants. For the average German retiree, occupational pensions do not play a major role in providing old-age income. Neither do individual retirement accounts, but there are important exceptions from this general picture. Broadly speaking, the German pension system—as it was created in 1972 and as it shapes the current retirees' income—is a monolith. This will change because of the reform described later. Some typical features of the German system, however, such as the benefit formula that is strictly linked to lifetime income and the resulting minor role of redistribution in the German pension system, will remain after the recent reforms.

Coverage and Contributions

The German public pension system features a very broad mandatory coverage of workers. Only the self-employed and, until 1998, workers with earnings below the official minimum earnings threshold (*Geringfügigkeitsgrenze*, which is 15 percent of the average monthly gross wage of all employees who paid contributions in that year; below this threshold are about 5.6 percent of all workers) are not subject to mandatory coverage.

Roughly 70 percent of the budget of the German public retirement insurance is financed by contributions that are administrated like a payroll tax, levied equally on employees and employers. Total contributions in 2003 were 19.5 percent of the first 5,100 euros of monthly gross income (upper earnings threshold, *Beitragsbemessungsgrenze*, is about twice the average monthly gross wage).[14] Technically contributions are split evenly between employees and employers. The contribution rate has been steadily rising since the late 1960s, and the upper earnings threshold has been used as an additional financing instrument. This threshold has increased considerably faster than wage growth.

Private sector pension benefits are essentially tax free. Pension beneficiaries do not pay contributions to the pension system and to unemployment insurance. However, pensioners have to pay the equivalent of the employees' contribution to the mandatory health and long-term care insurance. The equivalent of the employers' contribution to health insurance is paid by the pension system.

The remaining approximately 30 percent of the social security budget is financed by earmarked indirect taxes (a fixed fraction of the value-added tax and the new "eco-tax" on fossil fuel) and a subsidy from the federal government. The subsidy is also used to fine-tune the PAYG budget constraint because the system has a reserve of only about 14 days worth of benefits expenditures (as of spring 2004). As opposed to a "unified budget" such as in the United States, transfers can be made from the government to retirement insurance, but not the reverse.

Benefit Types

The German public retirement insurance provides *old-age pensions* for workers aged 60 and older; *disability benefits* for workers below age 60, which at the statutory retirement age are converted to old-age pensions at age 65; and *survivor benefits* for spouses and children. In addition, preretirement (that is, retirement before age 60) is possible through several mechanisms using the public transfer system, mainly unemployment compensation. We begin by describing old-age pensions.

Eligibility for Benefits and Retirement Age for Old-Age Pensions

Eligibility for benefits and the minimum retirement age depend on which type of pension applies to the worker. The German public retirement insurance distinguishes five types of old-age pensions, corresponding to normal retirement and four forms of early retirement. Table 22.2 shows the minimum retirement age for all pension types as it was until the late 1990s.

This complex system was introduced by the 1972 social security reform. One of the key provisions was the introduction of "flexible retirement" after age 63 with full benefits for workers with a long service history. In addition, retirement at age 60 with full benefits became possible for women, the unemployed, and older disabled workers. *Older disabled workers* referred to those workers who cannot be appropriately employed for health or labor market reasons and are age 60 or older. There were three ways to claim old-age disability benefits. One had to (1) be physically disabled to the extent that one is unable to work at least 50 percent, or (2) pass a strict earnings test, or (3) pass a much weaker earnings test. The strict earnings test was passed if the earnings capacity is reduced below the minimum earnings threshold for any *reasonable* occupation (about 15 percent of average gross wage, *Erwerbsunfähigkeit*, or EU). The weaker earnings test was passed when no vacancies for the worker's *specific* job description were available and the worker had to face an earnings loss of at least 50 percent when changing to a different job (*Berufsunfähigkeit*, or BU). In contrast to the disability insurance for workers below age 60 (see below), full benefits were paid in all three cases. This definition of disability and the associated earnings tests were changed as a part of the Riester Reform in 2001, and the term *disability* now applies in general only to health restrictions and no longer to labor market reasons.[15]

Because of the 1992 social security reform and its subsequent modifications, the age limits of early retirement will gradually be raised to age 65. These changes will be fully phased in by the year 2017, almost all changes, however, will be effective by 2011. The only distinguishing feature of types B and C of "early retirement" will then be the possibility to retire up to three years earlier than age 65 if a sufficient number of service years (currently

Table 22.2. Old-Age Pensions (1972 legislation)

Pension type	Retirement age	Years of service	Additional conditions	Earnings test
A Normal	65	5		No
B Long service life ("flexible retirement")	63	35		Yes
C Women	60	15	10 of the years of service after age 40	Yes
D Older disabled	60	35	Loss of at least 50 percent earnings capability	Yes
E Unemployed	60	15	1.5 to 3 years of unemployment (has changed several times)	Yes

Source: Authors' compilation.

Note: This legislation was changed in the reform of 1992. Changes first became effective between 1997 and 2001 (for the different pension types) and will be gradually phased in until 2017. Almost all changes will be effective by 2011.

35 years) has been accumulated. As opposed to the pre-1992 regulations, benefits will be adjusted to a retirement age below age 65 in the fashion described below.

OLD-AGE PENSION BENEFITS

Benefits are strictly work-related and quite close to actuarially fair and free from redistribution, very different from the United States.[16] The German system does not have benefits for spouses the way the U.S. system has.[17] Benefits are computed on a lifetime basis and adjusted according to the type of pension and the retirement age. They are the product of four elements: (1) the "earning points" (EP) that reflect the employee's relative earnings position, (2) the employee's years of service life (SY), (3) adjustment factors (AF) for pension type and (since the 1992 reform) retirement age, and (4) a macroeconomic reference pension value—the "current pension value" (PV). The annual value of a pension $P_{t,i}$ in year t for pensioner i is thus computed as follows:

$$P_{t,i} = EP_i * SY_i * AF_i * PV_t \qquad (22.1)$$

The first three factors make up the personal pension base; the fourth factor determines the income distribution between the current workers and the stock of pensioners. The combination of the first three factors is unique to the German pension system and provides a strong actuarial link between lifetime income and pension benefits—hence redistribution plays only a minor role. The current reform process will not change this. Rather, the cost-cutting reforms since 1992 all concentrate on the fourth factor and redefine how changes in the average earnings by workers affect the average pension. Note that the formula is applied to the entire stock of pensioners, not only to new entrants. Hence the German system is time-oriented, not cohort-oriented. This crucial difference from other pension systems—notably the Italian one—makes reform easier if equal burden sharing is an agreed upon principle among voters.

Earning points (EP). These are expressed as a multiple of the average annual contribution (roughly speaking, the relative income position) in each historical working year: one EP corresponds to average earnings in that year, 0.5 EP to 50 percent of average earnings, and 2 EPs to earnings twice as large as average earnings in that year.

Years of service life (SY). These comprise years of active contributions plus years of contributions on behalf of the employee and years that are counted as service years even when no contributions were made at all. They include, for instance, years of unemployment, years of military service, three years for each child's education for one of the parents, some allowance for advanced education, and so on. Unlike the case in many other countries, there is neither an upper bound of years entering the benefit calculation nor can workers choose certain years in their earnings history and drop others.

Adjustment factors (AF). This factor is one for a normal old-age pension. Before 1999, it included several adjustments to disability pensions. Depending on the type of disability pension, AF took on values between 0.25 and 1. Since about 2000, AF has a second element. For old-age pensions, it represents the adjustment of benefits to retirement age that are currently being phased-in (see table 22.3).

Current pension value (PV). This value is the crucial link between workers' earnings and pensioners' benefits. The PV is indexed to the annual changes in the level of wages and salaries net of pension contributions, and thus it enables pensioners to share in the rising prosperity generated by the economy. This link between changes in workers' earnings and pensioners' benefits is specified as a mathematical benefit indexation formula. Typical for the

Table 22.3. Adjustment of Public Pensions by Retirement Age

| | *Pension as a percentage of the pension that one would obtain if one had retired at age 65* | | | | |
| | Germany | | United States | | |
Age	pre-1992[a]	post-1992[b]	pre-1983[c]	post-1983[d]	Actuarially fair[e]
62	100.0	89.2	80.0	77.8	80.5
63	100.0	92.8	86.7	85.2	86.3
64	100.0	96.4	94.4	92.6	92.8
65	100.0	100.0	100.0	100.0	100.0
66	107.2	106.0	103.0	105.6	108.1
67	114.4	112.0	106.0	111.1	117.2
68	114.4	118.0	109.0	120.0	127.4
69	114.4	124.0	112.0	128.9	139.1

Source: Börsch-Supan and Schnabel (1999).

Note: a. GRV 1972–92; b. GRV after 1992 reform has fully phased in (after 2011); c. U.S. social security (OASDHI) until 1983; d. U.S. social security after the 1983 social security reform has fully phased in; e. Evaluated at a 3 percent discount rate, 1992/94 mortality risks of West German men and an annual increase in net pensions of 1 percent.

philosophy of the German public pension system, this mathematical formula, verbatim, is part of the law.

In the past the stability of this formula created a sense of actuarial fairness, so that workers perceived the contributions largely as insurance premia. However, this changed when the formula was altered several times since 1992. Until 1992, pensions were indexed to gross wages, between 1992 and 1998 to net wages, and in 1999 and 2000 to the respective previous year's rate of inflation. The perception of discretionary changes and the prospect of further reductions in the pension generosity has led to a great deal of dissatisfaction with the German pension system, in particularly among younger workers. Surveys show that by 2001, contributions were largely perceived as taxes.[18] Nonetheless and inevitably, changes in the benefit indexation formula are one of the main elements of the current cost-cutting reforms. Indexation to the average net labor income from 1992 until 1998 solved some of the problems that were created by indexation to gross wages until 1992.[19]

The German public pension system has provided a generous benefit level for middle-income earnings. The net replacement rate for a worker with 45 earning points was 70.5 percent in 1998.[20]

Unlike the U.S. social security system, the German pension system has only a little redistribution—as is obvious from the benefit computation.[21] The low replacement rates for high incomes result from the upper limit to which earnings are subject to social security contributions—they correspond to a proportionally lower effective contribution rate. The only element of redistribution in the individual benefit computation formula was introduced in 1972. The 1972 legislation stipulated that an annual earnings point could not fall below 0.75 before 1972, provided a worker had a service life of at least 35 years. A similar rule was introduced in the 1992 reform: between 1973 and 1992, earning points below 0.75 were retroactively multiplied by 1.5 up to the maximum of 0.75, effectively reducing the redistribution for workers with income positions below 50 percent. In 2001, this system was abolished in favor of a guaranteed minimum pension (*Grundsicherung*) at the level of social assistance plus 15 percent.

Before 1992, adjustment of benefits to retirement age was only implicit via SY. Because benefits are proportional to the SY, a worker with fewer SY will get lower benefits. With a constant income profile and 40 SY, each year of earlier retirement decreased pension benefits by 2.5 percent, and vice versa. The 1992 social security reform is changing this gradually (see figure 22.5). Age 65, the "normal retirement age," is thus acting as the "pivotal age" for benefit computations. For each year of earlier retirement up to five years, and if the appropriate conditions in table 22.2 are met, benefits will be reduced by 3.6 percent (in addition to the effect of fewer service years). The 1992 reform also introduced rewards for *later* retirement in a systematic way. For each year of retirement postponed past the mandatory retirement age, the pension is increased by 5 percent in addition to the "natural" increase by the number of service years.

Table 22.3 displays the retirement-age-specific adjustments for a worker who has earnings that remain constant after age 60. The table relates the retirement income for retirement at age 65 (normalized to 100 percent) to the retirement income for retirement at earlier or later ages, and compares the implicit adjustments made after 1972 with the total adjustments made after the 1992 social security reform is fully phased in. As references, the table also displays the corresponding adjustments in the United States and actuarially fair adjustments at a 3 percent discount rate.[22]

Although neither the German nor the U.S. system were actuarially fair prior to the reforms, the public retirement system in Germany as enacted in 1972 was particularly distortive. There was less economic incentive for Americans to retire before age 65 and only a small disincentive to retire later than at age 65 after the 1983 U.S. reform, while the German social security system at those times tilted the retirement decision heavily toward the earliest retirement age applicable. The 1992 reform has diminished but not abolished this incentive effect, as a comparison of the sixth and the third column of table 22.3 shows.

DISABILITY AND SURVIVOR BENEFITS

The contributions to the German retirement insurance also finance disability benefits for workers of all ages and survivor benefits for spouses and children. To be eligible for *disability benefits*, a worker must pass one of the two earnings tests described earlier for the old-age disability pension. If the stricter earnings test is passed, full benefits are paid (*Erwerbsunfähigkeitsrente*, or EU). If only the weaker earnings test is passed and some earnings capability remains, disability pensions before age 60 are only two-thirds of the applicable old age pension (*Berufsunfähigkeitsrente*, or BU). In the 1970s and early 1980s, the German jurisdiction has interpreted both rules very broadly, in particular the applicability of the first rule. Moreover, jurisdiction also overruled the earnings test during disability retirement. This led to a share of EU-type disability pensions of more than 90 percent of all disability pensions. Because both rules were used as a device to keep unemployment rates down, their generous interpretation has only recently, in the context of the Riester reform, led to stricter legislation.[23]

Survivor pensions are 60 percent (after 2001, 55 percent) of the husband's applicable pension for spouses who are age 45 and over or if children are in the household (*große Witwenrente*), otherwise 25 percent (*kleine Witwenrente*). Survivor benefits are therefore a large component of the public pension budget and of total pension wealth. Certain earnings tests apply if the surviving spouse has her own income—for example, her own pension. This is only relevant for a very small (below 10 percent) share of widows. As mentioned before, the German system does not have a married couple supplement for spouses of beneficiaries. However, most wives acquire their own pension by active (own employment) and passive contributions (years of advanced education and years of child education).

Preretirement

In addition to benefits through the public pension system, transfer payments (mainly unemployment compensation) enable what is referred to as *preretirement*. Labor force exit before age 60 is frequent: about 45 percent of all men call themselves retired at age 59. Only about half of them retire because of disability; the other 50 percent make use of one of the many official and unofficial preretirement schemes.

Unemployment compensation has been used as preretirement income in an unofficial scheme that induced very early retirement. Workers entered such a scheme much earlier than age 60 and were paid a negotiable combination of unemployment compensation and a supplement or severance pay. A pension of type E (see table 22.2) could then start at age 60. As the rules of pensions of type E and the duration of unemployment benefits changed, so did the "unofficial" retirement ages. Age 56 was particularly frequent in the Federal Republic of Germany because unemployment compensation is paid up to three years for elderly workers; it is followed by the lower unemployment aid. Earlier retirement ages could be induced by paying the worker the difference between the last salary and unemployment compensation for three years; and for further years the difference between the last salary and unemployment aid—it all depended on the "social plan" that a firm would negotiate with its workers before restructuring the workforce.

In addition, early retirement at age 58 was made possible in an official preretirement scheme (*Vorruhestand*), in which the employer received a subsidy from the unemployment insurance if a younger employee was hired. The first (and unofficial) preretirement scheme was very popular and a convenient way to overcome the strict German labor laws, but few employers used the (official) second scheme.

Retirement Behavior

The retirement behavior of entrants into the German public retirement insurance system closely reflects changes in the institutional environment. This is an important finding, summarized by figure 22.2. The figure shows the uptake of the various pathways to old-age pensions,[24] including the disability pathway, (adding to 100 percent on the vertical axis) and its development over time (marked on the horizontal axis). Most of these changes are in response to benefit adjustments and administrative rule changes, in particular the tightening of the disability screening process. The fraction of those who enter retirement through a disability pension has declined and was 29 percent in 1998. Only about 20 percent of all entrants used the "normal" pathway of an old-age pension at age 65.

The average retirement age in 1998 was 59.7 years for men and 60.7 years for women. These numbers refer to West Germany. In East Germany, retirement age was 57.9 years for men and 58.2 years for women. The average retirement age has dramatically declined after the 1972 reform (see figure 22.3). We interpret this as a clear sign of a policy reaction since it does not coincide with labor demand effects generated by the rise in unemployment.[25] The most popular retirement age is age 60 (see figure 22.4). The close correspondency/accordance of the development of the average retirement age with the pathways in table 22.2 is another clear sign of a behavioral response to the incentives created by the pension system, in particular the change of the peaks and spikes after the 1972 reform.[26]

Civil Service Pensions

About 90 percent of the German labor force is enrolled in the system described in the previous section. About one-third of the self-employed are self insured (3 percent of the labor force), and another 7 percent are civil servants. Civil servants are exempted from the public pension system. They do not pay explicit contributions for their pensions as the other employees in the private and public sectors do.[27] Instead, the "gross" wage for civil servants is lower than the gross wage of other public sector employees with a comparable education. Civil servants acquire pension claims that are considerably more generous than those described in the previous section, and they have rather distinctive early retirement

Figure 22.2. Pathways to Retirement, 1960–2002

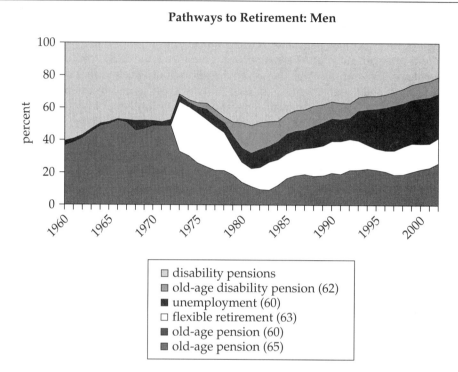

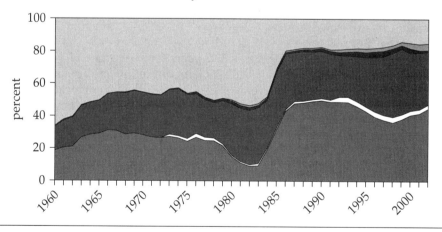

Source: VDR (2002).

Figure 22.3. Average Retirement Age, 1960–1995

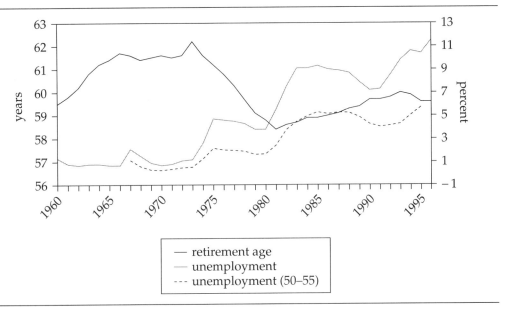

Source: VDR (1997) and BMA (1997).

Note: Retirement age is the average age of all new entries into the public pension system; *unemployment* is the general national unemployment rate; *unemployment (50–55)* refers to unemployed men age 50–55.

Figure 22.4. Distribution of Retirement Ages, 1970, 1975, 1980, and 1995

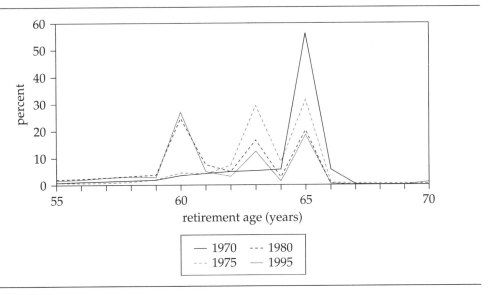

Source: VDR (1997).

incentives. Although the private sector pensions described above have undergone an incisive reform process (see the next main section), civil servants have largely been protected from benefit cuts so far.

Eligibility: Pathways to Retirement for Civil Servants

There are three pathways for civil servants: the *standard* option, the *early* option, and the *disability* retirement option. The standard retirement age is 65. Before July 1, 1997, the early retirement age for civil servants was 62, and thus one year less than the early retirement age for workers with a long service life in the social security system. In 1997, the early retirement age was raised to 63. Discount factors for early retirement were phased in linearly between the years 1998 and 2003, and reached 0.3 percentage points per month of early retirement, the same as in the private sector and substantially smaller than actuarially fair.[28]

Filing for disability is a third pathway to retirement for civil servants. In the case of disability, a civil servant receives a pension that is based on his or her previous salary. The replacement rate depends on the number of service years reached before disability retirement and the number of service years that could potentially have been accumulated until age 60. For those who did not reach the maximum replacement rate before disability, one additional year of service raises the replacement rate by only one-third of a percentage point per year.

Computation of Civil Servants' Pensions

The standard pension benefit for civil servants is the product of three elements: (1) the last gross earnings level, (2) the replacement rate as function of service years, and (3) the new adjustment factors to early retirement. There are three crucial differences between civil servants pensions and private sector benefits. First, the benefit base is gross rather than net income as it was in the private sector between 1992 and 1998. In turn, civil servants' pensions are taxed the same way as any other income. Finally, the benefit base is the last salary rather than the lifetime average.

Last gross earnings level. Benefits are anchored to the earnings in the last position and then updated annually by the growth rate of the net earnings of active civil servants. If the last position was reached within the last two years before retirement, the pension is based on the previous, lower position. Due to the difference in the benefit base, gross pensions of civil servants are approximately 25 percent higher (other things being equal) than in the private sector.

Replacement rate. The maximum replacement rate is 75 percent of *gross* earnings—considerably higher than the official replacement rate of the private sector system, which is around 70 percent of *net* earnings. The replacement rate depends on the years of service. High school and college education, military service, and other work in the public sector are also counted as service years. For retirement after June 1997, the college education credit is limited to 3 years.

Before 1992, the replacement rate was a nonlinear function of service years. The replacement rate started at a value of 35 percent for all civil servants with at least five years of service. For each additional year of service between the 10th and the 25th year, the increment was 2 percentage points. From the 25th to the 35th year, the annual increment was 1 percent. Thus the maximum replacement rate of 75 percent was reached with 35 service years under the old rule. This is much more generous than the private sector replacement rate of 70 percent, which requires 45 years of service.

New adjustment factors to early retirement. For persons retiring after January 1, 1992, the replacement rate grows by 1.875 percentage points for each year of service. Thus, the maximum value is reached after 40 years of service. However, there are transitional modifications to that simple rule. First, civil servants who reach the standard retirement age (usually age 65) before January 1, 2002, are not affected at all. Second, for younger civil servants, all claims that have been acquired before 1992 are conserved. These persons gain one additional percentage point per year from 1992 on. All persons who have acquired 25 service years before 1992 have reached 65 percentage points and would also have gained only one additional point per year under the old rule. Only persons with less than 25 service years in 1991 can be made worse off by the reform. The new proportional rule applies only if it generates a higher replacement rate than the transitional rule.

The generosity of gross pensions received by civil servants vis-à-vis private sector workers is only partially offset by the preferential tax treatment of private sector pensions. Since civil servants' pensions are taxed according to the German comprehensive income taxation, the net replacement rates of civil service pension recipients depends on their position in the highly progressive tax schedule. In general, the net replacement rate with respect to the preretirement net earnings is higher than 75 percent and thus considerably more generous than the net replacement rate in the private sector.

Incentives to Retire for Civil Servants

Currently, most civil servants reach the maximum replacement rate by the age of 54. Persons who have started to work in the public sector before the age of 23 have reached a replacement rate of 75 percent when taking into account the disability rules. This also holds for civil servants, who—like professors—receive lifetime tenure late in their life cycle. For those groups the starting age is usually set to age 21. Additional years of service beyond the age of 54 increase pensions only if the civil servant is promoted to a position with a higher salary. Retirement incentives therefore strongly depend on promotion expectations.

For persons who cannot expect to be promoted after age 54, the pension accrual is zero or very small. For those who have already reached the replacement rate of 75 percent, the accrual of the present discounted pension wealth is negative. Since the replacement rate is 75 percent of the gross earnings in the last position before retirement, the negative accrual of postponing retirement by one year is simply 75 percent of the last gross earnings. This is equivalent to a 75 percent tax on earnings.

For persons who expect to climb another step in the hierarchy, the gross wage increase is on average 10.5 percent. This raises the pension by approximately 10 percent. To cash in the higher pension, the civil servant has to defer retirement by at least one year.[29] In this case the social security wealth increases 10 percent through the effect of higher pensions and decreases by 5 percent through the effect of pension deferral; the pension accrual is positive. If the civil servant has to wait several years for the next promotion (or for the promotion to have an effect on pension claims) the accrual of working becomes negative; hence, it makes no financial sense to keep working.

Retirement Behavior of Civil Servants

The retirement behavior of civil servants reflects the very generous disability and early retirement rules. The average retirement age for civil servants in the year 1993 was age 58.9 and thus about one year lower than in the private sector. Disability is the most important pathway to retirement for civil servants: 40 percent of those who retired in the year 1993 used disability retirement. Almost one-third used the early retirement option at the age of 62. Only about 20 percent of civil servants retired at the regular retirement age of 65.

PART B: THE GERMAN PUBLIC PENSION SYSTEM— HOW IT WILL BECOME AN NDC LOOK-ALIKE

The German Pension Reform Process

After the remarkable expansion of the German pension system after 1972, four dates mark the pension reform process in Germany: 1992 and 2001 have seen two major pension reforms, with a further strengthening of the 2001 reform in 2004. A reform due to become law in 1999 failed after federal elections, but some elements were resurrected in the 2004 reform. In addition, there was a constant flurry of smaller adjustments in between.

From its beginning, the point system (see the subsection on benefit types) can be regarded as a first and important element of the NDC approach. Together with the central measure of the 2004 reform, the sustainability factor, and the almost actuarial adjustment factors introduced in 1992, the German PAYG system will almost perfectly emulate an NDC system from the year 2005 on.

The 1992 Reform

The first main change of the 1992 reform was to anchor benefits to net rather than to gross wages. This implicitly reduced benefits since taxes and social security contributions have increased, reducing net relative to gross wages. This mechanism will become particularly important when population aging speeds up, since it implies an implicit mechanism of burden sharing between generations.

The second important element in the 1992 reform was the introduction of "actuarial" adjustments to benefits to retirement age and an increase in the "normal" retirement ages for all pension types, except disability pensions (age 63), to 65. These changes have been described earlier and are displayed in figure 22.5 (including their 1999 speed-up). They will reduce incentives to retire early, although the "actuarial" adjustments are not actuarially neutral in a mathematical sense except when a very low discount rate is applied in the computation of what constitutes actuarial neutrality.[30] The introduction of benefit adjustments to retirement age in Germany mimics the automatic benefit adjustments within an NDC system approach, where benefits are adjusted to retirement age by the annuity formula. However, in contrast to an NDC system, the adjustments in the German system have been set discretionarily and are not directly linked to changes in life expectancy. They are about 1.5 percentage points lower than current life tables and a 3 percent discount rate would imply.

The 1999 Reform

The 1999 pension reform was supposed to lower the replacement rate according to a pre-specified "demographic factor"—a function of life expectancy plus several correction factors. The reform was revoked after the change of government in 1998. A side effect of this reform, which was not revoked, was a gradual change of eligibility ages for pensions for women and unemployed persons (types C and E in table 22.2) from age 60 to age 65. This change will be fully implemented by 2017, and effectively leaves a "window of retirement" for healthy workers only if they have at least 35 years of service. As opposed to the arrangements shown in table 22.2, there will be no distinction between men and women (after the year 2015); unemployment-retirement will be abolished (after the year 2007); and part-time retirement (which was largely taken in two "blocks" of full-work and subsequent full-retirement) will be impossible (after the year 2007). Figure 22.5 depicts the new eligibility regulations and adjustment paths for the various pension types described before in table 22.2. These changes were largely unnoticed by the population. They will change the effective retirement age by around 2 years from about age 60 to age 62.[31]

**Figure 22.5. Retirement Age with and without "Actuarial" Adjustments
(1992 and 1999 reforms)**

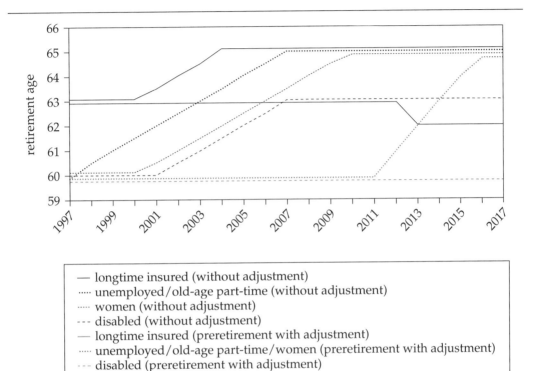

— longtime insured (without adjustment)
····· unemployed/old-age part-time (without adjustment)
····· women (without adjustment)
--- disabled (without adjustment)
— longtime insured (preretirement with adjustment)
····· unemployed/old-age part-time/women (preretirement with adjustment)
--·- disabled (preretirement with adjustment)

Source: Authors' compilation.

The Riester Reform in 2001

On May 11, 2001, a new pension reform act was ratified in Germany. This is popularly referred to as the *Riester reform* after the then labor minister, Walter Riester. The 2001 reform is a major change in the system. It will change the monolithic German system of old-age provision to a genuine multipillar system. The most important aspect of the reform, which came into effect on January 1, 2002, is a partial substitution of PAYG-financed pensions by funded pensions. The reform aimed to achieve three main objectives:

- **Sustainable contribution rates.** The key objective of the Riester reform was to stabilize contribution rates and thus (1) to limit further increases in nonwage labor costs and (2) to achieve a fairer balance of intergenerational burdens. The law actually states that contribution rates to the public retirement insurance scheme must stay below 20 percent until 2020 and below 22 percent until 2030 while the net replacement rate must stay above 67 percent. Failure must precipitate government action.
- **Secure the long-term stability of pension levels.** Pensions will be gradually reduced from the current level of 70 percent of average net earnings to around 67–68 percent by the year 2030. At the same time, however, the Riester reform changed the computational procedure for the reference earnings, now subtracting a fictitious 4 percent of gross earning to be invested into the new, funded, supplementary private pensions. This differs from the definition of net earnings that applied prior to the

reform, as it means that actual PAYG pension levels will fall by a larger margin (by some 10 percent to about 63.5 percent) than suggested by the new definition.

- **Spread of supplementary private pension savings.** The decline in public pensions is expected to be offset by supplementary (occupational and private) pensions. To achieve this aim, supplementary pensions are subsidized, either by tax deferral and tax deduction, or by direct subsidies to individual and occupational pension plans. These supplementary pensions are, however, not mandated.

Table 22.4 gives an overview over the main changes. The next subsection describes in detail how costs in the PAYG pillar are cut. The emerging gap is supposed to be filled by private individual and occupational pensions. The following subsections describe the subsidies for the private supplementary funded pensions and the changes in occupational pension. An assessment of the likely economic success of the Riester reform follows in the next main section.

The PAYG Pillar: Reducing the Replacement Rate

The calculation of the current monthly pension value PV_t for a specific year t takes account of the development of the earnings of all workers (see equation 22.1). This procedure is intended to guarantee that the "standard pension replacement rate" remains stable and does not fall behind the development of current average earnings.[32] Before the 2001 reform, the objective of safeguarding standards of living in old age was considered to be met if pensions were worth 70 percent of average net earnings. Thus the pension level more than maintained the purchasing power of the level of pension entitlements acquired

Table 22.4. Overview of the Core Elements of the Riester Reform

Measure	Content	Pillar
Introduction of a needs-oriented basic income	Minimum social security guarantee for old age; reduction in earning capacity secured by means of needs-oriented basic income	0
New adjustment formula	Reduction in pension level by about 10 percent	1
Abolition of occupational incapacity pensions	Discontinuation of occupational incapacity pensions; replacement by two-tier general invalidity pension	1
Reform of women's and survivors' pensions	Modification of income rules for survivors' pensions; introduction of "pension splitting for married couples"	1
Reformed framework for occupational pensions	Introduction of a legal right to convert salary into pension contributions; relaxation of investing rules; introduction of pension funds; DC plans permitted	2
Establishment of funded (voluntary) supplementary pension provision	Introduction of individual retirement accounts; rules for the recognition of financial services products eligible for state subsidies (Retirement Pension Contracts Certification Act); provision of state subsidy; introduction of deferred taxation	3

Source: Authors' compilation.

when a person retires. Until the 2001 reform, the German pension system was essentially run by adapting the contribution rate to this 70 percent standard replacement rate.

In 2001, the Riester reform introduced a rather complex new adjustment formula, which relates changes in the pension value (PV_t) to lagged changes in gross income (AGI_t), modified by the actual contribution rate to public pensions (π_t) and a fictitious contribution rate to the new private pension accounts (AVA_t), gradually increasing from 0.5 percent in 2003 to 4 percent in 2009. In addition, a somewhat awkward "sensitivity factor" d_t was introduced. It is 100 until 2010, then decreases to 90, which effectively increases the sensitivity of PV to increases in π after 2010. It thus simply decreases the replacement rate after 2010:

$$PV_t = PV_{t-1} \frac{AGI_{t-1}}{AGI_{t-2}} \frac{\dfrac{d_t}{100} - AVA_{t-1} - \tau_{t-1}}{\dfrac{d_t}{100} - AVA_{t-2} - \tau_{t-2}}. \tag{22.2}$$

The complex design of the formula reflects the balance between the two opposing aims of the reform: to keep the contribution rate below a fixed level (20 percent until 2020, 22 percent until 2030), and to keep the redefined standard replacement level above 67 percent until 2030. Both conflicting aims are part of the German pension law. If any of these aims are violated, the law precipitates government action, such as the introduction of the reform commission in 2003. Note that the awkward jump in the sensitivity factor d_t reflects the aims since the system dependency ratio is still flat until 2010 and then quickly rises (see figure 22.1).

The New Funded Pillar: Introducing Supplementary Funded Pensions

A crucial component of the Riester reform is the introduction and significant promotion of supplementary funded private pensions to fill the pension gap created by the reduction of the replacement rate. The objective is to offer incentives for people to take out supplementary private pension cover that, in the long term, should compensate for the future cuts in public pensions. However, there will be no legal mandate for people to invest in additional private schemes. These Riester pensions can be occupational or individual pensions. Since many restrictions apply, it remains to be seen how many workers actually start building up private pensions.

The main restriction on supplementary pensions is on payment plans. Since additional private pension schemes are intended to supplement or replace benefits from the public pension scheme, the government decided that incentives will be available only for investment vehicles that guarantee payment of a life annuity payable from the date of retirement. Investment vehicles that provide for lump-sum disbursements are not subject to state subsidies.[33] This restriction has already met with considerable criticism in the public debate as it excludes other forms of provision for old age (such as investments in old-age or nursing homes).

The incentives provided by the state can take two forms: direct savings subsidies or tax-deductible special allowances. The tax authorities automatically compute which of the two forms versions is most advantageous.

Direct savings subsidy. All dependently employed and certain self-employed workers who pay personal contributions to a certified retirement pension policy are entitled to receive a direct retirement savings subsidy. The subsidy is paid directly into the beneficiary's saving account. A basic subsidy and a child subsidy for each child for which child benefits were received during the previous year is paid. Child subsidies are payable to the mother. In the case of married couples, both partners receive a basic subsidy if they have each taken out their own supplementary private pension policy. In addition, nonentitled partners (such as mothers not in paid employment) are also entitled to receive the full subsidy for their own retirement pension policy provided that the respective married partner subject to compulsory insurance contributions has paid his or her minimum personal contribution to their supplementary retirement pension policy (see below).

Table 22.5 shows the maximum incentive subsidies available as of 2002. To qualify for the maximum subsidy, the beneficiary must invest a specified percentage of his or her gross earnings (denoted as "savings rate"). This percentage increases until 2008 in four steps (*Riester-Treppe*). The percentage is applied to the actual earnings level, capped at the same cap as the PAYG contributions (about two times average earnings). If less money is invested, the state subsidy is reduced accordingly. The scheme is complicated by the fact that the subsidy is included in the savings amount. Hence, the actual savings rate necessary for the maximum subsidy is lower than the percentages indicated in the second column of table 22.5. In turn, certain minimum amounts are necessary (see table 22.6).

Tax deductible special expenses. Alternatively, qualifying retirement savings can be deducted as "special allowances" from income taxes. This is usually more advantageous for workers with higher-than-average earnings. Saving rates, caps, and so on are the same as in the subsidy case. Table 22.7 shows the maximum tax-deductible contributions to private retirement savings accounts.

Table 22.5. Direct Savings Subsidies

From ... on	Savings rate	Basic subsidy in euros/year	Child subsidy in euros/year
2002	1 percent	38	46
2004	2 percent	76	92
2006	3 percent	114	138
2008	4 percent	154	185

Source: Authors' compilation.

Table 22.6. Minimum Savings (euros/year)

Year	No child	One child	Two or more children
2002–4	45	38	30
As of 2005	90	75	60

Source: Authors' compilation.

Table 22.7. Maximum Savings (euros/year)

From ... on	Tax deductible special expenses in euro/year
2002	525
2004	1.050
2006	1.575
2008	2.100

Source: Authors' compilation.

Criteria for individual pension plans eligible for subsidies/tax relief. Individual retirement accounts qualify for state promotion only if they meet criteria laid down in the new Certification of Retirement Pension Contracts Act (AltZertG). This act contains a long list of rules that makes the system complex for customers and potential insurers alike. Qualifying pension plans require certification by the Federal Financial Markets Authority (*Bundesanstalt für Finanzdienstleistungs- und Finanzmarktaufsicht*), which will be granted automatically if they fulfill the following preconditions:

1. The investor must be committed to making regular, voluntary pension contributions.
2. Pension benefits may be paid out only when the beneficiary reaches the age of 60 at the earliest or upon reaching retirement age.
3. At the beginning of the disbursement phase, the accrued pension contributions (inclusive of subsidies) must be guaranteed (that is, the nominal rate of return must be nonnegative).
4. Pension payments must guarantee lifelong benefits that retain or increase their nominal value—that is, they must be in the form of a life annuity or disbursement plan linked to lifelong annual installments.
5. The disbursement plan must continue to provide benefits until the beneficiary reaches the age of 85 and subsequently provide a life annuity guaranteed by the capital available at the beginning of the disbursement phase.
6. Supplementary survivor's coverage must not have features that offset the original plan.
7. Initial commission and administrative charges must be spread equally over a period of at least 10 years.
8. The investor must be informed about the following issues before taking out the policy: the level and distribution over time of commission and administrative costs, the cost of switching to a different policy, the costs of financial management, and the costs involved in changing to a different insurer.
9. The investor must be informed once a year during the term of the policy about how his or her contributions are being used, capital formation, costs, and yields, and also about whether and to what extent the insurer takes account of ethical, social, and ecological investment criteria.
10. The investor must have the right to suspend contributions during the saving phase, to allow the policy to continue running without making additional contributions, or to terminate the policy by serving three months notice to the end of the quarter.
11. Policy rights may not be assigned or transferred to third parties. Claims to pension benefits cannot, as a result, be bequeathed.

Products eligible for subsidy support and into which old-age pension contributions and the proceeds on such contributions may be invested include pension insurance and capitalization products, bank accounts with accumulated interest, and shares in growth and distributing investment funds. These products are offered by life insurance companies, banks, capital investment companies, financial services institutions, and securities services companies.

Deferred taxation. Although old-age pension contributions will be tax exempt during the saving phase, pension payments during the benefit phase will be taxed in full as normal income. This applies to all benefits regardless of whether these accrue from contributions, subsidies, or capital gains. One may regard this as another form of subsidy, since taxes occur later in life (hence, an implicit tax credit) and usually at a lower rate due to progressivity.[34]

State Promotion of Occupational Pension Schemes

The Riester reform remained largely inexplicit on the role of occupational pensions versus individual accounts. Occupational pensions have traditionally played a minor role in Germany, particularly in comparison with other countries. Demand for participation in occupational pension schemes has also been falling in recent years.[35] On the other hand, occupational pensions may provide a psychological substitute for mandated private pensions. To strengthen occupational pensions, additional (implicit and explicit) subsidies were introduced with the Riester reform.

The most important change that results from the Riester reform is the general right of the worker to convert part of the salary directly into contributions to pension plans. This applies regardless of whether the contributions are paid by the employer or the employee. Arrangements may be based both on gross and net pay. If they are based on net pay, there is a large implicit subsidy since the so-converted salary may not only be subject to deferred taxation but can also be exempt from social security contributions, at least until 2008. If they are based on gross pay, contributions may enjoy the same direct subsidies or tax relief as contributions to individual accounts, as long as the occupational pensions meet certain criteria that are less restrictive than the criteria for individual pension plans. Which contribution rules apply depends on the chosen investment vehicle and the incentives they attract (see below and table 22.4). Collective bargaining agreements, however, have precedence over the right to convert salary. This means that an employee covered by a binding collective agreement is entitled to convert his or her pay into pension only if this is explicitly provided for in the terms of the collective agreement. This rule makes sure that employers and unions can impose their own rules on occupational pension plans.

Investment vehicles and eligibility for Riester subsidies/tax relief. The Riester reform also introduced pension funds as a vehicle for occupational pensions—an investment vehicle that is widely used in other countries, but was previously not permitted in Germany. There are now five different investment vehicles in German occupational pension schemes (see table 22.8 for an overview of their features). Only three of these schemes are eligible for Riester incentives: (1) direct insurance, (2) staff pension insurance, and (3) pension funds. As the employer has to provide the employee with the chance of benefiting from the Riester incentives, this means—especially for smaller companies—that some companies now have to restructure their pension schemes.

An Assessment of the Riester Reform

Will the recent reforms, particularly the Riester reform, solve the problems of the German public pension system? An important and still open question is whether the new voluntary supplementary private pensions, the "Riester pensions," will be accepted by the German workers who were used to the all-caring public system. This is the topic of the next subsection. The subsection following then asks whether the new supplementary private pensions will suffice to offset the cuts in the PAYG pillar if workers actually participate, and the final subsection of this assessment of the Riester reform combines these results and poses the main question: Will the Riester reform put the German system of old-age provision on a stable and lasting new foundation?

Will the Riester Pensions Actually Take Off?

Since the new pensions are voluntary, one of the most debated issues in the context of the Riester reform is the question of whether workers will actually overcome the temptations

Table 22.8. Types of Occupational Pension Systems

Features	Investment Vehicles				
	Direct pension promise (Direktzusage)	Benefit funds (Unterstützungskasse)	Direct insurance (Direktversicherung)	Staff pension insurance (Pensions-kasse)	Pension funds (Pensionsfonds)
Tax on contributions	Tax free		1. Flat-rate tax 2. Fully taxed but Riester subsidy/tax deductible expense	1. Flat-rate tax 2. Fully taxed but Riester subsidy/tax deductible expense 3. Tax free until 4% of BMG	1. Fully taxed but Riester subsidy/tax deductible expense 2. Tax free until 4% of BMG
Tax on benefits	Fully taxed		1. Tax on returns only 2. Fully taxed	1. Tax on returns only 2. Fully taxed 3. Fully taxed	1. Fully taxed 2. Fully taxed
Investment	Internal		External		
Investment rules	None		Acc. Insurance Supervisory Act		None
Insolvency scheme	Membership in pension insurance fund (PSV)		No		Membership in PSV
State supervision	No		Federal Insurance Authority (Bundesaufsichtsamt für das Versicherungswesen)		

Source: Authors' compilation.

Note: BMG = earnings threshold (Beitragsbemessungsgrenze).

to procrastinate. How many will build up supplementary pensions? How much will they save? At this point, only one year since their introduction, it is too early to tell. It took about 5 years to popularize a general subsidized dedicated savings program (*Vermö-genswirksame Leistungen*, directly deducted from payroll), which now enjoys almost universal participation. In the United States, individual retirement accounts (IRAs) needed at least as long to be accepted by a large share of households. In this section, we look at the Riester pension's design and incentives to understand who is likely to take it up and who is not.

The depth of Riester incentives. Two aspects need to be considered when assessing the benefits offered by Riester incentives: the subsidies/tax exemptions during the contribution phase and any tax-related advantages or disadvantages that arise during the disbursement phase. The direct subsidies during the contribution phase are very deep for those who have relatively low incomes and those who have children. The reverse is the case for the tax-deductible special allowances, due to the progressive tax system. Here, households with higher incomes benefit more. This results in a U-shaped relation between subsidies and income, visible in figure 22.6, which shows the subsidy as a percentage of savings in the form of the new supplementary pensions.[36]

For lowest-income households, the subsidy is almost as large as the contribution itself. Even for the well-to-do, subsidy rates are high: around 40–50 percent. Given these deep subsidies, uptake is likely to be high.

Figure 22.6. Depth of Subsidies to Riester Pensions

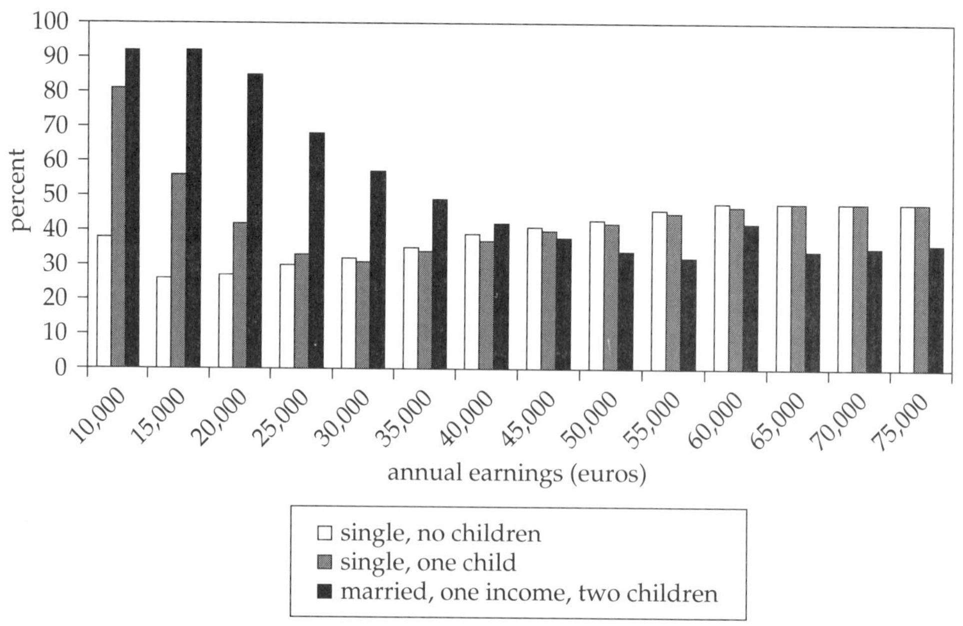

Source: Deutsche Bundesbank (2002).

Note: Direct subsidy tax advantage as a percentage of savings in form of the new supplementary pensions.

The image of figure 22.6, however, is misleading insofar as this U-shaped curve is flattened out during the disbursement phase when pension benefits will be taxed. This flattening effect is due to the impact of progressive taxation. Taxation will not affect pensioners in the lower half of the income distribution because their pension income is below a generous exemption for retired households. It will, however, considerably reduce the effective lifetime subsidy to households with incomes above average.

The form of the Riester incentives. Although the depth of the Riester incentives makes the Riester pensions rather attractive, the Riester pension is less flexible than other retirement investment products.

One of the main drawbacks is that most of the capital has to be annuitized and can therefore not be used as collateral or bequeathed. The argument lacks a certain logic since the very objective of the Riester pensions is to provide annuity income to fill the pension gap emerging from the reduced PAYG pillar. In our opinion, the widely voiced argument is a clear indication that most workers have not yet realized that they will depend on the Riester pensions for a reasonable retirement income.

The extensive certification requirements that severely restrict the scope of private providers to develop new private insurance products and that lead to higher costs is also disadvantageous. Certain cost items can result in total costs of up to 20 percent, compared with around 10 percent for a normal capital sum life insurance policy.[37]

What is more, the certification rules serve merely to create a formal product standard without creating the transparency needed to compare different investment vehicles and the relative rates of return they offer. As a result, customers are often not in a position to make truly informed private investment decisions. The guarantee of the nominal value of contributions does ensure that, on retirement, at the very least the nominal capital saved is available as pension capital. However, there are no rules that prescribe the sort of pension dynamization that is needed to ensure that the value of pension benefits paid out from the saved capital can be maintained over the long term. Nondynamized Riester benefits will very quickly lose their value, even at very modest rates of inflation.

Preliminary evidence on take-up rates. First survey results show that demand for Riester products is sluggish: only around 9 percent had actually taken out a policy by mid 2002; a further 16 percent planned to conclude a policy by the end of 2002. By early summer 2003, however, the take-up rate had increased to about 35 percent of all eligible workers.

This comes during a growing trend for workers to enroll in supplementary pension plans. Only around half of those planning to enroll in such plans are considering doing so in the framework of a Riester policy. The other half prefer other savings and insurance products, and/or occupational pensions.[38]

Moreover, many households, especially in the higher income brackets, may merely restructure their existing pension plans to reap Riester subsidies. At this point we do not have much hard evidence on such a substitution. Should these households have a fixed pension target, financing state subsidies via general taxation can actually have perverse effects that lead to a lower savings rate.[39]

Mandatory private pensions? Surveys have shown that a large section of the population would actually welcome the introduction of mandatory supplementary private pensions.[40] This preference may be explained by savers' lack of confidence in their ability to exercise the discipline needed to build up additional old-age provision by themselves and the fiscal externality imposed by those who speculate on general social assistance rather than save.

The argument generally cited in favor of mandatory supplementary old-age provision are poverty in old age and adverse selection on the insurance market.[41] Poverty in old age, however, is currently not an important problem in Germany. This may change in the future because of the benefit cuts, but it has been addressed by the Riester reform through the introduction of the new minimum income guarantee.

As far as adverse selection is concerned, compulsory provision could lead to a monopoly position being established by a single provider if this product and the offers it generates prove to be unattractive for smaller competitors, in which case coercion would bring about even less rather than more product variety.

Finally, making supplementary pensions mandatory will give the savings a tax-like character and may therefore create negative incentive effects.[42] The very idea of reducing the tax and payroll-tax-like contribution burden to stimulate economic growth would then be jeopardized.

Will the Riester Pensions Fill the Pension Gap?

The main point of introducing the Riester pensions was to compensate for the reductions in the PAYG public retirement insurance scheme. Model calculations show that an envisaged savings rate of 4 percent of gross income is, in principle, sufficient to close the gap that will open up in old-age provision as a result of the cuts in state pensions. Figure 22.7 illustrates the growing pension gap (defined as the difference between today's and forecasted future gross pension levels) and the level of additional benefits provided by the Riester pension based on different assumptions regarding rates of return.

Although the Riester pensions can fill the pension gap in the long run, they are, however, not sufficient for the older cohorts. Younger cohorts born after 1970 will be in a posi-

Figure 22.7. Filling the Pension Gap

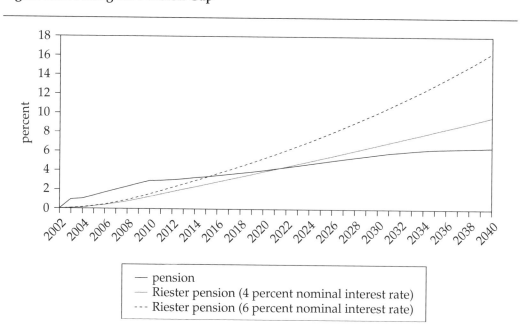

Source: MEA calculations based on the Rürup commission's demography and labor market projections.

tion to build up even higher pension entitlements than was previously the case, thanks to their supplementary pension savings. Older cohorts, however, will need to save more than the envisaged maximum saving rates in table 22.5 to close this gap entirely during the time still available to them. Obviously, rather than a slow increase to a fixed 4 percent of gross income, initial saving rates have to be high and be tailored to each cohort.[43]

Given successful take-up, the future composition of retirement income will be quite different from the current monolithic one. Figure 22.8 outlines this development by birth cohort in the year of their retirement under the assumption that the insured cohorts have adhered to the recommended Riester savings rates of table 22.5.

Figure 22.8 shows that even at full uptake, the German PAYG system will remain the dominant pillar for old-age provision. Riester pensions will make up about 35 percent of state organized retirement income. Should other income sources (currently about 15 percent of total retirement income) stay as they are, this would yield a share of PAYG pensions in total retirement income at about 55 to 60 percent. Some crowding out of existing occupational pensions and other private pensions by the new Riester pensions is likely, however, as mentioned earlier.

Will the Riester Reform Stabilize the German Pension System?

Of course, the main litmus test of the Riester reform is whether the shift from PAYG to a partially funded pension system will stabilize the contribution rates for the younger generation with acceptable replacement rates for the older generation. The Riester reform actually was quite courageous in writing into the law that the standard pension replacement level must not fall below 67 percent and at the same time that the contribution rate must not exceed 20 percent until 2020 and 22 percent until 2030. Can these promises be kept?

Figure 22.8. Composition of Retirement Income by Birth Cohort

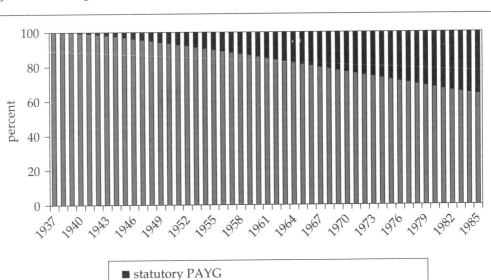

Source: MEA calculations based on the Rürup commission's demography and labor market projections.

The answer is—quite unambiguously—no. Our answer is based on the "official" demography and economic projections adopted by the Rürup commission and the Ministry for Health and Social Security.[44] We look first at standard replacement rates.[45] Model calculations of the long-term impact of pension adjustments demonstrate that, as a result of the new Riester adjustment formula, future pension levels will fall more than first predicted by the government (see figure 22.9).[46] They will fall below 67 percent very quickly, and eventually reach 62 percent.

The scale of this reduction also clearly demonstrates that the pension benefits provided by the PAYG public retirement insurance scheme will not be sufficient in themselves—that is, without supplementary pension provision—to safeguard pensioners' standards of living in old age.

Although the new adjustment formula will in effect bring about a larger reduction in pension levels than was perceived by public opinion, the most dramatic difference between promise and current projection relates to the objective of stabilizing contribution rates. Figure 22.10 depicts our projection for the long-term development of contribution rates prior to and after the reform.

Although the Riester reform substantively reduces the contribution rate to the PAYG pillar, Figure 22.10 shows that the 20 percent line will be exceeded by 2014, and 22 percent by 2022.

The apparent failure of the Riester reform to reach its main objectives—stabilization of the contribution rate at acceptable pension benefit levels—was not accidental. As a matter of fact, the overoptimistic demographic and economic assumptions were chosen in a fragile political compromise between reformists and unions that enabled the Riester reform package to pass the parliamentary hurdles.

Figure 22.9. Development of Pension Levels prior to and after the 2001 Reform

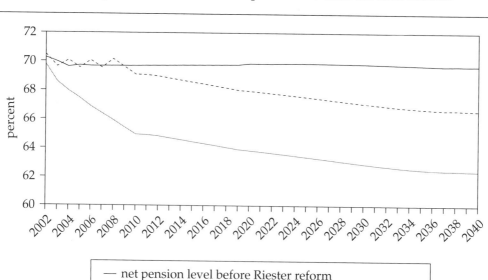

- — net pension level before Riester reform
- — net pension level after Riester reform
- --- net pension level after Riester reform (new definition)

Source: MEA calculations based on the Rürup commission's demography and labor market projections.

Figure 22.10. Contribution Rates prior to and after the 2001 Reform

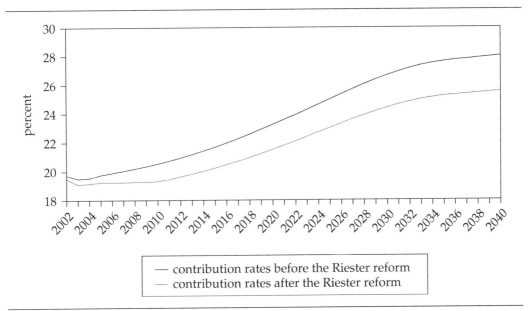

Source: MEA calculations based on the Rürup commission's demography and labor market projections.

New Efforts: The 2003 Proposals

When it became obvious that the Riester reform measures would not suffice to meet the contribution rate and pension level targets, a new reform commission, the Commission for Sustainability in Financing the German Social Insurance Systems, popularly referred to as the Rürup commission after its chairman, Bert Rürup, was established in November 2002.[47] Its twin objectives are those of the Riester reform: to stabilize contribution rates while at the same time ensuring appropriate future pension levels.

The Rürup commission met in 2003 very different circumstances than Riester faced in 2001. Unexpectedly high unemployment rates and the poor performance of the German economy with extremely low growth rates precipitated a short-run financial crisis of the pension system and created a sense of urgency for reform. Moreover, the electorate became increasingly aware that stabilizing social security contributions in total labor compensation is essential for enhancing future growth. This paradigm shift away from thinking in pension claims toward thinking in financing possibilities had a noticeable impact on the commission's reform proposals.

In addition, the commission profited from the fact that the Riester reform had already paved the way for a more forceful shift from PAYG financed first-pillar pensions to funded second- and third-pillar pensions.

Reform Proposals

The reform proposal, published at the end of August 2003, comprises two major elements plus several accompanying measures. The first main element is a gradual increase of the normal retirement age from 65 to 67 years; the second is a modification of the pension benefit indexation formula linking benefits to the system dependency ratio. The first element is accompanied by adjustments to the various early retirement ages, and the second element is accompanied by a revision of the Riester pension regulations. Although the main two elements directly serve to achieve the desired stabilization of contribution rates, the accompanying measures keep the system of pathways to retirement balanced and address some of the widely criticized aspects of the newly introduced second- and third-pillar pensions.

Increase of the normal retirement age. The commission proposes to increase the normal retirement age from 65 to 67 years. The increase is slow and gradual, starting in 2011 with monthly steps such that age 67 will be reached in 2035. This increase corresponds to two-thirds of the projected change in life expectancy at age 65. It will therefore simply offset future increases in the total value of accumulated benefits generated by a longer pension recipiency duration. The reasoning behind this increase in retirement age is that the prolonged life span necessitates a commensurate increase in working life unless the pension system is continuously being expanded.

To prevent substitution into early retirement and disability pensions as a result of the increase in the retirement age, the commission also proposed to increase the early retirement ages (to the same extent and on the same schedule as the normal retirement age) and to increase the actuarial adjustments for disabled and long-term insured workers. Since there were additional worries about the coverage for workers subject to extreme physical wear and tear due to long years of hard work, a new pension type was introduced to make it possible for workers with a service life of at least 45 years to retire two years earlier, however, with additional actuarial adjustments.

Change of the benefit indexation formula: The "sustainability factor." The commission proposes to extend the Riester benefit indexation formula by a new factor, the *sustainability factor*. This factor reflects the development of the relative number of contributors to pensioners, the system dependency ratio, which is the most important long-term determinant of pension financing.[48] The new pension formula looks as follows:

$$PV_t = PV_{t-1} \frac{AGI_{t-2}}{AGI_{t-3}} \frac{1 - \delta_{t-2} - \tau_{t-2}}{1 - \delta_{t-3} - \tau_{t-3}} \left(\left(1 - \frac{PQ_{t-2}}{PQ_{t-3}} \right) \alpha + 1 \right) \qquad (22.3)$$

where PQ = [pensioners/(contributors + unemployed)]. *Note:* The lags are due to data availability.

It includes the sustainability factor in the inner brackets, weighted by α, and replaces the one-time shift in the somewhat awkward "sensitivity parameter" d_t (see the earlier section on the Riester reform). If $\alpha = 0$, the current Riester pension adjustment formula would remain unchanged. If $\alpha = 1$, the new indexation formula would imply a purely income-oriented pension benefit adjustment policy. The commission set the value of α at one-quarter, thereby fulfilling the Riester objectives of keeping the contribution rate under 20 percent until 2020 and under 22 percent until 2030.

The new pension formula will lead to further decreases in pension benefit levels vis-à-vis the path planned by the Riester reform. In contrast to the proposed demography factor in the failed 1999 reform attempt, the sustainability factor considers not only the development of life expectancy but also the entire demographic development (including changes in migration and notably in birth rates), as well as the development of the labor market. This is important as the inevitable reduction of the working-age population can be compensated by a higher labor force participation of women and elderly workers. The introduction of the sustainability factor thus allows directly linking pension adjustments to the crucial factors determining pension financing—namely, the number of contributors and benefit recipients. In doing this, the sustainability factor incorporates a self-stabilizing feedback mechanism into the system similar to the notional rate-of-return mechanism in NDC systems.[49]

Higher second- and third-pillar pensions would compensate for this decrease. Since the uptake of the funded supplementary Riester pension has been modest so far (as was mentioned earlier), the commission proposed a host of administrative changes to occupational and private pensions to make the system easier to handle and thus more popular. Among these are the expansion of the group of entitled persons to all tax payers, dynamic pension benefits, and increased transparency in the private pension provision. These administrative changes accompany the proposed introduction of an exempt-exempt-taxed (or EET) regime of ex post taxation.[50]

Long-Term Effects of the 2003 Reform Proposals

Are the reform proposals by the Rürup commission sufficient to counteract the foreseen consequences of demographic change and stabilize the system? Will it keep the contribution rate below the targets set by Riester, and at the same time generate a level of pension income that, taking all pillars into account, corresponds to today's level? This subsection presents a projection of the main components of the reform proposals and takes a look at their long-term effects.[51] Figures 22.11 and 22.12 illustrate how the introduction of the sustainability factor and the increase of the retirement age affect contribution rates and pension levels for varying values of α.

Figure 22.11. The Effects of the Sustainability Factor on the Development of Contribution Rates

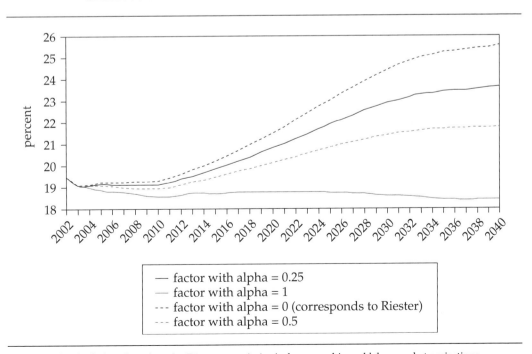

— factor with alpha = 0.25
— factor with alpha = 1
--- factor with alpha = 0 (corresponds to Riester)
--- factor with alpha = 0.5

Source: MEA calculations based on the Rürup commission's demographic and labor market projections.

Figure 22.12. The Effects of the Sustainability Factor on Pension Levels

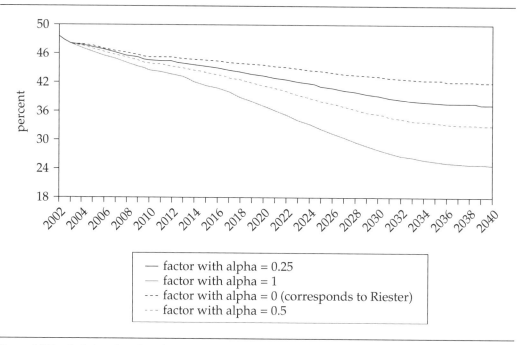

Source: MEA calculations based on the Rürup commission's demographic and labor market projections.

If α = 1, the sustainability factor generates a purely income-oriented pension benefit policy. The contribution rate will remain stable while benefits will decline to around 30 percent of gross earnings.

A weighting factor α of 0.5 would spread the additional financial burden created by the increasing dependency burden more equally between contributors and beneficiaries. It results in a contribution rate of 20.1 percent in 2020, 21.4 percent in 2030, and a benefit level in 2030 of around 37 percent of gross earnings.

The commission's reform targets are just met when α is set equal to 0.25. It results in a contribution rate a little lower than 23 percent in 2030, while the level of pensions is just over 40 percent of gross earnings.

Taking account of the increase in the normal retirement age to 67, which increases pension benefits according to the German benefit formula, and adding second- and/or third-pillar pensions, the Rürup proposal manages to deliver an income level for retirees that is comparable to today's income level—however, only after about 2030 (see figure 22.13). This projection assumes a saving rate of 4 percent into second- and third-pillar pensions from 2009 on, starting in a stepwise fashion according to table 22.5.

Figure 22.13 quite clearly shows the crux of all transition models: the transition generation will have to pay extra to maintain their total retirement income when the income from PAYG pensions is reduced. More refined transition models show that a saving rate of 8 percent is sufficient for the cohort with the highest transition burden.[52]

The 2004 Reform

Most of the Rürup proposals, and most significantly the introduction of the sustainability factor, were passed by the German parliament on March 31, 2004. The shift in the retire-

Figure 22.13. Total Pension Level Including Private Riester Pensions

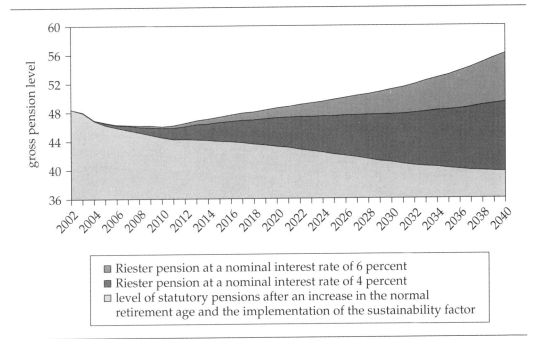

- Riester pension at a nominal interest rate of 6 percent
- Riester pension at a nominal interest rate of 4 percent
- level of statutory pensions after an increase in the normal
  retirement age and the implementation of the sustainability factor

Source: MEA calculations based on the Rürup commission's demographic and labor market projections.

ment age, however, was not legislated. Since the commission proposed that the phasing-in period should start in 2011, it was decided that there was no need for immediate legislative action.

The politics of shifting the retirement age are clearly not favorable. According to survey results by Boeri, Börsch-Supan, and Tabellini (2001; 2002; forthcoming), raising the retirement age is one of the most unpopular pension reform options in Germany (see figure 22.14).

An interesting result of this survey is that this option is particularly unpopular among those who are least informed about the costs of the current pension system. Hence, while early retirement is a well appreciated social achievement among Germans, awareness of the costs of early retirement may moderate the opposition to increasing the retirement age.

Another lesson from this survey is that the success of a reform depends on the flexibility in the hard choice between a later retirement age and a lower PAYG pension level, supplemented by private pensions that cut into consumption. As long as pensions are calculated in an actuarially neutral fashion, taking all side effects to the economy into account, there is no need for a "normal retirement age," and workers can decide themselves between working longer and saving more. The recent experience in the United States in the aftermath of the bubble burst appears to indicate that workers are quite aware of this substitution. Flexibility minimizes the opposition to reform proposals relative to proposals that make cuts in only one direction—say, increasing the normal retirement age.

At this point, the German system is not actuarially neutral from the point of view of workers who decide about their retirement age. [53] As much as the government shied away from legislating the prospective increase in retirement age, it did not touch the current lack of actuarial neutrality. Both steps have met fierce opposition from unions and pensioner

Figure 22.14. Popularity of Pension Reform Options

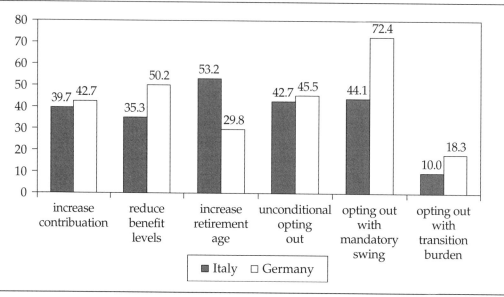

Source: Boeri, Börsch-Supan, and Tabellini (forthcoming).

advocacy groups, and, interestingly, the last step has also been opposed by the employers' union, since it increases the costs of severance.

Conclusions

The first part of this chapter described the generous German pension system, as it was in place between 1972 and the end of the 1990s. It generated early retirement ages and high replacement rates, but at high costs to society in the form of a large cost percentage of GDP (about 12 percent) and high contribution rates (about 28 percent of gross income, of which 19.5 percent was in direct contributions and 8.5 percent in indirect contributions for state subsidies financed by general taxes).

The Riester reform in 2001, described in the second part of this chapter, attempts to reduce the tax and contribution burden by transforming the monolithic PAYG system to a multipillar system with subsidized or tax-privileged private pensions in individual accounts or as occupational pensions. The reform is an important first step toward solving the demographic problems confronting the pension system. It does not, however, stabilize the public PAYG pillar in the coming decades.

This instability precipitated the creation of the reform commission chaired by Rürup. In contrast to the Riester reform, this commission took the political risk of proposing a rise in the normal retirement age and a further reduction in long-term benefits at the same time. As a major innovation, this reduction was rationalized by linking benefits to the system dependency ratio. It therefore provides an automatic stabilizer and de facto converts the defined benefit system to a system that mimics an NDC system. Although this mechanism became law in 2004, the change in retirement age was postponed. Hence, the slow but steady reform process of the German pension system is likely to continue as the German population ages.

Notes

1. Table 22.1 summarizes the history of the German public pension system.

2. Average retirement age in a given year is the average age of those workers receiving public pension income for the first time (VDR 2002).

3. This replacement rate is defined as the current pension of a retiree with a 45-year average earnings history divided by the current average earnings of all dependently employed workers. It is different from the replacement rate relative to the most recent earnings of a retiring worker, which are usually higher than the life-time average.

4. This figure is arrived at using the same replacement rate concept as in endnote 3.

5. At least 35 years.

6. See OECD (2001).

7. See OECD (2001). The OECD dependency ratio relates persons age 65 and older to persons between ages 15 and 64.

8. See Prognos (1987).

9. See Börsch-Supan (1998; 2000a) and Schnabel (1998) for descriptions of the problems, and Birg and Börsch-Supan (1999) and Börsch-Supan (1999) for concrete reform proposals.

10. Cutler and Sheiner (1998).

11. The commission is named after its chairman. The commission's charge was to make proposals for pension, health, and long-term care reform. One of the authors of this chapter, Axel Börsch-Supan, cochaired the pension reform subcommission.

12. "Notional defined contribution" and "non-financial defined contribution" should be understood to have the same definition.

13. This and the following section are updated versions of Börsch-Supan et al. (2004).

14. This average is about 20 percent less in the German Democratic Republic. One euro has a purchasing power of approximately 1 U.S. dollar. (as of September 2003, the exchange rate was 1.1 euro per 1 U.S. dollar).

15. There are still exceptions to the strict link to health problems as a consequence of case law spoken by the labor courts.

16. The main redistribution in Germany occurs through early retirement; see discussion below.

17. There are, of course, survivor benefits.

18. See Boeri, Börsch-Supan, and Tabellini (2001).

19. Nevertheless, wage rather than cost-of-living indexation makes it impossible to finance the retirement burden by productivity gains.

20. The official government computations, such as the above official replacement rate (*Rentenniveau*), assume a 45-year contribution history for what is deemed a "normal earnings history" (*Eckrentner*). In fact, the average number of years of contributions is about 38 years. In turn, however, many pensioners with short earnings histories had above-average earnings. Hence, about half of all entrants have 45 earnings points or more.

21. See Casmir (1989) for a comparison of the systems of the United States and Germany.

22. The actuarially fair adjustments equalize the expected social security wealth for a worker with an earnings history starting at age 20. A higher discount rate yields steeper adjustments.

23. See Riphahn (1995) for an analysis of disability rules.

24. See Jacobs, Kohli, and Rein (1990) for this concept.

25. Cf. Börsch-Supan and Schnabel (1998).

26. Cf. Börsch-Supan (2000b).

27. Civil servants are also exempt from unemployment insurance contributions, since civil servants have a life-time job guarantee. The government pays a certain fraction of health expenses of the civil servant and his or her dependents (ranging from 50 to 80 percent). The rest has to be covered by private insurance.

28. Very specific rules apply to some civil servants. For example, the regular retirement age for police officers is age 60; for soldiers it is even lower and depends on their rank.

29. For the higher earnings to take effect on pensions, civil servants are usually required to work for several years after the promotion.

30. Actuarial computations depend on a discount or interest rate that makes payments made or received at different points in time commensurable. Usually, a rate of 3 percent is assumed, sometimes 4 or 5 percent. The German computations rest on a discount rate of about 1 percent.

31. See the projections on the change of retirement age by Berkel and Börsch-Supan (2004).

32. The reader is reminded that the term *replacement rate* may be misleading. In the German context, it does NOT refer to last earnings before retirement. Rather, the "standard replacement rate" refers to the pension of a worker who had 45 earnings points, divided by the average net earnings of all current workers.

33. If a lump-sum payment is chosen, all subsidies have to be reimbursed to the tax authorities.

34. See Börsch-Supan and Lührmann (2000). The "tax credit" feature depends on the an income or consumption tax point of view.

35. See Ruppert (2000).

36, We use the word *subsidy* for both the direct subsidy and the tax-deductible special allowance.

37. See Stiftung Warentest (2002).

38. See Leinert (2003).

39. See Börsch-Supan and Lührmann (2000).

40. See Boeri, Börsch-Supan, and Tabellini (2001; 2002; Forthcoming).

41. See Börsch-Supan (2002).

42. See Summers (1989).

43. See the proposals by Birg and Börsch-Supan (1999) and Börsch-Supan (2002).

44. The demographic projections (fertility, mortality, migration) are considered realistic by academic demographers, while the economic assumptions (growth, employment) are considered slightly optimistic.

45. The reader is reminded that the standard replacement rate does NOT relate to the LAST earnings before retirement. Rather, the "standard replacement rate" refers to the pension of a worker, who had 45 earnings points, divided by the average net earnings of all current workers.

46. See also Bonin (2001) and Prognos (2001).

47. The commission was in charge of making reform proposals for the pension system, health care, and long-term care insurance. We only refer to the pension proposals.

48. Strictly speaking, the sustainability factor will link benefits to the "equivalized system dependency ratio" to avoid distortions created by extremely low contributions and/or pension benefits. This ratio standardizes the number of pensioners by converting standard pensions into the number of "equivalence pensioners." The number of "equivalence contributors" is likewise calculated by standardizing the average earner.

49. See Börsch-Supan (2006).

50. A parallel commission, also headed by Bert Rürup, proposed to keep pension contributions and capital gains tax exempt (symbolized by the two *E*s in EET), and to tax benefits (symbolized by the *T* in EET). See Börsch-Supan and Lührmann (2000).

51. The official projections of the reform commission are presented in Kommission für die Nachhaltigkeit in der Finanzierung der Sozialen Sicherungssysteme (2003): Abschluß-bericht. Bundesministerium für Gesundheit und Soziale Sicherheit, Berlin. (http://www.bmgs.bund.de/deu/gra/themen/sicherheit/kommission/index.cfm).

52. See Birg and Börsch-Supan (1999).

53. See Börsch-Supa n and Schnabel (1999).

References

Berkel, B., and A. Börsch-Supan. 2004. Pension Reform in Germany: The Impact on Retirement Decisions, *Finanzarchiv* 60 (3): 393–421.

Birg, H., and A. Börsch-Supan. 1999. *Für eine neue Aufgabenteilung zwischen gesetzlicher und privater Altersversorgung*. Berlin: GDV.

BMA (Bundesministerium für Arbeit und Sozialordnung). 1997. *Statistisches Taschenbuch*. Bonn: Bundespresseamt.

Boeri, T., A. Börsch-Supan, and G. Tabellini. 2001. "Would You Like to Shrink the Welfare State? The Opinions of European Citizens." *Economic Policy* 32: 7–50.

———. 2002. "Would You Like to Reform the Pension System? The Opinions of European Citizens." *American Economic Review* 92: 396–401.

———. Forthcoming. "How Would You Like to Reform Your Pension System? The Opinions of German and Italian Citizens." In *The Politics and Finance of Social Security Reform*, ed. R. Brooks and A. Razin, Kluwer.

Bonin, H. 2001. "Will it Last? An Assessment of the 2001 German Pension Reform." Institute for the Study of Labor (IZA), IZA Discussion Paper 343, Bonn.

Börsch-Supan, A. 1998. "Germany: A Social Security System on the Verge of Collapse." In *Redesigning Social Security*, ed. H. Siebert, 129–59. Tübingen: J.C.B. Mohr (Paul Siebeck).

———. 1999. "The German Retirement Insurance System." In *Pension Reform in Six Countries*, ed. A. Börsch-Supan and M. Miegel, 13–38. Berlin, Heidelberg: Springer.

———. 2000a. "A Model under Siege: A Case Study of the Germany Retirement Insurance System." *The Economic Journal* 110 (461): F24–45.

———. 2000b. "Incentive Effects of Social Security on Labour Force Participation: Evidence in Germany and Across Europe." *Journal of Public Economics* 78: 25–41.

———. 2002. "Incentive Effects of Social Security Under an Uncertain Disability Option" In *Frontiers in the Economics of Aging*, ed. D.A. Wise, 281–310. Chicago: University of Chicago Press.

———. 2006. "What Are NDC Pension Systems? What Do They Bring to Reform Strategies?" In *Pension Reform: Issues and Prospects for Non-Financial Defined Contribution (NDC) Schemes*, ed. R. Holzmann and E. Palmer, chapter 3. Washington, DC: World Bank.

Börsch-Supan, A., and M. Lührmann. 2000. *Prinzipien der Renten- und Pensionsbesteuerung*. Bad Homburg, Frankfurter Institut – Stiftung Marktwirtschaft und Politik.

Börsch-Supan, A., and R. Schnabel. 1998. "Social Security and Declining Labor Force Participation in Germany." *American Economic Review* 88 (2): 173–8.

———. 1999. "Social Security and Retirement in Germany." In *Social Security and Retirement Around the World*, ed. J. Gruber and D. A. Wise, 135–80. Chicago, London: University of Chicago Press.

Börsch-Supan, A., R. Schnabel, S. Kohnz, and G. Mastrobuoni. 2004. "Micro Modelling of Retirement Choices in Germany." In *Social Security Programs and Retirement Around the*

World: Micro-Estimation, ed. J. Gruber and D. A. Wise, 285–344. Chicago: University of Chicago Press.

Casmir, B. 1989. *Staatliche Rentenversicherungssysteme im internationalen Vergleich.* Frankfurt: Lang.

Cutler, D., and L. M. Sheiner. 1998. "Demographics and Medical Care Spending: Standard and Non-Standard Effects." Mimeo, Harvard University, Cambridge, Massachusetts.

Deutsche Bundesbank. 2002. "Kapitalgedeckte Altersvorsorge und Finanzmärkte." Monatsbericht Juli, Frankfurt am Main.

Gruber, J., and D. A. Wise, eds. 2004. *Social Security Programs and Retirement Around the World: Micro-Estimation.* Chicago, London: University of Chicago Press.

Jacobs, K., M. Kohli, and K. Rein. 1990. "Germany: The Diversity of Pathways." In *Time for Retirement: Comparative Studies of Early Exit from the Labor Force*, ed. M. Kohli, M. Rein, A.-M. Guillemard, and H. van Gunsteren, 181–221. Cambridge, New York: Cambridge University Press.

Kommission für die Nachhaltigkeit in der Finanzierung der Sozialen Sicherungssysteme. 2003. Abschlußbericht. Bundesministerium für Gesundheit und Soziale Sicherheit, Berlin. http://www.bmgs.bund.de/deu/gra/themen/sicherheit/kommission/index .cfm.

Leinert, J. 2003. "Die Riester-Rente: Wer hat sie, wer will sie: Vorausbewertung einer repräsentativen Umfrage zum Vorsorgeverhalten der 30- bis 50-Jährigen." Bertelsmann Stiftung Vorsorgestudien 18, Gütersloh, 2003, p. 14.

OECD (Organisation for Economic Co-operation and Development). 2001. *Ageing and Income: Financial Resources and Retirement in 9 OECD Countries.* Paris: OECD.

Prognos. 1987. "Gesamtwirtschaftliche Entwicklungen und Gesetzliche Rentenversicherung vor dem Hintergrund einer schrumpfenden Bevölkerung." Prognos AG, Basel.

———. 2001. "Reformoptionen für die gesetzliche Rentenversicherung: Auswirkungen der Rentenreform 2001 und die Verteilung der Umstiegskosten." Prognos AG, Basel.

Riphahn, R. T. 1995. "Disability Retirement Among German Men in the 1980s." *Münchner Wirtschaftswissenschaftliche Beiträge*, Nr. 95-20, Ludwig Maximilians Universität München.

Ruppert, W. 2000. *Betriebliche Altersversorgung,* ed. Institut für Wirtschaftsforschung (ifo), München.

Schnabel, R. 1998. "Rates of Return of the German Pay-As-You-Go Pension System." *Finanzarchiv* 55 (3): 374–99.

———. 1999. "Opting Out of Social Security: Incentives and Participation in the German Public Pension System." SFB504-Discussion Paper 99-42, University of Mannheim, Mannheim.

Stiftung Warentest. 2002. "Riester-Rentenversicherungen: Die Lücke schließen." FINANZtest.

Summers, L. 1989. "Some Simple Economics of Mandated Benefits." *American Economic Review* 79 (2): 177–83.

VDR (Verband deutscher Rentenversicherungsträger). 1997. www.vdr.de.

———. 2002. *Die Rentenversicherung in Zeitreihen.* Frankfurt am Main.

Chapter 23

The Spanish Pension System: Issues of Introducing NDCs

Carlos Vidal-Meliá and Inmaculada Domínguez-Fabián*

THE RACE TO REFORM PENSION SYSTEMS IN MANY COUNTRIES over the last few years has been such that, as Valdés-Prieto (2002) points out, the problems of pension reform have begun to dominate economic policy.

The main reforms proposed and applied can be summarized as parametric reforms of the pay-as-you-go (PAYG) system, changes to other (mainly capitalization) systems, and systems combining funded systems and PAYG, as proposed chiefly by the World Bank. Reform trends championed by the main international organizations can be found in papers by Gillion (2000), Holzmann (2000), and Queisser (2000).

One of the most important recent innovations in pension reform has been the introduction of "notional defined contribution" (NDC)[1] accounts in some countries, namely, Italy (1995), Latvia (1996), the Kyrgyz Republic (1997),[2] Poland (1999), Brazil (1999),[3] Sweden (1999), and Mongolia (2000). According to Williamson (2004), other countries such as China and Russia are also seriously thinking about introducing them.

The European Union (EU), the World Bank, and the Organisation for Economic Cooperation and Development (OECD), along with various Spanish researchers,[4] have all strongly recommended an in-depth revision of the Spanish public pension system. All are agreed that, at least in the long term, the financial viability of the system is seriously at risk. One valid possibility could be the introduction of notional accounts, as first suggested by Mateo (1997) and taken up in more detail by Devesa and Vidal (2004) and Vidal, Domínguez, and Devesa (2004, 2005).

In this chapter we will provide an objective technical assessment of the current situation of the contributory pension system in Spain and its prospects for the future. We will then look into the possibility of introducing a system of NDC accounts. The structure of the chapter is as follows: after this introduction, in the next section we explain the basic elements upon which the current system is based and show its main indicators; in the following section we set out the fundamental problems of the current system and look at the

* Vidal-Meliá is professor of financial economy at Valencia University (Spain) and an independent consultant-actuary; Inmaculada Domínguez-Fabián is assistant professor of social security at the University of Extremadura (Spain).

Revised version. The authors would like to thank Enrique Devesa-Carpio, Pierre Devolder, Peter Hall, and Ana Lejárraga-García for their help. The support and suggestions we received from Robert Holzmann were particularly useful. Any errors are entirely due to the authors.

most relevant research work, the conclusions of which will give us a clear idea of the system's financial sustainability. The next section includes a number of reasons that a notional accounts system could be a valid alternative for reforming the current system; in the section that follows we discuss which formula or group of formulae would best fit the profile of contributor-beneficiary risk and what the transition process would be; and finally we present our conclusions.

The Public Pension System in Spain

In this section we show the main features of the Spanish social security system and supply some key data. The current system provides the following types of protection:

- Contributory social insurance programs, organized along occupational lines. These programs award benefits to compensate for revenue no longer earned because of sickness, accident, unemployment, family responsibilities, disability, old age, or death. The amount payable depends on how much has been contributed over how long. This type of protection is financed by contributions from employees and/or employers, and is run by the state.
- Noncontributory protection, the purpose of which is to provide financial cover for disability, old age, unemployment, and family responsibilities. The amount payable is the same for everyone and conditional upon the beneficiary's lack of resources. This type of protection is financed and run by the state through taxation.
- A universal benefit basically consisting of healthcare and social services, open to everyone and financed at present through a mixed system of social security contributions and money from the state. There are plans to finance it in future through general revenues alone.
- Alongside the previous three types of state-run protection, there also exists a complementary system of privately run protection. Its most visible forms are friendly societies, group life insurance, and pension plans and funds.

This chapter will concentrate mainly on the first type of system, the contributory social insurance programs. The contributory system is structured in different "regimes" or systems, each of which covers a group of workers of a particular type. These special systems, as will be seen later on, cause a great many problems because they are all different. At present the following systems exist:

1. General System. This is the essential nucleus of the system as a whole and includes all employees over 16 not included in another "special system." The general system accounts for 60 percent of pensions and 75 percent of contributors. Its spending on pensions was 6.49 percent of GDP in 2003. This regime has a surplus of 1.08 percent of GDP.
2. Special System for the Self-Employed. This includes everyone who works for themselves or is not dependent on an employer (apart from those covered by the special systems for agricultural or fisheries workers). It accounts for 17 percent of contributors and pays out around 13 percent of pensions. Its spending on pensions was 0.84 percent of GDP in 2003. This regime has a surplus of 0.25 percent of GDP.
3. Special System for Agricultural Workers. This includes all those who normally work in agriculture, in forestry, or with livestock. It covers those who are employed by someone else as well as those who have their own smallholdings. It accounts for 21 percent of pensions and 7 percent of contributors. Its spending on pensions was 1.31 percent of GDP in 2003. This regime has a huge deficit of 1.12 percent of GDP.

4. Special System for Fisheries Workers. This includes all employed and self-employed workers involved in fisheries activities on land and at sea. It accounts for 1.8 percent of pensions and 0.46 percent of contributors. This regime has a deficit of 0.15 percent of GDP.

5. Special System for Coal Mining. This applies to all those employed to work in coal mines. It accounts for just 0.1 percent of contributors but pays 1 percent of pensions. This system has a deficit of 0.13 percent of GDP.

6. Special System for Domestic Staff. This covers those who provide exclusively domestic services for one or more heads of family. The services must be provided in the house where the head of family lives, and a wage or payment must be received in exchange. This regime accounts for 1.14 percent of contributors and pays out 2.8 percent of pensions. It has a deficit of 0.13 percent of GDP.

7. Apart from the special systems mentioned above, there are others covering civil servants, the armed forces, and the judiciary. The most important of these is the system for civil servants.

Coordination between the general and the various special systems is assured because the system is based on the following principles: (1) a common legal basis for the system as a whole, (2) unique one-off registration details regardless of transfers between systems, and (3) reciprocal calculation of quotas between the partial systems that make up the system as a whole.

The most relevant rules for determining the amount of retirement pension are:

- The pension base is calculated according to contributions made during the last 15 years of work. Contributions for the 24 months immediately prior to retirement are taken at nominal value, while previous contribution rates are revalued in line with the retail price index (RPI) for the months up to and including the 25th month before retirement. From this date the period of contribution rates taken at nominal value begins.

- In the case of the general system, the pension is determined by applying the corresponding replacement rate to the pension base. This is variable according to the number of years contributed. A sliding scale is applied, starting at 50 percent after 15 years of contributions, rising by 3 percent for every additional year from the 16th to the 25th, and by 2 percent from the 26th year up to a maximum of 100 percent for 35 years. When retirement pension is first claimed after age 65, a rate of 100 percent is applied plus an additional 2 percent for every full year contributed after that age, always assuming that 35 years contributions have already been paid. The minimum retirement age is 60 years.

- The replacement rate is reduced by between 6 percent and 8 percent for each year the retirement age is brought forward from the legal retirement age of 65.

- The pension increases annually in line with the RPI.

Table 23.1 can be used to analyze the evolution of one of the most significant variables for understanding the main problem faced by the Spanish pension system: the ratio between the number of contributors and the number of pensions. As far as the totals are concerned, a downward trend can be seen until 1996, but from then on the totals begin to increase. These variations are similar to those within the general system (it should not be forgotten that this is the system with the greatest relative weight) and the special system for domestic workers (although the upward trend in this system began later), but unlike those in the other systems, where the trend is still downward. The recovery of the general system is due to a much higher rate of growth in the number of contributors than in the

Table 23.1. Ratio of the Number of Contributors to the Number of Contributory Pensions

Year	General[5]	Self-employed	Agricultural workers	Coal mining	Fisheries	Domestic staff	Total
1980	3.39	3.84	1.22	0.84	1.67	4.13	2.46
1985	2.81	3.11	1.04	0.74	1.40	2.29	2.11
1993	2.65	3.10	0.74	0.44	0.96	0.86	1.83
1994	2.46	3.08	0.72	0.41	0.89	0.78	1.77
1995	2.44	3.07	0.71	0.38	0.73	0.73	1.77
1996	2.39	3.03	0.71	0.36	0.68	0.71	1.76
1997	2.40	2.99	0.72	0.34	0.65	0.70	1.78
1998	2.47	2.99	0.72	0.28	0.63	0.69	1.83
1999	2.58	3.01	0.73	0.26	0.62	0.72	1.91
2000	2.69	3.00	0.72	0.24	0.62	0.74	1.98
2001	2.77	2.97	0.72	0.22	0.61	0.76	2.04
2002	2.82	2.94	0.73	0.20	0.59	0.87	2.08
2003	2.85	2.93	0.75	0.19	0.58	0.93	2.12
2004	2.88	3.00	0.70	0.17	0.57	0.91	2.16
2005 (May)	2.98	3.04	0.71	0.15	0.56	1.26	2.24

Source: Ministerio de Trabajo y Seguridad Social (1995); http://www.mtas.es.

number of pensions. Nevertheless, the figures still give cause for concern. The improvement in the ratio seen in 2005 is due mainly to the regularization of illegal immigrants carried out in the first quarter of the year.

Future Perspectives for the Spanish Pension System

After a brief description of the main features of the public pension system in Spain, we analyze its future perspectives from the point of view of politicians, social agents, public opinion, and experts, and then discuss its main problems and some of the measures put forward for solving them.

At the beginning of the 1990s, as Jimeno (2002) explains, the effects of the economic recession on the public budget and the need to carry out a certain amount of fiscal consolidation imposed by the requirements of the Treaty of Maastricht meant that "anxiety" over the pensions problem became more acute. Much research was carried out concerning the system's financial viability. In the papers published, which relied basically on simulation models, there is an almost general consensus that the current pension system would suffer serious problems in the short term if steps were not taken to correct the deviations that would come about mainly because of the aging of the population. Another problem is that the system does not offer good labor incentives[6] for continuing to work.

Public opinion has been very concerned about the political use of the pension problem as an electoral weapon. According to Pérez-Díaz, Álvarez-Miranda, and Chuliá (1997), there was growing awareness that there was a problem with pensions, even a gradual conviction that reforms were necessary and that the system in its current form could not go on indefinitely. As Alvira, García, and Blanco (1996) noted, a great many people were worried about the future of their retirement revenue, and the public welfare system was seen in a negative light. Only those who had already retired had a positive opinion about the public system. During the economic expansion of the last few years there has been massive job creation and record numbers of affiliates have been registered. This has lifted much of the pressure off the public purse and has meant that the "pension problem" has shifted to a secondary level.

The Spanish government admits only the possibility of carrying out parametric type reforms in the sense described by Holzmann, Orenstein, and Rutlowski (2003). At present there is an atmosphere of unbridled joy because for the first time ever the reserve fund amounts to approximately 1.43 percent of GDP, with record numbers of contributors on the books. According to official sources, there are three measures considered essential for safeguarding the financial sustainability of the system:

1. The reference period for calculating the amount of pensions should be extended to cover the entire working life.
2. The money needed to cover the shortfall in some pensions and bring them up to minimum levels should be provided through general taxation.[7] In other words, this explicit redistribution should be carried out through the noncontributory system since it is still paid for with the surplus from contributions, around 4,132 million euros in 2003, or 0.63 percent of GDP. Thirty percent of pensioners receive the minimum pension.
3. There has to be a reduction in the avalanche of early retirements, which are preventing the real retirement age from being raised.

We will be looking at a number of studies in which some very different methodologies are used to "prove" that the pension problem in Spain really is important despite the fact that the current government, like the previous governments and the trade unions, deny the size of the problem. This is because pension system reform is tremendously unpopular and the effects are visible only in the long term, far beyond the planning horizon of the government and trade unions, both of which tend to concentrate on the short term.

The issues analyzed are the following:

- Demographic projections
- Implicit debt
- Intragenerational fairness
- The financial solvency of the system.

Demographic Projections

According to Jimeno (2002), the general features of population aging in Spain are:

- *Increased life expectancy*, which has risen by more than 9 years—from 69.85 years in 1960 to 79.08 in 2000—and which will bring about an increase in the number of people over 65 as a proportion of the total population.
- *The decrease in birthrate*, which in Spain has taken place later but with greater intensity and speed than in other countries, will also contribute to reducing the relative weight of the working-age population over the next 50 years.
- *Immigration*, which over the last five years has risen at an unprecedented rate in Spain, and could mitigate the reduction in working-age population.

Although it is uncertain how these demographic variables might develop in the future, it appears inevitable that the ratio between the sizes of older and younger cohorts will increase noticeably during the first half of this century, even under the most optimistic scenarios. In this respect, the projections of the National Institute of Statistics (Instituto Nacional de Estadística, INE) (2001) imply that the ratio between the population over 65 and the population between 20 and 64 will increase from 27 percent in 2001 up to 36 per-

Table 23.2. Population Projections for Spain 2002–50 Based on the 2001 Census by the National Institute of Statistics: Hypothesis I or Central Scenario

| Year | Immigrants (a) | Average number of children | Life expectancy at birth | | Population at 31 December (in millions) |
			Women	Men	
2002	227,000	1.279	83.07	75.72	40.683
2003	204,000	1.308	83.27	75.83	40.935
2004	181,000	1.327	83.39	75.94	41.167
2005	160,000	1.361	83.55	76.05	41.379
2010	160,000	1.424	84.35	76.58	42.359
2020	160,000	1.424	85.10	77.27	43.378
2030	160,000	1.424	85.10	77.65	43.369
2040	160,000	1.424	85.10	77.65	42.744
2050	160,000	1.424	85.10	77.65	41.200

Source: http://www.ine.es.

cent in 2025, reaching approximately 60 percent in 2050. These projections are shown in table 23.2 in revised form so as to incorporate recent changes in mortality, birthrates, and immigration in the second half of the 1990s.

Montero (2000) analyzes the effects the progressive aging of the population will have on financing social security in Spain. She confirms that if current contribution rates remain constant, the government will not be able to guarantee future retirees current levels of pensions. For this guarantee to be achieved, the contribution rate will have to be increased by 10 points, up to 36.4 percent of wages. According to the author, increasing the age of retirement will enable current pension levels to be maintained without having to increase contribution rates.[8]

Implicit Debt

Bonin, Gil, and Patxot (2001) estimate the implicit debt[9] built up by the current pension system in 1996 to be 175.7 percent of the GDP for that year. As a continuation of the work done in that study, Gil and Patxot (2002) explore the possibility of introducing reform policies on the revenue side so as to lessen the strong demographic dependence of social security revenue. They conclude that the severity of the demographic crisis makes this type of measure clearly insufficient for restoring the intergenerational equilibrium. They also point out that if the current configuration of the pension system is maintained indefinitely, this will be likely to transfer to future generations a volume of debt that would vary between 167 percent and 206 percent of the GDP for 1996. To overcome this gap in sustainability, revenue would need to be increased by between 3.97 percent and 4.89 percent of GDP every year.

The above calculation is an underestimate for two main reasons:

1. Early retirement is assumed to be eliminated under this scenario.
2. This scenario does not take into account the special system for civil servants.

Redecillas (1996) estimates the implicit debt as of December 31, 1994, at 2.1 times the GDP, excluding the special system for civil servants (which is another 0.3 times the GDP), while Abio, Bonin, Gil, and Patxot (1999) estimate it at twice the GDP for 1996. This debt grows sharply over time. According to Redecillas (1996), the pension rights of the social security (pensioners) grew from 0.9 times GDP in 1989 to 1.04 times five years later, at the rate of almost 3 percentage points of GDP per year.

Intragenerational Fairness

Another aspect to be taken into account in a contributory pension system is intragenerational fairness, which should be understood to mean that all members of the same generation should be able to obtain a similar return on contributions paid, independently of the sector in which they were employed. The way the social security system in Spain is divided into a series of special systems leads to differences in the way individuals of the same generation are treated. Monasterio, Sánchez, and Blanco (1996) analyze the different options used by contributors to maximize their revenue and "beat the system." So far, in July 2005, no legislation has yet been passed to counteract most of the problems described.

On the subject of intragenerational fairness, Bandrés and Cuenca (1998) examine to what extent the modifications adopted for retirement pensions achieve one of the aims declared in the 1997 legislation (the most important pension legislation of recent years): strengthening the system's fairness.

To do this they analyze the amount of variation between the pensions payable to and the contributions paid by pensioners retiring under the terms of the 1997 law (Law 24/1997). The quantification is done mainly by using the transfer component, which is defined as that part of the pension received that exceeds the amount of a pension maintaining actuarial equilibrium between contributions and pension, and which, therefore, can be interpreted as a transfer. This enables the entire intergenerational transfer that new pensioners receive to be quantified, as well as the different intragenerational transfers by the social security system. An empirical study is carried out on the cohort of pensioners who started to receive pensions in 1993. The results appear in tables 23.3 and 23.4.

The retirement pension reforms approved in 1997 would reduce the transfer component from 28.55 percent of total pensions under 1985 legislation to 21.65 percent if the new method of calculation were applied to 1993 pensions.

The repercussions on the various separate systems are very different: although the special systems appear to be almost unaffected by the new regulations, the transfer component of the general system would be reduced from 20.51 percent to 11.55 percent, which

Table 23.3. Transfer Components and Real Internal Rate of Return (IRR), Law 26/1985 (by system as a percentage of total pensions paid)

| System | Initial neutral pension | Total transfer | Transfer component | | IRR (real) |
			Transfer to initial pension	Minimum complement	
General	79.49	20.51	18.25	2.26	3.86
Self-employed	48.48	51.52	38.48	12.88	8.76
Agricultural workers (employed)	36.36	63.64	55.15	8.49	8.93
Agricultural workers (self-employed)	31.76	68.24	55.90	12.34	10.58
Domestic staff	24.54	75.46	50.08	25.39	16.10
Total	71.45	28.55	24.13	4.42	4.70

Source: Bandrés and Cuenca (1998).

Note: Law 26/1985 is the law regulating pension calculations in force until 1997.

Table 23.4. Transfer Components and Real Internal Rate of Return, Law 24/1997 (by system as a percentage of the total pensions paid)

| System | Initial neutral pension | Total transfer | Transfer component | | IRR (real) |
			Transfer to initial pension	Minimum complement	
General	88.45	11.55	7.55	4.00	3.15
Self-employed	50.37	49.63	28.01	21.62	8.44
Agricultural workers (employed)	37.51	62.49	46.69	15.80	8.75
Agricultural workers (self-employed)	32.82	67.18	46.30	20.88	10.36
Domestic staff	25.39	74.61	35.97	38.64	15.79
Total	78.35	21.65	13.86	7.79	4.06

Source: Bandrés and Cuenca (1998).

Note: Law 24/1997 is the law regulating pension calculations in force from 1997.

means we can assume that this is the system the reform was aimed at. A reduction in the rate of return can also be seen for the different systems, although the greatest reduction comes about in the general system.

Financial (Actuarial) Solvency of the System

Another way of focusing on the problem of pension systems is based on work carried out by Samuelson (1958) and Aaron (1966). Although this work was done many years ago, it is still completely valid and widely quoted in the literature. It concludes that a pension system financed by PAYG or through intergenerational transfers will be viable in the long term only if its internal rate of return (IRR) does not exceed the growth rate of earnings plus the stable growth rate of the contributing population, that is, if it does not exceed the growth of the system's tax base. Therefore the financial viability of the PAYG system will be linked to average economic growth sustainable in the long term, and this in turn will be the benchmark for setting the sustainability of the system. Devesa, Lejárraga, and Vidal (2000, 2002) calculate the real IRR of the general system. The average value of the IRR—around 4.25 percent for retirement ages close to the legal age of retirement—is much higher than the average GDP over the last 30 years (1970–2000), an annual accumulative rate of around 3 percent. It can be concluded that, should average economic growth not reach a certain level, the current configuration of the retirement pension system in Spain is not sustainable in the Samuelson-Aaron sense.

Jimeno (2002), bringing a previous work up to date (Jimeno 2000), also arrives at similar conclusions by using a simple formula to analyze the components of pension costs. The study forecasts pension costs in relation to GDP in 2025 and 2050 based on certain assumptions about the future evolution of the four factors shown.

The forecast of pension costs is represented in three scenarios. Two of these scenarios determine the percentage of spending in relation to GDP; one of the scenarios determines what the percentage ratio between average pension and average output should be to maintain a certain level of spending on pensions in relation to GDP. The results are shown in table 23.5 and lead us to conclude that maintaining spending on pensions in relation to GDP at acceptable levels, even in the most favorable scenario, would require a reform to the regulations governing the way pensions are calculated. At the same time the scenarios

Table 23.5. Forecast Spending on Pensions for 2025 and 2050

2001			
Population between 20 and 64 (in millions)	25.2		
Population over 65 (in millions)	6.9		
Number of pensions (in millions)	7.7		
Employment (in millions)	16.0		
Pensions/population over 65	1.12		
Population over 65/population between 20 and 64 (%)	27.4		
Rate of employment (%)	63.5		
Average pension/average output (%)	17.1		
Spending on pensions/GDP (%)	8.3		
2025			
Population between 20 and 64 (in millions)	26.0	26.0	26.0
Population over 65 (in millions)	9.4	9.4	9.4
Number of pensions (in millions)	10.5	10.8	10.8
Employment (in millions)	16.9	18.2	19.2
Pensions/population over 65	1.12	1.15	1.15
Population over 65/population between 20 and 64 (%)	36.2	36.2	36.2
Rate of employment (%)	65	70	70
Average pension/average output (%)	17	20	20.2
Spending on pensions/GDP (%)	10.6	11.9	12
2050			
Population between 20 and 64 (in millions)	23.3	23.3	23.3
Population over 65 (in millions)	12.8	12.8	12.8
Number of pensions (in millions)	14.3	14.7	14.7
Employment (in millions)	15.1	16.3	17.2
Pensions/population over 65	1.12	1.15	1.15
Population over 65/population between 20 and 64 (%)	60	60	60
Rate of employment (%)	65	70	70
Average pension/average output (%)	17	20	12.2
Spending on pensions/GDP (%)	17.6	19.7	12

Source: Jimeno (2002).

also show that there is an urgent need to set up alternative ways of financing pension costs. However, as the author points out, resorting to alternative sources of finance (general revenues, for example) is not exempt from problems, since a significant increase in the weight of general taxation in financing pension costs would substantially alter the essence of the social security contributory programs by breaking the existing link between contributions and benefits.

The last study analyzed here is by Alonso and Herce (2003), in which they continue, expand, correct, and modify their previous studies.[10] Recent population forecasts have been drawn up by the National Institute of Statistics for a horizon of 2050 taking into account scenarios that include immigration, something which up to now has not been considered in Spain. They analyze the consequences of immigration on forecasts for costs and revenue for the Spanish contributory pension system by establishing a central projection and then analyzing its sensitivity to different hypotheses regarding immigration, growth in output, and different ways of calculating the pension base.

The work of Alonso and Herce (2003) is developed using the MODPENS (Modelo de Pensiones) model (similar to the World Bank's PROST model) by the Fundación de

Economía Aplicada (FEDEA).[11] The basis for this study is the demographic and macroeconomic scenarios in which the hypotheses are established—the former already described in comments about the study by Jimeno (2002). MODPENS is an accounting model that does not consider behavior reactions. Apart from this limitation, the model is useful because of the information it supplies about the different systems and numbers of affiliates and pensioners by age and sex.

Conditional upon the assumptions being fulfilled, the results shown in table 23.6 suggest that, despite the census of the immigrant population implied by the most optimistic assumptions, long-term spending on pensions will continue to be appreciably greater than revenue from contributions, although in the short and medium term the amount of money in the system may show a marked increase. Naturally, the greater the migratory fluxes are, the smaller the financial insufficiency will be and the later it will appear. Similarly a rapid advance in output will defer the time and size of the system's financial insufficiency because pensions cannot capture output gains in the same proportion as salaries can, which would imply the relative impoverishment of pensioners. Job creation will sooner or later run up against a lack of manpower despite the steady influx of immigrants, and immigration cannot be depended upon for the system's long-term financial sufficiency even though it may have been its mainstay in the recent past. Finally, increasing the period for calculating the pension base of the pension has appreciable effects depending on the number of years taken into account. Faced with a problematic long-term central scenario, extreme scenarios as good or bad as desired can be considered, but they will be even more improbable.

All the studies analyzed have highlighted three issues:

- The current configuration of the pension system is not the best possible.
- Financial solvency cannot be achieved with the current system.
- The current system is not actuarially fair.

The situation described in this section, following the philosophy that big problems need big solutions, caused radical reforms to be proposed. The reforms concentrated on the progressive abandonment of the PAYG system and a move toward a funded system. The idea behind these reforms was that pensions would be guaranteed with a larger amount than they are in the current system and, in addition, the reforms would stimulate savings and economic growth. Bailén and Gil (1996) and Piñera and Weinstein (1996) were the first to propose these reforms. According to them, changing the system would remove the state's commitment to pay pensions from the state's accounts, would provide better individual pensions at a lower cost than the current system, and would increase personal savings, the accumulation of private capital, and economic growth.

Another proposal was put forward by Herce, Sosvilla-Rivero, Castillo, and Duce (1996). They defend the argument that the transition to a mixed system is not only possible but desirable because it would enable those workers who wanted to partially withdraw from the PAYG system and deposit part of their contributions in a private pension fund in such a way that, on retirement, they would receive revenue made up of the sum of both pensions. According to the authors, the advantage of their system over one of total substitution is twofold. On the one hand, there would be less coercion toward participants since no worker would lose the option of remaining within the social security system. On the other hand, the transition from the current PAYG model to the mixed model would be easier to finance as the reduction in monies entering the public system would not be extremely high because no worker would stop making contributions to social security.

Along similar lines, Herce (2001) again proposes that the partial privatization of public pensions could bring net advantages for future pensioners, and so radical reform of the

Table 23.6. Projections for the Spanish Contributory Pension System 2003–50, Central Scenario

	2003	2004	2005	2010	2015	2020	2025	2030	2035	2040	2045	2050
Affiliated workers[a]	16,448	16,777	17,113	18,333	19,146	19,416	19,303	18,870	18,115	17,133	16,240	15,767
Unemployed[b]	657	615	568	365	282	286	284	278	266	252	239	232
Number of pensions[c]	7,894	7,998	8,098	8,164	8,584	9,176	9,955	10,830	11,712	12,432	12,856	12,761
Ratio affiliates/pensioners	2.08	2.10	2.11	2.25	2.23	2.12	1.94	1.74	1.55	1.38	1.26	1.24
Income from contributions[d]	10.67	10.65	10.62	10.53	10.50	10.50	10.50	10.50	10.49	10.48	10.47	10.46
Spending on pensions[e]	9.75	9.75	9.74	9.33	9.71	10.40	11.42	12.71	14.29	15.87	17.12	17.23
Surplus or deficit	0.92	0.90	0.89	1.21	0.79	0.10	−0.92	−2.21	−3.80	−5.39	−6.65	−6.77
Accumulated fund or debt[f]	1.43	2.33	3.23	8.67	14.04	16.82	15.53	8.18	−7.26	−32.72	−68.46	−109.1

Source: Alonso and Herce (2003); authors.

a. Annual average in thousands.
b. Annual average in thousands. The Department of Employment (Instituto Nacional de Empleo, INEM) makes contributions for them to social security at the minimum contribution rate.
c. At the end of year, in thousands. Currently there are around 1.1 pensions to each pensioner.
d. As a percentage of GDP, including contributions for temporary incapacity.
e. As a percentage of GDP, including benefits for temporary incapacity, industrial injury, industrial disease, and administration costs.
f. The surplus for each year is added to that of the year before, or the deficit is subtracted. Returns on the fund or interest on debt are included in each case. The real interest rate is assumed to be 3 percent. This amount is not the implicit debt, which would clearly be far higher.

pension system should be undertaken as soon as possible. However, he makes no definite proposal as to how the transition should be made.

The reform proposals above have been rejected for five main reasons:

1. They meet with the unanimous opposition of all political parties and trade unions.
2. It would not be easy to take on the transition costs because of the enormous implicit debt accumulated.
3. Maintaining the current market (complementary system) and commission structure would mean high administration costs for contributors.[12]
4. The bad experiences associated with the real returns achieved by the private pension plan system over the last few years have made the Spanish population generally skeptical about the functioning of capital markets.
5. As mentioned before, there has been massive job creation and record numbers of affiliates registered with the government over the last few years, and this has meant that the "pension problem" has shifted to a secondary level.

Issues Surrounding the Introduction of a System of NDC Accounts

As described in the previous section, various proposals for reforming the pension system have been put forward and rejected in recent years. The aim of this section is to measure the effect that pension formulae based on notional account philosophy would have had on the initial amount of retirement pension and on the system's IRR if they had been introduced in Spain.

The first study to truly link the Spanish contributory pension system with notional accounts is the one by Devesa and Vidal (2004). They simulate the effect that would have been brought about by introducing regulations similar to those applying to the first and/or second pillar in the reformed pension systems of Brazil, Italy, Latvia, Poland, and Sweden. The simulation uses data for Spain for the following variables as benchmarks for calculating the pension: variation in the RPI, variation in average earnings (AEI), variation in the nominal GDP, and the total social security contributions index (TSSCI). The evolution of the variables used for this calculation can be seen in figure 23.1. A great degree of volatility can be seen over the years, with the highest values being reached in the mid-1970s.

Table 23.7 shows the ratio between the initial pension in Spain with the current regulations and the initial pensions that would have been provided by retirement formulae based on NDC contribution accounts as an approximation of the rules for calculating applied in Brazil, Italy, Latvia, Poland, and Sweden.

The value underlined in table 23.7 indicates that a person in Spain who retires at age 65 after contributing for 25 years obtains an initial pension 2.25 times greater than would have been obtained under Brazilian regulations. As can be seen, the ratio between the pension calculated according to rules in force in Spain in 2003 and the pension calculated with the data for Spain but using the calculation rules from countries with notional account systems does not fluctuate much according to the number of years contributed.

The fact that pensions are indexed according to different variables and different coefficients makes the initial pension an unsuitable element for comparison, and therefore "forces" comparisons to be made with reference to the IRR (see table 23.8 for data on the IRR). Its value, calculated according to the rules in force in Spain for 2003, is much higher than the other values obtained by applying the rules from other countries except in the case of 10 years of contributions. This is because according to those rules, pension entitlement in Spain starts only after 15 years of contributions. The highest IRR in Spain is for 15

Figure 23.1. Historical Evolution of the Various Arithmetic Rates in Spain, 1961–2004

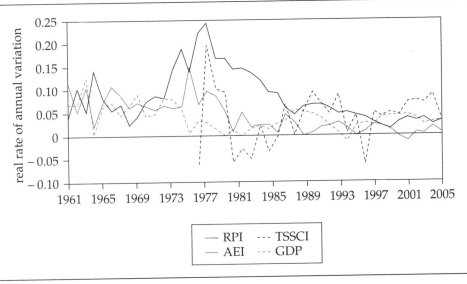

Source: Vidal, Domínguez, and Devesa (2005).

Table 23.7. Ratio between the Initial Pension in Spain (current system) and the Initial Pension Using Calculation Rules from Notional Formulae Applied in Other Countries

Years contributed	Brazil	Italy	Latvia	Poland	Sweden
15	2.23	2.83	2.77	4.09	2.49
20	2.22	2.48	2.51	4.14	2.43
25	2.25	2.27	2.47	4.30	2.39
30	2.26	2.14	2.31	4.32	2.24
35	2.30	2.08	2.19	4.37	2.11
40	2.19	1.86	1.93	4.09	1.85

Source: Devesa and Vidal (2004).

Note: Retirement age 65 and last salary equal to 100 percent of maximum pensionable earnings for 2002.

years of contributions, and it decreases from then on. The real IRR for women is always higher than for men because the amount of pension is the same but the probability of survival after retirement age (used for calculating the real IRR) is greater. It is also useful to note that under no set of rules does the IRR exceed 3.6 percent. This is the value of the average growth of GDP in Spain over the last 40 years and connects with the maximum value that should be shown by the IRR of a PAYG pension system for it to be sustainable in the Samuelson-Aaron sense.

According to the data in table 23.9, the replacement rate in all cases increases with an increase in the age of retirement. However, according to the real IRR, the results are not so

Table 23.8. IRR According to Number of Years Contributed, Men and (Women)

Years contributed	Brazil	Italy	Latvia	Poland	Spain[13]	Sweden
10	3.01 (4.22)	0.61 (1.91)	0.96 (2.26)	−0.45 (0.93)	—	2.09 (3.33)
15	2.57 (3.61)	1.15 (2.24)	1.44 (2.54)	−0.44 (0.76)	7.75 (8.58)	1.91 (2.97)
20	2.26 (3.17)	1.67 (2.61)	1.75 (2.69)	−0.46 (0.61)	6.54 (7.27)	1.78 (2.71)
25	2.04 (2.85)	2.00 (2.82)	1.75 (2.59)	−0.49 (0.49)	5.82 (6.47)	1.76 (2.59)
30	1.90 (2.66)	2.13 (2.87)	1.91 (2.68)	−0.45 (0.46)	5.34 (5.95)	1.93 (2.68)
35	1.81 (2.52)	2.21 (2.91)	2.11 (2.82)	−0.38 (0.49)	5.07 (5.64)	2.15 (2.84)
40	1.74 (2.42)	2.36 (3.01)	2.32 (2.98)	−0.29 (0.54)	4.63 (5.17)	2.37 (3.02)

Source: Devesa and Vidal (2004).

Note: Retirement age 65 and last salary equal to 100 percent of maximum pensionable earnings for 2002.

Table 23.9. Real Internal Rate of Return (IRR) and Replacement Rate (RR) for Retirement Age (X_r), with 35 Years of Contributions, Men and (Women)

(X_r) (years contributed)	IRR RR (%)	Brazil	Italy	Latvia	Poland	Spain	Sweden
60	IRR	1.56 (2.19)	2.26 (2.86)	2.01 (2.63)	−0.26 (0.50)	3.69 (4.22)	2.31 (2.90)
(35)	RR	31	38	34	17	56	38
61	IRR	1.61 (2.26)	2.21 (2.83)	2.03 (2.67)	−0.29 (0.50)	4.06 (4.59)	2.28 (2.89)
(35)	RR	33	39	36	18	63	39
62	IRR	1.65 (2.32)	2.23 (2.86)	2.05 (2.71)	−0.31 (0.50)	4.37 (4.91)	2.25 (2.88)
(35)	RR	34	40	37	19	71	40
63	IRR	1.70 (2.38)	2.24 (2.90)	2.07 (2.74)	−0.33 (0.49)	4.65 (5.20)	2.21 (2.87)
(35)	RR	36	42	39	19	78	41
64	IRR	1.76 (2.45)	2.26 (2.93)	2.09 (2.78)	−0.36 (0.49)	4.90 (5.45)	2.18 (2.86)
(35)	RR	38	43	40	20	85	42
65	IRR	1.81 (2.52)	2.21 (2.91)	2.11 (2.82)	−0.38 (0.49)	5.07 (5.64)	2.15 (2.84)
(35)	RR	40	44	42	21	92	43
66	IRR	1.86 (2.59)	2.24 (2.95)	2.13 (2.86)	−0.40 (0.48)	4.96 (5.55)	2.11 (2.83)
(35)	RR	42	46	44	22	92	45
67	IRR	1.92 (2.66)	2.27 (2.99)	2.15 (2.89)	−0.43 (0.48)	4.84 (5.45)	2.08 (2.81)
(35)	RR	44	48	46	23	92	46
68	IRR	1.98 (2.74)	2.19 (2.93)	2.18 (2.93)	−0.45 (0.47)	4.71 (5.34)	2.05 (2.79)
(35)	RR	47	49	48	24	92	48
69	IRR	2.05 (2.81)	2.14 (2.90)	2.20 (2.97)	−0.47 (0.46)	4.58 (5.22)	2.01 (2.78)
(35)	RR	50	51	50	25	92	49
70	IRR	2.12 (2.89)	2.18 (2.93)	2.23 (3.01)	−0.49 (0.45)	4.43 (5.10)	1.98 (2.76)
(35)	RR	53	53	53	26	92	51

Source: Devesa and Vidal (2004).

Note: Last salary equal to 100 percent of maximum pensionable earnings for 2002.

clear. With the Swedish rules, according to the IRR, deferring retirement age is penalized more. No clear incentive to retire later exists under Italian rules either. Brazilian and Latvian regulations do give favorable treatment to deferring retirement age. Polish rules are a special case: the real IRR for men is negative due to the way the initial pension is calculated, and becomes lower and lower, while for women it is positive and practically constant. In the case of Spain, the real IRR reaches its maximum at age 65.

From table 23.10 it can be seen that the replacement rate is once again increasing according to retirement age in all cases. If the values for the real IRR are taken as a benchmark, the results are clearer than they are from table 23.9. Generally speaking, the value of the real IRR now increases with retirement age under the rules of those countries with a notional accounts system. With the rules applied in Brazil and Latvia, the favorable treatment given on deferring retirement age can be seen more clearly. Polish rules continue to

Table 23.10. Real Internal Rate of Return (IRR) and Replacement Rate (RR) for Retirement Age (X_r), with Different Numbers of Years Contributed, Men and (Women)

(X_r) (years contributed)	IRR RR (%)	Brazil	Italy	Latvia	Poland	Spain	Sweden
60 (30)	IRR RR	1.63 (2.30) 29	2.18 (2.82) 33	1.82 (2.49) 30	−0.32 (0.48) 16	3.79 (4.36) 50	2.12 (2.76) 33
61 (31)	IRR RR	1.66 (2.34) 31	2.14 (2.80) 35	1.87 (2.56) 32	−0.34 (0.48) 17	4.15 (4.72) 58	2.12 (2.78) 35
62 (32)	IRR RR	1.70 (2.39) 33	2.17 (2.83) 37	1.93 (2.62) 34	−035 (0.48) 18	4.46 (5.02) 66	2.12 (2.79) 37
63 (33)	IRR RR	1.73 (2.43) 35	2.20 (2.87) 40	1.99 (2.68) 36	−0.36 (0.48) 19	4.71 (5.27) 75	2.13 (2.81) 39
64 (34)	IRR RR	1.77 (2.47) 37	2.24 (2.92) 42	2.05 (2.75) 39	−0.37 (0.48) 20	4.93 (5.49) 84	2.14 (2.82) 41
65 (35)	IRR RR	1.81 (2.52) 40	2.21 (2.91) 44	2.11 (2.82) 42	−0.38 (0.49) 21	5.07 (5.64) 92	2.15 (2.84) 43
66 (36)	IRR RR	1.85 (2.57) 43	2.27 (2.96) 47	2.17 (2.89) 45	−0.39 (0.49) 22	5.11 (5.69) 92	2.16 (2.86) 46
67 (37)	IRR RR	1.89 (2.62) 45	2.33 (3.03) 51	2.24 (2.96) 48	−0.39 (0.50) 24	5.15 (5.76) 92	2.18 (2.88) 49
68 (38)	IRR RR	1.94 (2.66) 48	2.28 (2.99) 53	2.31 (3.03) 52	−0.39 (0.50) 25	5.19 (5.82) 92	2.19 (2.91) 52
69 (39)	IRR RR	1.98 (2.71) 52	2.27 (2.98) 56	2.38 (3.10) 56	−0.39 (0.51) 27	5.23 (5.88) 92	2.21 (2.93) 55
70 (40)	IRR RR	2.03 (2.76) 55	2.34 (3.05) 60	2.45 (3.17) 60	−0.39 (0.51) 28	5.28 (5.94) 92	2.23 (2.95) 58

Source: Devesa and Vidal (2004).

Note: 30 years contributions for a retirement age of 60, increasing the number of years contributed by 1 as retirement age is deferred by 1 year. Last salary equal to 100 percent of maximum pensionable earnings for 2002.

give slightly decreasing negative values for men, with slightly increasing positive values for women.

As we have just shown, the introduction in Spain of notional retirement formulae similar to those applied in some other countries would have the effect of noticeably reducing the amount of pensions currently in payment, which have been calculated using pension formulae based on traditional defined benefits. The current theoretical replacement rate for someone retiring at 65 with 35 years of contributions would change from 92 percent to a range of values between 42 percent and 44 percent, depending on the formula chosen. In addition to this, the real theoretical IRR expected from the contributions would change from more than 5.35 percent to less than 2.5 percent with any of the formulae applied. These values are in greater harmony with the real average growth of GDP in Spain over the last 40 years (3.6 percent), which should undoubtedly be the reference for the system to aim at to be financially viable in the Samuelson-Aaron sense. At the same time, it could be the justification for introducing a notional accounts system in Spain.

Another positive effect of introducing this type of retirement formula in Spain could be to slow down the trend toward early retirement. The current formula, which applies decreasing weight to the years of contributions paid, does not encourage later retirement.

Similarly, if the notional accounts system had been adopted, the current system would have built up extensive reserves which, according to Alonso and Herce (2003), would enable the future "lack of manpower" to be considered more calmly.

It seems clear, therefore, that introducing a notional accounts system would to a great extent correct the deficiencies seen in the Spanish system. This reform should aim at achieving as far as possible the following objectives:

1. Narrow the relationship between contributions and benefits—that is, increase the actuarial fairness of the system.
2. Carry out redistribution in the most transparent way possible.
3. Reduce the risk of political manipulation.
4. Reach a financial stability that would stand up to the demographic and economic changes that affect the system itself.
5. Mitigate or weaken the disincentive to work which is present in the current system.
6. Eliminate or minimize the actuarial deficit of the system.

It is difficult for parametric reforms to achieve the above aims. Such reforms also tend to just patch things up to keep them going long enough to be handed on to other governments and generations, since they usually involve a series of mild measures that lengthen and complicate pension calculation via countless partial, transitory arrangements.

Finally, another interesting objective—the generation of financial savings managed by the private sector—could be achieved by strengthening the complementary systems and/or rerouting part of the contributions toward a funded system, which would enable sources of retirement revenue and the risks inherent in the pension system in general to be diversified.

Proposal: A New Formula for Calculating Retirement Pension and the Transition Process

If the introduction of a notional accounts system was being seriously considered for the beneficial effect it would have on the system as a whole by notably improving its financial viability and generating greater work incentives, one important question remains. Given that the risk is transferred explicitly to the contributors and beneficiaries, the question would be to determine the formula for calculating the pension that would best fit the degree of risk aversion of the contributor-beneficiary. The notional rates that would be used to revalue both the contributions and the pensions therefore need to be determined.

The methodology used was developed in the paper by Vidal, Domínguez, and Devesa (2004, 2005), who quantify the aggregate economic risk to which the beneficiary would be exposed if it were decided to introduce a retirement pension system based on notional account philosophy in Spain. For this they used scenario-generation techniques to make projections of the factors determining the real expected IRR for the beneficiary according to 16 retirement formulae based on the RPI, the GDP, the AEI , and the TSSCI. These projections are based on Herce and Alonso's macroeconomic scenario for 2000–50 (2000a) and include information about the past performance of the indexes and the time period for which the forecast is wanted.

The models used to calculate the initial retirement pension and its later variation based on the system of NDC accounts are shown in table 23.11.

The results for the average expected replacement rate for each of the formulae proposed can be seen in table 23.12.

After 40 years of contributing, the formula that provides the best replacement rate is the one for around 46.5 percent. This is in sharp contrast to the replacement rate currently supplied by the system, which is around 92 percent. If the notional accounts system was applied, in the best of cases the initial pension would reach 51 percent of that obtained under the present PAYG system in Spain. If people started work at 20 instead of 25, these replacement rates would be slightly higher, reaching 49 percent in the case of group 1.

Much of this difference can be attributed to the way the current pension calculation formula is designed. If the whole working life was considered when calculating the pension

Table 23.11. Formulae for Calculating the Initial Pension and Its Later Variation

Model	Revaluation of the contribution base	Notional rate for contributions	Notional rate for pensions
1	RPI	GDP	RPI
2	RPI	AEI	RPI
3	RPI	GDP	RPI +/– GDP differential
4	RPI	GDP	RPI +/– AEI differential
5	RPI	AEI	RPI +/– GDP differential
6	RPI	AEI	RPI +/– AEI differential
7	RPI	TSSCI	RPI
8	RPI	TSSCI	RPI +/– TSSCI differential
11	AEI	GDP	RPI
12	AEI	AEI	RPI
13	AEI	GDP	RPI +/– GDP differential
14	AEI	GDP	RPI +/– AEI differential
15	AEI	AEI	RPI +/– GDP differential
16	AEI	AEI	RPI +/– AEI differential
17	AEI	TSSCI	RPI
18	AEI	TSSCI	RPI +/– TSSCI differential

Source: Vidal, Domínguez, and Devesa (2004).

Note: RPI (retail price index); GDP (gross domestic product); AEI (average earnings index); and TSSCI (total social security contributions index).

Table 23.12. Average Expected Replacement Rate (retirement age 65)

Average expected replacement rate	Model	Group
46.43%	11 13 14	1
46.39%	1 3 4	2
46.36%	12 15 16	3
46.33%	2 5 6	4
41.27%	17 18	5
41.24%	7 8	6

Source: Vidal, Domínguez, and Devesa (2004).

base—as is advisable in contributory systems that aim at proportionality—instead of taking the last 15 years of contributions into account, then the replacement rate would have been about 75 percent for a person retiring at age 65 with 40 years of contributions.

The results obtained for the average expected IRR are shown separately for men and women in table 23.13, along with the percentage of expected deviation from the IRR for each model. Five basic aspects of results obtained for average expected IRR and expected deviation need to be highlighted:

1. The analysis of the average IRR shows clear differences between the rates for men and women. This discrepancy comes about because the joint average life expectancy of men and women at retirement age was used when calculating the initial pension. Because women have a higher life expectancy than men, the expected return on contributions for women is much higher.

2. If tables 23.12 and 23.13 are compared, no clear relation between the replacement rate and the IRR can be seen. This is because the replacement rate refers exclusively to the initial pension and, in addition, the contribution effort made is not taken into account. The IRR, however, relates all the probable inflows and outflows, and takes into account how the pension can vary over time.

3. There are only very small differences between the real average expected IRR for both men and women in the first 10 models. This seems to indicate that the participant-beneficiary could choose any of these models using his or her degree of risk aversion as a basis for making the decision.

4. The values obtained for the real IRR appear to be surprisingly low, but in fact they are not that low as the calculation is being considered a priori. The values will increase proportionally as the contributor is assumed to grow older. With similar assumptions, and assuming current Spanish legislation constant for the whole time

Table 23.13. Average Internal Rate of Return (IRR) and Expected Deviation for Men (M) and Women (W) (retirement age 65)

Model	IRRM average	IRRM deviation	% Dev M	IRRW average	IRRW deviation	% DevW
14	0.02492	0.01148	46.06%	0.03441	0.01192	34.64%
5	0.02491	0.01203	48.31%	0.03440	0.01364	39.65%
16	0.02490	0.01331	53.45%	0.03437	0.01372	39.90%
6	0.02489	0.0133	53.43%	0.03437	0.01349	39.26%
15	0.02489	0.01208	48.53%	0.03437	0.01234	35.92%
3	0.02488	0.01022	41.08%	0.03436	0.01065	31.00%
1	0.02486	0.00796	32.02%	0.03435	0.00823	23.94%
13	0.02485	0.01035	41.64%	0.03433	0.01057	30.79%
11	**0.02483**	**0.00791**	**31.84%**	**0.03433**	**0.00819**	**23.86%**
12	0.02482	0.00991	39.90%	0.03431	0.00997	29.07%
17	0.02111	0.01186	56.19%	0.03065	0.01169	38.14%
7	0.02101	0.01164	55.42%	0.03064	0.01166	38.04%
8	0.02097	0.01651	78.73%	0.03064	0.01682	54.89%
_18_	_0.02097_	_0.01651_	_78.74%_	_0.03064_	_0.01682_	_54.91%_
2	0.02046	0.00666	32.57%	0.02970	0.00667	22.47%
4	0.01926	0.00729	37.84%	0.02845	0.00755	26.56%

Source: Vidal, Domínguez, and Devesa (2004).

period considered, the real IRR would be 4.05 percent and 4.93 percent for men and women, respectively. However, it would be best to qualify the above figures since the value of the IRR in the defined benefit PAYG system does not include possible future reductions in its value—it is calculated in a system in which financial equilibrium is presupposed. Future pensioners will probably have to make greater contributions (through tax increases) and/or receive smaller pensions. In other words, if the defined benefit system intends to respect its acquired commitments to members, it must be because available financial resources exist to cover the system's future deficit. If these funds were used in the notional accounts system, this would provide a larger pension, thereby reducing the IRR differential.

5. The average values undergo deviations. This implies that those models that generate a greater deviation of the IRR relative to the average IRR are riskier. The listing in order of deviation is the same for men and women as they depend on the same volatility factors. Model 18 shows the highest risk in terms of typical deviation, while model 11 has the least. In general terms, IRR deviation for women is greater than for men.

The results in bold in table 23.13 for model 11 are those that are less volatile for both men and women, whereas model 18 is the most volatile and so its results have been underlined instead.

To summarize, it can be concluded from what has just been set out that:

• The a priori average expected IRR for both men and women, following any of the formulae tested based on representative indices of relevant macroeconomic variables, is quite clearly lower than the IRR awarded today on contributory retirement pensions by current Spanish legislation. The envisaged replacement rate in the most favorable formula reaches barely 50.5 percent of that obtained today. This highlights the profound structural actuarial imbalance present in the current configuration of the defined benefit retirement pension system in Spain.

- The preferred models for both male and female beneficiaries who are neutral to risk are 14 and 5, in descending order. The first of these capitalizes the contributions in line with the expected evolution of the GDP; the second follows the AEI. In both cases the pensions can participate in the probable upward fluctuations of the salaries index as foreseen above.

Some contributor-beneficiaries with a different risk profile may prefer retirement formulae different from those in the paragraph above. It would be possible to provide a certain degree of freedom of choice of the preferred formula according to the contributor's perception of risk and the evolution and forecast pathway of the indices. Involving individuals in making decisions about the model they consider most suitable will make them much more committed to the NDC system. Nevertheless, this individual choice would have to be subject to the financial sustainability of the system in the Samuelson-Aaron sense.

The transition from the current system to one of notional accounts should not pose any technical problems, since the Spanish social security system has a reliable computerized register of each contributor's employment history. Thus, to respect the acquired rights of those who are close to retirement age, the changeover to the new system should be carried out in such a way that pensions are calculated taking both systems into account using coefficients that would depend on date of birth, similar to the way it is done in Sweden.

The notional accounts model suggested for Spain should incorporate additional control elements for the solvency of the system as a whole. These could include, for example, a maximum annual level of deficit as a percentage of the GDP, or a maximum accumulated level of deficit over five years, also as a percentage of the GDP. And so that contributors and initial pensions do not bear the brunt of the adjustment effort, pensions already in payment could be reviewed periodically to take into account any possible changes in mortality rates. Any of the formulae put forward in this section would be acceptable and could be chosen by the contributor as long as applying them brought about an annual or accumulated deficit below the level eventually set by law. A stabilizing mechanism could also be incorporated similar to the one established in Sweden.[14] However, as we point out in our conclusions, more research would need to be done into this matter.

Following Holzmann (2006), to achieve a better coordinated pension system in an integrated Europe—and making the most of the fact that Spain already has a noncontributory pillar—this noncontributory pillar should be transformed into a zero pillar of social or noncontributory pensions that provides minimum income support for the vulnerable elderly. Eligibility for the noncontributory pension will naturally be means-tested, but in a more demanding and rigorous way than is done at present in Spain.

As with the contributory pillar, a means-tested guaranteed minimum pension should also be maintained, with the complement of the contributory pillar to bring it up to minimum levels being financed through taxation. Accurately setting the relation between the amount of the minimum pension and the pension that the zero pillar could provide would be of the utmost importance. The possibility of contributors having a free choice as to the age they retire could bring about an excessive number of early retirements that, in turn, could put pressure on the authorities to increase the amount of the guaranteed minimum pension. Palmer (2001) shows that there is empirical evidence that people tend to retire as soon as they are allowed to, and so it should not be made possible for early retirement to be decided freely. One of the main problems of the Spanish pension system is that the real average retirement age is around 62 years. This is because of permissive legislation that in many cases allows early retirement. The possibility of early retirement should be eliminated. At first the minimum retirement age should be maintained at 65 as long as enough has been accumulated in the notional account to give entitlement to the minimum pension. If the accumulated amount in the notional account is not sufficient, the person will have to continue working until age 70.

Alonso and Herce (2003)[15] state that the contributory pension system will go into deficit from the year 2020. Around 2020, therefore, would be the best time for the notional accounts system to be fully in place.

Despite being technically possible, the process of introducing the notional accounts system in Spain could not be immediate mainly because it would be unviable from the political point of view today. As mentioned above, neither the previous government nor the government in power since the general elections of March 14, 2004, consider any but parametric reforms. Increasing the way the pension base is calculated to cover the whole of working life, which almost all political parties think is a good idea, has been under discussion for more than two years and is still far from being agreed upon. In addition to this, the way notional accounts work is unknown to both politicians and the main opinion makers in Spain.

A less radical proposal, but one that could be politically possible, would be the one shown in table 23.14. This proposal is more in line with the transition process followed in Italy and Sweden than that in Latvia. The transition proposal suggested would mean both systems functioning side by side over a 20-year period, after which the notional accounts system would take over completely. This should be accompanied by a change in the way the amount of pension is calculated, so as to increase the pension base to cover the whole of the individual's working life and eliminate the possibility of retiring before age 65. Combining both systems would imply an improvement on the forecasts made by Alonso and Herce (2003), deferring the expected deficit and increasing the system's solvency for a time horizon of 20 years.

Various modifications could be made to the basic proposal above depending on the degree of political acceptance, which in Spain would be a rather thorny issue. The two main modifications are:

- Extend the transition period to 40 years, for example, in which case the change in the amounts of pension would be much more gradual. As a consequence, however, the benefits of the change would be also seen only gradually.
- Calculate the retirement pension following notional philosophy, but take into account acquired rights when calculating the initial notional capital.

Table 23.14. Timetable for Adapting to Pension Reform in Spain

Year of retirement	Pension received from the notional accounts system (%)	Pension received from the current system [a] (%)
2005	0	100
2006	5	95
. . .	. . .	. . .
2023	90	10
2024	95	5
2025	100	0

Source: Authors.

a. The number of years taken into account to calculate the pension base would start increasing by one year from 2005.

Conclusions and Future Research

In the light of all the arguments looked at here along with the research referred to, it seems clear that the main conclusion is that there is a need to carry out some kind of far-reaching reform of the contributory pension system in Spain.

The discussion should therefore revolve around the type of reform to be applied rather than whether its introduction should be recommended.

A reform in the shape of a notional accounts system applying to the Spanish contributory system as a whole (counting all the various systems, including the special system for civil servants) could enable the six objectives surrounding the introduction of a system of NDC accounts to be achieved. This reform would mean reducing the amount of pensions and IRR, but it would have the effect of giving the system greater credibility and greater long-term financial equilibrium, thereby avoiding constant piecemeal reforms. The objective of generating financial savings managed by the private sector could be achieved by strengthening the complementary systems and/or rerouting part of the contributions toward a funded system, which would enable sources of retirement revenue and the risks inherent in the pension system in general to be diversified.

Given that the risk is transferred explicitly to the contributor-beneficiary, great care would have to be taken over the design of the actual formula for calculating retirement pension. As was seen in the previous section, if contributor-beneficiaries who are neutral to risk are to be rewarded, contributions should be capitalized in line with the evolution of the GDP or the AEI. Pensions could participate in the upward fluctuations above the rate forecast of the index of variation in salaries. On the other hand, if the design of the formula were to reward contributor-beneficiaries who are more averse to risk, then the formula would be similar as regards contributions, but pensions would simply be adjusted in line with the RPI.

In response to one of the criticisms usually made against notional account systems—that contributors take on the risk of the evolution of the index and are subject to a risk-return trade-off they have not chosen; that is, their aversion to risk is not taken into account the way it is in private capitalization funds—it would be best if there were a menu of retirement formulae available, such as those put forward in the previous section. This way contributors could change the index used to capitalize their contributions every so often (every three or five years, for example) according to their perception of risk and the evolution and anticipated pathway of the indices. Involving individuals in making decisions about the models they consider most suitable will make them much more committed to the NDC system. This does not mean that there are no mechanisms to safeguard the financial equilibrium of the system in case of economic and/or demographic shocks. In practice, as mentioned above, some countries have mechanisms to stabilize the system in case serious financial imbalances appear.

Finally, bearing in mind that this is the first proposal for introducing a notional accounts system in Spain and given the special features of the current pension system and the country's idiosyncrasies, at least three aspects regarding the possible introduction of notional accounts need to be researched more deeply and carefully:

1. To evaluate more precisely the impact that introducing a notional accounts system could have on current contributors, there is a need for a sufficiently wide representative sample of their real wage histories (and contribution bases). An analysis of this information could also be very useful for deciding how to carry out the definitive proposal for harmonizing the different occupational schemes.
2. The proposed measures for financial stability in case of short-term financial imbalances should be more precisely defined.

3. Spanish public opinion, social agents, politicians, and even economists and actuaries are unaware of how notional accounts work. To test the political viability of the reform, an opinion poll would need to be carried out to find out how acceptable the proposal made in this study would be.

Notes

1. "Notional defined contribution" and "non-financial defined contribution" should be understood to have the same definition.

2. The Kyrgyz Republic's scheme, Palmer (2006), is incompletely designed regarding the rate of return, although the long transition period will allow plenty of time to improve the system design.

3. This is not exactly a notional accounts system.

4. These researchers include Alonso and Herce (2003), Barea and Gónzalez-Páramo (1996), Bonin, Gil, and Patxot (2001), Devesa, Lejárraga, and Vidal (2000, 2002), Durán and López-García (1996), Gil and Patxot (2002), Herce (1997, 2001), Herce and Pérez-Díaz (1995), Herce and Alonso (2000a, 2000b), Jimeno (2003, 2002, 2000), Jimeno and Licandro (1999), Mateo (1997), Meneu (1998), Montero (2000), and Piñera and Weinstein (1996).

5. The ratio between contributors and number of pensions is not strictly comparable for the last few years—from 1990 onward—as there has been a change in the way the data are broken down to calculate it.

6. This problem of a lack of good labor incentives is not dealt with here. There is a great deal of literature on the (dis)incentives of the jobs market generated by the current pension system. On this subject, see Boldrin, Dolado, Jimeno and Peracchi (1999), Boldrin, Jiménez-Martín and Peracchi (1999, 2000a, 2000b), Diamond (2001), Jiménez-Martín and Sánchez (2000, 2001), and Jimeno (2000).

7. The money needed to cover any shortfalls is the amount added to the pension if it is less than the minimum pension guaranteed under the general system.

8. As shown by Boldrin, Dolado, Jimeno and Peracchi (1999), much of the increase in spending on pensions that came about in many EU countries during the last quarter of the 20th century was due to lowering the effective age of retirement.

9. The *implicit debt* is comprised of the accrued-to-date liabilities. These represent the present value of pensions to be paid in the future on the basis of accrued rights; neither the future contributions nor the accrual of the new rights they imply are considered. For the terminology on pension liabilities, see Holzmann (1998).

10. See especially the studies by Herce and Alonso (2000a, 2000b); Herce (2001) and Herce and Pérez-Díaz (1995). The authors consider it natural that exercises in projections should be repeated at regular intervals to take into account new economic and demographic circumstances, changes in legislation, improvements in methodology, and the need to explore new hypotheses.

11. FEDEA (Fundación de Economía Aplicada) is a private, nonprofit institution that obtains part of its operating resources from a capital fund set up by its sponsors. Its objective is to carry out studies that contribute to the analysis, diagnosis, and discussion of Spanish economic problems, applying the principles of economic analysis and using rigorous scientific methods and independent judgment.

12. See Devesa, Rodríguez, and Vidal (2002a, 2000b, and 2003).

13. In Spain, 10 years of contributions do not give entitlement to a pension, so the IRR is therefore zero.

14. See Settegren (2001).

15. See table 23.5 for the main forecasts of Alonso and Herce (2003).

References

Aaron, H. 1966. "The Social Insurance Paradox." *Canadian Journal of Economic Review* 30 (3): 371–4.

Abio, G., H. Bonin, J. Gil, and C. Patxot. 1999. "El impacto intergeneracional de la reforma de las pensiones en España: Un enfoque de contabilidad intergeneracional." ("The Intergenerational Impact of Pension Reform in Spain: An Intergenerational Accountancy Approach.") *Cuadernos Económicos de ICE* 65: 110–16.

Alonso, J., and J. A. Herce. 2003. "Balance del sistema de pensiones y boom migratorio en España. Proyecciones del modelo MODPENS de FEDEA a 2050." ("Outcome of Pension System and Migratory Boom in Spain. Forecasts of the Model MODPENS from FEDEA to 2050 FEDEA.") Working Paper 03-02, FEDEA.

Alvira, F., J. García, and F. Blanco. 1996. "Jubilación, Planes de Pensiones y Opinión Pública." ("Retirement, Pension Funds and Public Opinion.") *Perspectivas de Sistema Financiero* 56: 83–90.

Bailén, J. M., and Gil, J. 1996. "Transitional Effects of a Pension System in Spain." Working Paper 96-24, FEDEA.

Bandrés, E., and A. Cuenca. 1998. "Equidad Intrageneracional en las pensiones de jubilación. La reforma de 1997." ("Intragenerational Fairness in the Retirement Pension. The 1997 Reform.") *Revista de Economía Aplicada* 6 (18): 119–40.

Barea, J., and J. M. González-Páramo. 1996. "Pensiones y prestaciones por desempleo ("Pensions and Unemployement Benefits.") Working Paper Fundación BBV, Bilbao.

Boldrin, M., J. Dolado, J. Jimeno, and F. Peracchi. 1999. "The Future of Pension Systems in Europe: A Reappraisal." *Economic Policy* 29: 283–323.

Boldrin, M., S. Jiménez-Martín, and F. Peracchi. 1999. "Social Security and Retirement in Spain." In *Social Security Programs and Retirement around the World*, ed. J. Gruber and D. Wise, 32–46. Chicago: University of Chicago Press for the NBER.

———. 2000a. "Micro-modelling of Retirement Behavior in Spain." Unpublished. Mimeo.

———. 2000b. "Sistema de Pensiones y Mercado de Trabajo en España." ("Pension System and Labor Market in Spain.") Report for the Fundación BBVA, Madrid.

Bonin, H., J. Gil, and C. Patxot. 2001. "Beyond the Toledo Agreement: The Intergenerational Impact of the Spanish Pension Reform." *Spanish Economic Review* 3 (2): 111–30.

Devesa, J. E., A. Lejárraga, and C. Vidal. 2000. "The Internal Rate of Return of the Pay-As-You-Go System: An Analysis of the Spanish Case." *Centre for Pensions and Social Insurance*. Research Report 33/2000, Birkbeck College and City University of London.

———. 2002. "El tanto de rendimiento del sistema de pensiones de reparto." ("The Internal Rate of Return of the Pay-As-You-Go System.") *Revista de Economía Aplicada* 10 (30): 109–32.

Devesa, J. E., R. Rodríguez, and C. Vidal. 2002a. "Assessing Administration Charges for the Affiliate in Individual Accounts Systems." Working Paper EC 2002-09, Instituto Valenciano de Investigaciones Económicas (IVIE).

———. 2002b. "Los costes de administración para el afiliado en los sistemas de pensiones basados en cuentas de capitalización individual: Medida y comparación internacional." ("Administration Costs for the Aaffiliate in Individual Account Systems: Assessment and International Comparison.") Working Paper 171/2002, Fundación para la Investigación Económica y Social (FUNCAS).

———. 2003. "Medición y comparación internacional de los costes de administración para el afiliado en las cuentas individuales de capitalización." ("Administration Costs for the Affiliate in Individual Account Systems: Assessment and International Comparison.") *Revista Española de Financiación y Contabilidad*. 32 (116): 95–144.

Devesa, J. E. and C. Vidal. 2004. "Notional Defined Contributions Accounts (NDCs). What Effect Would They Have Had on the Spanish Pension System?" *Moneda y Crédito* 219: 61–103.

Diamond, P. 2001. "Issues in Social Security with a Focus on Spain." *Universitat Pompeu Fabra*. Lección de Economía, October 29, 2001.

Durán, A., and M. A. López García. 1996. "Tres análisis sobre la Seguridad Social: Un comentario." ("Three analyses about Social Security: A Remark.") *Papeles de Economía Española* 69: 39–51.

Gil, J., and C. Patxot. 2002. "Reformas de la financiación del sistema de pensiones." ("Financing Pension System Reform.") *Revista de Economía Aplicada* 28 (10): 63–85.

Gillion, C. 2000. "The Development and Reform of Social Security Pensions: The Approach of the International Labour Office." *International Social Security Review* 53 (1): 35–62.

Herce, J. 1997. "La reforma de las pensiones en España: aspectos analíticos y aplicados." ("The Pension Reform in Spain: Applied and Analyzed Aspect.") *Moneda y Crédito* 204: 105–59.

———. 2001. "La privatización de las pensiones en España." ("Privatization of the Pensions in Spain.") Working Paper 01-01, FEDEA.

Herce, J., and J. Alonso. 2000a. "La reforma de las pensiones ante la revisión del Pacto de Toledo." ("The Pension Reform after the Revision of Toledo Pact.") *Colección Estudios Económicos* (19) *"La Caixa."* Barcelona.

———. 2000b. "Los efectos económicos de la Ley de Consolidación de la S.S. Perspectivas financieras del sistema tras su entrada en vigor." ("The Economic Effect of the Law of Consolidation of Social Security: Financial Perspectives after Its Starting Application.") *Hacienda Pública Española* 152 (1): 51–67.

Herce, J., and V. Pérez-Díaz. 1995. "La reforma del sistema público de Pensiones en España." ("The Public Pension Reform in Spain.") Working Paper 4, "La Caixa," Barcelona.

Herce, J. A., S. Sosvilla-Rivero, S. Castillo, and R. Duce. 1996. "El futuro de las pensiones en España: hacia un sistema mixto." ("The Future of the Pension in Spain: Going to a Mixed System.") Monografía 8, Servicio de Estudios de "La Caixa," Barcelona.

Holzmann, R. 1998. "Financing the Transition to Multipillar." *Pension Reform Primer*. Washington, DC: World Bank.

———. 2000. "The World Bank Approach to Pension Reform." *International Social Security Review* 53 (1): 11–34.

———. 2006. "Toward a Coordinated Pension System in Europe: Rationale and Potential Structure." In *Pension Reform: Issues and Prospects for Non-Financial Defined Contribution (NDC) Schemes*, ed. R. Holzmann and E. Palmer, chapter 11. Washington, DC: World Bank.

Holzmann, R., M. Orenstein, and M. Rutkowski. 2003. *Pension Reform in Europe: Process and Progress*. Washington, DC: World Bank.

Jiménez-Martín, S., and A. R. Sánchez. 2000. "Incentivos y reglas de jubilación en España." ("Retirement Incentives and Regulation in Spain.") *Cuadernos Económicos de ICE* 65: 45–88.

———. 2001. "The Effect of Pension Rules on Retirement Monetary Incentives with an Application to Pension Reform in Spain." Working Paper 01-36, *Universidad Carlos III*.

Jimeno, J. F. 2000. "El sistema de pensiones contributivas en España: Cuestiones básicas y perspectivas a medio plazo." "[The Spanish Contributory Pension System: Basic Questions and Perspective in a Short Time.]" Working Paper 02-15, FEDEA.

———. 2002. "Demografía, empleo, salario y pensiones." ("Demography, Job, Wage and Pensions.") Working Paper 02-04, FEDEA.

————. 2003. "Incentivos y desigualdad en el sistema español de pensiones contributivas por jubilación." ("Incentives and Inequalities in the Spanish Contributory Pension of Retirement System.") Working Paper 02-13, FEDEA.

Jimeno, J. F., and O. Licandro. 1999. "La tasa interna de rentabilidad y el equilibrio financiero del sistema español de pensiones de jubilación." ("The Internal Rate of Return and the Financial Balance of the Spanish Pension System.") *Investigaciones Económicas* 23 (1): 129–43.

Mateo, R. 1997. *Rediseño general del sistema de pensiones español.* (New Design of the Spanish Pension System.) Pamplona: Ediciones Universitarias de Navarra.

Meneu, R. 1998. "Equilibrio Financiero de las Pensiones de Jubilación en España 1995–2030." ("Financial Equilibrium of the Retirement Pension in Spain 1995–2030.") *Revista de Economía Aplicada* 6 (17): 157–69.

Ministerio de Trabajo y Seguridad Social. 1995. *La Seguridad Social en el umbral del siglo XXI.* (The Social Security at the Beginning of the 21st Century.) *Colección Seguridad Social*, 14. Madrid.

Montero, M. 2000. "Estructura demográfica y sistema de pensiones. Un análisis de equilibrio general aplicado a la economía Española." ("Demography Structure and Pension System.") *Investigaciones Económicas* 24 (2): 297–327.

Monasterio, C., I. Sánchez, and F. Blanco. 1996. "Equidad y Estabilidad del Sistema de Pensiones Español." ("Fairness and Stability of the Spanish Pension System.") *Serie Economía Pública.* Bilbao: Fundación BBV.

National Institute of Statistics (Instituto Nacional de Estadística, INE). 2001. "Proyecciones de población calculadas a partir del Censo de 2001." ("Population Projections Based on the 2001 Census.") INE, Madrid.

Palmer, E. 2001. "Financial Stability and Individual Benefits in the Swedish Pension Reform Model." *Asociación Internacional de la Seguridad Social*, Seminario de Actuarios y Estadísticos, Montevideo, 21–22 de noviembre de 2001.

————. 2006. "Conversion to NDCs—Issues and Models." In *Pension Reform: Issues and Prospects for Non-Financial Defined Contribution (NDC) Schemes*, ed. R. Holzmann and E. Palmer, chapter 9. Washington, DC: World Bank.

Pérez-Díaz, V., B. Álvarez-Miranda, and E. Chuliá. 1997. "La opinión pública ante el sistema de Pensiones." ("Public Opinion about the Pension System.") Working Paper 10, "La Caixa," Barcelona.

Piñera, J., and J. Weinstein. 1996. *Una propuesta de reforma del sistema de pensiones en España.* (A Proposal of Pension System Reform in Spain.). Madrid: Círculo de Empresarios.

Queisser, M. 2000. "Pension Reform and International Organizations: From Conflict to Convergence." *International Social Security Review* 53 (2): 31–45.

Redecillas, A. 1996. "Los compromisos financieros del Estado y de la seguridad social relativos a pensiones." ("The Financial Commitment of the State and the Social Security in Relation to Pensions.") *Serie Economía Pública.* Bilbao: Fundación BBV.

Samuelson, P. 1958. "An Exact Consumption-Loan Model of Interest with or without the Social Contrivance of Money." *The Journal of Political Economy* 66 (6): 467–82.

Settergren, O. 2001. "The Automatic Balance Mechanism of the Swedish Pension System— A Non-Technical Introduction." http:www.rfv.se/english.

Valdés-Prieto, S. 2000. "The Financial Stability of Notional Account Pensions." *Scandinavian Journal of Economics* 102 (3): 395–417.

————. 2002. "Políticas y mercados de pensiones." ("Pensions, Markets, and Policies.") *Ediciones Universidad Católica de Chile*, Santiago de Chile.

Vidal, C., I. Domínguez, and J. E. Devesa. 2004. "Economic Risk to Beneficiaries in Notional Defined Contribution Accounts (NDCs)." Working Paper 219-04, Fundación para la Investigación Económica y Social (FUNCAS).

———. 2005. "Subjective Economic Risk to Beneficiaries in Notional Defined Contribution Accounts (NDCs)." *Journal of Risk and Insurance.*

Williamson, J. B. 2004. "Assessing the Pension Reform Potential of a Notional Defined Contribution Pillar." *International Social Security Review* 57 (1): 47–64.

Chapter 24

Reforming Social Security in Japan: Is NDC the Answer?

*Noriyuki Takayama**

JAPAN ALREADY HAS THE OLDEST POPULATION IN THE WORLD. It has built a generous social security pension program but, since 2002, the income statement of the principal pension program has turned into a deficit. Its balance sheet suffers from huge excess liabilities, and distrust of the government commitment on pensions is growing. The Japanese are increasingly concerned with the incentive-compatibility problem.

This chapter investigates whether and how NDC schemes would help Japan and whether they are politically feasible. Before going into discussion, the chapter gives a brief sketch of Japanese social security pension program and summarizes Japan's major pension problems, while pointing out anticipated demographic changes and several basic facts about pensions.

Brief Outline of Pension Provisions before the 2004 Reform

Since 1980, Japan has repeated piecemeal pension reforms every five years, mainly because of great stresses on financing social security caused by anticipated demographic and economic factors. Since then, too-generous pension benefits have been reduced step by step, along with an increase of the normal retirement age from 60 to 65. The pension contribution rate has been lifted gradually as well. Yet current pension provisions still remain generous, and the system faces serious financial difficulties in the future.

Japan now has a two-tier benefit system, providing all sectors of the population with the first-tier, flat-rate basic benefit. The second-tier, earnings-related benefit applies only to employees.[1] The system operates largely like a pay-as-you-go (PAYG) defined benefit program.

The flat-rate basic pension covers all residents aged 20 to 60. The full old-age pension is payable after 40 years of contributions, provided the contributions were made before 60 years of age. The maximum *monthly* pension of 66,200 yen at 2004 prices (with a maximum number of years of coverage) per person is payable from age 65.[2] The benefit is indexed automatically each fiscal year (from April 1) to reflect changes in the consumer price index (CPI) from the previous calendar year. The pension may be claimed at any age between 60

* Noriyuki Takayama is professor of economics at Hitotsubashi University, Tokyo, and director general and CEO of the Project on Intergenerational Equity (PIE).

and 70 years. It is subject to actuarial reduction if claimed before age 65, or actuarial increase if claimed after age 65.

Earnings-related benefits are given to all employees. The accrual rate for the earnings-related component of old-age benefits is 0.5481 percent per year, and 40 years of contributions will thus earn 28.5 percent of career-average monthly real earnings.[3]

The career-average monthly earnings are calculated over the employee's entire period of coverage, adjusted by a net-wage index factor and converted to the current earnings level. The full earnings-related pension is normally payable from age 65 to an employee who is fully retired.[4] An earnings test is applied to those who are not fully retired. The current replacement rate (including basic benefits) for take-home pay or net income is about 60 percent for a "model" male retiree (with an average salary earned during 40 years of coverage) and his dependent wife. Its *monthly* benefit is about 230,000 yen.

Equal percentage contributions are required of employees and their employers. The contributions are based on the annual standard earnings including bonuses. The total percentage in effect before October 2004 was 13.58 percent for the principal program for private-sector employees (Kosei-Nenkin-Hoken, or KNH). Nonemployed persons between the ages of 20 and 60 years pay flat-rate individual contributions. The rate in effect before April 2005 was 13,300 yen per month. For those who cannot pay for financial reasons, exemptions are permitted. The flat-rate basic benefits for the period of exemption are one-third of the normal amount.

Under the current system, if the husband has the pension contribution for social security deducted from his salary, his dependent wife is automatically entitled to the flat-rate basic benefits, and she is not required to make any individual payments to the public pension system.

The government subsidizes one-third of the total cost of the flat-rate basic benefits. There is no subsidy for the earnings-related part. The government pays administrative expenses as well. The aggregate amount of social security pension benefits will be around 46 trillion yen in 2004, equivalent to about 9 percent of GDP.

Demography and Its Impact on Financing Social Security

In January 2002, the Japanese National Institute of Population and Social Security Research (NIPSSR) released its latest population projections. These indicate that the total population will peak at 128 million around 2006 and then begin to fall steadily, decreasing to about 50 percent of the current number by 2100.

The total fertility rate (TFR) was 1.29 in 2004. There is still little sign that the TFR will stabilize or return to a higher level. Yet the 2002 *medium variant* projections assume that it will record the historical low of 1.31 in 2006 and will gradually rise to 1.39 around 2050, progressing slowly to 2.07 by 2150. The number of births, currently about 1.12 million in 2003, will continue to decrease to less than 1.0 million by 2014, falling further to 0.67 million in 2050.

Japan already has one of the oldest populations in the world, and the long life expectancy of Japanese people means that Japan is now experiencing a very rapid aging of its population. The number of elderly (age 65 and above) is 25.5 million in 2005. It will increase sharply to reach 34 million by 2018, remaining around 34–36 million thereafter until around 2060. Consequently the proportion of the elderly will go up very rapidly from 20.0 percent in 2005 to 25.3 percent by 2014, rising further to more than 30 percent by 2033.

In Japan, 70 percent of social security benefits are currently distributed to the elderly. Along with the ailing domestic economy, the rapid aging will certainly put more and more stresses on financing social security.

In May 2004, the Ministry of Health, Labor and Welfare, Japan, published the latest estimates of the cost of social security broadly defined—that is, including pension, health, and social welfare benefits—using the 2002 population projections of the NIPSSR. According to the latest estimates, the aggregate cost of social security is 17.2 percent of GDP in 2004. It will steadily increase to 24.3 percent by 2025 if the current provisions for benefits remain unchanged.

Of the various costs of social security, that of pensions predominates, amounting to 9 percent of GDP in 2004, with further increase to 11.6 percent by 2025. The cost for health care is 5.2 percent in 2004, but this will rapidly rise to 8.1 percent by 2025.

The Japanese economy is still reeling from the effects of its burst bubble, and the decline in population will soon be reflected in a sharp decline in young labor, in a falling savings rate, and in a decrease in capital formation, all of which will contribute to a further shrinking of the country's economy.

Some Basic Facts about Pensions

Any pension reform proposal must take into account the basic facts about pensions. Among others, the following five facts are especially crucial.

Persistent Deficit in Income Statement
Since 2002, the KNH has been facing an income statement deficit. It recorded a deficit of 1.3 trillion yen in 2002, and the deficit was 5.1 trillion yen in 2004. It is estimated that the deficit will persist for a long time, unless radical changes are made in the KNH financing.

Huge Excess Liabilities in the Balance Sheet
The KNH balance sheet is shown in table 24.1. In calculating the balance sheet, we assumed that:

1. Annual increases in wages and CPI are 2.1 percent and 1.0 percent respectively in nominal terms, while the discount rate is 3.2 percent annually
2. The current contribution rate of the KNH, 13.58 percentage points, will remain unchanged in the future
3. The period up to year 2100 is taken into account.

Table 24.1 indicates that as of March 31, 2005, there will be excess liabilities of 550 trillion yen, which is a quarter of the total liabilities.[5]

Part One of table 24.1 shows assets and liabilities accrued from past contributions, and Part Two shows those accrued from future contributions. Table 24.1 implies that as far as the future is concerned, balance sheet of the KNH has been almost cleaned up. The funding sources of the current provisions will be sufficient to finance future benefits, and the only task left is to slim down future benefits by 4.5 percent.

But if we look at Part One of table 24.1, things appear quite different. The remaining pension liabilities are estimated to be 800 trillion yen, while pension assets are only 300 trillion yen (a funded reserve of 170 trillion yen plus transfers from general revenue of 130 trillion yen). The difference is quite large—about 500 trillion yen, which accounts for the major part of excess liabilities in the KNH.

Five hundred trillion yen is more than 60 percent of Part One liabilities, equivalent to about 100 percent of GDP of Japan in 2004. In the past, too many promises about pension benefits have been made, but sufficient funding sources have not been arranged. The Japanese have enjoyed a long history of social security pensions. However, contributions made in the past have been relatively small, resulting in a fairly small funded reserve. Consequently,

**Table 24.1. Balance Sheet of the KNH before Reform as of March 31, 2005
(yen, trillions)**

1. Part One	
Assets	
Financial reserves	170
Transfers from general revenue	130
Liabilities	
Pensions due to past contributions	800
Excess liabilities	500
2. Part Two	
Assets	
Contributions	920
Transfers from general revenue	130
Liabilities	
Pensions due to future contributions	1,100
Excess liabilities	50

Source: Author's calculations.

the locus of the true crisis in Japanese social security pensions is how to handle the excess liabilities of 500 trillion yen that were entitled from contributions made in the past.

Pension Contributions: Heavy Burdens Outstanding

One of the principal issues in Japanese public debates has been how to cut down personal and corporate income tax. But recently the situation has changed drastically. Social security contributions (for pensions, health care, unemployment, work injury, and long-term care) are 55.6 trillion yen (15.2 percent of national income) for fiscal 2003. This is apparently more than all tax revenues (43.9 trillion yen) of the central government for the same year. Since 1998, the central government has acquired more from social security contributions than from tax incomes. Looking at further detail, we find that revenue from personal income tax is 13.8 trillion yen and from corporate income tax is 9.1 trillion yen, while revenue from social security pension contributions stands out at 29.0 trillion yen. Needless to say, the last places a heavy burden on the public. The Japanese now feel that social security pension contributions are too heavy; they operate as the most significant factor in determining the take-home pay from the gross salary. On the other hand, corporate managers have begun to show serious concerns about any further increases in social security contributions.

Overshooting in Income Transfer between Generations

It may seem amazing that today in Japan the elderly are better off than those aged 30 to 44 in terms of per capita income after redistribution (see figure 24.1). Undoubtedly there is room for reduction in benefits provided to the current retired population.

Increasing Drop Out Rate

In the past 20 years the Japanese government has made repeated changes to the pension program, increasing social security pension contributions and reducing benefits by raising the normal pensionable age while reducing the accrual rate. Further such piecemeal reforms will most likely follow in the future.

Figure 24.1. Per Capita Income by Age in Japan

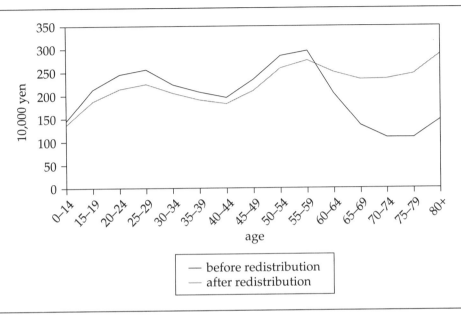

Source: Ministry of Health and Welfare, Japan (1996).

Many Japanese feel that the government is breaking its promise. As distrust about government commitment builds up, concern about a "credibility problem" is also growing.

In 2002, nearly 50 percent of nonsalaried workers and persons with no occupation dropped out from the basic level of old-age income protection, owing to exemption, delinquency in paying contributions, or nonapplication (figure 24.2 shows the increasing rate of delinquency).

Figure 24.2. Drop Out Rate from Social Security Pensions (nonemployees)[a]

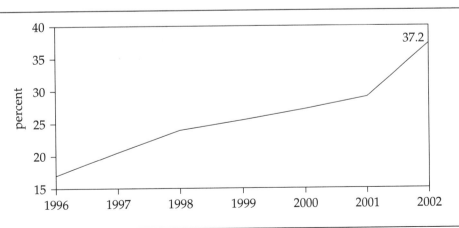

Source: Ministry of Health, Labor and Welfare, Japan (2003).

a. Delinquency in paying pension contributions.

Employers are also carefully trying to find ways to avoid paying social security pension contributions. Indeed, the aggregate amount of the KNH contributions has been decreasing since 1998, in spite of no change in the contribution rate.

Any further escalation in the social security contribution rate will surely induce a higher drop-out rate.[6]

The 2004 Pension Reform: Main Contents and Remaining Difficulties

In February 2004, Japanese government submitted a new pension reform bill that passed the Diet in June 2004. The main contents of it are:

- The KNH contribution rate is to rise by 0.354 percentage points every year from October 2004, reaching 18.30 percentage points by 2017. After 2017, it will be kept at 18.30 percentage points.
- Social security pension benefits will be further reduced by 0.9 percent in real terms every year for the next 20 years. Consequently, the replacement rate for the "model" male retiree and his dependant wife will decrease step by step from the current 60 percent to 50 percent by 2023. This is because of the introduction of a "demographic factor" that takes into account the decreasing rate of the total number of the actively working population and longer life expectancy.
- Transfers from general revenue are to be increased from one-third to one-half of the basic benefits by 2009.
- The earnings test is to be relaxed before age 65, while a new earnings test is introduced for those of age 70 and over.
- An earnings split between husband and his wife is to be introduced on divorce.
- More taxes are levied on pension benefits from 2005 on.
- There is no plan for any further increases in the normal pensionable age above 65.

The policy measures adopted in the 2004 pension reform bill will induce huge *excess assets* of 420 trillion yen in the Part Two balance sheet whereby offsetting excess liabilities of the same amount in Part One balance sheet, as shown in table 24.2. The huge excess assets of the Part Two balance sheet indicates that future generations will be forced to pay more than the anticipated benefits they will receive. Their benefits will be around 70 percent of their contributions and taxes, on the whole.

It seems as if we cut a paper not with scissors but with a saw. Younger generations are most likely to intensify their distrust of the government. The incentive-compatibility problem or the drop-out problem will become graver. The management (Nippon Keidanren) and trade unions (Rengo) both oppose any further increases of more than 15 percentage point in the KNH contribution rate.

Is the Swedish-Type NDC Applicable to Japan?

The Ministry of Health, Labor and Welfare, Japan, shows a great interest in switching the system to a Swedish-type NDC. It believes, however, that the switch can become realistic only after the KNH contribution rate reaches the peak level in 2017.

Switching to the Swedish-type NDC can be introduced in Japan very soon, however, if we *separate* the "legacy pension" problem from building a sustainable pension system for the future. The legacy pension problem of Japan looks like *sunk costs* in the economic perspective. This problem can be solved not by increasing the KNH contribution rate but by introducing a new 3 percent earmarked consumption tax and by an intensive interjection of the increased transfers from general revenue (see table 24.3). Needless to say, the current

Table 24.2. Balance Sheet of the KNH after Reform as of March 31, 2005 (yen, trillions)

1. Part One	
Assets	
Financial reserves	170
Transfers from general revenue	150
Liabilities	
Pensions due to past contributions	740
Excess liabilities	420
2. Part Two	
Assets	
Contributions	1,200
Transfers from general revenue	190
Liabilities	
Pensions due to future contributions	970
Excess assets	420

Source: Ministry of Health, Labor and Welfare, Japan (2004a).

generous benefits have to be reduced more or less by the same percentage as implemented in the 2004 pension reform bill.

For the Part Two balance sheet, which relates to future contributions and promised pension benefits entitled by future contributions, a switch to NDC is quite advisable. The KNH contribution rate would be kept unchanged at the current level of 13.58 percentage points. The notional rate of return should be endogenous, following a Swedish-type automatic balancing mechanism.

With the NDC plan, the incentive-compatibility problem can be avoided. Indeed, every penny counts in the NDC, and this would be the most important element when we switch to an NDC plan. It will be demonstrated to the public that everybody gets a pension equivalent to his/her own contribution payments.[7]

The NDC is expected to be rather neutral to the retirement decisions. The labor force participation rate for the elderly Japanese men remains at a considerably high level (71.2 percent of those aged 60 to 64 were working in 2003) compared with other developed countries, however. The shift to NDC can induce later retirement also in Japan, but its effect may not be so significant.

A move to NDC leads to lower replacement rates at age 65. This can be compensated for by working longer to age 67 or so, or by more voluntary saving. The Japanese government has decided to provide more tax incentives to the existing defined contribution plan from October 2004 onward.[8]

The supplementary benefit, the guaranteed pension, in Sweden was implemented as a provision for ensuring adequate income after retirement. It was also expected to work as a "shock-absorber" against social and economic risks. In Sweden, this benefit is solely dependent on pension income, and not on comprehensive income (including asset income, wages, and salaries), with no means-testing.

These Swedish arrangements for guaranteed pensions may be problematic in Japan, where income reporting to the tax bureau apparently differs among occupational groups. That is to say, income for wage-and-salary earners is usually fully reported, whereas

Table 24.3. Balance Sheet of the KNH: An Alternative as of March 31, 2005 (yen, trillions)

1 Part One	
Assets	
Financial reserves	170
Transfers from general revenue	290
Earmarked consumption tax	280
Liabilities	
Pensions due to past contributions	740
Excess liabilities	0
2 Part Two	
Assets	
Contributions	920
Transfers from general revenue	50
Liabilities	
Pensions due to future contributions	970
Excess liabilities	0

Source: Author's calculations.

income for self-employed persons is often underreported. Underreporting of income means less pension benefits from the NDC pillar, leading to more benefits in the guaranteed pension if Japan were to follow the Swedish system. This looks unfair to the eyes of salaried men. There should be special arrangements for nonemployed persons when a guaranteed pension is introduced in Japan.

Concluding Remarks

The Japanese are increasingly concerned with the "taste of the pie" rather than the "size of the pie" or the "distribution of the pie." When it comes to social security pensions, the most important question is whether or not they are worth buying at all.[9] How big or how fair the pensions are has become a secondary concern. The basic design of the pension program should be incentive-compatible. Contributions should be much more directly linked with old-age pension benefits, while an element of social adequacy should be incorporated in a separate tier of pension benefits financed by sources other than contributions.

The author believes that a Swedish-type NDC arrangement will be the only way for Japan to overcome urgent difficulties in its current pension system. Of course, the switch to NDC schemes has to be accompanied by other proper measures for handling the legacy pension problems of Japan.

Notes

1. A detailed explanation of the Japanese social security pension system is given by Takayama (1998, 2003b).

2. 1,000 yen = US$8.87 = euro 7.39 = UK£5.11 = SKr69.80 as of July 27, 2005.

3. A semi-annual bonus equivalent to 3.6 months salary is typically assumed.

4. The normal pensionable age of the Kosei-Nenkin-Hoken, or KNH, is 65, though Japan has special arrangements for a transition period between 2000 and 2025. See Takayama (2003b) for more details.

5. Excess liabilities of all social security pension programs in Japan as of the end of March 2005 amounted to around 650 trillion yen, which is equivalent to 1.3 times the 2004 GDP of Japan.

6. Contributions to social security pensions operate as "penalties on employment." Further hikes in the contribution rate will drastically damage domestic companies, which have been facing megacompetition on a global scale, and thereby exert negative effects on the economy, inducing a higher unemployment rate, lower economic growth, lower saving rates, and so on. Further increases in the contribution rate will also be sure to decrease take-home pay of actively working people in real terms, producing lower consumption and lower effective demand.

7. See Könberg (2002), Palmer (2003) and Settergren (2001) for more details.

8. See Takayama (2004) for more details.

9. See Takayama (2003a).

References

Könberg, B. 2002. "The Swedish Pension Reform: Some Lessons." DP-46, Project on Intergenerational Equity, Institute of Economic Research, Tokyo: Hitotsubashi University.

Ministry of Health and Welfare, Japan. 1996. *The 1996 Income Redistribution Survey* [in Japanese], Tokyo: Ministry of Health and Welfare, Japan.

Ministry of Health, Labor and Welfare, Japan. 2003. *The 2003 Statistical Abstract of Social Security in Japan* [in Japanese], Tokyo: Ministry of Health, Labor and Welfare, Japan.

————. 2004a. *The 2005 Financial Recalculation of the KNH* [in Japanese], Tokyo: Ministry of Health, Labor and Welfare, Japan.

————. 2004b. *The Estimates of The Cost of Social Security* [in Japanese], Tokyo: Ministry of Health, Labor and Welfare, Japan.

Palmer, E. 2003. "Pension Reform in Sweden." In *Taste of Pie: Searching for Better Pension Provisions in Developed Countries*, ed. N. Takayama, 245–69. Tokyo: Maruzen, Ltd.

Settergren, O. 2001. "The Automatic Balance Mechanism of the Swedish Pension System." Riksförsäkringsverket, Sweden. http://www.rfv.se.

Takayama, N. 1998. *The Morning After in Japan: Its Declining Population, Too Generous Pensions and a Weakened Economy.* Tokyo: Maruzen, Ltd.

————. 2003a. *Taste of Pie: Searching for Better Pension Provisions in Developed Countries.* Tokyo: Maruzen, Ltd.

————. 2003b. "Pension Arrangements in the Oldest Country: The Japanese Case." In *Taste of Pie: Searching for Better Pension Provisions in Developed Countries*, ed. N. Takayama, 185–217. Tokyo: Maruzen, Ltd.

————. 2004. "Changes in the Pension System." *Japan Echo* 31 (5): 9–12.

Contributors

Juha M. Alho is a professor of statistics at the University of Joensuu, Finland, and author (with B. D. Spencer) of a forthcoming book: *Statistical Demography and Forecasting* (Springer). He has written extensively on stochastic methods of population forecasting. juha.alho@joensuu.fi

John Ameriks is a senior investment analyst at the Vanguard Group, where he conducts research regarding household portfolio choice and savings behavior. He has authored studies on a variety of topics including household savings adequacy, income strategies for retirees, life-cycle portfolio allocation, financial planning and wealth accumulation, and the retirement and annuitization decisions of individuals participating in account-based retirement plans. john_ameriks@vanguard.com.

Nicholas Barr is a professor of public economics at the London School of Economics and the author of numerous books and articles, including *The Economics of the Welfare State* (OUP, 4th edition, 2004). He has spent periods of leave at the World Bank, working on social safety nets in the post-communist transition countries, and at the IMF. Since the late 1980s, he has been active in debates about pensions and higher education finance, advising governments in transition countries, and in the United Kingdom, Australia, Chile, China, and New Zealand. N.Barr@lse.ac.uk

Axel H. Börsch-Supan is director of the Mannheim Research Institute for the Economics of Aging (MEA) and a professor for macroeconomics and public policy at the University of Mannheim, Germany. He is chairman of the Council of Advisors to the German Economics Ministry and chaired the Pension Reform Unit of the German Social Security Reform Commission, which introduced the "Sustainability Reform" of the German public pension system in May 2004. Börsch-Supan coordinates the EU-sponsored Survey of Health, Aging and Retirement in Europe (SHARE); is a research associate at the National Bureau of Economic Research (NBER) in Cambridge, Massachusetts, USA; and a member of the Berlin-Brandenburg Academy of Sciences and the German Academy of Natural Sciences. axel@boersch-supan.de.

Sarah M. Brooks is an assistant professor of political science at Ohio State University. She has been a consultant for the World Bank on a study of the political economy of pension reform and has carried out research on the adoption and diffusion of structural pension reforms around the world. She is completing a book manuscript, *Social Protection and the Market*, which examines the making of structural pension reforms in Latin America. brooks.317@osu.edu

Agnieszka Chłoń-Domińczak is currently deputy minister in the Ministry of Social Policy in Poland. She completed her Ph.D. on the issue of aging populations and its impact on pension systems. She was a member of a pension reform team in Poland, preparing the reform of 1999. She has cooperated on various projects related to pension systems with the World Bank, the International Labor Organization (ILO) and the OECD and is the author of several publications within the field. Agnieszka.Chlon-Dominczak@mps.gov.pl

Peter Diamond is an institute professor at Massachusetts Institute of Technology. He was chair of the Panel on Privatization of Social Security of the National Academy of Social Insurance, 1996–98, whose report, "Issues in Privatizing Social Security," has been published by MIT Press. He has consulted about social security to the United States and the World Bank, and has written about the social security systems of Chile, China, Germany, Italy, the Netherlands, Spain, and Sweden as well as the United States. His recent books are *Taxation, Incomplete Markets and Social Security*, *Social Security Reform* and *Saving Social Security: A Balanced Approach* (with Peter R. Orszag). pdiamond@mit.edu

Inmaculada Domínguez-Fabián is an assistant professor of social security at the University of Extremadura (Spain). She is an expert on the study of both private and public pension systems from an economic and actuarial point of view, and has written a number of publications on the subject. idomingu@unex.es.

Bernhard Felderer is professor of economics in Cologne, Germany, and director of the Institute for Advanced Studies in Vienna, Austria. He has held various academic positions in Germany, has done research and teaching in the United States and the former Soviet Union, and has published widely in the areas of macroeconomics, economic policy, and pension economics. He is a member of the Pension Reform Commission of the Austrian government. felderer@ihs.ac.at

Elsa Fornero is a professor of economics at the University of Turin and Director of CeRP (Center for Research on Pensions and Welfare Systems, Turin). She has been a member of the Italian Government Commission of independent experts for the assessment of the Italian Social Security reform (2000–1) and of a team of evaluators in the area of pension reform at the World Bank (2003). She is an op-ed writer for the Italian economic daily *Il Sole-24 ore*, and the author of numerous writings, mainly in the fields of household economics, pensions, and savings. elsa.fornero@unito.it

Daniele Franco is director of the Public Finance Division in the Research Department of the Bank of Italy and previously served as Economic Adviser at the European Commission. He has contributed to international working groups on pension issues. He is the author of several articles on public pensions, fiscal sustainabilty, and generational accounting. daniele.franco@bancaditalia.it

Elaine Fultz is the senior specialist in social security, International Labor Organization, Subregional Office for Central and Eastern Europe, Budapest. There she manages a regional technical cooperation project that has produced many studies of social security reform in the region. Prior to joining the ILO, she worked on the staff of the Subcommittee on Social Security of the Committee on Ways and Means in the U.S. House of Representatives, where she was responsible for Congressional oversight of the U.S. Social Security Administration. She holds a Ph.D. from the Wagner School of Public Service at New York University. fultz@ilo-ceet.hu.

Marek Góra is a professor at the Warsaw School of Economics. He was a co-designer of the new Polish pension system and a leader of the team working on the Polish pension reform. He is an economic adviser to the President of Poland and to the Minister of Finance. He has worked as an adviser on pension policy for a number of foreign governments and is the author of numerous publications within the field. Marek.Gora@sgh.waw.pl

Sandro Gronchi is a full professor of economics at La Sapienza University of Rome. He also teaches Economics of Social Security for the Master's course in Public Economics. In July 2002, at the request of the Italian Ministry for the Economy, he was appointed Temporary Lecturer at the Ministry's newly founded School of Economics and Finance. In the early 1990s he proposed an NDC reform program for the Italian pension system, and in 1995 he was appointed consultant to the Government with the task of developing a bill for such a reform. He is now consultant on social security issues to the President of the National Council for Economy and Labour. Sandro.Gronchi@Uniroma1.it

Anna Hedborg holds a degree in economics. Following an earlier career within the Swedish Confederation of Labor, she held a number of top-ranking positions in government and public administration. She was one of two Social Democratic Party representatives in the Pension Working Group, which created the Swedish pension reform. The legislation was passed in the late spring of 1994, and with a change of government in the autumn of 1994, Hedborg became Deputy Minister in charge of Social Insurance. In this capacity, she initiated and chaired the Implementation Group for the reform. In 1996, she became Director General of the National Social Insurance Board (called the State Social Insurance Agency as of 2005), which was responsible for the practical implementation of the reform. In 2005, she left her position at the National Social Insurance Board to become the Government's special investigator on the Future of Social Insurance.

Robert Holzmann is director of the Social Protection Department of the World Bank. His department is in charge of the conceptual and strategic Bank work in the area of social risk management, and it leads the Bank's work on pension reform. Before joining the Bank, he was professor of economics and director of the European Institute at the University of Saarland, Germany; professor of economics at the University of Vienna, Austria; senior economist at the IMF; and principal administrator at the OECD, Paris. His research on and operational involvement in pension reform extends to all regions of the world, and he has published 24 books and more than 100 articles on social, fiscal, and financial policy issues. RHolzmann@worldbank.org

Reinhard Koman holds a Ph.D. in Economics and is currently working as an economist at the Institute for Advanced Studies in Vienna. He was an expert in the Committee on Long-Term Pension Sustainability and the Pension Reform Commission of the Austrian government. He has worked as an adviser on pension policy for the Austrian government and is the author of several publications within the field. Reinhard.Koman@ihs.ac.at.

Bo Könberg is governor of the county of Sörmland, Sweden. He was the minister for health and social insurance in 1991–94, when he led the Working Group on Pensions that created the Swedish pension reform. He has been a member of the Implementation Group for the Swedish Pension Reform, created in 1994 and consisting of representatives of the five political parties supporting the pension reform and which continued to meet to steer the implementation of the reform. Könberg has also been the group leader of the Liberal Party in the Swedish Parliament. He was an adviser in the pension reform processes in Latvia and Poland, and has spoken freqently on Swedish pension reform in countries around the world. bo.konberg@d.lst.se

Agneta Kruse is senior lecturer at the Department of Economics, Lund University. She was an expert in the Swedish government's Pension Committee. Her research focus is on pensions, especially on the effects of pension design on distribution and on risk sharing between generations. agneta.kruse@nek.lu.se

Jukka Lassila is research director at the Research Institute of the Finnish Economy (ETLA). He has studied pension policies and evaluated reforms in Finland and Lithuania. He is Scientific Coordinator in the EU 5th Framework research project "Demographic Uncertainty and the Sustainability of Social Welfare Systems," and has published several articles within the field. Jukka.Lassila@etla.fi.

Ronald Lee is professor of demography and economics at the University of California, Berkeley, and director of the university's Center on the Economics and Demography of Aging, which is funded by the National Institute of Aging. After teaching economics for eight years in the Economics Department at the University of Michigan and also working at the Population Studies Center, he joined the Department of Demography at U.C. Berkeley in 1979, with a joint appointment in the Economics Department. He has held the presidency of the Population Association of America. He has also chaired the population and social science study section for the U.S. National Institutes of Health and is a former chair of the Committee on Population at the National Academy of Sciences in the United States. He holds a Ph.D. in economics from Harvard University. rlee@demog.berkeley.edu

Florence Legros is a professor of economics at the University Dauphine in Paris. She does research on issues connected with aging, pensions, social policies, and savings and their effects on economic growth and financial flows. Legros served as an expert in the French Prime Minister's Pensions Advisory Council and works as a Scientific Adviser in Caisse des depots et consignations, a major French financial actor in the field of pensions. She also chairs the prospective council of AF2I (French association of institutional investors) and works for various international organizations in the field of retirement, pensions, and macroeconomics. As a specialist of retirement pension schemes, savings, and financial markets, she has written numerous publications, papers, and books dealing with these topics. Florence.legros@dauphine.fr

Assar Lindbeck is a professor of international economics at the Institute for International Economic Studies (IIES), Stockholm University, and at the Research Institute of Industrial Economics (IUI). His research focuses on macroeconomics and the analysis of the welfare state. Recent studies include the interaction between economic incentives and social norms. Recent publications on pensions are: "Pensions and Contemporary Socioeconomic Change," in *Social Security Pension Reform in Europe*, ed. M. Feldstein and H. Siebert, 19–44 (University of Chicago Press, 2002) and "The Gains from Pension Reform" (with Mats Persson), *Journal of Economic Literature* XLI: 74–112, March 2003. Assar.Lindbeck@iies.su.se

David Lindeman has worked on both public and private retirement income policy from several perspectives in a career that encompassed 25 years with the U.S. federal government (including executive director of the 1994–97 Quadrennial Social Security Advisory Council of the U.S. government and director for policy and research of the Pension Benefit Guaranty Corporation); the World Bank, where he advised on pension policy in many countries; and recently the OECD, where he has helped develop core standards for private pension regulation and supervision. david_lindeman@msn.com

Bernd Marin is executive director of the European Centre for Social Welfare Policy and Research, affiliated with the United Nations in Vienna. He is a comparative social scientist working and publishing widely on the sustainability of welfare and social security systems, more recently on innovative employment initiatives, health and disability policies, and pension reforms. He also serves as an expert and policy advisor to various governments, intergovernmental, and nongovernmental organizations on aging and pension issues. marin@euro.centre.org

Boguslaw D. Mikula is a researcher in the Division for Analysis at the Swedish Social Insurance Agency. He has worked with actuarial modeling and evaluations in the context of the Swedish pension reform. Recently he was an expert in the Swedish government's Committee of Inquiry on the Surplus in the National Pension System. He has also worked as an expert on modeling social insurance systems for a World Bank project in Latvia. danne.mikula@socialagency.se

Marek Mora works at the European Commission, Directorate-General for Economic and Financial Affairs, as country desk economist responsible for the Czech Republic. He has published several articles on the pension reform issues. Marek.Mora@cec.eu.int

Sergio Nisticò is a professor of economics at the University of Cassino (Italy) where he teaches Microeconomics, History of Economic Thought, and Social Insurance Economics. Since 2004 he has been a member of the Board of Directors of the University Master Programme in Advice for Labour and Social Security Issues. s.nistico@caspur.it

Edward Palmer is a professor of social insurance economics at Uppsala University and head of the Division for Research at the Swedish Social Insurance Agency. He was an expert in the Swedish government's Working Group on Pensions that formulated the Swedish pension reform and was a member of the government's implementation group. He has worked as an adviser on pension policy for a number of governments around the world and is the author of numerous publications within the field. Edward.Palmer@abc.se

Monika Queisser works on retirement systems and policies, disability, and other social protection issues in the Social Policy Division of the OECD. Prior to joining the OECD she worked at the World Bank's Financial Sector Development Department in the pensions and insurance group. She has worked with governments in Africa, Asia, Eastern Europe, and Latin America and has published several articles and studies on pension reform issues. Monika.Queisser@oecd.org

David Robalino is a senior economist at the World Bank, working in the Middle East and North Africa Human Development Department since July 2002. In this position he is involved in pension reform dialogue in essentially all countries in the region. He is the author of *Pensions in the Middle East and North Africa Region: Time for Change,* the first comprehensive report on pensions in the Middle East and North Africa, published in 2005. He also served on the Presidential Commission for Social Security Reform in Ecuador between 1994 and 1995. DRobalino@worldbank.org

Michal Rutkowski is director of the Human Development Department in the Middle East and North Africa Region of the World Bank. In the period 1997–2004, while in the Europe and Central Asia Region of the World Bank, he was responsible for pension policy reforms in the countries of the region as Sector Manager for Social Protection and then Director of the Human Development Department. In 1996–97, as director of the Office for Pension Reform in Poland, he was a co-author of the Polish pension reform that was subsequently implemented. He has worked as an adviser on social protection policies for a number of governments around the world. MRutkowski@worldbank.org

Nicola Sartor is a professor of economics in the Department of Economics at the University of Verona, Italy. A main area of her filed of research is public finance and pension policy issues. Nicola.sartor@univr.it

Ulrich Schuh is the head of the Department of Economics and Finance at the Institute for Advanced Studies in Austria. He has worked for several years at the Ministry of Finance of Austria. He joined the Institute for Advanced Studies in Vienna in 1999 and has since then published a number of articles in the field of Public Sector Economics and Labor Economics. He is a member of the Austrian commission to safeguard the financial stability of the Austrian pension system. schuh@ihs.ac.at

Ole Settergren is director of the Pensions Department at the Swedish Social Insurance Agency. While working for the Ministry of Health and Social Affairs he proposed a method of securing the financial stability of the new Swedish pension system. Assisted by Hans Olsson and Boguslaw D. Mikula, he led the research preceding the legislation of this method and penned the government bill "The Automatic Balance Mechanism." He developed the accounting principles that have been used since 2001 in the *Annual Report of the Swedish Pension System* and is its editor. ole.settergren@socialagency.se

Sandra Stabiņa is the head of the Division of Social Policy Monitoring and Forecasts at the Finance Management Department at the Ministry of Welfare of Latvia. She has worked with pension reform in Latvia and the social policy monitoring system in the ministry, and has also been an author of the "Social Report" produced periodically by the Ministry of Welfare. Sandra.Stabina@lm.gov.lv

Annika Sundén is a senior economist at the Swedish Social Insurance Agency. Previously Dr. Sundén was the associate director of research at the Center for Retirement Research at Boston College. She has also worked as an economist at the Federal Reserve Board in Washington, DC. Her research interests include the economics of social insurance, retirement, and household savings behavior. She earned her B.S. from the Stockholm School of Economics and her M.S. and Ph.D. in labor economics from Cornell University. annika.sunden@socialagency.se

Ingemar Svensson is a senior researcher at the Division for Research at the Swedish Social Insurance Agency. He has worked with evaluations and projections for the Swedish old-age and disability pension reforms and the Latvian pension reform. He has also contributed to the research about the effects of income security systems for retirement behavior. Ingemar.Svensson@socialagency.se

Noriyuki Takayama is a professor of economics at Hitotsubashi University, Tokyo. He is also director general and CEO of the Project on Intergenerational Equity (PIE). He has published numerous books and articles in international publications, including *Econometrica* and *American Economic Review,* and he edited the book entitled *Taste of Pie: Searching for Better Pension Provisions in Developed Countries.* He worked as a key player on the pension policy of Japan. takayama@ier.hit-u.ac.jp

Salvador Valdés-Prieto is a professor of economics at Catholic University of Chile and a researcher at the Centro de Estudios Públicos, Santiago. He is an expert in pension reforms in Latin America, has participated in the design of several subsequent reforms to the Chilean pension system, and has been a consultant to the World Bank. He has published a number of articles in journals and several books in the field, the last of which is a university-level textbook on *Pension Polices and Markets* (2002). svaldes@faceapuc.cl

Tarmo Valkonen is the head of the Unit in Public Finance Research at the Research Institute of the Finnish Economy (ETLA). Among other roles, he has been an expert in the steering group for the preparation of the Finnish Government Report on the Future, 2004. His most recent publications assess macroeconomic and welfare implications of fiscal and pension policy under demographic uncertainty. tarmo.valkonen@etla.fi

Inta Vanovska was a member of the working group under the Latvian Welfare Reform Project elaborating the legislative foundation for the new three-pillar pension system and providing economic evaluation of the pension policy based on a macrosimulation model's projections. As head of the Division of Economic Analysis and Forecasts and later the head of the Division of Pension Policy under the Ministry of Welfare in Latvia, she has made a notable contribution to the development of pension reform over the past ten years. Currently she is working at the State Social Insurance Agency of Latvia and is in charge of the Division of International Services. Inta_Vanovska@hq.vsaa.lv

Carlos Vidal-Meliá is a professor of financial economy at Valencia University (Spain) and an independent consultant-actuary. He has worked as an adviser on employer and personal pension schemes as well as a financial economist for small firms. He has also published several papers on public and complementary pension reforms, administration charges for the affiliate in individual accounts systems, and the demand for life annuities. carlos.vidal@uv.es

R. Kent Weaver is a professor of public policy and government at Georgetown University and a senior fellow in the Governance Studies Program at the Brookings Institution. He is the author of numerous works on welfare state politics including *Ending Welfare as We Know It* (Brookings, 2000) and *Automatic Government: The Politics of Indexation* (Brookings, 1988). kweaver@brookings.edu

Christina Benita Wilke is a research fellow in the area of social politics at the Mannheim Research Institute for the Economics of Aging (MEA). She supported Professor Axel Börsch-Supan in his work for the Commission for Sustainability in Financing the German Social Insurance Systems that elaborated the reform proposal for the 2004 German pension reform, and has published several papers on the German pension system. Since June 2004 she has also been a representative member of the Enquete-Commission Demographic Change—Challenges for State Policy of the State of Baden-Wuerttemberg. Wilke@mea.uni-mannheim.de

Index